V&R

BORIS REPSCHINSKI

The Controversy Stories in the Gospel of Matthew

Their Redaction, Form und Relevance
for the Relationship Between the
Matthean Community and Formative Judaism

VANDENHOECK & RUPRECHT
IN GÖTTINGEN

Forschungen zur Religion und Literatur
des Alten und Neuen Testaments

Herausgegeben von
Wolfgang Schrage und Rudolf Smend

189. Heft der ganzen Reihe

Die Deutsche Bibliothek – CIP-Einheitsaufnahme

Repschinski, Boris:
The controversy stories in the Gospel of Matthew:
their redaction, form and relevance for the relationship
between the Matthean community and formative Judaism / Boris Repschinski. –
Göttingen: Vandenhoeck und Ruprecht, 2000
(Forschungen zur Religion und Literatur des Alten und
Neuen Testaments; H. 189)
ISBN 3-525-53873-1

Preface

With a mixture of pride and gratitude I present this study of the Matthean controversy stories. Whether the pride is justified the readers might decide for themselves. But my gratitude is amply warranted by the many people who have helped along the way. First among them is Prof. Thomas H. Tobin, who directed this study with much wisdom and insight. He was always willing to discuss any questions at great length and more than once helped to avoid simplistic solutions to complicated problems. Similarly, Prof. Wendy J. Cotter was a well of wisdom in the field of Q studies. Furthermore, her appreciative criticism opened up a number of possibilities to re-interpret some of the material presented here. Prof. Frans J. van Beeck completed the original dissertation committee at Loyola University Chicago, where this thesis was defended in March 1998. Prof. Daniel J. Harrington first woke my interest in the Gospel of Matthew. Yet despite much good advice there are sure to remain some inconsistencies, oversights, or mistakes. These, of course, remain my own. Also my own is the sometimes clumsy or faulty use of the English language.

Gratitude is also due to the editors of the *Forschungen zur Religion und Literatur des Alten und Neuen Testaments*, Profs. Wolfgang Schrage and Rudolf Smend. I appreciate their acceptance of this study into the series. The Jesuit Community at the University of Innsbruck contributed generously towards the printing of this volume.

The appearance of an English study in a German series made for some peculiarities, particularly with regard to abbreviations. These follow Siegfried M. Schwertner, *Internationales Abkürzungsverzeichnis für Theologie und Grenzgebiete*. 2nd ed. (Berlin, New York: Walter de Gruyter 1992).

Finally, it took a great number of friends to complete this study. They listened to early attempts at formulating arguments they often had little interest in; they dealt with the good and the bad times of research, and were still expected to offer solace and support. For the many who did, Phong H. Pham must be mentioned. To him this book is dedicated.

Contents

8   Contents

List of Tables

I. *Forschungsbericht*: Matthew and Judaism

One of the recurring topics in modern biblical scholarship includes the question of authorship and audience of a particular text. Answers to these questions provide some insight into the social and historical location of the community that is reflected in the text. Depending on the answers to these questions a more or less clear picture emerges of a community that defines itself by a given text. The picture is less clear if one assumes that the authors, or the final editors, of a particular work are merely interested in collecting previously formed material into a whole. Yet the advent of redaction criticism showed how the final editors worked with sources, but gave them their own creative shape and interpretation. With the acceptance of the editorial work as creative the communities reflected therein take on more distinct features.

The gospel of Matthew provides a case in point. While it has always been realized that the gospel is to a large extent informed by Jewish traditions as well as the Jesus traditions, careful attention reveals that these traditions are not just taken over indiscriminately, but are shaped into a literary work of considerable coherence and creativity. With this creativity, however, a major problem arises: If the gospel interprets its Jewish traditions, what then is the gospel's precise relationship to the Judaism contemporary with it? As the following survey of modern critical scholarship will show, this question has not found an easy solution, despite several different methods applied to the problem. While the development of critical methods has helped in formulating the problems of Matthew's social history, certain solutions have remained elusive.

1. The Traditional View: Matthew as a Jewish Gospel

Beginning with the earliest patristic witnesses, the gospel of Matthew has traditionally been regarded as a Christian writing of Jewish origin and flavor. The patristic tradition sees at least some connection between the gospel of Matthew as we know it today, and a disciple of Jesus. About the year 130 C.E. Papias claimed that Matthew put together sayings in the Hebrew language.[1] Papias was followed

---

[1] Papias is quoted in Eusebius: *H. E.*, 3.39.16: "Matthew collected the oracles (τὰ λόγια) in the Hebrew language, and each interpreted (ἡρμήνευσεν) them as best he could."

by Irenaeus,[2] Origen,[3] Eusebius,[4] and others.[5] Yet none of them actually ever saw this Hebrew collection of λόγια, or provided an explanation for its supposed translation into Greek.[6]

Early commentaries on Matthew sometimes took the patristic evidence at face value. On their authority, Bernhard Weiss put together a biography of Matthew which relates missionary endeavors in Ethiopia and Macedonia, his vegetarianism as a form of strict Jewish asceticism, and his natural death in either Ethiopia or Macedonia.[7] Weiss concluded that the present gospel of Matthew has an intimate relationship with the Hebrew sayings that Papias mentioned.[8] Since he assumed that

---

[2] Irenaeus is also quoted by Eusebius: *H. E.*, 5.8.2: "Now Matthew published among the Hebrews also a written gospel (καὶ γράφην ἐξήνεγκεν εὐαγγελίου) in their own tongue ..." The translation here is slightly modified from the Loeb edition. Irenaeus subsequently states that Matthew was written before Mark. Eusebius here quotes Irenaeus: *Adv. Haer.*, 3.1.1.

[3] Origen, quoted by Eusebius: *H. E.*, 6.25.4: "... that first was written (πρῶτον μὲν γέγραπται) [the gospel] according to Matthew, who was once a tax collector but afterwards an apostle of Jesus Christ, who published it for those who from Judaism came to believe, composed as it was in the Hebrew language."

[4] Eusebius: *H. E.*, 3.24.6: "Yet nevertheless of all those who had been with the Lord only Matthew and John have left us their recollections, and tradition says that they took to writing perforce. Matthew had first preached to the Hebrews, and when he was on the point of going to others he transmitted in writing in his native language the gospel according to himself, and thus supplied by writing the lack of presence of himself ..." Nepper-Christensen discusses the patristic evidence concerning Matthew at some length. Poul Nepper-Christensen: *Das Matthaeusevangelium. Ein judenchristliches Evangelium?* AThD 1 (Aarhus: Universitetsforlaget, 1958), 37–75. In an appendix he collects the ten relevant texts (pp. 210–211). For the sake of completeness Jerome must be mentioned as another who hands on the tradition of Matthew as a gospel written for the Hebrews.

[5] Eusebius also mentions that a certain Pantaenus, teacher of Clement of Alexandria, went on a missionary journey to India and there found converts made by Bartholomew who were in the possession of a Hebrew gospel of Matthew (*H. E.*, 5.10.3).

[6] Jerome: *De Viris Illustribus* 12, is the first one to claim to have seen such a gospel and made a copy of it: "Matthaeus, qui et Levi ex publicano apostolus ... primus in Judaea propter eos qui ex circumcisione crediderant, Evangelium Christi Hebraicis litteris verbisque composuit: quod quis postea in Graecum transtulerit, non satis certum est. Porro ipsum Hebraicum habetur usque hodie in Caesariensi bibliotheca, quam Pamphilus martyr studiosissime confecit. Mihi quoque a Nazaraeis, qui in Beroea urbe Syriae hoc volumine utuntur, describendi facultas fuit." In a later work (*Commentarius in Evangelium secundum Matthaeum*, 2.12), Jerome also claims to have translated it: "In evangelio, quo utuntur Nazaraeni et Ebionitae (quod nuper in Graecum sermone transtulimus, et quod vocatur a plerisque Matthaei authenticum) homo iste ..." The accuracy and integrity of Jerome has sometimes been questioned as "einer der schamlosesten und hinterlistigsten literarischen Schwindler und Freibeuter, die es je gegeben hat." Alfred Schmidtke: *Neue Fragmente und Untersuchungen zu den judenchristlichen Evangelien*, TU XXXVII (Leipzig: Teubner, 1911), 67.

[7] Bernhard Weiss: *Das Matthäus-Evangelium*, ATLA monograph preservation program 1987–2274. (Göttingen: Vandenhoeck und Ruprecht, 1898), 1–2.

[8] "Gleichwohl muss es als eine durch die kirchliche Überlieferung ausser Zweifel gesetzte Thatsache angesehen werden, dass unser Evangelist in engster Beziehung zu einer mit dem

Matthew is dependent on Mark he proposes that the statement of Papias refers to an ancient source that was incorporated into the later form of the gospel.[9] Weiss summarized the gospel's purpose as a writing that tries to prove Jesus as the Messiah to Jews who do not live in Palestine and hence need a translation of Hebrew names.[10]

Heinrich Julius Holtzmann argued for the Jewish character of the gospel of Matthew from internal arguments. Holtzmann came to the conclusion that the gospel has a Jewish-Christian community in view.[11]

But the Jewishness of the gospel also had its doubters early on. Already Eduard Reuss contended in 1860 that the gospel was merely a pastiche of traditional material which did not allow for a judgment of the position of the final text towards Judaism.[12] As interesting as Reuss' thesis was he lacked the appropriate methodology to sift the material according to the various sources that he assumed. Therefore, his solution was largely ignored.

The analyses of Holtzmann and Weiss laid the groundwork for much of the discussion that followed. Weiss already noted the difficulty of connecting the gospel

---

apostolischen Ansehen des Matthäus als des Verfassers bekleideten Hebräischen (Aramäischen) Urschrift steht." Weiss: *Das Matthäus-Evangelium*, 4.

[9] "Diese älteste Apostelschrift nun ist es, die dem nachmals von ihr aus weiter ausgearbeiteten Evangelium den Namen des Apostels als Urhebers, den Namen εὐαγγέλιον κατὰ Ματθαῖον, verschaffte und bewahrte. Sie ist in unserem Evangelium am vollständigsten und treuesten erhalten, aber auf Grundlage des Markusevang. und einzelner mündlicher Überlieferungen zu einer vollständigen Geschichte Jesu ausgearbeitet worden." Weiss: *Das Matthäus-Evangelium*, 11.

[10] Weiss: *Das Matthäus-Evangelium*, 14–15.

[11] He lists as arguments: the beginning of the genealogy with Abraham (1:1–2), the missionary instruction to the disciples to go only to the house of Israel (10:6), the "Unverbrüchlichkeit des Gesetzes" and the concomitant "Herleitung allen Übels aus der Trübung des Gesetzes durch die Tradition" (5:20; 15:3.6), the justification through the works of the law (7:19–23; 12:33–37; 19:17; 21:34.41; 25:3), the "auf die Spitze getriebene Heiligung des Sabbats" (24:20), the elevation of Peter, the sayings of Jesus concerning the temple characterized as lies (26:61), the description of Jesus as king of the Jews, the local and temporal modifications of the parousia (10:23; 16:28), the concept of the eschatology with the end of the world as the end of Israel (24:3.22; 10:23) and the rebirth of the twelve tribes of Israel (19:28), changes undertaken by the evangelist to allude to the Old Testament (21:5; 26:15; 27:34), the fulfilment quotations, the resurrection of the souls of the pious (27:52), the theme of Moses and the exodus in the infancy narrative, and the theme of Jesus as the Messiah underlying the whole narrative. Heinrich Julius Holtzmann: *Die synoptischen Evangelien: ihr Ursprung und geschichtlicher Charakter*, ATLA monograph preservation program 1987–1158. (Leipzig: Wilhelm Engelmann, 1863), 377–384.

[12] "Das Evangelium nach Matthäus, wie es vorliegt, ist also nicht eine Parteischrift, sondern eine Sammelschrift, die aus den, dem Vf. zugänglichen, Quellen das Material der Geschichte treu und fleissig zusammenliest. Sofern das Letztere im Einzelnen die Farbe eines bes. religiösen Gesichtspunktes trägt, klebte dieselbe ihm schon an, ehe es hier verwendet wurde, und sie ist nicht der Grund der Aufnahme oder Ausschließung gewesen." Eduard Reuss: *Geschichte der heiligen Schriften, Neuen Testamentes* (Braunschweig: C. A. Schwetschke und Sohn (M. Bruhn), 1860), 182.

with a disciple of Jesus and at the same time assuming some sort of dependence on Mark. This becomes a problem of even greater proportion if one assumes a Gentile background for Mark.[13] The question arises why a supposed eyewitness would use a gospel of such different ideological slant. Some tried to solve the difficulty by relinquishing Markan priority,[14] so that the gospel of Matthew is identical with the document referred to by Papias.[15] For Schlatter the main conflict of the gospel was a fight against Judaism as Jesus is crucified because of his "Absage an das Rabbinat."[16]

Benjamin W. Bacon offered a further twist on the interpretation of Matthew as a Jewish gospel. He saw the groupings of discourses with a repetitive closing formula (7:28; 11:1; 13:53; 19:1; 26:1) as an attempt by the evangelist to give the gospel the form of "Torah" of Jesus that appeared to the interpreters of the 2nd century as an apostolic rebuttal of the Jews.[17] In his early article Bacon proposed his theories in a series of questions. His later studies develop these questions into a coherent theory of the gospel as an apologetic writing.[18]

---

[13] Graham N. Stanton: "The Origin and Purpose of Matthew's Gospel. Matthean Scholarship from 1945 to 1980," in: *Aufstieg und Niedergang der Römischen Welt*, ed. W. Haase und H. Temporini (Berlin, New York: Walter de Gruyter, 1985), II.25.3:1911.

[14] Adolf von Schlatter: *Der Evangelist Matthäus. Seine Sprache, sein Ziel, seine Selbstständigkeit: Ein Kommentar zum ersten Evangelium*, 6th edition (Stuttgart: Calwer, 1963). He assumes that the gospel pre-dates any separation between Judaism and Christianity. He writes concerning the author: "Da aber Mat. schon vor seiner Berufung im Dienst des Herodes in Geldgeschäften tätig war, war er damals nicht mehr Knabe, und wir brauchen nach dem Tod Jesu nicht mehr als rund zwanzig Jahre, damit Mat. in der Lage sei, als Presbyter zur Kirche zu reden. Das stimmt auch mit der Benützung seiner Arbeit durch Mark. und Luk. überein" (p. 304). In more recent scholarship Schlatter's view on authorship has been abandoned except for the commentaries by Gaechter and Gundry. Paul Gaechter: *Das Matthäusevangelium. Ein Kommentar* (Innsbruck: Tyrolia, 1963); Robert H. Gundry: *Matthew. A Commentary on His Handbook for a Mixed Church Under Persecution*, 2nd ed. (Grand Rapids: Eerdmans, 1994), 609–623. Gundry, however, sees no reason to abandon dependence on Mark because of Matthean apostolic authorship.

[15] Schlatter writes: "Der gemischte Charakter des lukanischen Textes bekommt … eine einheitlichere Erklärung, wenn für Lukas neben seiner besonderen Quelle der Text des Mat. zugrunde gelegt wird." P. 50: "Es ist aber unmöglich, den Bericht des Mat. aus dem des Mark. herzuleiten." Schlatter: *Matthäus*, 237.

[16] Schlatter: *Matthäus*, 664. He goes on to write: "Indem Jesus dies [23:2–3] anerkennt, begründet er die Verwerfung des Pharisäismus durch ein starkes Bekenntnis zur Schrift, wie er auch 15,3 für das Gebot Gottes gegen die Überlieferung der Alten stritt. Der Einrede, der Satz sei judaistisch, Jesus könne ja Jude bleiben, wenn er gegen diese pharisäischen Tendenzen nichts einwende, antwortet der Satz: es gibt im Menschen noch anderes als Gedanken und Lehren, nämlich Wollen und Tat, und hier findet sich das, was Jesus vom Pharisäer trennt" (p. 665). The Matthean community becomes the community that is more faithful to the Jewish traditions than Pharisaic Judaism.

[17] Benjamin W. Bacon: "The 'Five Books' of Matthew Against the Jews," *The Expositor* 25 (1918): 56–66.

[18] Benjamin W. Bacon: *Studies in Matthew* (New York: Holt, 1930).

A further development on the interpretation of the gospel of Matthew as a thoroughly Jewish document was offered by Ernst von Dobschütz.[19] Dobschütz was convinced that Matthew is "ein durch die Schule der Rabbinen gegangener Judenchrist, ein konvertierter jüdischer Rabbi,"[20] possibly of the school of Yohanan ben Zakkai. He was persuaded by the frequent repetitions in the gospel. The stereotypical phrases in the gospel point to the deeper Jewish content that is revealed in the gospel's attention to the Jewish Law and its correct interpretation, and to the institution of Peter as a Christian chief rabbi in 16:17–19. If the universal mission of 28:18 reveals more than Jewish interests it is to be interpreted as a later amendment of a Jewish-Christian source.

With these remarks a trend in Matthean scholarship becomes already visible: With the acceptance of the gospel's dependence on Mark the theory of the evangelist as the Jewish disciple of Jesus becomes much less credible. The Jewish traits of the gospel must be explained differently. Von Dobschütz and Bacon offered a way out of this dilemma by linking the content of the gospel to the atmosphere of post-second-temple Judaism. By placing the community of the gospel into the context of Jewish developments after 70 C.E. the gospel becomes part of what Jacob Neusner much later called "Formative Judaism."[21] This places greater emphasis on the final edition of the gospel than the previous historicizing attempts by Holtzmann, Weiss, or Schlatter. The community of Matthew is thus seen as taking a greater role in the shaping of the Jesus traditions it received.

2. Towards the Beginnings of Redaction Criticism

The hermeneutical shift toward the internal evidence continued to be sharpened. George D. Kilpatrick published the first major study of Matthew since Bacon.[22] In a chapter entitled "The Gospel and Judaism" Kilpatrick contrasted Mark and Matthew sharply. For Kilpatrick, Mark reflects the atmosphere of "Jewish Palestine before the war" while Matthew is much more reflective of the Judaism that worked

---

[19] Ernst von Dobschütz: "Matthäus als Rabbi und Katechet," *ZNW* 27 (1928): 338–348. He is convinced of Markan priority, following the efforts of Holtzmann, Weiss, Jülicher, Wernle, und Wellhausen. Heinrich Julius Holtzmann: *Lehrbuch der neutestamentlichen Theologie*, 2 vols., ed. Adolf Jülicher and Walter Bauer, Sammlung theologischer Lehrbücher. ATLA monograph preservation program 1987–0091. (Tübingen: J.C.B. Mohr (Paul Siebeck), 1911); Paul Wernle: *Die synoptische Frage*, ATLA monograph preservation program 1986–0463. (Freiburg: J.C.B. Mohr (Paul Siebeck), 1899); Julius Wellhausen: *Einleitung in die drei ersten Evangelien*, ATLA monograph preservation program 1986–3594. (Berlin: Georg Reimer, 1905).

[20] Dobschütz: "Matthäus als Rabbi und Katechet," 347.

[21] Jacob Neusner: *Formative Judaism*, 5 vols. (Chico: Scholars Press, 1982–1985).

[22] George D. Kilpatrick: *The Origins of the Gospel According to St. Matthew* (Oxford: Clarendon, 1946).

out its program at Jamnia.[23] Kilpatrick's key argument was the phrase "their synagogue."[24] The phrase is distinctively Matthean[25] and bears witness to the conflict surrounding the development of the *birkat-hamminim*. Kilpatrick suggested almost in passing that this conflict was within Judaism.[26]

The first forceful challenge to Matthew as a Jewish gospel came from Kenneth W. Clark.[27] After the initial statement of his thesis Clark examined several aspects of the gospel in more detail. First Clark pointed to evidence for the expulsion of the Jews from the kingdom. The texts he quoted in support are 8:12;[28] 12:20;[29] 21:43;[30] and 28:16–20,[31] the mission to the gentiles. Other indications were that in 22:41–46 the Messiah is seemingly not the son of David. In ch. 23 there is an outright denunciation of the Jewish leaders, and in ch. 24 judgment is turned against Israel.

Clark went on to consider the supposed evidence for Matthew's Jewishness on two levels: Scripture and the language of the gospel. Firstly he analyzed the scripture quotations. He pointed out that there are quotations as well in Luke and other obviously gentile writings of the New Testament. He attached no significance to the fulfilment formula and suggests that the Hebrew text seems by no means unambiguously the source for Matthew.[32] Secondly, the supposed Jewish language of the gospel cannot stand closer examination. The term "kingdom of Heaven" is not used to avoid the pronunciation of the divine name, since "God" is used profusely elsewhere. Furthermore, Matthew uses the term φυλακτήρια for the prayer tassels, while the LXX consistently uses the term ἀτάλευτον. The Matthean usage reflected for Clark gentile superstition and the magic of amulets. Matthew uses Hellenistic terms for the evil one[33] while other to Clark's mind entirely Jewish authors like Mark and Paul use the Semitic σατανᾶς consistently and exclusively.[34]

---

[23] Kilpatrick: *Origins*, 106. He maintains that the Jewish features of the gospel are not necessarily reflective of earlier sources but could be a re-Judaization of originally gentile material.

[24] It occurs in the gospel 5 times in this form: 4:23; 9:35; 10:17; 12:9; 13:54. Once it occurs as "your synagogues" (23:34). "Synagogue" without a possessive qualifier occurs in 6:2, 5.

[25] Kilpatrick: *Origins*, 110–112. He thinks that the phrase appears outside of Matthew in Mk 1:23, 39 and Lk 4:15 as an assimilation of the textual traditions to the distinctively Matthean idiom.

[26] "It is significant that the attitude to Judaism displayed by the book enabled the community to take over so much from Judaism, and at the same time it radically distinguished the church from the synagogue." Kilpatrick: *Origins*, 123.

[27] Kenneth W. Clark: "The Gentile Bias of Matthew," *JBL* 66 (1947): 165–172.

[28] "But the sons of the kingdom will be thrown into the outer darkness."

[29] "... until he brings judgment to victory..."

[30] " ... the kingdom of God shall be taken from you and given to a people bringing forth fruit"

[31] Especially Mt 28:19: "Go, therefore, and make disciples of all the nations ... "

[32] Clark: "The Gentile Bias of Matthew," 168.

[33] Πονηρός, πειράζων, διάβολος.

[34] As far as Paul is concerned, Clark is mistaken. Paul uses Σατανᾶς (Rom 16:20; 1 Cor 5:5, 7:5; 2 Cor 2:11, 11:14, 12:7), but not consistently: In 1 Thess 3:5 ὁ πειράζων appears. Mark is now often considered a Gentile. His ethnic background is at least a matter of debate.

This is in keeping with the avoidance of other semitic expressions[35] and Matthew's alleged misunderstanding of the terms "Hosanna" and "Golgotha." These misunderstandings reflect an earlier stage in the tradition where the Jewish influence would have been stronger.[36] Clark's merit lies in raising the question and pointing to valid objections against a too easily accepted view of Matthew as a Jewish gospel. Some of his assertions also pre-empt the historicizing views of later redaction critics.

Poul Nepper-Christensen devoted a monograph to Matthew's alleged Jewishness.[37] In a first step he analyzed the patristic evidence. He showed that the patristic sources rely on the statement of Papias who, according to his reporter Eusebius, is of doubtful trustworthiness. The connection between the gospel of Matthew and the statement by Papias is even less credible.[38] This is borne out by the impossibility of showing Matthew to be a translation from the Hebrew. Even the Old Testament quotations are as often different from the Hebrew as they are close to it.[39] Like Clark, Nepper-Christensen did not attach significance to the fulfilment quotations.[40] Similarly, he discounted any typology of Jesus as the New Moses or New Abraham since the Sermon on the Mount develops in antithetical fashion. Neither here nor in the temptation story is Moses expressly mentioned, and the mountain has no greater significance than as a geographical reference.[41] The express command to the disciples to a mission only within Israel (10:5) is offset not only by Jesus' own attention to Gentiles (8:5; 15:21) but also by the final missioning in 28:19. Likewise Jesus' claim to be sent only to Israel (15:24) is somewhat offset by his granting the request of the Canaanite woman. Nepper-Christensen concluded that while the author might have been Jewish, the addressees of the first gospel were not.[42]

---

[35] Βοανέργες, ταλιθα κούμ, κορβᾶν, Βαρτιμαῖος, ῥαββοῦνι, Ἀββα.

[36] Clark concluded that Matthew "was persuaded that the Christian gospel, originally delivered to the Jews, had been rejected by them as a people; that God had now turned his back upon Judaism and chosen the largely gentile Christianity. The two strains of the gospel reflect these two stages in God's plan to save his chosen people." Clark: "The Gentile Bias of Matthew," 172.

[37] Nepper-Christensen: *Matthaeusevangelium*.

[38] Nepper-Christensen: *Matthaeusevangelium*, 35–75.

[39] Nepper-Christensen relies here on the study of Stendahl that appeared in its first edition in 1954. Krister Stendahl: *The School of St. Matthew and its Use of the Old Testament*, ASNU XX. 2nd ed. (Lund: CWK Gleerup, 1968).

[40] He points to the evidence of their presence in the obviously gentile gospel of John: "Man hat also nicht das Recht ... zu behaupten, daß der Erfüllungsbegriff im Matth. etwas über die ersten Leser aussagt." Nepper-Christensen: *Matthaeusevangelium*, 162.

[41] Nepper-Christensen: *Matthaeusevangelium*, 177, esp. n.75.

[42] "Der jüdische Horizont ... enthüllt uns also das jüdische Milieu, dem das Matth. entstammt. Darum also hat man aus dem zweifellos vorhandenen jüdischen Hintergrund des Matth. irrtümlich die Schlussfolgerung gezogen, dass die Schrift für die Juden oder Judenchristen verfasst war." Nepper-Christensen: *Matthaeusevangelium*, 201.

Reuss, Clark, and Nepper-Christensen made important contributions to the contextualization of Matthew's gospel by casting doubt on the alleged Jewish background of Matthew. They did this by asserting that the Jewish material in the gospel must be relegated to a historical period earlier than the final edition of the gospel. For Reuss, this early material was pasted together in a haphazard manner that lets one retrace the Jewish history of the gospel, but not its final relationship to Judaism. Clark thought that the side-by-side of Jewish and Gentile material reflects two stages of early Christianity: a first stage within Judaism, and a second stage after the rejection by Judaism and the acceptance by Gentiles. Nepper-Christensen refers to the Jewish material as a reflection of the earliest stages of the Matthean community, and of the historical Jesus.

However, subsequently the separation of Gentile and Jewish material according to historical layers needed refinement. Had their critical studies so far revealed some glaring contradictions in the gospel that defied a simplistic explanation as the Jewish-Christian background, their solution of a separation of the contradicting material into historical layers was based on a historical-critical view of the evolution of early Christianity. Such an argument, however, is to a large extent extrinsic to the gospel itself. It does not set the individual sayings or pericopes into the greater context of the gospel as a whole. The advent of redaction criticism in Matthean studies opened up new avenues of research. Redaction criticism enabled the researcher to analyze the gospel in terms of its own literary development and rationale for composition by comparing it to its sources.[43] In this way, redaction criticism marked a stricter application of intrinsic arguments.

3. Redaction Criticism Proper and the Background of Matthew's Gospel

The term "redaction criticism" refers to two quite distinct methods of investigation. The first method concentrates on the changes the evangelist made to his sources. Behind this approach stands the conviction that these changes reveal a consistent theological position and a purpose for the writing under investigation. The second method concentrates on the overall achievement of a writer by looking at the

---

[43] G. Bornkamm wrote the first redaction-critical article on the gospel of Matthew. Günther Bornkamm: "Die Sturmstillung im Matthäusevangelium," in: *Das Matthäus-Evangelium*, ed. J. Lange (Darmstadt: Wissenschaftliche Buchgesellschaft, 1980), 112–118; first published in *WuD* (1948) 49–54. In it he remarks: "Wir haben in der neueren Synoptikerforschung gelernt, die Einzelperikope, das einzelne Wort und die einzelne Tat Jesu als die primären Daten der Überliefernung anzusehen ... Man wird jedoch sorgfältiger, als es vielfach bisher geschehen ist, auch nach den Motiven der Komposition der einzelnen Evangelien fragen müssen ... Ohne Frage haben die Evangelisten weithin einfach als Sammler gearbeitet ... Um so wichtiger ist die Festellung bestimmter theologischer Absichten ..." (pp. 116–117).

overall structure, or on sub-units and their placement within a writing. This variation in method is called composition criticism.[44] The redaction of the structure or structures within the writing comprises both incorporation and variation of sources, and thus, it is alleged, reveals the theological stance of the final redactor. Both methods are not exclusive of each other. The two articles by Günther Bornkamm that sparked redaction criticism in Matthean studies cover both methods. While the first article[45] is an exercise on the changes Matthew made to his source, the second[46] is a tour de force covering large parts of the whole gospel.

While redaction criticism forced Matthean scholars to look at the internal evidence for either the Jewishness or the Gentileness of the gospel, it failed to resolve the issue one way or the other. In the following pages, the various redaction-critical approaches to Matthew's gospel are therefore divided up into those that favor a Gentile background for the gospel and/or its author, and those that favor a Jewish environment. Then some mediating positions will be considered. This division will allow for the main arguments on all sides to stand out more clearly. Preceding the exposition of the various solutions special attention will be devoted to Bornkamm as the pioneer of the method.

3.1 Redaction Criticism Proper: Günther Bornkamm

Günther Bornkamm pioneered redaction criticism for the gospel of Matthew with his article on Mt 8:23–27, the storm on the lake. Behind the new method stands the realization that the gospels are not just a collection of sources but exhibit a

---

[44] The term was coined by William G. Thompson: *Matthew's Advice to a Divided Community. Mt. 17, 22–18, 35*, AnBib 44 (Rome: Biblical Institute Press, 1970). Other works that placed an emphasis on composition criticism are: William G. Thompson: "Reflections on the Composition of Mt 8:1–9:34," *CBQ* 33 (1971): 365–388; Peter F. Ellis: *Matthew: His Mind and His Message* (Collegeville: Glazier, 1974); O. Lamar Cope: *Matthew. A Scribe Trained For the Kingdom of Heaven*, CBQ.MS 5 (Washington: The Catholic Biblical Association, 1976); Jack D. Kingsbury: *Matthew: Structure, Christology, and Kingdom* (Philadelphia: Fortress, 1975); David E. Garland: *The Intention of Matthew 23*, NTS 52 (Leiden: Brill, 1979); Jack D. Kingsbury: "The Developing Conflict Between Jesus and the Jewish Leaders in Matthew's Gospel: A Literary-Critical Study," *CBQ* 49 (1987): 57–73; Jack Dean Kingsbury: *Matthew as Story*, 2nd ed. (Philadelphia: Fortress, 1988); Ulrich Luz: *The Theology of the Gospel of Matthew*, New Testament Theology (Cambridge, New York: Cambridge University Press, 1995). The emphasis on the total achievement of a particular writer arose out of the insight that while traditional redaction criticism was important, it ran the danger of concentrating on the changes a redactor made to his/her sources while not taking seriously the material that a redactor would incorporate unchanged from the sources.

[45] Bornkamm: "Sturmstillung."

[46] Günther Bornkamm: "Enderwartung und Kirche im Matthäusevangelium," in: *Das Matthäusevangelium*, ed. J. Lange (Darmstadt: Wissenschaftliche Buchgesellschaft, 1980), 224–264; first published in *The Background of the New Testament and its Eschatology (Studies in Honor of C. H. Dodd)* Cambridge 1956.

theological program.[47] Bornkamm used the pericope of the stilling of the storm to exemplify the theological motivation of Matthew's gospel. His point of departure was the comparison of Matthew with its sources. In a later essay Bornkamm extended the new method by examining large parts of the first gospel in a tour de force.[48] During this investigation he returned to Kilpatrick's view of Matthew's community as Jewish Christian and found support for it in the pericope of the temple tax.[49] He adduced yet another argument for the Jewishness of the gospel with his observation that the Matthean community lacks a structured organization as an individual body with functions and structures distinct from Judaism.[50] Thus Bornkamm concluded that the struggle with Israel in Matthew's gospel is as yet "ein Kampf *intra muros*."[51]

However, even the redaction-critical method did not solve the enigma of the gospel between Judaism and Gentile Christianity. This emerged most forcefully when eventually Bornkamm partially reversed his position on Matthew's relation to Judaism.[52] In the meantime, others grasped the new methodology to argue for Clark's and Nepper-Christensen's thesis of a separation between Matthew's community and Judaism.

---

[47] "Die Evangelisten greifen eben nicht auf irgendein Gemeindearchiv zurück, wenn sie die Worte und Taten Jesu weitergeben, sondern sie schöpfen aus dem Kerygma der Gemeinde und dienen diesem Kerygma. Weil Jesus Christus nicht eine Gestalt der Vergangenheit ist und also ins Museum gehört, kann es für die urchristliche Überlieferung auch nicht ein 'Archiv' geben, in dem sie gehütet wird." Bornkamm: "Sturmstillung," 112.

[48] Bornkamm: "Enderwartung."

[49] "Aber auch die Tempelsteuerperikope (17,24–27), unmittelbar vor der Gemeinderede eingefügt, steht unverkennbar im Dienst seines Kirchenverständnisses. Sie zeigt, daß die Gemeinde, die Matth. repräsentiert, noch im Verbande des Judentums steht und die Besteuerung der jüdischen Diasporagemeinden für sich selbst durchaus nicht ablehnt, sondern anerkennt, freilich im deutlichen Bewußtsein ihrer eigenen Sonderstellung: Jesu Jünger zahlen die Tempelsteuer als die freien Söhne, nur um nicht Ärgernis zu geben." Bornkamm: "Enderwartung," 227.

[50] He writes that "eine Ekklesiologie, orientiert an der Kirche als einer selbstständigen, empirisch umgrenzten Größe, nur in sparsamsten Anfängen zu erkennen ist." Bornkamm: "Enderwartung," 245.

[51] Bornkamm: "Enderwartung," 246.

[52] In 1970, Bornkamm wrote with regard to Matthew 18:19–20 that the Matthean community asserts its independence: "Die 'Rede' Mt 18 erweist sich damit als ein bedeutendes Dokument der spannungsvollen Begegnung hellenistischer und judenchristlicher Traditionen. Matthäus und seine Gemeinde setzen das hellenistische, aus dem Judentum bereits herausgewachsene und auf neuen Grund gestellte Christentum voraus, aber sie widerstehen einem nicht nur vom Judentum, sondern auch von den Geboten des irdischen Jesus sich emanzipierenden Enthusiasmus und verteidigen die Kirche als Jüngerschaft und Nachfolge." Günther Bornkamm: "Die Binde- und Lösegewalt in der Kirche des Matthäus," in: *Die Zeit Jesu: Festschrift für Heinrich Schlier*, ed. Günther Bornkamm and Karl Rahner (Freiburg, Basel, Wien: Herder, 1970), 106. Thus Bornkamm reversed himself on one of the major issues that undergirded his earlier hypothesis of Matthew's as a Jewish community, namely the question of community organization.

3.2 Redaction Criticism Proper: Matthew as a Gentile Gospel

At about the same time that Nepper-Christensen's study appeared, Georg Strecker and Wolfgang Trilling came to similar conclusions.[53] Strecker began by dismissing the external evidence for the Jewishness of the gospel as too tenuous to be reliable. The internal evidence is conflicting, when on the one hand Jesus exhorts his disciples to follow the words of the Pharisees (23:2–3), on the other hand warns them against their teaching (16:11–12).[54] The paradox is intensified by the interpretation of the law, given in the antitheses, in a way stricter than the tradition (5:21–48). But the Pharisees as such are typified as opponents of Jesus, and therefore, 16:11–12 cannot be minimized in its importance. Strecker solved the tension by assigning the conflicting material to different layers within the tradition. The Jewish material of the gospel became part of a developmental stage of the gospel that included some of the Matthean *Sondergut*.[55] Strecker concluded that "die jüdischen Elemente Ergebnis der Gemeindeüberlieferung sind."[56] Matthew's semitisms must be considered part of the tradition of the community and should not be assigned to the latest stage of the redaction.[57]

According to Strecker, Matthew's interest in the law extends only to its applicability as an example for the ethical exhortation of the community.[58] The gospel's attitude to the Gentiles shows that they have displaced the Jews as the chosen people.[59] The evidence for this lies in the Gentile mission of 28:19, and in

---

[53] Strecker points out that the first draft of his work was ready at about the same time as Trilling's and Nepper-Christensen's studies. Georg Strecker: *Der Weg der Gerechtigkeit. Untersuchung zur Theologie des Matthäus*, 3rd edition (Göttingen: Vandenhoeck & Ruprecht, 1971), 15, n. 5; W. Trilling: *Das wahre Israel: Studien zur Theologie des Matthäus-Evangeliums*, SANT 10, 3rd ed. (München: Kösel, 1964).

[54] Jeremias saw this "unconcerned juxtaposition of conflicting traditions" as the major stumbling block of any successful redaction criticism of Matthew's gospel. Joachim Jeremias: *New Testament Theology*, trans. S. H. Hooke (New York: Scribner, 1971), 307, n. 1.

[55] "Die Spannung ist also nicht aufzulösen. Sie erklärt sich aus der traditionsgeschichtlichen Überlagerung. Dies aber weist das judaisierende Element der Tradition zu, ohne daß es noch für den Redaktor charakteristisch sein kann." Strecker: *Weg*, 16.

[56] Strecker: *Weg*, 18.

[57] Strecker: *Weg*, 20–21. Here Strecker follows Kilpatrick: *Origins*, 104–105.

[58] As one example of the ethical re-interpretation of the Law Strecker analyzes the Matthean redaction of 15:20: For Matthew "ist die rituelle Observanz nur noch Kennzeichen der Juden, er selbst lehnt sie eindeutig ab ... Indem Matthäus [23:25–26] Lk 11:40 streicht und in V. 26 redigiert, hat er diesen Gedanken kräftig betont. Der 'Becher' hat nur noch übertragene Bedeutung, als Bild für den Menschen, dessen Inneres gereinigt werden muß, damit (!) sein Äußeres rein wird. Da hier ein finales Verhältnis angedeutet wird, kann das Äußere nicht mehr das rituelle, sondern allein das sittliche Tun umschreiben." Strecker: *Weg*, 31–32.

[59] Strecker admitted Matthean uses of the "jüdisch abwertende Sprachgebrauch" of ἔθνη and ἐθνικός. He submits that these uses refer to unconverted Gentiles and reflect Matthew's sources. Strecker: *Weg*, 33.

the parable of 21:33–46 that offers a consistent working out of its Markan source in terms of salvation history.[60] Strecker concluded that Matthew's "theologischer Standpunkt" is found among the Gentiles. This starting point allows for the Jewish tradition only in as far as it can be absorbed into a now gentile, early catholic world view.[61]

While Strecker separated the Jewish history of Matthew from the Gentile situation of the community, Wolfgang Trilling situated this historical progression within a theological framework.[62] He assumes with Strecker that the Jewish material must be relegated to historical phase of the community. But he went on to explain that the continued interest in this historical tradition is only explainable if the now Gentile community defines itself with the help of these traditions. The gentile community of Matthew now views itself as the true Israel.[63]

Trilling viewed the parable of the tenants in the vineyard (21:33–45) and the account of the proceedings before Pilate (27:15–26) as key passages showing that Israel rejected the mission of Jesus and, therefore, incurred collective guilt.[64] The kingdom is given to a new people,[65] the church takes the place of Israel.[66] Trilling reaches the culmination of his argument with the examination of the two "ecclesia"-passages (16:18; 18:17).[67] Their careful examination led Trilling to

---

[60] Strecker: *Weg*, 33–34.

[61] Strecker: *Weg*, 34.

[62] Later on Strecker develops a deeper appreciation for history as a theological theme in the gospel of Matthew. He sees the time of Jesus at the center of the narrative that looks back upon the time of preparation and looks forward to the time of the church. The time or preparation is shaped by patriarchs and prophets, while the time of the church is characterized by the mission to the Gentiles. Strecker does not explain the exact nature of the interaction between these three times in detail, and thus fails in this scheme to account for the importance of the Jewish controversies in the gospel for the community's present life. See: Georg Strecker: "Das Geschichtsverständnis des Matthäus," *EvTh* 26 (1966): 219–30; English translation: Georg Strecker: "The Concept of History in Matthew," in: *The Interpretation of Matthew*, ed. Graham N. Stanton (Philadelphia: Fortress, 1983), 67–84.

[63] Trilling: *Das Wahre Israel*.

[64] Trilling: *Das Wahre Israel*, 60.

[65] "Irgendein anderes Einzelvolk neben Israel kann aber auch nicht gemeint sein. Welches Volk sollte das sein? So kommt offenbar nur die religiöse Bedeutung in Frage, nämlich ein anderes Gottesvolk als das auserwählte Israel, ein ἔθνος ἅγιον wie in 1 Petr. 2,9." Trilling: *Das Wahre Israel*, 61.

[66] "Weil Jesus nur zu Israel gesandt ist, dieses ihn aber abgewiesen hat, trifft es die Verwerfung, während die Heidenvölker seinen Platz im Reiche Gottes einnehmen werden. Und umgekehrt: Damit Israel unentschuldbar sei und seine Schuld eindeutig festgestellt werden könne, muß Jesus nur zu ihm gesandt sein ... Der Messias ist der *Messias Israels*. Etwas anderes ist für ihn gar nicht denkbar. Das ist nicht eine 'judenchristliche' Tendenz, sondern eine theologische Notwendigkeit." Trilling: *Das Wahre Israel*, 105.

[67] Trilling: *Das Wahre Israel*, 143–163. He comes to the conclusion: "Doch geht die ganze Tendenz [des Matthäusevangeliums] dahin, diese Ekklesia Christi als das wahre *Volk Gottes* zu erweisen und mit ihm zu identifizieren. Wie Gottes Königtum und 'das Reich des Menschensoh-

assume a much less strict division between Jewish Christianity and Gentile Christianity than Strecker. Matthew's community as the true Israel shows that ideologically Judaism is still very much a lively and important part of Matthean Christianity: "Leserkreis und letzter Verfasser legen von einer Geisteshaltung Zeugnis ab, die weder typisch judenchristlich noch typisch heidenchristlich genannt werden kann."[68]

Douglas Hare rejected Trilling's conclusions concerning the community as the true Israel.[69] His main argument rests on his interpretation of the parable of the wicked tenants which Trilling also examined at some length. Hare argued that 21:43, and especially the mention of ἔθνος, is a Matthean addition to Mk 12:1–12. This implies that the kingdom is not transferred from the false Israel to the true Israel, but to "*another people*, non-Israel."[70] This new people is the church which also includes Jewish Christians. However, the new people draws its identity not from Jewish or Gentile affiliation but from its relationship to Jesus as the Messiah and thus defines itself christologically.[71]

It is perhaps the strength of Hare's argument that he can allow for a final redactor who is Jewish. While it was the anti-Pharisaic sentiment that convinced Clark of Matthew as a Gentile,[72] Hare is convinced by the strength of this sentiment that Matthew is a Jew who has followed the Messiah and is at odds with the majority of his nation who has rejected Jesus.[73]

Sjef van Tilborg advanced the study of the gentile bias in Matthew with an in-depth study of one particular issue, the Matthean approach to the Jewish leaders.[74] He treated the leaders not according to their social status as Pharisees, Sadducees, or scribes, but according to the epithets given in the gospel. In this sense the investigation became a counterpoint to a christology of the titles of Jesus. Tilborg investigates in particular the epithets "hypocrites," "evil people,"[75] "liars." He showed that these epithets are introduced by the final redactor. The indictment

---

nes' ineinandergeschoben und sachlich fast zur Deckung gebracht werden, so geschieht es auch zwischen dem Volk Gottes und der Ekklesia Jesu, so deutlich auch die verschiedenen Strukturen dieser verschiedenen Größen erkennbar bleiben" (p. 162).

[68] Trilling: *Das Wahre Israel*, 224.

[69] Douglas R. Hare: *The Theme of Jewish Persecution of Christians in the Gospel According to St. Matthew* (Cambridge: Cambridge University Press, 1967).

[70] Hare: *Persecution*, 153.

[71] "It is in this relationship to the Messiah which marks off the new People of God as distinct from the nation which rejected him." Hare: *Persecution*, 162.

[72] Clark: "The Gentile Bias of Matthew," 166.

[73] "Whereas the Gentile Luke speaks of the synagogue with the detachment natural to one for whom it is a foreign institution, Matthew speaks as one for whom it has only recently become an alien institution." Hare: *Persecution*, 165–166.

[74] Sjef van Tilborg: *The Jewish Leaders in Matthew* (Leiden: Brill, 1972).

[75] He overlooks 22:10 where "evil people" enter into the hall of the wedding feast alongside the "good." This weakens the force of the Jewish leaders being addressed as "evil people." In other places even those who follow Jesus are called "evil people" (cf. 5:10).

through titles is underscored by the emphasis on the leaders' guilt in the passion narrative, while the guilt of the Gentiles is lessened. Matthew must be seen as defending Gentile Christianity and being of Gentile origin himself.

John P. Meier followed up on these arguments with a study devoted to Matthew's use of the law.[76] Meier tried to distinguish between two questions: The first is whether the community of the gospel was or still is Jewish. To this Meier answers negatively and sums up the research up to this point, relying heavily on the evidence collected by Hare. However, for Meier there was a second question that begs for an answer: Was the final redactor a Jew or a Gentile? Meier concluded that Matthew was a Gentile for several reasons.

The first group of arguments could be summed up as mistakes about Jewish religion and institutions. One example, pointed out already by Strecker,[77] is Matthew's supposed misunderstanding of a *parallelismus membrorum* in the quotation of Zech 9:9 in 21:5. There the evangelist introduces two animals because of the "theological purpose of literal fulfilment."[78] Another example is the reference to the Sadducees in 22:23, where Meier read a Matthean misunderstanding of the Sadducean teaching concerning the resurrection. While in Luke and Mark the Sadducees are unmistakably identified as not believing in the resurrection, in Matthew the phrase λέγοντες μὴ εἶναι ἀνάστασιν means, according to Meier, a simple report of "what these particular Sadducees were thinking or saying as they approached Jesus."[79] From this Meier concluded Matthean ignorance of Sadducean traditions before and after 70 C.E. Similarly the reference to "the teaching of the Pharisees and Sadducees" (16:12) betrays a Matthean misunderstanding of the differences between Pharisaic and Sadducaic teaching and doctrine by lumping the two groups together indiscriminately.

A second group of Meier's arguments rested on the fact that Matthean language betrays a less Semitic background than Mark. Meier mentions the omission of εὐθύς, of ἄρχεσθαι with infinitive, and of many Aramaic loan words. Meier admitted that the evidence does not really cut either way.[80] Matthew might have been a Gentile, or he might have been a Hellenistic Jewish Christian. But Meier suggested that a proper distinction between a Hellenistic Jewish Christian and a Gentile Christian can no longer be made.[81]

---

[76] John P. Meier: *Law and History in Matthew's Gospel*, AnBib 71 (Rome: Biblical Institute Press, 1976).

[77] Strecker: *Weg*, 73–75.

[78] Meier: *Law*, 16–17. Meier claims that such a mistake is "much more intelligible in a Gentile redactor than in a converted Jewish rabbi or in a well-educated Jewish-Christian" (p. 18).

[79] Meier: *Law*, 19.

[80] Meier: *Law*, 20–21.

[81] Meier argues this with a reference to Siegfried Schulz: *Die Stunde der Botschaft* (Hamburg: Furche, 1967), 162. Meier: *Law*, 21

3.3 Redaction Criticism Proper: Matthew as a Jewish Gospel

While the new methodology of redaction criticism opened up the possibility of rethinking Matthew's position towards Judaism, arguments for a Jewish context of the gospel were refined as well. Reinhart Hummel relied frequently on approaches developed by Kilpatrick and his teacher Bornkamm.[82] But Hummel believed that contrary to Kilpatrick, the gospel must be viewed as written before the *birkat-hamminim* became part of the synagogue liturgy. The inclusion of the pericope concerning the temple tax (17:24–27) and the explicit endorsement of the payment of this tax was for Hummel a sign "der bewußten Zugehörigkeit zum jüdischen Verband."[83] Matthew's community is most probably developing its own life and identity, but it is still part of the association of synagogues.[84]

William D. Davies tried to place Matthew's gospel within Judaism, following Bornkamm and using his very phrase *intra muros*.[85] Davies approached the problem of the Matthean historical context with a painstaking reconstruction of Judaism in the early years after the destruction of the temple, the Jamnian period. Davies proposed cautiously that "Jamnian Judaism was consciously confronting Christianity" in an attempt at the "self-assertion of a faith determined to survive" after the fall of Jerusalem.[86] This opens up the question whether Matthew too was consciously confronting such a Judaism. Davies found a partial solution to this problem in the Sermon on the Mount as the Christian answer to Jamnia.[87]

Michael D. Goulder related Matthew with the Jamnian movement less directly.[88] He perceived the gospel as something akin to a Jewish midrash that might have been used in a lectionary cycle. But he maintained that Matthew was written before the crisis caused by the *birkat–hamminim* had its full impact. Goulder thought that Matthew "belongs to the Jewry and expects to be persecuted for his heterodoxy."[89]

Shortly after Davies' and Goulder's studies two articles were published that urged greater caution in the appeal to the council of Jamnia and to the *birkat–hamminim*.[90] Both articles point out that the historical data leading to a theory of a council of Jamnia are rather insecure. Jamnia was probably less important to early Christianity than either Davies or Goulder assumed.

---

[82] Hummel: *Auseinandersetzung*.

[83] Hummel: *Auseinandersetzung*, 32.

[84] Hummel: *Auseinandersetzung*, 159.

[85] William D. Davies: *The Setting of the Sermon on the Mount* (Cambridge: Cambridge University Press, 1966), 290, 332.

[86] Davies: *The Setting of the Sermon on the Mount*, 286.

[87] Davies: *The Setting of the Sermon on the Mount*, 315.

[88] Michael D. Goulder: *Midrash and Lection in Matthew* (London: SPCK, 1974).

[89] Goulder: *Midrash and Lection*, 152.

[90] Günther Stemberger: "Die sogenannte 'Synode von Jabne' und das frühe Christentum," *Kairos* 19 (1977): 14–21; Peter Schäfer: "Die sogenannte Synode von Jabne. Zur Trennung von Juden u. Christen im ersten/zweiten Jh. n. Chr," *Jud* 31 (1975): 54–64; 116–124.

Schuyler Brown argued that it was the gentile mission that was the most controversial issue between Judaism and Matthew's Christianity.[91] He maintained that the distinctively Matthean phrase "their synagogues" implies Matthew's community as holding distinct religious meetings without separating themselves consciously from Judaism.[92]

3.4 Redaction Criticism Proper: Mediating positions

Between the two extreme positions of Matthew's relationship to Judaism more mediating positions arose as well. Charles F. D. Moule asserted that the community of Matthew lived so close to antagonistic Judaism that it needed to defend itself against Jewish attacks and in the process came to define itself in Jewish terms. In the end, Christianity becomes the true Judaism as opposed to the false Judaism of Pharisaic tendencies.[93]

Eduard Schweizer first noted that the exclusion from the synagogue that Lk 6:22 alludes to is not present in its Matthean description of more general abuse and persecution in 5:11. This could be taken as evidence that the break was not yet complete.[94] However, this view conflicts with other hints at persecution of a much more concrete nature in 10:23 and 23:34. Thus while the association with Judaism is close, the relationship is no longer *intra muros*.[95]

3.5 Evaluation of the Evidence

It is now possible to evaluate the arguments for and against the Jewishness of the gospel of Matthew. In a first step the external evidence is briefly touched upon. In a second part the internal evidence of the gospel will be examined. The evidence of the redaction-critical methods will be summarized and evaluated. This summary will enable an assessment of the redaction-critical method, its values, its limitations, and ways of going beyond a purely redaction-critical approach.

---

[91] Schuyler Brown: "The Matthean Community and the Gentile Mission," *NT* 22/23 (1980): 193–221.

[92] "The absence in the gospel of any explicit reference to excommunication, even where such a reference is present in a Lucan parallel (Luke vi 22; cf. Mt. v 11), suggests a date before the decision at Jamnia. Furthermore, it would be difficult to believe that Matthew would have allowed a recommendation of Pharisaic teaching (Mt. xxiii 2f.) to stand in the gospel if his community had definitely separated from Judaism." Brown: "The Matthean Community and the Gentile Mission," 216.

[93] Charles F. D. Moule: "St. Matthew's Gospel: Some Neglected Features," in: *Studia Evangelica II*, 91–99. TU 88 (Berlin: Akademie-Verlag, 1964).

[94] Eduard Schweizer: *Matthäus und seine Gemeinde*, SBS 71 (Stuttgart: Stuttgarter Bibelgesellschaft, 1974), 11–12.

[95] Schweizer: *Matthäus und seine Gemeinde*, 36–37.

3.6 Evaluation of the External Evidence

The discussion of Nepper-Christensen showed that the external evidence can be reduced to a judgment concerning the statement made by Papias as reported by Eusebius. But nagging questions remain.[96] Papias reports the title "Gospel according to Matthew" and so presupposes it as known already around the turn of the century. This means that Papias was of the opinion that Matthew ordered the gospel in a Hebrew manner and was its author.[97] However, the title "gospel" as a description of the book about the deeds and sayings of Jesus is perhaps not borne out by the work itself.[98] Even if Papias meant the gospel proper with his phrase τὰ λόγια this might not have been so for predecessors of Papias who handed on this phrase.[99] Thus it is possible that there is a reference to a source that might have been incorporated into the final redaction of Matthew, and the Q tradition might fit this picture.[100] This theory has been proposed already by Friedrich Schleiermacher in a modified form where he sees Matthew as the author of the source of sayings that formed the basis of the gospel.[101]

---

[96] In recent years, Kürzinger and Kennedy have worked to rehabilitate Papias as a reliable source. Josef Kürzinger: "Das Papiaszeugnis und die Erstgestalt des Matthäusevangeliums," *BZ* 4 (1960): 19–38; Josef Kürzinger: "Irenäus und sein Zeugnis zur Sprache des Matthäusevangeliums," *NTS* 10 (1963): 108–115; George A. Kennedy: "Classical and Christian Source Criticism," in: *The Relationships Among the Gospels: An Interdisciplinary Dialogue*, ed. W. O. Walker, TUMSR 5 (San Antonio: Trinity University Press, 1978), 125–155. Fuller discussions of these positions can be found in the commentaries by Luz and Davies and Allison. William D. Davies and Dale C. Allison: *A Critical and Exegetical Commentary on the Gospel According to St. Matthew*, 3 vols., ICC (Edinburgh: T. & T. Clark, 1988–1997), 1:11–17; Ulrich Luz: *Das Evangelium nach Matthäus*, 4 vols., EKK I (Zürich: Benziger, Neukirchener, 1985–), 1:77.

[97] See Luz: *Matthäus*, 1:77. Luz argues that the preposition κατά denotes authorship, since Papias makes the same note about Mark. In the latter case the preposition cannot be understood otherwise since Mark is without apostolic authority and otherwise quite unknown. If one dismisses the note of Papias then one must assume that the gospel of Matthew bore another title earlier in its history. The small time frame makes this unlikely.

[98] The word "gospel" occurs 4 times in Matthew, three times in the phrase "gospel of the kingdom" (4:23; 9:35; 24:14) and once as "this gospel" (26:13). The last occurrence might possibly refer to a book, the other occurrences most certainly do not. Luz argues that this denotes the higher age of the title compared with the gospel in its final form. Luz: *Matthäus*, 1:77.

[99] Davies and Allison: *Matthew*, 1:17.

[100] Thomas W. Manson: *The Sayings of Jesus, as Recorded in the Gospels According to St. Matthew and St. Luke* (London: SCM Press, 1949), 15–20.

[101] "Also muß λόγια in jener Stelle auch so gefaßt werden, und man sieht daraus, daß Matthäus gar nicht ein Evangelium geschrieben hat, sondern nur diese λόγια, und daß es nachher viele an Werth verschiedene ἑρμηνεῖαι derselben gegeben hat. Ob dies nun Übersetzungen oder Erklärungen waren, ist nicht völlig zu entscheiden, aber viel wahrscheinlicher ist, daß ἑρμηνεύειν hier "erklären" heißt." Friedrich Schleiermacher: "Einleitung ins Neue Testament. Aus Schleiermachers handschriftlichem Nachlasse und nachgeschriebenen Vorlesungen, mit einer Vorrede von Dr. Friedrich Lücke," in: *Friedrich Schleiermachers sämmtliche Werke; 1. Abt., 8. Bd.*, ed. G. Wolde, ATLA Monograph Preservation Program 1989–3032 (Berlin: G. Reimer, 1845), 241.

These issues raise questions about an easy dismissal of Papias. Yet even if one discounts all the above arguments the question still remains: How did Papias come up with the assertions he made? If there is any credence at all to the supposition that Papias did not make this up on his own, then he knew of a tradition which saw Matthew as an author for Jews who believed in Jesus. However one may value the patristic witness, it points into the direction of a Jewish background for Matthew's gospel. This, then, turns the argument back even more forcefully to the internal evidence.

3.7 Evaluation of the Internal Evidence

The various internal arguments for or against the Jewishness of Matthew and his community can be summarized in three groups: the language of the gospel, the gospel's familiarity with Jewish matters, and the polemics against the Jews. As will be seen, none of the arguments proves decisive in one or the other direction.

3.7.1 Critique: The Language of the Gospel
As has been seen, some scholars suppose that the Jewishness of Matthew and his community presupposes that the author of the gospel must have been fluent in either Hebrew or Aramaic. Conversely, it is supposed that if it can be shown that the final redaction of the gospel is devoid of any traces of these languages, the author must have been a Gentile.

However, it is treacherous to conclude from Matthew's "good Greek"[102] that he had no knowledge of a Semitic language. Davies and Allison point out that the Greek of Matthew hardly measures up to the polished style of Josephus whose mother tongue was Aramaic,[103] and they assemble an impressive list of Semitisms still found in the gospel.[104] If Matthew is a scribe after the model of 13:52,[105]

---

[102] Most authors today agree that Matthew was written in Greek, and that there is little evidence to support the notion that it is a translation from an original in a Semitic language, be that Hebrew or Aramaic. The language of the gospel is even a "finished Greek" according to Davies and Allison: *Matthew*, 1:25. Matthew's Greek is good only by comparison with, e.g. Mark. However, the Greek of the first gospel is not as accomplished as the style of Josephus. Allen maintains that the gospel's Greek "lacks distinction" and is mediocre. Ward C. Allen: *A Critical and Exegetical Commentary on the Gospel According to St. Matthew*, ICC, 3rd ed. (Edinburgh: T. & T. Clark, 1912), lxxxvi. Davies and Allison agree with this view with some exceptions where Matthew shows "ability to write on occasion accomplished Greek (e.g. 17.24–7)" (p. 1:72).

[103] Davies and Allison: *Matthew*, 1:25.

[104] Davies and Allison: *Matthew*, 1:80–85. Davies and Allison note especially the asyndetic use of λέγει the preference for direct speech, increases in parallelisms, the frequent use of the Genitive. Davies and Allison: *Matthew*, 1:85. See also: Goulder: *Midrash and Lection*, 116–21. These Semitisms lead Luz to state: "Die zahlreichen Berührungen der Sprache des Matthäusevangeliums mit der Septuaginta und mit jüdischen Spracheigentümlichkeiten weisen auf einen judenchristlichen Verfasser." Luz: *Matthäus*, 1:63.

[105] Cope: *Matthew*.

perhaps even in the sense of a city scribe with some learning of literature,[106] he can be expected to have a decent command of Greek. However hypothetical such speculations must remain,[107] the gospel exhibits a command of the language that renders any attempt to identify it as a translation obsolete. On the other hand, this command of Greek does neither exclude this possibility, nor does it lead to the automatic conclusion that Matthew must have been a Gentile. The question behind such criticism is, however, of another nature: Is it necessary to assume that the Jewishness of the final redactor must necessarily be reflected in his or her ineptness in the Greek language? Philo and Josephus, roughly contemporary with Matthew, seem to indicate otherwise.

Thus the argument from the language of the gospel only proves that Matthew had a fair command of Greek. It says nothing about his ethnic background or his religious affiliation.

3.7.2 Critique: Matthew's Lack of Jewish Background

Behind the argument over the language of the gospel stands the larger issue of Matthew's lack of familiarity with a Jewish background in general. Several items in the gospel have been marshaled to make this point. The fact that Jesus seemingly rides two donkeys into Jerusalem (21:7) is certainly odd.[108] It might be an interest in the literal, and thus misunderstood,[109] fulfillment of the scripture quotation of Zech 9:9 that appears in 21:5, as Meier suggests. Meier claimed christological motives for this mistake.[110] He concluded that such a misunderstanding is "much more intelligible in a Gentile redactor than in a converted Jewish Rabbi or in any well-educated Jewish Christian."[111] Since neither the quotation nor the two animals occur in Mk 11:7, the mistake in Matthew reflects on the final redactor.

However, other explanations seem possible. Matthew shows a general interest in the number two. He uses it 41 times in his gospel, Mark only 18 times, and Luke

---

[106] Goulder: *Midrash and Lection.*

[107] Stendahl goes into a similar direction with his postulation of a Matthean school that stands behind the fulfillment quotations and the gospel. Stendahl: *School of St. Matthew.* While it is quite possible that there is a tradition behind the quotations the evidence for such a school as the author of the whole gospel is slim. But however this may be, the gospel itself has knowledge of Christian scribes (see also 23:34), and Matthew builds on the work of such scribes whose work becomes visible behind the fulfillment quotations. See: Luz: *Matthäus,* 1:61, 134–141.

[108] The quotation reads: ἤγαγον τὴν ὄνον καὶ τὸν πῶλον καὶ ἐπέθηκαν ἐπ' αὐτῶν τὰ ἱμάτια, καὶ ἐπεκάθισεν ἐπάνω αὐτῶν.

[109] The quotation of Zech 9:9 speaks only of one animal. However, it is mentioned twice in the form of Hebrew parallelism: "... riding on an ass, on a colt, the foal of an ass."

[110] Meier: *Law,* 17. Strecker assumes that Matthew is unaware of any christological implications of the quotation of Zech 9:9 mainly because he does not make a connection of the riding Messiah with Moses, as later Rabbinic interpretations do. Strecker: *Weg,* 76, esp. n.3.

[111] Meier: *Law,* 18. However, presumably even Gentiles do not ride two donkeys at the same time.

30 times. Occasionally Matthew doubles Markan events or persons.[112] Thus the problem of the two donkeys might be more a question of the number two and less of the odd literal fulfillment. A completely different explanation is offered by Gundry: He contends the phrase ἐπάνω αὐτῶν does not refer to the two animals but to the ἱμάτια that the adoring crowds offer Jesus. The Matthean redaction would be due to a christological enhancement of the scene.[113] Yet Gundry does not provide a solution to the problem. Matthew has just explained that the garments lie on top of both animals. If Jesus now sits on the garments, he still rides two donkeys.[114] On the other hand, Gundry is probably right in asserting that there is evidence for a christological point here.

Firstly, Matthew uses ἤγαγον for φέρουσιν (Mk 11:7) and thus clarifies that the disciples are walking, and that, consequently, Jesus is the only one in the pericope who rides. Furthermore, through the use of ἐπικαθίζω[115] the riding of Jesus resem-

---

[112] See, e.g., 20:29–34 ‖ Mk 10:46–51; 8:28 ‖ Mk 5:2; 26:57–68 ‖ Mk 14:57. Matthew also doubles the healing of the blind man with 9:27–30, and he reports two storms on Lake Gennesareth (8:24–27; 14:24–33).

[113] Gundry goes on to claim: "Though Jesus sat on top of the garments only on the colt, the association of the garmented mother makes a kind of wide throne. Indeed widening the throne to play up Jesus' royal majesty appears to underlie Matthew's importation of a second animal and his knowing breakup of the synonymous parallelism of Zech 9:9." Gundry probably goes too far in assuming, because of a lack of a possessive pronoun, the ἱμάτια of 21:7 to mean not the clothing of the onlookers, but saddle equipment. Gundry: *Matthew*, 409. This exegesis is somewhat doubtful since there is no evidence outside of this pericope to suggest that ἱμάτια could take on the meaning of saddle cloths. They quite probably refer to the outer garments of the onlookers, which does not necessarily invalidate Gundry's point: The phrase then just means that Jesus sat on the cloths. See Walter Bauer, et al.: *A Greek-English Lexicon of the New Testament and Other Early Christian Literature* (Chicago: University of Chicago Press, 1961), 376; Henry George Liddell and Robert Scott: *A Greek-English Lexicon*, 9th ed., with a revised supplement (Oxford: Clarendon, 1996), 829.

[114] Menninger, too fails to account for the cloths lying on both animals. While he is right in saying that Jesus' riding two animals is illogical and fails to account for the common sense of the reader, he highlights the problem rather than solving it. Richard E. Menninger: *Israel and the Church in the Gospel of Matthew*, AmUSt.TR 162 (New York: Peter Lang, 1994), 38. Meier already accounted for the possibility of the second αὐτῶν referring to the garments. Meier: *Law*, 17, n. 101.

[115] See Davies and Allison: *Matthew*, 3:123. The verb is a hapax legomenon in the NT, but occurs in the LXX; Davies and Allison refer to 1 Kings 1:38.44 where Solomon rides an ass to be anointed king. This suggestion relies to some extent on 21:9 where the crowd recognizes Jesus as the Son of David. In Mk 11:9 the shout is considerably different. However, the significance of the parallel with Solomon is somewhat weakened when one considers the other occurrences of the word in the LXX: Rachel riding a camel and sitting on her household idols (Gen 31:34); the uncleanness of everything a ritually unclean woman sat on (Lev 15:20); the flight of David's sons on mules after Absalom had killed Amnon (2 Sam 13:29); David's description of God like riding on a Cherub (2 Sam 22:11); Jehonadab riding with Jehu in a chariot (2 Kings 10:15). Thus the word is attested in the LXX in such a variety of circumstances that the incident of Solomon riding to his coronation should be used with utmost caution to infer a parallel with Mt 21:7. However,

bles an enthronement. Secondly, Matthew parallelizes the action of covering the animals with cloths, and Jesus sitting on them:

καὶ ἐπέθηκαν   ἐπ᾽ αὐτῶν   τὰ ἱμάτια

καὶ ἐπεκάθισεν   ἐπάνω αὐτῶν.

If Matthew tries to make a christological point here, the issue of the two donkeys is not conclusive. To say that Matthew was simply ignorant about the Hebrew *parallelismus membrorum* assumes that he would have chosen to forego his christological emphasis had he known about the rhetorical figure. However, the redaction of the verse shows that Matthew did not just lack knowledge, he had an agenda in shaping this verse: The introduction of the second animal, the creation of his own parallelism, and the description of the disciples walking and Jesus riding into Jerusalem creates a clearer picture of a messianic arrival in Jerusalem.[116] But even if it is conceivable that Matthew did not understand synonymous parallelism as a form of Hebrew poetry,[117] such an opinion does not, by itself, warrant the extension of this judgment to a general lack of knowledge concerning Judaism.

Similarly Meier makes too much of the phrase Σαδδυκαῖοι λέγοντες μὴ εἶναι ἀνάστασιν (Mt 22:23).[118] The Matthean participial construction is one of Matthew's favorite ways of editing Mark.[119] Since Matthew cannot be accused of misrepresenting the Sadducees in this instance, the argument from Matthew's redaction is specious.

Likewise, "the teaching of the Pharisees and Sadducees" (16:12) is hardly an indication of Matthew's lack of knowledge concerning the doctrinal differences between Pharisees and Sadducees. Again Meier must be faulted here for taking the saying out of its context for an interpretation that bypasses Matthew's intentions.

---

notable is the fact that the compound is used only here, and that 19:28 speaks of the Son of Man enthroned with καθίζω + ἐπὶ θρόνου δόξης αὐτοῦ. This formula is repeated in 25:31, again speaking of the Son of Man enthroned for judgment. The combination of καθίζω + ἐπὶ occurs only once more, in 23:2, where it describes the Pharisees sitting on the κάθεδρα of Moses. In all these instances the combination of καθίζω + ἐπὶ denotes a special honor.

[116] Witness the highly significant change in the shouts of the crowd. In Matthew, the people immediately recognize Jesus as the Son of David.

[117] Menninger denies this and tries to show that Matthew knew how to work a *parallelismus membrorum* as it occurs in Hebrew poetry by referring to 5:39–40; 6:19–21; 6:22–23; 7:24–26; and 10:24–25. Menninger: *Israel and the Church in the Gospel of Matthew*, 37. Closer examination of these passages reveals that they are indeed working a closer parallelism than the sources provide. However, a distinct parallelization of two members expressing the same reality is lacking.

[118] McNeile, like Davies and Allison, also draws attention to the fact that some old manuscripts have οἱ after Σαδδυκαῖοι: ℵ² K L Θ 0107 565 *pm* bo arm eth and others. Davies and Allison: *Matthew*, 1:32; Alan H. McNeile: *The Gospel According to St. Matthew* (London: Macmillan, 1915), 320. This article would render Meier's argument obsolete.

[119] See 3:16; 8:23, 25, 27; 13:3, etc.

In 16:1–4 Pharisees and Sadducees appear together asking for a sign from heaven. This pericope is followed by a discussion of the little faith of the disciples (16:5–12) who do not understand Jesus when he talks about the leaven of the Pharisees and Sadducees. In the discussion the leaven of Jesus' opponents becomes the counter-sign to the loaves of the feeding of the five thousand. The object of this discussion remains the little faith of the disciples and their need for greater faith. Matthew's discussion of the leaven of his opponents remains somewhat incomprehensible, which is mirrored in the fact that Jesus and his disciples talk at cross purposes.[120] But the redaction of the ending of this pericope (16:11–12) shows that Matthew himself saw the need to explain at least what the leaven of the Pharisees and Sadducees was: their teaching. As this and the preceding pericope deal with themes of faith and unbelief it is hard to draw the conclusion that Matthew now would make a statement concerning a common doctrine of these groups. It is more probable that their teaching concerns their attitude toward Jesus.[121] And in this they turn out to be united in unbelief.[122] Meier's arguments, however, stretch the text to include a topic that had not been discussed before, and that does not turn up again. Given the context, this stretch is not necessary.

3.7.3 Critique: Matthew's Anti-Jewish Polemics and the Rejection of Israel

More serious redaction-critical arguments against Matthew as a Jewish gospel concern the at times fervent anti-Jewish polemics of the gospel. This question has been approached on different levels. With a view towards contemporary theology Lloyd Gaston claimed that Matthew loses credibility because of his nowadays unacceptable attitude of antisemitism. This antisemitism, so Gaston, is foreign to Jesus. Gaston appealed to Luther's dictum "urgemus Christum contra scripturam."[123] Other writers situate the harsh language in the near or distant past of the Matthean community, or as part of a still ongoing struggle within the community. Simon Légasse noted that harsh language is not only a characteristic of Matthew's treatment of his Jewish opponents, but also of the denunciations of unfaithful community members. The harsh language characterizes Jesus in a prophetic

---

[120] Luz: *Matthäus*, 2:447. Luz, with tongue in cheek, gives a synopsis of the solutions that have been proposed to explain the difficulties inherent in the logical progression from the lack of bread to the leaven of Pharisees and Sadducees.

[121] Davies and Allison note: "Matthew does not here have doctrinal particulars in mind. He is simply thinking of the Jewish leaders as co-conspirators in the plot against Jesus and as partners in the attempt to put the church out of business." Davies and Allison: *Matthew*, 2:592.

[122] "The 'teaching of Pharisees and Sadducees' is no more telling than the 'righteousness of scribes and Pharisees' (5:20) in describing shared doctrine. The only implication is of shared error." Davies and Allison: *Matthew*, 1:32.

[123] Lloyd Gaston: "The Messiah of Israel as Teacher of the Gentiles," *Interp* 29 (1975): 40. Newport calls the accusations against the Jews "indefensible." Kenneth G. Newport: *The Sources and Sitz im Leben of Matthew 23*, JSNT.S 117 (Sheffield: Sheffield Academic Press, 1995), 65.

mode.[124] Graham Stanton has pointed to the possibility that Matthew tries to characterize his community as the one faithful to the traditions, opposing the "majority, unfaithful and rebellious Israel."[125]

The redaction-critical attempts of Strecker, Trilling, Meier, Hare, among others, tried to establish the anti-Jewish polemic of the gospel as an early part of the *Traditionsgeschichte*. Strecker assumed that the antitheses of ch. 5 and their conflict with 16:11–12 proved that the statement concerning the Pharisaic teaching authority (23:2–3) must belong to an earlier tradition.[126] Meier assigned these verses to a layer of tradition that concerned only the earthly ministry of Jesus but became void after the resurrection.[127] Others have held that Matthew composed the verses,[128] or at least incorporated them deliberately. Jeremias saw the rhetoric of irony in these verses.[129] According to Hill, Matthew used these verses in order to underline the subsequent denunciation of Pharisees and scribes in ch. 23.[130] Powell argued that the text reflects a situation in which the Torah is taught orally; believers must learn the Torah not from scrolls but from teaching heard in the synagogue. Matthew's audience is thus exhorted to learn the Torah, but to pay no heed to the hypocrisy of the Pharisees who do not do what they teach.[131]

---

[124] Simon Légasse: "L'Antijudaïsme dans l'évangile selon Matthieu," in: *L'évangile selon Matthieu. Rédaction et Théologie*, ed. M. Didier, BEThL 29 (Louvain: Gembloux, 1971), 417–428. Matthew polemicizes against Christians in 23:8–12; 22:11–14; 13:36–43, 47–50, with references to Christians as hypocrites in 7:5 and 24:51. The latter two texts come from Q; in 7:5 Matthew parallels Lk 6:42; while in 24:51 he parallels Lk 12:46. In 7:5 the reference to Christians as hypocrites appears in Q. In 24:51 the reference replaces a comparison with the "unfaithful."

[125] Graham N. Stanton: *A Gospel for a New People* (Louisville: John Knox, 1993), 150. Stanton sees a parallel with an interpretation of the history of Israel that sees the Prophets as representatives and advocates of the faithful minority against a majority that has left the ways of the Lord. See also Odil H. Steck: *Israel und das gewaltsame Geschick der Propheten*, WMANT 23 (Neukirchen-Vluyn: Neukirchener, 1967).

[126] He writes: "23,3f. ist mit großer Wahrscheinlichkeit ein vormatthäisches Logion, das Matthäus wie das Spruchgut des Kontextes in dem von ihm benutzten Exemplar der Logiensammlung vorgefunden hat." Strecker: *Weg*, 16. Beare leads this argument to its inevitable conclusion by asserting that the saying has no meaning for Matthew. Francis W. Beare: *The Gospel According to Matthew* (Oxford: Blackwell, 1981), 448. Gnilka suggests that the saying is taken over from tradition and receives restricted validity only inasmuch as the Pharisees and scribes teach Moses as true "Wiedergabe des AT oder ihre richterliche Tätigkeit ... Als die öffentlichen Hüter der Ordnung hatten sie Autorität." Gnilka: *Matthäus*, 2:274.

[127] Meier achieves this by comparing 23:2–3 to 10:4–5, where he sees a similar tradition at work. Meier: *Law*, 199.

[128] Gundry maintains that the composition has, "as usual," the antinomians in view. Gundry: *Matthew*, 454–455.

[129] Jeremias: *Theology*, 210.

[130] David Hill: *The Gospel of Matthew*, NCeB (London: Marshall, Morgan & Scott, 1972), 310.

[131] Mark A. Powell: "Do and Keep What Moses Says (Matthew 23:2–7)," *JBL* 114 (1995): 419–435.

The antitheses, on the other hand, are not really abolishing the teaching that has been received; they radicalize it. The antitheses in themselves are not an indictment of the kind of Pharisaic teaching mentioned in 23:2–3. Pharisees and scribes are later held accountable for their hypocrisy (ch. 6), and this same accusation recurs in ch. 23 when Pharisees and scribes are accused of teaching one thing and doing another (23:3).[132] As a consequence the antitheses, and the indictment of scribes and Pharisees in chs. 6 and 23 share both a high regard for the Law and an indictment of scribes and Pharisees as hypocritical teachers. While it is possible, perhaps even probable, to see these passages as material that Matthew received from his tradition, it is less convincing to argue for a concomitant diminishment in importance of these passages. Quite the contrary, if Matthew integrated both the reverence for the Law and the indictment of hypocrites on such a large scale both in the Sermon on the Mount and in ch. 23 it cannot be held that he merely did so out of regard for tradition.

This poses the problem of the possible contradiction between 23:2–3 and 16:11–12 even more forcefully. The latter verses are part of a whole story (16:5–12) that warns against the "leaven of the Pharisees and Sadducees" (16:6) as a danger to the "little faith" (16:8) of the disciples. In Mark's gospel (8:14–21) the story serves as the occasion to reiterate the theme of the disciples' lack of faith.[133] It is prominently displayed and illustrated in the pericope (8:17–18, 21). Matthew redacts the story significantly. He amends the lack of faith to little faith and inserts that the disciples finally understood (16:12). Instead he concentrates on the image of the leaven and moves to explain it. Matthew excises Herod from the story and substitutes the Sadducees (16:6). In vv. 11b–12, which are entirely without parallel in Mark, he repeats the warning against the leaven of Pharisees and Sadducees and explains it as their teaching.[134] However, their teaching in this context might not necessarily be their interpretation of the Law. Just preceding the present pericope Matthew relates how the Pharisees and Sadducees sought a sign from Jesus, displaying obvious unbelief and a malignant attitude towards Jesus.

---

[132] Chapters 6 and 23 are very much related in their common accusations against the Pharisees and scribes. The accusation is only that they do not do what they teach, and Matthew calls them on this hypocrisy. For this reason, among others, Newport sees ch. 23 and the Sermon on the Mount as belonging to the same strand of traditions within the gospel. Newport: *Matthew 23*, 157–176.

[133] In Mark the story is probably redactional. The pericope makes two obvious cross-references. In v. 19 it alludes to the feeding of the five thousand, in v. 20 to the feeding of the four thousand. These references make an independent existence of the pericope unlikely. Joachim Gnilka: *Das Evangelium nach Markus*, 2 vols., EKK II (Zürich, Einsiedeln, Köln, Neukirchen: Benziger, Neukirchener, 1978–1979), 1:309. Furthermore, the mention of the Herodians and the Pharisees together recalls 3:6.

[134] The identification of "leaven" with "teaching" might be the reflection of an Aramaic wordplay between *hămîrā'* (leaven) and *'amîrā'* (teaching). See Athanase Negoita and Christophe Daniel: "L'enigme du levain," *NT* 9 (1967): 306–314.

Thus the leaven which is their teaching is probably, in this context, their scepticism concerning Jesus. As a consequence, the teaching of 16:11b–12 is different from the teaching implied in 23:2–3.[135] Thus it is not necessary to use the contrast between these two sayings to relegate either one of them to a tradition now meaningless to Matthew. He preserved both statements, and both exhibit enough Matthean redaction to prohibit such precipitous judgments. It is likely that Matthew saw both statements as expressing his community's relationship to the Jewish leaders, albeit in different circumstances.[136]

Further redaction-critical evidence can be adduced to buttress the contention that Matthew is still in vivid dialogue with the Judaism of his time. The beatitudes in the Sermon on the Mount contain at the end a reference to persecution and vilification.[137] Matthew reproduces his source Q fairly closely,[138] but does not include the statement of Q that the persecution includes "casting their name out as evil,"[139] perhaps a reference to the expulsion from the synagogue.[140] These verses

---

[135] Davies and Allison maintain that 16:5–12 is about the differences between Jewish leaders and Christians, while 23:2–3 is about what they have in common. For them the two passages are complementary. Davies and Allison: *Matthew*, 2:593. Luz maintains the tension between the two passages without trying to explain it. Luz: *Matthäus*, 2:449–450.

[136] Powell proposes that the issue at stake in 23:2–3 is not the conflict between teaching and acting that leads Matthew to oppose the Pharisees, but their quoting the law (λέγειν), to which the disciples should pay attention, and their interpretation of the law (ποιεῖν) against which the disciples should guard themselves. Powell: "Do and Keep."

[137] Matthew 5:11–12: "Blessed are you when men revile you and persecute you and utter all kinds of evil against you falsely on my account. (12) Rejoice and be glad, for your reward is great in heaven, for so men persecuted the prophets who were before you." It need not be considered here whether 5:11–12 are, in fact, beatitudes, and whether these verses contain one or two beatitudes. A summary of the research can be found in Hans Dieter Betz: *The Sermon on the Mount. A Commentary on the Sermon on the Mount, Including the Sermon on the Plain (Matthew 5:3–7:27 and Luke 6:20–49)*, Hermeneia (Minneapolis: Fortress, 1995), 105–109.

[138] Betz: *Sermon*, 147–153.

[139] Lk 6:22–23: "Blessed are you when men hate you, and when they exclude you and revile you, and cast out your name as evil, on account of the Son of man! 23 Rejoice in that day, and leap for joy, for behold, your reward is great in heaven; for so their fathers did to the prophets." Catchpole offers a cogent analysis of the beatitude in Q 6:22–23 and includes references to other scholarly works. David R. Catchpole: *The Quest For Q* (Edinburgh: T. & T. Clark, 1993), 90–94. He argues, with the majority of Q scholars, that the beatitude entered Q as part of a young stratum because of its use of the second rather than the third person, because of its focus on the disciples rather than a general audience, because of its length and elaboration, and because of its christological focus. He writes: "[Here] the editor allows us a glimpse of a situation within the community of Israel. That situation had developed 'because of the son of man.' What that means is not that other Israelites object to the teaching of Jesus as such ... but that the Son of man is Jesus, an equation established with some effort and care elsewhere in Q" (p. 94). Catchpole interprets the phrase "they cast out your name as evil" as an insult rather than an expulsion from the synagogue. Tuckett basically agrees with the theory of a late development of the beatitude, but offers 6:23c as a gloss, which would make the beatitude itself at least earlier than the gloss. Christopher M. Tuckett: *Q and the History of Early Christianity. Studies on Q* (Peabody:

are a commentary on the preceding beatitude 5:10 which seems to be thoroughly Matthean in content.[141] If this is so, then Matthew has expanded considerably on a theme found in Q. It seems unlikely that such an expansion would be prompted by a reflection on the history of the community without a strong impact of this persecution on the community contemporary with Matthew. Stanton is probably right to suggest that "already at the beginning of the Sermon on the Mount, we sense that the evangelist's community is under great pressure from scribes and Pharisees."[142]

This impression is strengthened by the identification in ch. 6 of hypocrites with Pharisees and scribes. Q described hypocrites who are betrayed by their practices of almsgiving, prayers, and fasting, as examples to be avoided. Only Matthew makes the connection with the Pharisees and scribes to whom he has already drawn attention in the redactional 5:10 and 5:20.[143] This connection is still more drawn out in ch. 23. This redactional activity of Matthew makes an interpretation of these verses in a historical perspective unlikely.

Hendrickson, 1996), 247. Tuckett considers the phrase concerning the casting out in detail, yet in the end does not make a judgment whether it should be assigned to Q or to later Lucan redaction. In any event, Tuckett follows Hare in suggesting that regardless of its place in Q or Luke, the phrase does not imply official expulsion from the synagogue but merely verbal abuse (p. 299). Hare: *Persecution*, 53.

[140] Strecker has argued that this verse reflects on the expulsion of Jewish Christians from the synagogue. Georg Strecker: *Die Bergpredigt: Ein exegetischer Kommentar* (Göttingen: Vandenhoeck & Ruprecht, 1984), 46. However, Betz suggests a form of "social expulsion" more likely, although he remains unclear on the precise implications of such a social ostracism. Betz: *Sermon*, 580. If Q's version indeed refers to an expulsion from the synagogue it is likely that Matthew's redaction is quite significant. However, it is by no means certain that Q referred to an expulsion from the synagogue in this instance.

[141] Benno Przybylski: *Righteousness in Matthew and His World of Thought* (Cambridge, New York: Cambridge University Press, 1980), 80–87; Robert Guelich: *The Sermon on the Mount: A Foundation For Understanding* (Waco: Word Books, 1982), 155–161; Strecker: *Bergpredigt*, 44; Luz: *Matthäus*, 1:200. Arguments are the introduction of "righteousness as a Matthean term and the formation of an *inclusio* through the phrase "theirs is the kingdom of the heavens" that is also found in 5:3. To these arguments general wordstatistics can be added. Davies and Allison: *Matthew*, 1:459. Not so Betz: *Sermon*, 142–145. He sees in this verse the theology of the Sermon on the Mount, but not of Matthew as redactor. He argues with the widely known theme of the persecution of the righteous in the first century and the lack of any connection to the death and resurrection of Jesus.

[142] Stanton: *Gospel*, 150.

[143] Meier: *Law*, 108–119; Davies and Allison: *Matthew*, 498; Luz: *Matthäus*, 1:230. Again claiming coherence with the Sermon on the Mount in general but not Matthean theology, Betz disagrees. Betz: *Sermon*, 191. However, he can not satisfactorily explain the Mattheanisms of γάρ, περισσεύω, δικαιοσύνη. Luz: *Matthäus*, 1:38, 39, 48. Tere are also the parallels with 7:21 and 18:3 concerning the negatively formulated entrance into the kingdom. These formulations lead beyond a restriction to the theology of the Sermon on the Mount.

While the debate may have been lively, the line that decides whether this was a debate *intra* or *extra muros* is much harder to draw. While the beginning of the Sermon on the Mount exhibits interaction with the Pharisees and scribes, this interaction seemingly takes place in the situation of persecution. Thus it is quite possible that Matthew polemicizes against this persecution after the "parting of the ways," as it were.[144] Several passages at least indicate such a possibility. The story of the Centurion of Capernaum (Mt 8:5–13 || Lk 7:1–10) has its origin in Q.[145] Both Luke[146] and Matthew redact the story to a considerable extent. Matthew enlarges Jesus' reaction with material found elsewhere in Q.[147] This redaction culminates with the assertion that "many will come from east and west to sit at table with Abraham, Isaac, and Jacob," while "the sons of the kingdom will be thrown into the outer darkness; there men will weep and gnash their teeth" (8:11–12 || Q

---

[144] Graham N. Stanton: "Matthew's Christology and the Parting of the Ways," in: *The Parting of the Ways A.D. 70 to 135. The Second Durham-Tübingen Research Symposium on Earliest Christianity and Judaism (Durham, September 1989)*, ed. James D. G. Dunn, WUNT 66 (Tübingen: Mohr (Siebeck), 1992).

[145] Catchpole writes that it "is hardly possible to overestimate the importance for Q of this apophthegmatic miracle story and the theology it aims to articulate." Catchpole: *Quest*, 281. There is little debate among Q scholars over the inclusion of the story. Kloppenborg offers a reasonable reconstruction, as do Catchpole (pp. 281–308) and Tuckett. John S. Kloppenborg: *Q Parallels. Synopsis, Critical Notes & Concordance*, Foundation and Facets Reference Series (Sonoma: Polebridge Press, 1988), 48–51; Tuckett: *Q*, 285–86. Catchpole argues that the pericope is redactionally inserted between the blocks Q 6:20–23, 46–49 and 7:18–35. He suggests that the two blocks framing the story of the centurion are heavy with the same christological implications of Son of man and Lord, and show literary links with the centurion's speech. Consequently, Catchpole argues, the story shows that "John's question [in Q 7:18–35], and therefore the christological issue of Jesus as coming one and Son of man, arises directly from what has just happened, namely the miracle described in Q 7:1–10" (p. 281). Catchpole proffers this argument to defuse Kloppenborg's suggestion that the centurion's story is part of a Q them of the displacement of Israel. Kloppenborg argues that the story "is to be seen in the context of Q's polemic against Israel's lack of recognition of the authority of Jesus and his message, and Q's interpretation of Gentile faith as *Unheilszeichen* for Israel." John S. Kloppenborg: *The Formation of Q. Trajectories in Ancient Wisdom Collections*, Studies in Antiquity and Christianity (Philadelphia: Fortress, 1987), 120.

[146] Catchpole argues convincingly, with a discussion of the relevant scholarly literature, that the Lucan reference to the emissaries (7:3–6a, 7a) is most likely redactional. Catchpole: *Quest*, 293–298.

[147] The material is found in Q 13:28–29. Its present place in Matthew owes to the Matthean redaction. Catchpole: *Quest*, 284. Matthew may well preserve the original order of the banquet and the outer darkness, while Luke reverses it. This is suggested by Luke's awkward position of ἐκεῖ (13:28). Kloppenborg: *Formation*, 226–227; Tuckett: *Q*, 194. The saying clearly contrasts the gentiles in the kingdom and the Jews in the outer darkness; Tuckett argues that this saying is one of the instances for the appearance of the displacement of Israel in Q as a theme.

13:28–29). The people from the east and west might be Gentiles, while the sons of the kingdom might stand for the whole of Israel.[148]

But nagging doubts about the judgment on Israel remain: It seems curious that a banquet that excludes the whole of Israel would be presided over by Abraham, Isaac, and Jacob.[149] Furthermore, the only other reference to the sons of the kingdom in 13:38 is quite positive and even less clearly a description of the whole of Israel. Thus even if the saying is Q had originally a displacement of Israel in mind, for Matthew this need not be the case. Matthew places the saying into the context of the centurion's faith in Jesus. Thus for Matthew it is the faith in Jesus which is the deciding issue for the presence at the banquet. By placing the saying of the sons of the kingdom into the context of the faith of the centurion Matthew is able to reassess the condemnation to outer darkness as one primarily based of faith in Jesus and not by a gentile replacement of Israel.

A similar reinterpretation of a Jewish displacement theme seems to be at work in the parable of the wicked tenants (21:33–43). While the parable itself occurs in Mark as well, the crucial v. 21:43 is added by Matthew: "Therefore I tell you, the kingdom of God will be taken away from you and given to a nation producing the fruits of it." This addition has often been taken to imply the rejection of Israel.[150]

---

[148] Trilling writes: "Es scheint sich durch 8,11f zu bestätigen, daß Matthäus eine Endbekehrung Israels nicht im Blick hat ... Der Spruch ist bei Matthäus wesentlich *Gerichtswort*." Trilling states that the verses must be reckoned as redactional because of their contextualization with the Centurion, the phrase "sons of the kingdom," and the heightened literary contrast between those inside and those outside. Trilling: *Das Wahre Israel*, 88–89.

[149] Behind this argument lies the difficulty of deciding what exactly the emphasis of this *logion* is. If it is the sharing of the Gentiles in the kingdom, then the argument stands. Harrington: *Matthew*, 114, 116. However, if the emphasis lies on the judgment, it might be possible to take this saying as a wholesale condemnation of Israel. Luz: *Matthäus*, 2:15–16. Luz argues the pivotal importance of this passage because its phrases recur throughout the gospel. This is certainly true, but they do not recur in the context of the condemnation of Israel: See "the sons of the kingdom" in 13:38 where they are righteous. Thus the phrase does not necessarily refer to the whole of Israel. "The outermost darkness" connected with "weeping and gnashing of teeth" occurs in 22:13 and 25:30, and the latter phrase alone in 13:42, 50; 24:51. All these occurrences are Matthean redaction, yet only 8:12 can be construed as a rejection of the whole of Israel. It seems more likely that it is a condemnation of what is condemned in the other passages, too: the rejection of Jesus.

[150] Jeremias offers a concise statement of this position: "The vineyard is clearly Israel, the tenants are Israel's rulers and leaders, the owner of the vineyard is God, the messengers are the prophets, the son is Christ, the punishment of the husbandmen symbolizes the ruin of Israel, the 'other people' (Matt. 21:43) are the Gentile church." Jeremias: *Parables*, 70. Stanton, among others, sees this verse as "the clearest indication that Matthew's community saw itself as a separate and quite distinct entity over against Judaism." Stanton: *Gospel*, 151. Stanton echoes a long line of distinguished interpreters: Hubert Frankemölle: *Jahwebund und Kirche Christi*, NTA 10 (Münster: Aschendorff, 1974), 247–256; Rolf Walker: *Die Heilsgeschichte im ersten Evangelium*, FRLANT 10 (Göttingen: Vandenhoeck & Ruprecht, 1967), 79–83; Strecker: *Weg*, 110–111; Trilling: *Das Wahre Israel*, 55–65. A review of interpretations and methods is given by Klyne Snodgrass: *The Parable of the Wicked Tenants*, WUNT 27 (Tübingen: Mohr, 1983).

But the difficulties inherent in such an interpretation are obvious: If the vineyard is clearly Israel, the punishment of the husbandmen cannot be the destruction of Israel. The parable distinguishes clearly between the fruitful vineyard and the tenants who do not deliver the fruit to its rightful owner. As a consequence, it is much more likely that the expression ἀφ' ὑμῶν (21:43) refers to Jesus' partners in conversation, the chief priests and Pharisees. They realize that Jesus is speaking about them, and Matthew makes this clear in another redactional addition (21:45). If this is so, the logic of the parable is much more coherent if interpreted as talking about a change in leadership for Israel, not about her complete rejection.[151] Furthermore, this Matthean redaction then appears as a consequent application of a pattern already apparent in Matthew's version of the Baptist's sermon. Matthew reports John's indictment of the brood of vipers who do not bear the fruit of repentance (3:7–10). The sermon is found already in Q 3:7–9. But Matthew introduces the Pharisees and Sadducees as its audience, and puts up with some inconsistencies.[152] As a consequence the sermon of the Baptist is no longer a wholesale condemnation but directed against Jewish leaders. Similar observations can be made for Mt 19:28.[153] Consequently, while Matthew speaks of a people bringing fruit as the new tenants in 21:43, he does not speak of another people but of a different group of people without envisioning another nation.[154] Notable is also that no explicit mention is made of the Gentiles.[155] Rather than a replacement of Israel with the

---

[151] Gundry thinks of the judgment as an eschatological event. Gundry: *Matthew*, 428. Several other authors suggested that the punishment might be an allusion to the destruction of Jerusalem 70 C.E. This is argued with a reference to the following parable of the wedding banquet and Matthew's redactional addition of the king's war against his opponents (22:7). Charles H. Dodd: *The Parables of the Kingdom* (New York: Scribner, 1961), 96–102; Gnilka: *Matthäus*, 2:229; Harrington: *Matthew*, 302; Davies and Allison: *Matthew*, 3:184. In this case, the allusion of the parable would be to the replacement of the Jewish leaders by the Matthean community.

[152] These inconsistencies are pointed out by Catchpole: "The speech as a whole is a call for repentance, a call to baptism. Consequently, Matthew's 'many Pharisees and Sadducees' (v. 7a) do not really fit an audience for the speech, nor do those who have already responded by being baptized (vv. 5–6/Mark 1:5)." Catchpole: *Quest*, 8. Tuckett agrees with this assessment, but points out that the Lucan version of the audience as those come for baptism is equally fraught with difficulties. He concludes that the speech was probably addressed to those refusing baptism altogether, without specifically mentioning that they are Sadducees. Tuckett leaves it open whether Pharisees might have been mentioned in Q. Tuckett: *Q*, 109–116.

[153] The verse occurs also in Q 22:30. Yet it is probably no longer possible to infer it precise meaning in Q. Catchpole sees it in the context of a mission to Israel. Catchpole: *Quest*, 290. Tuckett merely asserts that those with Jesus will be judges over Israel. Tuckett also follows Kloppenborg in thinking that the Q version comprises Lk 22:28–30. Tuckett: *Q*, 163; Kloppenborg: *Formation* 164–165.

[154] Harrington: *Matthew*, 303. Matthew uses ἔθνος as a description for the Gentiles usually in the plural. In the singular it occurs only here and in 24:7 where it clearly denotes a nation, but not Gentiles. Harrington's interpretation can only be accepted with this caution.

[155] Anthony J. Saldarini: *Matthew's Christian-Jewish Community* (Chicago, London: University of Chicago Press, 1994), 243 n. 58. These difficulties have lead Ernst Lohmeyer to

Gentiles the passage suggests a replacement of the Jewish leaders with the church and Christ as the cornerstone (21:42).[156] The parable can be coherently interpreted without an appeal to Gentiles. The new tenants are the disciples of Jesus, the Matthean community.

A similar point can be made for the following parable of the wedding banquet (22:1–14 || Lk 14:15–24). In Matthew's version of the parable two sets of servants are sent with an invitation to the feast. The punishment meted out to those persecuting the second servants is sometimes interpreted as the rejection of Israel.[157] But again some arguments give pause: Matthew's redaction subtly shifts the focus from Q's emphasis on the disenfranchised who finally participate at the banquet (Lk 14:22) to a question of power and authority. Matthew's version of the banquet is a wedding feast given for the son of the king (22:2).[158] Matthew thereby introduces a christological sub-text into the parable that makes the response a response to the message of Jesus.[159] Concomitant with a christological emphasis is the expansion on the violent nature of the response to the invitation,[160] a close connection with the story of the wicked tenants. The difference between those who refuse to come and those who attend is not their status as subjects of the king but merely their obedience to the king.[161] This throws sufficient doubt on the proposition that

---

interpret the vineyard as the Temple and cult. Ernst Lohmeyer: "Das Gleichnis von den bösen Weingärtnern (Mark 12:1–12)," *ZSTh* 18 (1941): 242–259. He abandoned this interpretation in his commentary since the context of the parable did not lend itself for such an interpretation.

[156] Stanton suggests that the cornerstone should be interpreted as the people to whom the vineyard is given, namely the church. This interpretation has much to recommend it. However, it does not, as Stanton thinks, imply the rejection of Israel. Its consequence would be the replacement of the leaders with the church. But the vineyard would remain Israel. Stanton: *Gospel*, 151–152.

[157] Stanton argues that the first set of servants refers to the prophets while the second set refers to the rejected cornerstone by invoking the language of 21:39. Stanton sees in the punishment meted out to those persecuting the second set of servants the theme of rejection of Israel reiterated. The verse is comparable to the punishment promised in 23:34. Stanton: *Gospel*, 153.

[158] Gundry suggests that Matthew changes from the poor, crippled, lame and blind found in the Lucan version for a simple reason: "Matthew has thrown the city to the flames and can no longer write of such beggars; so he generalizes ..." Gundry: *Matthew*, 438. This ingenious argument cannot convince: Would not the mass destruction of a city produce more destitute than any banquet hall could hold?

[159] Overman: *Church and Community*, 300.

[160] Tuckett: *Q*, 146–147.

[161] The exact nature of the version in Q is difficult to ascertain. In Luke the servants finally go outside the city for guests who are not citizens. This can be read as an inclusion of Gentiles. Matthew does not report the outward movement, and thus all are subjects of the king. However, the general disagreement of the vocabulary between Matthew and Luke makes it quite difficult to establish Q's version. These differences have led some to dismiss the presence of this parable in Q entirely, although the agreement in plot and some verbal agreement suggest that the parable was present in Q. Kloppenborg: *Q Parallels*, 166.

Matthew has a division between Israel and the Gentiles in view.[162] The parable does not explain the Gentile part of the church but the mixed reception accorded to Jesus by Israel.[163] The parable of the vineyard and the parable of the great banquet are indeed as parallel as Stanton suggests, but their theme is not the rejection of Israel. It is a warning to the leaders of Israel to whom the parable is addressed (21:45; 22:1). Matthew uses this parable to connect a number of different themes: Those invited first reject the invitation to join the feast in honor of the son, just as they killed the son in the preceding parable. The Jewish leaders reject the ministry and message of Jesus. By this rejection they bring upon themselves the wrath of the king who destroys their city.[164]

Another example that illustrates the supposed anti-Jewish polemic of Matthew can be found in the last woe of ch. 23. This chapter contains some of the most vitriolic attacks against Pharisees and scribes of the whole gospel and suggests many problems concerning its compositional tradition.[165] There is little doubt that

---

[162] For Saldarini this is the decisive argument against the rejection of Israel in this passage: "If the king is understood as God, then the people invited are Israelites." A strong support for this view comes from the fact that the Gentiles are not mentioned as such in this parable. Saldarini: *Matthew's Christian-Jewish Community*, 63.

[163] Harrington: *Matthew*, 308.

[164] Overman concludes: "This important passage [of the destruction of the city] is only in Matthew. It is clearly a thinly veiled reference to the first revolt against Rome, the destruction of Jerusalem, and the anger of the foreign rulers. Matthew connects the revolt, the destruction of Jerusalem, and the wickedness of local leaders with the death of Jesus ... The same reckless tenants who killed Jesus are related to those leaders who opposed the foreign king, brought about Jerusalem's destruction, and now oppose Judaism." Overman: *Church and Community*, 300–301. Overman thinks that the king of the parable is identical with the Roman imperial power. This, to my mind, cannot convince, simply because of the introduction of the son's wedding feast. However, Overman might be correct in supposing an allusion to the burning of Jerusalem in 22:7. See also: Harrington: *Matthew*, 306; Gnilka: *Matthäus*, 2:239. Gundry opposes this because according to 28:19 Jesus sends the disciples onto the Gentile mission directly after the resurrection, whereas if the present passage were to reflect the destruction of Jerusalem such a mission would be possible only after the destruction of Jerusalem. This seems to be an over-interpretation of the parable from his perspective of the writing of the gospel before the war of 65–70 C.E. Gundry: *Matthew*, 437.

[165] Newport offers a review of the prevalent scholarship on the compositional theories of ch. 23. He himself argues that the chapter, together with the Sermon on the Mount, was almost entirely composed previous to the final redaction of the gospel. In order to make this suggestion plausible Newport abandons the two source hypothesis and suggests that Q, whether it existed or not, had no influence on the composition of ch. 23. Newport: *Matthew 23*, 15–61. Newport's assessment is largely dependent on his view that the *Sitz im Leben* of ch. 23 is entirely different from Matthew's gospel in its final stage. He assumes a Jewish community for ch. 23, while positioning the gospel itself in a Gentile context. Yet Newport fails to explain why a document so different from the overall purpose of the gospel would be incorporated in the first place. His argument is too weak to dismiss the two source hypothesis entirely.

ch. 23 incorporates a number of sayings also found in Q,[166] perhaps already as a block within Q, especially the material that now occurs in Lk 11. However, one might agree with Davies and Allison who "despair of reconstructing a common Q source."[167] Others have attempted such reconstructions, yet with widely divergent results.[168] For the present purposes it is sufficient to note that the vituperative language used by Matthew was already present to some extent in the sources. This is particularly true for the woes. The use of this kind of language in both Q and Matthew, as well as in Luke, only emphasizes the conventional nature of the polemic[169] branding those heaped with invective as "opponents, and such things should be said about them."[170] The nature of the invective rhetoric of ch. 23 in itself is not a sure sign of a parting of Matthew's Christianity from Judaism.

The last woe (23:29–36) is especially harsh in its vilification of the opponents. They are likened to those who killed the prophets before them (23:30) to whom "prophets and wise men and scribes" (23:34) are sent, only to be persecuted and killed. But retribution will "come upon this generation" (23:36). The forms of persecution recall 22:6, and the parallel is without doubt intended.[171]

The variation in wording between Matthew and Lk 11:47–51 is so considerable that certainty about its version in Q remains elusive. Yet the woe is redacted to address Pharisees and scribes (23:29). Similarly, the warning against the impending wrath is one that is issued to the Pharisees and scribes (23:35). Almost as an

---

[166] The parallels with Luke are extensive throughout the chapter: v. 4 || Lk 11:46; vv. 6–7a || Lk 11:43; 20:46; v. 11 || Lk 22:26 || Mk 9:35, 10:43–44; v. 12 || Lk 14:11, 18:14; v. 13 || Lk 11:52; vv. 23–24 ||Luke 11:42; vv. 25–26 || Lk 11:39–41; vv. 27–28 || Lk 11:44; vv. 29–43 || Lk 11:47–48.

[167] Davies and Allison: *Matthew*, 3:283.

[168] It is easily recognized that Matthew assembled a number of sayings also found in Lk 11. This consists of the material of the woes. Thus it is possible that the material in Lk 11 was originally of one section in Q, which Matthew then amplified with other Q material. But the differences between Mt 23 and Lk 11 are great as well. Two of Matthew's woes do not appear in Luke at all (vv. 15–23), and Luke's parallel to Matthew 23:25–26 is not a woe. Furthermore, even in the common material there is a significant divergence of wording and order. Despite these difficulties attempts at a reconstruction of Q based on Lk 11 have been made. Gnilka: *Matthäus*, 2:282; James M. Robinson: "The International Q Project Work Sessions 12–14 July, 22 November 1991," *JBL* 111 (1992): 504–505. Kloppenborg not only offers a reconstruction but also a tradition history behind the development: stage 1 included 11:42, 39–41; stage 2 consists of the addition of 11:43, and stage 3 adds 11:44, 47–48, 52. Kloppenborg: *Formation*, 139–147. Catchpole follows Kloppenborg in discerning a tradition history. Catchpole: *Quest*, 256–279.

[169] This has first been emphasized by Johnson through a considerable array of parallels in Greco-Roman literature. Davies and Allison repeat the argument and add to its force through a considerable body of parallels found in Jewish sources. Luke T. Johnson: "The New Testament's Anti-Jewish Slander and the Conventions of Ancient Polemic," *JBL* 108 (1989): 419–441; Davies and Allison: *Matthew*, 3:258–260.

[170] Luke T. Johnson: "The New Testament's Anti-Jewish Slander and the Conventions of Ancient Polemic," *JBL* 108 (1989): 441.

[171] Stanton: *Gospel*, 154.

afterthought the judgment is then said to come upon "this generation."[172] The context suggests that "this generation" is not suddenly the whole of Israel,[173] which does not have a place in the attack against Pharisees and scribes. It is rather a reference to the Pharisees and scribes still under attack.[174] It could well be an allusion to the destruction of Jerusalem again.[175] The judgment itself does not necessarily imply total rejection. Furthermore, the judgment is brought about by the guilt and murder of the Pharisees and scribes.

The final saying that will be examined here is the cry of all the people that Jesus' blood be on them and their children (27:25). It is a verse crucial for the interpretation of the gospel and has been held responsible for the Christian charge of Jewish responsibility for the death of Jesus.[176] The verse echoes the language of 23:35.[177] In its present form it contains some of Matthew's favorite language.[178] The verse has no parallel in the other synoptic gospels. The probability that Matthew composed this verse is high, and the care with which the verse is integrated into the surrounding narrative suggests that Matthew wanted to make a point here: Pilate washes his hands, proclaims his innocence, and asks the crowd to take charge themselves (27:24). They do just that by answering in unison (πᾶς ὁ λαός) in a solemn formulation in which they seem to condemn themselves.[179] At last here the

---

[172] Similar warnings to "this generation" are issued in 11:16; 12:39, 41–42; 16:4; 17:17; 24:34. In these references the phrase refers to the direct opponents of Jesus in the narrative, not to the whole of Israel.

[173] Against e.g. Gnilka: *Matthäus*, 2:302. Gnilka claims that "der bereits bekannte Begriff richtet sich immer auf Israel." It might be argued that this is so for 11:16, though there the reference is much too indistinct to be certain. In 12:39, 41–42 the saying concerning "this generation" which is "evil and adulterous" is directed against Pharisees and scribes and not the whole of Israel. In 16:4 the saying is directed against Pharisees and Sadducees who cannot interpret the signs of the times. In 17:17 the epithet is addressed to the man who brings his son to Jesus after the disciples failed to heal him. The "faithless and perverse generation" is not specified. Is it the disciples who could not heal for lack of faith (17:19)? Thus Gnilka's argument falls apart. "This generation" cannot mean unequivocally Israel only.

[174] Gundry: *Matthew*, 472.

[175] Gnilka: *Matthäus*, 2:302; Harrington: *Matthew*, 328–329. Harrington suggest that the rhetoric of this passage is of a prophet speaking within and to his people Israel.

[176] Karl Heinz Rengstorf: *Kirche und Synagoge: Handbuch zur Geschichte von Christen und Juden I* (Stuttgart: Klett, 1968), 33–34; Joseph A. Fitzmyer: "Anti-Semitism and the Cry of 'All the People' (Mt 27:25)," *TS* 26 (1965): 668; Vincent Mora: *Le refus d'Israël. Matthieu 27,25*, LeDiv 124 (Paris: Cerf, 1986).

[177] Mt 23:35a reads: ὅπως ἔλθῃ ἐφ' ὑμᾶς πᾶν αἷμα δίκαιον ἐκχυννόμενον ἐπὶ τῆς γῆς. Matthew 27:25b reads: τὸ αἷμα αὐτοῦ ἐφ' ἡμᾶς καὶ ἐπὶ τὰ τέκνα ἡμῶν. Mt 23:35 has a remote parallel in Lk 11:50–51.

[178] The phrase ἀποκριθεὶς ... εἶπεν and the word πᾶς. Gundry: *Matthew*, 565.

[179] According to Luz, "Matthew 27:25 is a case of staged dogmatics" that clarifies the final rejection of Israel as it stands self-condemned. Luz: *Theology*, 135.

"transferral of the kingdom from the Jewish people to the church"[180] seems accomplished.[181]

The argument for the final rejection of Israel in this verse hangs on several issues. Firstly, the question remains whether Matthew wanted to construct a theological statement here, or whether he uses λαός interchangeably with ὄχλος.[182] Probably the change from the repeated use of ὄχλος in the preceding material to λαός in 27:25 has some significance. The whole weight of the verse in recalling 23:35 seems to suggest this. If this is so, then the primary objective of this change would be the underlying irony in the fulfillment of the prophecy in 23:35 and the acceptance of the punishment in 27:25 through the destruction of Jerusalem in the year 70.[183] But if this is the primary sense of the verse, then the question of complete repudiation by and rejection of Israel recedes into the background.[184] It is not necessary to postulate synonymity between λαός and ὄχλος to suggest that the theme of ultimate rejection of Israel is not present in 27:25. It suffices to see this verse as a possible explanation for the destruction of Jerusalem that Matthew here and elsewhere connects with the death of Jesus. The verse can be interpreted quite literally: The guilt for the execution of Jesus brought down his blood on the Jews before Pilate in the destruction of Jerusalem. The absence of a complete repudiation of Israel in the rest of the gospel suggests this interpretation.

---

[180] Gundry: *Matthew*, 565.

[181] Frankemölle: *Jahwebund und Kirche Christi*, 210–211; Strecker: *Weg*, 116–117; Gnilka: *Matthäus*, 2:458–459, see this verse in combination with 21:43 as a loss of Israel's prerogatives in salvation history. Israel is replaced by the church. Trilling: *Das Wahre Israel*, 72–73, sees the verse as a *theologoumenon* that preserves the possibility of historicity. It is not quite clear how it is possible that Matthew on the one hand means "das auserwählte, heilige Bundesvolk als solches" and on the other hand implies that they all congregated in the space outside the praetorium. These positions imply that Matthew shifts deliberately from an amorphous crowd (ὄχλος in 27:15, 20, 24) to the whole of Israel (πᾶς ὁ λαός). See McNeile: *Matthew*, 413.

[182] The latter has been argued by Saldarini: *Matthew's Christian-Jewish Community*, 32–33. He suggests that the term "people" is not a term that is used unequivocally by Matthew. He suggests that in many passages "people" refers to those ruled by Jewish leaders (e.g. 2:4; 21:23; 26:3, 47; 27:1). At the beginning of the gospel the term is used to denote Israel "in a possibly theological sense" (1:21; 2:6; 4:16, 23). None of the passages cited by Saldarini is completely convincing, however. Harrington: *Matthew*, 392. It seems more probable that when Matthew uses "people" he has in view more than just the crowd in attendance, or the people ruled by Jewish leaders. For example, it seems unlikely that Matthew would use the term in two different senses within the space of one pericope as the analysis of Saldarini would assume for 2:4 and 2:6.

[183] Harrington: *Matthew*, 392–393; Saldarini: *Matthew's Christian-Jewish Community*, 33.

[184] This relieves also of contortions to explain that in this phrase really the leaders are meant, not Israel as a whole: "Thus Matthew excoriates an actual political and social segment of Jerusalem, not the people of Israel as a symbolic whole ... 'All the people' in 27:25 is not a term burdened with salvation-historical weight, but a social and political description of the main body of Israel associated with the center: Jerusalem and its leadership." Saldarini: *Matthew's Christian-Jewish Community*, 33.

The theme of the rejection of Israel can be proposed only in the context of the turn to the Gentiles. The key reference for this is the great commission to the disciples at the end of the gospel (28:16–20).[185] The crux of the interpretation is the phrase πάντα τὰ ἔθνη of v. 19b. The question is whether this phrase must be interpreted as "all the Gentiles" or as "all the nations" including Jews.[186] The question is not so much, then, whether the Gentiles are included or not. They are. But if "all the Gentiles" is the correct translation the gospel takes a turn from the mission that excludes the Gentiles (10:5) to a mission that excludes the Jews.[187] If "all the nations" are meant, the gospel would then conclude with an inclusion of the Gentiles that has been prepared in earlier pericopes: the Gentile magi who are the first to worship Jesus (2:11), the Gentile women and man in the genealogy of Jesus (1:2–16), the centurion of Capernaum (8:5–13), the Canaanite woman (15:21–28).[188]

Matthew uses ἔθνος in both singular[189] and plural,[190] and in the adjectival form.[191] In some instances the word becomes clearly pejorative as a reference to outsiders who do not know how to pray (6:7) or love their enemies (5:47), and who have base cares about their livelihood (6:32). Saldarini points out that this use is similar to the Greeks' pejorative use of this word for non-Greeks or ill-mannered

---

[185] For further discussions of the sources, structure and christology of the passage see: Gerhard Friedrich: "Die formale Struktur von Mt 28, 18–20," *ZThK* 80 (1983): 137–183; Benjamin J. Hubbard: *The Matthean Redaction of a Primitive Apostolic Commissioning: An Exegesis of Matthew 28:16–20*, SBL.DS 19 (Missoula: Scholars, 1974); Jack D. Kingsbury: "The Composition and Christology of Matt 28:16–20," *JBL* 93 (1974): 573–584; Joachim Lange: *Das Erscheinen des Auferstandenen im Evangelium nach Matthäus. Eine traditionsgeschichtliche und redaktionsgeschichtliche Untersuchung zu Mt 28, 16–20* (Würzburg: Echter, 1973); Bruce J. Malina: "The Literary Structure and Form of Matt. XXVIII. 16–20," *NTS* (1970); Jane Schaberg: *The Father, the Son, and the Holy Spirit. The Triadic Phrase in Matthew 28:19b*, SBL.DS 31 (Chico: Scholars, 1982); Jean Zumstein: "Matthieu 28:16–20," *RTL* 22 (1972): 14–33.

[186] Hare and Harrington argue the former, Meier argues the latter. Douglas R. Hare and Daniel J. Harrington: "'Make Disciples of All the Gentiles' (Mt 28:19)," *CBQ* 37 (1975): 359–369; John P. Meier: "Nations or Gentiles in Matthew 28:19?" *CBQ* 39 (1977): 94–102.

[187] Already Weiss proposed that "der Befehl 10,5f. ist also nicht bloß erweitert ... sondern zurückgenommen ..." because the story of the watch at the tomb shows the complete rejection of the resurrection by the whole of Israel. Weiss: *Das Matthäus-Evangelium*, 508. So also Walker: *Die Heilsgeschichte im ersten Evangelium*, 111–113; Lange: *Erscheinen*, 302–305. Walker sees the main argument in the perceived opposition to παρὰ τοῖς Ἰουδαίοις in 28:15. Harrington seems to fudge on the issue in his commentary. He still argues that the phrase needs to be translated as "Gentiles," and he acknowledges the implication of the exclusion of Jews. But this cannot be synchronized with his assertion that the gospel is written for and within a Jewish community. Thus his assertion that church and synagogue are only "on the way to separation" cannot convince. Harrington: *Matthew*, 416.

[188] Gundry: *Matthew*, 595.

[189] In 21:43 and twice in 24:7.

[190] In 4:15; 6:32; 10:5, 18; 12:18, 21; 20:19, 25; 24:9, 14; 25:32; 28:19.

[191] In 5:47; 6:7.

and uneducated folk.[192] Matthew uses the word sometimes to simply refer to non-Jews without any value judgment (10:5). Sometimes it is not quite clear whether Matthew refers with this term to Gentiles or to all nations including the Jews (10:17; 24:7). In 20:25 Matthew opposes the "rulers of the nations" who lord it over their subjects with a model of service (20:26–27). In this passage ἔθνη does not fit into the Jew-Gentile opposition but refers more to opposition between the "insiders and outsiders vis-à-vis Matthew's group."[193] This makes an interpretation of 28:19 as referring only to Gentiles unnecessary. A further note on the translation as "all the Gentiles" might illustrate this point. If indeed the phrase were to be translated thus, does it invalidate the earlier mission to the house of Israel (10:5)? This seems unlikely since the mission to Israel appears as only the beginning of the mission to the nations even in ch. 10 (εἰς μαρτύριον αὐτοῖς καὶ τοῖς ἔθνεσιν 10:18).[194] Consequently, with 28:19 the restrictive mission to the house of Israel (10:5) is finally over. Matthew now includes everyone as the addressee of the mission of the disciples: the Gentiles, who have throughout been a part of Matthew's story, but also Israel.

3.8 Summary: The Redaction-Critical Evidence

It is now possible to summarize some of the results which the redaction-critical scepticism concerning Matthew as a gospel of a Jewish community of believers in Jesus has brought to light. The features of the gospel emphasizing a turn toward the Gentiles have been brought out quite clearly. The assumption that Matthew was a Palestinian Jew composing a gospel for a Palestinian audience has been sufficiently undermined so that the Jewish character of the gospel can no longer be naively assumed. The conflicts of Matthew's Jesus with some Jews have been highlighted, and these conflicts are acrimonious enough to warrant careful attention in assessing the social setting of the gospel.

The attempt to isolate the Jewish material of the gospel and assign it to an early level of the tradition behind the gospel has, in my view, failed. Consistently it has been shown that Matthew redacts his sources with some care even in the passages dealing with Jewish material. The attention given to the last beatitude, the consistent treatment of the opponents of Jesus as hypocrites, the redaction of the story of the Centurion of Capernaum, the evil tenants and the wedding banquet, all exhibit considerable reworkings by the final redactor. In these, Matthew deals with material concerned with the place of Jews in the kingdom. This Matthean sensibility makes it impossible to relegate such material simply to tradition. The tradition that Matthew received is worked to his purposes. The only valid conclusion is that this

---

[192] Saldarini: *Matthew's Christian-Jewish Community*, 79.
[193] Saldarini: *Matthew's Christian-Jewish Community*, 80.
[194] Gnilka: *Matthäus*, 2:508: "Der Auftrag zu gehen hebt die Einschränkung auf Israel (10, 5b) auf, besagt aber nicht den ausdrücklichen Ausschluß Israels."

material still interests Matthew. A characterization of the Matthean community as Gentile with some old roots within Judaism has to bypass this evidence. Similarly, much speaks for the assumption that the final redactor was quite familiar with Jewish issues, arguments, and sensibilities. This cannot be used to dismiss the difficulties presented by, e.g., 16:12 or 27:24. These verses speak of a deeply rooted conflict between Matthew and at least some Jews. Yet it is possible to incorporate these statements into an interpretation of the gospel as a Jewish-Christian writing.

Some of the most biting rhetoric in the gospel is reserved for Jewish leaders. Consistently they turn up as people who do not understand, who want more signs, who attack Jesus, and who are finally responsible for his death. Redaction-critical examination reveals how Matthew has sharpened these conflicts and added to them. But while the distinction between disciples and opponents in the gospel is quite sharp, it is much harder to discern whether this distinction can be drawn along the dividing line between Jews and Gentiles. While Matthew does not spare words in castigating Jewish leaders, it must remain open whether he actually saw those leaders as representative of the whole of Israel. Much of the criticism of these leaders revolves around their hypocrisy of not doing what they say (ch. 23) and thus proving to be false leaders (15:14).

The issue of a Jewish or Gentile audience for the gospel of Matthew shows the limitations of redaction criticism quite clearly. While the method can approximate themes and topics in the gospel, it needs to be amplified with a methodology that helps in reconstructing the social setting of the gospel. Redaction criticism needs, by its very nature, to stay close to the text in the examination of older and newer material that make up the present text. But the reconstruction of a community needs other tools as well. Attempts have been made to amplify redaction criticism with narrative approaches.[195] Occasionally these attempts try to tackle directly the issue

---

[195] Thompson argues that the redaction-critical method cannot just work with individual pericopes but must take into account the place of the pericopes within the overall narrative of the gospel. He called this approach "composition criticism." Thompson: *Matthew's Advice*. It is the first inkling of what later has been called "narrative criticism." Pioneering studies of narrative criticism are: Jack D. Kingsbury: "The Figure of Jesus in Matthew's Story: A Literary-Critical Probe," *JSNT* 21 (1984): 3–36; Kingsbury: *Matthew as Story*. A later sub-category of narrative criticism is "reader-response-criticism." Richard A. Edwards: *Matthew's Story of Jesus* (Philadelphia: Fortress, 1985); Richard A. Edwards: *Matthew's Narrative Portrait of Disciples. How the Text-Connoted Reader is Informed* (Harrisburg: Trinity Press International, 1997). An integration of the two is attempted by David B. Howell: *Matthew's Inclusive Story. A Study in the Narrative Rhetoric of the First Gospel*, JSOT.SS 42 (Sheffield: JSOT Press, 1990). A further development of narrative criticism pays attention to rhetorical devices and strategies. Their investigation has developed into its own sub-category of "rhetorical criticism." See Burton L. Mack and Vernon K. Robbins: *Patterns of Persuasion in the Gospels*, Foundations and Facets: Literary Facets (Sonoma: Polebridge, 1989); Burton L. Mack: *Rhetoric and the New Testament* (Minneapolis: Fortress, 1990); *Persuasive Artistry: Studies in NT Rhetoric in Honor of George Kennedy*, ed. Duane F. Watson (Sheffield: JSOT Press, 1991).

of the social setting of the gospel of Matthew.[196] However, the most influential studies concerning themselves with the social situation of the gospel have tried to incorporate into their investigation the help of, for want of a better term, sociological aids.

4. Sociological Approaches: Matthew's Community as a Sectarian Jewish Writing

In more recent scholarship the community of the first gospel is increasingly presented as a Jewish sectarian group in opposition to other groups within the movement of formative Judaism in the period immediately following the Jewish War. The terms "formative Judaism" and "sectarian movement" need some explanation.

The phrase "formative Judaism" has been popularized by Jacob Neusner.[197] It denotes the reorganization and consolidation of Judaism after the destruction of the temple. The agents of this consolidation were a coalition of groups that survived the war. Probably best suited to this task were Pharisees and scribes, who were not as closely associated with the temple even before its destruction. Since the destruction of the temple the center of worship shifted towards local associations, synagogues, and a concomitant emphasis on the observation of the Law. This process was, of course, gradual, and perhaps even at times fluid. It laid the groundwork for the emergence of the rabbinic movement in subsequent centuries. A crystallization point of this movement was the foundation of the late Pharisaic/early rabbinic school of Jamnia, idealized in later rabbinic writings. The implication of this state of affairs in Judaism of the immediate post-Temple period is that, while Pharisees and scribes were certainly prominent and growing in stature, there was still room for a wide variety of approaches to the restoration of a Jewish identity. Consequently, the Matthean group can be imagined as a Jewish group in opposition to the Pharisaic/rabbinic movement, just as other groups might have been in conflict with this "fledgling coalition of forces" before it outmaneuvered its competitors.[198]

---

[196] Burnett uses the implied author theory to show, unsuccessfully, that Matthew uses the term "father" for God in order to make a polemical statement against Jewish opponents. Thus Matthew supposedly proves himself and his community to be Gentile. Fred W. Burnett: "Exposing the Anti-Jewish Ideology of Matthew's Implied Author: The Characterization of God as Father," *Semeia* 59 (1992): 155–191.

[197] A concise summary of Neusner's often published position is found in: Jacob Neusner: "The Formation of Rabbinic Judaism: Yavneh from 70–100," in *ANRW* II,19,2:3–42.

[198] David C. Sim: *Apocalyptic Eschatology in the Gospel of Matthew*, MSSNTS 88 (Cambridge; New York: Cambridge University Press, 1996), 183–184.

The notion of "sectarian movements" has been prominent in sociological discussions of New Testament writings for a while.[199] A sect is defined by its peculiar relationship to a parent body. L. Michael White has proposed the following cross-cultural definition: A sect is

> a deviant or separatist movement within a cohesive and religiously defined dominant culture. Thus despite expressed hostilities and exclusivism, the sect shares the same basic constellation of beliefs or 'worldview' of the dominant cultural idiom.[200]

Joseph Blenkinsopp has proposed a description of a sect that varies to some extent from White's, but also shares some features in common. It illustrates the extraordinary difficulty in defining a sectarian body.[201] Blenkinsopp writes:

> A sect is not only a minority, and not only characterized by opposition to norms accepted by the parent-body, but also claims in a more or less exclusive way to be what the parent-body claims to be. Whether such a group formally severs itself, or is excommunicated, will depend largely on the degree of self-definition attained by the parent-body and the level of tolerance obtaining within it.[202]

---

[199] White traces the concept back to Ernst Troeltsch, who published his seminal work in 1911. White traces the influence of studies by Troeltsch and Max Weber. He points out that both worked from a hypothesis of Judaism as the "national church" from which Christian groups diverged as sects. This hypothesis has been shown as inadequate, yet many of their observations are still useful. L. Michael White: "Shifting Sectarian Boundaries in Early Christianity," *BJRL* 70 (1988): 8–9.

[200] White: "Sectarian boundaries," 14.

[201] This difficulty reflects the nature of sociological studies. On the difficulty of defining sectarianism see Peter L. Berger: "The Sociological Study of Sectarianism," *Social Research* 21 (1954): 467–485. As Max Weber has repeatedly emphasized, sociological studies do not uncover laws with an applicability to any and all situations. Sociology is a heuristic science that allows one to notice things already present in the evidence that might be otherwise overlooked. Max Weber: *On the Methodology of the Social Sciences*, trans. E. A. Shils and H. A. Finch (Glencoe: The Free Press of Glencoe, 1949), 90. For the study of Matthew such sociological models enable an interpretation of the evidence in the gospel in terms of social models. As Stanton writes, "at best, they may provide support for particular historical hypotheses or reconstructions. In short, they enable us to read Matthew's gospel more sensitively by clarifying its social setting." Stanton: *Gospel*, 87. However, it is methodologically inadmissible to use sociological models in order to fill in gaps of knwoledge concerning first century groups, as does John Gager: *Community and Kingdom. The Social World of Early Christians* (Englewood Cliffs: Prentiss, 1983), 4.

[202] Joseph Blenkinsopp: "Interpretation and Sectarian Tendencies: An Aspect of Second Temple History," in: *Jewish and Christian Self-Definition*, ed. Ed P. Sanders (Philadelphia: Fortress Press, 1981), 1–2. This definition has become the working hypothesis for a number of scholars. J. Andrew Overman: *Matthew's Gospel and Formative Judaism. The Social World of the Matthean Community* (Minneapolis: Fortress Press, 1990), 6–34; Stanton: *Gospel*, 85–107. Blenkinsopp notes that sociologists of religion have found it extremely difficult to come up with a clearly defined and widely accepted definition of a religious sect. He therefore suggests that his is not a definition but a description.

The application of such sectarian models to the Matthean church is fraught with difficulties. Our knowledge of first century communities in general, and the Matthean group in particular, is sketchy and often based on "disciplined imagination" rather than hard verifiable facts.[203] The preceding section shows just how much of the reconstruction of a Matthean community is subject to possibly ambiguous interpretations of the gospel. Consequently, authors who wish to portray Matthew's community in terms of a Jewish sect attempt to establish critical controls for this theory by comparison with other groups who might conceivably called sects. One such group is the community of Qumran.[204]

Several criteria are put forward in support of a hypothesis of Matthew as a writing of a sectarian group. Most of these relate to Matthew's relationship with the supposed parent body of Judaism in its formative stage. Among these criteria is a distinct distancing from the parent body.[205] Matthew parts with the Pharisaic strands of Judaism (21:43; 23), and the controversy stories bear witness to the distance between Matthew and the Jewish leaders. Matthew's group perceives itself under threat from opposing groups (5:10–12; 10:17–18; 21:41–45; 22:6–7). A similar distancing from the parent body can be observed in the Qumran community.[206] The distancing is expressed not only in different views but also accompanied by a generous use of invective against the parent group.[207] Stanton comments on the striking similarity between Matthew and the Damascus Document not only in their use of invective, but also in their perceived threat of persecution from the parent body and the initiation of the sectarian group through a charismatic leader.[208] Besides the evidence of the Damascus document Overman mentions 1 Enoch, Psalms of Solomon, 2 Baruch, and 4 Ezra as examples of sectarian writings within Judaism.[209]

---

[203] Stanton: *Gospel*, 87.

[204] Overman: *Matthew's Gospel*, 9–10; Stanton: *Gospel*, 91–107; Saldarini: *Matthew's Christian-Jewish Community*, 13–18; Sim: *Apocalyptic Eschatology in the Gospel of Matthew*, 182–192.

[205] White: "Sectarian boundaries."

[206] The beginning of the Damascus Document draws a sharp line between those who "understand the actions of God" and those "who spurn him" (*CD* 1,1–3). Subsequently, a very sharp line is drawn between the community members who follow the Teacher of Righteousness and seek God with a perfect heart, and the part of Israel that has not followed the teacher and thus ended up transgressing the covenant, because they "sought easy interpretations, chose illusions, scrutinized loopholes, chose the handsome neck, acquitted the guilty and sentenced the just, violated the covenant, broke the precept, colluded together against the life of the just man, their sould abominated all those who walk in perfection, they hunted them down with the sword and provoked the dispute of the people. And kindled was the wrath" (*CD* 1, 18–21).

[207] Blenkinsopp studies such strategies in other early Jewish and Christian writings as well. Blenkinsopp: "Sectarian Tendencies."

[208] Stanton: *Gospel*, 96.

[209] Overman: *Matthew's Gospel*, 9–12. Harrington notes that an important feature connecting 2 Baruch, 4 Ezra and Matthew is the search for a response to the catastrophe of the destruction

Social conflict theories have pointed to polemical language as a further criterion in discerning the sectarian nature of a group. Rather than an indication of historical distance, polemics is a sign of the ideological proximity of two groups at odds with one another over the same issues.[210] The more acrimonious the debate the closer the two groups are. Applied to the Matthean community this theory explains to some extent the vigorous nature of the attack against Jewish leaders in the gospel. Tilborg has shown how Matthew treats the Jewish leaders stereotypically without much differentiation between the various groups of leaders, and how this treatment is rooted in the redactional activity of Matthew.[211] For the Matthean community this means that it still maintains a close, if adversarial, association with the parent body, in this case Judaism. At the same time, it vies for the role of leadership,[212] and for the claim to rightful interpretation of the tradition,[213] with those that it attacks in the gospel. This explains to some extent the reservations of Matthew against the synagogue. The phrase "their synagogues" obviously indicates a mixed relationship with them: On the one hand they are identified as the place where the Jewish leaders that the gospel attacks hold sway. On the other hand, Jesus teaches even in those synagogues. The Matthean community expresses its ambiguous role within Judaism yet without the association of the Pharisaic movement with the distinction between the συναγωγή αὐτῶν and its own ἐκκλησία. When Matthew, therefore, indeed

---

of the temple. With this assertion he comes close to Overman, though with a slightly different emphasis: While Overman stresses the future of Judaism, Harrington stresses the question of theodicee. At the heart of both emphases is the central problem: "Judaism would have to adjust to these realities or die out." Harrington: *Matthew*, 12.

[210] See Lewis A. Coser: *The Functions of Social Conflict* (New York: Free Press, 1964), 67–72. Coser's analysis has been by in large accepted by a number of scholars. Benno Przybylski: "The Setting of Matthean Anti-Judaism," in: *Anti-Judaism in Early Christianity*, ed. Peter Richardson and David Granskou (Waterloo: Wilfrid Laurier University Press, 1986), 199; Overman: *Matthew's Gospel*, 146–147; Stanton: *Gospel*, 98–99. Saldarini expands on this theory with an analysis of social groups and deviancy. Saldarini: *Matthew's Christian-Jewish Community*, 84–123, and the references given there.

[211] And yet van Tilborg is unable to interpret this tendency appropriately: "If one wishes to call the Jews who have refused to be converted hypocrites, evil people, murderers and impostors, there must be a fairly great and satisfactory distance on a historical level. This idea held by Mt can only be explained as being held by someone who, if he happened to come face to face with them, was still so absorbed in his own ideas that he had lost sight of reality." Tilborg: *The Jewish Leaders in Matthew*, 171. The characterization of such a Matthew as "armchair theologian" has been suggested by Sim: *Apocalyptic Eschatology in the Gospel of Matthew*, 185. A similar affliction ails the portraits of Matthew by Hare and Meier. Hare: *Persecution*; Meier: *Law*.

[212] Anthony J. Saldarini: "Delegitimation of Leaders in Matthew 23," *CBQ* 54 (1992): 649–680.

[213] Overman: *Matthew's Gospel*, 149. He writes: "The Matthean community, like several other communities in this period, claims to be the true Israel, the only faithful body, and fulfillers of the divine plan and law." With this statement Overman returns to the phrase coined by Wolfgang Trilling. Here, however, the struggle goes on within the greater body of Judaism, while Trilling saw the title conferred on a now Gentile community.

parts ways with the synagogue, it is a very limited parting: He does not imply a separation from what he understands as Judaism.

A final criterion for the suggestion of the Matthean group as a sect concerns its own legitimation and the concomitant delegitimation of the parent body. The study of this criterion originated again with sociological approaches to religion,[214] but has been put to use in New Testament studies.[215] The connection between legitimation and delegitimation is pronounced. Polemic is used to denounce the parent group and differentiate the sect. Legitimation also includes the claim that the sect preserves the tradition and orthodoxy, while the parent group has gone astray and left the tradition. Consequently, the sect does not view itself as innovatory but as "the legitimate heir to shared traditions."[216] The new group has divine authority on its side. Saldarini has applied this model of interpretation successfully to Matthew 23 and the polemics it contains.[217] Similar observations can be made about the polemics contained in the Damascus Document. The examination of the controversy stories will show how far Matthew carried his view of the parent group as unfaithful to the traditions.

Several indicators in the gospel show how much Matthew is still steeped in a Jewish background, and how much there is a rivalry between his community and other groups within Judaism. The Matthean group contained scribes, much like the Jewish leadership under attack in the gospel. Such scribes are among those for whom martyrdom is predicted (23:34), and scribes "trained for the kingdom of God" (13:52) are found in this community. The reference to "their scribes" indicates perhaps a rivalry between the scribes of the opposing faction and of the Matthean camp along the lines of the distinction between "their synagogues" and the church.[218] It is still sometimes argued that Matthew himself is such a scribe.[219] The title "rabbi" might be an indication of the kind of rivalry that these scribes encountered: The opponents love being called "rabbi," but Jesus instructs his disciples to avoid this title (23:7-8). Among the disciples it is only Judas who calls Jesus by this title (26:25, 49 || Mk 14:46). Matthew excises this title when it is used in Mark's gospel by Peter (17:4 || Mk 9:5; 21:20 || Mk 11:21) or Bartimaeus (20:33 || Mk 10:51). If the Pharisees and scribes of the opposition were indeed appropriating the title for themselves, then Matthew distances himself again from the

---

[214] Peter L. Berger: *The Social Construction of Reality. A Treatise in Sociological Knowledge* (Garden City: Doubleday, 1966); Peter L. Berger: *The Sacred Canopy. Elements of a Sociological Theory of Religion* (Garden City: Doubleday, 1967).

[215] An example is Francis B. Watson: *Paul, Judaism, and the Gentiles, A Sociological Approach*, MSSNTS 56 (Cambridge: Cambridge University Press, 1986).

[216] Stanton: *Gospel*, 105.

[217] Saldarini: "Delegitimation."

[218] Sim: *Apocalyptic Eschatology in the Gospel of Matthew*, 188.

[219] A detailed and recent discussion of this issue can be found in: David E. Orton: *The Understanding Scribe: Matthew and the Apocalyptic Ideal*, MSSNTS 25 (Sheffield: JSOT Press, 1989), 166–174.

Pharisaic movement by avoiding the title studiously.[220] Such a distance explains also the injunction to listen to what the Pharisees have to say and follow it without imitating their deeds (23:2–7). It is not the law that is at stake for Matthew, it is its interpretation that seems so utterly falsified by the hypocrisy of Pharisees and scribes.[221]

The limits of such a sociological approach to the question of Matthew's place *intra* or *extra muros* of Judaism are quite obvious. We have only the gospel of Matthew to make any judgment. Thus we can come to some understanding how Matthew saw his community's place in the various contemporary forms of Judaism. But the other side of the argument is missing. It is unclear how the movement of formative Judaism reacted to Matthew's claims. It is conceivable that Matthew was still debating when his conversation partners had already left him. The theory of the Matthean community as a Jewish sect offers some insight into the self-perception of the community. However, no converse evidence of how the parent body saw the Matthean community is available. Without evidence from the other side of the debate the riddle will probably never be solved with any certainty.

On the other hand, the sociological approach clarifies Matthew's relationship with Judaism better than redaction criticism could do on its own. While redaction criticism could unearth some of the distinctly Matthean material as having its roots in the Jewish context of Matthew the sociological approach designed a hypothetical framework within which this evidence can be understood. Thus the two methodologies are not mutually exclusive, they are complementary. The social model of Matthew's community as a sect within Judaism is dependent to a large extent on the redaction-critical evidence of the gospel even while going beyond it. Much of this evidence can be better understood in terms of sectarianism. The latter model makes the attempts of historicizing models of Strecker and Meier unnecessary and reveals them as anachronistic.

A completely different sociological model arises out of the comparison with associations and sodalities of varying size that were common in the Roman empire.[222] Such associations, sometimes referred to as *collegia*, were mostly voluntary associations for social purposes.[223] Comparison with such associations

---

[220] Overman: *Matthew's Gospel*, 46–48.

[221] Powell: "Do and Keep."

[222] Ramsay MacMullen: *Roman Social Relations* (New Haven: Yale University Press, 1974), 72–87.

[223] The preponderance of such organizations to turn into political groups led the Roman authorities to limit such associations to basically three types: professional associations of people with common trades, religious associations formed for the worship of a specific god, and burial societies formed mainly among the urban poor to help them afford decent funerals. The organizational structure of these associations tended to reflect military or political models. John E. Stambaugh and David L. Balch: *The New Testament in Its Social Environment*, LEC (Philadelphia: Westminster Press, 1986), 124–126.

has had some influence in New Testament studies, albeit with mixed success.[224] Thus it is perhaps not surprising that the study of ancient *collegia* has had virtually no influence on current Matthean scholarship. The study of Matthew's community as a sect, on the other hand, has been helpful in explaining the nature and function of the polemic language of the first gospel. It has also revealed some of the limitations of reconstructing the social history of the Matthean community. It points out that it is anachronistic to attempt to draw very distinct borderlines around Judaism, Jewish Christianity, and Gentile Christianity. Rather than a monolithic entity, Judaism in the first century gives a variegated and multifaceted impression that makes it difficult to speak of a clear parting of the ways.

5. Matthean Scholarship Reflected in Recent Commentaries

Until about 20 years ago the "finest"[225] commentary on the gospel of Matthew was available only in French.[226] The standard commentary in English remained that of Ward C. Allen, whose third edition was published in 1912.[227] However, the recent surge of interest in the first gospel has lead to a surge of major and minor commentaries on Matthew.[228] These commentaries reflect both the methodological

---

[224] Wayne Meeks considered the sodalities as a model for the urban communities that were the recipients of the Pauline literature. Wayne A. Meeks: *The First Urban Christians. The Social World of the Apostle Paul* (New Haven: Yale University Press, 1983), 77–80. Ultimately, he rejected the idea for four reasons that he draws from the Pauline literature. Firstly, he observes that the Christian communities were exclusive in a way that the ancient sodalities were not. The "baptism into Christ ... was intended ... to supplant all other loyalties" (p.78). Secondly, Christian groups were much more inclusive in terms of social stratification of their members. Thirdly, Meeks points out that there is practically an "almost complete absence of common terminology for the groups themselves or their leaders" (p.79). Finally, Meeks observes that the extralocal links between Christian communities have no counterpart in the ancient sodalities, even if these served deities known beyond the confines of a particular locale.

[225] Graham N. Stanton: "Matthew's Gospel: A Survey of Some Recent Commentaries," *BiTr* 46 (1995): 131.

[226] Pierre Bonnard: *L'évangile selon Saint Matthieu*, CNT 1 (Neuchatel, Delachaux & Niestle, 1963).

[227] Allen: *Matthew*. Another major commentary in English was provided by McNeile: *Matthew*.

[228] In this small survey, commentaries on parts of the gospel are ignored, largely for the sake of brevity. Several excellent commentaries on the Sermon on the Mount have appeared and created their own genre of commentary. Noteworthy are especially: Guelich: *Sermon*; Strecker: *Bergpredigt*; Jan Lambrecht: *The Sermon on the Mount: Proclamation and Exhortation*, GNS 14 (Wilmington: Glazier, 1985); Betz: *Sermon*. Furthermore, Raymond Brown has written masterful commentaries on both the infancy and the passion narratives in Matthew. While the commentary on the infancy narratives keeps the Matthean portion separate from the Lucan account, in the commentary on the passion narrative Brown hesitatingly decided to juxtapose the accounts of the four gospels incident by incident. However, Brown keeps a constant eye on the distinctive accents

developments and the diverse positions concerning the location of the Matthean community with regard to Judaism in the first century. In this short survey, the positions of the major commentaries will be outlined first. Then a number of the smaller commentaries will be highlighted briefly.

5.1 The Major Commentaries[229]

Having just come to a conclusion, the commentary by William D. Davies and Dale C. Allison represents an outstanding achievement that is sure to remain a standard reference for many years to come.[230] The commentary is traditional in its emphasis on close attention to the micro-textual issues, with comments on structure and sources usually preceding detailed exegeses of individual words and phrases. Wider theological issues that are raised by the text are usually treated in perceptive concluding observations at the end of each section. Davies and Allison view Matthew as a Jewish gospel.[231] Consequently, one of the emphases in the exegesis is the reference to Jewish, and often rabbinical, parallels.

Ulrich Luz, a Swiss scholar writing in German, is currently engaged in another major commentary.[232] While the commentary takes a traditional approach to the

---

and narrative flow of each gospel. Raymond E. Brown: *The Birth of the Messiah: A Commentary on the Infancy Narratives in the Gospels of Matthew and Luke*, AncB.RL 1, 2nd ed. (New York: Doubleday, 1993); Raymond E. Brown: *The Death of the Messiah: From Gethsemane to the Grave. A Commentary on the Passion Narratives in the Four Gospels*, AncB.RL, 2 vols. (New York: Doubleday, 1994).

[229] The four commentaries chosen for this survey are representative. They are chosen for their outstanding achievements and illustrate how, in recent years, the discussion over the place of Matthew in Judaism has not abated. Nevertheless, the positions outlined here have drawn together more closely. Matthew's affinity to Judaism is no longer under suspicion, nor is it doubted that the Jewish tradition is still the major intellectual framework for the first gospel. The disputed question is whether Matthew reflects the break with Judaism as already accomplished or as yet waiting in the wings. All commentaries in this survey agree that the event is very close. Other commentaries that fit the category are: Walter Grundmann: *Das Evangelium nach Matthäus*, ThKNT (Berlin: Evangelische Verlagsanstalt, 1968); Gerhard Maier: *Das Matthäusevangelium*, 2 vols., Bibel-Kommentar (Neuhausen, Stuttgart: Hänssler, 1979); Alexander Sand: *Das Evangelium nach Matthäus*, RNT (Regensburg: Pustet, 1986); Rudolf Schnackenburg: *Das Matthäusevangelium*, 2 vols., NEB.NT (Würzburg: Echter, 1985, 1987); Hubert Frankemölle: *Das Matthäusevangelium*, 2 vols., (Düsseldorf: Patmos 1997, 1999).

[230] The introduction to the third volume explains how Davies and Allison shared the work between themselves. Davies and Allison: *Matthew*, 3:ix.

[231] In the retrospect in their third volume, Davies and Allison acknowledge the advances made by the social studies of deviancy and sects, and write: "... we incline to believe that despite its positive association with Gentile Christians, Matthew's community was still a deviant Jewish association." Davies and Allison: *Matthew*, 3:695.

[232] Luz's commentary was first projected to comprise of two volumes. With the appearance of the second volume it became clear that a third volume was needed. This third volume appeared in December 1997. However, now a fourth volume is projected. An English translation is scheduled to appear in the Hermeneia series. Luz: *Matthäus*.

exegesis of the text,[233] its distinguishing feature is a detailed history of effects in which the author describes the influence of a passage on the theological and ethical traditions of the church through the centuries.[234] The history of effects is often concluded with usually perceptive observations about the possibilities of interpreting the text in the life of the church today. Luz views the gospel of Matthew as a writing that emanated from a Jewish-Christian community. However, in the wake of the destruction of Jerusalem this community regarded the mission to Israel as completed and turned towards the Gentile mission. Consequently, the author and his community are no longer in dialogue with synagogal Judaism.[235] For Luz, the gospel no longer makes an appeal to Israel for conversion.

The commentary by Donald Hagner, though comprising two volumes, is somewhat smaller in scope than either Davies and Allison or Luz.[236] Hagner tries to solve the problem of Matthew's relation to contemporary Judaism by focusing on both the particularism and the universalism of the gospel.[237] Hagner contends that it is wrong to try play the mission to Israel against the mission to the Gentiles. Thus he comes to the conclusion that Matthew reflects a Jewish-Christian community that had to deal with the unbelief of the greater part of Israel and the turn to the Gentiles for the Christian mission.[238] With this view Hagner reads the gospel foremost as an apologetic writing for the legitimation and use of a community that sees itself as the inheritor's of God's promises to Israel charged to make disciples of all nations.

Joachim Gnilka's fine commentary describes the position of the Matthean community as a Hellenistic-Jewish group with its own coherent tradition of interpreting the Law. On the other hand, the conflict with the synagogue indicates

---

[233] Most pericopes are dealt with first according to structure, then according to sources, finally by verse by verse exegesis. A summary recaps the salient points of the exegesis. Luz is less comprehensive in the citation of rabbinical parallels than Davies and Allison.

[234] Luz published a separate monograph detailing the rationale for the inclusion of the history of effects in his major commentary and the hermeneutical problems this method tries to address. Ulrich Luz: *Matthew in History. Interpretation, Influence, and Effects* (Philadelphia: Fortress, 1994). Luz also published a slim volume on the theology of Matthew. Luz: *Theology*.

[235] Luz writes: "Matthäus rechnet nicht damit, nicht-christliche jüdische Leser seines Evangeliums zu finden. Nur so wird es verständlich, daß die jüdischen Führer und auch die Rolle des jüdischen Volkes so weitgehend typisiert werden konnten." Luz: *Matthäus*, 1:71.

[236] Donald A. Hagner: *Matthew 1–13*, Word Biblical Commentary 33A (Dallas: Word Books, 1993); Donald A. Hagner: *Matthew 14–28*, Word Biblical Commentary 33B (Dallas: Word Books, 1993).

[237] Hagner: *Matthew 1–13*, lxvi–xi.

[238] "Matthew's original readers were in this unenviable position, in a kind of 'no man's land' between their Jewish brothers and sisters, on the one hand, and gentile Christians, on the other, wanting to reach back for continuity with the old and at the same time to reach forward to the new work God was doing in the largely gentile church – simultaneously answerable, so to speak, to both Jews and Gentiles." Hagner: *Matthew 1–13*, lxx.

that the community is heading for the break with contemporary Judaism.[239] For Gnilka, this break is not yet a reality, though inevitable. Given his position, Gnilka's commentary is close to Davies and Allison in its reliance on references to Rabbinic sources to clarify where Matthew's community might have diverged from Judaism of its time.

5.2 Medium Length Commentaries

If major commentaries have appeared at a welcome rate, medium length commentaries have proliferated. By in large they take positions similar to those of the major commentaries with regard to the question of Matthew and Judaism. However, they do so from different perspectives. These commentaries can basically be divided into two groups according to their methodologies.

The first of these groups accords Matthew a redaction- and historical-critical treatment that by now has become traditional.[240] Wolfgang Trilling built on his earlier work in his commentary, but emphasizes pastoral and homiletical approaches, as does Leon Morris.[241] David Hill's commentary was the first English commentary to set out the redaction-critical method in a commentary.[242] Robert Gundry's always stimulating commentary uses a strict redaction-critical approach through comparison of Matthew with Mark. The second edition includes a defense of some of the more idiosyncratic points Gundry makes.[243] Daniel Harrington uses a redaction-critical approach to place the gospel within Judaism in its early formative period.[244] Lesser commentaries include those of Albright and Mann, and of Beare.[245] J. Andrew Overman has worked his earlier study on the sectarian nature of the Matthean community into a coherent treatment of the gospel restating his position on Matthew's Jewishness,[246] as did Meier a more than a decade earlier.[247]

---

[239] Gnilka: *Matthäus*, 2:530–534.

[240] Stanton: "Commentaries," 138.

[241] Wolfgang Trilling: *The Gospel According to St. Matthew*, trans. K. Smyth (New York: Herder & Herder, 1969); Leon Morris: *The Gospel According to Matthew*, Pillar Commentary (Grand Rapids: Eerdmans, 1992).

[242] Hill: *Matthew*.

[243] Among these idiosyncrasies is the thesis that Matthew was used by Luke. Furthermore, Gundry argues that Matthew wrote with an eye to the controversy with the Jewish leaders and the persecution under Nero. These assumptions lead him to popose a date for Matthew between 65 and 70 C.E., but before the destruction of Jerusalem. Gundry: *Matthew*.

[244] Harrington: *Matthew*.

[245] William F. Albright and Charles S. Mann: *Matthew*, AncB 26 (New York: Doubleday, 1971); Beare: *Matthew*.

[246] Overman: *Church and Community*.

[247] John P. Meier: *The Vision of Matthew. Christ, Church and Morality in the First Gospel*, Theological Inquiries (New York, Ramsay, Toronto: Paulist, 1979).

The second group of medium length commentaries grew out of compositi-on-criticism as a particular emphasis within the redaction-critical method. Hand in hand with the emphasis on composition went a certain disenchantment with the results of source-critical analyses in view of the resurgence of the Griesbach hypothesis. Thus some commentators shifted the emphasis to the analysis of the text as a literary unit. Major themes of such criticism involve plots and sub-plots of a writing, as well as the portrayal of characters. Modern literary criticism has been a major force behind this methodological reshaping.[248]

Representative of this approach is Jack Dean Kingsbury. He distances his method considerably from redaction criticism by professing that his interest lies in the story itself, not in the usual topics of the historical-critical or redaction-critical methods of locating the community of the evangelist in the social world of the first century.[249] However, even Kingsbury himself does not evade these questions, and thus is closer to redaction-criticism than he admits. Kingsbury places the community of Matthew outside of Judaism.[250] Margaret Davies is less successful in her literary treatment of Matthew,[251] as is Daniel Patte.[252] More successful narrative approaches to Matthew are provided by Garland and Carter.[253] Carter views the Matthean community "in transition out of the synagogue" building a new identity around the person of Jesus.[254]

---

[248] For a summary of the new literary criticism see Mark Allan Powell: *What is Narrative Criticism?* (Philadelphia: Fortress, 1990).

[249] "To approach Matthew's story as a unified narrative, however, is to attend to the very story it tells ... one temporarily takes leave of one's familiar world ... and enters into another world that is autonomous in its own right ..." Kingsbury: *Matthew as Story*, 2. Yet on occasion, he will admit that inferences concerning the readers can be made by "glances at Mark or Luke or at other historical data" (p. 147).

[250] Kingsbury includes, at the end, a chapter on the community of Matthew, where he describes it as a group of Jewish and Gentile Christians "outside the orbit of official Judaism." Kingsbury: *Matthew as Story*, 156.

[251] Davies falls short at crucial points of the gospel, e.g. in her comments on 5:17–20. Margaret Davies: *Matthew*, Readings: A New Biblical Commentary (Sheffield: JSOT Press, 1993).

[252] Patte takes a different literary approach by focusing on a structuralist perspective. He assumes that Matthew expounds on his convictions by stating them clearly, but also by stating clearly what he does not want to say. Thus Matthew uses tensions and oppositions to express his main points. Daniel Patte: *The Gospel According to Matthew. A Structural Commentary on Matthew's Faith* (Philadelphia: Fortress, 1987), 6. Yet often the tensions seem labored, and often they are absent. Thus they do not provide a helpful matrix for understanding the gospel. Patte's footnotes reference some standard secondary literature, yet often without bearing on his comments in the main body of the commentary.

[253] David E. Garland: *Reading Matthew: A Literary and Theological Commentary on the First Gospel*, Reading the New Testament (New York: Crossroads, 1993); Warren Carter: *Matthew: Storyteller, Interpreter, Evangelist* (Peabody: Hendrickson, 1996).

[254] Carter: *Matthew*, 92.

5.3 Summary

The commentaries reviewed here offer a bird's eye view of the *status quaestionis* concerning Matthew's relationship with Judaism. The harsh distinction between Jews and Gentiles of early redaction criticism has given way to a more fluid perception of Matthew's gospel reflecting the transition from Judaism to a Gentile church. Even when scholars come down one way or the other on the dividing line the impression remains that this line was much less clear to Matthew than commentators today would like it to be.

6. The Proposition of this Study

Matthew's relationship with Judaism has been a focal point for understanding much of the gospel's social history throughout its modern critical investigation. The acrimonious debates between Jesus and the Jewish leaders in the gospel bear witness to the conflictual nature of this relationship. In the search for a better understanding of the conflict between Matthew and his Jewish opponents it becomes necessary to analyze this conflict in greater depth. This study proposes to proceed with such an analysis. The point of departure for this investigation will be the controversy stories themselves. They will be analyzed for the redaction that Matthew accords these stories. In observing how Matthew shapes these stories of Jesus at odds with his opponents among the Jewish leaders Matthew's particular issues will reveal themselves. They will be analyzed for the particular literary form that reveals itself in these stories. The assumption behind this investigation is that the form of these stories will reveal how Matthew employs them in the narrative progression of the gospel.

But the redaction- and form-critical analysis of these stories must be placed in the wider context of the literature roughly contemporary with Matthew's gospel. In searching out parallels it will hopefully become clear that these stories are employed in accord with the literary conventions of the time. Once these conventions are identified they will reveal additional information about the description of the conflict with the Jewish leaders in the gospel of Matthew.

Once this information is gathered it will then be possible to return to the beginning of this study and ask once more the question: Was the Matthean community *intra* or *extra muros* of Judaism?

II. The Matthean Redaction of the Controversy Stories in Chapter 9

Before the redaction-critical examination of the controversy stories can begin an inventory of these stories needs to be established at least briefly. More thoroughgoing form-critical deliberations will follow in chapter 6. They will concentrate on the Matthean development of the form, and thus will follow the redaction-critical analysis. Yet a few remarks are in order with regard to the choice of stories treated in this study. They conveniently begin with Rudolf Bultmann as one of the most influential form-critics of this century.[1]

Bultmann established criteria for the treatment of the controversy stories as a form[2] and catalogued as controversy stories the Matthean pericopes 9:2–8, 10–13, 14–17; 12:1–8, 9–14, 22–37, 38–45; 15:3–9; 16:1–4; 19:3–9; 21:23–27; 22:15–22, 23–33, 34–40, 41–46. Bultmann catalogued 13:53–58 and 21:14–17 as biographical apophthegms.[3] Yet Bultmann pointed out the very close relationship between controversy stories and biographical apophthegms[4] and further noted that these stories exhibit hostile behavior by the opponents of Jesus in these stories. Consequently, they will be included in the following analysis, although with the reservation that they must be tested by the complete form-critical analysis of chapter 6. As a result, the redaction-critical analysis will cover 17 stories. Those of

---

[1] Rudolf Bultmann: *The History of the Synoptic Tradition*, 2nd ed., trans. John Marsh (New York: Harper, 1968).

[2] Bultmann called the stories "controversy dialogues" and dealt with them in the context of apophthegms. This reflects his view that at the origin of these stories is the dominical saying, while the development into a story is secondary, and, in the case of controversy dialogues, even the product of an increasing tendency in the church. Bultmann: *History*, 11–61. Bultmann saw four elements in a controversy dialogue: As a point of departure such pericopes provide an action or attitude (1) which is used by opponents (2) in an attack by question or accusation (3). The attack is followed by a reply (4), often including a counter-question or a scripture quotation. He did not view a narrative setting or conclusion as essential to the controversies (pp. 39–41) as he grouped them among the sayings material. Bultmann only admitted legends and miracles as narratives. It ought to be pointed out that Bultmann is not entirely consistent in the application of the criteria regarding controversy dialogues. Thus he qualifies Mt 21:41–46 as a controversy dialogue (p. 53), even though the pattern of attack and reply is not present. The attack in this story is made by Jesus, and the reply is missing.

[3] Bultmann: *History*, 31, 34.

[4] Consequently, Bultmann sees them as sub-groups of the larger category apophthegms. Bultmann: *History*, 56–57.

Mt 9 will be treated in chapter 2, the stories of Mt 12 in chapter 3, the stories of Mt 13–19 in chapter 4, and the stories of Mt 21–22 in chapter 5 of this study.

1. Introduction

In the controversy stories the attitudes of the gospel of Matthew with regard to the Jewish leaders are most tangible. A redaction-critical examination of these stories reveals the particularly Matthean interest in the Jesus' quarrels with the Jewish leaders. In other words, if authors like Strecker and Meier are right in their "historicizing" view of the gospel's relationship with Judaism, the redaction-critical analysis ought to reveal that the Matthean interest in these stories lies in the tradition about Jesus' conflict with the Jewish leaders rather than in an updating of these stories for the purposes of illuminating the community's struggle with such opponents. On the other hand, should the redaction focus on an interpretation of these stories with a view towards their applicability to the community, such a historicizing view fails. In this case, it is much more likely that the conflict between Jesus and his opponents finds its continuation in a conflict between the community of the gospel and the successors of the opponents of Jesus. The controversy stories, then, express part of the life experience of the Matthean community. These redaction-critical conclusions would also have important consequences for the analysis of the social setting of the entire gospel.

Matthew takes over most of his controversy stories from the gospel of Mark. Most of them appear in Matthew in three distinct blocks. The first block consists of a triad[5] of controversy stories. It comprises the story of the healing of the paralytic and the ensuing controversy with some Scribes (9:1–8 || Mk 2:1–12), the controversy over Jesus' association with the tax collectors and sinners on the occasion of the call of Matthew (9:10–13 || Mk 14–17), and the controversy over the fasting of John's disciples and of the Pharisees (9:14–17 || Mk 2:18–22). The second block occurs in ch. 12 and contains two Sabbath controversies (12:1–8, 9–14 || Mk 2:23–28; 3:1–6), and two controversies dealing with the authority of Jesus: the first is a defense against the accusation that Jesus is in league with Satan (12:22–37 || Mk 3:22–30), the second concerns the demand for a sign (12:38–42 || Mk 8:11–12). The two pairs are set off from one another by the quotation of Is 53 (12:15–21). Then, four isolated controversies follow in the narrative: The rejection of Jesus in Nazareth (13:53–58 || Mk 6:1–6a), a discussion of the tradition of the

---

[5] Matthew is fond of arranging his material in triads. It is possible to detect the threefold structure in the major discourses. Davies and Allison: *Matthew*, 1:60–72, 86–87. Apart from the triad in ch. 9 the two pairs of controversy stories in ch. 12 can viewed as parts of two triads, and the controversies of 22:14–40 are a triad that Matthew takes from Mark and appends with another controversy that is markedly different in character. A full discussion of this feature will be given below.

elders with the example of the washing of the hands before meals (15:1–9 || Mk 7:1–13), a doublet of the demand for a sign (16:1–4 || Mk 8:11–12), and a discussion concerning divorce (19:3–9 || Mk 10:2–12). A third and final block of controversy stories appears after the entrance into Jerusalem (21:14–17, without parallel in the other synoptics; 21:23–27 || Mk 11:27–33; 22:15–22 || Mk 12:13–17; 22:23–33 || Mk 12:18–27; 22:34–40 || Mk 12:28–34; 22:41–46 || Mk 12:35–37a). This final block of the Matthean controversy stories is interwoven with the parable of the fig tree cursed and explained (21:18–22 || Mk 11:15–17, 20–24), the parables of the two sons (21:28–32), of the wicked husbandmen (21:33–46 || Mk 12:1–12), and the parable of the wedding banquet and the man without a wedding garment (22:1–14).

The first block of controversies in ch. 9 follows the narrative sequence of Mk 2:1–22. After the controversies in ch. 9 Matthew discontinues the Markan sequence, to take it up again only in 12:1–32 (Mk 2:23–3:30), with the exception of Mk 3:13–19, used already in ch. 10, and the omission of 3:20–21. Furthermore, Matthew inserts 12:17–21, a fulfillment quotation of Is 42:1–4. The large break in the Markan sequence means that Matthew shifts a considerable amount of source material and effects a breakup of much of the Markan sequence between Mk 1–6. However, with the end of ch. 13 Matthew returns to the narrative sequence provided by Mark, and the following controversy stories follow in the same places in the narrative. The significant break with the Markan sequence in the early chapters needs to be accounted for. It will be examined in chapter 7 of this investigation.

The following pages will deal with these controversy stories one by one. The particular focus of the examination will be on their individual Matthean redaction. Thus the stories will be analyzed for the changes and emphases Matthew gives them. The underlying rationale for the individual examination of the stories is the attempt to uncover particular themes and patterns that emerge from these stories as a whole. Thus after the individual examination of the stories a summary review will draw attention to recurring phrases, themes, and emphases in the Matthean redaction. After these patterns emerge it will it be possible examine the stories in their specifically Matthean narrative and thematic context.

As must already be obvious, this investigation takes the Two Source theory as a working hypothesis. The theory itself is not under investigation here. In addition, whether Matthew and Luke each operated with a different version of Mark and Q is equally tangential to the present analysis. That possibility is certainly acknowledged. However, the present investigation of the controversy stories deals mainly with stories in Matthew that are also part of the Markan tradition. The possibility, therefore, that Luke used a slightly different version of Mark need not detain us. The obvious minor agreements will be pointed out. They will be noted and discussed when they are relevant to the order of priority assumed by the two source theory. However, the latter will serve as the working hypothesis.

With the two source hypothesis assumed, it will be useful to examine at least briefly the main issues that underlie the sources of the Matthean narratives. Therefore, after the discussion of an individual Matthean pericope a short summary of the main issues for the Markan parallel will be attempted in a separate section. This will throw more light on the twist that Matthew gives these stories. In cases where the sources for a Matthean narrative are woven together from Mark and Q such a separate investigation will be omitted for the sake of brevity. Furthermore, the mere fact that Matthew combines sources is enough evidence for the the particular Matthean interest in the stories at hand. Relevant points in the sources will be incorporated into the main section of the analysis of Matthew.

2. Matthew 9:2–8

The first Matthean controversy story occurs at the occasion of the healing of a paralytic (Mt 9:1–8 ‖ Mk 2:1–12 ‖ Lk 5:17–26). The story marks the return to Capharnaum which is qualified as Jesus' own city (9:1).[6] Matthew thus takes up the narrative thread of miracles that had been interrupted with his crossing of the Lake of Galilee (8:18, 23) to the "other side" (8:18). The small journey had given opportunity for sayings about discipleship (8:19–22) that were illustrated by the storm on the lake (8:24–27) and the Gadarene demoniac (8:28–34). The disciples-hip sayings have introduced the first "son of man" saying (8:20); the storm on the lake brought up the question of the identity of Jesus (8:27), and the story of the Gadarene demoniac brought the first inkling of rejection of Jesus (8:33–34). The following triad of controversy stories weaves these themes much more closely together.

The first controversy story revolves around a paralytic. Matthew describes a paralytic being brought to Jesus.[7] He drops the colorful details about the number

---

[6] Strack and Billerbeck suggest that this refers to the full citizenship of Jesus which he would have acquired after a stay of 12 months. Hermann Leberecht Strack and Paul Billerbeck: *Kommentar zum Neuen Testament aus Talmud und Midrasch*. 4 vols., (München: Beck, 1956), 1:493–494. However, this is unconvincing since the gospel does not really show any interest in the civil status of Jesus, either here or elsewhere. It is perhaps enough to assume that Capharnaum was the city associated with Jesus. The reference here serves mainly to keep Jesus on the move.

[7] Matthew introduces the story with καὶ ἰδού (9:2), a minor agreement with Luke (5:18). Matthew's and Luke's general proclivity to use this particle (62 times in Matthew against 7 times in Mark and 57 times in Luke) makes this of little if any significance. Davies and Allison: *Matthew*, 2:87; Gundry: *Matthew*, 162. In Mt 9:2–8 it serves as a marker to divide the story into parts. In 9:2 it marks the meeting between Jesus and the paralytic and his companions. In 9:3 it introduces the meeting between Jesus and the Scribes. Here it is not paralleled by Mark or Luke. The third marker, again not paralleled by either Mark or Luke, occurs with τότε in 9:6 and introduces the return of Jesus to the paralytic. Thus the καὶ ἰδού in 9:2 is satisfactorily explained as a structural element in the Matthean story that is probably redactional.

of the porters, their attempts to reach Jesus through the courtyard, and their ingenuity in digging through the roof of the house where Jesus is teaching (Mk 2:3b–4).[8] Matthew merely states that some people brought a paralytic on a bed[9] to him. While Mark interprets the whole sequence of actions leading to the presentation of the paralytic before Jesus as a sign of their faith, the details are no longer important to Matthew.[10] Thus he concludes the setting of the scene with the Markan remark that Jesus saw their faith and spoke to the paralytic.[11] The

---

[8] Lohmeyer suggested that this lack of colorful detail points to the fact that Matthew had a tradition different from Mark's of the same story. Ernst Lohmeyer: *Das Evangelium des Matthäus*, KEK.S (Göttingen: Vandenhoeck & Ruprecht, 1956), 169. However, in the remaining material there is often word by word agreement between Matthew and Mark. The suggestion of a different tradition cannot explain this satisfactorily. It is much easier to assume that Matthew deleted some of the colorful detail, as he is wont to do in other circumstances as well. The preceding story of the Gadarene demoniac, e.g., displays similar editorial activity of Matthew. Thus Lohmeyer's argument really rests only on the extent of the Matthean cuts. This is an argument from silence that is not supported by the evidence of what is left of the Matthean story.

[9] Matthew added ἐπὶ κλίνης to Mk 2:3, as did Lk 5:18. The phrase replaces the reference to the paralytics's pallet (κράβαττος) in Mk 2:4. The congruence with Luke has led to some discussion concerning a connection between Matthew and Luke independent of Mark. William R. Farmer: *The Synoptic Problem: A Critical Analysis* (New York: Macmillan, 1964), 133–134; Frans Neirynck: "Les accords mineurs et la rédaction des évangiles. L'épisode du paralytique (Mt IX 1–8 / Lc V 17–26, par. Mc II 1–12)," *EThL* 50 (1974): 15–30. The expression is fairly common: In the Septuagint it occurs 4 times without and 11 times with a definite article modifying κλίνης. The Septuagint does not use the word κράβαττος. The Markan κράβαττος is consistently avoided by both Matthew and Luke: Mark uses it 5 times; on no occasion is the word taken over by either of the side referents. However, Luke is not averse to using the word in Acts 5:15 together with κλινάριον, and 9:33 alone. Somewhat damaging to the view of this word as a minor agreement is the fact that Matthew and Luke use it in different grammatical constructions: In Luke it is attached to φέροντες, while Matthew attaches it to βεβλημένον. Davies and Allison appeal to the phrase βεβλημένον ἐπὶ τὴν κλίνην in Mk 7:30 as influencing Mt 9:2. Davies and Allison: *Matthew*, 2:87. This seems farfetched since the context as well as the case of κλίνη in Mk 7:30 are different. Furthermore, the presence of a definite article and the different syntactical arrangement in Mark counter-indicates dependence. While the agreement between Luke and Matthew is surprising, it is not puzzling, and it does not warrant to posit a literary dependence of one on the other.

[10] This is perhaps odd, as Davies and Allison remark. They point out that "everywhere else in Matthew that a person's faith is commented upon it is in view of what he or she has said or because of his or her persistence (8.10; 9.22, 29; 15.28)." For this reason they question Matthean familiarity with Mark's account. Davies and Allison: *Matthew*, 2:88. Yet it is not quite clear this is what the argument actually proves. The parallels cited by Davies and Allison are not part of a controversy story. It is possible that the context of a controversy story here imposes its own significance upon the Matthean account. The abbreviations, then, indicate Matthew's focus on the conflict rather than unfamiliarity with Mark's account. Perhaps it is best to assume that the fact that the party comes to Jesus is enough for Matthew to interpret this as a sign. Luz: *Matthäus*, 2:36.

[11] The only change in Matthew's phrasing is the substitution of the historic present in Mark (λέγει) with the Aorist (εἶπεν). This constitutes another minor agreement with Lk 5:20. Neyrinck

endearing appellation "child" remains[12] and is augmented by the encouraging "take heart."[13] The encouragement that Jesus offers heightens a marked contrast with his approach to the Scribes. Jesus goes on to speak the word of forgiveness of sins in the Markan phraseology.

Verse 3 begins with another καὶ ἰδού that marks a turn in the story toward the Scribes who suddenly appear. Again Matthew omits detailed circumstantial descriptions such as their sitting (Mk 2:6). Significantly Matthew changes their behavior from a "questioning in their hearts" (Mk 2:6) to a "saying to themselves."[14] The questioning of Jesus' activity in Mark leads to a judgment in Matthew. This is emphasized by the omission of the Markan explanation for the discontent of the Scribes.

Mark explains the opposition of the Scribes by referring to their view of the forgiveness of sins as the prerogative of God alone.[15] Matthew omits this reference. But he probably does not do so because he sees the opposition of the Scribes motivated differently. Matthew makes it clear in Jesus' answer to the Scribes that they misunderstood the power to forgive sins (9:6).[16] Thus the rationale for the

---

and Luz consider Matthean redaction unlikely in view of a dominical saying. Neyrinck: "Le Paralytique," 223–225; Luz: *Matthäus*, 2:36 n.7. However, a redaction seems likely because its result is the parallelization of εἶπαν in v. 3, εἶπεν in v. 4, and the twice used εἶπειν in v. 5. Gundry: *Matthew*, 162. For both Matthew and Luke the emendation of the historical present in Mark is not surprising.

[12] It occurs only here in Matthew's gospel as a term of endearment. A similar phrase, with the same word of encouragement, occurs in 9:22: θάρσει θύγατερ.

[13] Theissen has remarked upon the theme of encouragement in miracle stories. Gerd Theissen: *Miracle Stories of the Early Christian Tradition*, trans. F. McDonough (Philadelphia: Fortress, 1983), 58–59.

[14] Davies and Allison contend that this change makes the phrase "more decisive." Davies and Allison: *Matthew*, 2:90–91. Luz contends that they merely grumble "innerlich" and not out loud. Luz: *Matthäus*, 2:37. Gnilka perceives them as "tuscheln" among themselves as a group. Gnilka: *Matthäus*, 1:326. Gaechter has the Scribes thinking. Gaechter: *Das Matthäusevangelium*, 287. Gundry argues for "within themselves" as prompted by Mk 2:8. Gundry: *Matthew*, 163. Gundry is probably right to assume that the phrase does not mean a grumbling out loud with their group, but that the protest is internal, since Mark uses ἐν ἑαυτοῖς and ἐν ταῖς καρδίαις αὐτῶν synonymously. This is clarified by Matthew himself in 9:4 when the result of their activity is called ἐνθυμήσεις.

[15] Cf. Is 43:25.

[16] So argued by Davies and Allison: *Matthew*, 2:91. Luz argues that Matthew omits this reference because it would no longer have been understandable for Matthew's Jewish-Christian community why the forgiveness of sins would have been blasphemy since they believed regardless that God was working in and through Jesus. Luz: *Matthäus*, 2:37. This argument does not seem to hold up to closer scrutiny, however. In other controversy stories the opposition is quite vocal about why they oppose Jesus, and the argument at least on one level deals with these accusations. In the accusations of Jesus' opponents the power of Jesus is revealed.

Scribes' accusation may be the same as in Mark.[17] The omission of Matthew cannot be explained by a dissatisfaction with the explanation offered by Mark. It must be assumed that Matthew had another purpose in mind when he abbreviated. Perhaps the accusation was indeed familiar for Matthew's community so that it needed no further expansion. However, it is more probable that the narrative purpose of Matthew's abbreviations throughout the pericope becomes apparent here. The reduction of the encounter with the paralytic to a bare outline, and the omission for the reason of the Scribal discontent, make the accusation of the Scribes stand out much more clearly. The focus of the story is no longer a discussion about the possibility or impossibility of Jesus' forgiveness of sins, as it was in the Markan pericope. The conflict itself takes precedence, and the actual item of contention becomes secondary and is no longer explained as part of the accusation of blasphemy. Thus the opposition of the Scribes is highlighted in its starkness precisely because it is not amplified or explained. This kind of opposition legitimizes Matthew's added description of the opponents' thoughts being evil (9:4). The Scribes' opposition to Jesus is very different from that of the Gadarenes who asked Jesus to leave their country without questioning his authority. It also makes the redaction of Matthew crucial, as we shall see, to the understanding of the following stories of conflict between Jesus and his opponents. The accusation of blasphemy, then, becomes the first climax of the story.

This climax is accentuated by the stark use of "that one blasphemes." The accusation anticipates the final explanation for the death of Jesus: Because Jesus is seen as blaspheming he is sentenced to death by the Jewish leaders (26:65).[18] Thus this first controversy story forms an inclusion for the struggle of Jesus with his opponents. The first accusation also indicates in retrospect that the conflict between Jesus and the Jewish leaders was irreparable right from the beginning. The lines are clearly drawn. It is the Scribes who distance themselves from Jesus with the accusation and the derogatory οὗτος.

---

[17] Gaechter brings the problem to the point when he writes: "Durch die Absolutheit, mit welcher Jesus Sünden vergab, stellte er sich im Grunde genommen in dieselbe Beziehung zur Sünde wie Gott." Gaechter: *Matthäusevangelium*, 287.

[18] This parallels the arrangement by Mark. In Mark the accusation of blasphemy is also the first to be made against Jesus in a controversy story (2:7) that becomes the final rationale for Jesus' death (14:64). However, Matthew elaborates on this inclusion that covers the controversies of Jesus by a repetition of the charge in 26:65, by a more precise verbal congruence between 9:3 (βλασφημεῖ) and 26:65 (ἐβλασφήμησεν ... ἴδε νῦν ἠκούσατε τὴν βλασφεμίαν) than Mark (βλασφημεῖ in 2:7, ἠκούσατε τῆς βλασφεμίας in 14:64), and by the lack of Mark's explanatory remarks in 9:3. The Markan arrangement is analyzed by: Peter von der Osten-Sacken: "Streitgespräch und Parabel als Formen Markinischer Christologie," in: *Jesus Christus in Historie und Theologie. Neutestamentliche Festschrift für Hans Conzelmann zum 60. Geburtstag*, ed. Georg Strecker (Tübingen: Mohr (Siebeck), 1975), 378–380.

Jesus' rejoinder in 9:4–6 begins with a small redactional change from ἐπιγνούς ὅτι to καὶ ἰδών[19] for a parallelization with 9:2.[20] "In his spirit" is dropped as unnecessary, and twice the root διαλογιζ- is replaced by ἐνθυμε-. Because Matthew left out Mk 2:7, there is nothing to discuss. Thus Matthew is concerned with the inner thoughts of the Scribes. It is probably beside the point to speculate whether Jesus' knowledge of the Scribes' thoughts was "paranormal or telepathic."[21] More to the point is the explicit characterization of the Scribes' thoughts as evil and Jesus' immediate knowledge of their thoughts. While Jesus offers a "Take heart, child" to the paralytic, the Scribes are revealed as evil even in Jesus' first words to them.

From 9:5 on Matthew follows more closely the formulations of Mark, with only slight modifications. He leaves out "to the paralytic" and the command "and take your pallet" for brevity. In v. 6 the phrase "on the earth" is moved.[22] Somewhat weightier is the question whether 9:6 is an aside to the reader or a continuation of the speech of Jesus. Mark on occasion makes such asides (7:3–4, 19c; 13:14). In Mark's gospel the title "son of man" appears only twice before the confession of Jesus as the Messiah in 8:29, here and in 2:28. After the confession the title occurs frequently. Both early occurrences can be interpreted as asides to the reader and

---

[19] Some manuscripts have εἰδώς instead of ἰδών. The latter is the *lectio difficilior* since "seeing their thoughts" would have invited the correction "knowing." Bruce M. Metzger: *A Textual Commentary on the Greek New Testament*, 2nd ed. (New York: United Bible Societies, 1994), 19–20. Furthermore, the parallelism with 9:2 supports ἰδών.

[20] Davies and Allison: *Matthew*, 2:90.

[21] So proposed by Davies and Allison: *Matthew*, 2:92. In a story where the lame walk again the ability of Jesus to read his opponents thoughts can only be of minor interest. Apart from this, the continuation of the story shows that the community exercised the same forgiveness of sin as Jesus did, so they would have been familiar with such controversies.

[22] Several explanations for this change provided by Davies and Allison are unlikely. If it stresses the fact that the son of man has already appeared, how does it do so more forcefully than Mark's formulation with the phrase at the end of the sentence (Mk 2:10)? If it indicates the earthly ministry of the son of man the same question arises. There is probably no contrast implied between earth and heaven since the latter does not appear in the pericope at all. The suggestion that Jesus is the only one to forgive sins on earth is not supported by the implication of 9:8 of precisely such a ministry within the community and the fact that the authority to bind and loose lies with the community in 18:18. Davies and Allison: *Matthew*, 2:93. Lange suggests that the shift in the formulation is motivated by a close affinity to 28:18–20 since the phrase now moves closer to ἐξουσία: "Jedenfalls entsteht so bei Matthäus eine Akoluthie und Struktur, die sich mit der von Mt 28,18–20 stärker berührt und wohl nicht beziehungslos neben der dort gefundenen Formulierung steht" Joachim Lange: *Das Erscheinen des Auferstandenen im Evangelium nach Matthäus. Eine traditionsgeschichtliche und redaktionsgeschichtliche Untersuchung zu Mt 28, 16–20* (Würzburg: Echter, 1973), 64. But this possibility is farfetched, and there is no real correlation of terms between the phrases 9:6 and 28:18–20. It is probably best not to read much into this change. Luz: *Matthäus*, 2:37 n.14.

would, if this were true, lend greater consistency to the gospel of Mark.[23] But Matthew does not follow the scheme of Mark in his early chapters, and the title was used by Jesus for himself already in 8:20. Thus even if Mark's use of the phrase is perhaps an aside,[24] the Matthean version need not be so.[25]

The forgiveness of sins is, as in Mk 2:10, associated with the power of the son of man. This power may be understood as both the ability and the authority of the son of man. It is possible that on one level the Scribes notice that Jesus speaks of himself and are embittered by this. On another level the community probably realizes the association of the son of man with Dan 7:13–14 and sees the power to forgive sins in relation to the eschatological judgment of which the son of man is the sign.[26]

Matthew inserts a τότε to mark the return of the paralytic into the narrative and leaves out "I say to you" (Mk 2:11), changes the imperative "rise" into a circumstantial participle in order to achieve greater parallelism with the actual description of the rising man in 9:7, again substitutes κλίνη for κράβαττος, and creates a parallelism with 9:6 by describing how the man went home εἰς τὸν οἶκον αὐτοῦ.[27]

In the conclusion of the story (9:8) Matthew again takes greater liberty with Mark. The conclusion is highlighted by separating it better from the miracle through the use of the particle δε that substitutes for the Markan connector ὥστε. But more

---

[23] So Davies and Allison: *Matthew*, 2:93. The question of authority in connection with the son of man plays a role in Mark only in 2:10 and 2:28. Thus these early son of man sayings are fundamentally different from the others found in Mark and lend themselves to an interpretation as rhetorical asides to the reader.

[24] Several authors argue against taking the verse as an aside: Morna Hooker argued that here a dominical saying is preserved, with allusions to Dan 7:13–14. Morna D. Hooker: *The Son of Man in Mark. A Study of the Background of the Term "Son of Man" and Its Use in St. Mark's Gospel* (Montreal: MacGill University Press, 1967). Lindars argues similarly, but from a conjectured Aramaic original. Barnabas Lindars: *Jesus Son of Man* (London: SCM Press, 1982).

[25] Against Davies and Allison, who conclude from the Markan version that Matthew must be an aside as well. Davies and Allison: *Matthew*, 2:93.

[26] So Luz: *Matthäus*, 2:37. The association with 16:19 and especially 18:18 makes this a very probable assumption. Matthew uses the term "son of man" in the polemics against Jewish authorities in 9:6; 11:19; 12:8, 32, 40. In all cases the opponents of Jesus do not associate the term with the claim of the association with Dan 7:13–14. However, the formation of 28:16–20 is probably an indication that at least the Matthean community knew of this association and used it for its catechetical purposes. This is borne out by the fact that most "son of man" sayings in the gospel are sayings addressed to the disciples. In this context the son of man is often coming in judgment: 10:23; 13:41; 16:27–28; 19:28; 7 times in 24:27–25:31; these judgment sayings are by far the majority of the "son of man" sayings in Matthew's gospel.

[27] Matthew uses repetitive phraseology occasionally to show that an order of Jesus is carried out to the letter: See 1:24–25; 2:13–14, 19–20. The phenomenon is perhaps connected with Matthew's general interest in the theme of obedience. Luz: *Matthäus*, 2:37. On the other hand, Matthew's use of repetitive phraseology goes far beyond that. Davies and Allison have accumulated a list of such phrases. Davies and Allison: *Matthew*, 1:88–92.

significantly Matthew changes the Markan πάντας to οἱ ὄχλοι. With this distinction Matthew creates another group of people in this story besides the paralytic and his friends and the Scribes. He introduces the crowds who react to the miracle. Mark's formulation leaves it open whether the Scribes join in the praise or not. In Matthew they definitely do not. They remain adversaries. Matthew also conveys that Jesus brought the crowds to see his side of the argument. But Matthew is not yet done. He repeats the theme of power that already appeared in 9:6 as the power of the son of man. The power that God gives becomes the rationale for the admiring crowds. This power was defined in 9:6 as the power to forgive sins. Its reappearance in 9:8 steers the admiration of the crowd into the direction of forgiveness of sins, and away from the miracle. Mark 2:12 phrases the admiration of all as an admiration for what they saw. This is presumably the miracle, since the forgiveness of sins is not immediately visible, nor is it mentioned. The Markan formulation is at least ambivalent. Matthew makes it clear that the admiration is directed to the power to forgive sins.

This power, however, is now predicated of people, τοῖς ἀνθρώποις.[28] This remarkable phrase is probably a hint that the power to forgive sins finds its continuation in the practice of the community.[29] Such a view is seconded by the power to bind and loose that is first given to Peter (16:19) and then extended to the whole community (18:18).[30] The whole story becomes a story in which not just the activity of Jesus is under discussion, but also the practice of the community.

The redactional activity of Matthew can now be summarized: Matthew structures the story better than Mark through καὶ ἰδού (9:2.3) and τότε (9:6) into three parts, with a conclusion marked by δε. Within the first two parts some people act (the paralytic and his companions) or speak (the Scribes) and elicit a response from Jesus that is introduced in both cases by καὶ ἰδὼν ὁ Ἰησοῦς. In the first case Jesus sees the faith, in the second their innermost evil thoughts. In the third section suddenly it is Jesus who acts first. The response, again introduced by καί and a circumstantial participle (ἐγερθείς), is the healing of the man. In the central section

---

[28] The assumption that the plural here might be an indication of a collective understanding of "son of man" seems unwarranted and has fallen out or use. For such an argument see McNeile: *Matthew*, 116–117.

[29] Such a view is not without opponents. Luz reports that Calvin saw this reference as an error on the part of the crowds, but the power is only given to Jesus. Luz: *Matthäus*, 2:38 n. 18. This argument is still repeated by Lohmeyer: *Matthäus*, 169. Schenk has argued that the words are constructed as a *dativus commodi* and must be translated as "for the benefit of humans." Wolfgang Schenk: "'Den Menschen' (Mt 9,8)," *ZNW* 54 (1963): 272–275. This is probably impossible because such a translation would imply a similar construction in 10:1; 21:23; and 28:18. But in all these places a *dativus commodi* is impossible.

[30] This argument was first proposed by Schlatter: *Der Evangelist Matthäus*, 301. Highly influential in popularizing the thesis was: Heinrich Greeven: "Die Heilung des Gelähmten nach Matthäus," *WuD* 4 (1955): 74–78.

the Scribes are revealed as evil, and their isolation becomes apparent when the crowds in the conclusion side with Jesus and his community.[31]

The circumstances recede into the background, the miraculous part of the story is lessened. Clearly Matthew is interested in the healing primarily in so far as it becomes a supporting argument for the power to forgive sins, and it becomes an argument from the minor to the major issue.

The argument from the minor to the major is a common rhetorical device. The Roman Quintilian, a rhetorician at the courts of Vespasian, Titus, and Domitian, lists it among the arguments in the rhetorical art.[32] Quintilian was a contemporary of Matthew and a rhetorician who preferred the style of Cicero to later developments in rhetoric embodied by the speeches of Seneca.[33] Although he is the first rhetorician to include the argument *a minore ad maius* in a systematic treatise of the rhetorical art,[34] his conservative taste as well as the didactic nature of his *Institutio Oratoria* lead to the conclusion that this particular argument was already common in his time.

In Jewish circles the argument was likewise used. The argument from the minor to the major is included in the 7 *middot* of Rabbi Hillel.[35] These *middot* were probably not invented by Hillel but represent a "collation of the main types of argument in use at that time."[36] The first of these is the *qal-wa-ḥomer*, the argument from the lighter, or less significant, to the weightier, or more significant. The argument can also go from the weightier to the lighter. In the interpretation of the Law this rule is valid with one exception. It cannot justify greater punishment.

It is probably futile to try to trace the Matthean argument to either the Greco-Roman tradition of rhetoric or the Rabbinic rules of interpreting the Law.

---

[31] The present structural analysis departs slightly from the one proposed by Davies and Allison, who do not see τότε as a structural marker in the story and therefore have the second couplet conclude with the healing word of Jesus, while the third couplet consists of the rising of the man and the reaction of the crowd. Davies and Allison: *Matthew*, 2:86. This analysis, however, must explain the difficulty in the change of audience and re-introduction of the paralytic in the middle of the second couplet. Gnilka proposes the same scheme and encounters the same difficulty. He even draws unwitting attention to it: "Strukturell ist die Erzählung in drei Szenen gegliedert. Sie sind jeweils durch besondere Personengruppen geprägt." Gnilka: *Matthäus*, 1:324–325.

[32] Quintilian: *Inst.*, 5, 10, 87.

[33] For a biography of Quintilian and a characterization of his rhetorical art see: George A. Kennedy: *A New History of Classical Rhetoric* (Princeton: Princeton University Press, 1994), 177–186.

[34] Heinrich Lausberg: *Handbuch der Literarischen Rhetorik. Eine Grundlegung der Literaturwissenschaft*, 3rd ed. (Stuttgart: Franz Steiner, 1989), 219.

[35] The *middot* are transmitted in several versions: They are related in *t.Sanh* 7.11 (Z. 427), in the introduction to the *Sifra* (W. 3a), and in *ARN* A37. In *Sifra* they are joined with the later 13 rules of Rabbi Ishmael. Hermann Leberecht Strack and Günther Stemberger: *Introduction to the Talmud and Midrash*, trans. M. Bockmuehl (Minneapolis: Fortress, 1992), 19–23.

[36] Strack and Stemberger: *Introduction*, 19.

There may have been a connection between these two traditions, but it is probably no longer traceable.[37] The argument would have appealed to people from a Greco-Roman background as well as readers with a background in Jewish legal debates.

As the details of the miracle recede into the background the acting persons become more prominent. At the heart of the story is the conflict between Jesus and the Scribes. Matthew makes it clear that at the beginning of the conflict lies the internal attitude of the Scribes. This attitude implies a rejection of the son of man. That makes their thoughts evil. This evil is brought into the open by Jesus' challenge to them. At the same time, the Scribes are described more clearly as opposed not only to Jesus, but also to the crowds who accept the power to forgive sins. The final editorial remark opens the controversy towards the Matthean community.

The extensive redaction of the story makes it unlikely that Matthew reported the incident out of nostalgia for bygone times, or just because he found it in the gospel of Mark. The redactional opening to the community at the end of the story implies that the issue was an issue in Matthew's community. The heightening of the controversial aspect of the story suggests that the issue was still debated with some opponents of a practice of forgiveness as a ministry of the community. The opponents, here characterized as Scribes, seem to be outsiders of the Matthean community since they appear in contrast to Jesus as well as to the admiring crowds. The redaction of the story leads to the conclusion that the debate between Jesus and the Scribes was in some fashion a contemporary one for the Matthean community.

2.1 The Markan Pericope

It has been argued that the Markan story that stands behind the Matthean account is itself comprised of two sources. Behind such an assumption lies the realization that the controversy in this pericope is interwoven with a miracle.[38] It has been

---

[37] David Daube has argued that the *middot* of Hillel owe something to the principles of Hellenistic rhetoric that were adopted in Roman legal interpretation. David Daube: "Rabbinic Methods of Interpretation and Hellenistic Rhetoric," *HUCA* 22 (1949): 239–264. Daube's argument rests mainly on the observation that Hillel's teachers Shemayah and Abtalion were proselytes who had studied and taught in Alexandria. This argument presumes that the *middot* did not grow out of a wide consensus of the early rabbis, but were composed by Hillel under the influence of his teachers. This, however, can neither be proven, nor is it likely.

[38] This is already argued by Bultmann: *History*, 14–16. He argues that there is no real connection between miracle and controversy (p. 15). Hultgren calls this story a non-unitary conflict story and defines non-unitary conflict stories as stories "in which the opponent's question, and usually some other narrative element are a secondary construction, composed to give a setting for a dominical saying (authentic or not) which originally circulated independently." For the pericope at hand this would assume that Mk 2:10 circulated, at least in part, independently before the integration into the context of the controversy. Arland Hultgren: *Jesus and His Adversaries: The Form and Function of the Conflict Stories in the Synoptic Tradition* (Minneapolis: Augsburg,

frequently argued that the controversy and the miracle represent two different strands of tradition.[39] One reason for holding this view is the easily removable controversy section of the pericope: If 2:5b–10 is removed the narrative gains a smoothness as a simple miracle story that would also explain the "all" of 2:12 since the Scribes are no longer present in his story, and the absence of a reference to forgiveness in 2:12.

However, difficulties with such a deconstruction remain.[40] Though it is true that the resulting miracle story reads smoother than the present version, the remainders of such a deconstruction could hardly have existed on their own. They do not form a coherent narrative.[41] On the other hand, it is hardly conceivable that such an important issue as the forgiveness of sins could have been part of this miracle early on without ever influencing its narrative progression beyond 2:6–9.[42]

Much of these arguments must necessarily remain speculation, and it is not necessary for our purposes to present a final judgment on the issue. However, the problem of Mk 2:1–12 reveals the uneasy side-by-side existence of a miracle and a controversy that defies facile explanations. Matthew dealt with this problem in his redaction.[43] The tighter structuring of the whole pericope ties the miracle and the controversy together with a clear emphasis on the latter. The changed ending integrates the crowds admiration with the issue of forgiveness of sins. Finally, Matthew's deletions affect only the miraculous part of the story. He makes a

---

1979), 100. However, the independence of this saying can perhaps be suggested, yet its integration into the surrounding material does not give any literary grounds for an independent use of the saying. While Hultgren's definition is useful, it is preferable to suspend judgment on the supposed priority of some elements over others within this particular story. If, as will be discussed in chapter 6, the controversy stories are a subgroup of chreia then one deals with a literary form in which the dominical saying, authentic or not, is as much part of the form as the opponent's question. Thus the dominical saying cannot be separated from the setting of the conflict story on form-critical grounds.

[39] Wrede seems to have been the first to propose such a theory. William Wrede: "Zur Heilung des Gelähmten (Mc 2.1ff.)," ZNW 5 (1904): 354–358. For further bibliographical information consult. Hultgren: *Adversaries*, 135 n.24. More recently the theory has been proposed by Pesch and Klauck. Rudolf Pesch: *Das Markusevangelium*, 2 vols., HThK (Freiburg: Herder, 1977), 1:151–152; Hans-Josef Klauck: "Die Frage der Sündenvergebung in der Perikope von der Heilung des Gelähmten (Mk 2.1–12 parr.)," BZ 25 (1981): 223–248.

[40] For a bibliography of opponents of the deconstruction see: Hultgren: *Adversaries*, 136 n. 27.

[41] Hultgren tries to solve the issue by asserting that the present form of the narrative originated with the miracle story of 2:1–5a. 11–12, which was "expanded by *composing* 2:5b–10." In this way the controversy was the important issue for the redactor, while the miracle was the earlier tradition. Hultgren: *Adversaries*, 107.

[42] This is the argument of Theissen: *Stories*, 164.

[43] For this reason Greeven seems correct in his assumption that the consistency and rationality of the Matthean redaction of the healing of the paralytic make it unnecessary to assume a source for Matthew that is related to, yet different from the present Mark. An *Urmarkus* need not be assumed for this pericope. Greeven: "Heilung."

decision about what is important in the source, and the miracle becomes primarily an occasion. Matthew's redaction of the address to the paralytic becomes the foil by which the controversy with the Scribes stands out even more forcefully. At the center of Matthew's structure and redaction is the controversy in which the miracle is the minor part of the argument that proves the major issue of the power of Jesus to forgive, and of the continuation of this power within the community. The controversy takes precedence, and with it the figure of Jesus assumes a stronger profile, while the opponents are revealed in their wickedness.

2.2 Summary of the Matthean Redaction in 9:2–8

The trends of the Matthean redaction in 9:2–8 can now be summarized briefly. They concern both the structure of the story and the content of the story.

▸ Matthew inserts structural elements to divide the story into three distinct parts and a conclusion. The elements include corresponding particles as well as parallelizations of similar elements in the three parts.

▸ Matthew abbreviates the story chiefly in its setting. The miracle gives way to a greater emphasis on the controversy.

▸ The accusation of the Scribes is paralleled to the accusation made by the Sanhedrin in 26:65, and thus expresses already the irreconcilable differences between Jesus and his opponents.

▸ Matthew's redaction distinguishes between the Scribes and the crowds in the audience of Jesus. While the Scribes react negatively, the crowds react positively. The story portrays the Scribes and the crowds at variance with each other.

▸ Matthew's redaction extends the controversy explicitly to the praxis of the community.

3. Matthew 9:9–13

Matthew continues the narrative thread of Mark with the story of the call of Matthew, the meal with tax collectors and sinners and the controversy of Mt 9:9–13 ‖ Mk 2:13–17. He creates a closer proximity to the controversy over the forgiveness of sins by leaving out Mark's summary report of Jesus teaching the crowds (Mk 2:13). This leads to the explicit mention of Jesus as subject in 9:9. Matthew substitutes for "Levi son of Alphaeus" (Mk 2:14) with "a man called Matthew."[44]

---

[44] The reasoning behind this change of name, and probably person, is of only tangential interest to the following controversy story. It is possible that Matthew preferred to include a disciple of the circle of the twelve into this vocation story; in effect, this creates a closer affinity with the vocations in 4:18–22. The ascription of the authorship of the gospel to this Matthew are not warranted by the text. For a fuller discussion see: Gnilka: *Matthäus*, 1:330–331.

The Markan emphasis on the immediate obedience of the tax collector is taken over.

In v. 10 the scene is briefly set up for the ensuing controversy. Jesus reclines at table in the house whose ownership is no longer important to Matthew.[45] The beginning of the actual controversial issue is highlighted by the insertion of ἰδού. The tax collectors and sinners are introduced a little more smoothly than in Mark through the insertion of ἐλθόντες. An impression of a very casual affair arises, at which more and more people show up.[46] Matthew also distinguishes Jesus and the disciples more clearly from the sinners through the insertion of ἰδού and ἐλθόντες (9:10). While the meal begins with Jesus alone (αὐτοῦ ἀνακειμένου), the outcasts drop in on the meal (πολλοὶ τελῶναι καὶ ἁμάρτολοι ἐλθόντες συνανέκειντο). The disciples appear, as in Mk 2:15, closely associated with Jesus (τῷ Ἰησοῦ καὶ τοῖς μαθηταῖς αὐτοῦ). Consequently, the insertion of the participle gives the impression that Jesus and his disciples are engaged in a ministry to those who come to them for table fellowship.

Matthew is no longer interested in repeating the number of the participants of the feast (Mk 2:15c).[47] The information would be interruptive in the account of the controversy story. Perhaps Matthew is also not interested in shaping a ceremonious event out of the meal with sinners and tax collectors.[48] Quite possibly, however, the

---

[45] The confusing possessive pronoun αὐτοῦ in Mk 2:15 does not help to clarify whether Jesus reclines in his own house, or whether he reclines in Levi's house. Lk 5:29 likewise sees the difficulty Mark presents. He solves the problem by creating a feast that Levi prepares for Jesus in Levi's house.

[46] Matthew achieves this by first describing that Jesus reclined with Matthew. The other guests are introduced then through καὶ ἰδού ... ἐλθόντες συνανέκειντο.

[47] Matthew frequently deletes Markan γάρ-clauses. Of 35 of such Markan constructions Matthew retains 10, reshapes 9, and deletes 16. The deletions can be categorized according to their appearance in Mark: "(1) explicative comments awkwardly attached ... (2) disedifying and unnecessary revelations about the inferior state of the disciples and followers of Jesus ... (3) information obvious to the reader by its context ... (4) afterthoughts of new information interruptive of the account ..." Wendy J. Cotter: "For It Was Not The Season For Figs," *CBQ* 48 (1986): 64. Mk 2:15c belongs to the fourth category.

[48] Gnilka supposes that the table fellowship depicted in this verse is a small image for the community. He then jumps to the conclusion that this was "die in der Gemeinde geübte Tischgemeinschaft von ehemaligen Juden und Heiden, die von der Synagoge kritisiert wurde (vgl. Gal 2, 11 ff)." Gnilka: *Matthäus*, 1:332. Gnilka probably goes too far in his reasoning here. There is no evidence that any of the sinners or tax collectors were Gentile. Furthermore, when Matthew leaves out the reference that the group of disciples was large he diminishes the significance this meal might still have had for Mark. Similarly Hummel assumes that "Matthäus hat in der Berufung des jüdischen הארץ עם durch Jesus die Berufung der Heiden vorgebildet gesehen. Darum kann angenommen werden, daß er in 9, 9–13 die Gemeinschaft von Juden und Christen im Auge hat." Hummel argues this because the acceptance of tax collectors and sinners into the group around Jesus must have been as offensive to the opponents of Jesus as the acceptance of Gentiles. Hummel: *Auseinandersetzung*, 39. But closer scrutiny does not bear this out. Matthew never uses tax collectors, sinners, and Gentiles interchangeably or together. And Hummel's

omission reflects merely Matthew's penchant for abbreviating Mark. There might be also a possibility that the omission of the many reflects a situation in the Matthean community and its rather limited success of the ministry to Israel.[49]

The opponents of Jesus are introduced through καὶ ἰδόντες + Nominative (9:11). A small change of the word order found in Mk 2:16 creates a structural element that parallels καὶ ἰδού + Nominative in 9:10. Matthew also corrects "the Scribes of the Pharisees"[50] to Pharisees and omits the repetitive mention of the meal with tax collectors and sinners. Instead, he moves immediately to the objection raised by the Pharisees to the disciples. The question becomes slightly more pointed by the insertion of διὰ τί for ὅτι.[51] A more important addition is recognition of the Pharisees that Jesus is "your teacher."[52] This is an ironic twist in the story, since it turns out that the teacher of the Matthean community knows the scriptures better than the Pharisees. And while the Pharisees accept that Jesus is the teacher of the community, they do not accept him as their own teacher when they refuse to learn the meaning of Hos 6:6 (see 12:7).

The riposte of Jesus is introduced with ὁ δέ which serves to mark a greater contrast than Mark achieves in 2:17. The answer is further highlighted by leaving out the unnecessary αὐτοῖς ὅτι. The answer of Jesus is given in three parts. The first repeats the Markan saying of the physician, the second enjoins the Pharisees to go and learn the meaning of Hos 6:6, and the third repeats Mark's saying that Jesus came to call not the righteous but sinners. The three sayings are clearly distinguished from one another by the insertion of δε into the second and γάρ into the third (9:13).

The redaction of the pericope reveals again Matthew's eye for structuring his narrative. With καὶ ἰδού, καὶ ἰδόντες, and ὁ δὲ ἀκούσας Matthew sharpens the

---

connection between the tax collectors and sinners and the Jewish עם הארץ is questionable. At issue here is probably the ease with which Jesus and his disciples sat at table with sinners. An argument for Gentile participation in the Matthean church cannot be inferred from this pericope. Gnilka takes up Hummel's arguments. Gnilka: *Matthäus*, 1:332.

[49] This would assume a situation of the community as sectarian within the larger parent body of Judaism as proposed by Overman and taken up by Saldarini. Overman: *Matthew's Gospel*, 6–34; Saldarini: *Matthew's Christian-Jewish Community*, 11–26.

[50] Perhaps "Pharisäische Schriftgelehrte," suggested by Joachim Gnilka: *Das Evangelium nach Markus*, EKK II,1–2 (Zürich, Einsiedeln, Köln, Neukirchen: Benziger, Neukirchener, 1978–1979), 1:103, 106. Mark might have had in mind an attempt to tie his controversy stories together more tightly since the previous story contained Scribes as opponents, while the next story contains Pharisees in conjunction with disciples of John (2:18).

[51] This redaction is probably motivated by 9:14 ‖ Mk 2:18. The two stories are thus more intimately linked. Matthew uses the same construction also in 13:10 (red.); 15:2; 15:3 (red.); 17:19 (red. from Markan ὅτι); 21:25.

[52] "Teacher" is not an adequate title for Jesus in Matthew. It is only opponents of Jesus who call him teacher: 8:19 (the prospective disciple is not accepted); 9:11; 10:24; 10:25; 12:38; 17:24; 19:16; 22:16; 22:24; 22:36; 23:8; 26:18. See also: Janice C. Anderson: *Matthew's Narrative Web: Over, and Over, and Over Again*, JSNT.S 91 (Sheffield: JSOT Press, 1994), 118–119.

threefold structure of the story of setting, objection, and riposte. The same threefold structure is emphasized in the actual answer of Jesus. Matthew achieves this through the insertion of small particles, but also through the omission of material that he regards as repetitive or interruptive. As in the previous controversy story the emphasis on the structure helps to focus attention on the controversy and its participants. The amplification of the answer of Jesus draws attention to his stature, while the Pharisees again stand out more prominently than in the account of Mark because of their correct identification and the omission of the unnecessary circumstances.

Matthew's additions are significant. The Pharisees recognize that Jesus is a teacher. While the title has a negative connotation here, as throughout the gospel, it has an additional function here: It prepares for the second element of the answer of Jesus that begins with πορευθέντες δὲ μάθετε.[53] As the Pharisees recognize that Jesus is a teacher, they are enjoined by him to learn the meaning of Hos 6:6. Occasionally the argument is made that Matthew saw in this quotation a hint that the official cult was invalidated by the acts of mercy enjoined by the gospel.[54] However, by the time that Matthew was writing the temple had been destroyed, and the reference to sacrifices would seem somewhat pointless.[55] Furthermore, Hos 6:6

---

[53] Strack and Billerbeck see here "ein rabbinischer Schulausdruck" formed after צא למד. Strack and Billerbeck: *Kommentar*, 1:499. Their sources are few and late (*Seder ElijR* 18; *NuR* 8 (149a), as well as varied (*Av* 2,9 employs the plural). It is only remotely possible that Matthew knew of this expression as a formula. However, it is impossible to ascertain this.

[54] Already so proposed by Lohmeyer: *Matthäus*, 173. Strecker similarly observes that the "zeremonialgesetzlichen Schranken hinfällig sind und nur noch die sittlichen Normen gültig sind." Strecker: *Weg*, 32. Meier is more concrete in extending such observations to the social setting of Matthew in the Gentile world: "Indeed, the 'lax' attitude of Jesus toward stringent religious observance marks a break with both the disciples of the Baptist and the Pharisees. It could not be otherwise, for the eschatological bridegroom has come to the marriage feast to claim his people as a bride." Meier: *Vision*, 72.

[55] So argued by Schlatter: *Matthäus*, 307–308. The story related about Yohanan ben Zakkai and his pupil Joshua contains a significant parallel: In it Joshua mourns the passing of the temple as the place where atonement for sins was received. Yohanan consoles him with the reference to Hos 6:6 and saying that in the place of the temple there is another way to receive forgiveness: mercy. The story is related in both versions of Aboth Rabbi Natan. In version A the story is related in ch. 4 and given a context in which Yohanan and Joshua travel from Jerusalem and see the ruins of the temple. It is further annotated with the examples of David and Daniel in order to illustrate the quotation of Hos 6:6. Judah Goldin: *Abot de Rabbi Natan A*, YJS X (New Haven: Yale University Press, 1955), 34–35. In version B the story is given without context and illustration in 8,22. Anthony J. Saldarini: *The Fathers According to Rabbi Nathan (Abot de Rabbi Natan) Version B*, SJLA 11 (Leiden: Brill, 1975), 75. This double attestation in *ARN* is probably the result of a common oral tradition before the two traditions of *ARN* A and *ARN* B parted ways and developed separately into written tractates. If this is so, there are the problems of how far back such an oral tradition reached, whether such a tradition might have any significance for the interpretation of Matthew, and whether Matthew might have been aware of such an interpretation of Hosea in the light of the destruction of the temple. If so, the accusation that the Pharisees do

itself does not bear out such an interpretation in terms of an antithesis between mercy and cult.[56] Given Matthew's view on the keeping of the Law (5:17–18), this line of interpretation is highly unsatisfactory.

The text form of the quotation, ἔλεος θέλω καὶ οὐ θυσίαν, can be attributed to Matthew himself.[57] If Matthew inserted the quotation, the question is whether the charitable conduct towards others really exhausts the meaning of ἔλεος, and whether it can be shown that the sacrifices are truly a logical opposite. The word is a translation of the Hebrew חֶסֶד which denotes covenant loyalty, devotion and fidelity to Yahweh.[58] If Matthew translates and inserts a quotation that comes out of a context of covenant loyalty in the prophet Hosea,[59] it seems probable that this meaning passes on to the context that Matthew gives the quotation now.

If the quotation derives its meaning primarily from its context in Hosea, then the reference to sacrifices becomes clearer as well. The context in Hosea did not intend to abolish the sacrificial cult in its entirety. It merely pointed out that this cult was useless if it was not an expression of the covenant faithfulness that should permeate all aspects of Israel's life.[60] Thus mercy and sacrifice are not mutually exclusive, but complement each other, as sacrifice and cult are a part of the covenant faithfulness enjoined upon Israel. For Matthew this meant that the Pharisees were unable to go from the smaller good to the greater virtue. While they were bound to the cultic observances, they could not make the step towards true covenant faithfulness.

---

not understand the meaning of Hos 6:6 and refuse to learn it gains added significance. However intriguing such speculations are, they remain just that: speculations.

[56] Hos 6:6b clarifies that 6a does not contain an antithesis but is built around the concept that mercy must accompany sacrifice in order to validate it. Similarly the *TargHos* 6:6 interprets the verse in this way. Strack and Billerbeck: *Kommentar*, 1:499. Thus both the original meaning and an interpretation much later than Matthew argue not the illegitimacy of the sacrifice, but the complementary nature of mercy.

[57] The majority of the LXX manuscripts read ἤ instead of καὶ οὐ. The Matthean form of the text is found only in LXX B and Origen, and the probability that the Matthean version is a pre-Christian assimilation to the original Hebrew is very slim, since Or[lat] supports ἤ, while Or supports καὶ οὐ. A more complete discussion can be found in: Robert H. Gundry: *The Use of the Old Testament in St. Matthew's Gospel* (Leiden: Brill, 1967), 321. The upshot of this discussion is that Matthew's rendering seems independent from the LXX.

[58] Hill points out that the word occurs only three times in Matthew, once here, once in the parallel quotation 12:7, and once more in 23:23, where it appears in the context of an allusion to Mic 6:8 and is again the equivalent of the Hebrew חֶסֶד. David Hill: "On the Use and Meaning of Hosea VI. 6 in Matthew's Gospel," *NTS* 24 (1977): 109.

[59] To illustrate the context a little, a fuller quotation is given here: Hos 6:4–7: "What shall I do with you, O Ephraim? What shall I do with you, O Judah? Your love is like a morning cloud, like the dew that goes early away. 5 Therefore I have hewn them by the prophets, I have slain them by the words of my mouth, and my judgment goes forth as the light. 6 For I desire steadfast love (חֶסֶד) and not sacrifice, the knowledge of God, rather than burnt offerings. 7 But at Adam they transgressed the covenant; there they dealt faithlessly with me."

[60] Davies and Allison: *Matthew*, 2:105.

Accordingly, the Pharisees remain unable to understand the *qal-wa-ḥomer* arguments that Jesus makes again and again.

It is improbable, then, that Matthew uses the quotation as a prophetic word that speaks of the abolition of sacrifices by an act of mercy of the eschatological messenger of God.[61] The introduction that Matthew accords this quotation as an invitation to the Pharisees to go and learn its meaning does not support this view.[62] Matthew uses the quotation as a source of halakha. This means that the table fellowship with the sinners and tax collectors is not a mere setting aside of social boundaries, as radical as that may be. Jesus, in his surprising communion with sinners, is faithful to the covenant that is enjoined by God. By extension, the Pharisees who are objecting to this behavior are not just criticizing Jesus, they suddenly become unfaithful to the very covenant that they try to uphold.[63] The Pharisees become, in more modern words, ironic and tragic figures in the narrative. By their very desire to uphold proprieties they turn away from the covenant, and their professed love for the Law becomes like a morning cloud, like the dew that evaporates quickly to give way to dryness (cf. Hos 6:4).

Beyond the question of the exact meaning of the quotation its embedding in the narrative needs to be taken into account. Jesus tells the Pharisees to learn the quotation's meaning, and in 12:7 it turns out that they have not done so. This quotation, then, prepares for a deepening of the conflict because the Pharisees do not do what Jesus teaches. Thus Luz is probably correct in inferring that the thrust of the quotation is not so much paraenetic as it is christological. The address of Jesus as teacher prepares for this, and indeed he gives a teaching that Pharisees ought to understand since it concerns the interpretation of the scripture. At the same time, the pericope as a whole illustrates well Jesus' grasp of the quotation: In his sharing of a meal with sinners Jesus proves that he has understood Hósea perfectly.[64]

The embedding of the quotation between the two sayings in Mark bears this out. On one end of the quotation Jesus compares himself to a physician who tends to the sick, on the other end he is the one who came to call sinners like the paralytic in the preceding pericope. The prominent middle place of Hos 6:6 puts both these statements into perspective: Jesus is so, and acts so, because it is enjoined by God himself, and he has understood the scripture. The Pharisees' opposition is not just opposition to Jesus, it is opposition to the scriptures, and, therefore, to the will of

---

[61]   Against Lohmeyer: *Matthäus*, 174.

[62]   Hill: "Hosea VI. 6," 111.

[63]   While Hill points out the covenant faithfulness of Jesus, he fails to see the quotation here in its context within a controversy. He does not draw out the implications of the quotation for the Pharisees. This is somewhat surprising since Hill characterized Jesus' use of it as halachic, and surely a halakha does not just apply to Jesus? Hill: "Hosea VI. 6," 110–111.

[64]   Luz points out how from now on the ill will address Jesus with ἐλέησον in 9:27; 15:22; 17:15; 20:30–31. Luz: *Matthäus*, 2:45.

God himself. And along with their refusal to understand the scripture comes the inability to understand who Jesus is and what he does. The controversy is thus highly charged with christological motifs in a way lacking in Mark.

3.1 The Markan Pericope

The question of the historicity of the described events has featured prominently in the scholarly discussion of this pericope. Some have supposed that behind the story as Mark tells it lies an actual event in the life of Jesus that concludes with a historical dominical saying.[65] This has been disputed on several grounds,[66] yet is only marginally important for the present discussion.

The connection between the call of Levi and the meal in the house is somewhat uneasy, since the ownership of the house is not clarified, nor Levi mentioned again in the scene of the meal. In addition, the call of Levi is almost certainly modeled on the call of the four disciples in 1:16–20. Thus it is quite possible that Mark connected the two stories which might have existed separately before him.[67] Markan redaction seems equally responsible for the explanatory mention of the extent of Jesus' following in 2:15c through a γάρ-clause.[68] Thus while the Markan account reveals some editorial activity, even if some pre-Markan or historical background

---

[65] So, e.g. Vincent Taylor: *The Gospel According to St. Mark* (London: Macmillan, 1952), 203–207. Behind this thesis lies Taylor's general assumption that redactional activity in Mark shows signs of great care to discover the historical truth.

[66] The arguments that speak against the historicity of the event are firstly the unlikely situation of Jesus eating with his disciples and sinners and tax collectors in a house in which the Pharisees are present as well. Hultgren: *Adversaries*, 109–111. This argument is weak and speculative. Firstly it departs from Hultgren's claim to argue form critically. Secondly, it is quite possible that the objection of the Pharisees was raised on the occasion of the dinner, but not during it. Thus the Pharisees might have seen the people gather for a dinner, but not have been part of the actual affair, or not been present in the house. Gnilka: *Markus*, 1:103–104. Weightier is Bultmann's observation that the formation of the controversy stories in general shows a tendency to insert the Pharisees and Scribes as opponents of Jesus. Bultmann: *History*, 52. Another argument rests on the construction of the verb "to come" + infinitive in 2:17b as a form that is found sometimes in material that cannot be "assigned confidently to the earliest stage of the tradition." Hultgren: *Adversaries*, 109–110. As sayings of Jesus this construction occurs in Mk 10:45; Lk 12:51 ∥ Mt 10:34; Lk 12:49; 19:10; Mt 5:17. It also occurs in summary sayings: Lk 9:56; 1 Tim 1:15. Hultgren considers Mk 2:17b just such a summary that might be the product of the community's reflection on the ministry of Jesus.

[67] Gnilka provides a detailed discussion of the tradition of this pericope that is summarized here. Gnilka: *Markus*, 1:104.

[68] On the γάρ-clauses as a feature of Markan style see: Charles H. Bird: "Some Γάρ-Clauses in St. Mark's Gospel," *JThS* 4 (1953): 171–187; Cotter: "Figs."

cannot be ruled out entirely.[69] But such a historical background might have been only in the association of Jesus and disreputable people[70] around a table.

The redactional elements of the Markan pericope reveal a particular aim that is highlighted in the addition of 15c. The disciples, already present in the story in 15b, are emphasized by their number.[71] Thus the disciples gain an importance that leads to the supposition that the story served a specific purpose in the Markan community. The community needed to defend itself against charges that its membership was disreputable.[72] Mark strengthens this defense by adding to the appeal to the ministry of the earthly Jesus with an emphasis on the large number of his disciples. Verse 17 bolsters this argument with a dominical saying.

The Matthean redaction reveals an additional development. The weakening of the emphasis on the community in Matthew's version achieves a re-orientation of the story. In the place of the Markan appeal to Jesus to defend a community against charges of impropriety Matthew decides to focus on the argument between Pharisees and Jesus. While the Pharisees recognize that Jesus is a teacher, he takes up this epithet and becomes a teacher to the Pharisees. Thus Matthew achieves a clearer christological focus of the story by playing Jesus against the Pharisees. Jesus becomes a powerful teacher who knows the scriptures much better than the Pharisees. The focal point is no longer the improper constitution of the community. It now is Jesus, who is accepted by some as the teacher, and is rejected by others. While the conflict with the Pharisees takes center stage, the legitimization of the community through a dominical saying is still present. But it becomes more pointed in its accusation against the Pharisees as those who think themselves righteous and are, therefore, not called (cf. 9:13). Matthew has not re-invented Mark's story. But he has shifted its balance from the embattled community to the Pharisees who reject Jesus.

3.2 Summary of the Matthean Redaction in 9:9–13

Matthew's redaction of the meal with tax collectors and sinners concerns the structure of the story as well as its content.

▶   The abbreviations create a closer proximity to the preceding controversy story.

---

[69] Hultgren describes that "general reminiscences about the conduct of Jesus" form the historical background of this story. Hultgren: *Adversaries*, 111.

[70] Whether such disreputable people actually included tax collectors and sinners may be disputed. Both groups seem to occur as a formula: cf. Mt 11:19, Lk 15:1. Gnilka: *Markus*, 1:104.

[71] Gnilka suggest that the redactional nature of 15c leads to the "Verdacht, daß er die in 15b und 16 eingetragen hat." Gnilka: *Markus*, 1:104.

[72] Hultgren writes: "The entire story, then, including its dominical sayings, must have been composed and put to use in a time and place in which the church was attacked by opponents on the grounds that its fellowship was suspect." Hultgren: *Adversaries*, 110.

▸   The structural redaction divides the story more succinctly into setting, objection, and riposte. The opposition is more clearly defined, the objection more pointed, the riposte better structured.

▸   Matthew distances Jesus and the disciples from the meal with the tax collectors and sinners and thus achieves a distinction between the community and the outcasts.

▸   Matthew achieves a clearer christological focus of the controversy through the address "teacher" and the insertion of Hos 6:6 into the answer of Jesus and thus describing him as a teacher of scripture.

▸   Matthew emphasizes the conflict within the narrative.

4. Matthew 9:14-17

The question of the table fellowship with sinners and tax collectors is immediately followed by a pericope concerning the practice of fasting among the disciples of Jesus (Mt 9:14-17 || Mk 2:18-22).[73] Matthew follows the Markan version closely, but he brings some editorial activity to bear on this story. The connecting τότε (9:14) ties the story more closely to the preceding material. The impression is that the meal with the sinners gave rise to the present discussion as well. The reader can imagine Jesus in the house of the meal until he gets up in 9:19. This would locate the dialogues of eating with sinners and of the disciples' fasting practice in the same room, a narrative device to sharpen the cohesion of the stories.[74] This immediate connection also cleans up some of Mark's misunderstandings: Matthew makes clear that it is John's disciples who ask the question.[75]

The story has traditionally been classified as a controversy story.[76] Yet the introduction of the Baptist's disciples as questioners of Jesus is somewhat

---

[73]   The *Didache* indicates a similar controversy. In 8:1 it states that "hypocrites fast on Monday and Thursday. Christians, therefore, should fast on Wednesday and Friday."

[74]   This makes it doubtful that we are to imagine actual events. The Markan association of the stories is much less concise. Matthew tells not a story of "a day in the life of Jesus." Richard A. Edwards: *Matthew's Story of Jesus* (Philadelphia: Fortress, 1985), 30. Matthew is interested in the growing opposition to Jesus in its immediacy.

[75]   Mk 2:18 introduces a third party of people which actually comes to Jesus and asks the question. Grammatically it could be the association of Pharisees and John's disciples. But in the question that begins the controversy they are referred to in the third person. Thus it is likely that those who come to ask the question remain anonymous, taken out of the crowd that surrounds Jesus.

[76]   Bultmann and Dibelius classified the Markan story and its parallel in Matthew as a controversy. Bultmann: *History*, 18-19; Martin Dibelius: *From Tradition to Gospel* (New York: Scribners, 1934), 96. This assessment has been followed by many. Hultgren: *Adversaries*, 78-82; Hagner: *Matthew 1-13*, 242; Patte: *Matthew*, 130; Luz: *Matthäus*, 2:46; Davies and Allison: *Matthew*, 2:107. Gnilka does not comment of the form. Gnilka: *Matthäus*, 1:335.

surprising in Matthew's gospel, since they do not appear again as part of the opposition against Jesus.[77] Similarly, the questioners in Mk 2:18 are not immediately identifiable as hostile. They only report what they see the disciples of John and the disciples of the Pharisees do. This raises at least the possibility of classifying the story as a scholastic dialogue.[78] But Matthew's mention of the Baptist's disciples is a redactional clarification that also introduces the Pharisees. In Mk 2:18 some people approach Jesus (ἔρχονται) whose question makes it clear that they are not the disciples of John, nor the disciples of the Pharisees. They are a third party which speaks of those who fast in the third person (νηστεύουσιν). Matthew 9:14 maintains the setting of the dialogue with questioners who approach Jesus (προσέρχονται), but decides to phrase the question in the first person (νηστεύομεν). Consequently, Matthew achieves greater directness by eliminating the third party. In a next step Matthew corrects Mark by replacing the disciples of the Pharisees in Mark simply with Pharisees. They are already in place from the previous controversy. The only remaining group mentioned by Mark are the disciples of John who in Matthew now approach Jesus to become the questioners. Thus Matthew still remains close to his source Mark while clarifying a confused situation.

The consequence of this redaction is a sharpening in the question Jesus is asked. This sharpening lies in the tighter structure of the question. It no longer contains the double "the disciples of" used by Mark. Furthermore, the question changes from "they fast, but your disciples do not fast" to "we and the Pharisees fast, but your disciples do not fast." The question changes from one that might be interpreted as a request for information to a challenge. This challenge is heightened by the association of the questioners with the Pharisees, who are known to be hostile from the previous controversy story. Consequently, the Matthean version of the story

---

[77] In 11:2 they appear as emissaries of the imprisoned Baptist to inquire of Jesus whether he is "the one to come." But their question is not hostile, and they leave, seemingly content with the answer Jesus gives. Consequently, Bultmann classifies this story as a scholastic apophthegm. Bultmann: *History*, 54. In 14:12 the appear again to tell Jesus of the Baptist's violent death. The latter remark indicates some friendliness between Jesus and the disciples of John.

[78] Bultmann refers repeatedly to the very close relationship between scholastic and controversy dialogues. Bultmann: *History*, 39, 54. He writes: "The essential difference between them is that in the scholastic dialogues it is not necessary to have some particular action as the starting-point but for the most part the Master is simply questioned by someone seeking knowledge" (p. 54). In both Mark's and Matthew's story such an immediate action is absent from the story. Furthermore, in Mark's story the questioners are anonymous and thus cannot be classified as hostile, while in Matthew the questioners are the disciples of the Baptist. They, too, are not otherwise hostile in Matthew's gospel. Thus the classification of these stories as controversy or scholastic dialogues tends to focus around the perceived hostility in the question and response. Thus Bultmann, e.g., refers to an attack on the disciples and their defense by Jesus in Mark's story (p.19).

concerning fasting is much more clearly a controversy story than the Markan version.[79]

On the surface the elimination of "the disciples of the Pharisees" might be explainable by the inconsistency of Mark's usage of "disciples of Pharisees" and "Pharisees" in the same verse.[80] However, Matthew made a similar change in 9:11 when he replaced "the Scribes of the Pharisees." Thus the Matthean redaction, while clearing up Markan confusion, is also consistent in focusing on the Pharisees[81] who in this instance have something in common with John's disciples.[82] The disciples of the Baptist, however, recede into the background through the use of the simple personal pronoun. The Pharisees appear as the real opponents of Jesus.

The challenge in Matthew is more concise than in Mark. Matthew clarifies the speakers with "we" and follows it with a concomitant change in the syntactical structure. He qualifies the opponents' amount of fasting by inserting πολλά.[83] The insertions marks more clearly than Mark the distance between the disciples of John and the Pharisees on the one hand, and the disciples of Jesus on the other. From Mt 6:16–18[84] the reader already knows that the disciples of Jesus fast. However, Mt 6:16–18 is special Matthean material, while the present controversy is taken over

---

[79] This is not to say that Mark's story is not a controversy. As in Matthew Mark mentions the Pharisees in the question, and as in Matthew the Pharisees are known to be hostile in Mark. However, the Matthean identification of the opponents with the Pharisees makes the controversial character much more pronounced. Gnilka views Mark's story as a "Mischgebilde" with elements of a controversy dialogue. Gnilka: *Markus*, 1:113.

[80] Textual analysis of Mk 2:18 supports this. The nominative of "Pharisees" in 18a, though supported by the major manuscripts, is by some manuscripts replaced with a Genitive, and some manuscripts of the Western tradition supply "disciples of the Pharisees." The "disciples of the Pharisees" in 18c are in some minor manuscripts replaced by "Pharisees" only. While the official reading is not seriously put in doubt by the variants, the variants nevertheless attest to the incongruence of the present reading.

[81] Against Davies and Allison who think that the change is not explainable apart from a "desire for brevity." Davies and Allison: *Matthew*, 2:108.

[82] Luz remarks rightly that this association is somewhat surprising since John the Baptist is normally more closely associated with Jesus. This distinguishes the passage from 14:12 and makes the disciples of John here another of the Jewish groups who distance themselves from Jesus and who in 9:2–17 "den Bruch zwischen Jesus und Israel einleiten." Luz: *Matthäus*, 2:47.

[83] This qualifier is absent in important manuscripts (אֲ* B) and thus not a sure reading. There is a possibility that this qualifier was introduced by later manuscripts. It seems unlikely, however, that the non-parallel reading is a later scribal emendation. More likely, the divergent manuscripts אֲ* and B omitted πολλά because it is missing in Mark. This is borne out by a considerable number of similarly ancient witnesses to the presence of πολλά. See also Metzger: *Textual Commentary*, 20.

[84] Mt 6:16–18: And when you fast, do not look dismal, like the hypocrites, for they disfigure their faces that their fasting may be seen by men. Truly, I say to you, they have received their reward. 17 But when you fast, anoint your head and wash your face, 18 that your fasting may not be seen by men but by your Father who is in secret; and your Father who sees in secret will reward you.

from Mark. As a consequence Matthew ends up with an inconsistency between these two passages. The present controversy describes the disciples as not fasting, while Jesus defends their practice. It reflects the Markan account. This raises the questions of why Matthew would accept such an inconsistency, and what weight the question of fasting carried for him.

The answer to this problem might conceivably be found in the Matthean redaction of the question itself. Matthew used the question to shape the story more clearly as a controversy story. Thus it seems likely that for Matthew the point of the story lay not so much in the problem of a fasting or non-fasting community, but in the problem of allegations made against the community that needed an answer. Mark's story of the question about fasting provided Matthew with an opportunity to show his community attacked by opponents and defended by Jesus. The christological focus of the riposte bears this out.

Jesus' answer draws on three parables already found in Mark: the bridegroom, the unshrunk patch on an old garment, and the new wine in old skins. The first answer is slightly edited in Matthew. Instead of fasting the wedding guests mourn (9:15 ‖ Mk 2:19). Matthew draws attention to this change by positioning the verb πενθεῖν before the mention of the bridegroom, thus enhancing parallelism with the following clause. The change to mourning might be an allusion to 6:16–18 where fasting bears the outward signs of mourning, and to the beatitude of 5:4. It also draws attention to the focus on the bridegroom. Fasting might be a religious practice, but mourning is much more directed towards a person.

A christological interpretation of the parable of the bridegroom is the most likely. The disciples know that Jesus is the bridegroom.[85] Thus the change to "mourning" emphasizes the christological implications of the original question: While Jesus is with his disciples they have no reason to mourn. However, it remains unclear when the time for mourning will come. If the christological interpretation offered by the identification of Jesus with the bridegroom is correct, the time of mourning is one of the absence of Jesus. But again Matthew is inconsistent with other passages of his gospel. The time of the absence of Jesus could be the time between the resurrection and the parousia.[86] However, the disciples carry the promise of Jesus' continued presence (28:20). The two allegories of 25:1–30 understand the time between the resurrection and the parousia as a time of the absence of Jesus, but the element of mourning is entirely absent from these accounts.[87] While the interpretation of the absence of Jesus as the time after the

---

[85] See esp. 22:1–14; 25:1–13.

[86] Gundry explains that the fast is a practice interrupted only by the "brief interlude of Jesus' ministry." Gundry: *Matthew*, 171.

[87] Davies and Allison see the time of mourning precisely as "the days of eschatological affliction" because of the phrase "the days will come" and their eschatological significance elsewhere. However, Davies and Allison have to draw on parallels outside of Matthew to come to this conclusion. Davies and Allison: *Matthew*, 2:110–111. Their argument is strengthened by an

resurrection and before the end of times seems preferable, its inconsistency with 28:20 is noted.[88] Thus Jesus' answer may reflect a general practice in the community that was grounded perhaps in a christological reasoning reflected in the reference to the bridegroom which is then enhanced by the use of πενθεῖν.[89]

The images of the patched cloth and the wine in wineskins (9:16–17) closely match the Markan account (2:21–22). But Matthew introduces stylistic changes.[90] The exact meaning of the contrast between the old and the new remains, as in Mark, rather unclear. The relationship to the question of fasting is not obvious, particularly since both contesting groups are fasting, albeit in different forms.[91] However, Matthew does give the two parables a different direction by the redactional insistence that "both are preserved" (9:17). This has often been taken to mean that both the old and the new are preserved.[92] Taken to its extreme, and applied to the present controversy, such an interpretation would imply that both the

---

appeal to the eschatological dimension of the parable of the wedding feast (22:1–14) and of the parable of the ten maidens (25:1–14). In both these parables, however, eschatological motives are woven around the theme of a marriage feast where the theme of mourning is absent.

[88] The inconsistency is considerably increased by the fact that 25:1–13, the parable of the ten maidens waiting for the bridegroom, and 28:20 are both Matthean special material. Perhaps the absence of Mark's ἐν ἐκείνῃ τῇ ἡμέρᾳ suggests that Matthew was not altogether comfortable with denoting the precise time for the disciples' fasting.

[89] Luz warns against an unwarranted theological over-interpretation. Luz: *Matthäus*, 2:47. This is correct. Firstly, Matthew abbreviates the Markan account. Secondly, the Markan version suggests that the three images that Jesus uses were connected already before Matthew, perhaps even before Mark. Matthew's faithfulness to his source need not be over-interpreted as to the precise theology of the fasting practices of the Matthean community. A parallel in *EvThom* 104 reveals that the question of fasting was connected to the image of the bridegroom in different traditions as well, and Jn 3:29 contains a similar reference to a bridegroom, his friends, and the joy they experience together. While a dependence of John 3:29 on the synoptic tradition as suggested by Davies and Allison seems unlikely, these various traditions reveal the widespread use of the bridegroom imagery to describe the relationship and its outward signs between Jesus and his disciples. Davies and Allison: *Matthew*, 2:111.

[90] In v. 16 Matthew introduces δε, making the connection with v. 15 firmer. He substitutes ἐπιβάλλειν for ἐπιράπτειν, perhaps because of ἐπίβλημα; the rarity of the latter makes the minor agreement ἐπιβάλλειν with Lk 5:36 plausible without questioning the two-source hypothesis. This change strengthens the relationship with v. 17, where βάλλειν occurs twice. In v. 17 Matthew uses an impersonal plural, perhaps a Semitism as suggested by Davies and Allison, while οὐδέ parallels the δε of v. 16. Matthew gives both wine and wineskins their own verb in 17bc and thus highlights the destructive force. Davies and Allison: *Matthew*, 2:113.

[91] Luz: *Matthäus*, 2:47.

[92] Davies and Allison maintain this position and give further references. Davies and Allison: *Matthew*, 2:114–115. Harrington infers that the "old" refers to "pre-A.D. 70 Judaism (the Hebrew Bible, Israel's history, the Temple, the land, and so forth), the addition may reflect Matthew's conviction that the traditions of pre-70 Judaism is best preserved by the movement around Jesus." Harrington: *Matthew*, 129. This puts the gospel into the struggle for leadership among various Jewish movements in the period of early formative Judaism. Yet the stress of this saying is not so much on the preservation of traditions as it is on the preservation of new wine and skins.

Pharisaic Jewish way and the Matthean Christian way can be preserved.[93] This seems, however, unlikely in view of the anti-Pharisaic polemic of the gospel as a whole, and in view of the present context of a controversy story. More likely is the interpretation that Matthew claims that both the skins and the wine are preserved, and both of them are new. His interest in the old garment and wineskins wanes once their incompatibility with the new is pointed out.[94] The parables of the cloth and the wine, then, both argue for the incompatibility of the new and the old. In terms of Matthew's community this means that their status as the community of Jesus implies new ways of expressing itself. Fasting is one issue where such a re-organization becomes visible, and is consequently challenged by the opponents of the community. The two parables point out very strongly that the Matthean community represents something entirely new that cannot be fit into the categories that the opponents of Jesus want to apply. This point is already made in the Markan version of the parables. However, Matthew strengthens it with the additional saying of the preservation of wine and skins.

4.1 The Markan Pericope

The Markan account exhibits several features which suggest that the story was redacted by Mark from pre-gospel traditions. Commentators have used them to establish a pre-Markan tradition of the story with varying results.[95] Some of these features indicate the particularly Markan interests in the story. The saying of the bridegroom is lengthy and seems somewhat interruptive of the flow of the parables, although in keeping with the tendency of other New Testament writings to describe

---

[93] Harrington comments briefly on this passage in an article that mainly analyzes the story of the rich young man (19:16–22). He comes to the conclusion that the gospel of Matthew contains the rudiments of a "two way theology" that grants equal salvation to both Jews and Christians. Daniel J. Harrington: "The Rich Young Man in Mt 19,16–22: Another Way to God for Jews," in *The Four Gospels 1992. Festschrift Frans Neirynck*, ed. Frans van Segbroeck, Christopher M. Tuckett, et al. (Leuven: Leuven University Press & Uitgeverij Peeters, 1992), 1425–1432.

[94] So Luz: *Matthäus*, 2:48.

[95] Several superficially noticeable breaks in the narrative are: In v. 18 Mark mentions both Pharisees and disciples of Pharisees; it is not immediately clear who the questioners are. Vv. 19b–20 seems interruptive in the progression of the parables of the bridegroom, the patch and the wine, particularly since the parables of the patch and the wine are not appended with a seam but follow immediately. The two parables of the patch and the wine are constructed as parallels with οὐδείς ... εἰ δὲ μή. Obviously they belong together. This suggests that they did not form part and parcel with the parable of the bridegroom, which is constructed in the form of a rhetorical question. Similarly, the conclusion in 22c beginning with ἀλλά seems added to the combination of the patch and wine parables. It is different in structure, interrupts the parallelism, and refers only to the parable of the wine. As a consequence, commentators are prone to attempt a reconstruction of the tradition behind the Markan account. Bultmann: *History*, 17–18; Dibelius: *Formgeschichte*, 62–63; Taylor: *Mark*, 210–211; Hultgren: *Adversaries*, 78–82; Gnilka: *Markus*, 1:112–113; Robert H. Gundry: *Mark. A Commentary on His Apology For the Cross* (Grand Rapids: Eerdmans, 1993), 133–134.

Jesus in terms of a bridegroom.[96] The conclusion of the story, "new wine into fresh skins" (2:22), is a possible Markan redaction. Similarly, the incongruous mention of the Pharisees and their disciples in 2:18 suggests that Mark has tinkered with the story. Thus while Mark combined traditional material, his hand seems evident as well.

The story exhibits a certain interest in the Pharisees. As the Pharisees throughout Mark's gospel are known as a hostile entity Mark's version of the dialogue concerning fasting moves into the direction of a controversy story. The questioners are not the Pharisees, nor the disciples of John who are also reported as fasting. But the comparison between the disciples of Jesus and the Pharisees is drawn, and the implication of this comparison is hostility between the two groups.

Mark also exhibits an interest in the bridegroom. Thus he moves to enhance the christological character of the story. Mark makes the argument that the rationale for the community to fast or not to fast rest on the presence or absence of Jesus. It is most likely that the day of the absence of the bridegroom is a veiled reference to the death and resurrection of Jesus and the community awaiting his return.

Finally, the addition to the parables of the patch and the wine shows that Mark was concerned with the distinctiveness of the community. He regarded the community as something new that needed new forms of expression. While Mark probably found this outlook already in his sources, he emphasized it to a great extent.

Despite the fact that the questioners of Jesus are not identified as hostile, the Markan pericope is generally taken to be a controversy story.[97] While this is probably correct it must be noted, however, that the story is also quite close to what Bultmann called the scholastic apophthegms. The reason for this is the absence of explicitly hostile questioners, which turns the story very close to a request for knowledge.[98] The story in Mark is certainly skirting the boundaries of form. At the same time, the presence of and emphasis on the Pharisees in the question denotes how this story moves into the direction of the controversy story.[99]

---

[96] Besides the Matthean evidence see 2 Cor 11:12; Eph 5:23–33; Rev 19:7–9; 21:9. In these instances the church is associated with the bridegroom as the bride.

[97] Bultmann's arguments are representative of the majority opinion: (1) The nature of the question is argumentative. (2) The situation depicted here is quite indefinite and has prompted the Matthean and Lukan redactions in the parallels. Nevertheless, a somewhat unsatisfactory situation of the story has been created. (3) The conduct of the disciples is questioned, and Jesus defends their actions. Bultmann: *History*, 18–19. Hultgren follows Bultmann and provides a relevant bibliography. Hultgren: *Adversaries*, 78–82. An already noted exception to the majority opinion is Gnilka: *Markus*, 1:113.

[98] See Bultmann's definition of scholastic apophthegms: Bultmann: *History*, 54.

[99] Hultgren is perhaps correct in stating: "The fact that the material is presented in the form of a conflict story indicates that the primitive church in Palestine was interested in distinguishing the basis for Christian fasting from that of Judaism in the light of the tradition that Jesus and his

In the light of these issues in the Markan account its Matthean redaction stands out as an attempt to give the story more coherence. The Pharisees become more prominent in the story, and they are more appropriately described. The controversial character of the story is emphasized by the omission of the anonymous questioners and by the creation of a greater distance between those who fast and the disciples of Jesus. The whole story thus gains a greater formal distinction as a controversy story not present as such in Mark's account. The focus on the practice of the community is further emphasized with the conclusion that both skins and wine are preserved. This saying ties together with the earlier accusation that the community's practice of fasting is a mark of deficiency. Thus the whole pericope gains more coherence.

4.2 Summary of the Matthean Redaction in 9:14–17

The Matthean redaction of this controversy again focuses on both structure and content of the story:

- ► Matthew constructs a closer connection with the preceding controversy story. The three controversies of ch. 9 thus appear as a narrative block.
- ► Matthew clarifies and emphasizes the opponents as Pharisees, who appear in collusion with the disciples of John.
- ► Matthew emphasizes the distance between the opponents and the disciples of Jesus.
- ► Matthew strengthens the focus on the community in his interpretation of the parables of the new cloth and the new wine in new skins.

5. Summary of Patterns in the Matthean Controversy Stories in Chapter 9

Several preliminary patterns in the Matthean redaction of the controversy stories can already be observed. Matthew is interested in the stories he inherited from Mark as far as they are controversy stories. Thus in each story the controversial character is highlighted. Matthew achieves this through several techniques.

In each case seen so far, Matthew eliminates circumstantial material. The healing of the paralytic makes this most obvious: The miraculous part of the story is severely trimmed, several figures that appeared in Mark's account are simply dropped, the setting of the pronouncement is kept to a bare minimum. This tendency can be observed to a lesser extent in the controversies over table

---

disciples did not fast during his ministry. Christian fasting is based on the absence of the Bridegroom, not Jewish tradition." Hultgren: *Adversaries*, 81–82.

fellowship with sinners and fasting. The Matthean omissions serve to highlight the controversy at the expense of the setting.

The emphasis on the controversies as such is further enhanced through structural clarifications and emendations of the source material. Matthew uses particles to distinguish more clearly the different parts of his stories as setting, opposition, and riposte of Jesus.

With the emphasis on the controversial character of these stories Matthew achieves a clearer focus on the participants in the conflict. In all three controversies the main opponents are Jewish leaders. In the healing of the paralytic Matthew characterizes the opposing Scribes more clearly by distinguishing them from the crowd. In the second and third story, Matthew is more concise in identifying the Pharisees as opponents. At the same time, Matthew is clear about the irreconcilability of the opposition to Jesus. Most pertinently this is shown by the reference to the opponents being evil (9:4), by the inclusion that is formed between the first controversy and the trial before the Sanhedrin, by the invitation to go and learn (9:13) which is subsequently rejected, and by the reference to the preservation of the new (9:17) that shows no concern for the preservation of the old.

Concomitant with the better identification of the opponents is the clearer characterization of Jesus. Most clearly this appears in the second story with its additional christological material, showing Jesus as the teacher of the Law who offers his expertise to the opponents (9:13). Yet Jesus is highlighted also in the perfect obedience of the paralytic (9:7), the admiration of the crowds (9:8), and the reference to mourning in the controversy over fasting (9:15).

A further pattern of Matthean redactional activity places the community in a prominent place. While the community praxis was already a matter for debate in the Markan controversy over fasting, Matthew makes the community even more closely a focus of his attention. In the first controversy he extends the praxis of forgiveness of sins to the community (9:8). In the third controversy he applies the sayings of the new and the old explicitly to the community and its preservation (9:17). In the middle controversy, Matthew removes the community from center stage. Yet he seemingly does so to preserve his community from the false impression that it comprises of sinners and tax collectors. Distancing his community from the meal with sinners while shifting the emphasis to the teaching of scripture lets Matthew preserve his community as one of greater righteousness. Consequently, the redaction-critical evidence shows that all three controversies have direct bearing on the Matthean community.

One item in the Matthean redaction has occurred only once so far but bears keeping in mind: In 9:8 Matthew introduces the crowds as the audience of the first controversy story. They react positively and thus distinguish themselves from the opponents of Jesus. In later controversies Matthew will expand on the motif of the crowds as opposed to the Jewish leaders.

III. The Matthean Redaction of the Controversy Stories in Chapter 12

After a long interruption Matthew resumes the narrative sequence of the Markan controversies (Mk 2:1–3:6) with the two Sabbath controversies of 12:1–14 (Mk 2:23–3:6). During the interruption Matthew presents further aspects of Jesus. He inserts the story of a double miracle (9:18–26 ‖ Mk 5:21–42), the healing of two blind men (9:27–31), and the healing of a dumb demoniac (9:32–34).[1] A summary of the activity of Jesus (9:35–38 ‖ Mk 6:6b, 34) leads to the missionary discourse of ch. 10 and the discourse of ch. 11.[2] In the miracle stories particular attention is given to the reaction that these miracles evoke in those healed or the witnesses.[3] The last miracle previews the opposition of the Pharisees that will become an explicit controversy in 12:24, provoking and repeating the same reaction from the

---

[1] The miracles of the two blind men and a demoniac (9:27–34) are doublets that are used more fully elsewhere (20:29–34 and 12:22–24).

[2] Chapter 10 varies the Markan sequence, even though some Markan material is incorporated, and ch. 11 portrays Jesus as teacher in various situations, without any parallels in Mark. The missionary discourse is assembled from material found in Mk 6:7–13, 30–31 and Q 10:2–16. Both sources contain a missionary discourse which Matthew used to assemble his own discourse. Furthermore, Matthew incorporates other Q material as well. Thus 10:26–33 originates in Q 12:2–9; 34–36 in Q 12:51–53; 37–39 is a composite from Q 14:25–27 and 17:33. Luz: *Matthäus*, 2:77–78; Dorothy J. Weaver: *Matthew's Missionary Discourse: A Literary Critical Analysis*, JSNT.S 38 (Sheffield: JSOT, 1990). Tuckett summarizes the discussion arising out of the double tradition of a missionary discourse in Q and Mark. Tuckett: *Q*, 183–188. Among the more marginal theories concerning the double tradition is Catchpole who believes in Markan dependence on Q. Catchpole: *Quest*, 151–188. While Matthew does not draw on Mark for ch. 11, Q is the source for almost all of the material here. James Edwards: "Matthew's Use of Q in Chapter Eleven," in: *Logia: Les paroles de Jésus. The Sayings of Jesus. Mémorial Joseph Coppens*, ed. J. Delobel and T. Baarda, BEThL 59 (Leuven: Uitgeverij Peeters, 1982), 257–275. The following parallels can be observed: The question of John the Baptist (11:2–6) appears in Q 7:18–23; Jesus' witness about the Baptist (7–19) appears in Q 7:24–35; the woes over the Galilean cities (20–24) appears in Q 10:12–15; the great thanksgiving to the Father (25–27) appears in Q 10:21–22. Matthew appends his own saying of Jesus' invitation to those who labor (28–30).

[3] In 9:26 Matthew adds the reference to the spreading of Jesus' fame throughout the district. The story of the two blind men is a doublet of 20:29–34. Again there is the added reference to the spreading of Jesus' reputation (9:31). The dumb demoniac is a doublet of 12:22–24 and contains, besides the negative reaction of the Pharisees that mirrors 12:24, the statement that "never was anything like this seen in Israel" (9:33).

Pharisees. In this sense the reactions that Matthew reports in the remainder of ch. 9 are somewhat preliminary in nature.

A first reaction to the power of Jesus is the empowering of the disciples with the same powers that Jesus has (10:1). This leads to their commissioning for a mission to the house of Israel (10:6). The mission to Israel incorporates an eschatological sub-text already present in Q. It determines the judgment over the towns of Israel at the end time (10:15.32–39).[4] Finally, the mission discourse strengthens the missionaries as representatives of Jesus himself (10:40–42) to a considerable extent over Q.[5] The discourse is permeated by a sense of urgency that demands from the disciples the proclamation of the gospel that the kingdom is at hand (10:7). This kingdom is revealed by the mighty deeds of the missionaries that are also the mighty deeds of Jesus (10:8). The gospel becomes intricately linked with the person of Jesus.

The urgency of the mission corresponds to a similarly pressing need for a response to the proclamation which will precipitate the eschatological judgment. A right answer to the missionary proclamation is primarily visible in the treatment of the missionaries (10:13–15.16–23.40–42). This treatment is the proof whether a person has received Jesus (10:40).

A second reaction to Jesus is shown in ch. 11. It shows Jesus teaching (11:1) and commenting on the various responses his teaching receives. Jesus answers the christological question of the disciples of John with a reference to Is 29:18 (cf. Q 7:22–23). He goes on to chastise the attendant crowds for their lukewarm reaction to the Baptist as the Elijah who is to come (11:14). Woes are pronounced against unrepentant cities in Galilee that are compared to Gentile cities who would have responded to the call for repentance (11:20–24). The insistence on the lack of repentance shows these cities deaf to the preaching of Jesus that includes a call for repentance (4:17).

Both the reference to John as the messenger who prepares the way and the lack of repentance among the Galilean cities focus the attention on the person of Jesus. In the midst of the negative appraisal by crowds and cities Jesus then makes a declaration of his identity and the nature of his own teaching: He is the Son of the Father, the revealer of the Father, and his yoke is easy (11:25–30).

---

[4] The relevant Q parallels here are: 10:12; 12:8–9, 51–52; 14:26–27. On the eschatology of these texts see: Tuckett: *Q*, 139–163. Tuckett provides a salient discussion with positions other than his as well.

[5] The conclusion of the missionary discourse in Q reads: "He who hears you hears me, and he who rejects you rejects me, and he who rejects me rejects him who sent me" (10:16). Thus Matthew 10:40 seems to have its source in Q 10:16, v. 41 seems to be Matthean special material, while v. 42 might be a reworking of the last verse of the otherwise omitted pericope Mk 9:38–41. Luz discusses the possibility and difficulty with this reconstruction. Luz: *Matthäus*, 2:149–150. Here it suffices to note that Matthew has considerably enlarged on a theme he found in Q's conclusion of the missionary discourse.

The long insertion into the Markan block of controversy stories is highly christological in nature. It is not a Matthean creation. Yet Matthew used his source Q to great effect in the preparation for the controversy stories of ch. 12. The focus on the acceptance of Jesus has been heightened with the insertion of the mission discourse and the discourse concerning the Baptist. The following controversy stories will have to take account of this development in the Matthean narrative.

1. Matthew 12:1–8

Matthew takes up Mark's narrative thread with the first of two controversy stories revolving around the Sabbath. Comparison with the two synoptic parallels Mk 2:23–28 and Lk 6:1–5 shows that Matthew has the longest text, while Luke reports the shortest. These differences in size revolve around Mk 2:27. Luke omits the reference to the Sabbath as made for man, not man for the Sabbath. Likewise, Matthew does not report Mk 2:27. Instead, he inserts 12:5–7. The omission of Mk 2:27 is a significant minor agreement that has led some to question the Two Source Hypothesis. Yet the abandonment of the two source hypothesis does not offer a better explanation of the omission of Mk 2:27 in both Matthew and Luke.[6]

Matthew begins his version of the controversy with a tighter connection to the previous material by inserting ἐν ἐκείνῳ τῷ καιρῷ[7] and smoothing out the Mar-

---

[6] Sanders suggested that the Lukan account is the oldest of the three because it represents the common denominator. Ed P. Sanders: "Priorités et dépendances dans la tradition synoptique," *RSR* 60 (1972): 534. Similarly, Matthew has been suggested as the source for the other narratives. Marco suggests that only Matthew 12:7 is a redactional addition, while Mk 2:27 is a replacement for Matthew 12:5–6. Mariano H. Marco: "Las espigas arrancadas es sábado (Mt 12,1–8 par)," *EstB* 28 (1969): 313–322. Benoit suggests rather ingeniously that Matthew and Luke represent older traditions despite their secondary literary development. Pierre Benoit: "Les épis arrachés (Mt 12,1–8 et par)," *SBFLA* 13 (1962/63): 81–87, 90–92. Both these reconstructions, however, must explain the Markan mistake of placing the Davidic episode in the times of Abiathar as secondary. This is highly questionable, since both Luke and Matthew excise it. Luz: *Matthäus*, 2:228. Similarly, a Markan dependence on Matthew might explain the absence of the rather Jewish sounding verses Matthew 12:5–7 in Mark's orientation towards a gentile audience; however, their replacement with Mk 2:27 is perhaps not less Jewish in flavor. Gnilka points to a similar saying in the rabbinic sources that is attributed to Rabbi Simeon ben Menasja who lived around 180 A.D. Gnilka: *Markus*, 1:123. This saying is too late to be of importance to the interpretation of Mk 2:27, even if the attribution were accurate. But Gnilka correctly asserts that Mark presents an argument that does not deal with the Sabbath in principle. The Sabbath is not abolished, but clarified. Such a saying, then, presumes a background in which the Sabbath is still of importance, regardless of whether this is found in the material that Mark used as his traditions, or whether it is formed by Mark.

[7] The same phrase was used to introduce the self-revelation of Jesus in 11:25–30. Thus the two pericopes share not just a temporal affinity, but also a formal affinity. The phrase is used again to introduce the episode of Herod's execution of John. The weight that Hicks attaches to the phrase

kan construction of ἐγένετο + infinitive. He clarifies that the disciples act out of hunger (12:1) and thus creates a closer affinity to David and his men (3).[8] The parallel between the disciples and David also explains the omission of χρείαν ἔσχεν in v. 3 (Mk 2:25).[9] The distracting phrase ὁδὸν ποιεῖν also is omitted.[10]

In v. 2 Matthew introduces the Pharisees with the contrasting particle δε and, as he does in 9:11, adds that they saw the event.[11] Thus the disciples' action is even more closely connected with the reproach of the Pharisees than in the Markan account. Matthew prefaces their comments with the Aorist εἶπαν rather than the Imperfect ἔλεγον.[12] The reproach itself mirrors the difficulty that both Luke and Matthew must have felt when they looked at the Markan construction where Jesus appears unaware of the disciples' action until the Pharisees point it out to him (cf. ἴδε in Mk 2:24). Luke solved the problem by dropping the distinction between the disciples and Jesus in the offensive action. Matthew decides to revise the construction more radically: He mentions explicitly οἱ μαθηταί σου, repeats ποιεῖν

---

here as the middle use of a threefold device is probably overstated. John M. Hicks: "The Sabbath Controversy in Matthew: An Exegesis of Matthew 12:1–14," *RestQ* 27 (1984): 80.

[8] So, e.g., already Hummel: *Auseinandersetzung*, 41. Schlatter contends that for Matthew the need of the disciples suspends the Law. But he also points out that such an interpretation does nothing to clarify the actual controversy with the Pharisees: "... der Pharisäismus [war] nicht überschritten und die Freiheit Jesu vom Gesetz verkannt." Schlatter: *Matthäus*, 392. But would Matthew indeed argue the freedom from the Law? Mt 5:17–20 and 23:2 seem to speak against this. Likewise, there is no evidence in the text to support the theory of Kilpatrick that the disciples broke the Law unintentionally. Kilpatrick: *Origins*, 116. The argument is not about the intention of the disciples, but about their actual deed. The hunger of the disciples, then, is foremost a parallelization with the hunger of David and his men. But it also serves to clarify the position of this deed within the confines of the Law precisely because Matthew creates a closer affinity with the men of David. For Matthew, the parallel between the disciples and the men of David is the only key to the argument that is borne out by the text.

[9] Against Luz: *Matthäus*, 2:228.

[10] Marco suggests that the phrase, a Latinism from *iter facere*, denotes in Mark that the disciples actually went into the field and made a path there. Marco contends that this is the infraction that the Pharisees objected to. Marco: "Espigas," 338–339. It is possible that in the pre-Markan development of the pericope it was actually the making of a way that constituted the Sabbath violation. This is supported by the fact that Mark does not mention the hunger of the disciples, but only the need of David and his men (2:25). Then the addition of the plucking of grain and the argument from David and his men are a secondary addition to the pre-Markan story. Gnilka suggests such a reconstruction. Gnilka: *Markus*, 1:119–121. Gundry comments characteristically: "The woods are full of mutually destructive theories regarding stages of tradition history leading up to the present pericope." Gundry: *Mark*, 148. Matthew then goes a step further and eliminates the question of making a way completely and focuses of the argument concerning the plucking of grain and its answer with scripture.

[11] The Matthean phrase is: οἱ δὲ Φαρισαῖοι ἰδόντες. Similarly in 9:11: καὶ ἰδόντες οἱ Φαρισαῖοι.

[12] This minor agreement with Lk 6:2 is an independent stylistic improvement.

in the relative clause, moves the mention of the Sabbath to the end of the sentence,[13] and finally removes τί denoting a question.

Thus the reproach of the Pharisees takes a much more severe form in Matthew: The question becomes an objection, emphasized by the ponderous repetition of ποιεῖν. If in Mark the Pharisees ask "what are they doing?" the objection in Matthew concerns much more the fact that what they are doing is unlawful on the Sabbath. The implicit accusation is that Jesus does not know the law. It is entirely directed against Jesus: The disciples are identified as those of Jesus, the accusation is directed against him, he is held responsible for the actions of his disciples.

The Pharisees take issue with the disregard that the disciples show toward the Sabbath.[14] The holiness of the Sabbath is not to be taken lightly, and their agitation seems justified. In his redaction of the Pharisees' objection Matthew accurately mirrors the seriousness of the situation. His redaction of the answer shows just how much more seriously Matthew takes the accusation.

As in v. 2 Matthew replaces a Markan καί with δε to enhance the contrast between Jesus and the Pharisees. The answer itself is structured into two scriptural problems that are each introduced with οὐκ ἀνέγνωτε (12:3, 5)[15] and a concluding judgment in three parts, introduced with λέγω δὲ ὑμῖν (12:6).[16] Possibly the

---

[13]   This is not a minor agreement with Luke, despite Luke's moving the Sabbath to the end of his sentence as well. Luke retains the plural construction τοῖς σάββασιν, while Matthew introduces the singular with a preposition: ἐν σαββάτῳ.

[14]   The pertinent texts that command the holiness of the Sabbath can be found in Gen 2:2, Ex 20:8–11; Deut 5:12–15; Neh 13:15–22; Is 56:6; etc. Davies and Allison point out the severity of the infraction: The disciples break a command that God himself kept (Gen 2:2; *Jub* 2:16–18) and that distinguishes Jew from Gentile. Davies and Allison: *Matthew*, 2:306. McConnell and Hicks suggest that the objection is rooted not directly on the Torah but on the rabbinic understanding of the Sabbath, the oral Torah. Richard J. McConnel: *Law and Prophecy in Matthew's Gospel: The Authority and Use of the Old Testament in the Gospel of Matthew* (Basel: Kommissionsverlag Friedrich Reinhardt, 1969), 69; Hicks: "Sabbath Controversy," 81. While this is possible, too little is known about the oral Torah to make a judgment on the issue. It seems safer to assume that the implication of the passage is that the Pharisees understood the disciples to infringe on the Sabbath command, and Jesus holds his own interpretation against theirs. It is also notable that while Jesus responds with a halachic argument, the objection of the Pharisees is simply stated as such without further explanation.

[15]   The structural function of this phrase in the development of the pericope explains to some extent the replacement of οὐδέποτε (Mk 2:25). It should not be regarded as a minor agreement, because Luke uses οὐδέ (6:3). Neither is it "kaum ... erklärbar." Luz: *Matthäus*, 2:228. With the omission of the rather emphatic οὐδέποτε Matthew shifts the emphasis on ἀνέγνωτε and the lack of scholarship which the Pharisees show in their objection.

[16]   This structure is a modified version of Gnilka's analysis. Gnilka sees the answer of Jesus in three questions and three statements ("Sentenzen"). The questions are 12:3,4,5, introduced with οὐκ ἀνέγνωτε, πῶς, and οὐκ ἀνέγνωτε respectively, while the statements are 12:6,7,8. Davies and Allison follow Gnilka's schematics. Gnilka: *Matthäus*, 1:442; Davies and Allison: *Matthew*, 2:304. However, the parallel use of οὐκ ἀνέγνωτε seems a strong structural marker in the pericope. Furthermore, the first two questions both relate to the story of David and are thus not

contrast between οὐκ ἀνέγνωτε and λέγω δὲ ὑμῖν is reminiscent of the antitheses (5:22, 28, 32, 34, 39, 44).[17]

The first question that Jesus asks the Pharisees is knowledge of the story of David. It is only slightly redacted by the omission of the High Priest Abiathar and the change to the plural "they ate"[18] in order to tighten the parallel between the companions of David and the disciples of Jesus. Mark made an error since the story, as related in 1 Sam 21:1–6, took place under the High Priest Ahimelech, father of Abiathar. A further Markan error is corrected by omitting that David gave of the bread to his men (Mk 2:26). The story in 1 Sam specifically records that David was alone. Perhaps Matthew was aware of these facts.[19] Matthew concentrates on the problem that eating the bread of the presence was not allowed for David and his men. Matthew is more precise than Mark in formulating the problem and reporting the story of 1 Sam.

Matthew then leaves out Mk 2:27 and replaces it with the second problem Jesus raises, after the mention of David and his men. Perhaps through association with the story of David in the house of God, Jesus asks whether the Pharisees did not read in the Law that the priests of the temple break the Sabbath and yet are not guilty of transgression (v. 5). This argument has several functions. It cannot have escaped Matthew that Mark's argument of David had various weaknesses. Firstly, it is not concerned at all with the Sabbath, but with the eating of forbidden bread.[20] The

---

truly separate elements in the narrative. The three "Sentenzen" of the second part of the answer are very different in character: While the outer statements seem like pronouncements, the inner part does not correspond structurally. Thus Gnilka's structure seems somewhat forced, and is is better to take the answer of Jesus a little more loosely in three parts with two problems posed and one compound judgment.

[17] Gundry suggest such a parallel, esp. with the second "have you not read" since it also makes reference to the Law, and since 5b and 6b supposedly "parallel" each other. Gundry: *Matthew*, 223. The latter parallel I fail to recognize. While the possibility of a throwback to the antitheses should not entirely be ruled out, it really rests only on the phrase λέγω δὲ ὑμῖν.

[18] The text here is only supported by two major manuscripts (א and B) and a few minor ones, while the majority of witnesses have "he ate." The weight of א and B speaks for the plural form. The variance in the other manuscripts is most easily explained by the assimilation to the singular of the other synoptics in the other manuscripts. This argument is strengthened by the omission of the men of David in the rest of the verse. They are, for Matthew, present in the process of eating. If the men were not eating with David, the whole point of the story would be lost completely.

[19] However, it is puzzling that both Matthew and Luke chose to correct Mark not by emendation but by omission. It is possible that Matthew abbreviated Mark just for the sake of brevity, as he is wont at times. This argument must remain speculation. However, since two Markan mistakes are corrected, it seems likely that Matthew knew of Mark's mistakes and chose to correct them by abbreviation. A small piece of supportive evidence is found in Lk 6:4. Even though Luke omits Abiathar, he does not seem to be aware that there were no men with David to whom he could have given the bread.

[20] Luz infers from Lev 24:8 that the incident took place on a Sabbath since this was the day when the Bread of the Presence was prepared in the Temple. Luz: *Matthäus*, 2:230. However, it is not clear whether this bread remained there for a while, or whether it was consumed

description of the incident in Mark leaves out several details important in 1 Sam.[21] Yet even with the abbreviations the argument about David does little to advance a solution to the problem under discussion.[22] Secondly, it is an argument that does not really touch on the Law itself since the Davidic incident was of merely haggadic significance. Such a haggadah might provide a legal challenge in explaining David's actions, but it was methodologically unsuitable for the purpose of establishing a halachic precept.[23]

---

immediately. 1 Sam 21:8 describes that the bread was replaced only when the new one was brought in. If the new bread was brought in on a Sabbath, it would lie there until the next Sabbath when it was replaced. Thus Luz's inference seems without much force. It would be surprising that a reference to the Sabbath, if there was one, was not made explicit by either Mark or Matthew. Luz points out that later rabbinic exegesis assumed that the bread was taken on a Sabbath, and that rabbinic arguments tried to excuse David's behavior with arguments similar to the hunger that Matthew mentions. But the rabbinic sources are considerably later than Matthew and should not be forced to make the point here. What remains of Luz's argument? There is the theoretical possibility of the Sabbath being presumed in Matthew's account of David. But it is not made explicit, and the expansion of Matthew's account with the argument from the priests in the temple make it unlikely that Matthew saw the Davidic incident as a compelling argument for the lawfulness of the disciples' actions on the Sabbath.

[21] The story as told in 1 Sam 21 does not seem to have a problem with David and his men eating the bread in question. The argument is about whether they meet the prerequisites for eating it. In this case it is sexual abstinence over a period of time. This observation is important because it raises the issue of the lawfulness of David's action as seen by the author of the passage in 1 Sam, and the later interpretation by the Rabbis. Davies and Allison catalogue eight possible interpretations of the force of the Matthean appeal to David, and five of them appeal to rabbinic writings or even the concept of the Oral Torah. Davies and Allison: *Matthew*, 2:310–311. The appeal to the Rabbis, however, only emphasizes the conundrum of interpretation: If there was such an obvious development of interpretation between the author of 1 Sam and the Rabbis, at which point did Matthew enter the fray? Unfortunately, there are no sources giving an interpretation that would back up a placement of Matthew within an inner-Jewish development of interpretation. Furthermore, it is probably ill judged to attempt an interpretation of the argument of the men of David independent of the argument of the priests on the Sabbath. Consequently, it seems more likely that Matthew saw the difficulties inherent in the analogy from the Davidic incident, and so he moved to append an argument that was much stronger in his eyes.

[22] This is argued by Davies and Allison: *Matthew*, 2:313. and repeats the argument made by Davies: *The Setting of the Sermon on the Mount*, 103–104. See also Luz: *Matthäus*, 2:229. He describes Mark's argument as "wenig stichhaltig." Daube explained that the Davidic incident served as a precedent for the actions of the disciples in the Law itself and cites Num 28:9–10. Daube: *NT and Rabbinic Judaism*, 67–69.

[23] This argument is made by: Davies: *The Setting of the Sermon on the Mount*, 103; Daniel M. Cohn-Sherbok: "An Analysis of Jesus' Arguments Concerning the Plucking of Grain on the Sabbath," *JSNT* 1979 (1979): 36. Daube writes: "It was of the essence of the rabbinic system that any detailed rule, any halakha, must rest, directly or indirectly, on an actual precept promulgated in scripture. It must rest on it directly or indirectly: that is to say, there was no need for a halakha to be laid down in so many words, so long as it could be derived from some precept by means of the recognized norms of hermeneutics. One of these norms, for example, was the inference *a fortiori* or as the rabbis termed it *qal-wa-ḥomer* ..." Daube: *NT and Rabbinic Judaism*, 68. Again

Thus the argument that Matthew introduces is much more useful in discussing the legalities involved in the Sabbath observance. By pointing out that the priests, though working in the temple, are not guilty of breaking the Sabbath, Matthew achieves several things.

Firstly, the argument remains with the problem of the infraction of the Sabbath observance. It is raised to a discussion of legal principles on the basis of established rules. First and foremost, the institution of the Sabbath itself is not at issue. The argument is about the implications of the Law for its day to day observance, not the Law itself. This is quite in keeping with Matthew's assertion that Jesus came to fulfill the Law, not to abrogate it (5:17). But the Law must be kept perfectly (5:18–20), and the disciples cannot be questioned by those who have shown themselves hypocrites.

But there is a further implication of the argument that Matthew adduces: The disciples of Jesus are suddenly lined up with the priests in the temple. This is not just a clumsy comparison.[24] The priests in the temple are exempt from the Sabbath rule because they serve in the temple and are thus in the presence of God. Consequently, there is at least one exemption from the Sabbath rule.[25] The temple service takes precedence over the Sabbath observance. This then allows Matthew to argue that when there is something more important than the temple, it consequently displaces the Sabbath observance as well. This he asserts in 12:6. Thus Matthew has here the halachic argument that eluded Mark in the comparison with David.[26]

The consequence of the comparison with the temple service is drawn in 12:6 which begins with λέγω δὲ ὑμῖν, a favorite Matthean phrase.[27] It continues with the assertion that in this situation there is something greater than the temple.[28] Matthew does not elaborate, and one is left to wonder what this greater thing could

---

the uncertainty of the applicability of rabbinic rules in the time of Matthew must be stressed. But it seems possible that the art of legal disputation developed by the rabbis had its roots in the Pharisaic movement that Matthew knew.

[24] Gundry contends that "the disciples' acting out of mere hunger does not compare well with the service of the priests obeying God's command." Gundry: *Matthew*, 224. Cohn-Sherbok writes that "unlike the priests, Jesus' disciples were not engaged in any sort of religious observance, nor were they serving Jesus by plucking ears of grain." Cohn-Sherbok: "Jesus' Arguments," 39.

[25] Davies and Allison: *Matthew*, 2:314.

[26] This is the argument *a fortiori* or *qal-wa-homer* that Daube called a "means of the recognized norms of hermeneutics." Daube: *NT and Rabbinic Judaism*, 68.

[27] Matthew uses λέγω [δὲ] ὑμῖν 59 times against Mark's 11 and Luke's 39 times. Luz: *Matthäus*, 1:44.

[28] Davies and Allison draw attention to the fact that it is greater than the temple and not the Law. It is not quite clear what this argument is supposed to show, except that Matthew stays within the logical parameters of the argument that he set up with the description of the priests in the temple. Davies and Allison: *Matthew*, 2:314.

be. The μεῖζον that Matthew uses is neuter in gender.[29] It is possible to take the neuter literally as referring to a thing, or abstract entity, and then interpret it variously as the kingdom, the love of God, Jesus' interpretation of the law, or the community of disciples and, by extension, the church.[30] If the μεῖζον is interpreted as referring to Jesus, however, the logical structure of vv. 5 and 6 becomes much more immediately relevant to the halachic argument: The priests logically relate to the temple in the same way as the disciples relate to Jesus. If the temple exempts the priests from the Sabbath regulations, then Jesus, being more than the temple, allows the disciples to pluck heads of grain on the Sabbath.[31] The formulation resembles those of 12:41–42, though πλεῖον is used there.[32] In addition, the assertion that the Son of Man is Lord even over the Sabbath (12:8) receives its force from the christological interpretation of μεῖζον. In turn, it serves the unity of the whole answer of Jesus if v. 6 is interpreted with the christological punch line of v. 8 in mind.

Verse 7 takes up once again the quotation Hos 6:6 that already marked the controversy in Mt 9:13. There Matthew exhorted the Pharisees to go and learn the meaning of the quotation. In its second, and again unparalleled, appearance this

---

[29] Although some manuscripts amend the neuter to the masculine singular μείζων and thus indicate that they see a christological claim in this passage. The manuscripts in question are C L Δ 0233 *f*[13] 1010 1424 *pm* lat. These variants are no challenge to the established text. They give, however, witness to a trend of a christological interpretation, at least in the later Alexandrian school where most of the above manuscripts originated.

[30] As representative of such a tradition of interpretation Luz makes a strong argument. He contends that the μεῖζον needs to be read in the light of the following v. 7. There Matthew takes up the argument from the priests in the temple with the word θυσία and supersedes it with mercy: "Das, was größer ist als der Tempel, ist also die Barmherzigkeit, die in Jesu Auslegung des Willens Gottes das Größte geworden ist. In seiner eigenen Zeit bildete wohl für Matthäus die Zerstörung des Tempels einen Hinweis darauf, wie wahr Jesus den Willen Gottes ausgelegt hatte." Luz contends that this interpretation ties together the statements of vv. 6 and 7 into a continuous argument of antipharisaic overtones by interpreting v. 7 as a "antipharisäische Zuspitzung des μεῖζον." Luz: *Matthäus*, 2:231–231. Luz succeeds in joining vv. 6 and 7 together more closely. However, this interpretation also comes at a cost: By interpreting μεῖζον as representative of the mercy advocated by Jesus Luz loses some of the logic inherent in the argument that connects vv. 5 and 6. The μεῖζον must fulfill the same logical function towards the disciples as the temple does towards the priests. However, the mercy does not do this. The mercy enters the argument because it is greater that the sacrifices. But the sacrifices are performed by the priests in the temple. Thus logically, mercy cannot be greater than the temple, because it is never compared with the temple. While the argument of Luz is certainly very attractive, it obscures the logical sequence between vv. 5 and 6.

[31] The christological interpretation of μεῖζον is adapted, without much explanation, by Davies and Allison: *Matthew*, 2:314. See also: Gnilka: *Matthäus*, 1:444. Gundry comments that the neuter "stresses the quality of superior greatness rather than Jesus' personal identity." Gundry: *Matthew*, 223.

[32] Luz argues, consistent with his interpretation of 12:6, that those formulations equally do not refer to Jesus. Luz: *Matthäus*, 2:231 n.37, 280–281.

quotation and exhortation are not just repeated. It is made clear that in the intervening period, which presumably gave the opportunity to do what Jesus asked, the Pharisees did not do so. Jesus brings the hypocrisy of the Pharisees to the point: While in their challenge they lay claim to the knowledge of the law, Jesus' answer shows that they have no clear knowledge of it: They did not read the story of David (12:3), they did not read the law (12:5), and now they did not read the prophet Hosea even when they were invited to do so. While in 12:3.5 there was an ironic undertone in the answer of Jesus, in 12:7 the accusation of Jesus turns more serious and reveals not just the ignorance of the Pharisees, but also their ill will and their conscious intention not to listen to either Jesus or the Law. By choice the Pharisees have abandoned the loyalty to the covenant with God that Hos 6:6 asked for. The Pharisees are shown to have abandoned God not only by lack of knowledge in the interpretation of the Law, but now by their unwillingness to study it.

At the same time, the argument of Hosea does not only serve to show the stubbornness of the Pharisees. It also throws light on the interpretation of Matthew concerning the Sabbath observance. Obviously Matthew felt that the quotation had some force in validating the Sabbath practice of the community. Matthew consciously subordinates the Sabbath observance to the covenant faithfulness of Hos 6:6.[33]

The consequence of the pharisaic stubbornness is a serious misjudgment. The Pharisees have ended up condemning the guiltless. With this phrase Matthew ties the link between the disciples and the priests in the temple even more closely. Matthew refers to the disciples as ἀναίτιοι, the word also used to describe the position of the priests in 12:5. The Pharisees, by condemning the guiltless, thus do not just condemn the disciples, but also pass judgment over the priests in the temple. Ironically, in their judgment they render themselves ridiculous. While they set out to defend the sanctity of the law, they end up to twist the law in a way that even the temple cult cannot survive. Matthew shows the Pharisees undermining the foundations of the Jewish nation whose leaders they claim to be. The Pharisees, in the repartee of Jesus, loose everything they claim to be: versed in the Law and the

---

[33] Stanton writes: "The Sabbath commandment is not abolished; it is subordinated to the kindness and mercy of God. In this way the conduct of the disciples is defended." Graham N. Stanton: "Matthew as a Creative Interpreter of the Sayings of Jesus," in: *The Gospel and the Gospels*, ed. Peter Stuhlmacher (Grand Rapids: Eerdmans, 1991), 259. This is only partly convincing. While the Sabbath is certainly to be interpreted in the light of mercy, it is not the mercy and kindness of God, but the concrete acts of mercy by the community that are an expression of the covenant faithfulness. This is the whole point of the quotation of Hos 6:6. The Pharisees do not show this mercy, and therefore they condemn the guiltless. In the following controversy the showing of mercy will be elaborated as doing good on the Sabbath, and by the concrete act of healing that Jesus performs on the man with the withered hand. Covenant faithfulness as concrete acts of mercy is the measure by which the Sabbath observance is to be interpreted.

Scriptures, knowledgeable about the destiny of Israel, destined to be leaders of their people.

In v. 8 Matthew returns to the narrative of Mk 2:28. He leaves out ὥστε and καί,[34] and moves "the Son of Man" to the end of the sentence. Overall, Matthew achieves a stylistic improvement with a succinct christological emphasis. Finally, the center of the argument is restated: While the Sabbath and its seeming violation by the disciples gave rise to a controversy with the Pharisees, the underlying argument concerned a question of authority. The Pharisees have been exposed as willfully ignorant of the scriptures, while Jesus emerges not only more knowledgeable concerning the scriptures, more skillful and profound in presenting a legal argument, but also more authoritative in rendering a legal precept. Thus he is truly Lord of the Sabbath. The Pharisees have been exposed as pretenders to a position they are not qualified to hold. The Markan assertion that the Son of Man, Jesus, is Lord of the Sabbath, is not just a statement of antagonism. The legal argument has shown that Jesus' claim is justified by his superior knowledge of the Law.[35] Furthermore, the repetition of Hos 6:6 shows that the Pharisees lack the proper prerequisite asked for by the Torah: They do not show mercy like Jesus who provides food for the hungry. The Pharisees are shown as having abandoned the covenant faithfulness by their faulty interpretation of the Sabbath regulations.

1.1 The Markan Pericope

Two issues in the Markan account of the pericope deserve special mention as they serve to highlight the Matthean redaction of the story. The first is the original setting of the controversy. Ed P. Sanders has forcefully argued that the story cannot be a reflection of a historical event in the ministry of Jesus: "Pharisees did not actually spend their Sabbaths patrolling cornfields."[36] Sanders draws attention to the surprising immediacy of action and response in the Matthean narrative. However, the Markan pericope is not quite that immediate and leaves room for speculation about the sequence of events and their time frame. Thus the Pharisees might have heard later, or have confronted Jesus later. Perhaps even by coincidence one of them might have seen the event. Pesch argues that the story must be historical on several grounds. Multiple attestation witnesses to a Sabbath practice of Jesus that

---

[34] The Markan use of καί has given rise to the speculation that the Son of Man saying originally concluded a cycle of pericopes from which Mark lifted the saying to conclude the Sabbath controversy. Gnilka: *Markus*, 1:121.

[35] According to Davies, Matthew's treatment of this controversy "presented a rabbinically more technical and, therefore, more forceful argument than Mark and Luke who have only made use of the example of David. This is another indication of the "'scholarly' *Herkunft* of Matthew." Davies: *The Setting of the Sermon on the Mount*, 456.

[36] Ed P. Sanders: "Jesus and the Constraint of the Law," *JSNT* 17 (1983): 20.

gave rise to controversy with Jewish authorities.[37] Pesch asserts that Mk 2:23–26 contains possible Semitisms[38] and treats of a situation that does not reflect early Christian practice, especially with the reference to hunger. The situation blends much better if a setting in the ministry of Jesus with his disciples is assumed. This includes that Jesus is made responsible for the actions of his disciples.[39] Finally, Pesch maintains that a "Sendungsbewußtsein" cannot be ruled out *a priori* for Jesus, since the self-referential comparison to David re-appears in Mk 12:35–37. In the final analysis, Pesch retains almost the whole pericope as a historical event in the life of Jesus.[40]

Hultgren has worked out a less radical approach that combines the assumption of a historical basis in the story with significant later developments to shape the story to the needs of the community.[41] He assumes a basic kernel of a controversy story (2:23–24.27). This controversy was created in the community from a probably authentic[42] saying of Jesus (2:27) when the community came under attack from the Pharisees[43] for failing to keep the Sabbath. This would explain the artificiality of the scene.[44] In a final development the apologetic function of the story was christologically developed with the addition of 2:25.26.28, when appeal was made not to the earthly Jesus but to the exalted Son of Man.

The various reconstructions of the development of the pericope reveal an underlying issue. Depending on the view one takes towards the historicity of the event that this story describes, the *Sitz im Leben* of the pericope for the community changes considerably. Pesch goes farthest in ascribing the Markan account to an

---

[37] Among these traditions are Mk 2:23–3:6 with their parallels, Luke's special tradition in 13:10–17 and 14:1–6, and the Johannine traditions of 5:1–18 and 9:1–41.

[38] Pesch names τί, εἰ μή, and a superfluous ἄρχομαι. Pesch: *Markusevangelium*, 1:183.

[39] Pesch cites Mk 2:18 and 7:5 as further evidence of such responsibility of Jesus. A similar point is made by David Daube: "The Responsibilities of Master and Disciples in the Gospels," *NTS* 19 (1972): 1–15. This particular argument is not very convincing. If the Christian community refers to the practice of Jesus in trying to establish its legitimacy, as the controversies of Matthew 9 have shown, then the situation would blend well with such a theological endeavor: The Sabbath practice of the disciples, exemplified by plucking the grain, could then be legitimized by the teaching of Jesus.

[40] Davies and Allison take up a similar path. They add to the arguments of Pesch by pointing out that the situation itself is so odd that it can hardly be used for a theological development of a teaching on Sabbath observance: "Hard cases make bad law, as the saying goes." Davies and Allison: *Matthew*, 2:305.

[41] Hultgren: *Adversaries*, 111–115.

[42] Hultgren: *Adversaries*, 114.

[43] Or perhaps from other Christian groups who were more faithful to the Sabbath than Mark's group was. Mt 5:19 might indicate such conflicts between various Christian communities.

[44] Hultgren points out that the dominical saying in 2:27 "is not dependent on the contextual situation to be comprehensible. It is likely to have been, prior to the composition of the story itself, a free-floating saying for which the narrative and the question of the Pharisees were composed." Hultgren: *Adversaries*, 114. This argument is thoroughly form-critical in its progression and goes back to Bultmann: *History*, 16–17.

event in the life of Jesus. But as he finds a historical event behind the narrative, he can no longer explain why this story was reported by Mark beyond its anecdotal character in the life of Jesus. The analyses of Sanders and Hultgren find the *Sitz im Leben* of this pericope in the ongoing struggle of the community, while the historicity of the event seems doubtful to them.[45] The *traditionsgeschichtliche Methode*, irrespective of its final outcome, contains a built-in conflict between the various layers of tradition it discovers, and plays them against each other.

Matthew's development of the Markan pericope sheds some light on these questions. As Matthew inserts a new argument into the controversy, and as he heightens the aspect of conflict between the Pharisees and Jesus, he solves some of the Markan puzzle. Obviously the story is not primarily a historical reminiscence any more, if it ever was such in Mark. The Matthean development shows that the *Sitz im Leben* of this story was, for Matthew, very much within the life of the community. Matthew felt the need to expand on the rebuttal of the Pharisees. As he does so, the Pharisees suddenly appear in much harsher light than in the Markan account: The question of the Pharisees in Mark could have been interpreted as somewhat benign, or at least interested in the discussion. Matthew shapes a very simple and hostile accusation. The rebuttal of the Pharisees is not just an argument concerning the Sabbath practice of the disciples, but it becomes an exposition of pharisaic hypocrisy and pretension that makes the christological conclusion of the pericope considerably more pointed. This leads to the conclusion that the Matthean community was, in fact, under attack for its Sabbath practice from more conservative Jewish quarters that were identified with the Pharisees. In such a struggle the identification of the disciples with the priests in the temple raises the question whether Matthew actually saw the disciples of Jesus as the replacement of the priestly class which had become meaningless after the temple was destroyed.[46] In

---

[45] The difficulty with the theory of Pesch is the failure to point to the place of the story within the gospel of Mark. Similarly, Davies and Allison contend that it "would seem to follow that Mk 2.23–26 was not freely created for the sole purpose of instructing Christians on how to treat the Sabbath ... Would not an early Christian, seeking to commend a Christian practice, have created a story whose implications are a little more patent?" Davies and Allison: *Matthew*, 2:305. This argument basically contends that the story must be historical because it has no obvious *Sitz im Leben* for the Markan community. But is this truly convincing? Mark's adaptation to the community in 2:27 and the christological addition in 2:28 show that the Markan community did make sense of the story; for Mark, the implications of the story were indeed patent: The story served to affirm the Lordship of Jesus as the Son of Man. This assertion expands christological implications of the parallel between David and his men and Jesus and his disciples.

[46] The formulation of this suggestion is consciously phrased in hesitant terms for two reasons. Firstly, the suggestion of a claim of the Matthean community to a priestly role rests solely on the identification of the disciples with the priests. However, this argument is primarily at the service of establishing the authority of Jesus as rightful interpreter of the Law. Thus the role of the disciples can perhaps easily be over-interpreted. Secondly, none of the secondary literature familiar to me ever made such a suggestion. It is more often asserted that the comparison between the priests and the disciples is somewhat unsuitable. However, it is precisely the jarring nature of

such a situation the disciples of Jesus, the Matthean community, would lay claim to leadership of the Jewish people which rendered the conflict with the Pharisees highly acrimonious. At the same time, it would propose Jesus as the replacement for the lost temple as a center around which the Jewish people could re-group.

The Matthean redactional expansion does not, in the end, answer the question whether Mark's controversy story is a historical reminiscence, a construction around a historical saying of Jesus, or a fictional treatment of a problem within the Markan or pre-Markan community. But Matthew shows that creative treatment of sources was possible. Matthew took a story he found in Mark, and reworked it to such an extent that its focus became very different. If such a reorientation of a story is possible for Matthew, then a similar process could be imagined for the Markan version. A discernible Markan *Sitz im Leben* of this story cannot *a priori* preclude its historicity, while its historicity does not exclude its particular application in the Markan community. The *traditionsgeschichtliche Methode*, then, must be limited to what it actually can do: discern layers of traditions within a narrative with some degree of probability. It cannot serve to establish meaning in a text. The boundaries between the traditions and the actual *Sitz im Leben* of this pericope within each of its layers are much more opaque than either of the above reconstructions let on.

Tied up with the question of the *Sitz im Leben* of the pericope as reported by Mark is the question of the christological direction that the pericope takes with the reference to the Son of Man in 2:28. The side by side reference to "man" and "Son of Man" in 2:27–28 has led some interpreters to believe that they are interchangeable, or at least originally were so.[47] However, if "man" and "Son of Man" are distinct terms, and if the latter is indeed a christological term, a theory of literary

---

this comparison that led, e.g., Gundry to pronounce its unsuitability, that gives pause to consider the possible implications of such a simile. Furthermore, the investing of the disciples with such high authority would be in keeping with a trend in the gospel. Matthew consistently gives his disciples more authority that either Luke or Mark do. There is a consistent parallel between the actions of Jesus and his disciples. In the missioning of the disciples Matthew employs the vocabulary that he uses to summarize the actions of Jesus (10:1 parallels 9:35 and 4:23–24). The authority of the disciples is most evident in their power to bind and loose (16:19; 18:18). Their actions are valid both on earth as in heaven, and the prayer of the community reflects their conviction that it is an image on earth of the heavenly order (6:10). Overman speaks of the community as a *mimēsis* of the heavenly society. Overman: *Matthew's Gospel*, 131.

[47] Torrey has translated the verses: "The Sabbath was made for man, and not man for the Sabbath; therefore man is master of the Sabbath." Conversely, Manson suggested: "The Sabbath was made for the Son of Man, and not the Son of Man for the Sabbath; therefore the Son of Man is lord also of the Sabbath." *The Four Gospels: A New Translation*, ed. & trans. Charles C. Torrey (New York: Harper & Row, 1933); Thomas W. Manson: "Mark 2:27f," *CNT* 11 (1947): 145. Beare follows Manson. Francis W. Beare: "The Sabbath Was Made for Man?" *JBL* 79 (1960): 130–136. Hay follows Torrey. Lewis S. Hay: "The Son of Man in Mark 2,10 and 2,28f," *JBL* 89 (1970): 69–75. But the change in the text that is needed to provide the unity of the two verses is too great to be justifiable.

development becomes almost inevitable.[48] Behind this theory of development lies the assertion that Jesus would not have used the term "Son of Man" for himself in order to make a christological assertion.[49] It does indeed seem convincing that the last argument of the controversy story in Mark reflects the community's appeal to Jesus as Lord.

While these issues remain significant in the debate over the Markan pericope, the Matthean redaction clarifies them considerably for its audience. Through the omission of Mk 2:27 the confusion between "man" and "Son of Man" is removed. Moreover, the Markan focus of the Sabbath is replaced by the focus on the parties to the dispute. Typical for the Matthean redaction of the controversy stories seen so far, Matthew concentrates on the conflict between the opposing factions, not on the issue that gives rise to the opposition. Thus the concluding statement that the Son of Man is Lord over the Sabbath receives a much more pointed christological emphasis than Mark achieved.[50] But Matthew also justifies this statement better than Mark by showing much more clearly that Jesus is a great teacher of the Law. Again Matthew shows a clearer concentration than Mark, and he does not hesitate to relegate side issues to the background of the story.

1.2 Summary of the Matthean Redaction in 12:1–8

The Matthean redaction concentrates on structural elements as well as on the clarification of the argument:

▸   Matthew connects the pericope tightly with the preceding material.
▸   Matthew structures the answer of Jesus into three distinct parts.
▸   Matthew describes the objection of the Pharisees more concisely than Mark. He reformulates the question into an objection and concentrates not on the Sabbath observance as such but on the particular action and its lawfulness.
▸   Matthew creates a closer affinity between the disciples and the men of David and uses more precision in the formulation of the problem raised by the parallel of David's men.

---

[48] The oddity of "man" and "Son of Man" beside each other is the starting point for Hultgren's evaluation of Mk 2:23–28. Hultgren: *Adversaries*, 113. Gnilka comes to the same conclusion. Gnilka: *Markus*, 1:120. It is probable that, as Gnilka asserts, the Sabbath question was debated in the community first with the help of 2:27. "Weil dieses aber nicht mehr als ausreichend angesehen wurde, erweiterte man es um den Menschensohnspruch."

[49] This is disputed by Gundry: *Mark*, 147.

[50] Luz brings this to the point when he writes: "V 8 hält für [die Gemeinde] fest, daß es in V 7 nicht um ein allgemeines Prinzip der Liebe und nicht um die Autonomie des Menschen überhaupt gegenüber dem Sabbatgebot geht, sondern um den von Jesus endgültig und verbindlich formulierten Willen des Vaters, des biblischen Gottes, der auch das Sabbatgebot einschließt." Luz: *Matthäus*, 2:233.

▶ Matthew introduces a second argument with the priests who offer sacrifices in the temple on the Sabbath. He goes on to identify the disciples with the priests.

▶ Matthew introduces a third argument with the re-appearance of Hos 6:6.

▶ Matthew uses all three arguments in the answer of Jesus to highlight the christological nature of the controversy. Jesus appears as teacher of the scriptures, as greater than the temple, and as Lord of the Sabbath.

2. Matthew 12:9–14

Matthew's narrative, paralleled by Mk 3:1–6, observes the usual stylistic[51] and structural redactional activity.[52] The structure of the Matthean account appears more controlled[53] and cohesive.[54] Through the omission of Mk 3:3 Matthew lets the miracle recede into the background and achieves a concentration on the central argument concerning the Sabbath observance.[55] Therefore Matthew changes Mark by turning the watchfulness of the Pharisees[56] (Mk 3:2) into a direct question (12:10) concerning the lawfulness of healing[57] on the Sabbath.[58] This change

---

[51] In v. 9: Μεταβὰς ἐκεῖθεν connects this story with 12:1–8. Matthew works similarly in 11:1 and 15:29. Since Matthew does not report Mk 1:21–28, πάλιν is omitted. The Markan εἰσῆλθεν εἰς is simplified to ἦλθεν εἰς. The synagogue is qualified as αὐτῶν. Verse 10: Matthew abbreviates the statement of the malady by replacing the clumsy Markan construction with ἰδοὺ and using the adjective rather than the perfect passive participle. The verb ἐπερωτάω is mostly used by Matthew to denote hostile questioning: See 16:1; 22:23, 35, 41, 46; 27:11. Only in 17:10 is it used for a question by the disciples. Verse 13: Matthew avoids the repetition of χεὶρ.

[52] The situation is introduced with καὶ ἰδοὺ (v. 10), δέ is used as a marker to introduce the answer of Jesus (v. 11) as well as the reaction of the Pharisees (v. 14); τότε marks the validating miracle (v.13). The objection of the Pharisees is moved into direct discourse.

[53] The actual controversy in this pericope is found in vv. 10b–12. The sick man is only the occasion for the controversy, and at the end serves the purpose of validating the pronouncement of Jesus by the completeness of his healing. See also Hummel: *Auseinandersetzung*, 44.

[54] Luz observes a "ringförmiges Schema" that revolves around the image of the sheep: Verse 9 and 14 are introduction and conclusion that are held together by the movement in and out of the synagogue. Vv. 10a and 13 contain the miracle and its setting, and correspond through catchwords: ἄνθρωπος, χεὶρ. Vv. 10bc and 12b contain the objection of the Pharisees and the direct response of Jesus, again connected by a catch phrase (ἔξεστιν τοῖς σάββασιν). Luz: *Matthäus*, 2:237.

[55] Gnilka writes that the "Intention der Bearbeitung ist deutlich erkennbar. Die Stellungnahme zum Sabbatgebot wird herausgearbeitet." Gnilka: *Matthäus*, 1:447. Luz adds that Matthew concentrates on the conflict with the pharisaic opponents. Luz: *Matthäus*, 2:238.

[56] Matthew does not mention the Pharisees until v. 14, when they leave the synagogue. However, the close connection with the preceding pericope suggests that the Pharisees are still the opponents of Jesus here. Mark's account equally does not mention the Pharisees until 3:6.

[57] The text contains a difficulty about whether to read θεραπεῦσαι or θεραπεύειν. The former, adopted by Nestle, is witnessed by ℵ D L W *pc*, the latter by B C Θ 0233 *f*[1.13] and the Majority text.

clarifies the character of the controversy: The subject matter is another discussion about the appropriateness of Jesus' actions in the eyes of the Law.

These changes combine to clarify the form of the controversy story. In Mark's account of the pericope, there is no question of the opponents, just their watchfulness to see whether Jesus might heal the man (Mk 3:2). And there is no pronouncement or riposte of Jesus, merely a question (3:4) to which the opponents do not answer. The miracle finally provokes hostile reaction and the plot to kill Jesus (3:6).[59] Matthew establishes more clearly the opponents' hostile question (12:10) as well as the riposte containing an argument from scripture and an apophthegmatic verdict (vv. 11–12). The miracle moves to the periphery of the controversy story (vv. 13–14).

The direct question also fits the pattern that Mt 12 moves to show the controversy with the Pharisees more pronounced than in ch. 9. The Pharisees are, for Matthew, more important than the man with the withered hand who is in the

---

Luz and Davies and Allison opt for the latter. Luz: *Matthäus*, 2:236; Davies and Allison: *Matthew*, 2:317 n. 37. Both commentaries suggest that the Aorist form is related to Lk 14:3 and an extraneous addition. However, Lk 14:3 seems more closely related to Mk 3:4 in its presentation of the problem as the question of Jesus, while, on the other hand, Matthew 12:10 presents the problem as the question of the opponents. Despite the change in construction Matthew still resembles Mk 3:2,4 with the phrase τοῖς σάββασιν, and especially Mk 3:4 with the addition of ἔξεστιν. Lk 6:6 and 14:3 use ἐν τῷ σαββάτῳ instead. Consequently, the Aorist θεραπεῦσαι in Matthew 12:10 might have been influenced by the Aorist ἀγαθὸν ποιῆσαι ἢ κακοποιῆσαι in Mk 3:4. Thus it is quite possible to read the Aorist in Matthew as influenced by the formulation in Mk 3:4. This lends plausibility to the reading of the manuscripts ‭א D L W *pc* and makes it unnecessary to view it either as a minor agreement or as extraneous. For the originality of θεραπεύειν speaks the parallel present tense of the infinitive in 12:12. This would create a nice parallelism between the problem presented by the opponents and the answer given by Jesus. However, a definitive judgment is perhaps no longer possible in view of the divergent manuscript traditions.

[58] Among the commentators Davies and Allison are alone in raising the question whether a healing on the Sabbath was actually allowed or not. Davies and Allison: *Matthew*, 2:318. Strack and Billerbeck list the appropriate parallels from rabbinic teaching: *Mek Ex* 31,13 (109a); *TShab* 15,17 (134). Strack and Billerbeck: *Kommentar*, 1:623–629. The consensus among the rabbis seems to be that healing is, in fact, unlawful, yet allowing for certain exceptions like immediate danger of death. The exceptions are not applicable in Matthew, and the question is not phrased to allow for casuistry. The answer, too, makes no distinctions. Furthermore, the evidence adduced by Strack and Billerbeck can hardly be applicable to Matthew since it is of such late origin. On the other hand, the question itself, and its controversial nature, seem to indicate that in the time of Matthew, and perhaps of Jesus, healing on the Sabbath was not considered a lawful activity. This is borne out by the opinion of the Qumran community, which seems to have observed a stricter enforcement of the Sabbath rules. S. T. Kimbrough: "The Concept of Sabbath at Qumran," *RevQ* 5 (1966): 483–502. A similarly strict observance of the Sabbath is reflected in *Jub* 2:50.

[59] Yet Bultmann still categorizes the Markan account as a controversy dialogue. He assumes 3:4 to be the riposte to the challenge implied in 3:2. Bultmann: *History*, 12.

foreground in Mark.[60] Finally, the use of the infinitive in the question not only correlates well with the answer that is given by Jesus in 12:12, it also generalizes the issue sufficiently that it can become a paradigm for the community. The Pharisees are no longer asking about Jesus healing this particular man on this particular Sabbath. The question becomes more generally applicable to the community.[61] The controversy, then, reflects not only Jesus' conflict with the Pharisees, it is also a mirror for the community.[62] At the same time, the controversial nature of this story presents a further step in the escalation of hostilities. Now it is no longer the action of the disciples that the Pharisees openly object to. This story sees them moving consciously against Jesus himself.

In 10c it becomes clear that the question of the Pharisees is no invitation to a learned disputation. Matthew repeats Mark's statement that the Pharisees' intention is to bring charges against Jesus, and thus again raises the stakes in the conflict with the Pharisees.[63] The answer of Jesus is threefold: one example in the form of a question (v. 11), one assertion, and a conclusion (v. 12). The example and the assertion are clearly distinguished by separate interrogative pronouns (τίς and πόσῳ), while the conclusion is suitably drawn with ὥστε.

The first part of Jesus' answer contains an example drawn from the experience of farmers: a sheep, having fallen into a pit, is lifted out of it on a Sabbath. The argument by example bears some semblance to Lk 14:5[64] and is likely taken from Q.[65] It is phrased as a rhetorical question (τίς ἔσται ἐξ ὑμῶν ἄνθρωπος).[66] This

---

[60] Interestingly, Luke also seems more interested in the controversy with the Pharisees. He inserts, before reporting that Jesus asked the man into the middle of the room, that Jesus knew the thoughts of the Pharisees and Scribes (6:8).

[61] If the reading θεραπεύειν were correct, it would underline the general nature of the question over the particular incident.

[62] Davies and Allison: *Matthew*, 2:318. Hummel already pointed out the significance of this story for the community: "*Das Streitgespräch begründet eine in der Gemeinde gültige, der pharisäischen Gesetzespraxis widersprechende Halacha über den Sabbat.*" Hummel: *Auseinandersetzung*, 45, emphasis original. Hummel, however, overlooked the possibility of strengthening his argument through the Matthean re-phrasing of the Pharisees' objection.

[63] The verb κατηγορέω is a technical term of judicial language that presupposes a court setting. Liddell and Scott: *A Greek-English Lexicon*, 926–927.

[64] Lk 14:5: "And he said to them, 'Which of you, having a son or an ox that has fallen into a well, will not immediately pull him out on a Sabbath day?'"

[65] Most scholars agree that such a saying was part of Q because of the substantial agreement between Matthew and Luke. John S. Kloppenborg: *Q Parallels. Synopsis, Critical Notes & Concordance*, Foundation and Facets Reference Series (Sonoma: Polebridge Press, 1988), 160; Tuckett: *Q*, 414. Schulz has argued that this saying does not accord well with Q' otherwise conservative attitude to the Law, and therefore cannot be part of Q. Siegfried Schulz: *Q – Die Spruchquelle der Evangelisten* (Zürich: TVZ, 1971), 41. Yet Schulz is too narrow in not allowing a casuistic interpretation in Q. Matthew's equally conservative attitude to the Law reports the saying in the context of this controversy. Consequently, it must have been regarded as a powerful argument in Jewish circles. Thus the saying does not conflict with a conservative attitude to the Law, and consequently cannot be dismissed on these grounds. The precise reconstruction of Q

response to the Pharisees implies that they actually ought to know the answer to their question. It also points out the hypocrisy of the Pharisees' accusation. Apparently they pull animals out of the pit on the Sabbath, or at least approve of the practice.[67] While the Pharisees thus show concern for animals, they do not do so for human beings. This question suggests that the Pharisees measure with two different scales. They do not know the mercy of the covenant (12:7).

The example itself recalls a situation of a farmer who has a sheep that falls into a pit.[68] Matthew uses it in a way that suggests to help this sheep is accepted practice.[69] The example seems to have been common among the contemporaries of Matthew's community. It existed in several versions.[70] The almost folkloric cha-

---

14:5 is hindered by textcritical difficulties in Luke's text. Manuscripts disagree who or what has fallen into the pit, "son" or "ox" or "ass" or one or another combination of these. Metzger: *Textual Commentary*, 138–139.

[66] See also Matthew 7:9 for the same construction. The formulation is sometimes seen as a semitism. Heinrich Greeven: "'Wer unter Euch ... ?'," *WuD* 3 (1952): 86–101; Matthew Black: *An Aramaic Approach to the Gospels and Acts*, 3rd. edition (Oxford: Oxford University Press, 1967), 118–119. The semitism can then be connected with the historical Jesus as "characteristic of Jesus." Davies and Allison: *Matthew*, 2:319. The latter seems an unwarranted inference since the saying is a halachic analogy that seems more suited to the Matthean context than to the *ipsissima vox Jesu* Luz: *Matthäus*, 2:237 n. 8. The Semitic phrase מִי־הָאִישׁ אֲשֶׁר is amplified by Matthew with ἐξ ὑμῶν, while the following material is not formulated as an imperative but as a rhetorical question. Betz in the commentary on the parallel 7:9 remarks that ἄνθρωπος is the key word in this question since "being a human being implies the obligation to act like one. This assumption is typical of the humanistic element in wisdom sayings." Betz: *Sermon*, 505. It is more probable that the formulation belongs to Matthew than to Jesus. It is possible that Matthew was informed by a Semitic language in the formulation, perhaps by way of wisdom literature. Matthew used this formulation elsewhere. It seems to have had a special appeal to Matthew. It served his purpose in this controversy in order to portray the Pharisees as hypocrites.

[67] Luz writes: "[Jesus] setzt damit eine selbstverständliche, nicht etwa umstrittene Praxis voraus." Luz: *Matthäus*, 2:238. However, Luz does not draw out the implications of such an established practice for the portrait of the Pharisees.

[68] Matthew post-positions ἕν after πρόβατον. This could imply that Jesus talks about a person who only has a single sheep. This interpretation is favored by Luz: *Matthäus*, 2:236. Davies and Allison do not want to take a position. Davies and Allison: *Matthew*, 2:319.

[69] The Essenes took a dim view of any such practices: See *CD* 11:13–14. Thus Matthew perhaps allows a view of a "nicht essenische, aber auch nicht rabbinische Sabbatpraxis." Luz: *Matthäus*, 2:238–239. Later rabbinic teaching allowed to help the animal by providing cushions so that it could climb out on its own, but forbade pulling it out. References in: Strack and Billerbeck: *Kommentar*, 629.

[70] Luke's version uses an ox for the example, while the Damascus Document refers more generically to an animal. The versions in Lk 13:15 and 14:5 bear witness to the fact that such examples were used in some quarters to explain the Sabbat practice of the early Christians. This is the function of the example in Matthew as well. It seems unwarranted, however, to assume that the Matthean version of this example has its roots in Q, suggested cautiously by Davies and Allison: *Matthew*, 2:316. While the Lukan parallels mirror the logical pattern of the example, the congruence in wording is minimal. This suggests that the pattern of interpretation was used across different Christian communities, while the actual wording was shaped locally. While this

racter of this example is underlined by Matthew's suggestion that it does not, on its own, provide enough of an argument to counter pharisaic opposition. Thus Matthew draws a halachic conclusion that incorporates a *qal-wa-ḥomer* argument.

Verse 12a states that a human being is worth much more than a sheep. The conclusion from the minor to the major is made explicit with πόσῳ.[71] Verse 12a is probably redactional. Matthew uses a similar argument in 6:26; 7:11, 10:31, and οὖν is one of his favorite particles.[72] The comparison of a human being to a sheep leads to the conclusion introduced with ὥστε. Observing a close parallel with the question, Matthew states that it is permissible to do good on the Sabbath.

Again Matthew observes the form of the minor to major argument in order to deliver a halachic judgment. The conclusion derives from Mk 3:4,[73] yet in a much more succinct form. Matthew shortens Mark's account in order to fit the words of Jesus to his formal argument. But he also extends the implications of Jesus' answer. Matthew has created a general rule concerning the Sabbath observance rather than simply raised a question as Mark does. The rule for the Sabbath now is entailed in the phrase καλῶς ποιεῖν. This rule corresponds to the needs of the community that were raised in the opening question of this controversy.[74]

Again Matthew does not move to suspend the Sabbath observance. He keeps the Sabbath in place, but moves to interpret it through a legal principle. As in the previous controversy, common ground with the Pharisees remains. Both Jesus and the Pharisees interpret the Law. However, the Pharisees are shown inept in their interpretation. In the previous controversy they did not know the Law and scriptures. Now they show themselves unable to draw a simple conclusion. When they admit to helping an animal on the Sabbath but question helping a person on the Sabbath, their interpretation of the law is shown up as a contradiction both illogical and immoral.

The general nature of the legal principle of Jesus is brought out by another subtle change Matthew makes. The question revolved around the possibility of healing during the Sabbath. In the general rule that the Matthean Jesus establishes, the net is cast wider: It is allowed to do good (καλῶς ποιεῖν). While this formulation is almost certainly inspired by Mk 3:4[75] the redaction also indicates that the Matthean version has its own rationale. Matthew distances himself even further from the incident that gives rise to the controversy. It is no longer the healing that is at stake.

---

assumption does not definitely exclude the saying from Q, it makes in harder to prove one way or the other.

[71] Several minor manuscripts add μᾶλλον to underline the conclusion (Θ, *f¹³*,33, 565, lat sy mae). The addition is perhaps inspired by 7:11.

[72] Davies and Allison: *Matthew*, 2:321; Luz: *Matthäus*, 1:46, 2:239.

[73] "Is it lawful on the Sabbath to do good or to do harm, to save life or to kill?"

[74] "Das Streitgespräch erhält ätiologische Bedeutung. Es legitimiert die Freigabe des Sabbats für die Liebestat gegenüber dem Pharisäismus." Hummel: *Auseinandersetzung*, 45.

[75] Mark has ἀγαθὸν ποιῆσαι ἢ κακοποιῆσαι.

Instead, Matthew proposes a general principle under which the Sabbath observance needs to be interpreted regardless of the situation at hand.[76] This general rule is applicable both in the community and among the Pharisees who question Jesus.

In v. 13 Matthew explains what καλῶς ποιεῖν means in the particular circumstances of the story that he narrates. Jesus turns to the man with the withered hand and performs a healing miracle.[77] The report is closely modeled after the Markan account in 3:5.[78] However, Matthew amends Mark to emphasize the completeness of the healing (ὑγιής ὡς ἡ ἄλλη).[79] Jesus is shown as a teacher whose halachic eloquence is supported by an act of power.[80]

But the teaching of Jesus has a second consequence: In v. 14 the Pharisees leave the synagogue to make plans for the destruction of Jesus. Matthew adapts Mark's version (3:6) slightly: εὐθύς drops out, as is usual for Matthew, and he substitutes ἔλαβον for ἐδίδουν, also usual for Matthew.[81] The most significant redaction is the omission of the Herodians as co-plotters of the Pharisees.[82] The easiest explanation for this omission is the fact that the Herodians are, up to now, an unknown factor in the Matthean narrative. In the end, they do not even play a significant part in the

---

[76] Luz interprets this as the "*grundsätzliche* Unterordnung des Sabbatgebots unter die Liebe" and connects it with the quotation of Hos 6:6 in the previous controversy story. Luz: *Matthäus*, 2:239. Davies and Allison elaborate: "καλῶς ποιεῖν is to do God's will. More concretely, it is to love one's neighbor, which is the chief commandment (cf. 7.12; 19.19; 22.39–40)." Davies and Allison: *Matthew*, 2:321. Similarly Hummel (cf. above). This is not necessarily convincing. This pericope, and the halachic conclusion it draws, make no reference to either love or the mercy described by Hos 6:6. The phrase καλῶς ποιεῖν does not appear anywhere else in the gospel, and the equation with doing God's will forces Davies and Allison to search elsewhere in the New Testament for substantiating evidence (Mk 7:37; Lk 6:27; Acts 10:33; 1 Cor 7:37–38; etc.).

[77] Davies and Allison mention a similar miracles in 1 Kings 13:1–10 and *TestXII.Sim* 2:11–14. Beyond the withered hand the similarities are scant, and verbal agreement is practically absent. Davies and Allison: *Matthew*, 2:321–322. However, the parallels indicate a similarity not drawn out by Davies and Allison: These miracles have in common their function as an affirmation of a prophecy or teaching. According to Gerd Theissen, the miracle can be classified as a "rule miracle" that reinforces sacred prescriptions. In this particular case, the miracle justifies the prescription to do good on the Sabbath. Theissen: *Stories*, 106–112.

[78] Matthew inserts τότε to mark the shift in the story and to emphasize the consecutive nature of the miracle as an explanation of the teaching just given. He adds σου, as does Luke.

[79] This redactional change enhances the effectiveness of the miracle in underlining the Matthean teaching. Matthew uses words he particularly likes. Gundry: *Matthew*, 228.

[80] It is probably this portrayal of Jesus as so superior to the Pharisees that prompts Matthew to omit the Markan reference to the feelings of Jesus as anger and grief (Mk 3:5). The equanimity of Jesus in the Matthean version also contrasts well with the Pharisees' plot to destroy Jesus. The Pharisees now abandon the argument over the Law and reach to demeaning methods. The miracle explains not only what it means to do good on the Sabbath. It also explains the meaning of the Hosea quotation of the previous controversy story.

[81] Cf. 22:15; 27:1.7; 28:12. See Gundry: *Matthew*, 228.

[82] Matthew also omits them from his account of Mk 12:13 (Mt 22:16).

execution of Jesus. Their hostility could not be explained at this point, and need not be explained for a later development.[83]

With this development Matthew achieves a twofold effect. The phrase συμβούλιον ἔλαβον presages grave consequences. The phrase will occur again in another controversy (22:15) and several times in the passion narrative (27:1,7; 28:12). Matthew signals that it will be controversies like this one that lead to the death of Jesus. While the teaching of Jesus is convincing and effective, it alienates the Pharisees to the point where they both plot and bring about the death of Jesus. At the same time, when Matthew shows the Pharisees as leaving the synagogue, he gives the story an ironic twist. The synagogue is the home-ground of the Pharisees, suitably described as αὐτῶν (12:9).[84] But the Pharisees cannot out-argue Jesus even on their own turf. Jesus proves himself to be greater than the Pharisees, not by working a miracle, but by being the better lawyer who can validate his decisions by a miraculous deed. As the great teacher of the Torah Jesus is validated before God by the success of the miracle. Matthew achieves this effect through the insertion of Q 14:5 into Mk 3:1–6.

2.1 The Markan Pericope

The Markan story of the man with the withered hand (3:1–6) is less distinctly organized than the Matthean parallel. Mark presents a mixture of a miracle story, a controversy story, and a pronouncement story. The lines between these elements overlap considerably.[85] This has led to the suggestion that the Matthean version with its clearer distinction between the forms is the older one.[86] However, it is hard

---

[83] Davies and Allison raise the question whether Matthew actually knew the identity of the Herodians and wanted to avoid thorny political issues, or whether he did not know them at all. Davies and Allison: *Matthew*, 2:322. There is no proof either way. Yet at the time of Matthew's writing the Herodians, at least of this story, had ceased to be significant and presented no thorny political problems. So Matthew might not have known them. Less speculative is the outcome of the omission: Matthew concentrates on the Pharisees as opponents. More helpful is their suggestion that Matthew wanted to concentrate on the Pharisees.

[84] Matthew consistently associates the synagogue with the opposition of Jesus by denoting it with the possessive pronoun "their" (4:23; 9:35; 10:17; 12:9; 13:54) or "your" (23:34). In the cases where "synagogue" is used without possessive pronoun, the context makes it clear that the synagogue is associated with people that oppose Jesus, or whom Jesus opposes (6:2; 6:5; 23:6). The synagogue is, for Matthew, a place of hostility against Jesus.

[85] Gnilka: *Markus*, 1:125. However, not so Bultmann: He called the Markan version an "organically complete apophthegm" if one omits 3:6. Bultmann: *History*, 12. In Mark, the miracle story intervenes in the conflict story because Mark has Jesus call the man with the withered hand into the midst of the congregation after the objection is mentioned (3:3). The controversy is not fully developed since the objection is never openly voiced. In this it resembles Mk 2:6. However, here Mark does not tell that Jesus knows their thoughts (cf. 2:8). There is no dialogue between the opposing factions. The pronouncement is actually given in the form of a question (3:4).

[86] So, e.g., Karl Kertelge: *Die Wunder Jesu im Markusevangelium. Eine redaktionsge-schichtliche Untersuchung*, StANT 33 (München: Kösel, 1970), 85.

to imagine the Herodians as a secondary addition, and the Matthean version of the story reflects well the way Matthew usually handles Markan source. It is harder to justify a Markan omission of Mt 12:11–12a on redactional grounds.

This evidence is supported by the general outline of the Markan account. The Markan argument seems somewhat unfocused. If the argument concerning healing o the Sabbath is an anecdote from the life of the historical Jesus, then his rejoinder does not at all capture the problem at hand: The man with the withered hand does not pose the problem of saving life or killing (Mk 3:4). If however, the controversy is constructed to reflect the conflict the Markan community experienced, the answer of Jesus seems equally out of place. Consequently, one area of discussion in the exegesis of the Markan pericope concerns the social setting for this controversy.[87] Possibly the question of Jesus is ironic in overstating the alternatives concerning the healing of a withered hand. The irony would be underlined by the reference to the Pharisees and Herodians who plot to destroy Jesus on the Sabbath (3:6).[88] Yet Mark does not make the connection obvious. The answer of Jesus refers to ἀποκτεῖναι, while the Pharisees and Herodians plot ὅπως αὐτὸν ἀπολέσωσιν. Several manuscripts, however, interpret Mark to make the connection between the

---

[87] Gnilka argues that the mixed form of the pericope yields the evidence for a late composition. Gnilka: *Markus*, 1,125. The frequent occurrence of Sabbath controversies in the synoptic gospels in general, however, seems to indicate that a historical precedent for at least this kind of controversy was rooted in the ministry of Jesus. Thus this could be a "weitgehend von der Erinnerung her gestaltete" story. Jürgen Roloff: *Das Kerygma und der irdische Jesus. Historische Motive in den Jesuserzählungen der Evangelien* (Göttingen: Vandenhoeck & Ruprecht, 1970), 64. Davies and Allison concur and add that the expression τίς ἔσται ἐξ ὑμῶν ἄνθρωπος is "an expression characteristic of Jesus," yet without further substantiation beyond the semitic nature of the expression. Davies and Allison: *Matthew*, 2:316–317, 1:681. It is telling that Roloff as well as Davies and Allison in their judgment concerning the historicity of the pericope concentrate on the fact that Jesus is at odds with the Pharisees over the Sabbath. This is, of course, a motif that occurs frequently enough in the gospels for the conclusion that is was indeed part of Jesus' ministry. While this argument provides good background for a judgment of the historicity of this pericope it does not actually decide the issue one way or the other. It must be shown convincingly that the answer given is actually an answer that would fit with a social setting in the historical ministry of Jesus. This both commentaries fail to do. They also fail to point out that their discussion of the issues presumes that a clean distinction between the ministry of Jesus and the interests of the community is indeed possible. This, however, is only possible if one assumes a fairly visible discontinuity between the historical Jesus and the communities that followed him. But if, as is likely, Jesus *and* the Markan community had to defend their Sabbath practice, it is harder to draw the line that divides historical reminiscence from composition for theological purposes.

[88] Gundry writes: The conclusion of 3:6 "ironically casts [the opponents] in the role of assassins who deserve the kind of death that Jesus will unjustly suffer because he saves life rather than killing people. Again ironically, the guardians of the Sabbath conspire to destroy the Lord of the Sabbath ... The forward position of αὐτόν, 'him,' heightens the irony." Gundry: *Mark*, 152.

answer of Jesus and the plot of the opponents by replacing ἀποκτεῖναι with ἀπολέσαι in Mk 3:4.[89]

The discussion of the social location is complicated by the possibility that Mk 3:1-6 is part of a collection of controversy stories that was one of the sources for Mark's gospel.[90] If this is so, the social setting of this controversy might be found neither in the ministry of the historical Jesus nor in the setting of the gospel of Mark, but bear witness to a stage of the community preliminary to that of the gospel. However, the lines between these various stages are not easily demarcated. The fact that Mark incorporated these stories indicates that they had some relevance for his community. Mark's work on 3:1-6 indicates that he saw it as a preparation for the cross and a reassurance of the audience of Jesus' innocence.[91]

However one wants to solve the Markan quandary, the Matthean redaction bears again witness to the skill with which Matthew adapted these stories to fit his own purposes. Matthew makes the story much more relevant to a discussion of various Sabbath practices that confronted his own community. Matthew's work shows that his community was still interested in the Sabbath to an extent where it needed to define its acceptable observance within the context of a community that had become Christian. Thus Matthew keeps the Sabbath in place and enjoins its keeping. But the keeping of the Sabbath command is now shaped by the teaching of Jesus. It has its purpose now in doing good. With arguments that derive from the Law Matthew counters Pharisaic charges of improper conduct on the Sabbath. As these charges are made against Jesus, Matthew shows how they are also made to include his community. Matthew makes Jesus the teacher of the Law who can expose the Pharisaic teaching as illogical and hypocritical, and propose an interpretation of the Law that is better argued and more humanely applied. Matthew's Jesus shows the way to the greater righteousness (5:17).

This teaching gives the community its arguments against opposition. By centering the story more clearly around the conflict Matthew draws attention to the still virulent opposition that the community faced. The legal argument that Matthew provides is suited for exactly this kind of conflict. It shows that the community is

---

[89] The manuscripts in question are: L W Δ Θ f[1.13] 28. 565. 700. 892. 1424 latt sy[s.p] sa[ms]. These manuscripts are a substantial group, even if they do not have enough force to question the reading of ἀποκτεῖναι seriously.

[90] For a discussion of the hypothesis that Mk 2:1-3:6 was originally a collection of conflict stories collected previous to the composition of the gospel see: Hultgren: *Adversaries*, 151-174. Hultgren comes to the conclusion that the five controversy stories in 2:1-3:6 were a collection previous to Mark, and that the collection had its own narrative flow already before Markan additions fitted it into the overall narrative purpose of the gospel. These additions consist mainly of 2:13-14, modeled after 1:16-20, and 2:21-22. They could have been added to make some of the conflict stories more understandable for a growingly Gentile audience. A more detailed analysis of the hypothesis of a pre-Markan collection and the reasons why Matthew might have broken it up follows in chapter 7 of this study.

[91] Gundry: *Mark*, 152.

not opposed to the Law, that it wants to keep the Law perfectly, and that it does so with an appeal to Jesus as a teacher of the Law whose authority surpasses that of the Pharisees. In the end, the Matthean community presents itself as more faithful to the Law and its observance. Its interpretation is such that it drives the Pharisees out of their synagogue, but it also explains that the enemy now plots destruction.

2.2 Summary of the Matthean Redaction in 12:9–14

The Matthean redaction of the healing of the man with the withered hand concerns itself with structure and content of the pericope:

- ► The structural work of Matthew achieves a greater cohesion of the story as a controversy story through the complete separation of miracle from controversy. The miracle is abbreviated and subordinated to the controversy. It becomes the illustration of the controversial issue.
- ► Matthew initiates the controversy with a direct question by the Pharisees.
- ► Matthew inserts an example and allows for the construction of a qal-wa-ḥomer argument.
- ► Matthew generalizes the conflict beyond healing to a general rule concerning the Sabbath observance. The generalizations make the controversy more applicable to the community.
- ► Matthew omits the Herodians and achieves a concentration on the Pharisees as opponents plotting the destruction of Jesus. Again this could be a reflection on the Matthean community.

3. Matthew 12:22–37

Matthew continues to follow the sequence of Mark.[92] After the controversy of the man with the withered hand Matthew models a summary statement (12:15–16) on Mk 3:7–12. It shows Jesus withdrawing,[93] but followed by many.[94] The Markan

---

[92] Matthew leaves out Mk 3:13–19 since he has used the material already in 10:1–4.

[93] This withdrawal of Jesus (ἀναχορέω) repeats itself in 14:13 and 15:21. Together with 13:36a and 16:4b it has led Luz to speak of a withdrawal of Jesus from Israel as the theme of 12:1–16:20. Luz: *Matthäus*, 2:225–226; Luz: *Theology*, 81–100. Matthew uses ἀναχορέω in 2:12–13. There it describes the departure of the magi who avoid Herod. In 2:14,22 it marks Joseph's move first to Egypt, then to the district of Galilee. In 4:12 Jesus reacts to the arrest of the Baptist by withdrawing to Galilee. In 9:24 Jesus orders the bystanders to withdraw from the room of the daughter of the synagogue official. In 12:15 and 14:13 Jesus withdraws, but great throngs follow him. In 15:21 Jesus withdraws to Tyre and Sidon to meet the Syro-Phoenician woman. In 27:5 it marks Judas' departure from the temple to hang himself. It seems that the word alone cannot be used to infer a coherent theme for 12:1–16:20 since its uses are not restricted to Jesus, or to this part of the gospel. Furthermore, 12:15; 14:13; 15:21 are all inspired by Mark (3:7; 6:32; 7:24), as is 16:4b that uses slightly different vocabulary. This leaves 13:36a to carry the burden

summary is amplified by a programmatic fulfilment quotation of Is 42:1–4.[95] The considerable difficulties in locating the origin and redaction of the quotation in Matthean tradition or redaction point to the looseness of its fit within its context. It points forward to the following controversy story by clarifying that it is the Spirit of God that rests on Jesus. And it points backwards by its reference to mercy and love embodied in the image of the bruised reed and smoldering wick.[96]

---

of the argument. But the withdrawal of Jesus is inspired here by the differentiation between public and private teaching. It is not prompted by any overt opposition to his teaching of the parables of the kingdom. The withdrawal in 12:15 is only preliminary, since Jesus returns immediately to enter into another controversy with the Pharisees. Kingsbury: *Matthew as Story*, 73. This makes Gnilka's position untenable: "Jesus, der Wissende, weiß um die Ränke seiner Gegner. Er verzichtet darauf, ihnen entgegenzutreten, sondern weicht zurück." Gnilka: *Matthäus*, 1:450.

[94] The withdrawal of Jesus leads to a separation of those who follow him and those who are in opposition to him. Thus the withdrawal is not a flight; it shows that, as a result of his powerful interpretation of the Law, people follow him. They do not follow the Pharisees who also left (12:14). The crowds that follow Jesus anticipate the formation of the church in Israel. Luz: *Matthäus*, 2:243. Gundry views the passage differently: He assumes that Matthew makes "Jesus an example of the fleeing he commanded his disciples to practice under persecution (10:23)." Gundry: *Matthew*, 228. However, in 10:23 the verb is φεύγειν, not ἀναχορεῖν.

[95] Scholars do not agree whether the quotation is Matthean redaction or stems from a source that Matthew incorporated into his gospel. The latter hypothesis is held by: Trilling: *Das wahre Israel*, 126–127; Strecker: *Weg*, 67–70; Barnabas Lindars: *New Testament Apologetic: The Doctrinal Significance of the Old Testament Quotations* (London: SCM Press, 1973), 144–152; Robert Hodgson: "The Testimony Hypothesis," *JBL* 98 (1979): 374. Reasons for this hypothesis include: The quote contains several Matthean *hapax legomena* (αἱρετίζω, ἐρίζω, κραυγάζω, συντρίβω, κατάγνυμι τύφω, νῖκος), the Christian testimonial collection of Papyrus Rylands Greek 460 includes Is 42:3–4, in the targumim the text receives a messianic interpretation, points of contact with the Matthean summary are scant (Jesus' silence) or absent, the quotation was possibly used in a pre-Matthean setting as a catechesis concerning baptism, resurrection, and the Gentile mission. For a full discussion of these possibilities see Davies and Allison, who regard the quotation as Matthew's original work. Davies and Allison: *Matthew*, 2:323. Their main arguments are: The textual form is not attested elsewhere; the quote is adapted to its present context; the phrase ὁ ἀγαπητός μου κ.τ.λ. shows assimilation to Matthew 3:17; 17:5; θήσω τὸ πνεῦμά μου ἐπ' αὐτόν not only recalls the baptism but also links up with the following question concerning the nature of the spirit that Jesus has; the double mention of the Gentiles is a major Matthean interest. Gnilka acknowledges that the quote fits into the Matthean context and concludes indecisively that its origin lies either in Matthew or in the school behind Matthew. He does no longer try to distinguish between the two. Gnilka: *Matthäus*, 453. Finally, Luz assumes that the quotation reached its present form before Matthew who can be credited with linking the quotation to the Markan summary. Luz: *Matthäus*, 2:244–246.

[96] For Cope, Is 42:1–4 is one of the mid-point texts of the gospel that are employed as "a key to the organization of a number of parts of the gospel." O. Lamar Cope: *Matthew. A Scribe Trained For the Kingdom of Heaven*, CBQ.MS, vol. 5 (Washington: The Catholic Biblical Association, 1976), 10. The connection between the quotation of Is 42:1–4 and the rest of ch. 12 is probably less of a structural nature than this statement leads one to believe. As Cope himself points out in his actual analysis of ch. 12 (pp. 32–52) the relationship between Isaiah and Matthew 12 is more thematic than structural. Cope relates Matthew 12:19 ("He will not wrangle nor cry

The function of the quotation can be assessed in this light. Mk 3:7–12 provided an interruption of the controversy stories through a very odd summary. It shows Jesus and his disciples as withdrawing, although unsuccessfully. Large multitudes follow them (v. 7) because of previous healings (v. 10), and Jesus is so pressed that he orders a boat readied (v. 9). With the crowds a large number of unclean spirits arrive and acknowledge him as the Son of God (v. 11). Jesus, however, commands them to silence (v. 12). Mark's summary shows Jesus beleaguered by the crowds, but only reacting to the evil spirits. Matthew shortens this summary considerably, but does not abandon it completely. He still shows Jesus withdrawing, yet followed by many (12:15). But then Matthew has Jesus address the situation by turning to heal many (v. 16). He omits the reference to the evil spirits, and somewhat weakens Mark's command not to make Jesus known. Matthew's presentation of Jesus is much more civil. Jesus is not pressed in by the crowds as their victim, and he turns to them when he sees their need. Furthermore, Matthew does not report the possibly embarrassing obeisance of the evil spirits. The events of the summary are then explained with a christologically focused[97] fulfilment quotation of Is 42:1–4.

---

aloud ...") to the withdrawal of Jesus, while Matthew 12:18 ("Behold, my servant whom I have chosen ...") with the controversy about the origin of Jesus' authority to exorcize, because the crowds ask whether Jesus might be the son of David. While I agree that the quotation serves as an interpretation of Jesus that helps to place the controversies of ch. 12, the controversies themselves probably also shed light on the use of the quotation. Cope's attempt to be more specific in relating particular phrases in the quotation to particular phrases in the rest of the chapter seem labored. For example, in order to relate 12:18 to the Beelzebul controversy, he first claims that the Targum of Isaiah proves that Matthew must have understood the verse as a Messianic reference, and that this was clear to his audience as well. This would be proven by the question whether Jesus is the son of David. Secondly, the promise of the Spirit for the servant relates to the argument of the Spirit of Jesus. Cope's first argument fails. The Targum is considerably later than the gospel, and therefore cannot be evidence to Matthew's understanding of Isaiah. Furthermore, the easy equation of Messiah with son of David is highly questionable, particularly since Matthew develops his own concept of the latter title in his gospel. Luz: *Matthäus*, 2:59–61. There remains the tentative connection between the Spirit of the quotation and the Spirit of the controversy. This connection is probably more by association than by an intentional structure. The controversy itself makes no reference to Isaiah. The value of the quotation for Matthew lies probably in its applicability to Jesus. It highlights, in the midst of controversy, who it actually is that the Pharisees reject: the humble servant of God.

[97] This does not entirely disagree with B. Rod Doyle. Doyle begins with Cope's argument that such quotations are midway texts and thus reflect both backward and forward; then he argues that the quotation bears a direct connection to the Pharisees in order "to contrast Jesus, the Servant of the Lord, with his opponents the Pharisees." B. Rod Doyle: "A Concern of the Evangelist: Pharisees in Matthew 12," *ABR* 34 (1986): 22. Doyle can argue this by playing up the contrast between Jesus and the Pharisees that develops in ch. 12. However, Doyle's attempt to link the Pharisees directly with the quotation are labored. The contrast between the Pharisees and Jesus is not in question, yet is also a Matthean creation in ch. 12. The Isaiah quotation itself, however, emphasizes the figure of Jesus without the contrast. To be sure, the difference in argument with Doyle is only one of emphasis.

Jesus is the humble servant doing God's will. Jesus is kind and merciful (11:28–29; 12:7, 12). The quotation offers an interpretation of Jesus as son of God[98] that provides a foil for the controversy stories surrounding it. As Jesus has shown himself to be the interpreter of scripture, now scripture is used to interpret him. The quotation highlights whom the Pharisees reject.

This sets the stage for 12:22–37 (cf. Q 11:14–26).[99] The controversy is introduced by the healing of a blind and dumb demoniac. The miracle was already used in 9:32–34 in a slightly modified form of Matthew's own composition. There the demoniac was only dumb. In the earlier occurrence the miracle gave rise to the accusation of the Pharisees that Jesus casts out demons by the prince of demons (9:34). But the early accusation of the Pharisees was not developed into a controversy story. Now the miracle is heightened by the addition of the blindness of the demoniac, while the accusation of the Pharisees prepares for a full development of a controversy story.

The structure of the story is simple.[100] The short miracle (12:22) gives rise to the ensuing controversy. Different reactions to the miracle are reported that center around the authority of Jesus. In 12:23 the crowds ask whether Jesus is the Son of David, while in 12:24 the Pharisees accuse Jesus of exorcizing by the Prince of demons. Verse 25 begins a long answer of Jesus that can be divided into two parts. The first part (12:25–30) consists of several sayings of Jesus (25–27). Verse 28 is the central argument against the accusation of the Pharisees, followed by the saying of the strong man (29) and the conclusion about being with Jesus or against him (30). The second part is clearly distinguished by διὰ τοῦτο and consists of two parts (12:31–32 and 12:33–37) that both contain a λέγω ὑμῖν (12:31.36) and both end in the reference to the last judgment (12:32.37).[101]

Within this structure Matthew constructs the argument in parallelisms. In 12:25 two parallel images are offered (πᾶσα βασίλεια ... πᾶσα πόλις), followed by their application in 12:26 to Satan. The construction of 12:27 and 28 with εἰ ἐγὼ ἐκβάλλω τὰ δαιμόνια each contains an antithetical parallelism that opposes Beelzebul to the Spirit of God. A similar antithetical parallelism is contained in 12:31–32. Furthermore, 12:33–37 also contain a number of opposing pairs. Noteworthy are also the three rhetorical questions marked by πῶς (12:26.29.34)

---

[98] Παῖς (Mt 12:18) refers to "child" much more often than to "servant." Liddell and Scott: *A Greek-English Lexicon*, 1289. In Matthew this is almost exclusively so. The only exception is 14:2, the παῖδες of Herod. In 24:49 Matthew reformulates and uses συνδούλους instead of παῖδας καὶ ... παιδίσκας. See Luz: *Matthäus*, 2:246. This interpretation of παῖς would strengthen a possible connection with the baptism of Jesus.

[99] See the discussion of the Beelzebul controversy in Kloppenborg: *Formation*, 121–127.

[100] Luz: *Matthäus*, 2:253.

[101] Davies and Allison take 31–32 as a separate section, as does Gnilka. Davies and Allison: *Matthew*, 2:334; Gnilka: *Matthäus*, 1:455. Their judgment represents only a minor shift in emphasis since both recognize the common elements that connects 31–32 with 33–37.

that help to unify the speech of Jesus. Thus the collection of sayings in 12:25–37 seems carefully composed.[102]

The question of sources for this incident is complicated because Matthew interweaves different traditions. The place of the controversy seems occasioned by Mk 3:22–40.[103] The most common hypothesis holds that Matthew combined the Markan text with the Beelzebul controversy of Q 11:14–23, following in general the outline of Q.[104] The major differences between Luke and Matthew are: a) The demoniac[105] is brought to Jesus in Matthew, while Luke just reports the healing. b) The person is dumb in Luke, blind and dumb in Matthew. c) The healing itself is reported more formally in Matthew with ἐθεράπευσεν ... ὥστε.[106] d) The reaction of the Matthean crowd is exaggerated into almost frenzied behavior (ἐξίσταντο)[107]

---

[102] Robbins concludes that the controversy story contains almost all steps necessary for a successful rhetorical argument according to Hermogenes. Vernon K. Robbins: "Rhetorical Composition and the Beelzebul Controversy," in: *Patterns of Persuasion*, ed. Burton L. Mack and Vernon K. Robbins (Sonoma: Polebridge, 1989), 185. For Harrington the speech is a "somewhat choppy one." Harrington: *Matthew*, 185. Gnilka is similarly sceptical concerning the success Matthew has in ordering the "Vielfalt von Einzelsprüchen und kleinen Spruchgruppen." Gnilka: *Matthäus*, 1:455. These two views are not necessarily exclusive of each other. It is possible to acknowledge the diversity of the sayings while still acknowledging that Matthew went to some lengths to mold them into a single discourse.

[103] Like Luke, Matthew omits the story of the accusation of insanity against Jesus by his relatives (Mk 3:19b–21), probably for the reason of its possibly embarrassing nature. Mark only reports the charge, he does not dispute or discredit it.

[104] Luz: *Matthäus*, 2:254. Downing has used the Beelzebul pericope to test the consequences of dispensing with Q and showed convincingly that this is not possible. F. Gerald Downing: "Towards a Rehabilitation of Q," *NTS* 11 (1964): 169–181. Catchpole reiterates Downing's arguments and reconstructs Q to have included the following elements: (1) the demoniac (2) who was dumb (3) and spoke after his cure by Jesus, (4) while the crowds marveled (5) and others spoke of the agency of Beelzebul. Catchpole suggests that the Matthean redaction added the blindness, the reference to the Son of David. Catchpole: *Quest*, 48–51. Kloppenborg provides a convincing reconstruction of the Q material behind this controversy. Kloppenborg: *Formation*, 121–127. See also Kloppenborg: *Q Parallels*, 90–93.

[105] Matthew: δαιμονιζόμενος; Luke: δαιμόνιον.

[106] Its doublet in 9:32–34 has a closer congruence of 9:33 with Lk 11:14. The healing is described with a circumstantial participle in both Luke and Matthew. Matthew adds λέγοντες κ.τ.λ. to report the reaction of the crowd.

[107] Davies and Allison argue that the use of ἐξίσταντο was suggested by the omitted Mk 3:21 and claim that the verb here has the weak sense of being astonished. Davies and Allison: *Matthew*, 2:334 n.5. Similarly Gundry: "Matthew not only compensates for his omitting the charge [of 3:21], but also changes the reference and meaning of the verb from the falsely supposed insanity of Jesus to the crowds' amazement ..." Gundry: *Matthew*, 231. The two arguments do not quite mesh. If the verb was suggested by Mk 3:21 reporting the family thinking Jesus mad, then why does it get weakened? Such a weakening would be all the more remarkable as it is a Matthean *hapax legomenon*. The doublet of 9:33 uses ἐθαύμασαν. This suggests that the verb, while perhaps suggested by Mk 3:21, is also a redactional element here without a weakened meaning. Matthew deliberately exaggerates the reaction of the crowd over its previous reaction to the same miracle.

while πάντες emphasizes the uniformity of the crowd's reaction. e) The Matthean crowd's reaction is verbalized into a question concerning the identity of Jesus: "Can this be the son of David?" (12:23). f) Matthew leaves out Q 11:16 as he uses this verse in the controversy over the demand of a sign (12:38).

The controversy follows the sequence of Mk 3:22–30. However, Q 11:15–23 has contributed greatly to the present form of the story in Matthew. Thus Matthew 12:22–37 appears as a passage taken from Q 11:14–32 which is integrated through rearrangements and insertions with Mark and Matthean special material. The Markan part of the story accounts for its place in the narrative sequence.[108] The following analysis of the Matthean text will try to verify this assertion.

The first impression is that the Matthean version of the miracle is an enhanced version of the miracle reported in 9:32–33. The elements remain the same, but are amplified: the disease of the possessed man, the reaction of the crowd, even their response shows development: In 9:33 the crowds were astounded and said: "Never was anything like this seen in Israel." In 12:23 they are beside themselves and raise the question of Jesus' identity.

The miracle in 9:32–33 is so closely related to Lk 11:14 that there is an almost certain literary relationship.[109] Therefore, 12:22–23 is also related to Lk 11:14 and can be assumed to be a re-working of material found in Q and used in ch. 9.

This re-working draws attention to several facets of the story. Jesus is regarded well, and so people bring the sick to him because by now they know of his healing power and compassion (12:15–21). And the excited crowds finally ask a christological question which focuses the following material closely on the person of Jesus.[110] The elements of healing, of the crowds' reaction, and of Jesus are taken to higher levels, emphasizing the attendant controversy. In 9:34 the Pharisees already brought up arguments against the authenticity of Jesus' healing the demoniac that were left unanswered. This time, the distance between Jesus' deed and the opposition is even greater, and can no longer be left unanswered.[111]

---

[108] The connection between the accusation that Jesus exorcizes through Beelzebul with the healing of the dumb demoniac seems to have existed already in Q.

[109] The most incisive argument for this relationship is the verbal agreement in the phrase ἐλάλησεν ὁ κωφός. καὶ ἐθαύμασαν οἱ ὄχλοι.

[110] Catchpole rightly points out that the introduction of the Son of Man saying is Matthean redaction of Q 11:14. Catchpole: *Quest*, 51. This is borne out by the introduction of the title into the story of the Canaanite woman (Mt 15:22, cf. Mk 7:25), and to the controversy of Mt 21:14–17.

[111] Against Luz, who argues that "die Leser sollten also nicht merken, daß Mt dieselbe Wundergeschichte aus Q zweimal braucht; es geht deshalb bei Mt auch um einen *Blinden*!." Luz: *Matthäus*, 2:254 n.18. This argument is unconvincing. The possessed man is not just blind, he is also dumb, repeating 9:33. Furthermore, it seems absurd to argue that Matthew writes to confuse his readers. Matthew wants to prepare his readers for the following controversy, and he does so by using old material, enhancing it, and finally answering the old challenge. One indication of this is that the charge that Jesus exorcizes through Beelzebul is not just dropped after 9:34. The reader is reminded of it in 10:25: "The placement and arrangement of these stories is crucial to the

The negative reaction of the Pharisees marks the beginning of the controversy story. The identification of the Pharisees as the opponents is further Matthean redaction.[112] Then he creates a curious construction. In Lk 11:15 it is perfectly clear that the objection of the opponents relates to the miracle that Jesus has just performed and stands in contrast with the reaction of the crowds. But Matthew has inserted the response of the crowds in direct discourse. Now he adds that the Pharisees heard this (12:24), and consequently they object to what they heard. Thus it is no longer the miracle that provokes a mixed reaction, as in Q, but the positive reaction of the crowds that upsets the Pharisees.[113] The accusation shows the full extent of the Pharisees' contempt by the emphatic placing of οὗτος and the Matthean construction οὐκ ... εἰ μή.[114] As in Luke and Mark the opponents make their charge in the third person, addressing the crowds rather than Jesus himself.[115] The charge is a very free reworking of the Markan phraseology.[116] It alleges that Jesus casts out demons by the prince of demons, Beelzebul.[117] The Pharisees try to

---

development of both plot and character in Matthew ... The implied reader reads each episode in the light of the other, in prospect and in retrospect." Anderson: *Web*, 175. A similar expansion of a doublet to move the plot forward is the stilling of the storm (8:23–27; 14:22–33). The convincing thesis of Anderson's book is to show how repetition has a conscious function in the Matthean narrative for the implied reader.

[112] Luke does not identify them: τινὲς δὲ ἐξ αὐτῶν. Mark does not report the miracle, and so the controversy follows immediately after the accusation of Jesus' family that he is mad. The accusers in Mark are Scribes from Jerusalem.

[113] Cf. Davies and Allison: "What the Pharisees are interested in above all, is keeping others from belief." Davies and Allison: *Matthew*, 2:335. So also: Gundry: *Matthew*, 232; Gnilka: *Matthäus*, 1:457. Not so: Luz: *Matthäus*, 2:258.

[114] A Semitism according to Davies and Allison: *Matthew*, 2:335.

[115] Gundry claims that the Pharisees speak to themselves. Gundry: *Matthew*, 233. This is not convincing since the Pharisees in their charge respond to the reaction of the crowds. Matthew heightens the situation of a fight over followers.

[116] Against Davies and Allison: "As with 9:34 and Lk 11:15b, there is no need to suppose influence from Mk 3:22 ..." Davies and Allison: *Matthew*, 2:335. The phrase in 9:34 is a complete rendering of Mk 3:22c. Lk 11:15b also repeats Mk 3:22c with the insertion of Beelzebul from 3:22b. In 12:24 Matthew can use Mk 3:22 more freely since he has already reported it in 9:34. The addition of οὗτος and the construction with οὐκ ... εἰ μή sharpens the accusation considerably and is thus in keeping with the redaction of the miracle preceding it. The construction with οὐκ ... εἰ μη occurs again in 14:17 and 15:24, and thus can be classified as a Mattheanism.

[117] It seems likely that in the first century this name had become one of several for Satan. Some minor manuscripts change the name to Beelzebub for all three synoptic gospels. The name perhaps derives from one of the ancient names for the Canaanite god Baal. On the problematic Semitic background of the name see the full discussion in: Davies and Allison: *Matthew*, 2:195–196. For the charge made by the Pharisees this discussion is only marginally interesting. The parallelisms of 12:26–28 show that Beelzebul is identified with Satan, and is the direct opposite of the Spirit of God.

discredit Jesus by denying that he works as an agent of God and claiming that he does his signs in direct opposition to God.[118]

The rejoinder of Jesus begins by stating that Jesus knew their thoughts (12:25) and responds to them. The statement is influenced by Q 11:17. The Matthean replacement of διανοήματα with ἐνθυμήσεις recalls Matthew 9:4 and is probably redactional.[119] The saying about the kingdom and house are a conflation of Q 11:17b and Mk 3:24–25.[120] Matthew achieves greater parallelism than Q,[121] and he is more succinct than Mark. The construction gives the impression of greater finesse and asserts Matthew's redactional freedom. Matthew adds the reference to the division within a city.[122] In v. 26 Matthew returns to the problem at hand by formulating, against Luke, but prompted by Mk 3:23, the proposition: Satan casts

---

[118] It is possible that such accusations against Jesus were common. Such an accusation would put Jesus in the company of magicians. A good collection of pertinent magical texts has been assembled by: Morton Smith: *Jesus the Magician* (San Francisco: Harper & Row, 1978), 21–80. However, the Greek magical papyri mostly date from the third to the fifth century C.E. and are thus only partially useful for comparison; only very few instances can be dated as contemporary with Jesus or Matthew. For a full discussion on the usefulness of the magical papyri and summaries of varying scholarly opinions, see: John P. Meier: *A Marginal Jew. Rethinking the Historical Jesus*, 3 vols., AncB.RL (New York, London, Toronto, Sydney, Auckland: Doubleday, 1992–), 2:537–541; Bruce J. Malina and Jerome H. Neyrey: *Calling Jesus Names: The Social Value of Labels in Matthew* (Sonoma: Polebridge, 1988), 3–4. Davies and Allison point out that such charges presuppose Jesus' uncontested success at exorcisms. Davies and Allison: *Matthew*, 2:336.

[119] Common are εἰδώς (9:4 has ἰδών) τὰς ἐνθυμήσεις αὐτῶν εἶπεν. The Lukan version 11:17a does not recall Lk 5:22a. It seems likely, then, that Luke preserves a more original version of the introduction to Jesus' answer. Luke has: αὐτὸς δὲ εἰδὼς αὐτῶν τὰ διανοήματα.

[120] Common with Lk 11:17b are: πᾶσα, ἐρημοῦται; common with Mk 3:24–25 are: the simple form of μερίζω (Luke uses the compound διαμερίζω), ἵστημι and the greater parallelism between kingdom and city/house. Matthean is the insertion of the city into the second example, thus amplifying the parallelism. Davies and Allison regard Markan influence as negligible. Davies and Allison: *Matthew*, 2:332. Luz agrees that Matthew combined his two sources. Luz: *Matthäus*, 2:254. On the whole Matthew has a longer text than Luke, but is shorter than Mark. The latter is achieved through the omission of words Matthew regarded as unnecessary: δύναμαι the repetition of the house in Mk 3:25.

[121] πᾶσα βασιλεία ... πᾶσα πόλις ἢ οἰκία; μερισθεῖσα καθ᾽ ἑαυτῆς ... μερισθεῖσα καθ᾽ ἑαυτῆς.

[122] Matthew adds πᾶσα πόλις to the group of similes and achieves a fine hierarchy of symbols: Kingdom, city, household. Gnilka suggests that the addition of πόλις could be a reference to the personal experience of the Matthean community in a large city. Gnilka: *Matthäus*, 1:458. This can easily be imagined since πόλις is one of Matthew's favorite redactional amendments: He uses it 14 times without parallel.

out Satan.[123] Matthew then can conclude: Satan is divided against himself, and his kingdom cannot stand.[124] Matthew achieves the rhetorical form of an enthymeme.[125]

In vv. 27–28 Matthew follows Q with only minor variations.[126] He asks for the implications of the preceding enthymeme with regard to Jesus' activity as exorcist: If Jesus exorcizes by the power of Satan, then how do the disciples[127] of the Pharisees do it? And if it is by the Spirit[128] of God, then the kingdom of God[129] has

---

[123] Mk 3:23 reads: πῶς δύναται σατανᾶς σατανᾶν ἐκβάλλειν; Davies and Allison hold that Matthew's version is the more original version of Q. Davies and Allison: *Matthew*, 2:337. But the careful crafting of the phrase and its parallelization throughout the pericope speak against this. The phrase εἰ ὁ σατανᾶς τὸν σατανᾶν ἐκβάλλει is carefully formed to take up a catch phrase first introduced in 12:24 (οὗτος οὐκ ἐκβάλλει ... εἰ μή) and repeated in 12:27 (εἰ ἐγὼ ἐν Βεελζεβοὺλ ἐκβάλλω) and 12:28 (εἰ δὲ ἐν πνεύματι θεοῦ ἐγὼ ἐκβάλλω). The verb ἐκβάλλειν becomes a key word in the passage.

[124] The use of the rhetorical question with the interrogative pronoun πῶς and the reference to the kingdom of Satan indicate that Matthew was more influenced by Q (see Lk 11:18) than by Mk 3:26. Further indications are ἐμερίσθη with Luke's διεμερίσθη against Mark's ἀνέστη, the omission of Mark's ἀλλὰ τέλος ἔχει.

[125] The enthymeme is a variation of the rhetorical form of a syllogism. The syllogism is the logically complete form of an argument that consists of all logically necessary parts of the argument. The enthymeme is a partial syllogism, in which one or some of the logically necessary parts of the argument are presumed. Lausberg: *Handbuch*, 198–200. In this particular case, Matthew's argument as a syllogism would need these elements: a) Every kingdom, city, and house divided against itself cannot stand. b) If Satan cast out Satan, he is divided against himself. c) Therefore, he cannot stand. d) Jesus stands. e) Consequently, Jesus does not cast out Satan through Satan. However, Matthew leaves out elements d) and e) because his audience can supply them for themselves. Hence Matthew constructs an enthymeme.

[126] Verse 27: insertion of καί, more emphatic position of ὑμῶν at the end of the sentence. Verse 28: substitution of "Spirit" for "finger" of God, possible insertion of ἐγώ (the textual witnesses to Lk 11:20 are not conclusive). Kloppenborg: *Q Parallels*, 90.

[127] Against Plummer, υἱοί does not imply natural sons here. Alfred Plummer: *An Exegetical Commentary on the Gospel According to St. Matthew* (London: R. Scott, 1915), 176–177. See Walter Bauer, W. F. Arndt, et al.: *A Greek-English Lexicon of the New Testament and Other Early Christian Literature* (Chicago: University of Chicago Press, 1961), 833–835.

[128] The introduction of the Spirit is probably redactional. Lk 11:20 has "finger." In this particular case the Spirit supplies redactional links backward to 12:18, the programmatic quotation of Is 42:1–4, and forward to the sin against the Holy Spirit, which in Luke does not occur until later (12:10). Thus Luke probably conserves the more original form of the saying.

[129] Noteworthy is Matthew's acceptance of "Kingdom of God" since his preference usually is "Kingdom of Heavens." In Matthew it occurs only here, in 19:24; 21:31; 21:43. Against Dunn, this is not an oversight. James D. Dunn: *Jesus and the Spirit. The Religious and Charismatic Experience of Jesus and the First Christians According to the New Testament* (Philadelphia: Westminster, 1975), 45. It stands in parallelism with πνεύματι θεοῦ and antithesis to βασιλεία αὐτοῦ. Davies and Allison: *Matthew*, 2:339. Patte suggest that the phrase is surprising, since Matthew did not use it before, and the comparison is even more powerful. Questionable is his conclusion that Matthew makes a conscious distinction between the "Kingdom of God" and the "Kingdom of Heavens," the former representing God's power, the latter his authority. Patte: *Matthew*, 177. Such an argument presses Matthew too far; after all, he received the formulation

appeared to them.[130] The argument of v. 27 is logically quite persuasive. It argues negatively what Jesus' exorcisms are not. The negative argument anticipates the positive argument of v. 28. Here Matthew implies that with the exorcisms of Jesus something qualitatively new happens: The kingdom of God becomes manifest. Matthew answers not only the accusations of the Pharisees with a logical argument (v. 27), he shows how Jesus' activity differs in quality from the Pharisees' disciples exorcisms (v. 28). But this assertion is beyond logical argument[131] and requires a decision. Matthew, in asserting this, anticipates v. 30.[132] The exorcisms of Jesus are a sign of the imminence of the kingdom, while at the same time they bind Beelzebul.[133]

Here Matthew can now insert Mark's saying of the strong man (Mk 3:27).[134] Matthew 12:29 amends Mark slightly to fit into the overall argument.[135] The

---

from his source. Furthermore, there is no evidence that the distinction between the power and the authority of God is Matthean.

[130] Again an expression (φθάνω) otherwise unfamiliar in Matthew. It probably is not to be taken as expressing sentiments different from 4:24; 10:8 (ἐγγίζω).

[131] The problem with Matthew's argument is that it obfuscates the actions of the Pharisees' disciples; if through the exorcisms of Jesus the kingdom of God has come upon them, why not by the exorcisms of their own group? Bultmann argues this way. Bultmann: *History*, 12. He is followed by, e.g., Perrin, and, more recently, by Meier. Norman Perrin: *Rediscovering the Teaching of Jesus* (New York: Harper & Row, 1967), 63–64; Meier: *Marginal Jew*, 2:410.

[132] So argued by Luz: *Matthäus*, 2:260–261.

[133] There has been some consensus among scholars that v. 28 and its parallel Lk 11:20 represent one of the original sayings of Jesus. The arguments for such a supposition rest mainly on a supposed lack of original connection with the surrounding context. The passage immediately following, about the strong man, occurs at roughly the same point in the Markan narrative sequence, yet the without the saying linking the exorcisms of Jesus with the kingdom of God. Thus the connection with the following material seems not original. The preceding material has sometimes been regarded as not connected as well. There is a curious shift in tone between the *ad hominem* argument of v. 27 against "you" who will be judged by "your sons" and the "you" who will be witnesses to the kingdom in v. 28. This discussion is summarized by Meier: *Marginal Jew*, 2:407–411. Meier comes to the conclusion that these "Jewish leaders who oppose and stigmatize Jesus' exorcisms would seem to be the one group to which the kingdom is not coming *via* Jesus' exorcisms. 'You' in v 28 seems to demand some other referent, such as Jesus' audience in general ..." (p. 409). The last argument is not entirely convincing. The connection between v. 27 and 28 evokes the curiously ironic situation that the kingdom of God is come upon the opponents of Jesus to a degree that makes their denial ridiculous. What remains of Meier's argument is a progressive redactional integration of the saying into its context. While Mark did not report the saying at all, it is present in Q, and Matthew reports it almost *verbatim* with only one change to integrate it more tightly with what precedes and what follows. While other contexts for this saying are imaginable, this is the only one we have.

[134] Luz comments that through the insertion of the definite article Matthew makes an allusion to the strong man as the opponent of God in Is 49:24–25. Luz: *Matthäus*, 2:261. For a short discussion of the history of the allegorical interpretation of the parable see his n. 71.

[135] Matthew creates the rhetorical question with πῶς, converts εἰσελθών into an infinitive and moves it to form a chiasm with ἁρπάσαι which necessitates a καί. He moves δήσῃ, perhaps to create a parallelism of verb + object between δύναται and δήσῃ.

rhetorical question is the second in the controversy. The first was asking how Satan's kingdom could stand. The implied answer was that it cannot. Now the question is how one can enter the strong man's house without binding him first. The implication is that in his exorcisms Jesus shows how to bind the strong man in order to plunder his house.[136]

The following verse (12:30)[137] does not advance the argument any further but states that there is a distinction between those who are with Jesus and those who are not: The former gather, the latter scatter. The statement has the mark of a conclusion of the argument, but it also calls for a decision to be either with Jesus or against him.[138] There is no room for a neutral attitude.[139] The double saying sits somewhat loosely in its context. The agricultural simile of gathering and

---

[136] Against Luz. His interpretation remains unclear. On the one hand he rejects any allegorical implications of the parable, and so rejects an interpretation that tries to fit the parable into the context of Jesus' answer in this controversy story ("Sie läßt im Hörer nur eine Ahnung aufblitzen"). On the other hand, he comments on the occasion of this parable that Jesus saw his exorcisms in the context of the eschatological battle against Satan and his dominion. He goes on to say that 12:29 points to the victory over Satan. Luz: *Matthäus*, 2:261–262. Also against Gundry, who argues that because Matthew switches from the Markan ἀλλ' to ἤ, Matthew indicates an alternative to Jesus' casting out demons by the Spirit of God. Thus the strong man is Jesus, his house are his disciples, and the saying as a whole refers to the church under persecution. The implication is that Satan cannot bind Jesus. Gundry: *Matthew*, 236. This interpretation is unconvincing since the controversy is not about persecution, it is about the authority by which Jesus casts out demons. Gnilka seems confused. On the one hand the parable speaks about Satan, "der wie ein Sklavenhalter die Menschen versklavt." On the other hand, he views the parable in apocalyptic terms and holds that "Jesus bezwingt ἐν πνεύματι θεοῦ." But there is no imagery of slavery here, and the binding of the strong man gives no inkling of a freeing of slaves. Gnilka: *Matthäus*, 1:459. Davies and Allison are correct in noting that ἤ makes v. 29 a variation of the argument presented in vv. 27–28. Davies and Allison: *Matthew*, 2:342. So also Harrington: "The point is that Jesus has already bound up Satan, and his exorcisms should be understood as signs of victory over Satan." Harrington: *Matthew*, 184.

[137] Its provenance is Q (Lk 11:23). Gundry assumes that the Matthean text relates to Mk 9:40 ("for he who is not against us is for us") as a token of acknowledgment for omitting the story of the strange exorcist (Mk 9:38–40). Matthew supposedly turns the statement into one relevant for a situation of persecution and adds a line to create parallelism. Luke is dependent on Matthew. Gundry: *Matthew*, 235. The assumed context of persecution is forced, it does not seem the decisive momentum here. Furthermore, it is not clear how the Matthean version reflects the supposed persecution better than Mk 9:40. Why would Matthew turn from "we" to "I" if he had persecution in mind? Gundry's argument seems specious.

[138] Luz calls the verse an "Entscheidungsruf." Luz: *Matthäus*, 2:262. Gnilka points out that the verse emphasizes its soteriological and christological relevance. Gnilka: *Matthäus*, 1:459.

[139] See Kloppenborg: *Formation*, 125–126. In Mk 9:40, a similar saying appears. However, in Mark those who are condemned are those who actively oppose Jesus; neutrality seems acceptable to Mark ("He who is not against me is for me."). The Q version opposes not only opposition, but neutrality. Tuckett makes the point that the opposition to neutrality is, in fact, also the point of the parable of the unclean spirits which, in Q, immediately followed Q 11:23. Tuckett: *Q*, 290–291.

scattering[140] seems disconnected after the image of kingdoms, cities, houses, and strong men. Despite this apparently flawed position of the saying in the context, it advances the argument even further: The verse emphasizes the christological implications for the allegations made against Jesus: Whoever accuses Jesus is among the scatterers. The exorcisms of Jesus become a call to decide whether to be on the side of Jesus or of Satan.

Thus the argument concerning the exorcisms is concluded. But Matthew draws out more of its implications. He begins the saying about the sin against the Holy Spirit with διὰ τοῦτο (12:31).[141] In 12:31–37 Matthew again creates an amalgam of Mark and Q.[142] The extensive Matthean redaction produces two antithetical couplets in "near synonymous parallelism" (vv. 31 and 32).[143] Their key is the parallel pairing of ἀφεθήσεται (31a and 32a) with οὐκ ἀφεθήσεται (31b and 32b).[144] The parallelism gives particular emphasis to the only redactional addition at the end of the passage: "not in this age nor in the age to come." It emphasizes Mark's statement that the sin is "eternal" (Mk 3:30).

---

[140] Some commentators see an image with an agricultural background here. Davies and Allison: *Matthew*, 2:343; Luz: *Matthäus*, 2:262; Gnilka: *Matthäus*, 2:459. While this is possible, it is not the emphasis. What is gathered or scattered by the decision to be for or against Jesus is the kingdom, the city, the house. Patte: *Matthew*, 178.

[141] Mark has ἀμήν.

[142] Verse 31 is a redaction of Mk 3:28 with the usual Matthean stylistic corrections: Matthew omits ὅτι, positions "sin" and "blasphemy" at the beginning after "all" in the singular, and omits the superfluous Markan relative clause. He changes "sons of men" to "men" in order to avoid confusion with the "Son of Man" of v. 32. The exception, blasphemy against the Spirit, is mentioned immediately. Verse 32a is a redaction of Q found in Lk 12:10. However, Matthew uses a construction with ὃς ἐάν inspired by the omitted relative clause in Mk 3:28 and in parallel with 32b. He uses κατά instead of εἰς, probably to be consistent with 12:30. Verse 32b reflects Mk 3:29a with its construction of ὃς δ' ἄν, again uses κατά, agrees with Mark in τοῦ πνεύματος τοῦ ἁγίου and with Luke in οὐκ ἀφεθήσεται. Matthew radically rephrases Mark in stating that such a person shall not be forgiven "either in this age nor in the coming age." Q 12:10, used in Matthew 12:32, perhaps was originally part of a continuous Q passage 12:8–10. Kloppenborg: *Q Parallels*, 122–125; Tuckett: *Q*, 291–293. The sayings are united by their harsh polemical rhetoric. If they belonged together in Q, Matthew has broken the sequence. He used Q 12:8–9 already in 10:32–33 as part of the missionary discourse.

[143] Davies and Allison: *Matthew*, 2:345.

[144] Cope considers the pair of couplets a proposition and conclusion, thus removing the parallelism at least on the logical level. However, since he takes v. 31 as proposition he claims that it is a "general rule which all could accept" and it is only the particular example of v. 32 that puts the Pharisees under the accusation of blasphemy. Cope: *Matthew*, 39. This seems doubtful on several grounds. First, διὰ τοῦτο introduces v. 31, not v. 32. To claim that only v. 32 is a conclusion is to mask this fact. Furthermore, it seems highly doubtful that v. 31 is acceptable as a generally accepted rule since 9:2 already voiced opposition to the forgiveness that Jesus offered. Verse 32c explicitly states that forgiveness in this age is included as much as forgiveness in the coming age.

The interpretation of the saying of the unforgivable sin remains puzzling in its Matthean context.[145] The original setting of the saying in Q might have had in view Christians or active persecutors.[146] Part of the problem is the distinction between a forgivable sin against the Son of Man and an unforgivable sin against the Spirit. This puzzle remains regardless of whether the saying goes back to Jesus or the early Christians[147] and is not made easier by that fact that it seems to contradict 10:33. The extensive Matthean redaction implies perhaps more than Matthew's sense of structuring his sources: It must be assumed that Matthew thought he made sense of this saying.[148]

---

[145] Davies and Allison admit to being "stumped." Davies and Allison: *Matthew*, 2:348. Luz remains dissatisfied with all explanations he found in the secondary literature and concludes that in all honesty he can only say that Matthew preserved a word from the tradition. Luz: *Matthäus*, 2:266–267.

[146] Kloppenborg gives a fine discussion of the possible ways of interpretation for the Q setting. He concludes that the Q text shifts from being addressed to Christians (Q 12:4–7) to being addressed to the recipients of the Christian message (12:8–10). He sees a parallel shift in Q 10:12, 13–15. Kloppenborg: *Formation*, 211–216. Tuckett disputes this claim on the grounds that the "presuppositions of the 'confessing/denying' vocabulary would seem to necessitate some kind of positive commitment of the part of the addressees." Tuckett: *Q*, 292 n. 19. However, I do not find Tuckett's claims convincing. It is not at all unlikely that the preaching to outsiders included some reference to confessing and denying Jesus and the Holy Spirit.

[147] Both Luz and Davies and Allison provide extensive discussions of the various theories that have been proposed. A first theory holds that the saying was formulated in the early Christian communities that made a distinction between the earthly ministry of Jesus as Son of Man and the Spirit that the churches experienced. Anton Fridrichsen: "Le péché contre le Saint-Esprit," *RHPhR* 3 (1923): 367–372; Heinz Eduard Tödt: *The Son of Man in the Synoptic Tradition*, trans. D. Barton (London: SCM Press, 1965), 119. But this does not accord with Matthew's other uses of the Son of Man. A second theory is a variation thereof: It claims the saying as dominical and the distinction between a sin against Jesus the man versus a sin against the Spirit as going back to Jesus himself. Theodor Zahn: *Das Evangelium des Matthäus*, Reprint of the 4th edition 1922 (Wuppertal: R. Brockhaus Verlag, 1984), 462; Schlatter: *Matthäus*, 411; Cope: *Matthew*, 35. Again the general Matthean usage of Son of Man speaks against this theory. Patte suggests that the sin against the Son of Man is forgivable because of the humility and meekness of Jesus and his refusal to impose himself in power (cf. 8:20; 9:6; 11:19; 12:8). Patte: *Matthew*, 178. Tuckett provides a rather labored interpretation of this verse in its Q setting. He sees the setting of 12:10 in the time of the preaching of Q. An earlier rejection of Jesus might be forgivable in the light of a renewed presentation of Jesus' message in the preaching of the Q Christians. Rejection of the latter will not be forgiven. Tuckett: *Q*, 293.

[148] Luz maintains that the Matthean redaction reveals how Matthew became unfaithful to the gospel message himself: "Der Evangelist läßt Jesus dieses Wort als Keulenschlag gegen 'die' bösen Pharisäer brauchen ... Hier ist etwas anderes passiert als das, was Jesus, dessen Gebote seine Jünger alle Tage bis ans Ende der Welt für die Völker zu verkündigen und zu leben haben, in der Bergpredigt meinte!" Luz emphasizes that his criticisms of Matthew are understood as a result of its history of effects. But this history, according to Luz, is grounded in the Matthean redaction. Luz: *Matthäus*, 2:267. This interpretation is misleading. It is precisely Matthew's interest to show how the Pharisees became unfaithful to the gospel message, and how they hardened their hearts.

One of the possible keys to understanding 31–32 lies in its introduction.[149] When Matthew begins the passage with διὰ τοῦτο λέγω ὑμῖν he makes clear that the saying is not just a general maxim, but that it applies directly to the Pharisees. Furthermore, the Matthean "therefore" implies that the saying has its relevance because it relates to the preceding argument. The saying of the sin against the Spirit is still part of the controversy with the Pharisees.

The next step in the interpretation must ask the question of emphasis. Even though Matthew presents the saying in two antithetical couplets, this does not mean that the lines in each couplet are of equal weight.[150] The second line of each couplet contains the reference to the Spirit. In the second couplet the Spirit is further described as holy. The Spirit, however, is the connection with the preceding material concerning Jesus' authority to exorcize. At the center of that discussion stood Jesus' assertion that he expels demons by the Spirit of God (12:28). Consequently it seems probable that for Matthew the emphasis is on the second line of each couplet.

The sense, then, seems to be this: The Pharisees accused Jesus of exorcizing by the power of Beelzebul. Matthew counters that Jesus expels the demons by the Spirit of God as a manifestation of the kingdom of God. Now he draws the consequence of this dispute: The Pharisees deny the Spirit of God in Jesus, and so they blaspheme against the Holy Spirit. They are guilty of a sin that is not forgivable. The breach that opened between the Pharisees and Jesus cannot be bridged either in this age nor in the age to come.

This interpretation does not alleviate the problem of interpretation posed by the forgivable sin against the Son of Man.[151] But it puts it into perspective. At issue is the sin against the Spirit. And the accusation that Jesus is in collusion with Satan is precisely this sin. The antithetical parallelisms heighten exactly this perception by pointing out all the things that could be forgiven, while the Pharisees pick on the one thing that cannot be forgiven.

Matthew continues the attack on the Pharisees. He resumes with an image he has used already in 7:16–20, the image of the tree and its fruit (12:33 ‖ Lk 6:43–45). The image was probably found in Q.[152] However, Matthew's version is considerably

---

[149] Gnilka makes this point forcefully and convincingly. Gnilka: *Matthäus*, 1:459–360.

[150] Kloppenborg makes the same point for the saying in Q. He also suggests that Matthew was not successful in integrating Q 12:10a fully into the gospel. Kloppenborg: *Formation*, 213.

[151] Gnilka hesitantly suggests 11:19 as a possible sin of this category. Gnilka: *Matthäus*, 1:460.

[152] See Lk 6:43–45: "For no good tree bears bad fruit, nor again does a bad tree bear good fruit; 44 for each tree is known by its own fruit. For figs are not gathered from thorns, nor are grapes picked from a bramble bush. 45 The good man out of the good treasure of his heart produces good, and the evil man out of his evil treasure produces evil; for out of the abundance of the heart his mouth speaks."

different.[153] The most important difference concerns the use of the parable of the good and the bad tree. In Lk 6:43–44a the image is used as a proverb. Matthew constructs it with the imperative ποιήσατε to use it as an exhortation. Consequently the proverbial imagery recedes almost completely into the background, while it becomes clearer that though the words are about the trees and their fruit, the saying is directed to the Pharisees as a description of their nature.[154] The redaction of Q 6:43–45 to apply directly to the Pharisees recalls a similar redaction Matthew made to Q 3:7–9 in 3:7–10.[155]

Strikingly, the command is not just to make tree and fruit good, but to make them either both good or both bad.[156] The point, then, is about consistency of tree and fruit, of inner and outer behavior of the Pharisees. The accusation implicit in the saying is that of hypocrisy. The command to make tree and fruit either good or bad is issued because the Pharisees lack this consistency. They continue to argue with Jesus even though it is by now clear that Jesus is the better interpreter of scripture. They continue to question, even though they have been shown to contradict their own words. The Pharisees are inconsistent and unreliable.

Verses 34–35 confirm the analysis. Jesus' attack becomes more forceful. The Pharisees are "offspring of vipers," a description familiar already from the Baptist's preaching (3:17). A rhetorical question (πῶς) asks how they can speak good when they are evil. The question probably does not imply that the Pharisees actually spoke good. The logic seems to be that their accusations against Jesus reveals them as being evil.[157] The following image (12:35) reinforces this logic further. Matthew uses a proverb, probably found in Q (Lk 6:45),[158] that he applies generally with a

---

[153] In 7:16–20 Matthew could not use Lk 6:45, but here he inserts it. Here Matthew does not report Lk 6:44b. He stays closer to the image than he did in ch. 7: the goodness or rottenness of tree and fruit correspond, while in 7 the adjectives were not parallel. Matthew changes the order of the parts of the saying to achieve greater parallelism. The saying in Lk 6:45c is moved to Mt 12:34b.

[154] Against Luz, who sees the image in 33 in neutral terms and its application to the Pharisees only in 34. Luz: *Matthäus*, 2:268. As an example of an interpretation that overlooks the imperative, Patte strays widely off the mark and from the text when he makes it a general exhortation to choose between authority and power. Patte: *Matthew*, 178.

[155] Although Tuckett tries to make a case for the presence of at least the Pharisees in the Q version. Tuckett argues that the crowds of Lk 3:7 are explainable as Lukan redaction, whereas the Sadducees are probably Matthean redaction. Q itself has a tendency to indict the Pharisees. Consequently, Matthew might be more faithful to Q in mentioning the Pharisees. Tuckett: *Q*, 109–116. As Tuckett himself admits (p. 116), this theory is highly speculative. It is discredited to some extent by the fact that Matthew is prone to emphasize the Pharisees as a hostile group in material both from Mark and from Q. Thus on balance, it is more likely that Matthew introduced the Pharisees into Q 3:7.

[156] Gundry: *Matthew*, 239.

[157] Luz: *Matthäus*, 2:268.

[158] Matthew again achieves greater parallelism than Luke because he inserts a second ἄνθρωπος and omits τῆς καρδίας. He also integrates it into the context by substituting ἐκβάλλει for προφέρει. Thus Matthew still stays with the original controversy about the exorcism.

return to the third person singular. The Pharisees can only take out evil from their treasure, but Jesus already has shown that he takes out good from his treasure because he exorcizes the demons. The wordplay with ἐκβάλλει seems intentional.

With vv. 36–37 Matthew concludes the controversy[159] in his own words.[160] He calls the eschatological judgment into view.[161] First he gives a general rule in the third person plural, stating that everyone will have to render account at judgment for every careless word spoken (v. 36). Then Matthew turns this rule into a direct warning in the second person singular: "By your words you will be justified, and by your words you will be condemned" (v. 37). The issue remains with the spoken word. It will become the grounds for the judgment. This is possible because it reflects the inner nature of the speaker. By implication, the Pharisees can expect a dire judgment since they have already uttered a more than careless word in the accusation against Jesus.[162] But the change of address in v. 37 implies a wider audience than the Pharisees alone.[163] The statement is more general and extends now to the crowds who gave the initial occasion for the controversy.[164] It is a demand for a decision for or against Jesus.

3.1 Summary of the Matthean Redaction in 12:22–37

Matthew crafted the controversy about the exorcism of Jesus from different sources with much skill. The controversy does not concern itself with the fact that Jesus worked miracles. It is concerned with accusations about the origin of these

---

[159] Luz: *Matthäus*, 2:269. Gnilka assumes that the conclusion is of halachic character. Gnilka: *Matthäus*, 1:461.

[160] The formal λέγω δὲ ὑμῖν supports this. The words πᾶς, ῥῆμα, ἄνθρωποι, ἀποδίδωμι, ἡμέρα κρίσεως, γάρ are favored by Matthew. Luz: *Matthäus*, 1:35–55. The finely constructed parallelism of v. 37 further indicates Matthew's hand.

[161] Gnilka: *Matthäus*, 1:461.

[162] Gundry points out the "poetic justice" that is meted out. Κατεδικάσατε recalls 12:7. There the Pharisees condemned the innocent, here they will be condemned at the last judgment. Gundry: *Matthew*, 241.

[163] Luz seems to think that the conclusion mitigates the impending judgment for the Pharisees. He argues that since the word ἀργός means "useless," it implies that every word must lead to a work. In Matthew, so Luz, this means a work of love. Thus the conclusion is applicable to the community, not just the Pharisees. The Pharisees become an example for the community. Luz: *Matthäus*, 2:269. The argument seems to read too much into the text. The accusation against the Pharisees is not that their words do not result in works of love. The Pharisees' accusation has marked them as evil. They cannot escape judgment. That an exhortation to the community might be implied by Matthew's use of the second person singular in v. 37 should not be excluded. But this does not imply that the Pharisees get off lightly.

[164] Against Gundry, who maintains that the verse simply "brings the issue down to the individual level" without specifying who these individuals might be. Gundry: *Matthew*, 241. The consistency with which Matthew has treated the Pharisees so far in the second person plural indicates that the focus now shifts.

miracles. And Matthew insists that the question arose because people began reacting favorably to Jesus' miracles against the opposition of the Pharisees. One of Matthew's most pointed redactions is the introduction of the Pharisees and the continuing reference to them throughout the passage as the addressee of Jesus' sayings.

The controversy with the Pharisees comes to a preliminary climax.[165] The discussion moves from the interpretation of the Law to the interpretation of the person of Jesus. Matthew is no longer satisfied to answer the allegations. He has now begun to draw out the consequences of these allegations for the Pharisees. It is no longer enough to state that the Pharisees are wrong. Now their reaction to Jesus marks them for eschatological judgment.

The controversy with the Pharisees receives a sharper context as well. Matthew takes great care in describing the controversy as the result of the onlooking crowds' reaction to Jesus. In this sense, the crowds become the middle ground between the opposing factions. While the Pharisees reject Jesus, and with him the kingdom of God, and while Jesus shows that the kingdom of God is made manifest in his exorcisms, the crowds are left to wonder about the identity of Jesus. Their undecidedness provokes the controversy. The care Matthew applies to the description of this situation might indicate a situation that the Matthean community found all too familiar. The important role of the crowds suggests that there was a struggle between the Matthean community and their opponents over the allegiance of the crowds. This would point to a situation of a struggle *intra muros* of Judaism. From the beginning the conflict between Jesus and his opponents seemed irrevocable. Now the conflict is brought to a new level: The opposition has committed the unforgivable sin, and consequently is threatened with judgment. For the narrative development of the gospel as a whole, however, the crowds become more important than the opponents. While the position of the latter is clear and seems to harden with every conflict story, the crowds are still undecided, and thus keep the narrative under suspense.

For Matthew, then, the heart of this controversy lies in the response to Jesus. He holds up the Pharisees as an example of a negative reaction and threatens them with eschatological judgment. But Matthew goes beyond the direct confrontation with the Pharisees and intimates that this judgment is not reserved for the Pharisees alone. The good and the bad will be judged, so everyone needs to heed the teaching about evil and useless speech. The disciples of Jesus are at odds with the Pharisees, and both are fighting for the allegiance of the crowds wavering between them. Matthew raises the stakes by relating their decisions to the judgment at the end of times. The continuing narrative must be watched for any signs that the crowds make up their minds in favor of, or against Jesus. Only then can it be finally determined

---

[165] Luz: *Matthäus*, 2:269.

whether the Matthean community considers itself still a serious contender in the struggle for leadership within Judaism.

The highlights of the extensive Matthean redaction in this controversy story are:

▸ The structural redaction achieves greater cohesion through the extensive use of parallelisms and rhetorical questions.

▸ Matthew introduces the Pharisees and shapes the controversy story into an attack specifically on them.

▸ The answer of Jesus is formulated in the rhetorical form of an enthymeme.

▸ The controversy receives its setting through the miracle story. However, the miraculous aspect of the story is not the object of the controversy.

▸ Matthew positions the crowd as the key factor in the controversy. The multitude occasions the controversy by its reaction to the miracle and provide the rationale for the controversy in the call, addressed to the crowd, to make a decision.

▸ Matthew emphasizes the christological aspect of the controversy through the re-orientation of the controversy as one over the crowds' suggestion of Jesus as Son of David, the emphasis on the knowledge of Jesus, and through the call to make a decision for or against him.

4. Matthew 12:38–45

The controversy concerning a sign demanded from Jesus, and the saying of the sign of Jonah, occur in a number of variations in the synoptic gospels. Matthew reports the controversy twice and both times connects it with the saying of Jonah (12:38–42; 16:1–4). Mark reports a similar controversy in 8:11–12, but he does not report the sign of Jonah. Luke reports the demand for a sign in the context of his form of the Beelzebul controversy (11:16) and reports the controversy over the sign of Jonah independently (11:29–32). Even John's gospel reports the demand for a sign (6:30).

The double occurrence of the demand for a sign in Matthew eases the question of sources for Mt 12:38–42 considerably. As has been seen before in the use of the quotation Hos 6:6 and the controversy surrounding the dumb demoniac, Matthew consciously uses doublets to advance his plot. Consequently, a first look must be directed at the doublet in 16:1–4 to see whether a narrative development takes place.[166]

---

[166] This approach is different from either Luz, or Davies and Allison, or Gnilka, or Gundry, who all approach Matthew 12:38–42 without such a comparison to the doublet. This is, in my opinion, a flawed approach. If it can be shown that the doublets are related by a narrative purpose, then it must be concluded that some of the Matthean peculiarities of the pericope are explainable as Matthean narrative devices, rather than dependencies or independencies from Mark and Q. For a general introduction to the narrative purposes of Matthean doublets see Anderson: *Web*.

The controversy in 16:1–4 is a composite that will be analyzed little later. Here it suffices to remark that 16:1, the demand for a sign, seems to be dependent on Mark 8:11.[167] It follows the Markan sequence and contains a number of congruencies which point to such a dependence.[168] Furthermore, Mk 8:11 agrees to a considerable extent with the Lukan demand in 11:16.[169] This makes it likely that Lk 11:16 is influenced by Mk 8:11, and that its placement is redactional.[170]

On the other hand, the response to the demand for a sign is much more worked out in what follows Lk 11:16 than Mark's version of the demand. In addition, the Lukan demand stands in the context of the Beelzebul controversy and does not introduce a distinct and separate controversy story. It is not too well integrated into the surrounding material that is obviously from Q and thus gives the expression that it interrupts the sequence. Furthermore, the saying in Q 11:29–32 is the answer that Matthew uses as the response to the demand for a sign (12:39–42). The Q saying 11:29 makes reference to the crowds seeking a sign, and it is perhaps incongruous that such a saying should exist without a concomitant demand for a sign in Q. Thus some Q scholars submit that Lk 11:16 is the demand for a sign that in Q prefaced Q 11:29–30.[171] While it is likely that such a demand existed, it remains doubtful how much Lk 11:16 actually resembles the original request in Q.[172] Thus a probable sequence of traditions leading up to the present pericope can be suggested. The demand for a sign was present in Q and Mark. Matthew used the Markan account

---

[167] Luz: *Matthäus*, 2:444; Davies and Allison: *Matthew*, 2:577; Gnilka: *Matthäus*, 2:39.

[168] The agreements are: πειράζοντες, σημεῖον, τοῦ οὐρανοῦ, and the mention of the Pharisees.

[169] Luke's version agrees with Mark in ἐζήτουν (Mark: ζητοῦντες) παρ' αὐτοῦ, πειράζοντες, σημεῖον, οὐρανοῦ. Luke does not report the Pharisees as those demanding a sign and introduces the the saying into another controversy, where it is secondary.

[170] Fitzmyer writes: "Luke himself has added 11:16 (using, indeed, a phrase from Mk 8:11)." Joseph A. Fitzmyer: *The Gospel According to Luke*, 2 vols., AncB 28–28A (New York, London, Toronto, Sydney, Auckland: Doubleday, 1983), 2:918. He adds that the use of ἕτεροι in 11:16 further indicates Lukan redaction as this is one of his favorite words (2:921).

[171] See the reconstructions and discussions in: Kloppenborg: *Formation*, 128–134; Harrington: *Matthew*, 188; Catchpole: *Quest*, 8; Gundry: *Matthew*, 243; Tuckett: *Q*, 36, 257. Kloppenborg argues "that request for a sign existed in Q as well as in Mark. The Q version of the request is considerably longer and more complicated than the Marcan one ..." (p. 128). This is, of course, true of the answer to the request. But the request itself is actually longer in Mk 8:11 than it is in Lk 11:16. However, the crux of the argument is whether one is willing to imagine Q 11:29–30 as an apophthegm independent from an actual request made in Q, or whether one assumes it to be part of a controversy story which needs the request formulated. On balance, it is quite likely that Q had some actual request prefacing 11:29. Luke might mirror this original request in 11:16. However, the formulation and its placement seem influenced by Lukan redaction, so that the wording in Q remains elusive. The importance of this discussion rests in the form of the Q material. If the request itself was absent, the Q material was an apophthegm with perhaps apologetic purposes. If the request was present, the material in Q was already a controversy story before Matthew. The complicated nature of Lk 11:16, however, will probably not allow for a certain answer.

[172] Kloppenborg never really addresses this issue. Kloppenborg: *Formation*, 128.

in 16:1–4. In 12:38 Matthew was using a large block of Q material that included a controversy over a demand for a sign. Matthew followed the sequence of Q at this point, while he later used it to shape Mk 8:11–12 into a doublet resembling the earlier material from Q. This development was occasioned by Matthew's penchant to use doublets. The presence of the demand for a sign in the double tradition prompted Matthew to use it as a doublet. The controversy in ch. 12, containing sayings material from Q 11:16, 29–32, thus influenced the controversy in ch. 16. Matthew defers the mention of the testing of Jesus to 16:1 to increase tension, the answer in 16:4 makes again reference to the "evil and adulterous generation" and the sign of Jonah is repeated.

A comparison between the different versions of the request shows that Matthew edited the demand for a sign. Matthew inserts Pharisees and Scribes as the opposition.[173] The Pharisees are already present from the previous controversy. Matthew makes no reference to the testing of Jesus in 12:38, and the sign is not specified as being from heaven.[174] The request of the opponents is redactionally introduced with "teacher," a title omitted from 16:1. Its use again carries an ironic undertone, as it did in 9:11, that is revealed fully in 16:1 when the opponents ask again for a sign, indicating that they have not learned at all. Jesus may be addressed as teacher, but his opponents do not learn from him. As in 9:11, the opponents use the title "teacher" in a belittling fashion.

Further redactional activity concerns the reversal of the order of the sayings about the men of Niniveh and the Queen of the South, probably in order to keep the sayings concerning Jonah together.[175] And Matthew inserts 12:40 to interpret the meaning of the sign of Jonah.

The answer of Jesus is suitably introduced as a response to the request for a sign (12:39). Matthew then departs from Q by stating that an "evil and adulterous generation demands a sign." Q states that "this generation is an evil generation because it seeks a sign." Matthew's statement is less sweeping than Q's. Those who seek a sign are evil and adulterous, and they are Pharisees and Scribes.[176] While the

---

[173] The Scribes occur 20 times in the gospel as a distinct group in opposition to Jesus. Of these, 10 occurrences mention them together with the Pharisees (5:20; 12:38; 15:1; 23:2, 13, 15, 23, 25, 27, 29). While the Scribes are not necessarily associated with the Pharisees, their being mentioned together is not unnatural for Matthew, either. Their introduction in 12:38 does not raise problems. The Pharisees possibly appear by way of Mk 8:11. Davies and Allison: *Matthew*, 2:351.

[174] Both these elements were probably present in Q already. Kloppenborg: *Q Parallels*, 98–101.

[175] Davies and Allison: *Matthew*, 2:351.

[176] This argument counters Davies and Allison, who maintain that there is a consistent use in Matthew's gospel of "generation" denoting the contemporaries of Jesus or Matthew. Davies and Allison: *Matthew*, 2:260–261. It seems, however, that in this instance it is the asking for the sign that makes the generation evil. Those asking are Pharisees and Scribes, and it makes little sense to extend the meaning of the word to any contemporaries of Jesus or Matthew on theological grounds. Quite the contrary, it would seem absurd to include the bystanders and the crowd that

target is more directly identified, the countercharge is sharpened. The adjective μοιχαλίς, introduced by Matthew, is probably used in its Old Testament sense of faithlessness to the covenant.[177] Matthew picks up the theme of covenant faithfulness that already undergirded the quotation Hos 6:6. As in Luke, Matthew states that no sign will be given except that of Jonah.[178]

But Mt 12:40 proceeds to give an interpretation of the sign of Jonah entirely different from Q 11:30. In Q the preaching of Jonah to the Ninevites is the sign.[179] Matthew sees the sign in Jonah's three days and three nights in the belly of the whale. He compares this experience of Jonah with the Son of Man who spends three days and three nights in the heart of the earth. Mt 12:40 has sometimes been regarded as a post-Matthean interpolation.[180] While a late interpolation seems

---

just reacted positively to a miracle of Jesus (12:23). The redaction of Jesus' answer would be incomprehensible, and the composition of the pericope as a controversy story would not make sense. This does not invalidate Lövestam's assertion that "this generation" alludes to the generation of the flood and the desert wanderings in the Old Testament, and thus in the New Testament signifies a group's relation to God. Evald Lövestam: "The ή γενεά αὕτη Eschatology in Mk 13.30 parr.", in Lambrecht: *Apocalypse*, 403–413.

[177] Relevant texts are Is 52:3; Jer 3:10; Ezek 23; Hos 1–3; 5:3–4.

[178] Matthew adds "the prophet."

[179] The text in Q does not make an explicit connection between Jonah and the death and resurrection of Jesus. Two other possibilities for interpretation of the sign of Jonah in Q exist. Since in Q the sign of Jonah is connected with the son of Man, the sign given to the evil generation might be the coming of the son of Man in judgment. On the other hand, it might also be the preaching of judgment given by the earthly Jesus and its continuation by his followers. Both possibilities are discussed by Kloppenborg, who suggests the second possibility as the more plausible one since it reconciles more easily with the story of Jonah who also preached judgment and effected repentance. Kloppenborg: *Formation*, 131–133.

[180] Most strongly it has been argued by Stendahl. Cope follows Stendahl in the main points. Stendahl: *School of St. Matthew*, 132–133; Cope: *Matthew*, 40–42. Stendahl's arguments can be summarized: a) Together with 13:14–15, the reference to "three days and three nights" is the only literal translation of the LXX in the gospel of Matthew. b) 12:40 seems to interrupt the sequence of 12:39–41, where the "evil and adulterous generation" parallels "the Ninevites" and "Jonah" parallels "one greater than Jonah." The addition of "prophet" indicates that Matthew was thinking of Jonah's teaching rather than his subaquarian sojourn. c) Justin Martyr quotes the passage in *Dialogue with Trypho* 107:1–2 without the reference to 12:40. d) all textual witnesses are from the third or fourth century. Stendahl concludes that 12:40 was an interpolation made after Justin quoted the text. Several arguments must be held against this thesis. a) There is no evidence in the textual witnesses that imply the possibility of an interpolation. If 12:40 were an interpolation, then at least some of the manuscripts could be expected to miss this verse. They do not. b) Perhaps Stendahl has wrongly identified 12:39–42 as the source for Justin's quotation. It is quite probable that Justin quoted 16:4. Arthur J. Bellinzoni: *The Sayings of Jesus in the Writings of Justin Martyr*, NT.S 17 (Leiden: E. J. Brill, 1967), 121. c) Stendahl implies that 12:41 is quoted by Justin, Cope corrects him by saying that it is not (p. 41 n.70). If 12:41 is not quoted by Justin either, why should it be considered less of an interpolation than 12:40? d) Justin clearly implies that the sign of Jonah referred to the cross and resurrection of Jesus, which Stendahl admits. A similar interpretation of the sign of Jonah is found in Tertullian *On Modesty* X. The most potent argument of Stendahl and Cope remains the interruptive nature of 12:40 when compared with vv.

unlikely the verse could be left out in its entirety without loss of narrative flow. Its counterpart in Lk 11:30, however, could not be left out at all without the reversal of the saying of the Queen of the South and the Ninevites.[181] This makes it likely that the Lukan form of the saying is the more original one. When Matthew switched the order of Q 11:31–32, Q 11:30 was no longer necessary, and it gave him the opportunity to give the sign of Jonah one more nuance: the death and the resurrection of Jesus. Consequently, the original order of the sayings of the Queen of the South and the Ninevites, as well as the interpretation of the sign of Jonah, seem better preserved in Luke.[182]

With the redaction of 12:40 Matthew achieves a greater concentration on Jesus. While the Lukan version highlights the repentance of the Ninevites, Matthew's comparison, faulty though it may be in detail,[183] draws a comparison between Jesus and Jonah that will be taken up later again.[184] The emphasis is no longer on the

---

39 and 41–42. It alone cannot overcome the unanimous textual witness. Thus it seems much more probable that 12:40 reflects Matthean redaction.

[181] See Kloppenborg: *Formation*, 130–132.

[182] Against Davies and Allison, this makes it improbable that 12:40 can be shown to originate with Jesus himself. Davies and Allison: *Matthew*, 2:356. It is equally improbable that Matthew preserves the original form of Q, as argued by Chow, both in the interpretation of the sign of Jonah and the order of the two sayings concerning the Ninevites and the Queen of the South. Simon Chow: "The Sign of Jonah Reconsidered: Matthew 12:38–42 and Lk 11:29–32," *Theology and Life* 15–16 (1993): 56–59. Chow's argument rests on the assumption that Q's version needs to imply the episode of the fish for a complete understanding of the sign of Jonah. This is not convincing.

[183] According to the narrative of Matthew, Jesus did not spend three days and three nights in the tomb. Davies and Allison appeal here to "poetic license." Davies and Allison: *Matthew*, 2:356. Luz is more precise in relating 12:40 to 27:63–64 where Matthew speaks of the resurrection of Jesus "after three days" and "on the third day" interchangeably. Luz: *Matthäus*, 2:278.

[184] Luz comments that Matthew's interpretation of the sign of Jonah follows "was für jeden Juden und der Geschichte Jonas am wichtigsten war: an seine Errettung aus dem Bauch des Fisches." Luz: *Matthäus*, 2:277. This assessment must be modified. Two narratives of the Jonah that are approximately contemporary with Matthew stress various elements of the Jonah story: In the *Lives of the Prophets* Jonah's family is given, but his mission is only mentioned cursorily, and the episode in the belly of the fish is not central at all. Instead, he is identified with the son of the widow of Zarephath whom Elijah raised from the dead. If anything, the relationship to his mother seems the most important aspect of the short narrative. Josephus mentions Jonah in the *Ant.* 9.10.2, §§204–214. For him the episode of the storm is important while the episode of the fish occurs almost as an afterthought. The sermon to the Ninevites, or Ninoites in Josephus' story, is altered as well: It becomes a prophecy foreseeing their loss of dominion over Asia. The repentance of the Ninevites is not mentioned at all. This is the more surprising since Josephus claims to set forth Jonah's "story as I found it written down" (214). An earlier mention of Jonah occurs in 3 Mac 6:8 where the episode of the fish is reported as central, while it is also mentioned that he was restored afterwards to his family; the sermon is not mentioned. Further mention of Jonah occurs in Tob 14:4, 8, but only in selected manuscripts. Here only mention is made of the reliability of Jonah's prediction of doom for Niniveh. These different texts bear witness to the fact that in Matthew's time Jonah had become a *topos* for discussion, but with varying emphases.

Ninevites who repented, but on Jonah himself. Consequently, the emphasis also shifts from the people of this generation to Jesus himself. While the resurrection of Jesus is not explicitly mentioned, it must be assumed with the time limit that the Son of Man spends in the heart of the earth.

With 12:41–42 the focus returns again to the generation that was indicted in 12:39. Matthew pre-positions the comparison of the Ninevites with this generation, but otherwise the Lukan and Matthean versions are quite congruent.[185] Both sayings conclude that there is πλεῖον here as compared to the preaching of Jonah or Solomon.[186] The christological focus that appeared in 12:40 makes a neutral interpretation improbable for the Matthean redaction, as it is similarly improbable in 12:6. Matthew is making a christological case in 12:40, and this case is continued throughout 41–42. He compares Jonah with Jesus in v. 40, and it seems natural to extend this comparison into v. 41 and, by extension, 42.[187] Thus, despite its neuter gender, πλεῖον must be interpreted as referring to Jesus. The rearrangement of the saying concerning Ninevites and Queen of the South suggests as much.[188]

The two sayings also draw attention to correct behavior in the face of Jesus: As the Ninevites, people are expected to repent, and like the Queen of the South, people are expected to come from afar to listen to Jesus. Both examples are drawn from Gentiles and heighten the embarrassing nature of the refusal of Pharisees and Scribes to listen to Jesus.[189] But the undertone of these sayings is more than

---

[185]   The only difference aside from the order of the two sayings is the Matthean omission of τῶν ἀνδρῶν in 12:42 and the concomitant change to αὐτήν instead of αὐτούς. This change can easily be explained with the parallelizing tendency of Matthew. He gains the double use of μετὰ τῆς γενεᾶς ταύτης in vv. 41 and 42.

[186]   Luz wants to interpret πλεῖον as a neuter again. He comments: "am wichtigsten aber ist, daß Matthäus hier nicht einen 'dogmatischen' christologischen Satz formuliert, sondern 'offen' auf das verweist, was in Christus an Israel geschieht: Das 'Mehr' konnte Israel erfahren; Matthäus erzählt davon in seiner Geschichte." Luz: *Matthäus*, 2:280–281. See also his comments on Mt 12:6.

[187]   Davies and Allison: *Matthew*, 2:358.

[188]   Davies and Allison bring up the interesting question whether behind these two sayings was a christological dimension already before they were incorporated into Matthew. Davies and Allison: *Matthew*, 2:358. Luke, preserving the older version of Q, is less clear on the point than Matthew, since he compares Jonah with Jesus in 11:30, but then continues to talk about the Queen of the South in 11:31, only to return to Jonah in 11:32. Thus, if there is a christological interpretation implied, it is less obvious. Alternately, πλεῖον could be a reference to the kingdom. Charles H. Dodd: *The Parables of the Kingdom* (New York: Scribner, 1961), 31. Fuller sees the preaching of Jesus compared to the preaching of Jonah. Reginald H. Fuller: *The Mission and Achievement of Jesus. An Examination of the Presuppositions of New Testament Theology*, SBT 12 (Chicago: Allenson, 1954), 34–35. Perhaps it is unwise to try to distinguish too clearly between the christological connotations of the sayings and other possible meanings in the Lukan account. After all, the kingdom was inextricably bound up with the preaching of Jesus.

[189]   Luz sees a foreshadowing of the post-resurrection Gentile mission of the Matthean church. Luz: *Matthäus*, 2:281. It is hard to assess this claim. On the one hand, it is probably significant that Jonah and Solomon both made great impressions on Gentiles. On the other hand,

embarrassing, it is threatening with the last judgment. The judgment will be rendered on the criterion whether this generation listens to Jesus or not. And the judgment will be rendered by Gentiles. If the Queen of the South honored Solomon by coming to him, and if the Ninevites humbled themselves in their repentance, they submitted to the superiority of Israel. But now they are called upon to render judgment on a generation that has become evil and adulterous and has left the covenant.[190]

Matthew closes the controversy with a saying of the unclean spirit returning with his friends to the clean house (12:43–45). The passage originates with Q,[191] and perhaps was connected there with the controversy over the exorcism of Jesus.[192] But Matthew inserts it now and makes the connection stronger by appending 45c: "So it shall be also with this evil generation." For Matthew this saying is a parable which speaks about his opponents.[193]

The exact meaning of the saying is difficult to ascertain, and a variety of proposed solutions seem forced onto the text.[194] But Matthew is clear in applying

---

these verses were not composed by Matthew, only used by him. Furthermore, the sayings serve to illustrate the judgment over this evil generation. If an allusion to mission to the Gentiles is implied, it is not in the foreground of its Matthean context.

[190] Luz rightly points out the shocking nature of this assessment of "this generation." Luz: *Matthäus*, 2:280.

[191] The saying lacks a parallel in Mark. Lk 11:24–26 and Matthew are in almost complete agreement except for: Verse 43: Matthew inserts δέ, has οὐχ εὑρίσκει for μὴ εὑρίσκον. Verse 44: Matthew might have inserted τότε, but the Lukan witnesses are not conclusive. Matthew moves ἐπιστρέψω, and uses a different compound: Luke has ὑποστρέψω. Matthew inserts σχολάζοντα. Verse 45: Matthew inserts μεθ' ἑαυτοῦ and moves ἑπτά. Matthew inserts οὕτως ἔσται καὶ τῇ γενεᾷ ταύτῃ τῇ πονηρᾷ.

[192] The Lukan parallel 11:24–26 follows directly upon the saying of the strong man.

[193] Originally this might not have been so. The saying itself does not give any indication that it is to be understood as a parable, nor does it imply any indication for a course of action. Luz: *Matthäus*, 2:281. Perhaps it was a straightforward warning for people who had benefitted from the exorcisms of Jesus. Davies and Allison: *Matthew*, 2:360.

[194] Hill assumes that it is a warning against the future directed to the community. Hill: *Matthew*, 221. This is unconvincing since the community did not feature prominently in the preceding verses, and since the evil generation has been identified as the Pharisees and Scribes. Gundry applies an allegorical interpretation and identifies the period of the absence of the spirit with the time of the righteousness of Pharisees and Scribes and the time of the return "represent[s] an outburst of multiplied evil on the part of the Scribes and Pharisees, an outburst that will falsify their righteousness." Gundry: *Matthew*, 246. While Gundry rightly identifies the Pharisees and Scribes as the evil generation, his explanation makes no sense at all. There is no period of righteousness for the Pharisees in Matthew. Fenton believes that "the possessed man stands for *this generation* of the Jews; the exorcism is the ministry of Jesus; the emptiness of the man is the unbelief and unrepentance of the Jews; and their *last state* is their condemnation at the last judgment." John C. Fenton: *The Gospel of St. Matthew*, PGC (Baltimore: Penguin, 1964), 133. But Fenton has to introduce the Jews that are not present in the pericope, and the saying itself is lacking any language resembling eschatological judgment. Strecker relates the two periods of the emptiness of the man and the return of the spirits to the resurrection of Jesus. Strecker: *Weg*,

the saying to this generation. In the narrative context it is not a reflection on what has already happened, but on what will happen to this generation (ἔσται). But what will happen to this generation? The οὕτως of v. 45 is not clear at all. Much of the sense of this saying depends on the identification of this generation with an item in the metaphorical saying.

Almost always "this generation" is identified with the man who is possessed and whose spirit is exorcized and then returns. This would fit neatly with the fact that Jesus is known as an exorcist. This has already led to some controversy in the gospel. A possibility arises that Jesus is teaching that his exorcisms are in one way or another provisional, that the person who has been exorcized needs to fill up the empty house with good deeds, or repentance, in order to keep the seven worse devils out.[195] But the identification of "this generation" with the possessed man is not without problems. If "this generation" is to be identified with the Scribes and Pharisees of 12:38 as represented by the possessed man of the parable, it does not make sense to speak of them being exorcized. Their opposition to Jesus has been clear from the beginning of the gospel, and the reader has never seen them as anything else but γεννήματα ἐχιδνῶν (3:7) and lacking in righteousness (5:20). But if one gives up on the connection between "this generation" and the opponents of 12:38, the whole construction of the controversy as including 12:43–45 falls apart. The repetitious use of "generation" throughout (12:39, 41, 42, 45) falls short of its unifying function for the controversy if its meaning changes.[196]

Another possibility remains. The actual subject of the saying 43–45 is less the possessed man than the spirit who wanders around and brings his colleagues. The narrative takes a much greater interest in the sojourn of the spirit than in the fate of the man, and the man is indeed only interesting in as much as he reflects the effects of the spirit and his friends. What happens if the opponents of 12:38 are identified with these spirits? This association is suggested by the text with the reference to the spirits more evil than the first one and the evil generation to whom the parable is applied (12:45). The opponents of Jesus go through a period of "waterless places" or little success, while Jesus exorcizes, or preaches the gospel. But they come back in greater numbers and occupy their old house. In a sense, this could be a reflection

---

105–106. Hummel sees a similar relationship to the destruction of the temple. Hummel: *Auseinandersetzung*, 126–127. Both interpret the saying *ex eventu* from their respective views of salvation history in Matthew; but there is little to bear this out in the actual text of the saying, and they must look elsewhere for confirmation. Similarly, Davies and Allison see the saying as a reflection of the evilness of Israel who has heard one greater than Solomon and not repented. Davies and Allison: *Matthew*, 2:360.

[195] As an example see Patte: *Matthew*, 181.

[196] Schlatter proposed a rather ingenious solution to this conundrum. He interprets by identifying "this evil generation" with the possessed man, but then maintains that these verses remain mysterious just like saying of Capernaum's exaltation (11:23), because it originates in the royal consciousness of Jesus. Schlatter: *Matthäus*, 421. Needless to say, such a theological interpretation goes beyond the confines of historical critical exegesis, and perhaps beyond the text itself.

of the experience of the Matthean community of the authority of Jesus. While Jesus has the authority to defeat the Pharisees and the Scribes, and while this is amply documented in the controversy stories, the experience of the community was that the evil spirits had returned home. Israel was once more in the hold of the Pharisees, and the authority of the Matthean community in Israel was severely diminished. The saying, then, would be a reflection on the context of the Matthean community, framed as a prophecy of Jesus (ἔσται) concerning the fate of a still unconverted Israel.[197]

Here it becomes apparent why it was important for Matthew to point out in 12:39 that Jonah was a prophet. As Jonah gave a prophecy of doom that led to the repentance of the Ninevites, Jesus, greater than Jonah, is giving a prophecy of doom that should lead to the repentance of his opponents, but it does not. Consequently, a severe denunciation of Pharisaic leadership is included as the reason for the horrible state of Israel in Matthew's time. Israel has become possessed by evil spirits, by an evil and adulterous generation, by the opponents of Jesus. For Matthew this might have been one explanation for the failure of Israel to follow Jesus even though it seemed positively inclined for a while.[198]

The advantage of this interpretation of the parable of the man possessed is the better incorporation of the present controversy into the context of Matthew 12. Throughout this chapter the accusations against Jesus and the counter accusations against the Pharisees rose to a higher pitch. In the analysis of the controversies of ch. 12 so far, this escalation could be attributed to the redaction of Matthew. If the opponents of Jesus now were identified with the evil spirits, the escalation would come to a fitting climax. The Pharisees and their collaborators are portrayed as opponents of Jesus who lead Israel astray, and the horrendous state of Israel after the failure to follow Jesus is now for all to see. The Pharisees are, metaphorically speaking, demons. If, however, "this evil generation" is to be interpreted as the Jews in general, or if "this evil generation" were the Pharisees interpreted as the possessed man in the parable, the climax would be given away and the saying would lose its logical force.

4.1 Summary of the Matthean Redaction in 12:38–45

Matthew's redaction is considerable in these verses due to the fact that he combines sources. The Matthean redaction shifts to a condemnation of Jesus' opponents on christological grounds. The highlights of the redaction are:

---

[197] Against Luz, who sees this future not in the present of the Matthean community but in the final judgment of 12:41–42. Luz: *Matthäus*, 2:282. Otherwise, Luz, too, identifies the "house" with Israel, but fails to pay any attention to the roving spirits.

[198] Important here is Matthew's treatment of the crowd as interested in Jesus, excited about him, even following him. Key texts that have already occurred at this juncture are: 4:25; 5:1; 7:28–29; 8:1; 9:8; 9:33. Most important is 12:23 where the people's interest becomes an acrimonious controversy between Jesus and the Pharisees.

- ▶   Matthew uses a doublet that has its own narrative purpose in the gospel.
- ▶   Matthew redirects the accusation of this generation being evil against the Pharisees and Scribes directly.
- ▶   Matthew interprets the sign of Jonah in directly christological terms by applying it to the resurrection of Jesus. Thus the demand for a sign becomes a christological challenge, while the answer becomes a christological pronouncement.
- ▶   Matthew appends the Q saying of the return of the evil spirit directly to the controversy and forms it into a severe indictment of the leadership of Pharisees and Scribes by comparing them to the evil spirits.

5. Summary of Patterns in the Redaction of the Matthean Controversy Stories in Chapter 12

The redaction-critical analysis of the controversy stories in ch. 12 reveals several patterns in Matthew's work. It can generally be observed once again that the foremost interest of Matthew lies in the conflict related in the stories. Consequently, he shortens material extraneous to the conflict, as e.g. the miracle in 12:9–14 and the demand for a sign in 12:38. On the other hand, Matthew exhibits several traits that sharpen the controversies.

The first is the already observed Matthean penchant for ordering his material and structuring it. Again Matthew uses particles to divide his stories more clearly into setting, objection or question, and answer. Furthermore, in three stories particular attention is given to the answers of Jesus. These answers appear in three parts. In the Sabbath controversies (12:1–14) this is achieved through the insertion of material not found in Matthew's sources, while in the controversy over the demand for a sign (12:38–45) Matthew appends the arguments from Jonah and the Queen of the South with the story of the roaming demons found in Q in a different setting. Only in the controversy over the authority of Jesus (12:22–37) does the answer of Jesus become more roaming.

The two stories concerning the keeping of the Sabbath elicit more examples of Matthew's command in arguing the Jewish Law. In the first controversy (12:1–8) Matthew again notices the deficiency of Mark's argument. Thus he corrects it and goes on to insert another argument more pertinent to halachic teaching. In the second story (12:9–14) Matthew argues from a presumed common practice and makes it applicable to the case of the man with the withered hand. In both stories, Matthew thus constructs a *qal-wa-homer* argument.

The christological significance of the controversies is heightened and sustained throughout the chapter. In the first story this is achieved through the statement that Jesus is more than the temple; the second story ends with the plot to kill Jesus; the third story makes the identity of Jesus as Son of David or Beelzebul the subject matter of the controversy; the fourth story contends that Jesus is more than Jonah and the Queen of the South with the emphasis on the comparison with Jonah, his prophecy, and his effect on the Ninevites. The christological significance of the controversy stories is even more palpable in ch. 12 than it was in ch. 9. In ch. 12, the controversy stories move from the interpretation of the Law by Jesus to the interpretation of the person of Jesus.

With the christological emphasis the portrait of the opponents of Jesus becomes even more desolate. They are described as Pharisees and Scribes, and are distinguished from the crowds. Furthermore, the omission of the Herodians (12:8) narrows the circle of opponents further. The Sabbath controversies show them not only to be inept in their interpretation of the Law, but to undermine the Jewish institutions they profess to uphold with their inability to interpret the Law correctly, and to live in accordance with their interpretation. But this ineptness is malicious since they not only refuse to learn what Jesus teaches, but also plot to kill him. The two later controversies heighten this impression. The opponents of Jesus now turn against him personally, accusing him of collusion with Satan and demanding legitimation through a sign. Consequently, the indictment of the opponents becomes more vigorous. The controversy stories become progressively more acrimonious. The indictment of the opponents includes proof of a false claim to leadership. The first two stories show concrete examples of how Pharisees and Scribes undermine the institutions of temple and Law by their false interpretations of the Sabbath laws. The accusations come to a climax with the more general accusations of committing the unforgivable sin against the Spirit by opposing Jesus, and through the denunciation of the opponents as roaming demons who destroy the house of Israel cleaned out by Jesus. Concomitant with the move of the controversies from the interpretation of the Law to the interpretation of Jesus the denunciation of the Jewish leaders is harshened.

As in ch. 9, the controversies of ch. 12 also relate to the experience of the Matthean community. The first Sabbath controversy has the praxis of the community as its starting point while the general rule concerning Sabbath praxis in the second story probably reflects the custom of the Matthean community. The Beelzebul controversy incorporates a call for discipleship, while the story of the demand for a sign contains an explanation for the unsatisfactory social situation of the Matthean community. Thus all stories reflect a concern of the Matthean community and cannot be dismissed as historical reminiscences.

As already seen in ch. 9, Matthew goes to some length to distinguish the opponents of Jesus from the crowds. Matthew now shapes one controversy, over the identity of Jesus as Son of David or Beelzebul, so that the positive reaction of the crowd becomes the matter of dissent. At the same time, the answer of Jesus in this controversy is perhaps the most expansive, if not rambling, refutation of the opponents. This represents a development in the narrative: While 9:28 noted the positive reaction of the crowds, 12:23 shows that this reaction was grounds for conflict. This redactional development indicates that, for Matthew, the fight over followers within Israel is not over. This argument needs to be confirmed by more evidence, and the following controversy stories need to be examined for such a conflict between Jesus and his opponents over the sympathy of Israel.

These patterns highlight how Matthew shapes material he found elsewhere. Matthew retells the stories of his sources with his own creative imagination and purpose.

IV. The Matthean Redaction of the Miscellaneous Controversy Stories in Chapters 13–19

Following the controversy stories of ch. 12 Matthew inserts the pericope of the Jesus' family seeking him out (12:46–50 ‖ Mk 3:31–35). Chapter 13 continues the portrayal of Jesus as the righteous teacher as Matthew presents a cluster of parables drawn from Mark and Q in a small discourse. At the conclusion of the discourse, Matthew presents the Markan account of Jesus rejection by the people of his home town (13:53–58 ‖ Mk 6:1–6a). With this account Matthew returns finally to the narrative sequence of Mark. From here on, he follows it closely.

After the parable discourse until the entry of Jesus into Jerusalem there are four pericopes which can be classified as controversy stories. All four stories have their source in Mark. Three stories follow the usual pattern of an objection brought against Jesus or his disciples by Jewish leaders, to which Jesus gives an answer: Matthew 15:1–9 (cf. Mk 7:1–13) is a controversy over ritual purity; Matthew 16:1–4 (cf. Mk 8:11–13) repeats the controversy over the demand for a sign; and Matthew 19:3–9 (cf. Mk 10:2–12) contains a controversy over the permissibility of divorce.

A fourth story breaks the pattern of debate between the Jewish leaders and Jesus. It is the report of the rejection of Jesus in his home town (Mt 13:53–58; cf. Mk 6:1–6a). Bultmann classified the story as a biographical apophthegm.[1] However, he admitted that the story contained elements of hostility, although he assumed that they were among the latest layers of the tradition.[2] Mark's account, however, clearly concentrates on a hostile reaction of Jesus' audience in Nazareth.

---

[1] At the origin of the pericope Bultmann assumes the saying of the prophet rejected at home, as it occurs in *P. Oxy.* 1,5. Bultmann: *History*, 31–32.

[2] Bultmann writes of the offense the townspeople take as a "surprising addition" and continues to ask the question: "Was there originally an account of some successful appearance of Jesus?" Bultmann: *History*, 31. He answers in the positive and concludes that the account in Mk 3:1–6a derives from two originals, one reporting success, the other reporting failure in the light of the later experience of the church. Yet Bultmann has to turn to Luke's account (Lk 4:16–30) for evidence for such a development. Yet it is highly unlikely that parts of the Markan account ever circulated as a story of the success of Jesus in Nazareth, particularly if, as Bultmann assumes, the origin of the pericope lies in the word of the rejected prophet. Gnilka gives a survey of the attempts to reconstruct a tradition history behind Mk 6:1–6a and finally rejects Bultmann's reconstruction in favor of a source for Mark that already included the hostile elements, which, as Gnilka argues, Mark extended. Gnilka: *Markus*, 1:227–229.

Several arguments speak against the classification of the pericope as a controversy story. Those who react against the teaching of Jesus are not otherwise known to be hostile. In fact, they do not appear before or after this story. Furthermore, their objection to Jesus is never quite made clear or definite. They take exception to Jesus' teaching, but this is a rather general criticism. They are reported to say that they know the family of Jesus, and this becomes their reason to question Jesus' wisdom and mighty works. Then they are reported to take offense, but this does not come up in direct discourse. Their opposition is curiously ill defined. These characteristics led Bultmann to reject the story as a controversy dialogue.[3]

On the other hand, the story bears enough resemblance to the controversy stories that it merits inclusion among the group. The reply of Jesus follows the criteria set down by Bultmann by being suitably pithy and metaphorical in its use of the title "prophet." Furthermore, despite the vagueness of the opposition, the townspeople are decidedly hostile. Matthew probably heightened this sense of hostility by mentioning in his introduction to the pericope that Jesus taught in"their" synagogue (13:53). The hostile elements in this story are pronounced already in Mark's account, and sharpened by Matthew. Consequently, the story is probably a mixed form with leanings towards a controversy story already in Mark's account. Matthew extends the controversial character slightly, and thus the story is included in the following analysis.[4]

The stories are grouped together in this chapter for the sake of convenience rather than their inherent cohesion as a group. As with previous stories, they will be examined for obvious Matthean redactional interests and patterns.

1. Matthew 13:53–58

The source for the story of Jesus' homecoming is Mk 6:1–6a. Matthew takes up the Markan narrative sequence with his rendition.[5] Matthew's editorial activity is slight.

---

[3] To recall Bultmann's definition, controversy dialogues need a distinct starting point in the particular action or attitude the opponents seize upon. Bultmann: *History*, 39–41.

[4] Davies and Allison agree in classifying this story as a controversy, "although it remains in many respects unique." Davies and Allison: *Matthew*, 2:453. Unfortunately, Hultgren does not deal with the story at all. Hultgren: *Jesus and His Adversaries*. Gnilka thinks that the form of Mk 6:1–6 is *sui generis*. Gnilka: *Markus*, 1:229.

[5] At this point, Matthew begins to follow Mark's narrative outline more closely than he did before. He no longer transposes Markan material as he did before, but follows the Markan sequence while adding to it with material from other sources, and occasionally leaving out some of the material in Mark. For a survey of Matthew's transposition of earlier material in Mark see chapter 7.

He begins the story with a formula that concludes the parable discourse (13:53).[6] Matthew substitutes μετῆρεν for ἐξῆλθεν (Mk 6:1), perhaps to avoid repetition when he uses ἐλθών in v. 54. Jesus leaves the house that he entered in 13:36. Matthew omits the reference to the disciples of Jesus (Mk 6:1) and the Sabbath (Mk 6:2) as immaterial.[7] He uses a participial construction for the arrival of Jesus in his own town[8] (13:54), and simply states that Jesus began teaching[9] in the synagogue.[10] Characteristically, Matthew adds the qualifier "theirs" to the

---

[6] Matthew uses this formula to conclude several discourses. It appears in 7:28–8:1; 11:1; 13:53; 19:1; 26:1. The formula consists of the phrase καὶ ἐγένετο ὅτε ἐτέλεσεν ὁ Ἰησοῦς which occurs in all five occurrences. The matter that is concluded appears once as τὰς παραβολάς (13:53), once as διατάσσων τοῖς δώδεκα μαθηταῖς (11:1), otherwise as τοὺς λόγους τούτους, once amplified with πάντας (26:1). Furthermore, in four cases the formula contains an indication that Jesus moves from the place of instruction to another place: καταβάντος δὲ αὐτοῦ (8:1); μετέβη ἐκεῖθεν (11:1), μετῆρεν (13:53; 19:1).

[7] Even in Mark's version, the disciples drop out of the story after their initial introduction. Similarly, the Sabbath is not part of the ensuing argument.

[8] The singular of "synagogue" suggests theat Jesus arrives not in his own country, but his own town. Gundry: *Matthew*, 282. This assumes that Jesus' town had only one synagogue. The Greek word πάτρις is ambiguous. Liddell and Scott: *A Greek-English Lexicon*, 1349. Luke is the only one among the synoptics who places this episode specifically in Nazareth (Lk 4:16). There is no indication that Matthew has Nazareth in mind. Matthew uses πάτρις only in this pericope. In this he follows Mk 6:1. It cannot be his birth place, since Bethlehem lies in Judea, and at this point Matthew's Jesus is still in Galilee. In view of 2:22–23 Nazareth is conceivable as Jesus' πάτρις and is so argued by Luz and Davies and Allison. Luz: *Matthäus*, 2:384; Davies and Allison: *Matthew*, 2:454. However, the lack of specificity in the Matthean text makes such an argument a mere hypothesis resting on the assumption that Matthew has a town in mind rather than a region. Since the redaction of Matthew indicates that he is not really interested in specific details in this story, it must be left open whether πάτρις refers to a city or to a region, Gundry's argment not withstanding. The trade of τέκτων of Jesus' father makes it plausible that the family of Jesus was known beyond the confines of a village like Nazareth.

[9] Matthew's use of the imperfect (ἐδίδασκεν) is probably inchoative and reflects Mark's use of ἤρξατο διδάσκειν (6:2). Gundry: *Matthew*, 282. Hagner suggests that its character is durative and indicates that Jesus taught for a while in Nazareth before the confrontation took place. Hagner: *Matthew 1–13*, 405. The former hypothesis has the advantage that it can be related to its source Mk 6:2. Mark describes Jesus' teaching as taking place on a specific Sabbath. If Matthew reflects Mark in his use of the imperfect, then the supposition that this teaching might have gone on over a certain length of time is unlikely. While the latter hypothesis is not unthinkable, there is nothing else in the text to support a lengthy stay of Jesus in Nazareth.

[10] Gundry maintains that it would have been clear to Matthew's readers that such teaching would have taken place on the Sabbath. Gundry: *Matthew*, 282. While this may be so, it is inconsequential. The omission of the reference to the Sabbath serves to bring the teaching of Jesus into focus. A similar effect is achieved by the omission of ἤρξατο. Noteworthy is also the fact that Jesus enters the synagogue for the last time in his ministry. Davies and Allison rightly caution against attaching too much weight to this fact, since this is taken over from Mark's narrative. Davies and Allison: *Matthew*, 2:455. Furthermore, while Jesus abandons the synagogue after 13:58, he continues his ministry to Israel. Jesus will conclude his public ministry in the temple.

synagogue.[11] His redaction achieves a clear and undistracted focus on the teaching of Jesus, while the reaction of Jesus' audience, introduced by ὥστε instead of καί,[12] is abbreviated. Matthew omits πολλοί (Mk 6:2) and thus gives the impression of a united reaction to Jesus' teaching. He abbreviates the Markan construction expressing the surprise of the audience by omitting ἀκούοντες (Mk 6:2). The direct discourse of the audience is streamlined into a construction emphasizing parallels: Twice Matthew uses πόθεν τούτῳ (13:54, 56), three times he uses οὐχ(ι) (13:55–56). Thus Matthew achieves a chiastic construction:[13]

Table 1: Chiasm in Matthew 13:54–56

a	54c	πόθεν τούτῳ ...
b	55a	οὐχ οὗτός ἐστιν ...
c	55b	οὐχ ἡ μήτηρ ... καὶ οἱ ἀδελφοί ...
b'	56a	καὶ αἱ ἀδελφαὶ αὐτοῦ οὐχί ...
a'	56b	πόθεν οὖν τούτῳ ...

The chiastic structure of the response of the people to the teaching of Jesus provides the basis for much of its Matthean redaction. Matthew omits the Markan construction with δοθῆσαι and the additional explanations of the powerful deeds

---

[11] Hagner states that the addition of "theirs" marks the synagogue not "as elsewhere (4:23), the synagogue of the Jews, thus reflecting a break with Judaism (contra Luz), but merely the synagogue of the people of Nazareth." He believes that the use of the synagogue here was occasioned by the reference to the teaching of Jesus. Hagner: *Matthew 1–13*, 405. On several levels this seems unlikely. Jesus is not at all averse to teaching outside the synagogue, be it on a mountaintop, in cities, or in the temple (5:2; 7:29; 11:1; 21:23; 22:16; 26:55). Thus the mention of the synagogue probably is not prompted by the teaching of Jesus. It is more likely that it is prompted by Mk 6:2. If this is so, the addition of αὐτῶν is significant. It alerts the reader, as it has before, that Jesus is treading hostile territory. In the gospel of Matthew the synagogue is not a neutral place. It is a place where hypocrisy is encountered (6:2, 5; 23:6), where conflict breaks out between Jesus and his opponents (12:9; 13:54), and where the disciples face persecution (10:17; 23:34). Even the mention of the synagogues in the generally positive summaries of 4:23 and 9:35 the distance from the synagogue is emphasized through αὐτῶν.

[12] Again a characteristic of Matthean redaction. Matthew uses ὥστε 15 times in his gospel. Of these, 14 times the passage is paralleled in Mark. Of the latter 14 occurrences, 11 times Matthew uses ὥστε while Mark prefers another construction (8:24, 28; 10:1; 12:12, 22; 13:54; 15:31, 33; 19:6; 24:24; 27:1), while in three instances Matthew parallels Mark (13:2, 32; 27:14). The only occurrence in exclusively Matthean material is 23:31.

[13] As further elements of this chiastic construction the surprise of the audience (v. 54b) and the offence they take (v. 57a) could be added. However, there is no verbal connection between these two elements. Therefore, they are not included in the table above. Davies and Allison add as the outermost elements of the chiasm the overture of Jesus coming home (vv. 53–54a) and the answer of Jesus (vv. 57b–58). Davies and Allison: *Matthew*, 2:451. These elements do not really correspond in either wording or content. While the overture serves to introduce the story, the answer of Jesus is an integral part of the conflict between Jesus and his audience.

(Mk 6:2). In Mk 6:3 Jesus is the carpenter,[14] in Mt 13:55 is the carpenter's son. While several explanations have been given to account for this change,[15] in the context it seems most likely that Matthew redacted the wording in order to remain with the pattern of establishing the familiarity of the Nazarenes with Jesus through acquaintance with his immediate family. Consequently, Matthew establishes a pattern of ὁ τοῦ τέκτονος υἱός, ἡ μήτηρ αὐτοῦ, καὶ οἱ ἀδελφοὶ αὐτοῦ, καὶ αἱ ἀδελφαὶ αὐτοῦ. In each case, then, Jesus is characterized only by his familial bond to others, and not by reference to who he is by himself. As the story continues, Matthew makes it clear that he considers such a characterization inadequate.

Matthew rephrases Mark's "the son of Mary" into "his mother is called Mary," Hellenizes the Markan "Joses" into "Joseph," and changes the order of the appearance of Simon and Jude. In v. 56 Matthew adds πᾶσαι and omits ὧδε, changes οὐχ into οὐχί and moves it, and repositions the verb to the end of the sentence. He inserts the repetition of πόθεν οὖν τούτῳ ταῦτα πάντα to conclude the chiasm.

The reaction of Jesus' audience is ironic, and its irony is heightened by the concise rendering of the Matthean redaction. The people witness the teaching of Jesus, and realize that there is wisdom and power in his teaching. And so inadvertently they admit to this wisdom and power (13:54c). However, their familiarity with the background of Jesus' family becomes an obstacle to acknowledging Jesus. Though facing wisdom and power through Jesus, they continue asking where such things come from. Herein lies the irony of Matthew: The people

---

[14] The Greek word τέκτων denotes an artisan whose materials are of wood or stone. Liddell and Scott: *A Greek-English Lexicon*, 1769. Thus a mason, woodworker, builder, or contractor could be implied. The precise meaning is probably irrelevant here. The epithet serves mainly to establish the familiarity of the Nazarenes with Jesus.

[15] Gnilka assumes that both the father of Jesus and Jesus himself were carpenters. Therefore, both Matthew and Mark are correct. Gnilka: *Matthäus*, 1:515. While this is possible, it fails to account for the reason that Matthew might have had in changing Mark. Menial labor might have been thought degrading, and thus the remark that Jesus was a carpenter could have been an embarassment. Thus Origen denied that Jesus was a carpenter in *Contra Celsum* 6, 34.36; quoted by: Luz: *Matthäus*, 2:385. But then it is surprising that Matthew did not drop the reference altogether. Perhaps the phrase "son of Mary" (Mk 6:3) had become a slur denoting illegitimate birth, as Stauffer argued. Ethelbert Stauffer: "Jeschu ben Mirjam: Kontroversgeschichtliche Anmerkungen zu Mk 6:3," in: *Neotestamentica et Semitica: Studies in Honor of Matthew Black*, ed. E. Ellis and M. Wilcox (Edinburgh: T. & T. Clark, 1969), 119–128. Matthew might have done some damage control with the reference to Jesus' father, and with the rewording into "is not his mother called Mary." Gundry proposes that Matthew's interest in the Davidic descent of Jesus has led him to make a reference to Jesus' father here. Gundry: *Matthew*, 283. However, it would seem a clumsy attempt, since neither David not Jesus' father are mentioned by name. Luz argues that the Matthean change originates with the complete lack of reference in the gospel to any professional activity of Jesus besides that of a wandering preacher. Luz: *Matthäus*, 2:384–385. Davies and Allison agree cautiously with Gnilka. Davies and Allison: *Matthew*, 2:457.

who seem to know Jesus so well are utterly amazed. Although the Nazarenes know all about the background of Jesus, when they are faced with his wisdom and power they take offense and manifest ἀπιστία (13:58).

The question about the origin of the wisdom and power of Jesus may have more sinister undertones as well. The origin of the power of Jesus was already the subject of discussion in 9:34 and 12:24. There the accusation was leveled against Jesus that he works exorcisms with the authority of Satan. But the emphasis here seems to lie on the twice used derogative τούτῳ (13:54, 55).[16]

In v. 57 Matthew reports the offense that the audience took, and the reply of Jesus, in the words of Mark.[17] He shortens the reply of Jesus by omitting Mark's "and among his own kin," most probably because of 12:49–50. There Matthew defined the disciples of Jesus as his true family.[18]

In v. 58 the most substantial of the Matthean redactions is made. While Mk 6:5–6a concludes the story with the statement that Jesus could do no miracles there except a few, and that he was astounded at their unbelief, Matthew simply states that Jesus did not do many miracles because of their unbelief.[19] With this redaction Matthew relates the inactivity of Jesus at home directly to the unbelief of his audience and shows Jesus' reticence as his choice. In Mark, the connection between the lack of miracles and the audience's unbelief is much less direct, while Jesus appears as almost powerless in the face of this rejection. While the Matthean formulation οὐκ ἐποίησεν ἐκεῖ δυνάμεις πολλάς may be an indication that Matthew was aware of the Markan contradiction between οὐκ ἐδύνατο ἐκεῖ ποιῆσαι οὐδεμίαν δύναμιν and the following list of exceptions introduced with εἰ μή, Matthew's version also highlights the conflict between those that took offense at Jesus and Jesus himself. Matthew is not diverted by Mark's exceptions, and the lack of miracles does not show Jesus as powerless, but appears as his decision.

---

[16]   Hagner: *Matthew 1–13*, 405.

[17]   Matthew substitutes δε for καί and εἶπεν for ἔλεγεν.

[18]   Davies and Allison argue that the response of Jesus makes no reference to the family of Jesus at all. Matthew omits the direct reference to Jesus' kinfolk, and πατρίδι and οἰκίᾳ are in synonymous parallelism and refer both to the Jesus' home. Davies and Allison see this tendency paralleled in Matthew's toning down of Mk 3:20–35. Davies and Allison: *Matthew*, 2:459. The argument of Davies and Allison is only partly convincing. It is much more probable that Matthew omitted the explicit reference to Jesus' kinfolk here because Matthew has previously redefined the family of Jesus as the disciples (12:49–50). Matthew prefaces the "little theodicy" of parables in ch. 13 with the story of Jesus' true family (12:46–60), and ends it with the offense taken in Nazareth. Thus the two stories form an *inclusio* for the discourse of ch. 13. Consequently, it is quite probable that Matthew's definition of the disciples as the family of Jesus works in 13:57 to displace the reference to the συγγενεύσεις in Mk 6:4. See also Hagner: *Matthew 1–13*, 404.

[19]   The Matthean πολλάς is probably an acknowlegment of Mark's εἰ μὴ ὀλίγοις ἀρρώστοις ἐπιθεὶς τὰς χεῖρας (6:5).

Jesus emerges as a much stronger figure.[20] Therefore, he is not surprised at their unbelief either (cf. Mk 6:6a).

If Jesus is highlighted in Matthew's account, the question about Jesus as prophet emerges more forcefully than in Mark. Does Matthew see Jesus as prophet,[21] or is the reference merely a proverbial description of the difficulty that Jesus faced at home?[22] Of the 37 uses of the word in Matthew's gospel only five refer to Jesus. Of these, four uses describe how the crowds see Jesus as a prophet. These references are all subsequent to the present one (14:5; 16:14; 21:11; 21:46). Twice the Jewish leaders are said to fear the crowds since they believe Jesus to be a prophet (16:14; 21:46). The confession of Peter (16:16) makes it clear that the crowd's appraisal of Jesus as a prophet is inadequate. Finally the controversy over the demand for a sign (12:38–45) compared Jesus with Jonah. Jonah is explicitly referred to as prophet, and even though Jesus himself gives a prophecy (v. 45) it is made clear that Jesus is more than Jonah. The function of the title for Jesus, then, seems to be mainly to describe an insufficient understanding of Jesus by the crowds. At the same time, the title proves as a finally ineffective deterrent for the leaders to move against Jesus.

This evidence makes it unlikely that Matthew viewed "prophet" as an adequate understanding of Jesus. Furthermore, the emphasis of this saying seems to rest not so much on the identification of Jesus as prophet, but on the rejection that he faced in his home.[23] And it is precisely the aspect of rejection inherent in prophetic activity that the Matthean Jesus takes up again later in 23:29–36 with a view to the persecution of the community. This evidence does not deny the prophetic nature of Jesus' ministry. But Jesus as prophet is not a major theme in the gospel, while the persecution of the prophets is such a theme that is variously applied to the prophets of old, to Jesus, and to the disciples. And intertwined with this theme is the constant reminder of Matthew that this or that word of one or another prophet has been fulfilled. The rejected prophets are proven true.

---

[20] Luz: *Matthäus*, 2:386.

[21] Davies and Allison assume that, for Matthew, the meaning of the saying "is that Jesus is not recognized for what he is, namely, a true prophet." Davies and Allison: *Matthew*, 2:460.

[22] Luz views the saying of the prophet rejected at home as "geläufige Erfahrung oder sogar Sentenz." Luz: *Matthäus*, 2:385. Davies and Allison take it as a proverb that expresses the true identity of Jesus as prophet. Davies and Allison: *Matthew*, 2:460. In this particular form the saying occurs only in the synoptic parallels Matthew 13:54, Mk 6:4, and Lk 4:24, though in a different formulation. Jn 4:44 preserves another variation of the saying, as do *EvThom* 31, *P. Oxy.* 1 recto. In the pagan tradition the sentiment of rejection in at home was sometimes applied to philosophers, Dio Chrysostom 47.6, Epictetus: *Diss.* 3.16. Apollonius of Tyana applied it to himself: *Ep.* 44. Cf. also Pindar: *Ol.* 12.13–16. Bultmann even quotes an Arabic proverb. Bultmann: *History*, 31. Thus the possibility that this saying is proverbial is rather well attested.

[23] Thus it is probably beside the point to argue, as Hagner does, that the title was apt in view of the teaching of Jesus. Hagner: *Matthew 1–13*, 406.

From here the full significance of the story becomes apparent: It is a story of rejection despite wisdom and miracles. But the culmination of this story lies in the reaction of Jesus. Matthew's redaction of the ending makes it clear that Jesus is not powerless in the face of rejection. On the contrary, Jesus answers with a rejection of his own: He refuses to do many mighty deeds. As in a previous controversy, unbelief cannot be averted by miracles (12:38–39). The offense taken remains curiously indescript, and no clear objection is voiced by the Nazarenes. Matthew is more than usual faithful to his source. Consequently, even though Matthew preserves the rejection of Jesus in his home, it cannot be used unequivocally to argue the rejection of Jesus in the whole of Israel.[24]

1.1 The Markan Pericope

The history of the tradition behind Mk 6:1–6a is a matter of debate. Bultmann sees the story as a prime example of how a freely circulating logion about a prophet rejected at home was developed into an idealized narrative of a biographical apophthegm.[25] However, it is also possible that the isolated logion of the prophet was secondarily inserted into the narrative of the rejection of Jesus at home.[26] The pericope's precise development is, however, of little consequence here.

Mark's story follows immediately after the healing of the daughter of Jairus and the woman with the hemorrhage (5:21–43). Thus the reference to the δυνάμεις τοιαῦται of Jesus (6:2) becomes an allusion to the miracles that Jesus just worked.[27] The Nazarenes fail to associate the wisdom of Jesus and the miracles that he works with a divine origin, or with Jesus' special status. For this reason, the Markan reference to the inability of Jesus to work miracles in Nazareth is completed by the mention of only a few minor miracles (6:5).[28] For Mark, the miracles are

---

[24] See Hagner: *Matthew 1–13*, 406. Hagner sees in this story a sign that the kingdom is transferred from Jews to Gentiles because the miracles of Jesus cannot be and are not used to overcome the faithlessness of the people in Nazareth. This, however, stretches the evidence severely. There is no indication that the Nazarenes are representative of the whole of Israel.

[25] Bultmann sees the oldest form of this logion in *P. Oxy.* 1,5: "No prophet is honored in his home town, no physician heals his acquaintances." Bultmann assumes that the second half of this saying gave rise to the narrative, while the acquaintances were changed into relatives. Bultmann: *History*, 30–31.

[26] Gnilka uses this argument and remarks that the phrase καὶ ἔλεγεν αὐτοῖς is a "Markinische Anreihungsformel." Gnilka: *Markus*, 1:228. This formula appears indeed 11 times in Mark (2:27; 4:2, 11, 21, 24; 6:4, 10; 7:9; 8:21; 9:1, 31; 11:17) and thus might be a Markan seam.

[27] Gundry suggests that the placement of the story suggests as one of its purposes the contrast with the preceding miracles of Jairus and the woman with the hemorrhage (Mk 5:21–43). Gundry: *Mark*, 289. See also Gnilka: *Markus*, 1:230.

[28] Gundry suggest another possibility: He maintains that Mark must ascribe some miracles to Jesus since there is a reference to miracles in 6:2. Furthermore Mark uses the phrase οὐδεμίαν ... εἰ μή also in 6:8 and 10:18. Thus Mark's point here is to say that there are only a few miracles taking place in Nazareth. "In a backhanded way then, Mark turns the fewness of miracles here

important in their relationship to the faith they evoke, or to the faith that prompts them.[29] In Matthew's account the miracles are much more removed. There are no miracles in the immediate vicinity of this pericope. The last miracle was the healing of the blind and dumb demoniac in 12:22, and this healing served as the opening of a controversy rather than as an illustration of the power of Jesus. The next miracle is the healing and feeding of the five thousand in Matthew 14:13–21, and these powerful deeds are offered to a crowd that follows Jesus (14:13).

Mark's context for the story, then, focuses on the miracles of Jesus. Matthew, however, focuses on the teaching of Jesus with the long parable discourse of ch. 13. For Matthew, the teaching activity is more important, and consequently Jesus seems rejected because his teaching provokes the Nazarenes, although they also mention the miracles. Both seem to them incongruous with Jesus' humble background.

The differences in the questions that the Nazarenes ask clarify the point. In Mark, the questions of Jesus' opponents focus on several things at once. They ask about the origin (πόθεν 6:2) of "all this" (ταῦτα). They proceed to ask about the nature of the wisdom and the miracles of Jesus (τίς ἡ σοφία ... καὶ αἱ δυνάμεις τοιαῦται 6:2). This three-pronged question about origin, wisdom, and miracles, mirrors perhaps the confusion faced by the Nazarenes.[30]

Matthew abbreviates Mark in these questions, as was seen above. In doing so, he also focuses the direction of the Markan questions. The character and nature of Jesus' teaching and miracles are no longer at issue. Matthew concentrates on the issue of origin. This particular issue is perhaps most pertinent in the face of objections relating to the family of Jesus. But this focus also heightens the impression already given in Mark, that Jesus' wisdom and miracles are not really contested. The Nazarenes are portrayed as looking for an explanation in the

---

into a testimony concerning the multitude of miracles ... elsewhere ... Here lies the main point: not unbelief itself, but the invalidation of unbelief by Jesus' astonishing words and deeds." Gundry: *Mark*, 293. The point is well taken.

[29] Ludger Schenke: *Die Wundererzählungen des Markusevangeliums* (Stuttgart: Katholisches Bibelwerk, 1974); Dietrich A. Koch: *Die Bedeutung der Wundererzählungen für die Christologie des Markusevangeliums* (Berlin: de Gruyter, 1975); Ernest Best: "The Miracles in Mark," *RExp* 75 (1978): 539–554.

[30] Gnilka: *Markus*, 1:230. Gundry assumes that for Mark these three questions are all aimed at the same thing. Thus he thinks that the question about the origin of "these things" is "prospective, for the next question specifies the things as Jesus' wisdom and miracles." He goes on to say, however, that the following questions concerning wisdom and miracles also ask about the character of these. Gundry is probably right in this. However, the formulation of these questions is different, and that is what is important in their assessment with regard to the Matthean redaction. Gundry also detects a chiasm in the first two questions: a) πόθεν τούτῳ; b) ταῦτα; b') καὶ τίς ἡ σοφία ἡ δοθεῖσα; a') τούτῳ. Gundry argues that because the miracles fall outside of this chiasm, they gain a special importance which prepares for 6:5. Gundry: *Mark*, 290. While this observation is an attractive piece in the argument for the importance of the miracles for Mark, the elements of the chiasm are not balanced enough to convince. The assumption of a chiasm rests merely on the repetition of τούτῳ.

immediate family of Jesus. Thus, they miss the point entirely. Instead, they take offense because they find wisdom and miracles unexpectedly in the familiar.

As before, Matthew's redaction emphasizes the christological aspect underlying the story in Mark. Matthew finds in the reaction of the Nazarenes something he had already observed in the Pharisees' demand for a sign: Signs, miracles, and even wisdom teaching, cannot overcome unbelief. Therefore, Matthew's Jesus is, unlike Mark's, not surprised.

1.2 Summary of the Matthean Redaction in 13:53–58

Matthew's redaction of the rejection of Jesus in his own town is moderate. However, several distinctively Matthean traits can be discerned:

▸ Matthew places the story after the parable discourse. Furthermore, the introduction reveals a clear and undistracted focus on the teaching of Jesus. The Markan interest in miracles is much reduced.

▸ The acquaintance of the Nazarenes with the family of Jesus is structured into a chiasm. Their opposition is tinged with irony.

▸ Matthew portrays Jesus as choosing not to do many powerful deeds. The story receives a stronger christological impact.

2. Matthew 15:1–9

After the rejection of Jesus in Nazareth, three pericopes and a summary follow. Chapter 14 begins with the violent end of John the Baptist (1–12), continues with Jesus' withdrawal and the feeding of the five thousand (13–21), and moves on to the miracle of Jesus walking on the lake (22–33). Matthew has expanded this last miracle with the episode of Peter walking on the lake that culminates in the disciples' worship and confession that Jesus is the Son of God (14:33). A summary of Jesus' return and healings in the region of Gennesaret concludes the chapter (34–35). After this turn in the gospel to faith and healings, the following controversy with the Pharisees and Scribes (15:1–9) is particularly disturbing. The disciples confessed Jesus as the Son of God. Following their confession they become the object of an acrimonious debate.[31]

The controversy 15:1–9 is part of a longer section in three parts, consisting of the controversy with Pharisees and Scribes (1–9), a teaching directed towards the crowds (10–11), and an instruction of the disciples (12–20). The sequence is

---

[31] Cope goes so far as to say that the material in 15:1–20 "is entirely unrelated to the preceding portion of ch. 14." Cope: *Matthew*, 53. This sentiment is echoed by Davies and Allison: *Matthew*, 2:517. They ignore the possibility that the contrast itself could be a narrative device. Furthermore, the disciples are a link between ch. 14 and 15:1–20. In the latter section the disciples both are the occasion for the controversy and are the recipients of the teaching of Jesus.

paralleled by Mk 7:1–23. Matthew tightens the overall structure of this section in the conclusion of 15:20. He refers back to the initial controversy concerning the consumption of food with unwashed hands and unifies the three scenes.[32] At the same time, the instruction of the disciples is prompted by their recounting to Jesus the objection of the Pharisees to the teaching of the crowds (15:12).[33] Thus the instruction of the crowds seems the center that holds the three scenes together.[34] Because Matthew has so tightly interwoven the controversy proper with instructional material, this material will have to be commented on inasfar as it sheds light on the Matthean approach to the problem of eating with unclean hands.

The Matthean redaction of the controversy story proper is extensive. It takes on two main characteristics. Firstly, Matthew omits the Markan description of circumstances and explanation of dietary laws. Secondly, Matthew transposes Jesus' answer to the Pharisees and Scribes by moving the quotation of Is 29:13 from the beginning (Mk 7:6b–7) to the conclusion of the controversy. The effect of this redaction is a tightening of the narrative structure of the controversy story and a parallelization with 9:10–13 and 12:1–8 where the scripture quotation also concludes the controversy story. This tightening of structure becomes obvious in the three pairs of narrative oppositions: In vv. 2a, 3a Matthew opposes Pharisees and Scribes to Jesus. In vv. 2b, 3b the disciples transgress the tradition of the elders, while the Pharisees transgress the commandment of God. In vv. 4a, 5a God commands, while the Pharisees say something different. A less obvious fourth pair of opposites consists in the command of God to honor one's parents (15:4) while the prophecy of Isaiah (15:8–9) sees through this "honor" as one of lips only, not of hearts.[35]

Matthew radically revises the approach of the Pharisees and Scribes. He begins in v. 1 (Mk 7:1) by substituting τότε for καί, and uses προσέρχονται instead of συνάγονται.[36] Matthew mentions Pharisees and Scribes summarily as being from

---

[32] Davies and Allison: *Matthew*, 2:516.

[33] Davies and Allison see the instruction of the disciples as a commentary on the instruction of the crowds. Davies and Allison: *Matthew*, 2:516.

[34] Gnilka: *Matthäus*, 2:18. Gnilka sees the instruction of the crowds as "Gleichnis." This seems to be a reflection on Mk 7:17: "... his disciples asked him about the parable." However, Matthew excises the reference to the instruction of the crowd as parable and instead has the disciples make reference to the Pharisees' offense at the teaching given to the crowd (15:12). Gnilka's commentary on 15:10–12 is somewhat unclear on the matter. On page 24 one gets the impression that 15:10–11 contain a *halakha* contrary to that of the Pharisees. Yet this is not convincing, either. The verses do not contain a precept of the Law, or derived from the Law. And Matthew does not report the statement of the Markan parallel that Jesus thus declared all foods clean.

[35] This analysis is taken from Patte: *Matthew*, 216–217. The first three pairs seem quite convincing, the fourth pair is less succinct and lacks clarity.

[36] Both substitutions are a preference of Matthean diction. Gundry goes so far as to say that the use of "προσέρχονται connotes respect, implies Jesus' lordship ..." Gundry: *Matthew*, 302. However, the context of the controversy does not bear this out, and the lexical entry of the word

Jerusalem and presents them as a single front opposing Jesus.[37] Then Matthew omits Mk 7:2–4. He sees no need to report that the opponents saw Jesus' disciples eat with unclean hands. The Jewish practice of washing one's hands before a meal apparently does not need explanation for Matthew.[38] He turns immediately to the discussion on the topic.[39] Mark's confusingly broad extension from the washing of hands to purification and washing of cups and vessels and the "many other traditions" (7:4) detracts from the argument at hand, and possibly Matthew felt uncomfortable with Mark's extension of the argument.

The question raised by the opponents of Jesus (Mt 15:2) is a slight revision of Mk 7:5. Like Mark, Matthew's question begins with διὰ τί, but then moves the disciples forward. Matthew emphasizes that the practice of the disciples is at stake. He substitutes παραβαίνουσιν for περιπατοῦσιν κατά. This change emphasizes the parallelism with the counter-question of Jesus in 15:3. The object of the disciples' transgression is, as in Mk 7:5, the tradition of the elders (τὴν παράδοσιν τῶν πρεσβυτέρων). The explanation of the transgression is fuller in Matthew than in Mark, because Matthew left out Mk 7:2–4. Matthew's description of the disciples eating with unclean hands combines Mk 7:5 with the gist of Mk 7:2.[40] Matthew inserts ὅταν to denote that the practice of the disciples to eat without washing their hands was not a singular incident[41] but a customary procedure. Thus Matthew insists that the opposition of the Pharisees and Scribes was not merely a singular incident, but was raised against a custom among the disciples of Jesus. The Pharisees and Scribes oppose the tradition of the elders to the customs of the Matthean community.

---

bears witness to a wide variety of uses, including a hostile connotation. Liddell and Scott: *A Greek-English Lexicon*, 1511.

[37] In Mk 7:1, the Pharisees seem already in place, while "certain Scribes" come up from Jerusalem. Matthew here puts the pair of Pharisees and Scribes in this order, probably because of Mark's influence. Gundry: *Matthew*, 302. Matthew's omission of the distinction between the Pharisees and certain Scribes is probably due to Mk 7:5: καὶ ἐπερωτῶσιν αὐτὸν οἱ Φαρισαῖοι καὶ οἱ γραμματεῖς. Matthew sometimes drops definite articles with these groups of people (23:13, 15, 23, 25, 27, 29). Thus their omission here is probably not significant.

[38] Davies and Allison: *Matthew*, 2:519. Taylor argues that Mk 7:3–4 is an interpolation that was not present in Matthew's copy of Mark. He maintains that the explanation of these verses is historically incorrect and exaggerates with the reference to all Jews. Vincent Taylor: *The Gospel According to St. Mark* (London: Macmillan, 1952), 335. Gundry mistakenly reports Gnilka holding Taylor's position. Gundry: *Mark*, 361; Gnilka: *Markus*, 1:227.

[39] Gundry: *Matthew*, 302.

[40] The points of contact are: οὐ νίπτονται (Mk 7:2: ἀνίπτοις); χεῖρας (Mk 7:2, 5: χερσίν); ἐσθίωσιν (Mk 7:2, 5: ἐσθίουσιν); ἄρτον (Mk 7:5: τὸν ἄρτον). Davies and Allison: *Matthew*, 2:521.

[41] The word means "whenever" or "in each instance when" with the connotation of both an indefinite future and of events likely to recur. Liddell and Scott: *A Greek-English Lexicon*, 1264. An allusion to the feeding of the five thousand is unlikely, *pace* Davies and Allison: *Matthew*, 2:521.

The word παράδοσις here refers not directly to the Law, but to traditions outside of the Law.[42] These traditions seem to have been associated particularly with the Pharisees. Josephus reports on the religious customs of the Pharisees as παραδόσεις that were rejected by the Sadducees.[43] Similarly, the Qumran community seems to have known such traditions of Pharisees but rejected them.[44] Consequently, it must be assumed that these traditions of the Pharisees[45] were

---

[42] In the gospels it is only Matthew and Mark who use the word, and only in the context of this passage. Matthew uses it three times (15:2, 3, 6), while Mark uses it five times (7:3, 5, 8, 9, 13). Paul uses the word to describe Jewish traditions (Gal 1:14), but also transfers it to Christian traditions (1 Cor 11:2). As Christian tradition it is also used in 2 Thess 2:15, 3:6; and in Col 2:8 it denotes pagan religious traditions.

[43] In *Ant.* 13.6, § 297: "For the present I wish merely to explain that the Pharisees had passed down (παρέδοσαν) to the people certain regulations handed down by former generations and not recorded in the Law of Moses, for which reason they were rejected by the Sadducean group, who hold that only those regulations should be considered valid which were written down, and that those which had been handed down (παραδόσεως) by former generations need not be observed." He also writes in *Ant.* 17.41: "There was also a group of Jews priding itself on its adherence to ancestral custom (τοῦ πατρίου) and claiming to observe the laws of which the Deity approves, and by these men, called Pharisees, the women (of the court) were ruled." However, there is a probability that Josephus here cites his source Nicolaus of Damascus; see the note in the Loeb edition. Josephus reports in his *Vita* 2, § 12 that he joined the Pharisees. Thus he would be familiar with their teaching on the παράδοσις and would not claim that the Pharisees were hypocrites by only pretending to observe the Law. Overman: *Church and Community*, 224.

[44] See 1QH 4.14-15: "Teachers of lies and seers of falsehood have schemed against me in a devilish scheme, to exchange the Law engraved on my heart by You for the smooth things which they speak to your people." In the scrolls of Qumran Pharisees are ridiculed as seekers of smooth things because of their abandoning the strict interpretation of the Law as advocated by the Teacher of Righteousness and his disciples, the community of Qumran. James C. VanderKam: *The Dead Sea Scrolls Today* (Grand Rapids: Eerdmans, 1994), 107. Baumgarten has used 1QH 4.14-15 in particular to show how the Qumran community leveled a charge against the Pharisees similar to that found in Matthew and Mark, namely that the Pharisees exchange the Law for their traditions. Baumgarten further adduces 4QMMT as evidence. Albert I. Baumgarten: "The Pharisaic-Sadducean Controversies about Purity and the Qumran Texts," *JJS* 31 (1980): 157-170. However, the evidence of 4QMMT is highly controversial. Schiffman has argued repeatedly that the Halakhic Letter reflects the origin of the Qumran sect as a group of Sadducean origin that found it hard to accept the abolition of the Zadokite High Priesthood by the Maccabees in the aftermath of their revolt. Thus the Halakhic Letter, according to Schiffman, has as its true opponents not the Pharisees but the Sadducean group remaining in Jerusalem and arranging itself with the new order. Yet Schiffman also states that the opponents in 4QMMT have the views that in mishnaic and rabbinic texts are attributed to the Pharisees. Lawrence H. Schiffman: "The New Halakhic Letter (4QMMT) and the Origins of the Dead Sea Sect," *BA* 53 (1990): 64-73; Lawrence H. Schiffman: "Origin and Early History of the Qumran Sect," *BA* 58 (1995): 37-48. If Schiffman's theory is accepted, the boundaries between Pharisees and Sadducees seem to have been, at least in the estimation of the Qumran sect, less along halakhic than along social lines.

[45] Gnilka equals these traditions to the "oral Torah" that served as the fence to avoid violation of the written Torah. Gnilka: *Matthäus*, 2:21. For a discussion of the oral Torah see. Hermann Leberecht Strack and Günther Stemberger: *Introduction to the Talmud and Midrash*, trans. M.

controversial at least before the destruction of the temple. They probably continued to be so for a time after.[46] For Matthew the opposition of the Pharisees and Scribes here raises one particular item of their tradition to a matter of principle; the issue of washing hands before a meal becomes an example of the Matthean community breaking with Pharisaic tradition.[47] Behind the question of accepting their tradition the Pharisees and Scribes ask a different question: Why do the disciples of Jesus not accept the authority of the Pharisees and Scribes?[48] The story becomes a dispute over the difference between the Judaism of the Pharisees and the observance of the disciples. The question of the Pharisees is loaded with innuendo.

The issue under discussion emphasizes this to a large extent. The earliest attestations we have for a regular Jewish ritual of washing hands before a meal are Mk 7:1–5 ‖ Mt 15:1–2. Perhaps Jn 2:6 alludes to the same practice.[49] The Jewish Scriptures refer to the need of cleaning one's hands in the context of a person suffering from a bodily discharge. This washing of hands prevents spreading the impurity to others (Lev 15:11). Ex 30:17–21 exhorts the priests to wash their hands and feet before entering the tent of meeting. This practice seems to have continued in the temple, as Josephus reports ritual washing of hands in the context of the priestly functions in the temple.[50] In the later accounts of the Mishnah the washing of hands becomes more common,[51] but it is improbable that this custom was generally accepted already in the first century. It appears, then, that the washing of hands as reported by Mark and Matthew was, in the first century, a Pharisaic custom, not a general rule within Judaism.

The answer of Jesus (15:3) goes directly to the heart of the objection. Matthew does not use the quotation of Is 29:13 first, as Mark does (7:6b–7). He first uses the counter-argument given in Mk 7:8–9 and shapes it to parallel the question of

---

Bockmuehl (Minneapolis: Fortress, 1992), 35–49. Their conclusion is that it "is undeniable that such a tradition alongside Scripture must already have existed in the biblical period" (page 36). But the relationship of this oral Torah to the tradition of the Pharisees is less clear.

[46] Albert I. Baumgarten: "The Pharisaic *Paradosis*," *HThR* 80 (1987): 63–78. One of the pieces of evidence for a continued rivalry between Pharisees and Sadducees is a passage in *ARN* A, 5: "but the Sadducees said, 'It is a tradition among the Pharisees to afflict themselves in this world; yet in the world to come they will have nothing.'" Goldin: *ARNA*, 39.

[47] Gnilka: *Matthäus*, 2:21.

[48] Overman writes: "This conflict story is really a dispute over local tradition and authority. Who will control behavior, possess legal authority, and determine what is proper or improper interpretation." Overman: *Church and Community*, 222–223.

[49] Jn 2:6: "Now six stone jars were standing there, for the Jewish rites of purification (κατὰ τὸν καθαρισμὸν τῶν Ἰουδαίων), each holding twenty or thirty gallons." This suggestion is made by Luz: *Matthäus*, 2:420–421.

[50] See Josephus *Ant.* 8.6, §§ 86–87; 12.13, § 106. Josephus speaks of a pool of water called ocean that was used by priests to wash hands and feet before service at the altar.

[51] See *m.Shab.* 1.4; 13b–14b; *p.Shab.* 1,3d.40. According to these references, the washing of hands was one of the 18 agreements between Hillel and Shammai. According to *t.Demai* 2.11 the washing of hands is a condition for acceptance among the ranks of the Pharisees.

Pharisees and Scribes (15:2) precisely : He inserts διὰ τί, repeating the rhetorical question, he inserts καὶ ὑμεῖς,[52] paralleling the subject οἱ μαθηταί σου, and repeats the verb παραβαίνειν. Thus as the Pharisees accused the disciples of transgression, so Jesus accuses the Pharisees of transgression. Their lack of observance is treated in the juxtaposition of the command of God with their tradition. Matthew insists on the tradition being theirs.[53] This allows him to heighten the contrast between τὴν ἐντολὴν τοῦ θεοῦ and τὴν παράδοσιν ὑμῶν. The implicit accusation against the Pharisees and Scribes is, then, not just between Law and tradition, but it is between God and them. Matthew argues that the practice of the disciples does not follow the tradition of the Pharisees because the Pharisees do not follow the commandment of God.

Matthew is aware that the accusation leveled against the Pharisees and Scribes needs to be buttressed. So he goes on to give the example of the putative Pharisaic tradition of Corban and contrasts it with one of the ten commandments. Again Matthew edits significantly. He changes the Markan introduction to the example to read ὁ γὰρ θεὸς ἐνετείλατο λέγων, emphasizing that Matthew is not about to attack the Law itself.[54] The actual quotation of the commandment is the same as in Mk 7:10, with the exception that Matthew excises the possessive pronoun σου.[55] The quotation of the decalogue is amplified, as in Mark, with the punishment enforcing the commandment to honor one's parents. It is an almost verbatim rendering of LXX Ex 21:16[56] that Matthew takes from Mark.

In 15:5 Matthew contrasts the commandment of God with the behavior of the Pharisees. He changes Mk 7:11 only slightly. The clumsy Markan construction ἐάν ... ἄνθρωπος is changed to the simplified ὃς ἄν, the Markan mention of κορβᾶν, ὅ ἐστιν δῶρον is abbreviated into δῶρον. In 15:6 Matthew draws the conclusion of his argument. He replaces Mk 7:12 and returns to the consequence that the

---

[52] The position of ὑμεῖς is emphatic. Davies and Allison: *Matthew*, 2:522.

[53] Matthew has τὴν παράδοσιν ὑμῶν; Mk 7:8 speaks of τὴν παράδοσιν τῶν ἀνθρώπων. Mk 7:9 has: Καλῶς ἀθετεῖτε τὴν ἐντολὴν τοῦ θεοῦ, ἵνα τὴν παράδοσιν ὑμῶν στήσητε.

[54] Mark reads: Μωυ σῆς γὰρ εἶπεν. Matthew's text is transmitted in variants. The reading adopted here occurs in ℵ*.2 C L W 0106 f syʰ and the Majority text. A different version (ὁ θεὸς γὰρ εἶπεν) is found in ℵ¹ B D Θ 084 f¹.¹³ 700. 892 pc lat syˢ.ᶜ.ᵖ· co; Irˡᵃᵗ Cyr, and accepted by the Nestle-Aland text. The variant is explainable as an assimilation to Mark. Davies and Allison: *Matthew*, 2:522. Gnilka accepts the variant. Gnilka: *Matthäus*, 2:18. Metzger argues the reading accepted here is influenced by v. 3, while the variant should not be taken to reflect Mark because Mark has a different subject to εἶπεν. Metzger: *Textual Commentary*, 31. This argument does not take into account Matthew's penchant for parallelisms, which is particularly obvious in this pericope. Matthew might have consciously imitated the formulation of LXX Deut 5:16: τίμα τὸν πατέρα σου καὶ τὴν μητέρα σου ὃν τρόπον ἐνετείλατό σοι κύριος ὁ θεός σου.

[55] Mark uses the possessive pronoun σου twice, once after father, once after mother. In this he follows the LXX version of Deut 5:16. The LXX version of Ex 20:12 has σου only once. Matthew's version without any possessive pronouns is an abbreviation and parallelization with the following phrase. Davies and Allison: *Matthew*, 2:523.

[56] "ὁ κακολογῶν πατέρα αὐτοῦ ἢ μητέρα αὐτοῦ τελευτήσει θανάτῳ."

offering of the gift has for the commandment of God. Emphatically Matthew states that "most certainly he will not honor his father" (οὐ μὴ τιμήσει τὸν πατέρα αὐτοῦ).[57]

While the example shows how the Pharisees and Scribes do away with one particular commandment, the implications of this example are finally drawn out in more general terms (15:6). The opponents of Jesus void the word of God by their traditions. Matthew's redactional changes to Mk 7:12 are of stylistic nature.[58] Having proven that the Pharisees and Scribes put their traditions above the Law, Matthew does not need the confusing Markan addition that they do so with many other things (7:13b). Matthew keeps to the argument introduced by the Pharisees themselves.

The tradition of Corban and its significance in the first century are difficult to assess.[59] Originally the word referred to a sacrifice or offering. But over time it shifted its meaning to something that was withdrawn from common usage. This withdrawal was effected by its dedication to the temple. Such practices were known among the contemporaries of Matthew.[60] The Mishnah explains how such a dedication was sometimes a legal fiction.[61] As such, the dedication would not actually entail any kind of sacrifice. However, the Mishnah also reports that at some stage in the tradition allowance was made for ill considered Corban vows. The example of the honor that one owes to father and mother is specifically mentioned.[62] The Mishnaic evidence, however, does not permit us to draw conclusions concerning the practice of Corban vows in the first century. It merely shows how

---

[57] Some manuscripts add ἢ (or καί) τὴν μητέρα αὐτοῦ: C L W Θ 0106 f¹, the Majority text, and others. It is possible to imagine equally the insertion by a Scribe prompted by the preceding verses, and the accidental omission by passing from αὐτοῦ to αὐτου. The manuscripts slightly weigh in favor of omission. For this reason, the Nestle-Aland text does not include the mother in the verse. Metzger: *Textual Commentary*, 31. A certain decision is impossible.

[58] Matthew inserts a καί with consecutive overtones, ἀκυρόω becomes the main verb instead of the Markan participial construction. Matthew inserts διά for the Markan construction with the dative, and he leaves out the ponderous ἢ παρεδώκατε.

[59] Albert I. Baumgarten: "*Korban* and the Pharisaic Paradosis," *JANES* 16 (1984): 5–17.

[60] Josephus: *Ant.* 4.5 § 73, makes an allusion to people offering themselves as Corban and redeeming themselves by payment to the priests; in *C. Ap.* 1.22 § 167, he reports that Theophrastus knew of Corban as a Jewish oath. In this particular context it is not clear whether Corban refers to a person or to material possessions. Josephus names Corban in both cases explicitly and provides δῶρον as translation. In Qumran the practice might have been known as well; see *CD* 16.14–15, though here the word Corban is not used. *CD* treats things vowed to the altar in the general context of oaths: "No man shall vow to the altar anything unlawfully acquired. Also, no Priest shall take from Israel anything unlawfully acquired. And no man shall consecrate the food of the house to God, for it is as He said, *Each hunts his brother with a net* (or *votive-offering*)." The allusion in italics is to Micah 7:2. In the general context of oaths the document is very clear that oaths do not supersede the Law. In this the Damascus Document argues similarly to Matthew.

[61] See *m.Ned.* 3.11.

[62] See *m.Ned.* 9.1.

the practice developed over time, without pinning down the development to specific dates. Thus the information gleaned from Mark and Matthew is more pertinent. Behind the gospels the assumption seems to be that the Pharisees and Scribes considered the Corban vow to outweigh the commandment to honor one's parents. It is difficult to ascertain whether the opinion held by Mark and Matthew accurately represents the Pharisaic position since the description is given within a controversy that must allow for some bias in the evidence.

In 15:7–9 Matthew finally uses the quotation from Isaiah (Mk 7:6b–7) to conclude the controversy story. In its introduction (15:7) Matthew makes a few changes that reflect his own stylistic preferences: He moves ὑποκριταί forward and puts it into the vocative case, as he does frequently in ch. 23. "Isaiah" moves to the end, followed by λέγων.[63] The whole introduction is shorter and more concise, while at the same time more combative. The quotation itself follows Mark verbatim except for the transposition of the demonstrative οὗτος after λαός.[64] The quotation provides a good conclusion for Matthew's argument as it contrasts outer and inner honor of God, while the criterion that makes their honor of God superficial is their adherence to precepts, not of the Law, but of human origin.

The controversy story offers Matthew another opportunity to show that his community is faithful to the Law. In this apology[65] of its view of the Law the community attacks the interpretation offered by the Jewish leaders who try to supplement the Law through their tradition. Matthew's version of the controversy story shows a well argued defense of its practice, while it explains at the same time the Pharisaic opposition as motivated not by concern for the Law or for God, but by concern for their traditions and their leadership. The Pharisees and Scribes have opposed themselves to God by elevating their own traditions to an authority where they oppose the Law of God.

Matthew continues after the conclusion of the controversy story with an instruction of the crowd, and later of the disciples. In this instruction he continues to make the point about eating with unclean hands, and his own conclusion at 15:20 ties the material together. Matthew follows Mark in these instructions, even though he redacts some of the material. But Matthew also has a remarkable interpolation in 15:12–14. The disciples remark on the offense that the Pharisees take,[66] and Jesus

---

[63] Mark has ὡς γέγραπται.

[64] The Matthean word order is closer to the LXX of Is 29:13 than Mark. Davies and Allison: *Matthew*, 2:525. On the whole the quotation seems closer to Septuagint than to the Masoretic text. However, both beginning and ending are newly formed. Gnilka: *Matthäus*, 2:24. The LXX reads: ἐγγίζει μοι ὁ λαὸς οὗτος τοῖς χείλεσιν αὐτῶν τιμῶσίν με ἡ δὲ καρδία αὐτῶν πόρρω ἀπέχει ἀπ' ἐμοῦ μάτην δὲ σέβονταί με διδάσκοντες ἐντάλματα ἀνθρώπων καὶ διδασκαλίας.

[65] Overman: *Church and Community*, 227.

[66] At this point of the narrative the Scribes drop out. This is probably an indication that in the whole discussion 15:1–20 the Pharisees are the real opposition that Matthew faces. The presence of the Scribes (15:1) is merely a nod to Mark as the source. Davies and Allison rightly point out

answers them with sayings about the plants not planted by the Father and the blind guides.[67] The two parables are separated by the exhortation of the disciples to leave the Pharisees be (15:14). On occasion this has been taken as an expression for the separation of the church from the synagogue.[68] But such an explanation needs to account for the curious fact that Matthew omits Mk 7:19b. Mark interprets the controversy to mean that all foods are clean. Matthew does not do so, even if the argument that he takes from Mark could be construed to imply this as a consequence.[69] But the Matthean argument is not really about what foods are clean and what foods are unclean. The controversy takes the washing of hands before a meal only as an example of the more general Pharisaic traditions. Thus the possible ritual defilement does not originate with the food, but with the lack of cleanliness before dinner. Matthew preserves this aspect much better than Mark. Similarly, an explanation of this interpolation should not assume that Peter and the disciples have just been taught about the kingdom of God and the origin of evil.[70]

However, another explanation is possible. The Matthean insistence that the disciples are concerned about offending the Pharisees is somewhat odd. It has not appeared before in the gospel, and it will not do so again. The exhortation to leave the Pharisees be is surrounded by two parables. After these parables Matthew inserts 15:15 to have Peter ask for an explanation of the parable. While this redaction certainly reflects Mk 7:17, where the disciples ask for an explanation of the parable, the context is entirely different. In Mark, the disciples ask for an explanation of a parable that has been given to the crowds: Mk 7:15 and the apodictic saying that "there is nothing outside a person which by going into him can defile him." Arguably it is not a parable at all, but a ruling concerning purity.[71] In

---

that it is not the Jews as a whole who are offended. "Matthew's Jesus is not attacking Judaism as a whole but only the Pharisaic tradition." Davies and Allison: *Matthew*, 2:532.

[67]   The latter simile has a parallel in Lk 6:39. Thus it might come from Q. Davies and Allison: *Matthew*, 2:533. In the Lukan context the blind guides are disciples; in Matthew they are Pharisees. Gundry asserts that the saying about the trees not planted by the Father has a parallel in Lk 17:6. Gundry: *Matthew*, 306. But the two sayings really have only the motif of the tree and its uprooting in common, and the verbal agreements exhaust themselves in the verbs uprooting and planting. Both context and application are too different to speak of a literary relationship. Scribes and Pharisees are also blind guides in Mt 23:16, 24. Kloppenborg suggests that Lk 6:39 was part of Q. There, he asserts, the saying was probably not a direct attack against the Pharisees. Kloppenborg: *Formation*, 184.

[68]   Gundry: *Matthew*, 307.

[69]   Argued by Gundry: *Matthew*, 308.

[70]   Patte appeals to 13:11 to make his point. Patte: *Matthew*, 219. However, the immediate context makes such an appeal questionable.

[71]   Gundry points out that for Mark, "παρβολή has come to refer not only to comparative statements but also to puzzling ones." Gundry: *Mark*, 354. He cites the arguable passage 3:23 as another example. While his example might not bear him out, Gundry has nevertheless called to attention that Mk 7:15 lacks the comparative dimension of a usual parable. It is not a simile, but a judgment on the rules of purification.

Matthew, the demand for an explanation follows the parable of the blind guides. Thus Matthew gives Peter a reason to ask for an explanation of the parable by actually inserting one, and before that, another one, followed by the command to leave the Pharisees alone. Thus when Peter now asks for an explanation of the parable, he no longer asks about eating with clean or unclean hands, he asks about the saying concerning blind guides leading the blind. Peter is interested in the status of the Pharisees. Matthew explains their position by having Jesus relate the teaching about the things that make and make not unclean.

Matthew's redaction is not easily explained with a reference to the separation of church and synagogue. If the relationship between the two is still as close as the controversy story lets on, it might be possible to infer, instead of a separation, that the Pharisaic movement held a certain attraction for, or power over, some of the members of the Matthean community. Both the Matthean community and the Pharisaic movement were highly concerned with the interpretation of the Law as the linchpin for Judaism after the destruction of the temple. It is entirely possible that the Pharisaic interpretation of the Law in the light of their traditions might have held an attractive solution to the re-formation of Judaism after 70. In this case the controversy story might have been less persuasive than desired by Matthew. Thus he felt compelled to add the command to leave the Pharisees alone, and the warning about the blind guides, the Pharisees, leading the blind into the pit. The Matthean interpolation, then, is a warning for the community. The disciples are cautioned not to fall into the trap that the Pharisees lay for themselves. Matthew's community is asked to hold fast to the Law, but not to give in to the temptation to amplify it with Pharisaic traditions.[72]

2.1 The Markan Pericope

The narrative of Mk 7:1–13, the source for Matthew 15:1–9, is far less smoothly constructed than the Matthean narrative. At several points it becomes clear that Mark's controversy is composite. After the introduction of the Pharisees and Scribes as observing the supposedly unclean meal of the disciples, Mark inserts a little parenthesis that purports to give information on this and other practices of ritual purity of Jesus' opponents. But the parenthesis is aggressive, since it expands these customs from the Pharisees to "all the Jews" (7:3). And it is historically incorrect to expand these rules of ritual purity to all Jews. However, this parenthesis interrupts the narrative thread from vv. 2–5, and so in v. 5 a certain repetitiveness

---

[72] Luz has a similar insight when he writes that Matthew 15:1–20 documents some of the struggle over legitimization for leadership after the destruction of the temple: "Innerjüdisch kann man also das Mt-Ev als eines der wenigen erhaltenen Dokumente antipharisäischer Reaktion in der Zeit nach der Tempelzerstörung bestimmen." Luz: *Matthäus*, 2:421.

occurs.[73] In v. 8, after the quotation of Isaiah, Mark has the apodictic statement that Jesus' opponents leave the commandment of God to hold fast to human traditions. This apophthegm works as a good conclusion to the controversy story. However, Mark then begins, in v. 9, with καὶ ἔλεγεν αὐτοῖς, one of his favorite seams.[74] And what follows is in essence a second answer to the objection of the Pharisees and Scribes, in slightly different words. In this second answer, Mark now incorporates the example of Corban (7:10–13). He concludes this second answer with another broad sweep at the opponents by stating: "And many such things you do" (7:13). In Jesus' first response, Mark opposed "human tradition" (7:8). In the second answer, they suddenly become "your tradition" (7:9).[75]

Beyond the controversy itself, the Markan narrative exhibits a several other inconsistencies. The controversy begins with the issue of washing one's hands before a meal (7:2). But as the narrative progresses, the issue of purity is transferred to vessels in the parenthesis 7:3–4, then expanded to include "everything" (7:15),[76] and finally restricted again to clean and unclean food (7:19). Thus Mark takes the tradition of washing hands and in his argument expands it to include finally all rules about food purity. With this trend Mark distinguishes his community not just from Pharisaic forms of Judaism. With the repudiation of all food laws Mark sets his community apart from Judaism itself.

Matthew reverses this trend. When faced with the sweeping statement of Mk 7:15 he omits οὐδέν ἐστιν ... ὃ δύναται κοινῶσαι and replaces it with τὸ εἰσερχόμενον εἰς τὸ στόμα (15:11). He omits Mark's reference to the purity of all foods, and in his conclusion qualifies the discussion again to refer to the washing of hands only (15:20). Matthew's redaction actually seems to bring the story closer to what might have been its pre-Markan state. Matthew also levels out the inconsistencies of Mark. The sweeping parenthesis concerning all the Jews is left out, and two parables are added that reflect specifically on the Pharisees. Matthew

---

[73] Gnilka: *Markus*, 1:276–277. The repetitions are in the introduction to the question, where the Pharisees and Scribes are mentioned again. It is also significant that the parenthesis does not make any mention of the Scribes. This gives further indication of the controversy story and the parenthesis being of different sources. On resumption as a literary device see Urban C. von Wahlde: "*Wiederaufnahme* as a Marker of Redaction in Jn 6:51–58," *Bib* 64 (1983): 542–549.

[74] Gnilka assumes that because of this formula Mark here works traditional material into his narrative. Gnilka: *Markus*, 1:227.

[75] Gnilka assumes that for this particular reason the second answer must be the older one in the tradition: "Die Jesusantwort spiegelt noch die unmittelbare Konfrontation mit den Gegnern wider, wie die Anrede "eure Überlieferung" erkennen läßt." Gnilka: *Markus*, 1:277.

[76] Because of this, Gnilka sees 7:15 as an originally independent dominical saying. Gnilka: *Markus*, 1:284. Its original meaning was the exclusion of all cultic purity laws. Gundry considers the saying more in its context and concludes that it refers to food only. But the "saying marks a progression from the question of *how* to eat to the question of *what* to eat." Gundry: *Mark*, 354. Gnilka's suggestion is somewhat to be preferred since the saying is wide open and not, at least in its wording, restricted to food. Even the mention of "mouth" does not alter this since Mark obviously interprets the saying as a parable (7:17).

stays with the initial objection throughout the narrative, and he never deviates from dealing with the initial opponents, except for narrowing them down to the Pharisees only.

Accordingly, Matthew not only creates a more coherent story. He also locates his community differently. Mark's broad attacks against all Jewish purity laws set him outside of Judaism. Matthew carefully avoids this. His redaction reveals that his real concern is with the opposition between the tradition of the Pharisees and the Law of God. This opposition between Law and tradition allows Matthew to portray the teaching of Jesus as the doctrine that is more faithful to the Law. In his pairs of opposites Matthew aligns Jesus, the Law, and God, while on the opposite side the Pharisees and their traditions are set against God. Consequently, Matthew 15:19 amends the list of vices given in Mk 7:21–22 to conform with the second part of the decalogue.[77] Matthew warns his community against deviation from Jesus, the Law, and God. Pharisaic tradition leads only into the pit. While Matthew takes over the Markan notion that purity and impurity are to be judged on moral grounds, Matthew does not extend this judgment to the entire system of ritual purity, but confines himself consciously to the washing of hands as representative of the tradition of the Pharisees.

2.2 Summary of the Matthean Redaction in 15:1–9

Besides the usual attention paid to the structural cohesion of the story, Matthew situates the story differently from Mark:

▸ Matthew integrates the controversy proper much more tightly with the following material. The structure of the story itself is tightened through the transposition of material and the introduction of contrasting pairs.

▸ Matthew omits much circumstantial material. In particular he seems to assume that his readers know about dietary laws.

▸ Matthew emphasizes that the objection of the opponents is directed against the customary practice of the Matthean community.

▸ Matthew counters the objection by showing several times that the tradition of the Pharisees and Scribes are opposed to the command of God. The opponents are the ones shown to have distanced themselves from Judaism proper through their traditions.

---

[77] Klaus Berger: *Die Gesetzesauslegung Jesu: Ihr historischer Hintergrund im Judentum und im Alten Testament. Vol. I: Markus und Parallelen*, WMANT 40 (Neukirchen-Vluyn: Neukirchener Verlag, 1972), 503. Matthew uses murder, adultery, theft, and false witness in the same order as Ex 20:13–16 and Deut 5:17–20. He also mentions evil thoughts, fornication, and slander. These three are also mentioned in Mark's catalogue. Gnilka suggests that evil thoughts and slander are particularly relevant for Matthew because of the accusations of the Pharisees. Gnilka: *Matthäus*, 2:26.

▶   Matthew resists the Markan trend of separating his community from
        Judaism. The Matthean community is shown as more faithful to the Law
        than the opponents.
▶   The claim to the greater faithfulness of the community rests on the teaching
        authority of Jesus who teaches the commandments of God.

3. Matthew 16:1–4

After the controversy concerning purity Matthew follows closely Mark's narrative
sequence. Jesus leaves for the district of Tyre and Sidon (15:21). Matthew
continues the story of Jesus with the great faith of the Canaanite woman that brings
Jesus to heal her daughter (15:22–28 ‖ Mk 7:24–30). A summary (15:29–31), in
place of Mark's healing of the deaf-mute (Mk 7:31–37), has Jesus return to the
Lake of Galilee. Jesus ascends a mountain and is seated there (15:29), perhaps in
an allusion to the beginning of the Sermon on the Mount (5:1–2). The summary
places special attention on the healing activity of Jesus and takes care to note how
the dumb speak, the maimed are made whole, the lame walk, and the blind see.
Matthew seems to allude to the fulfillment of an earlier statement (11:5) as well as
to Is 35:5–6.[78] Jesus then feeds the four thousand (15:32–38 ‖ Mk 8:1–9).
Afterwards, he returns to Galilee, to the region of Magadan (15:39 ‖ Mk 8:10).[79]

As in Mark, the controversy of 16:1–4 (Mk 8:11–13) disrupts this positive
atmosphere of faith, miracles, and eschatological fulfillment once again. Pharisees
and Sadducees wish to see a sign from heaven. Their malice is unrestrained. Matthew used similar material in 12:38–45. There this controversy was lengthy and
accompanied by several answers of Jesus, ending in the saying of the unclean spirit
returning with his friends to the house he had left. There Matthew used a large
amount of material he found in Q. This time, Matthew uses the controversy in a
short form that is much closer to the controversy in Mk 8:11–13. Matthew rewords
the Markan introduction to the story slightly. In 16:1 he adds the Sadducees[80] and

---

[78] Davies and Allison: *Matthew*, 2:566.

[79] Magadan is not otherwise attested. Mk 8:10 has Jesus reach Dalmanutha at this point,
equally unknown otherwise. The place caused considerable confusion even among various
manuscripts, who attest to Melagada, Melegada, Magaida, Magedan, Magdala, Mageda in place
of Dalmanutha. Variants for Magadan include Magdala, Magalan, and Magedan.

[80] The addition is probably motivated by the following pericope. In Mk 8:14–21, the
instruction on the leaven of the Pharisees and of Herod follows. Matthew repeats this story, but
replaces Herod with the Sadducees (16:5–12). This explains their entry into 16:1–4: Matthew
introduced them into the controversy to give the whole of 16:1–12 more cohesion. Perhaps the
substitution made eminent sense to the Matthean community with the demise of Herodian
importance after the destruction of the temple. The Sadducees, however, lack distinguishing
features since they are grouped with the Pharisees. They appeared already in 3:7 as those
castigated by John the Baptist, also grouped with the Pharisees. In the controversies with Jesus
they appear here for the first time and remain important throughout ch. 16 where Jesus warns his
disciples against the yeast of Pharisees and Sadducees (16:6, 11–12). The Sadducees reappear in

improves the style.[81] A significant addition to the request of the opponents is the phrase ἐπιδεῖξαι αὐτοῖς. It seems Matthean in origin and is not reported by either Mark or Luke. Matthew makes sure that the audience understands that what the opponents are seeking is a special sign (σημεῖον) for them, a legitimation from heaven directed particularly at the opponents of Jesus.[82] The Pharisees and Sadducees seek a special favor that sets them apart from the crowds. After the feeding of the four thousand it is the leaders that ask for another sign, not the multitude.[83] By the same token, they also admit that the miracles that Jesus has worked in the preceding chapter are not sufficient for them. It seems as if they still believe that those miracles are not worked by the Spirit of God but through the authority of Beelzebul (cf. 12:22–30).[84] The Pharisees and Sadducees fail to interpret the miracles of Jesus as signs from heaven.

Contrary to the earlier version of the controversy story, Matthew here reports, following Mark, that the malicious intent of the opponents of Jesus is obvious in their attempt to test Jesus. The word πειράζειν recalls the temptation story where Satan was described as πειράζων (Matthew 4:3).[85]

Verses 2b–3 present a special textcritical problem. They contain a saying, present as the first part of Jesus' answer, about interpreting the signs of the sky in forecasting the weather. A good portion of manuscripts omits this saying. The short

---

the Jerusalem controversy over the resurrection (22:23) where they alternate with the Pharisees as opponents (22:34). Only in this pericope are they distinguished from the Pharisees. Consequently, Matthean interest in the Sadducees as a group distinct from the Pharisees should not be overestimated.

[81] Matthew leaves out ἤρξαντο συζητεῖν, perhaps because the reference to πειράζειν already marks the conflict. He substitutes ἐπερώτησαν for ζητοῦντες and makes it the main verb of the sentence. The verb is a favorite of Matthew's. Gundry: *Matthew*, 677. The approach of the Pharisees and Sadducees and their testing of Jesus become participial constructions. Matthew changes ἐξῆλθον into προσελθόντες and moves πειράζοντες before the main verb. The request for the sign is, as in Mark, in indirect discourse. Here Matthew changes the preposition, from ἀπό to ἐκ.

[82] Matthew, following Mark, does not use σημεῖον to denote miracles of Jesus. The word is used to denote eschatological occurrences and events that accompany the end of times (24:3, 30), but that can also be ambiguous (24:24). T. Francis Glasson: "The Ensign of the Son of Man (Matt XXIV.30)," *JThS* 15 (1964): 299–300. It also is the sign by which Judas will make Jesus known to the band arresting Jesus in Gethsemane (26:48).

[83] Gundry sees the significance of ἐπιδεῖξαι αὐτοῖς in the parallel to ἐπερώτησαν. Gundry: *Matthew*, 322. The parallel, however, is not a striking literary device since it is restricted to the prefix. It is more likely that Matthew appends the phrase in order to accentuate the evil intent of the opponents of Jesus. Luz: *Matthäus*, 2:444–445. Gnilka thinks that the addition expresses a wish for a more concrete sign. Gnilka: *Matthäus*, 2:39. But it is not clear what he means by that.

[84] The point made here is emphasized by the mention of a sign ἐκ τοῦ οὐράνου, following Mk 8:11. The phrase was replaced in the earlier version 12:8 with ἀπό σοῦ. It seems that the Pharisees and Sadducees do not trust the signs from Jesus, namely the miracles worked earlier.

[85] Both Mark and Luke make reference to the testing of Jesus during his temptation, albeit in different phraseology: πειραζόμενος ὑπό τοῦ σατανᾶ [διαβόλου] (Mk 1:13; Lk 4:2).

text is attested by some very good manuscripts, though with a geographical emphasis in Egypt.[86] The textual evidence is not conclusive.

A rule for interpreting the weather is given in Lk 12:54–56.[87] However, there are significant differences between the two versions. The Lukan parallel occurs in quite a different context: the instruction of the crowds. The rules themselves differ considerably in content. Furthermore, the two passages have only very few words actually in common.[88] The Matthean version has several parallels in Antiquity that are closer than Luke in the formulation of the rules.[89] Thus the differences in both wording and content between Matthew and Luke, the parallels in other literature

---

[86]   The witnesses can be divided according to text type. The Alexandrian witnesses C L Δ 33 892 1241 include 2b–3, ℵ B sa bo^pt Origen omit it. Among the Caesarean witnesses, N Θ f¹ 565 700 1071 geo Eusebius include the saying, while f¹³ 157 267 1216 2430 arm omit it. In the Western text the saying is attested in D it Diatessaron Hilary Juvencus, and not attested in syr^c,s. The Byzantine manuscripts K W Π *et al.* Chrysostom attest the saying, while V X Γ do not. The external evidence for either reading, then, is almost equal. The short version was known early and predominated in Egypt. This is borne out by the Coptic version and by Origen. Furthermore, the short version also seems to have been known early on in Syria. However, the Western tradition offers no evidence for the short version of the text at all. Its reading became known in the East around the fourth century. The external evidence of the manuscripts is not a sure guide to the antiquity of either reading, but merely a witness to different regional developments. Donald A. Hagner: *Matthew 14–28*, Word Biblical Commentary 33B (Dallas: Word Books, 1993), 453; Toshio Hirunuma: "Matthew 16, 2b–3," in: *New Testament Textual Criticism: Its Significance for Exegesis. Essays in Honor of Bruce M. Metzger*, ed. Eldon J. Epp and Gordon D. Fee (New York: Oxford University Press, 1981), 35–45.

[87]   The text in Lk 12:54–56 reads: Ἔλεγεν δὲ καὶ τοῖς ὄχλοις, Ὅταν ἴδητε [τὴν] νεφέλην ἀνατέλλουσαν ἐπὶ δυσμῶν, εὐθέως λέγετε ὅτι Ὄμβρος ἔρχεται, καὶ γίνεται οὕτως· 55 καὶ ὅταν νότον πνέοντα, λέγετε ὅτι Καύσων ἔσται, καὶ γίνεται. 56 ὑποκριταί, τὸ πρόσωπον τῆς γῆς καὶ τοῦ οὐρανοῦ οἴδατε δοκιμάζειν, τὸν καιρὸν δὲ τοῦτον πῶς οὐκ οἴδατε δοκιμάζειν; The Matthean text 16:2b–3 reads: Ὀψίας γενομένης λέγετε, Εὐδία, πυρράζει γὰρ ὁ οὐρανός· 3 καὶ πρωΐ, Σήμερον χειμών, πυρράζει γὰρ στυγνάζων ὁ οὐρανός. τὸ μὲν πρόσωπον τοῦ οὐρανοῦ γινώσκετε διακρίνειν, τὰ δὲ σημεῖα τῶν καιρῶν οὐ δύνασθε;

[88]   In the weather rules themselves there is no agreement at all. In the conclusion about reading the signs of the times the congruence rests with τὸ ... πρόσωπον ... τοῦ οὐρανοῦ; the word for the discernment differs. In Luke, the opponents cannto read τὸν καιρὸν δὲ τοῦτον; in Matthew they cannot discern τὰ δὲ σημεῖα τῶν καιρῶν. Luz: *Matthäus*, 2:444. The lack of verbal agreement in the weather rules themselves, and the differences in their application to the opponents of Jesus, caution against an easy assignation of this material to Q; against Hagner: *Matthew 14–28*, 453–454.

[89]   Similar rules for interpreting the weather are given by Pliny the Elder: *Naturalis Historia*, 18, 78; Aratus: *Phaenomena*, 858–871; Virgil: *Georgics*, 1. 438–456; Aristotle: *Problems*. 4. 26, 8. Aristotle's *Problems* is generally regarded as spurious, sometimes dated as late as the 5th or 6th century. Luz claims that Matthew's disputed rule belonged to the most widely known in Antiquity. Luz: *Matthäus*, 2:443–444. While this may be so, it must be noted that the witnesses adduced by Luz are all of the northern part of the Mediterranean world.

of Antiquity and the textual uncertainty concerning Matthew's version speak against a common origin in Q.[90]

The next question to be asked is whether the saying exhibits any traits of a possible Matthean redaction. It can be lifted out of its context without any loss of narrative flow. The passage does not seem to have influenced its context. It does not occur in the Markan parallel, nor does it appear in Matthew 12:38–39.[91] The saying itself exhibits some parallelisms, but without Matthew's usual clarity.[92] Another indicator for a late addition of 2b–3 might be the verb πυρράζω which is not otherwise attested until the Byzantine period.[93] Thus the editorial activity of Matthew cannot be shown convincingly.[94]

If the Matthean saying is a later gloss, some account must be given of why it was inserted, and why in this particular form that is so different from Luke's. Luke's version is explainable through its Palestinian setting. Clouds from the West are clouds developed over the Mediterranean, and they promise rain. Wind from the South comes out of the desert and is suitably hot. However, the signs of the weather in Matthew point to a more northwestern origin.[95] Thus it is possible that

---

[90] Kloppenborg deals briefly with this text. Kloppenborg: *Formation*, 152. He does not make a judgment whether this text actually occurred in Q or not, but points out the text-critical difficulties attending Matthew 16:2b–3. However, he also points out that the theme of the appropriate response to the impending judgment bears some resemblance to Q 3:7–9, "which likewise presupposes the nearness of the end and chastises the impenitent for their lack of response to what, in the mind of the speaker, are the obvious signs of the end." Tuckett concurs with the scepticism concerning the text's place in Q. Tuckett: *Q*, 158.

[91] Luz says that this might be an argument for the originality of the long form. Some textual witnesses might have erased 2b–3 in order to adjust the passage to the parallels. Luz: *Matthäus*, 2:444.

[92] Gundry notes the following: "When it becomes evening" corresponds to "early in the morning," "you say, fair weather" and "you say, today, stormy weather." In 3bc corresponding elements are: "You know how to discern the face of the sky" and "you are not able [to discern] the signs of the times." But the Greek formulations are actually not quite parallel: ὀψίας γενομένης relates to πρωΐ, λέγετε; εὐδία corresponds to σήμερον χειμών; finally γινώσκετε διακρίνειν corresponds to οὐ δύνασθε. Thus the parallels that Gundry lists are such only in content. One parallel alone remains: the twice used πυρράζει γάρ. The parallel formulations that Matthew uses so frequently, are conspicuously absent. Gundry then tries to make the case that the Matthean material is a redaction of Q as found in Lk 12:54–56. This is entirely unconvincing, even though Gundry tries hard to explain how Matthew would be led to substitute almost the entire vocabulary found in Luke. It escapes Gundry that, with the change of the vocabulary in Matthew, the signs become indicative of a different weather pattern than that described in Luke. Gundry: *Matthew*, 323.

[93] The entry in Liddell gives only Matthew 16:2 as reference. Liddell and Scott: *A Greek-English Lexicon*, 1558. BAGD gives only Byzantine writers. Bauer, Arndt, et al.: *A Greek-English Lexicon*, 731.

[94] If Matthew were truly to draw on Q/Luke for this saying it would be highly surprising that he would leave out the vocative ὑπόκριται that he uses so frequently elsewhere.

[95] Gnilka: *Matthäus*, 2:40.

the saying was inserted later, perhaps prompted by the similar saying in Lk 12:54–56. The context might have been the association between the demand for a sign and the signs of the times in v. 3. When it was inserted, however, a different situation was accounted for through the adjustment of the weather rules for a different geography. This would account for the fact that the insertion is best attested by the manuscripts of the Western tradition. While the weather rules given in Matthew are not applicable to Egypt, and thus may be an indication why Egyptian manuscripts excised them if they were originally part of the text, they are not indicative of a Palestinian or Syrian setting either. The weather rules of Matthew reflect a setting in the northern regions of the Mediterranean world. Whether 2b–3 are a later gloss, or whether they are part of the original text of Matthew, can no longer be determined with certainty. But what evidence there is slightly favors the hypothesis of a later interpolation.

Thus the answer of Jesus is given in vv. 2a, 4. As in 12:39 it is introduced with ὁ δὲ εἶπεν αὐτοῖς, omitting the emotional sigh of Jesus (Mk 8:12). The answer itself repeats verbatim the answer of 12:39. From this earlier occurrence it is clear that Matthew does not condemn the contemporaries of Jesus wholesale, but that his criticism is limited, in this case, to the Pharisees and Sadducees. "This evil and adulterous generation" refers to the Pharisees and Sadducees only, as only they are addressed (αὐτοῖς), and only they seek a sign. Again, only the sign of Jonah is offered. Here Jonah is not expressly described as prophet. Matthew then repeats the note of Mk 8:13 that Jesus left. However, Matthew uses his own words. He substitutes καταλίπων for ἀφείς, omits πάλιν ἐμβάς and moves εἰς τὸ πέραν to the next pericope beginning with 16:5 with the result that the saying concerning the leaven of the Pharisees and Sadducees (Mt 16:5–12 ‖ Mk 8:14–21) takes place not in the boat, as in Mark, but on the shore.

Matthew does not move the struggle between Jesus and his opponents further along. He sharpens the conflict slightly by the reference to the opponents as tempters, and by the fact that Jesus leaves them at the end of the story. The story also points out that Jesus' authority is still not accepted by his opponents. Even though in an earlier controversy the signs of Jesus and his authority to work them have been discussed, the context suggests that the Pharisees and Sadducees have not learned well. But that was to be expected, since they did not learn from their instruction on Hosea 6:6 either (cf. 12:7).

3.1 The Markan Pericope

The Markan controversy story in 8:11–13 contains few surprises. Matthew followed the narrative sequence of Mark. As a consequence, both share the context after the feeding of the four thousand. The pericope of the leaven of the Pharisees and Herod follows. The opponents of Jesus in Mark are the Pharisees, Matthew added Sadducees. Mark exhibits all the traits of a controversy story.

Mark connects the setting and the objection with a little wordplay introducing the Pharisees (συζήτειν αὐτῷ ζητοῦντες παρ᾽ αὐτοῦ).[96] A further connection between setting and question is established by positioning the remark that the opponents ask the question in order to test[97] Jesus after the actual question. The question itself is the demand for a sign from heaven, briefly reported in indirect discourse. The sign that the Pharisees demand must be distinguished from the miracles of Jesus. Mark speaks of σημεῖα not as miracles, but as eschatological signs.[98] The Pharisees do not demand another miracle, but ask for divine legitimation of Jesus.

In Mk 8:12 Jesus' answer is prefaced with the remark that Jesus sighed deeply in his spirit (ἀναστενάξας τῷ πνεύματι αὐτοῦ).[99] Then Jesus asks why this generation seeks a sign. The question is followed by the pronouncement, introduced through ἀμὴν λέγω ὑμῖν, that no sign will be given it. The generation is probably not an extension to the contemporaries of Jesus but a description of the faithless Pharisees who are the ones seeking a sign.[100] The Matthean redaction presses this point much further.

Mark concludes in v. 13 with the departure of Jesus. It contains the reference to Jesus leaving the Pharisees, but also mentions his embarkation and departure for the other side of the lake.

Matthew has expanded Mark's narrative only slightly. On the formal level, Matthew has distinguished the setting and the question of the opponents more

---

[96] According to Gundry, this wordplay emphasizes the contest between Jesus and the Pharisees. Gundry only sees συζητεῖν and ζητοῦντες as the wordplay and does not include the pronomina. Gundry: *Mark*, 401.

[97] The Pharisees are described as tempters (πειράζοντες), putting the Pharisees on the side of Satan. See 1:12–13, and Gundry: *Mark*, 404. Martin thinks that the Pharisees want to entice Jesus to sin. Ralph P. Martin: *Mark: Evangelist and Theologian* (Grand Rapids: Zondervan, 1973), 168–169. However, in 1:12–13 the temptation of Satan is not defined as such an enticement. More probable is the demand for a prophetic or messianic legitimation. Gnilka: *Markus*, 2:306. Such a legitimation would be different from 1:12–13, where the temptation of Jesus is not clearly defined in its purpose.

[98] See Mk 13:4. Similarly, in 13:22 the signs are distinguished from miracles (τέρατα). Usually, Mark refers to miracles of Jesus as δύναμεις. The longer ending of Mark refers to σημεῖα as miracles of the disciples attending their missionary activity (16:17, 20), but the longer ending is usually regarded as a later addition.

[99] Gundry sees this groaning as "gathering and concentrating inner power to make a pronouncement prophetically heavy with judgment." Gundry: *Mark*, 404.

[100] Against Gnilka, who cites the parallel of the generation of the flood (Gen 7:1) and of Moses (Ps 95:10). This generation "meint jeweils das lebende Geschlecht in seiner sich dem Anspruch Gottes verweigernden Haltung ..." Gnilka: *Markus*, 2:307. Thus the Pharisees would represent "this generation." But the text itself makes no explicit reference to an extension to the contemporaries of Jesus. Furthermore, Mark uses the term often in a more limited sense: In 8:38 the term seems to exclude disciples of Jesus who are not ashamed of him; in 9:19 it might just be a reference to faithless disciples failing to cast out a demon. Consequently, "this generation" may just refer to the Pharisees here. Gundry: *Mark*, 4–6.

clearly. Another emphatic Matthean redaction is the more aggressive answer of Jesus that changes the Markan question into a statement that this generation is evil and adulterous. The Markan distinction between the question and the pronouncement of Jesus, separated by "amen I tell you," disappears in Matthew. Instead, the answer of Jesus is more clearly unified. Since Matthew uses this controversy story of Mark twice, his intent to discredit the opponents of Jesus is quite clear. Mark's version is less clear in applying the epithet "generation" to the Pharisees. But it is quite possible that Matthew understood Mark in this way. Thus the editorial activity of Matthew does not re-invent the story, but it does sharpen it.

3.2 Summary of the Matthean Redaction in 16:1–4

The Matthean redaction of this pericope is slight and only sets a few accents different from Mark's version:

- ▶ Matthew's version is briefer. The second use of this controversy accentuates the malignance of the opponents.
- ▶ The portrait of the opponents of Jesus is more severely critical.
- ▶ Matthew more clearly separates the leaders of Israel from the crowds.
- ▶ Matthew adds the reference to the sign of Jonah.

4. Matthew 19:3–9

With the beginning of ch. 19 Matthew ends the discourse on the ordering of the church (Mt 18) with his usual concluding formula (19:1–2). This time it is slightly amplified to include a short summary of the healing activity of Jesus and a reference to large crowds who follow Jesus. The conclusion follows Mk 10:1, with the exception of Matthew's reference to the healing activity.[101] The impression arises that Jesus is a successful teacher and healer who attracts many followers.[102] Now Jesus leaves Galilee, never to return. His efforts now take place in Judea and move toward Jerusalem.[103] As seen before, this picture of the successful ministry of Jesus

---

[101] Mk 10:1 reports that Jesus "taught, as was his custom." Matthew probably omits the reference to teaching since he just concluded a teaching discourse. Thus Matthew reports Jesus as healing, as he does in most of his summaries (cf. 4:23–25; 9:35–38; etc.). The same change occurred in 14:14 || Mk 6:34. Gundry rightly regards ἐθεράπευσεν as a Mattheanism which serves as authentification of the instructions of ch. 18. Gundry: *Matthew*, 376.

[102] Matthew seems to heighten the success of the ministry of Jesus against Mark. In Mk 10:1, crowds gather to Jesus. Matthew 19:2 adds πολλοί, and the crowds follow Jesus. Matthew no longer says that Jesus healed some from among the crowds (14:14), but seemingly heals them all. Thus he achieves a portrayal of the crowds as disciples. Gundry: *Matthew*, 376.

[103] In Mk 10:1, the region beyond the Jordan and Judea are distinct. Matthew omits this distinction so that the impression arises that Judea, in Matthew's eyes, extended east of the Jordan. Gnilka: *Matthäus*, 2:151. While this seems incorrect in terms of political administration, some

is interrupted by a controversy (Mt 19:3–9). This time, Pharisees come to challenge Jesus over the practice of divorce and its regulation in the Mosaic law that has its source in Mk 10:2–12.

The redaction of Matthew follows Mk 10:2–12 closely, but makes several significant changes in the structure of the story. The order of argument changes, first citing Genesis, then answering the Mosaic regulation of divorce. The result is that Matthew can begin the answer of Jesus with οὐκ ἀνέγνωτε, a much more forceful counter-accusation of Jesus.[104] In order to introduce the Mosaic rule Matthew has the Pharisees ask a question that tries to counter the argument from Genesis. Finally, Matthew uses the saying concerning the adulterousness of divorce in the controversy with the Pharisees, not in the discussion with the disciples, as Mk 10:10–11 does. Matthew uses the framework of the instruction of the disciples to introduce his own saying of the eunuchs for the sake of the kingdom (19:10–12). Thus the question of divorce is dealt with entirely in the framework of the controversy with the Pharisees, while the disciples are the object of an instruction on the issue of celibacy.

In v. 3 Matthew begins, following Mk 10:2, with the approach of the Pharisees, and inserts αὐτῷ.[105] He moves πειράζοντες αὐτόν forward and thus ends the exposition with the question of the Pharisees. The question itself, as in Mark in indirect discourse, has ἀνθρώπῳ for ἀνδρί, uses the definite article with the wife, and adds the possessive pronoun. Matthew then amplifies the question with the phrase κατὰ πᾶσαν αἰτίαν. While the grammar is ambiguous to whether the phrase is supposed to mean "for any reason" or "for every reason" the context favors the latter alternative.[106] With this change Matthew signals that the question is not concerned with the general permissibility of divorce, as was the case in Mark. Matthew's version of the Pharisaic question aims at the possible grounds for divorce and thus hones in on the problems posed by the law.[107] The answer of Jesus

---

evidence shows that Judea was sometimes regarded as extending to the east of the Jordan, perhaps because of the number of Jews living in the area (Strabo: *Geography*, 16. 2,21; Tacitus: *Histories*, 5. 6). However, Matthew is interested in the fact that Jesus turns toward Judea now, regardless of the geographical intricacies. Hagner: *Matthew 14–28*, 543.

[104] Matthew is fond of this phrase: see 12:3; 12:5; 19:4; 22:31. It occurs only in controversies.

[105] Gundry sees this as evidence for the stronger christological emphasis in Matthew. Gundry: *Matthew*, 376.

[106] Hagner: *Matthew 14–28*, 547.

[107] Hagner: *Matthew 14–28*, 547; Gnilka: *Matthäus*, 2:152. Gnilka places the controversy in the context of "Gemeindeproblematik." While it is quite possible that the question of divorce occupied the community of Matthew to some extent, the passage here treats it in the context of a controversy with people outside of that community. The instruction of the disciples that follows in vv. 10–12 takes a different direction. Gnilka also states that this question "visiert die mögliche Ausnahme an." Gnilka's formulation is informed by the answer of Jesus. However, the Pharisees give no indication of an exemption to a rule. For them, divorce is taken for granted, and the question reveals this. Thus their question shows the chasm between Jesus' answer and the Pharisees' opinion, it does not anticipate Jesus' answer. Gnilka thinks that the answer changes

shows how wide the distance between the two parties of the controversy has become.

Jesus answers with the reference to Genesis found in Mk 10:6–9. He prefaces this reference with the phrase οὐκ ἀνέγνωτε (19:4). As earlier in 12:1–8, the Pharisees are shown to be deficient in their knowledge of scripture and its interpretation. The reference to Gen 1:27c (5:2); 2:24 and its interpretation (19:4–6) is an almost verbatim rendering of Mk 10:6–9.[108] Thus the first answer of Jesus does not really bear on the question, but summarizes his teaching on the insolubility of marriage.[109] Matthew points out that the Pharisaic question is really beside the point. The Pharisees are shown to be deficient in two respects. Firstly, they do not know their scriptures well. Secondly, their spotty knowledge of the scriptures reveals their deeper misunderstanding: If they had known Genesis they would not have asked about reasons for divorce. Gen 2:24 shows, in Matthew's interpretation, both that divorce is not possible, and that the Pharisees are inept interpreters of the Law. Matthew achieves this picture of the Pharisees not so much by redacting the answer of Jesus, but by redacting the question of the Pharisees.

The synoptic argument is somewhat surprising. After all, the texts in Genesis speak about creation more than they speak about the ordering of marriage. In a sense, the Pharisees in their appeal to Moses offer the more predictable interpretation of marriage law. However, the Qumran community offered a similar interpretation of Gen 1:27 to support its ruling on marriage.[110] In the Qumran

---

the connotation of the tempting of Jesus. He maintains that in Mark the Pharisees want to tease Jesus into an answer against the Law. In Matthew the tempting only connotes the general disbelief of the Pharisees. In this Gnilka is probably correct. While the question of the Pharisees shows how far they are from faith in the teaching of Jesus, the reference to the temptation also qualifies the position of the Pharisees as evil.

[108] The changes are: Matthew inserts ὅτι following "have you not read," exchanges the Markan κτίσεως for ὁ κτίσας. In v. 5 he inserts καὶ εἶπεν referring to the creator (cf. 15:4), against Gundry, who sees Jesus as the speaker here. Gundry: *Matthew*, 378. Matthew uses ἕνεκα instead of ἕνεκεν, omits the possessive pronoun after "father", and uses κολληθήσεται πρός instead of προσκολληθήσεται πρός. In v. 6 Matthew puts μία at the end of the sentence to make the parallel with v. 5. In Mk 10:7 there is a text-critical problem concerning the phrase καὶ προσκολληθήσεται πρὸς τὴν γυναῖκα αὐτοῦ. The manuscripts do not give decisive evidence to the presence or absence of the phrase. It could be an interpolation prompted by Matthew 19:5 and the LXX of Gen 2:24. On the other hand, a scribal omission by jumping from καί to καί is possible as well. Metzger: *Textual Commentary*, 88–89. The use of προσκολληθήσεται πρός shows Markan diction, but it is impossible to decide the issue definitively. Furthermore, the issue is only marginal to the interpretation of Matthew.

[109] Gnilka: *Matthäus*, 2:152.

[110] See *CD* 4,20: " The 'builders of the wall' (Ezek 23:10) who have followed after 'Precept' – 'Precept' was a spouter of whom it is written, *They shall surely spout* (Mic 2:6) – shall be caught in fornication twice by taking a second wife while the first is alive, whereas the principle of creation is, *Male and female He created them* (Gen 1:27)."

document, the text is used to undergird their teaching of monogamy for life.[111] For Matthew, the text is used to illustrate the will of God. Through his creation God made clear that it is his will that man and woman be "one flesh." The phrase has an entirely positive connotation.[112] Matthew uses the interpretation of Genesis to establish the principle of the indissolubility of marriage. The Pharisaic counter-argument based on the Law of Moses becomes subsidiary to the principle of creation. As the principle does not allow for divorce, the Mosaic Law can then be used to show that the opponents of Jesus are less than perfect: The regulation of divorce by letter of dismissal was made because of their hardness of heart. For this reason, Matthew's use of Genesis as the first argument in his narrative is essential to his portrayal of the Pharisees: unfaithful and deviating from the purpose of God established in the order of creation.

Thus in v. 7 Matthew, unlike Mark, does not have Jesus ask about the Mosaic law.[113] Instead, the Mosaic ruling is presented as a counter-argument against Jesus. The Markan Pharisees who know the Law disappear. Instead, Matthew's Pharisees show themselves obstinate toward the teaching of Jesus. They ask the question why Moses commanded that a certificate of divorce be given. Matthew's phrasing is slightly different from Mk 10:4 because it is in the form of a question.[114] More significant is the Matthean use of ἐνετείλατο for ἐπέτρεψεν in Matthew 19:7. For Matthew it is important that here the Law is in view, and so he uses a technical term. But there is also a more decisive difference: Matthew is inspired here by Mk 10:5: ἔγραψεν ὑμῖν τὴν ἐντολὴν ταύτην. In 19:8 however, Matthew writes in the response of Jesus that Moses ἐπέτρεψεν ὑμῖν. He thus reverses the word order in Mark: In Mark, the Pharisees use the word "permit" while Jesus speaks of a "commandment." In Matthew, this is reversed: Jesus speaks of "permission," while the Pharisees speak of "command."

This seemingly slight change indicates how Matthew views the exchange with the Pharisees. The Pharisees look at the rule of Moses as a commandment that can be used against the argument of Genesis. Matthew looks at Moses' rule as a

---

[111] Gnilka cites this parallel and continues: "Eine gemeinsame Grundlage ist kaum in Zweifel zu ziehen." Gnilka: *Matthäus*, 2:153. Yet just because the *CD* and the synoptic gospels offer a similar application of Gen 1:27 one cannot infer a common tradition. The synoptic gospels use Gen 2:24, a passage missing in *CD* 4,20. Furthermore, the brunt of the argument in the gospels lies on Gen 2:24, not 1:27. Consequently, it seems easier to assume that the synoptic interpretation reflects one of the possible strands of interpretation current at the time, while the Pharisees obviously represent another.

[112] Paul uses the same phrase in a negative way in 1 Cor 6:16. There it denotes immoral sexual intercourse which is opposed to becoming "one spirit" with the Lord (6:17).

[113] See the Markan arrangement: In Mk 10:3 Jesus asks about the Mosaic Law, but in 10:5 he has to explain that it was for their hardness of heart, and only in 10:6 does Jesus finally get around to the real argument of the principles of Gen 1:27; 2:24.

[114] Matthean are: τί οὖν, the clarification that eliminates γράψαι for δοῦναι and thus explains that the divorce certificate stays with the woman.

permission that says more about the Pharisees' hard heart than it says about God's will. But the small change also shows Matthew's difficulty with the easy dismissal that Mark accorded the Mosaic Law. Matthew is not at all interested in changing the Law, and therefore he changes the technical term in Jesus' answer. In Matthew Moses permits an exception, he does not command divorce.[115] And because it is an exception, Matthew inserts a repetitious allusion to the principle of Genesis to bring the point home: "From the beginning it was not so."

With 19:9 Matthew concludes the controversy by repeating in shortened form the teaching he gave already in 5:31–32. Matthew leaves out 5:31, and the reference in 5:32 to ποιεῖ αὐτὴν μοιχευθῆναι. He keeps the statement, already in Mk 10:11, that anyone divorcing his wife and remarrying commits adultery.[116] Through the omission of ἐπ' αὐτήν the saying achieves a more general character; adultery is not tied up with the former wife, but stands on its own. But Matthew does insert μὴ ἐπὶ πορνείᾳ and thus parallels 5:32.[117] Matthew also generalizes the prohibition of divorce further by omitting the reference from 5:32 (ἐὰν ἀπολελυμένην). Consequently, in 19:9 any remarriage is considered adulterous, while in 5:32 the marriage of a divorced woman was considered adulterous. Thus the point of 19:9 is very different from 5:32. In 5:32 Matthew dealt with the prohibition of divorce from the woman's point of view: she becomes the adulteress, while the guilt of the man consists in making her one. Only the marriage to a divorcee makes also the man an adulterer. In 19:9 the man's point of view is considered; his divorce and remarriage constitute adultery.[118] Thus Matthew leaves out Mk 10:12. The case proposed by the Pharisees assumes that men divorce their wives, but not the other way around. This is certainly a reflection of Jewish practice at the time[119] and fits well with the situation of controversy with the Pharisees.

---

[115] Gundry: *Matthew*, 380.

[116] The Matthean redaction includes the shifting of this saying into the controversy story, whereas Mark reports it as an instruction of the disciples. Thus Matthew has λέγω δὲ ὑμῖν instead of καὶ λέγει αὐτοῖς. He inserts ὅτι and μὴ ἐπὶ προνείᾳ, and he omits ἐπ' αὐτήν.

[117] The wording there is slightly different: παρεκτὸς λόγου πορνείας. Some manuscripts assimilate 19:9 to 5:32 (P²⁵ B D f^1.13 and others), but this reading is not attested to an extent that would question the present version. Gundry: *Matthew*, 381.

[118] The differences between 5:31–32 and 19:9 lead Luz to claim that Matthew knew of two different versions of the prohibition of divorce. Luz: *Matthäus*, 1:269.

[119] The literature on this issue is rather large. For a sampling, see: David W. Amram: *The Jewish Law of Divorce According to the Bible and Talmud*, 4th ed. (New York: Hermon, 1968); Ludwig Blau: *Die jüdische Ehescheidung und der jüdische Scheidebrief: Eine historische Untersuchung*, 2 vols (Straßburg: Trübner, 1911–1912); Daube: *New Testament and Rabbinic Judaism*, 71–86; Boaz Cohen: *Jewish and Roman Law: A Comparative Study*, 2 vols. (New York: Jewish Theological Seminary of America, 1966), 1:377–408; Joseph A. Fitzmyer: "Divorce Among First-Century Jews," *ErIs* 14 (1978): 103–110; Irwin H. Haut: *Divorce in Jewish Law and Life*, Studies in Jewish Jurisprudence 5 (New York: Sepher-Hermon, 1983); Emil Schürer: *The History of the Jewish People in the Age of Jesus Christ (175 B.C. – A.D. 135)*, 4 vols., ed. Geza Vermes, Fergus Millar and Martin Goodman (Edinburgh: T. & T. Clark, 1973–1987), 2:485–486.

But the redaction of Matthew achieves still a further end. With the move of the saying into the controversy Matthew avoids the Markan situation of the disciples challenging Jesus' teaching. Thus Matthew restricts the opposition to Jesus' teaching on divorce to the Pharisees. The disciples receive further instruction, as in Mark, but 19:10–12 only notes the disciples' somewhat disappointed acceptance of this teaching, while the further instruction regards the eunuchs of the kingdom.

The Pharisaic argument of the letter of divorce refers to Deut 24:1–4.[120] The wording in this passage is ambiguous and depends to a large extent on the issue of indecency (עֶרְוַת דָּבָר) in 24:1. The phrase is attested only once more in the Hebrew Scriptures (Deut 23:14); there it does not refer to an infraction of a sexual nature.[121] The meaning of עֶרְוַת דָּבָר can refer either to a general offense given to the husband,[122] or specifically to sexual misconduct. The history of its interpretation reflects both the specific and the general interpretation.[123] In later Jewish writings, a growing tendency advocates the complete prohibition of divorce.[124] But other traditions seem to have favored a liberalization of divorce procedures. Among the rabbis these two tendencies were embodied by the schools of Hillel and Shammai.[125] The differing interpretations of Hillel and Shammai hinge on the interpretation of Deut 24:1 as either general or specific. In the general interpretation, indecency can

---

[120] Deut 24:1–4 "When a man takes a wife and marries her, if then she finds no favor in his eyes because he has found some indecency (עֶרְוַת דָּבָר) in her, and he writes her a bill of divorce and puts it in her hand and sends her out of his house, and she departs out of his house, 2 and if she goes and becomes another man's wife, 3 and the latter husband dislikes her and writes her a bill of divorce and puts it in her hand and sends her out of his house, or if the latter husband dies, who took her to be his wife, 4 then her former husband, who sent her away, may not take her again to be his wife, after she has been defiled; for that is an abomination before the LORD, and you shall not bring guilt upon the land which the LORD your God gives you for an inheritance."

[121] In Deut 23:12–14, the phrase refers to uncovered human excrement: "You shall have a place outside the camp and you shall go out to it; 13 and you shall have a stick with your weapons; and when you sit down outside, you shall dig a hole with it, and turn back and cover up your excrement. 14 Because the LORD your God walks in the midst of your camp, to save you and to give up your enemies before you, therefore your camp must be holy, that he may not see anything indecent (עֶרְוַת דָּבָר) among you, and turn away from you."

[122] The LXX translates עֶרְוַת דָּבָר as ἄσχημον πρᾶγμα. This reflects probably a decision of the translators to interpret the Hebrew phrase in a wider sense. The Greek might point to some legal matter as grounds for divorce, as in Susannah 63 (Theodotion): Χελκιας δὲ καὶ ἡ γυνὴ αὐτοῦ ᾔνεσαν τὸν θεὸν περὶ τῆς θυγατρὸς αὐτῶν Σουσαννας μετὰ Ιωακιμ τοῦ ἀνδρὸς αὐτῆς καὶ τῶν συγγενῶν πάντων ὅτι οὐχ εὑρέθη ἐν αὐτῇ ἄσχημον πρᾶγμα. Betz: Sermon, 247.

[123] For a survey see: Blau: Ehescheidung, 10–31; Berger: Gesetzesauslegung, 508–575.

[124] Mal 2:13–16, with the pronouncement that God hates divorce; Jub 3:4–8; 17:14; Sap 14:26; Sir 7:26; 28:15, yet different in 25:26; CD 4:20.

[125] See m.Git. 9, 10: "The school of Shammai say: A man may not divorce his wife unless he has found unchastity in her, for it is written, Because he hath found in her indecency in anything. And the school of Hillel say: [He may divorce her] even if she spoiled a dish for him, for it is written, Because he hath found in her indecency in anything." The translation is that of Herbert Danby: The Mishnah (Oxford: Oxford University Press, 1933), 321.

be anything that is not pleasing to the man, while in the specific interpretation indecency is of a particularly sexual notion.[126]

The difficulty for the interpretation of Jesus' answer in Matthew rests with the phrase μὴ ἐπὶ πορνείᾳ and the exact meaning of πορνείᾳ. A number of explanations are possible. Firstly, it could mean adultery, a wife's illicit sexual relation with a partner other than her husband.[127] Concomitant with the broader Hellenistic use of the word it could also refer to some general sexual misconduct.[128] If this is so, then the teaching of Jesus would basically agree with the teaching of Shammai. However, it can be objeced that Matthew seems to make a distinction between πορνεία and μοιχεία even in this passage, and the penalty for adultery in Deut 22:22 is not divorce but death. These objections are countered by the fact that the wider range of sexual offenses that might be included in πορνεία could very well account for the distinction between πορνεία and μοιχεία. Furthermore, there is considerable evidence that the death penalty for adultery was not strictly enforced during the first century, but replaced by compulsory divorce.[129]

A second possibility for the meaning ot πορνεία is a variation of the first in that it would refer to premarital unchastity.[130] Then Deut 22:13–21 would apply as frame of reference. Again the punishment for such an offense would have been death. However, Matthew describes a similar situation at the beginning of the gospel when Joseph considers sending Mary away without fuss (1:19). This interpretation explains well why the term μοιχεία is not used.[131] But it would seem odd for a community to formulate an exception to a general prohibition of divorce that would allow for pre-marital fornication but not post-marital adultery.[132] And a more generalizing understanding would make the choice of πορνεία equally understandable.[133]

---

[126]   The latter interpretation hinges on the meaning of עֶרְוַה. The word means "nakedness" or "pudenda" and thus influences the interpretation of Deut 24:1 to mean sexual indecency or adultery. Francis Brown et al.: *The Brown-Driver-Briggs Hebrew and English Lexicon. With an Appendix containing the Biblical Aramaic* (Peabody: Hendrickson Publishers 1997; reprinted from the 1906 edition), 788–789.

[127]   This would basically equate πορνεία with μοιχεία. Bauer has shown that in biblical Greek the μοιχ-root is mostly used to describe adultery perpetrated by men, while women's adulterous behavior is described with words of the πορν-root. Johannes B. Bauer: "Bemerkungen zu den matthäischen Unzuchtsklauseln (Mt 5,32; 19,9)," in: *Begegnung mit dem Wort: Festschrift für Heinrich Zimmermann*, ed. J. Zmijewski and E. Nellessen, BBB 53 (Bonn: P. Hanstein Verlag, 1980), 23–33. Matthew 19:9 predicates of a divorced and remarried man: μοιχᾶται.

[128]   Bauer, Arndt, et al.: *A Greek-English Lexicon*, 693.

[129]   Raymond F. Collins: *Divorce in the New Testament*, GNS 38 (Collegeville: Glazier, 1992), 191.

[130]   Anton Fridrichsen: *"Excepta fornicationis causa,"* SEÅ 9 (1944): 54–58.

[131]   Richard B. Hays: *The Moral Vision of the New Testament. A Contemporary Introduction to New Testament Ethics* (San Francisco: Harper, 1996), 354.

[132]   Guelich: *Sermon*, 204.

[133]   Hays: *Moral Vision*, 354.

A third possibility is the supposition that πορνεία refers to marriages prohibited by the provisions of Lev 18:6–18. These marriages would have been regarded as incestuous under the Law, but were legal under Hellenistic customs. With this assumption the Matthean text would parallel Acts 15:28–29 in its use of πορνεία.[134] The problem for the Matthean community would arise with the advent of converts from a Gentile environment that were already bound in such unions. Matthew then would require Gentile converts to abstain from such unions and seek a divorce. It would also imply that such a teaching would be far more restrictive than teachings current among the schools of either Hillel or Shammai.[135] However, the underlying reference to Leviticus does not quite fit with this presumed meaning. Lev 18 prohibits not just incest (6–18), but also intercourse during menstruation, adultery, homosexuality, and bestiality (19–23). Thus, if one assumes that πορνεία in Acts 15:28–29 and Matthew 19:9 refers to Lev 18, there is no reason to restrict its meaning to incestuous marriages.[136]

Thus not one of the three possible interpretations is entirely convincing. But it is probable that with the exception Matthew offers his community the possibility to allow for divorce on grounds related to sexual impropriety. The central statement of the pericope concerns the radical indissolubility of marriage. The exceptive phrase is logically a secondary element. Consequently, the exception can only

---

[134] Aidan Mahoney: "A New Look at the Divorce Clauses in Mt 5:32 and 19:9," *CBQ* 30 (1968): 29–38; Joseph A. Fitzmyer: "Matthean Divorce Texts and Some New Palestinian Evidence," *TS* 37 (1976): 197–226; Ben Witherington: "Matthew 5.32 and 19.9 – Exception or Exceptional Situation?" *NTS* 31 (1985): 571–576; Francis J. Moloney: "Matthew 19,3–12 and Celibacy. A Redactional and Form Critical Study," *JSNT* 2 (1979): 42–60. Mahoney argued that the Pharisees wanted to trap Jesus with the "insidious question ... directed toward the then current and divisive *cause célèbre* in this matter, the *affaire* Antipas-Herodias" (p.33). This assumes without question that the passage reports Pharisaic opposition to Jesus as it happened in the lifetime of Jesus. It does not answer why Matthew would have kept this for his community some 50 years later. Fitzmyer relates the use of πορνεία to the Qumran documents and assumes that the term here is a *terminus technicus* for marriages prohibited by Leviticus. Witherington offers a summary of the position.

[135] Moloney makes this point very strongly. Furthermore, he argues that the appeal to the incestuous marriages among Gentiles also provides an explanation for the eunuch-saying of 19:12. If in 19:3–9 Matthew makes a general argument concerning such marriages among Gentile converts, he then goes on to clarify in the eunuch-saying what the practical consequences for such people in the Matthean community are: They are required to live celibately. Moloney suggest this pericope as outlining the demands of radical discipleship. Moloney: "Celibacy," 46–48.

[136] Guelich adds another argument: "[H]ow could a community or an evangelist pursuing a more rigorous intensification of the Law than found among the rabbis require divorce in the case of the forbidden marriages of Lev 18:6–18 but exclude adultery that brought the death penalty in the Old Testament ... and required divorce among the rabbis?" Guelich: *Sermon*, 205; the argument is repeated by Hays: *Moral Vision*, 355. This argument is treacherous because it appeals to the theological program of Matthew. But the appeal could as easily be made by the proponents of the opposite argument: Because Matthew is so much more stringent in applying the exceptions for divorce he intensifies the Law.

explain itself through the destruction of the indissolubility. This seems to be given through sexual misconduct. Matthew's argument for the indissolubility of marriage rests on the two becoming one flesh. It is likely that the exception clause, then, refers to a transgression which destroys that unity and puts asunder what God has joined. This transgression is probably a denial of the unity of husband and wife by joining oneself to another flesh. Consequently, the exception referred to as πορνεία is probably adultery. If this is so, then Matthew has not really weakened his argument for the indissolubility of marriage. He still does not allow for divorce. The exception is merely a public acknowledgment of the fact that the unity of husband and wife is already destroyed through adulterous behavior.

The exception relates to a situation of the community in which the radical demands of discipleship were at odds with the realities of the community. The dependence of the passage on Mark with the appended exception seems to indicate that the Matthean community viewed the problem of divorce different from its Markan cousins on a practical level while, at the same time, keeping the principle behind the theology of marriage. Thus the exception, independent of its exact meaning, reveals a distinct "process of moral deliberation."[137]

This brief outline sets the controversy between Jesus and the Pharisees into context. Matthew advocates a narrow interpretation of the passage in Deuteronomy, and his addition of μὴ ἐπὶ πορνείᾳ seems to set him closer within the Jewish debate over divorce than Mark with the absolute impermissibility of divorce. The Pharisees represent the more liberal interpretation of divorce procedures. However, the Matthean prohibition of divorce is not a surprise to any informed Jewish audience. The debate was not new to them. Matthew's report of the controversy regarding divorce has its setting in Jewish debates over the issue. The mention of μὴ ἐπὶ πορνείᾳ clarifies that Matthew is concerned with the interpretation of the Deuteronomic עֶרְוַת דָּבָר. This nuance is lost in the Markan account. Matthew interprets Deuteronomy in the narrow sense, while the Pharisees are accused of poor knowledge and interpretation of the Law in the broader accusation. This controversy, then, positions the opposing factions squarely within Judaism. This argument is very weighty since Matthew used a Markan rendition of the story that lost the nuance of the argument already. Mark's interests with this story are elsewhere.

4.1 The Markan Pericope

Mark deals with the question of divorce after a short summary that connects Jesus' teaching activity with an inexact geographical orientation (10:1).[138] The treatment of divorce falls into two distinct scenes. The first is a controversy with the Pharisees (10:2–9) while the second contains an instruction of the disciples (10:10–12). The

---

[137] Hays: *Moral Vision*, 356.
[138] Gnilka: *Markus*, 2:70–71.

controversy is structured into a the question of the Pharisees (10:2), the counter-question of Jesus with its answer by the Pharisees (10:3–4) and the pronouncement of Jesus, illustrated with the reference to Gen 1:27 and 2:24 (10:5–9).

The initial question of the Pharisees is phrased in more general terms than in Matthew and prepares thus for the general answer of Jesus.[139] It is characterized as a question with which the Pharisees seek to tempt Jesus. The Pharisees want Jesus to commit himself to an answer that contradicts the Law of Moses.[140] Thus Jesus' counter-question asks for what is commanded (ἐνετείλατο) by Moses (10:3). And in his pronouncement Jesus refers to Deut 24:1 again as a commandment (τὴν ἐντολήν 10:5). Ironically, the argument of Jesus that divorce runs counter to the order of creation is, in fact, a repudiation of Jewish Law.[141] The commandment is written not because it is the word of God, but because it accommodates the hardness of hearts of Jesus' opponents (σκληροκαρδίαν ὑμῶν 10:5). Consequently, the argument from Genesis is not played against the argument from Deuteronomy as arguments from scripture that oppose one another, and where one is more important than the other. The contrast in Mark's account of the controversy lies in what is written by Moses ([Μωϋσῆς] ἔγραψεν 10:5) and what the will of God is embodied in creation (ἀπὸ δὲ ἀρχῆς κτίσεως ... ἐποίησεν 10:6). The contrast in 10:9 between what has been joined by God and what should not be separated by humans is already present in the contrast between the order of God's creation and the commandment of Moses' Law.

Mark does not make any attempt to save the integrity of the Law, and he seems quite unaware that the Mosaic regulation Deut 24:1 could be interpreted differently. For Mark the discussion of divorce is an occasion to show how Jesus, and consequently his community, have "broken" with the Law. The instruction to the disciples (10:10–12) bears this out. The disciples have difficulties understanding the pronouncement of Jesus, and so they ask him again in the privacy of the home.[142] The explanation that Jesus gives reflects a situation different from Matthew's: Mark accounts for a situation where it is not only possible for a man to divorce his wife,

---

[139] Mark does not mention κατὰ πᾶσαν αἰτίαν, but inquires to the general lawfulness of divorce, to which Jesus gives a general answer that does not allow for exceptions at all. Mark does not include μὴ ἐπὶ πορνείᾳ. Gnilka: *Markus*, 2:70.

[140] It does not matter much here whether the Pharisees are supposedly interpreting the Law narrowly or liberally. Since Judaism allowed for divorce in at least some cases, the question of the Pharisees is wrong in its assumptions. Gnilka: *Markus*, 2:71.

[141] Gnilka writes: "Der antijudaistische Charakter der Kontroverse ist offenkundig." Gnilka: *Markus*, 2:71.

[142] The phrase εἰς τὴν οἰκίαν denotes perhaps the instruction for the community, as Gnilka writes: "Das Schema der im Haus stattfindenden Sonderlehre für die Jüngerschaft ist in der Gemeindekatechese vorgeprägt." Gnilka: *Markus*, 2:69–70. Parallels are: 1:29; 2:15; 7:17; 9:28, 33; 14:3.

but also for a woman to divorce her husband.[143] Such a situation did not exist among Jews, but among a Gentile audience.[144]

Mark's treatment of the Law and of the situation of women attests to the situation of his audience within a Gentile environment. They did not feel bound by the Jewish Law. Therefore, Mark's appeal to the order of creation revealed in Gen 1:17, 2:24 cannot be rightly made as an appeal to Jewish Law. It does not matter to Mark whether the Pharisees know the Law or not. Equally unimportant is the possibility of arraying the argument from Genesis against the lesser regulation in Deuteronomy. The thrust of Mark's argument rests on the saying in 10:9. It closes the controversy powerfully. Furthermore, while the Pharisees disappear from the story, the disciples bring up the matter again. Thus the controversy which used the Jewish Law to make an argument about divorce here visibly becomes the background for an instruction for the gentile community.[145]

4.2 Summary of the Matthean Redaction in 19:3–9

Matthew's redaction of the controversy over divorce is extensive in it's re-positioning of the controversy in the context of an inner-Jewish debate.
- ▸ Matthew sets the controversy into the context of healings and of the admiration of the crowds.
- ▸ Matthew changes the Pharisaic question from one of the general permissibility of divorce to one about the possible grounds for divorce.
- ▸ Matthew emphasizes that Jesus knows the Mosaic Law.

---

[143] The variants in the manuscripts attest to the fact that the possibility of women divorcing their husbands was not widely accepted. The variants include: "if she divorces her husband and is married by another" (A vg sy^p.h, and the Majority text); "if she runs away from her husband and marries another" (D Θ f^13 etc.). These variants do not put much doubt on the present version, but attest to difficulties with the situation described in "if she divorces her husband and marries another."

[144] In the Greco-Roman world divorce was frequent and could be initiated by either partner in the marriage. Veyne writes: "Strictly speaking, it was not even necessary to notify an ex-spouse of the divorce, and cases are recorded in which husbands were divorced by their wives without their knowledge ... Divorce and remarriage were quite common." Paul Veyne: *The Roman Empire*, trans. A. Golhammer (Cambridge: Belknap Press of Harvard University Press, 1997), 34. For the legal and customary intricacies of divorce in the Greco-Roman world see Delling. He provides a detailed discussion with the concomitant references to authors in antiquity. Gerhard Delling: "Ehescheidung," in: *RAC*, ed. T. Klausner (Stuttgart: Hiersemann, 1959–), 4:707–719.

[145] Gundry writes concerning the progression from Pharisees to disciples: "But Jesus clamps [the arguments from scripture] together and draws an inference concerning that topic, an inference so powerful in its effect that the Pharisees vanish from the story." Gundry: *Mark*, 532. The argument presented here goes against Gnilka's view of the saying in Mk 10:11–12 as the Jesuanic saying which is the kernel of the tradition giving rise to the controversy story. Gnilka: *Markus*, 2:69–70. Yet it seems somewhat forced to assume that a saying which includes reference to Gentile practices of divorce is of the historical Jesus, while the community, whether Markan or pre-Markan, interpreted the saying in the light of the Jewish scriptures.

►   Matthew views the letter of divorce as an allowance for the hard heart of his opponents rather than a commandment in the Law.
►   Matthew removes the disciples from the controversy.
►   Matthew gives an exception to the general impermissibility of divorce in order to reflect the practice of his community.

5. Summary of Patterns in the Redaction of the Four Scattered Matthean Controversy Stories in Chapters 13–19

Matthew's redaction of the controversy stories treated in this chapter is congruent with the patterns established in chs. 9 and 12. Again Matthew restructures some of his material. In the story of Jesus' rejection in Nazareth Matthew creates a chiasm, in the controversy over ritual purity Matthew transposes material and integrates the whole story more successfully with the preceding narrative. The repeated controversy over the demand of a sign is more succinct, and in the story concerning marriage and divorce Matthew takes the objection of the disciples in Mark and attributes it to the opponents.

Matthew seemingly takes little interest in the rejection of Jesus at Nazareth. The redaction restricts itself mainly to the portrait of Jesus. Similarly, the demand for a sign is less redacted. However, Matthew's interest in the story can be deduced from its previous use. The controversies over purity and marriage are more thoroughly redacted to reflect the Matthean interests.

Matthew exhibits a clear interest in the Jewish Law. Thus he contains the argument over purity within the confines of the Law and resists the Markan trend to dismiss ritual purity entirely. The distinction between Pharisaic tradition and Jewish Law is clearer in Matthew than it is in Mark. Consequently, Matthew is adamant about the lawfulness of the praxis of his community. Similarly, Matthew reshapes the argument over the indissolubility of marriage to distinguish between what the Law commands and what Moses allows. These debates are shaped by Matthew to reflect on a situation where the community is in controversy with the Jewish leaders over the interpretation of the Law, but not over the general principle of the Law. Thus Matthew returns these debates to an inner-Jewish conflict and excises the elements that place the Markan versions outside of Judaism.

Accordingly, the community is portrayed as a community that keeps the Law faithfully. In keeping with this image Matthew can omit much of the explanatory material Mark provided in the controversy over purity. The opponents, however, become unfaithful to the Law because of their traditions as in the controversy over purity, or just unable to interpret the Law correctly, as in the controversy over marriage. The severity of the opponents failure is furthermore emphasized in the Matthean redaction of the controversy over the demand for a sign. In these stories the opponents are shown to undermine the foundations of Judaism while Jesus and his disciples emerge as the true adherents to the Law.

The portrait of Jesus in these stories receives greater dignity. Reacting to the opposition in Nazareth Jesus is not powerless but rather chooses to do few miracles. In the dispute over purity Jesus is shown to know the Law and to teach it as the word of God. Similarly the controversy over marriage portrays Jesus as versed in the Law and able to make distinctions that escaped his opponents.

Finally, the crowds play a less significant role here than they did in several previous controversy stories. In the controversy over the demand for a sign the crowds are more clearly distanced from the opposing parties than in Mark. The removal of the reference to the crowds, or to all Jews, is significant in containing the scope of the controversies. Jesus argues with the Jewish leaders, not with the Jewish people.

V. The Matthean Redaction of the Jerusalem Controversies

After the controversy over divorce Matthew continues to follow the Markan narrative sequence. The blessing of the children (19:13–15 || Mk 10:13–16) is followed by the account of the rich man and the teaching on discipleship (19:16–30 || Mk 10:17–31). Then Matthew inserts the parable of the laborers in the vineyard from his own special material (20:1–16), followed by a passion prediction and the request of Zebedee's sons (20:17–28 || Mk 10:32–45). The last incident before the entry into Jerusalem is the healing of two blind men (20:29–34 || Mk 10:46–52).

With ch. 21 Matthew begins the account of Jesus' stay in Jerusalem largely following Mark. This account can be divided into three parts with one chapter functioning as a narrative bridge: Chapters 21–22 (cf. Mk 11–12:37a) relate the final direct confrontation with the Jewish leaders. Chapter 23 (cf. Mk 12:37b–40) turns to an instruction of the crowds on the matter of the Jewish leaders. This is followed by chs. 24–25, an instruction to the disciples on the end of times (cf. Mk 13). Finally, chs. 26–28 (cf. Mk 14–16) relate the passion and resurrection of Jesus.

Chapters 21–22 are mainly concerned with Jesus' relationship to the leaders of Israel. These chapters begin with the entry of Jesus into Jerusalem (21:1–9 || Mk 11:1–10), but are dominated by six controversy stories (21:14–17; 21:23–27 || Mk 11:27–33; 22:15–22 || Mk 12:13–17; 22:23–33 || Mk 12:18–27; 22:34–40 || Mk 12:28–34; 22:41–46 || Mk 12:3–37a) that are interrupted by four parables: The parable of the fig tree: 21:18–22 || Mk 11:12–14, 20–26; of the two sons: 21:28–32; of the vineyard and its tenants: 21:33–46 || Mk 12:1–12; of the marriage feast and the guest without proper garment: 22:1–14 || Q 14:15–24. These parables are spoken to the leaders, who recognize that they are the target of these parables (21:45). As in Mark, the place of the controversies is the temple in Jerusalem where they end with the silencing of the leaders who no longer dare to ask Jesus questions (22:46).

In ch. 23 Matthew constructs a narrative connection between the controversy with the Jewish leadership and the instruction of the disciples. Chapter 23 is occasioned by Mk 12:37b–40. However, the charge against the leaders is greatly amplified by material from Q 11:39–52; 13:34–35 and from Matthew's own sources.[1] The characters in the narrative change. Jesus is still teaching in the

---

[1] Luz writes: "Mt hat aus seinen Quellen einzelne Verse benutzt, um einen ihnen gegenüber völlig neuen Text zu gestalten." Luz: *Matthäus*, 3:296.

Jerusalem temple, but his audience is now the crowds. Matthew typically inserts the disciples into the audience (23:1). Jesus' opponents become the object matter of the teaching. Jesus instructs crowds and disciples first about the hypocrisy of Pharisees and Scribes, then he turns to address them directly in the woes against them (23:13 || Q 11:52) and ends with a lament addressed to all of Jerusalem (23:37–39 || Q 13:34–35).

Chapters 24–25 (cf. Mk 13) contain the second part of Jesus' activity in Jerusalem. Matthew turns his attention to a last instruction of the disciples in the discourse on the end of times. As in Mark Jesus is no longer in the temple, but just outside Jerusalem. The instructions begin already on the way out of Jerusalem (24:1 || Mk 13:1). For a last time Jesus ascends a mountain: the Mount of Olives becomes the setting for the last discourse (24:3 || Mk 13:3). Before the Matthean conclusion of the discourse on the end (26:1), Matthew inserts Q material with an eschatological outlook into the discourse: The parable of the flood (24:37–44 || Q 17:26–35), of the good and wicked servants (24:45–51 || Q 12:41–46), of the ten virgins (25:1–13), of the talents (25:14–30 || Q 19:12–27)[2] and of the last judgment (25:31–46). As in ch. 23, Matthew uses his sources creatively to shape the discourse on the end of times.

The third part of Matthew's account of Jesus in Jerusalem contains the passion (26:3–27:66 || Mk 14:1–15:47) and Matthew's account of resurrection of Jesus (28:1–15) ending with the resurrection appearance in Galilee and the mission of the disciples (28:16–20).

This structure of the account of Jesus' days in Jerusalem is thus already a given of Mark's story.[3] However, Matthew enlarges the Markan structure by inserting material from Q and from his own material.[4] Thus Matthew shows that the Markan structure was able to convey his own interests and themes within the frame of the

---

[2] A parallel in Lk 19:12–27 is highly debated as a Q text. Tuckett, after a summary of the discussion, opts to include the parable in Q. Tuckett: *Q*, 92–96. Arguments against the inclusion of this parable in Q include: (1) Except for the direct discourse the verbal agreement is minimal. (2) Even within the common expressions there are divergences which are not easily explained by editorial activities of either Luke or Matthew. (3) In both Luke and Matthew the parable appears outside of Q blocks. (4) The present text would be the only elaborate parable in Q. See Migaku Sato: *Q: Prophetie oder Weisheit?* WUNT 2.29 (Tübingen: Mohr, 1988), 22.

[3] Mk 11–12 recount the entry of Jesus into Jerusalem and are dominated by controversies and the accompanying parables. Mk 13 contains the instruction of the disciples on the Mount of Olives regarding the last days, while the passion commences with Mk 14.

[4] Leading up to the passion narrative, Matthew inserts the parable of the two sons (21:28–32), the parable of the wedding banquet and the man without proper garment (22:1–14 || Lk 14:15–24), some of the instructions to the disciples (23:8–12), expands on the woes on the Pharisees and Scribes (23:13–26 || Mk 12:40 || Lk 20:47; 11:42–51), the lament over Jerusalem (23:37–39 || Lk 13:34–35), the parable of the flood and the time of the coming of the Son of Man (24:37–44 || Lk 17:26–36; 12:39–40), the parable of the good and of the wicked servant (24:45–51 || Lk 12:41–46), the parable of the ten virgins (25:1–13), the parable of the talents (25:14–30 || Lk 19:11–27), the parable of the last judgment (25:31–46), the passion prediction (26:1–2).

last days of Jesus in Jerusalem. The redactional activity of Matthew in the account of the controversy stories of chs. 21–22 will show some of this interest.

1. Matthew 21:14–17

After the solemn entrance into Jerusalem Matthew alters the sequence of the Markan narrative slightly by skipping the account of Jesus spending the night in Bethany and his return to the temple the next morning with the cursing of the fig tree along the way (Mk 11:11b–14). Matthew chooses not to separate the event of Jesus' glorious entry into Jerusalem from his takeover of God's temple. He heightens the significance of the people's acclamation at the entry of Jesus with the immediate recounting of the cleansing of the temple. Then Matthew inserts Jesus' healing activity and another acclamation of the people. These give rise to a controversy story (21:14–17).

As Jesus enters Jerusalem the question of his identity is brought up once more (21:10). Jesus is once again described as a prophet by the crowds (21:11), while during the solemn entrance he was already described as the Son of David (21:9). Immediately the cleansing of the temple follows (21:12–13 || Mk 11:15–17). Then Matthew constructs a controversy story (21:14–17) without parallels in Mark or Luke.[5] Thus the first Jerusalem controversy takes place on the day Jesus enters the city while in Mark the cleansing of the temple follows on the next day. From the beginning Matthew characterizes the ministry of Jesus in Jerusalem as controversial. Consequently, Matthew elaborates the hostile thrust of Mark's remark immediately following the cleansing of the temple that the chief Priests and Scribes sought to destroy Jesus (Mk 11:18) by replacing it with the controversy in Matthew 21:14–17. Matthew delays their counsel to put Jesus to death until after the last passion prediction (26:1–5).

The controversy proper begins with the statement that blind and lame people came to Jesus in the temple, and Jesus healed them (21:14). This activity of Jesus underlines his identity as the Son of David who was acclaimed during the solemn

---

[5] Contra Gundry. He assumes that in v. 16 "Matthew seems to revise some traditional material that appears also in Lk 19:39–44 (esp. vv. 39–40) just *before* Jesus' entry into Jerusalem ..." Gundry: *Matthew*, 414. This is, on the whole, not convincing. The opponents in Lk 19:39–40 are Pharisees, their opposition is worded differently, and the retort of Jesus is different in its allusion to Habakkuk 2:11. Gundry needs to import the children from the different context of 19:44, where they are described as τέκνα, while Matthew uses παῖδες. Thought to its logical end, the hypothesis of Gundry would assume that Luke preserves material of the tradition in 19:39–44, which Matthew then adapted for the present controversy. However, in the process Matthew would have shifted the context of the quarrel with the Pharisees, the persons who acclaim Jesus, and he would have dropped Lk 19:41–44 completely. This is too much to ask of such divergent material. Context and vocabulary show such differences between Luke and Matthew that no literary dependence or connection can still be shown persuasively.

entrance (21:9).[6] In 9:27 two blind men call Jesus "Son of David," in 20:30–31 the two blind men along the road from Jericho appealed to Jesus in the same way. Up to this point in the narrative Matthew applies the title to Jesus mostly in the context of healings.[7] Thus it is no surprise when the children in the temple witness the healings and call Jesus "Son of David" again (21:15). These children, and before them the blind men of 9:27 and 20:30–31, formulate a response to Jesus that stands in stark contrast to the rejection of Jesus at the hand of the Jewish leadership. This contrast was already highlighted in 12:22–24. In this pericope it returns again. In this way the controversy becomes an introduction to the discussion of the title in 22:41–46. The controversy stories of chs. 21–22 are thus unified in a thematic inclusion.[8]

Matthew does not comment on the presence of the blind, lame, and children in the temple (21:14: ἐν τῷ ἱερῷ) as unusual. Jewish custom of the time restricted their access to the temple significantly.[9] Perhaps one is to think of the maimed in the

---

[6] Hagner: *Matthew 14–28*, 601.

[7] Apart from the already mentioned occurrences in 9:27 and 20:30–31; the title is applied to Jesus in the genealogy, in 12:23 as a reaction of the crowd when Jesus heals a blind and dumb demoniac, in 15:22 the Canaanite woman appeals to Jesus with this title to ask for healing for her daughter. For a study on the connection between the Matthean use of "Son of David" and the healings see Dennis C. Duling: "The Therapeutic Son of David. An Element in Matthew's Christological Apologetic," *NTS* 24 (1977–1978): 392–410.

[8] Luz interprets the Matthean use of this title allegorically: "The 'little people' in Israel, then, recognize Jesus for what he is; they receive the miracles bestowed by the healing Messiah upon his people and respond to them. Opposite them stand, menacingly, the high Priests and Scribes, now in the precincts of their own temple (21:15–16). They will have absolutely nothing to do with the miracles of the Son of David ... Thus, the stories of Jesus' miracles, and the 'Son of David' title so closely connected with them, serve in Matthew's gospel to relate the conflict with Israel and hence the 'plot' of his story." Luz: *Theology*, 73–75. While Luz's analysis is persuasive, his conclusion is less than that. As Luz himself points out, it is Israel's leadership that rejects the title for Jesus, but those who acclaim him so are also Israelites. For Matthew, then, this conflict takes place within Judaism, between those little people of Israel and their leaders. The use of this title is certainly occasion for conflict in the gospel, but not "with Israel," but within her.

[9] See 2 Sam 5:8: "Therefore it is said, 'The blind and the lame shall not come into the house.'" The LXX translates: διὰ τοῦτο ἐροῦσιν τυφλοὶ καὶ χωλοὶ οὐκ εἰσελεύσονται εἰς οἶκον κυρίου. The formulation Mt 21:14 with its explicit mention of τυφλοὶ καὶ χωλοὶ ἐν τῷ ἱερῷ might be a direct allusion to this passage. See also Lev 21:18–19 for a similar prohibition with an expanded list of those prohibited in the temple. More contemporary sources from the Qumran community are even more restrictive: They do not allow the maimed any participation in the community of the saved; *1 QSa* 2:5–22: "And no man smitten with any human uncleanness shall enter the assembly of God; no man smitten with any of them shall be confirmed in his office in the congregation. No man smitten in his flesh, or paralyzed in his feet or hands, or lame, or blind, or deaf, or dumb, or smitten in his flesh with a visible blemish ... for the Angels of Holiness are with their congregation." Similar prejudices against the unclean and handicapped are expressed in *1 QM* 7:5–6; *CD* 15:15–17.

court of the Gentiles, the outer court.[10] But their presence is significant. It gives Matthew an opportunity to contrast Jesus with the Jewish leaders in a decisive manner: The leaders have introduced trade and commerce into the temple and have thus transformed it from a house of prayer into a den of thieves (21:13). Jesus acts decisively against this in two ways: he throws out the merchants and then turns his attention to the lame and blind whom he heals. Thus in a very practical way Jesus shows how the temple can become a house of prayer. For Matthew, the Jewish leaders have desecrated the temple, just as they earlier were guilty of abusing the Law. Jesus restores the temple to its rightful purpose, expressed in his healing activity. Through the healings of the blind and lame Jesus brings the temple into accord with the precept of 2 Sam 5:8 and restores a spotless people of Israel to the cleansed temple.[11] Thus the cry of the children "Hosanna to the Son of David!" (21:15) is not only the acclamation of the activity of Jesus as the healer of the blind and the lame, but also as the restorer of the temple and its people.

The chief Priests and Scribes are indignant at seeing the wonderful things (τὰ θαυμάσια). It is unlikely that these things only included the healing activity of Jesus.[12] The controversy is very closely connected with the preceding purging of the temple,[13] and the healing activity of Jesus is described only very briefly. Furthermore, Matthew uses the word θαυμάσια only here, while usually miracles are described as δυνάμεις.[14] Consequently, the θαυμάσια that Jesus works probably

---

[10] Hagner: *Matthew 14–28*, 600; Gnilka: *Matthäus*, 2:208. The scene of the healings in the temple follows immediately upon the protest of Jesus against the trading activity in the temple (21:21–13) and takes place in the same location; Matthew does not report Jesus moving to another place. Eppstein has argued that the High Priest Caiaphas had just recently introduced a market in the outer court of the temple in order to compete with several markets on the Mount of Olives that were run by the Sanhedrin. Victor Eppstein: "Historicity of the Gospel Account of the Cleansing of the Temple," *ZNW* 55 (1964): 42–58. This has been challenged because it is not clear why the chief Priests and Scribes should react so negatively to this action to the point of seeking to kill Jesus (Mk 11:18, 27–28), since they would have benefitted from Jesus' action. For a fuller critique of Epstein see Craig A. Evans: "Jesus' Action in the Temple: Cleansing or Portent of Destruction?" *CBQ* 51 (1989): 237–270. But regardless of the political intricacies behind the ownership of the market rights in the outer courtyard of the temple, the presence of traders there can be taken for granted. Consequently, the presence of blind and lame and children is perhaps not surprising, either.

[11] Hagner argues similarly, though less precisely: "The Messiah manifests the blessings of the kingdom precisely in the precincts of the temple ..., which is thereby transformed from a commercial center to a place of healing (one cannot but think of Matthew's earlier citation of Hos 6:6 [Matt 9:13; 12:7])." Hagner: *Matthew 14–28*, 601.

[12] Hagner: *Matthew 14–28*, 602; Gnilka: *Matthäus*, 2:208.

[13] Matthew uses καί to connect the two incidents one upon the other.

[14] Θαυμάσια is a hapax in the entire New Testament. Gundry surmises that it "makes a typically Matthean allusion to the OT, where it often appears in the LXX with ποιέω, as in the present verse." Gundry: *Matthew*, 413. This must remain speculation, since a hapax cannot be used to infer a Mattheanism. This is borne out by the Matthean use of the cognates. Θαυμάζω is inserted by Matthew only twice, in 15:31 and in 21:20. In both cases the verb denotes a reaction

included the cleansing of the temple, the healings, and the acclamation of the children.

The reaction of the Jewish leaders is specifically attributed to the chief Priests and Scribes.[15] The association between those two groups is already familiar to the reader[16] and thus probably not accidental. The first group that opposes Jesus in Jerusalem is the same that Herod called on to give him information on the birth of the Messiah (2:4).[17] There they knew about the origin of the Messiah but did not act on their knowledge. Furthermore, in the most recent passion prediction Jesus prophesied that it would be the chief Priests and Scribes who would put him to death (20:18). Now, just as at the beginning of the gospel, they are unable to interpret the wonderful things correctly, while the children in the temple precinct acclaim Jesus as the Son of David. The children show up the shortcomings of chief Priests and Scribes in interpreting the deeds and identity of Jesus. While the children acclaim Jesus, the Jewish leaders are vexed.

Verse 16 records very briefly the controversy dialogue. The leaders ask Jesus whether he hears what they are saying. Matthew deals with the authority of Jesus to cleanse the temple in a later controversy (21:23–27). The healings might be irksome to the authorities, but they are not contested. Thus the leaders pick on the chant of the children.[18] In this challenge the leaders oppose themselves to Jesus. But

---

to Jesus' deeds, in the former case healings, in the latter case the withering of the fig tree. Consequently, it is probable that θαυμάσια was chosen here because Matthew wanted to relate the reaction of chief Priests and Scribes not just to the miracles, but also to the cleansing of the temple. If Gundry is right in his assumption that the word here is prompted by θαυμαστή in 21:42 it is a further argument against the equation of θαυμάσια with miracles. In 21:42 θαυμαστή does not refer to miracles, but to the exaltation by God of the stone rejected by the builders. Schweizer constructs a more cogent argument for the restriction of the word to the miracles of Jesus. He points out that the quotation of Ps 8:3 is taken from the LXX without any changes. Furthermore, the term θαυμάσια "bezeichnet in der LXX Gottes Wundertaten." Hence, so Schweizer, the word refers to the healing of the blind and lame. Schweizer: *Matthäus*, 132–133. However, it is not clear why the reference to God's wonderful deeds in the LXX should exclude the cleansing of the temple. It is more likely that the both the cleansing of the temple and the healing of the maimed in the temple constitutes θαυμάσια both in the LXX sense of "Gottes Wundertaten" and for Matthew.

[15] Since Matthew omits Mk 11:18 and replaces the decision to put Jesus to death with the present controversy to follow on the cleansing of the temple, it is quite likely that Matthew used this grouping of chief Priests and Scribes because he found it in Mark. Gundry: *Matthew*, 413.

[16] See 2:4; 16:21; 20:18. Following this occurrence, the chief Priests are mentioned once more together with Scribes and elders (27:41; see also 16:21 for the same grouping); they are grouped only with the Elders (21:23; 26:3; 26:47; 27:1, 3; 27:12, 20), or with the Pharisees (21:45; 27:62), or with the Sanhedrin (26:59), and occur alone (26:14; 27:6; 28:11).

[17] Hagner: *Matthew 14–28*, 601.

[18] Hagner argues that the children had "little, if any, understanding of the meaning of their chant …" Hagner: *Matthew 14–28*, 602. This is not the point Matthew is trying to make. The leaders understand the implications of the acclamation, and therefore, bring it up in a challenge to Jesus.

the contrast between them and the children also becomes apparent. In a sense, the whole scene achieves an ironic twist in which the children arrive at some truth about Jesus while the Jewish leaders, who showed themselves knowledgeable about the king of the Jews in 2:2–6, do not recognize the Son of David here. Thus the children might be a Matthean metaphor for the community, to whom Jesus turned his loving attention before (18:2–10).[19]

The answer of Jesus is affirmative (ναί). He has heard what the children are saying and simply accepts their acclamation as Son of David without further explanation. Instead he accuses his opponents once more of lacking knowledge of the scriptures (οὐδέποτε ἀνέγνωτε).[20] The content is a quotation of Ps 8:3 (LXX).[21] The application of Ps 8 here finally gives the reason for the introduction of the children in v. 15 (ἐκ στόματος νηπίων).[22] The function of this quotation seems to be twofold. The children who were praising Jesus seem to be justified in their acclamations. By the same token, the Priests and Scribes are proven wrong in their indignation. The contrast between Israel and her leaders is once more accentuated. Just as Matthew contrasted the praise for Jesus during his solemn entrance into Jerusalem with the harsh criticism of the Jewish leaders during the cleansing of the temple, now in this controversy story the same praise for Jesus is contrasted with the indignation of the leaders. But as Jesus quotes the scripture, the leaders are proven wrong.

Secondly, the scripture quotation not only validates the shout of the children, but also emphasizes that this shout is validated by God himself. As the children acclaim Jesus, the Psalm makes it clear that this acclamation is not just child's play but a recognition of Jesus as the Son of David[23] endorsed by God himself. Consequently,

---

[19] Gnilka makes this connection. Gnilka: *Matthäus*, 2:208–209. If this association is legitimate, it might reflect Matthew's fascination with those humble as Jesus is humble (5:5; 11:29; 21:5). It also makes the connection with the revelation of the truth to νήπιοι in 11:25, where the babes stand for the Matthean community.

[20] Gundry claims that the phrase implies that the Priests and Scribes actually had read the passage. "Therefore, their unscriptural indignation stands condemned all the more." Gundry: *Matthew*, 414.

[21] The quotation is verbatim from the LXX. Instead of the word αἶνον the Hebrew has עֹז, meaning strength. For Hagner, this is an indication that the argument goes back to Matthew rather than Jesus. Hagner: *Matthew 14–28*, 602. This would accord with Stendahl's assessment that the Greek Psalter, or parts thereof, were part of the liturgy in the early Christian communities. Stendahl: *School of St. Matthew*, 134–135.

[22] A further argument against the hypothesis of Gundry that the children are a remnant of the tradition contained in Lk 19:44. Gundry: *Matthew*, 414.

[23] Davies and Allison argue that the point of the Psalm is not the acclamation of Jesus as Son of David but an allusion to Jesus as the New Moses. They argue that the same verse is used in *Sap* 10:21 in the context of the Exodus: When Israel crossed the Red Sea wisdom "made the babes speak clearly" (ὅτι ἡ σοφία ἤνοιξεν στόμα κωφῶν καὶ γλώσσας νηπίων ἔθηκεν τρανάς). The connection between Ps 8:3 and Ex 15 is further attested by the *Mekilta* on Exodus. Davies and Allison: *Matthew*, 3:142. If one discounts the evidence of the *Mekilta* as too late, the reference to

the introduction of the Psalm makes a christological statement. To acclaim Jesus as Son of David in the context of healings is a familiar feature in the gospel of Matthew. It takes on added significance, however, by its placement in the temple and underlines the fact that Jesus is the restorer and keeper of the temple, and not the Chief Priests and Scribes opposing him.

With the quotation of Ps 8:3 Matthew concludes the controversy story. In 21:17 he takes the sequence of Mark up again and reports Jesus going to Bethany to spend the night there (Mk 11:11b). However, Matthew edits this withdrawal significantly.[24] The abrupt departure might indicate a further note of condemnation of the chief Priests and Scribes.[25] Since Matthew does not mention the late hour which is the reason for Jesus' departure in Mk 11:11b, the departure is a comment on the preceding controversy. Matthew inserts that Jesus left his opponents (καταλιπὼν αὐτούς). He further clarifies that Jesus now is outside the city. While this local distance probably reflects the growing alienation between Jesus and Israel's leaders, Matthew does not portray the break with Jerusalem as final. The next day Jesus returns to Jerusalem, and the controversy stories continue.

With this first brief controversy story set in Jerusalem Matthew has established his narrative perspective. The Jewish leaders, although they remain in the temple, have shown themselves unworthy and inept guardians of the temple. On the other hand, Jesus was shown to be the true restorer of the temple, and to him the scriptures apply. Thus Matthew emphasizes right from the beginning of the Jerusalem controversies that his objective is the christologically motivated displacement of the Jewish leaders. He shows that for a true renewal, Judaism must listen to the children who acclaim Jesus as the Son of David. If others are left in charge, Judaism will come to ruin as the temple came to ruin under chief Priests and Scribes. Matthew establishes this theme right on the first day of Jesus' ministry in Jerusalem. The following controversies taking place in the temple precinct develop on this theme.

1.1 Summary of the Matthean Redaction in 21:14–17

The first of the Jerusalem controversies is a construct of Matthew that, together with 22:41–46, ties the conflict with the leaders of Israel together in an inclusion. The theme of this inclusion is the identity of Jesus and his rejection by the leaders. The Matthean redaction highlights this:

▸   Matthew constructs the controversy without the help of his sources.

Sap 10:21 cannot convince on its own strength since the parallel really only consists of the word νηπίων, albeit in a different construction, while στόμα is used with the blind. It is hard to imagine Matthew knowing the passage in Wisdom but foregoing the reference to the blind in this context. Thus Davies and Allison are mistaken. The endorsement of Ps 8:3 refers to the Son of David.

[24] Matthew omits Mark's mention of nightfall and the late hour. He also does not mention the Twelve. He inserts καὶ καταλιπὼν αὐτούς ... ἔξω τῆς πόλεως ... καὶ ηὐλίσθη ἐκεῖ.

[25] Hagner: *Matthew 14–28*, 602.

▶ Matthew ties together the deeds of Jesus in the cleansing of the temple and his healing activity with the admiration of the crowds and the acclamation of the children that he is the Son of David.

▶ The objection of Chief Priests and Scribes is occasioned by the deeds of Jesus on his first day in Jerusalem and voiced against the resulting acclamation by the children.

▶ Matthew's use of Ps 8:3 includes a high christological claim for Jesus.

▶ Jesus' reaction highlights the chasm between him and his opponents.

2. Matthew 21:23-27

After Jesus has spent the night in Bethany, he returns to Jerusalem, cursing a fig tree on the way. The fig tree becomes an opportunity for Jesus to teach on the efficaciousness about prayer (21:18-22). The next of the Jerusalem controversies follows immediately (21:23-27 || Mk 11:27-33) and concerns the authority of Jesus and the baptism of John. The redactional changes in Matthew are few. Matthew leaves out Mk 11:27a[26] The disciples disappear from the controversy.[27] The second day in Jerusalem begins with the cursing of the fig tree and continues with the controversies and parables in the temple.[28]

The setting of the scene in Matthew is slightly puzzling. On the one hand, he redacts Mark to show that the Chief Priests and Elders of the People approach Jesus as soon as he enters the temple.[29] On the other hand, Matthew also inserts the note that Jesus was already teaching (διδάσκοντι). Thus the Matthean setting of the scene shows the opponents of Jesus in a hurry to get to him, but also rude in interrupting him. While in Mk 11:27 a lingering Jesus is confronted by the opponents, in Matthew Jesus has taken up the active role of a teacher. He takes up the role he has assumed in the previous controversy story when he laid claim to replacing the leaders.

---

[26] "And they came again to Jerusalem."

[27] Mk 11:27: ἔρχονται.

[28] While the beginning of Jesus' ministry in Jerusalem seems tightly organized in terms of time and place, later on this organization is less strict. The second day consists of two parts: controversies, parables, and instructions in the temple (22:23-23:39), and the instructions of the disciples on the Mount of Olives (24:3-25:46). In between there is a short passage to mark the transition from Jerusalem to the Mount of Olives (24:1-2). The next indication of time is the remark that there are two days until Passover (26:2), while the next indication of location is the meal in the house of Simon the Leper in Bethany (26:6). Thus Matthew crams the ministry of Jesus in Jerusalem into two days.

[29] Mt 21:23 has ἐλθόντος εἰς, while Mk 11:27 has περιπατοῦντος ἐν.

Matthew omits the Scribes from Mark's list[30] and amplifies that the elders are "of the people."[31] The reference to the teaching of Jesus was probably important for Matthew in the context of the following controversy. In 7:29 the teaching of Jesus was described as the teaching of someone who possesses authority (ἐξουσία).[32]

The setting contains the major redactional activity of Matthew in the pericope. Other changes are mostly stylistic to allow for a greater balance in the narrative.[33] Two questions of the opponents are answered by two questions of Jesus.[34] The two questions of Jesus evoke two different possibilities in the deliberation of the opponents, marked by two clauses with ἐάν.[35] And the promise of Jesus κἀγὼ ὑμῖν ἐρῶ (21:24) is taken up again with οὐδὲ ἐγὼ λέγω ὑμῖν in 21:27. At the same time, it functions as an *inclusio* with the initial question of 21:23 through the

---

[30] Mk 11:27 mentions Chief Priests, Scribes, and Elders. The omission might be due to the fact that Matthew prefers the opponents of Jesus to appear either as one or as two groups. Matthew never has them occur as three different groups. Sand opines that the Scribes are omitted because the discussion does not concern the Law. Sand: *Matthäus*, 427.

[31] Matthew often refers to this group of Jewish leaders as πρεσβύτεροι τοῦ λαοῦ: 21:23; 26:3, 47; 27:1. Without the Genitive they are referred to in 16:21; 26:57; 27:12, 20, 41; 28:12. The Genitive is a redactional addition here, and in 26:47; 27:1. The Elders become more prominent in Jerusalem than they were before in the gospel. They become one of the main groups to push for the death of Jesus. Gnilka: *Matthäus*, 2:216.

[32] Gnilka: *Matthäus*, 2:216. However, in 7:29 the teaching of Jesus is contrasted with the teaching of the Scribes. Matthew omits the Scribes from this pericope. Thus the connection between 7:29 and 21:23 is not entirely convincing.

[33] In v. 23 Matthew changes Mk 11:28 καὶ ἔλεγεν αὐτῷ to λέγοντες. The Markan question of the opponents is made into a double question by substituting καί for ἤ. Matthew omits the clumsy ἵνα ταῦτα ποιῇς. In v. 24 Matthew inserts ἀποκριθείς, κἀγώ, and transposes to say λόγον ἕνα. He constructs a conditional relative clause with ὃν ἐάν to bring out more clearly the implication of the Markan construction with καί. He substitutes εἴπητε for ἀποκρίθητε, probably in order to parallel more closely the phrase οὐδὲ ἐγὼ λέγω ὑμῖν of 21:27. He inserts a second κἀγώ in order to create a parallelism, and takes ὑμῖν forward. In v. 25 the question of Jesus is clarified by inserting πόθεν ἦν. Consequently, Matthew has two questions instead of one. He omits the insistence of Jesus in Mk 11:30 ἀποκρίθητέ μοι. He substitutes οἱ δέ for καί to accentuate the contrast between Jesus and his opponents, and uses ἐν instead of πρός. He inserts ἡμῖν. In v. 26 Matthew uses ἐὰν δε for ἀλλά in order to parallelize the two alternatives in the deliberation of the opponents. For Matthew the fear of the opponents is part of their deliberation and thus parallelizes the second alternative more closely with the first. Consequently, Matthew uses φοβούμεθα instead of ἐφοβοῦντο. The identification of John as prophet is slightly altered to preserve it in direct discourse. Εἶχον becomes ἔχουσιν, and the clumsy Markan construction ὄντως ὅτι προφήτης ἦν is replaced by ὡς. This allows Matthew to move John to the end of the sentence. In v. 27 Matthew replaces the Markan historic present with εἶπαν and ἔφη, omits the name of Jesus and instead says καὶ αὐτός.

[34] Hagner: *Matthew 14–28*, 608. Gundry draws attention to the construction of the question of Jesus as a chiasm: a ἐρωτήσω, b ὑμᾶς, c κἀγώ, d λόγον ἕνα, d' ὃν ἐὰν εἴπητέ μοι, c' κἀγώ, b' ὑμῖν, a' ἐρῶ ἐν ποίᾳ ἐξουσίᾳ ταῦτα ποιῶ. Gundry: *Matthew*, 420.

[35] Gnilka: *Matthäus*, 2:215.

repetition of ἐν ποίᾳ ἐξουσίᾳ.[36] Matthew's narrative is more polished than its Markan counterpart.

The stylistic redaction of Matthew serves also to heighten slightly the portrait of Jesus as actively in command of the situation. The emphatic κἀγώ is inserted twice in 21:24[37] and corresponds to καὶ αὐτός in 21:27.[38] It is less probable that the inversion of word order to produce λόγον ἕνα ought to be seen in this light.[39] This heightening of the portrait of Jesus draws attention to the theme of authority that Matthew found already present in Mark's version of the story.

There is no question that Jesus in fact consistently acts with authority, as he has done before (7:29; 9:6; and again in 18:18).[40] Already in Mark, the opponents of Jesus in a way revive the old Beelzebul controversy by asking about the quality and origin of Jesus' authority.[41] Both questioners and location give the controversy an added urgency. The chief Priests and Elders are in charge of the temple, and they view Jesus as an intruder. Thus the actions of Jesus on the preceding day, the

---

[36] Hagner: *Matthew 14–28*, 609.

[37] Most Markan manuscripts insert κἀγώ before ὑμᾶς in 11:29. However, D W θ 28 565 it omit it, and so does NA[26]. If the Markan κἀγώ was absent, the parallel Lk 20:3 constitutes a minor agreement.

[38] Gnilka: *Matthäus*, 2:215.

[39] The phrase has a parallel in the LXX version of 2 Sam 3:13: καὶ εἶπεν Δαυιδ ἐγὼ καλῶς διαθήσομαι πρὸς σὲ διαθήκην πλὴν λόγον ἕνα ἐγὼ αἰτοῦμαι παρὰ σοῦ λέγων οὐκ ὄψει τὸ πρόσωπόν μου ἐὰν μὴ ἀγάγῃς τὴν Μελχολ θυγατέρα Σαουλ παραγινομένου σου ἰδεῖν τὸ πρόσωπόν μου. The Matthean parallel is perhaps striking, and has led some commentators to remark on it as expressing the christological function of drawing the parallel between David and Jesus. Lohmeyer: *Matthäus*, 306; Gnilka: *Matthäus*, 2:215. Davies and Allison merely point out the parallel without drawing christological conclusions. Davies and Allison: *Matthew*, 2:159. In the accusative case, this is the only parallel in the LXX. In the Nominative it occurs once more in 1 Kings 3:58. But in view of Matthew's freedom with Markan word order such a connection between the LXX and Matthew cannot be shown as inescapable. The parallel remains intriguing, but quite weak as an argument. However, if Matthew 21:14 can be viewed as an allusion to 2 Sam 5:8, the present possible parallel gains authority. In the end, the parallel is only one of two words out of a completely different context; the connection between 2 Samuel and Matthew is not an inevitable conclusion.

[40] See also 9:8; 10:1; 28:18 for this authority given to the disciples of Jesus.

[41] In the LXX, the word ἐξουσία renders the Hebrew מֶמְשָׁלָה and other derivatives of שׁלט and means right, freedom, permission in the juridical and civil sense. Such authority derives from God or from the Jewish Law. Werner Foerster: "ἔξεστιν κ.τ.λ.," *TDNT* 2:560–575. However, this use in the LXX is not consistent. Klaus Scholtissek: *Die Vollmacht Jesu: Traditions- und redaktionsgeschichtliche Analysen zu einem Leitmotif markinischer Christologie*, NTA 25 (Münster: Aschendorff, 1992), 31. It seems that a strictly legalistic view of the word cannot be sustained for Matthew, or the New Testament literature in general. Konrad Huber: *Jesus in Auseinandersetzung. Exegetische Untersuchungen zu den sogenannten Jerusalemer Streitgesprächen des Markusevangeliums im Blick auf ihre christologischen Implikationen*, fzb 75 (Würzburg: Echter, 1995), 46–52. However, the ironic nature of the pericope is partly underlined if one considers the legalistic meaning as at least implied.

cleansing and the healing, did not go unnoticed.[42] And his teaching is probably a further jab at the authority of Priests and Elders in the temple precincts[43] as he assumes a role they should fulfill. Jesus, then, riles the opponents by doing what they ought to be doing. He lodges his temple protest, and accuses them of having changed it from the house of God into a den of thieves. He heals in the temple, and it becomes an occasion for Jesus to expose their lack of knowledge of the scriptures. And now he teaches in the temple.[44] Thus Matthew's objection of the opponents to the authority of Jesus to do ταῦτα is cast wider than in his source Mk 11:28.

The conclusion of the controversy story follows Mark very closely. Jesus' answer (21:24–25) is more than a clever ploy to avoid an answer. It exposes the power of Jesus' actions and teaching by exposing the failure of Priests and Elders to give an authoritative teaching when asked for it. As in Mk 11:29–30 the leaders are given two choices for an answer, neither of them appealing. If they say that John's baptism was of divine origin, then the next question would be about their failure to believe him. In the context of the gospel this would mean that the leaders, if they believed in John, also needed to believe in Jesus, because John was the Elijah who preceded the Messiah (Mt 11:7–15; 17:11–13).[45] But the initial challenge of the leaders shows that they have closed that door already. Thus the first choice offered by Jesus is impossible for the opponents. Consequently, the second choice would be the honest one, to say that John's baptism was of human origin. However, in this the leaders fear the crowds who think otherwise. Thus they evade the question.

Ironically, the failure of the leaders to answer the question of Jesus gives an indirect answer to the quality and source of the teaching of Jesus.[46] The leaders fail to provide leadership. They fail to teach because of their own fears. In a sense, they fail to provide exactly what Jesus provides: teaching with authority. By exposing their own lack of authority, Jesus in effect assumes their place in the temple. As in the incident of the cleansing of and the healings in the temple Jesus again proves that he is that which the leaders assume to be, the rightful leader of the temple and, by extension, all the Jewish people. The chief Priests and the Elders, whom Matthew qualifies as τοῦ λαοῦ (21:23), loose their claim to true leadership of the people. As the chief Priests and Elders are shown to lack authority, Jesus is shown

---

[42] Hagner: *Matthew 14–28*, 609.

[43] Gnilka: *Matthäus*, 2:216.

[44] Thus Gnilka is right when he sees the main challenge to the "Lehre in Vollmacht." Gnilka: *Matthäus*, 2:216. However, this teaching with authority encompasses the deeds of authority of the preceding day. The verb ποιεῖς indicates that Jesus' teaching was not the only issue.

[45] Gnilka writes: "Johannes der Täufer ist in unserem Evangelium mit seiner Predigt, mit seiner Taufe und seinem Tod der Vorläufer Jesu. Er ist völlig auf Jesus hingeordnet." Gnilka: *Matthäus*, 2:217.

[46] Hagner points out how the teaching and authority of Jesus stand in direct continuity with that of John the Baptist. Hagner: *Matthew 14–28*, 609.

to carry the authority of God. This indirect answer to the question of Priests and Elders is, however, not accessible to them. In their failure to commit themselves to an answer, they cannot commit themselves to Jesus either. Hence it would be useless to give them a direct answer, and Jesus refuses to do so. As before, the Jewish leadership is exposed to the reader as inept and malevolent. They "do not know" (21:26).

2.1 The Markan Pericope

The controversy story[47] concerning the authority of Jesus occurs in the gospel of Mark after the return to Jerusalem (11:27–33). The disciples are mentioned in Mk 11:27, but disappear thereafter. Jesus walks around in the temple (περιπατοῦντος).[48] The Scribes are part of the opposition, alluding to the first passion prediction (8:31).[49] There is no explicit link with the cleansing of the temple, and thus the question of the opponents seems to regard the whole ministry of Jesus. On the other hand, the position of the narrative within the gospel of Mark seems to indicate that Mark viewed the objection as directed against Jesus' temple protest.[50] The

---

[47] Gnilka challenges the ususal supposition that the story is actually a controversy story in the proper sense. The starting point of his argument is the Rabbinic controversy story b.San. 65b. Gnilka asserts that Rabbinic controversy stories containing a counter-question use it to introduce an argument to which the opponents agree. For this reason the question concerning the baptism of John ought to elicit a positive answer, and not the indecision of the leaders that is actually found in Mark. Gnilka assumes that an original assent of the opponents was lost in the development of tradition. Gnilka: Markus, 2:136–137. Gnilka is probably stretching his evidence too far. The rabbinic evidence is considerably later in its final literary form, and thus should not be used to argue backwards concerning the literary form of Mk 11:27–33. It is probably sufficient that the question and its answer have a thematic relationship with the counter question and its answer. Huber: Jesus in Auseinandersetzung, 123. This thematic relationship is given by the divine origin of both the authority of Jesus and the baptism of John.

[48] Grundmann's conjecture that Mark associates Jesus with the philosophical school of the Peripatetics is probably without merit. Walter Grundmann: Das Evangelium nach Markus, ThHK 2 (Freiburg: Herder, 1974), 236. It is odd that Mark would not mention Jesus as teaching if he wanted to imply that Jesus is a Peripatetic. The other occurrences of this word in the gospel of Mark (2:9; 5:42; 6:48; 6:49; 7:5; 8:24; 12:38; 16:12) cannot be regarded as congruent with the use of the word as a terminus technicus.

[49] Gnilka writes: "Die vollständige Aufzählung der Fraktionen des Synhedrions (vgl. 8,31), dem über den Tempelhauptmann die Tempelpolizei unterstand (vgl. Apg 4,1), gibt dem Auftritt offiziellen Rang und stellt die Brücke zur Passionsgeschichte her." Gnilka: Markus, 2:138.

[50] See Gundry for an analysis of the pericope in the light of the cleansing of the temple only. He argues that only the temple protest is implied because of the position of the narrative. Gundry: Mark, 666. Gnilka argues otherwise. Gnilka: Markus, 2:138. The opponents object to ταῦτα (11:28). This could hardly be an objection to Jesus wandering around in the temple. The objection concerns what Jesus does, and so far in the gospel of Mark Jesus has taught without direct challenge to his teaching authority. This speaks for ταῦτα as a reference to the temple protest. On the other hand, the controversy is somewhat removed from the cleansing of the temple by the lesson of the fig tree and a night passed in Bethany, and the plural of ταῦτα is sufficiently

deliberation of the opponents concerning the question of Jesus is marked by an editorial comment mentioning that they were afraid of the crowds. The form of anakolouthon and asyndeton of this comment is highly dramatic.[51] The controversy ends with the refusal of Jesus to answer their question, as in Matthew.[52]

The most important difference between the Markan and the Matthean account of the controversy over the authority of Jesus lies in the respective position in the narratives. For Matthew, it is the second Jerusalem controversy, while for Mark it is the first. Mark starts the cycle of Jerusalem controversy with a challenge to the authority of Jesus, while Matthew begins with a challenge to Jesus that reflects on people who acclaim him as Son of David. In a sense, Mark heads the Jerusalem controversies with a treatment that is highly christological in nature. Matthew too begins with a treatment that is christological in its reference to the Son of David. But the Matthean order brings out more clearly the roles of Jesus as healer and teacher. Furthermore, Matthew also integrates the community in the form of the little ones who call Jesus Son of David. The first controversy of Matthew is not just a defense of Jesus, it is also a defense of the community.

Matthew then takes up the Markan narrative with this christological controversy and highlights some of the emphases already present in Mark. His addition of the teaching clarifies the direction of the opponents' attack, while the Markan editorial remark concerning the fear of the opponents becomes part of their deliberations to accentuate their deviousness. Matthew does not alter the direction of the controversy. Mark's narrative served Matthew's purpose.

2.2 Summary of the Matthean Redaction in 21:23–27

Matthew's story summarizes and highlights the accents given already in Mk 11:27–33. Such highlights and accents include:

▸   Matthew improves on Mark's style through a smoother narrative that includes parallelisms including the objection in the form of two questions, and omissions like the disciples.

---

indistinct in its reference to include more than just the cleansing of the temple. Thus the challenge to Jesus might broader here than Gundry admits. The opposition concerns the authority of Jesus to do things, and the cleansing of the temple could have been the action that precipitated the question, while it then is applied to the wider range of Jesus' ministry. Huber: *Jesus in Auseinandersetzung*, 57. The issue in Mark can no longer be settled with complete certainty. The Matthean redaction which inserts healings right after the cleansing of the temple, and which substitutes διδάσκειν for περιπατεῖν, presents a clarification in Matthew's context. Matthew thus understood ταῦτα to refer to more than just the cleansing of the temple: For him the objection encompassed the ministry of Jesus.

[51] Gundry: *Mark*, 658.

[52] Gundry, in accord with his overall approach to the gospel of Mark, writes: "Thus the dialogue ends with his overpowering [the opponents] in theological debate ... They lose face (a serious loss in near eastern culture). The shame to which [Jesus] puts the very ones who will get him crucified cancels the shame of his crucifixion." Gundry: *Mark*, 659.

▶   Matthew's main redactive activity is seen in the setting.
▶   Matthew notes the teaching activity of Jesus in the temple and thus has
    Jesus assume a role claimed by the Jewish leaders.
▶   Matthew has the opponents aware of their low motives in not answering
    Jesus.

3. Matthew 22:15-22

After the controversy concerning the authority of Jesus, Matthew inserts the parable
of the two sons (21:28–32), before he returns to the Markan sequence with the
parable of the wicked tenants (21:33–46 ∥ Mk 12:1–12). At this point Matthew
inserts the Pharisees into the group of opponents listening to the parables and
perceiving that the parable is spoken about them (21:45). Matthew also inserts that
the crowds held Jesus to be a prophet (21:45–46; cf. Mk 12:12). Again Matthew
interpolates a parable (22:1–10) into the Markan account. He takes the parable of
the marriage feast of the king from Q 14:15–23 and appends it with his own
postscript of the man without the wedding garment (21:11–14). The apparent
audience of all three parables is the group of Jesus' opponents which was
introduced in 21:23 and amplified with the Pharisees in 21:45. Thus Matthew
prepares for the controversy on paying taxes to Caesar with three parables. Mark,
on the other hand, has only one parable intervening.

Again Matthew redacts the setting of the controversy considerably. The recently
introduced Pharisees become the major agents in the Matthean setting. The opening
v. 22:15 provides an exposition not found in Mark. The Pharisees take counsel to
entrap Jesus in his talk.[53] The phrase συμβούλιον ἔλαβον recalls Matthew 12:14
∥ Mk 3:6 and draws attention to the evil intent of the Pharisees. In 12:14 the same
phrase was used to describe the Pharisees' plotting of Jesus' destruction.[54]

The Pharisees, then, send out their disciples to help in the entrapment of Jesus
(22:16). As in Mark, the opponents send for others. In Mark, the opponents are still
the members of the Sanhedrin of 11:27. Consequently, they can send for the
Pharisees (Mk 12:13). In Matthew, the main agents have become the Pharisees, so

---

[53]   Matthean are: τότε πορευθέντες οἱ Φαρισαῖοι συμβούλιον ἔλαβον. The following phrase
has its origin in Mk 12:13b. Matthew replaces ἵνα with ὅπως, retains αὐτόν, uses παγιδεύσωσιν
ἐν instead of ἀγρεύσωσιν. Gundry attributes the latter change to the relative frequency of παγιδεύω
in the LXX. Gundry: *Matthew*, 441. This is a possible, but not inescapable conclusion. Matthew's
word also describes more closely the intent of the Pharisees: The Markan ἀγρεύω refers generally
to hunting, while the Matthean παγιδεύω describes the more specific laying of a trap. Liddell and
Scott: *A Greek-English Lexicon*, 14, 1284.

[54]   Gundry: *Matthew*, 441.

they send for their disciples.[55] This change does not introduce a new group[56] but puts more emphasis on the Pharisees.[57] Matthew, like Mark, mentions the Herodians as well, though he inserts μετά.[58] The Pharisees are even more emphasized through the redaction that omits the Markan καὶ ἐλθόντες λέγουσιν αὐτῷ and replaces it with λέγοντες.[59] The nominative of the participle refers to the subject of ἀποστέλλουσιν, which is the Pharisees. The real opponents, then, are the Pharisees themselves, and not whoever they send.

Similar to the beginning Matthew also amends the conclusion (22:22). While Mark notes the amazement of "them" (Mk 12:17) Matthew clarifies that it is the opponents (ἀκούσαντες ἐθαύμασαν) who are amazed and mentions that they left Jesus and went away. This small redaction makes a good preparation for the Sadducees who appear in the next pericope.[60]

The redaction of the controversy proper reveals once again Matthew's sense of stylistic improvements.[61] Some of the typically Matthean accents in this pericope are

---

[55] Hagner claims that the disciples of the Pharisees "are mentioned only here in the NT." Hagner: *Matthew 14–28*, 635. This is not accurate. In Matthew 9:14 the Pharisees are a replacement for the disciples of the Pharisees that occur in Mk 2:18.

[56] Against Gnilka, who claims: "Die Formulierung ist ungenau, weil die Pharisäer keine Jünger um sich scharten. Wohl taten dies die Schriftgelehrten. Es wird somit an Schriftgelehrte pharisäischer Provenienz zu denken sein." Gnilka: *Matthäus*, 2:246–247.

[57] A similar redaction took place with the introduction of the disciples of John in 9:14, where the Pharisees were already in place. There as here, the Pharisees were the main agents in the Matthean controversy story.

[58] The Pharisees could hardly be supposed to commandeer the Herodians. The insertion of "with" maintains the association while glossing over the precise relationship with the Herodians. Gundry: *Mark*, 441.

[59] This reading is not completely assured. Several manuscripts (א B L 085) read λέγοντας. The accusative would make the participle agree with the disciples sent by the Pharisees. This is the reading accepted by Gundry: *Mark*, 442. However, the textual witnesses in favor of the nominative are strong (C D W Θ 0138 *f*.13 and the Majority Text). Hagner's assertion that the construction with the accusative is found nowhere else in Matthew is not accurate, cf. 21:15. Hagner: *Matthew 14–28*, 633. Nevertheless, the nominative must be given precedence because of its good attestation and its being the *lectio difficilior*.

[60] Gnilka: *Matthäus*, 2:246.

[61] In v. 16 Matthew moves Mk 12:14e forward, rearranges the word order, and replaces ἀλλ' with καί, to read καὶ τὴν ὁδὸν τοῦ θεοῦ ἐν ἀληθείᾳ διδάσκεις. This moves the emphasis slightly on the last statement of v. 16 that Jesus does not regard the positions of people. In v. 17 Matthew separates the question from the introductory remarks of v. 16 by inserting εἰπὲ οὖν ἡμῖν τί σοι δοκεῖ. He omits the repetitious δῶμεν ἢ μὴ δῶμεν. In v. 18 Matthew substitutes γνούς for εἰδώς, πονηρίαν for ὑπόκρισιν, and post-positions αὐτῶν. He omits the superfluous αὐτοῖς and takes up the Markan reference to hypcrisy by inserting ὑποκριταί into the address of Jesus. In v. 19 Matthew introduces more variety in the vocabulary by using ἐπιδείξατε instead of φέρετε and νόμισμα τοῦ κήνσου instead of δηνάριον. He omits ἵνα ἴδω as superfluous and uses προσήνεγκαν instead of ἤνεγκαν. Matthew inserts αὐτῷ δηνάριον. In v. 21 Matthew uses λέγουσιν instead of εἶπαν, and λέγει instead of εἶπεν because in v. 20 he took over the historic present tense from Mark, and now assimilates to it. Matthew inserts τότε and removes the repetitions mentioning of

due less to direct changes in Mark's version. Rather, they are provided by connotations that Matthew has previously established. When the Pharisaic questioners begin by calling Jesus "teacher" their inadequacy is already established. The title does not carry a positive meaning for Matthew.[62]

Consequently, what appears at first as a *captatio benevolentiae* immediately falls under suspicion by the address of Jesus as teacher. By now, Matthew has made it quite clear where he stands with regard to the Pharisees. Thus their attempt at complimenting Jesus is nothing more than part of the trap that they lay for him. Matthew corrects Mark's style by moving up the phrase "you teach truthfully" and closer to "you are truthful." He also emphasizes the ironic twist already present in Mark. The note that Jesus has no regard for the position of people is now at the end of the Pharisees' introduction. Perhaps the Pharisees intend to goad Jesus to say something critical about the emperor.[63] But what Jesus says ends up as a criticism not of the emperor but them. Matthew has certainly shown so far that Jesus has little regard for the position of the Pharisees. Thus their attempt to compliment him is clearly a failure, for the trap they have conceived becomes the pit into which they fall themselves. The Pharisees seem somewhat ridiculous. As this attempt is placed between Matthew's remarks that the Pharisees lay a trap for Jesus, and that Jesus knew of their maliciousness and then goes on to call them hypocrites, the irony is emphasized.

But even more ironic is the concession the Pharisees actually make. They acknowledge, for their own evil purposes, that Jesus teaches the way of God truthfully.[64] While this observation is as true for Mark as it is for Matthew, the first Gospel emphasizes this with the phrase, "Tell us then, what do you think." The Pharisees seem to acknowledge the teaching authority of Jesus while at the same time trying to entrap him in his very teaching.

Jesus' name. Matthew also inserts οὖν and thus necessitates a change in word order. The latter change parallelizes the things of Caesar with the things of God perfectly.

[62] It is a title used exclusively by opponents of Jesus: 8:19; 9:11; 10:24; 10:25; 12:38; 17:24; 19:16; 22:16; 22:24; 22:36; 23:8; 26:18. The disciples, though recipients of the teaching of Jesus, never call him this: In 8:19, a Scribe is rejected as disciple after calling Jesus "teacher," while in 19:16 the man who calls Jesus "Teacher" does not show enough commitment to become a disciple. In 9:11 the Pharisees use the title in a way that seems intended as ironic, since at the same time they criticize Jesus severely (cf. also 17:24). In 12:38 the address, used by Pharisees and Scribes, is accompanied by the demand for a sign. When the disciples in Mark call Jesus "teacher" Matthew usually changes Mark to read "Lord." See Mk 4:38 ‖ Mt 8:25; Mk 9:17 ‖ Mt 17:15. Matthew omits the title "teacher" without replacing it in Mk 10:35 ‖ Mt 20:20. In the story of the rich man Matthew keeps the title, since the man does not become a disciple: Mk 10:17 ‖ Mt 19:16. Matthew omits the story of the strange exorcist and thus does not report the address there: Mk 9:38. Conversely, Matthew introduces the title also into Mk 2:16 ‖ Mt 9:11. Thus the negative connotation of the title in Matthew is established.

[63] Hagner: *Matthew 14–28*, 635.

[64] Gnilka: *Matthäus*, 2:247.

Another clearly Matthean accent is the reference to Jesus' knowledge. Jesus knew about the secret discussions among the disciples (16:18; cf. 26:10). Similarly, Jesus was able to read the thoughts of his opponents (9:4) just like the faith of those approaching him (9:2). But most importantly, when the Pharisees took counsel (συμβούλιον ἔλαβον) on how to destroy Jesus, he knew this (γνοὺς 12:14–15). Thus Matthew's mention of Jesus knowledge here is important in establishing the conflict, but also in emphasizing the person of Jesus by again noting his extraordinary knowledge. While the Pharisees pretend to know Jesus as a truthful teacher and miscalculate badly, Jesus in turn knows them well. And while in 12:14 the Pharisees plotted the death of Jesus, and his knowledge led him to withdraw, here Jesus no longer withdraws, but answers the challenge.

These Matthean accents highlight the character of the agents of the story. The Pharisees become more prominent than they are in the Markan account, and the figure of Jesus gains stature by highlighting his knowledge. On the one hand are the opponents of Jesus, whose clearly evil intentions Matthew mentions and whom Jesus addresses as hypocrites (22:18). On the other hand there is Jesus whose knowledge exposes the Pharisees even before he answers them. Matthew's interests rest more in this accentuation of the agents in the controversy story, rather than in the actual issue of the controversy itself. The paying of taxes is of importance only because it shows the Pharisees in their usual bad light.[65] What matters is not so much whether or not to pay taxes,[66] but to give to God what is God's.[67] The short

---

[65] Derrett comes to the wrong conclusion that in obeying Caesar one obeys the Law of God. John D. Derrett: "'Render to Caesar ...'" in: *Law in the New Testament* (London: Longman & Todd, 1970), 313–338. There is no indication in the text that Matthew or Mark intend to enjoin obedience to Caesar. Derrett is one of a long line of interpreters who have taken this saying, along with Rom 13:7 and 1 Pet 2:17, to imply the duty of rendering honor and obedience to secular rulers. For a discussion, see: Leonhard Goppelt: *Die Freiheit zur Kaisersteuer: Christologie und Ethik* (München: Kaiser, 1968); Gnilka: *Matthäus*, 2:249–250. Such an interpretation has its earliest witness in Justin: *Apology* 1.17: "More even than others we try to pay the taxes and assessments to those whom you appoint, as we have been taught by him. For once in his time some came to him and asked whether it were right to pay taxes to Caesar ... [Justin narrates the pericope.] ... So we worship only God, but in other matters we gladly serve you." Similar interpretations were offered by Irenaeus: *Adv. Haer.* 3.8.1, and by Tertullian: *On Idolatry*, 15. It needs to be stressed that the pericope in Matthew as well as in Mark is not primarily about paying taxes, but about the conflict with the Pharisees. The interpretations of Justin, Irenaeus, and Tertullian probably illustrate that, while not enjoining the paying of taxes, the pericope probably just assumes it without further ado.

[66] Josephus reports that the Roman taxes were a controversial issue among the Jews of the time. The more extreme nationalists rejected the tax as a token of being subjected by the Romans, while other groups paid the tax. See *B.J.* 2, 118: " Under [Coponius'] administration, a Galilean, named Judas, incited his countrymen to revolt, upbraiding them as cowards for consenting to pay tribute to the Romans and tolerating mortal masters after having God for their lord." The Pharisees were probably among those consenting; cf. *Ant.* 18, 1–4. The same incident is reported there, though the issue there is a property assessment ordered by Quirinius. Such an assessment was most probably related to taxes, and Josephus writes: "Although the Jews were, at first,

description of the amazement of the Pharisees and their departure shows that they are not willing to do the latter. In leaving Jesus (ἀφέντες αὐτόν: 22:22) the Pharisees do not give to God what is belongs to him. They have become like the devil not only in testing Jesus[68] but also in leaving him.[69]

For Matthew it is probably important that the matter of controversy is framed in a question concerning the Law (ἔξεστιν 22:17 ‖ Mk 12:14).[70] It is on the

---

shocked to hear of the registration of property, they gradually condescended, yielding to the arguments of the High Priest Joazar, the son of Boethus, to go to no further opposition. So those who were convinced by him declared, without further shilly-shallying, the value of their property." If Josephus is right, this would imply an assent to paying taxes on the authority of the Jewish ruling class represented by the High Priest.

[67] Gnilka writes: "Die Pointe der Sentenz liegt aber im Nebeneinander von Kaiser und Gott. Dieses kann nicht als beschwichtigendes Nebeneinander gesehen werden. Wenn man die Basileia-Predigt mitberücksichtigt, erscheint die imperiale Macht in ihrer Vergänglichkeit, die Gottesherrschaft aber als die bleibende und endgültige." Gnilka: *Matthäus*, 2:248–250. Gnilka is less than clear here, though it seems that he implies that even though the construction of the apophthegm places in parallel Caesar and God, its actual meaning is the subordination of Caesar to God. For such an interpretation it is not necessary to refer to the general teaching on the kingdom in Matthew's gospel. As seen before, in such parallel sentences the weight is not distributed equally between the parts, but falls on the second. Myers wishes to see the καί connecting Caesar and God as adversative, thereby constructing a choice between Caesar and God. Ched Myers: *Binding the Strong Man* (Maryknoll: Orbis, 1988), 311–312. Such a construct does not have any further evidence in the text at all. Matthew is not opposing Roman rule. Giblin tries to account for the parallelism between Caesar and God with the observation that as far as Caesar is concerned, the pericope talks about his image on the coin. Therefore, the image of God on human beings (Gen 1:27) must be implied in the reference to God. Charles H. Giblin: "'The Things of God' in the Question Concerning Tribute to Caesar," *CBQ* 33 (1971): 510–527. However, the saying about the coin refers to the image and an inscription. The latter has no reference in Genesis. Giblin, therefore, refers to Prov 7:3; Jer 31:33, Is 44:5. But the parallels are unconvincing. In Proverbs, the son writes on his own heart, not God. In Jeremiah and Isaiah, God's writing on human hearts is an eschatological occurrence and not related to the creation. Furthermore, Jesus is not otherwise described as talking about humans in the image of God. Finally, the pericope does not contain an explicit reference to the image of God as an antipode to the image of Caesar.

[68] Compare πειράζων in 4:3 with τί με πειράζετε in 22:18.

[69] Compare τότε ἀφίησιν αὐτὸν ὁ διάβολος in 4:11 with καὶ ἀφέντες αὐτόν in 22:22.

[70] It is doubtful whether the legitimacy of the emperor's tax was indeed a burning issue in Pharisaic legal debates. While it is clear that the Zealots saw the paying of taxes as an abomination (Josephus: *B.J.* 2, 118) the Mishnah did not deal with the problem. Derrett: "'Render to Caesar ...'" 322–323. It is illegitimate to conclude from this that the Pharisees must have had "ein besonderes Interesse" concerning this question. Huber: *Jesus in Auseinandersetzung*, 189. It seems more appropriate to conclude that because the topic does not occur elsewhere in Jewish literature of the time or later as a matter of discussion on the Mosaic Law, interest might not have been all that great. The rabbinic discussions are more about political authority in general, and in general political authority is to be obeyed. This would include the payment of taxes. Josephus describes the issue in terms of nationalistic feelings more than as a test case for the Mosaic Law. Nevertheless, Matthew and Mark bring up this topic in reference to the Law.

interpretation of the Law that many of the Matthean controversies focus. Here Matthew focuses more clearly on the principle of the Law by omitting Mark's personalized comment "should we give or no?" (Mk 12:15). Again Matthew's Jesus emerges as the superior interpreter of the Law.

3.1 The Markan Pericope

The pericope of the controversy[71] of paying taxes to Caesar (Mk 12:13–17) has a fairly unified appearance.[72] The closing statement of Jesus could not very well have circulated independently of the story. The cohesiveness of the pericope is perhaps one of the reasons for the small extent of the Matthean redaction.

The *captatio benevolentiae* of 12:14b serves as a prologue to the controversy proper.[73] It is chiastically structured through the content as well as through correspondence of words:[74]

Table 2: The Chiasm in Mk 12:14b

a	διδάσκαλε
b	οἴδαμεν ὅτι ἀληθὴς εἶ
c	καὶ οὐ μέλει σοι περὶ οὐδενός
c'	οὐ γὰρ βλέπεις εἰς πρόσωπον ἀνθρώπων
b'	ἀλλ' ἐπ' ἀληθείας τὴν ὁδὸν τοῦ θεοῦ
a'	διδάσκεις

---

[71] Gnilka again disputes that this story is a controversy because "eine gegenteilige Auffassung der Kontrahenten wird am Anfang nicht zu verstehen gegeben." Gnilka: *Markus*, 2:151. With this statement Gnilka reflects the position of Bultmann, according to whom occasion and question of a controversy story must be thematically related. Bultmann: *History*, 40–56. However, Gnilka does not comment on the impact that mention of the hypocrisy of Jesus' opponents has on the form of the pericope. It is perhaps not explicitly mentioned that the opponents hold a contrary opinion, but their contrary action is obvious from the beginning in their attempt to entrap Jesus. Hultgren: *Adversaries*, 41–44. *EvThom* 100 presents the same question, but merely as a pronouncement of Jesus to a question from his disciples: "[The disciples] showed Jesus a gold coin and said to him: Caesar's men ask taxes from us. He said to them: Give the things of Caesar to Caesar, give the things of God to God, and give to me what is mine."

[72] For Hultgren, the pericope is an example of what he calls unitary controversy stories, stories in which the apophthegm is not independently useful. Hultgren: *Adversaries*, 75. He thinks that the question, the production of the coin, and Jesus' answer, are no longer distinguishable in terms of layers of tradition. Gnilka is slightly more careful. He realizes that v. 14 is somewhat overwrought: "In der Tat ließe sich der Begründungssatz: Denn Du blickst nicht auf die Person der Menschen, sondern lehrst in Wahrheit den Weg Gottes, entbehren." Gnilka: *Markus*, 2:151. However, Gnilka does not take into account the chiastic structure of this preamble to the actual question. The structure of the preamble is such that it seems impossible to isolate one element and assign it to a later part of the tradition.

[73] Huber: *Jesus in Auseinandersetzung*, 170. Derrett calls it a preamble. Derrett: "'Render to Caesar ...'" 314.

[74] Huber: *Jesus in Auseinandersetzung*, 170–171.

The frame is given by the teaching of Jesus (a, a'), while the inner members of the chiasm are somewhat repetitive and redundant in their second appearance, so that the *parallelismus membrorum* is perhaps reminiscent of Semitic poetic forms.[75] The text's arrangement is skillful in laying the focus directly on Jesus. The arrangement is also less ironic than in Matthew.[76] Matthew destroys this chiasm when he rearranges Mk 12:14.

In Mark's gospel, the address "teacher" is at this point new in the mouth of the opponents of Jesus. Up to now, only the disciples (4:38; 9:38; 10:35; 13:1) and those in need of assistance (5:35; 9:17; 10:17, 20) have used the title. Thus for Mark, it does not carry any negative connotations as it does in Matthew but is a laudatory title for Jesus.[77]

Consequently, the Markan version of the *captatio benevolentiae* raises the question of its purpose.[78] From Mk 12:13b the negative intentions of the opponents are clear (ἀγρεύσωσιν), and they are reiterated in v. 15 (ὑπόκρισιν). Thus it is likely that the preamble of the opponents serves to illustrate their hypocrisy.[79] Mark

---

[75] Taylor: *Mark*, 478; Huber: *Jesus in Auseinandersetzung*, 171.

[76] Gundry points out that the double answer of Jesus contains a corresponding chiasm: a τί; b με; c πειράζετε; c' φέρετέ; b' μοι; a' δηνάριον ἵνα ἴδω. Gundry: *Mark*, 693–694. The weak link in this argument is the lack of correspondence between a and a'. However, without a and a' the chiasm is still obvious, though it no longer corresponds to the chiasm of the compliment since it is now only two members strong.

[77] During the stay in Jerusalem, the opponents of Jesus appropriate the title to some extent. In 12:14, 19, 32 they call him teacher. Perhaps the title acquires a negative meaning from these passages, and ought to be taken as indicating the hypocrisy of Jesus' enemies here. Huber: *Jesus in Auseinandersetzung*, 173. The problem with such an interpretation is that the retrojective interpretation of "teacher" does then not just affect 21:14, but also the previous occurrences. While it is arguable that the title is insufficient for Mark to describe the person of Jesus, it is less convincing to infer hypocrisy for the disciples and those who come to him for assistance. Consequently, it probably easier to view the use of the title here and in the subsequent controversy stories as a polite address that fails to gloss over the hypocrisy of Jesus' opponents. Their evil intentions are more obvious from what they debate with Jesus than from how they address him. For a complete analysis of the title in Mark and its socio-cultural implications see Vernon K. Robbins: *Jesus the Teacher. A Socio-Rhetorical Interpretation of Mark* (Philadelphia: Fortress Press, 1984). He writes: "[Mark's gospel] was dominated by the cycle of relationships that emerges around a teacher who gathers disciple-companions; communicates and manifests his system of thought and action in their presence; and accepts arrest, trial, and death because he presents an alternative system of thought and action in a cultural setting dominated by an established legal system with political power" (p. 167). As a consequence, even the opponents recognize this relationship. In 10:46–12:44 Jesus is regularly recognized as a teacher, and, even by his opponents, "addressed in a manner appropriate for his social identity" (p. 166).

[78] Huber: *Jesus in Auseinandersetzung*, 183.

[79] Gnilka: *Markus*, 2:151. Stock emphasizes that the statement stands in contrast to all other statements of the opponents about Jesus. Klemens Stock: *Jesus – die frohe Botschaft. Meditationen zu Markus* (Innsbruck: Tyrolia, 1983), 106. According to Huber, the statement renders "den Eindruck ..., den das Lehren und Wirken Jesu auf die Menschen seiner Zeit, ja sogar auf seine Feinde gemacht haben." Huber: *Jesus in Auseinandersetzung*, 184. Stauffer writes that the verse

has identified the purpose behind the argument of Jesus is the attempt to entrap him (12:13). For that reason the positive statement cannot be separated completely from the hypocrisy of the opponents.[80] It is meant to be ironic and hypocritical. Because for Matthew the title "teacher" is a negative one throughout the gospel, he has sharpened the confrontational aspect of the opponents' question at the expense of the irony inherent in Mark's version.

When Matthew breaks up the chiastic arrangement of the Pharisaic compliment to rearrange it, he achieves a sharper focus on the opponents of Jesus. The elements that appear chiastically in Mark are directly parallelized in Matthew's arrangement. By placing the remarks about Jesus' disregard for human position or achievement to the end of the *captatio benevolentiae*, the opponents emerge with greater prominence. This is emphasized by the insertion of εἰπὲ οὖν ἡμῖν (22:17). With this transitional statement Matthew creates a connecting bridge between the *captatio benevolentiae* and the question of the Pharisees and Herodians. The Matthean Pharisees, even in their opening *captatio benevolentiae*, make it clear that they are less interested in Jesus' truthful teaching about the way of God, than in the controversy with Jesus. Consequently, for Matthew the opponents are not just hypocrites, they are malicious (22:18a). Ironically, the controversy revolves around the statement of the Pharisees that Jesus cares for no one's position. Matthew turns this statement against them in showing how little Jesus regards the position of the Pharisees. The final emphasis in the Matthean redaction of the opponents is the note that they left Jesus. While Matthew keeps the Markan observation that the opponents marveled, he also insists on the distance between Jesus and the opponents. As a controversy story, the Matthean version has a sharper edge than the Markan account and a clear focus on the opposing parties rather than the matter of paying taxes that gives rise to the controversy.

3.2 Summary of the Matthean Redaction in 22:15–22

The Matthean redaction picks up on topics already present in Mark's account and highlights them both stylistically and thematically:

▸   Matthew enhances the Markan narrative stylistically.

---

contains "eines der ganz herrlichen Zeugnisse über Jesus, ein ganz undogmatisches Urteil aus dem Mund seiner Feinde, eine rein protokollarische Feststellung wie Markus 1,27; Lukas 4,22; Matthäus 7,28ff; Johannes 7,46." Ethelbert Stauffer: *Christus und die Caesaren. Historische Skizzen*, 7th ed., (München: Kaiser, 1966), 104. Gundry probably is correct when he comments that the answer of Jesus proves the *captatio benevolentiae* both true and a ruse in the mouth of the Pharisees and Herodians. Gundry: *Mark*, 693.

[80] Huber tries to achieve just such a separation by claiming that the Markan remark concerning the hypocrisy of the Pharisees and Herodians refers to their question, not to their description of the teaching of Jesus. Huber: *Jesus in Auseinandersetzung*, 183–184. However, this does not convince entirely since the opening remark of the pericope (12:13) already infers an evil intention in the opponents.

- Matthew redacts the setting and the conclusion in order to focus more clearly on the Pharisees and their evil intent to entrap Jesus. To this end Matthew breaks up the Markan chiasm.
- Matthew increases the maliciousness of the Pharisees in the question through his connotations of the title "teacher.".
- Matthew heightens the knowledge and superiority of Jesus.
- With the note that the Pharisees leave Jesus they are associated with the tempter in the desert.

4. Matthew 22:23–33

Like Mark, Matthew follows the controversy over the payment of taxes with the controversy over the resurrection. He improves on the connection between the stories. In the previous story, Matthew had, unlike Mark, the Pharisees and Herodians leave (22:22). Now the Sadducees enter.[81] Matthew inserts that they came on the same day (22:23).[82] Matthew gives the impression that Jesus had to deal with a barrage of opponents to his wisdom. A crucial redaction takes place when Matthew introduces the opinion of the Sadducees that there is no resurrection. Matthew changes οἵτινες λέγουσιν (Mk 12:18) to λέγοντες. Meier has taken this change to indicate Matthew's lack of knowledge concerning the teaching of the Sadducees on the resurrection.[83] This argument, however, is inadequate, since it

---

[81] Matthew slightly modifies Mark by using προςῆλθον αὐτῷ instead of ἔρχονται ... πρὸς αὐτόν. Gundry claims that by adding the πρός to the verb Matthew highlights the dignity of Jesus. Gundry: *Mark*, 444.

[82] While Mark appends the story to the episode of the taxes simply with καί, Matthew has ἐν ἐκείνῃ τῇ ἡμέρᾳ. This phrase is unusual in Matthew and occurs only once more in 13:1, though with a different word order: ἐν τῇ ἡμέρᾳ ἐκείνῃ. In both cases a meaning beyond the time reference does not seem to be implied.

[83] He writes: "A second slip on the part of Mt seems to be his reference to the Sadducees in 22:23 ... The *hoitines* [in Mark] indicates who the Sadducees are as a group. It is a definition of the Sadducees' position, not just a description of what particular Sadducees were saying to Jesus at one particular moment ... Mt has made the attributive clause ... predicative, without any real difference from the *legontes* beginning vs. 24. *Legontes mē einai anastasin* no longer describes the basic position of the Sadducees, but simply reports summarily what these particular Sadducees were saying or thinking as they approached Jesus. Once again, the only viable explanation of this garbling of the Markan tradition is ignorance of the Jewish situation *before and after* A.D. 70. Neither before nor after that date could any well-educated Jew make such a mistake in describing the Sadducees." Meier: *Law*, 18–19. The major problem that arises with this argument is its separation from the context of Matthew's gospel as a whole. Meier chooses to deal with this particular redaction only in the change of meaning from Mark to Matthew. He does not address at all how the redaction might fit into the overall purpose of the first gospel in terms of language and style. Furthermore, Meier's argument rests on assumptions that cannot really be proven. The first is that Saducean teaching on the resurrection as a general doctrine ought to have been more

discounts other possible explanations for the Matthean redaction. The first thing of note is a textual variation that occurs at this point.[84] But apart from the caution caused by textual uncertainty, the abbreviation that Matthew achieves through the participial construction is a trait of the Matthean redaction in general. Furthermore, Matthew consistently uses λέγοντες to introduce direct discourse.[85] By introducing λέγοντες in 12:23 he achieves a parallel with 12:24. The first occurrence introduces the problem of faith in the resurrection, while the second occurrence introduces the problem of the Levirate marriage. The answer of Jesus shows that Matthew deals with both problems, first taking up the Levirate case (30), then

---

important, even for Matthew, than the situation in which the topic arises. Thus, because Matthew redacts the remark with the situation in mind, he cannot have known about the doctrine. However, such precedence of doctrine cannot be validated. In a second assumption, Meier argues that Matthew garbled Mark. However, the structure and meaning of the Matthean sentence are quite clear. There is a different emphasis, but no garbling. The Matthean version does not exclude the Markan statement about Sadducean doctrine. Thirdly, Meier regards Matthew as making a mistake. But he does not, he merely shapes the doctrinal to the situation. Fourthly, Meier must assume that the Sadducees were still important enough for Matthew to report their general scepticism with regard to the resurrection. However, by the time the gospel of Matthew was put into its final form some time in the late 80s, the Sadducees may have ceased to be a major force in Jewish life. Harrington: *Matthew*, 314. One indication for this is the shift of emphasis to the Pharisees from Josephus' earlier *War* to his later *Antiquities*. Similarly, the Pharisees become more important in the later gospels, while the Sadducees recede. There is no direct evidence that places the Sadducees in the period after the destruction of the temple. On the other hand, the inclusion of some priestly elements in the early parts of the Mishnah might point to an integration of the Sadducees' agenda into the developing formative Judaism. The assessment of such evidence, however, is highly speculative. Günther Stemberger: *Jewish Contemporaries of Jesus. Pharisees, Sadducees, Essenes*, trans. A. W. Mahnke (Minneapolis: Fortress, 1995), 140–147. Thus, the assumptions behind Meier's judgment are not convincing. It is quite possible that Matthew wanted to shape the controversy to the particular situation, and he felt that he could do so since the Sadducees, and with them their position, had lost ground after the destruction of the temple. In giving the controversy a shape that focusses on the situation, Matthew does not garble Mark, nor does he make a mistake in representing the opinion of the Sadducees as he found it in his source Mark. Matthew's focus on the particular Sadducees approaching Jesus seems, therefore, quite appropriate.

[84] Several early manuscripts (א[2] K L Θ f[13] and others) insert οἱ before λέγοντες. It is possible that this article was left out in other manuscripts through homoioteleuton following Σαδδυκαῖοι. On the other hand, the article might be an insertion through assimilation of the parallels. The decisive argument against the originality of the article is the fact that Matthew does not provide a similar explanation of Jewish customs elsewhere in his gospel. Metzger: *Textual Commentary*, 48. While this argument is quite convincing, the evidence of the manuscripts themselves is inconclusive. If the article was present Meier's argument would collapse. However, he does not address the textual problem. For the sake of completeness, several manuscripts add the article before Σαδδυκαῖοι (700 *pc*), while f[13] inserts the article both before and after Σαδδυκαῖοι.

[85] Gundry claims: "λέγοντες is a Mattheanism – 61,23." Gundry: *Mark*, 444. The participle occurs in the plural to introduce direct discourse 49 times in Matthew and 17 times in Mark. Among the Matthean occurrences the tense is always the present tense except in the parable of the ten virgins (25:9, 11). See also: Hagner: *Matthew 14–28*, 639; Gnilka: *Matthäus*, 2:251.

taking up the general question of the resurrection (31). Thus the introduction of λέγοντες in 12:23 serves a narrative purpose: it introduces the first problem parallel to the second problem, and Matthew deals with them in reverse order, thus creating a chiasm. Consequently, the first λέγοντες is crucial to the structure of Matthew's account. This structure, then, obviates Meier's problem. The Matthean chiasm can be broken down as follows:

Table 3: Chiastic Construction in Matthew 22:23–31

a	23b	general problem	λέγοντες μὴ εἶναι ...
b	24a	case study	λέγοντες Μωϋσῆς ...
c	29	Jesus' answer	ἀποκριθεὶς δὲ ὁ Ἰησοῦς ...
b'	30	case study	ἐν γὰρ τῇ ἀναστάσει ...
a'	31	general problem	περὶ δὲ τῆς ἀναστάσεως ...

At the same time, Matthew's focus on the particular Sadducees approaching him renders the controversy more confrontational than Mark's account. In Matthew, the Sadducees approach Jesus by denying the resurrection and at the same time presenting a preposterous scenario designed to render the possibility of the resurrection both ridiculous and contrary to the Law.[86] The focus on Jesus' opponents is entirely in keeping with the usual Matthean redaction of the controversy stories. As the Sadducees address Jesus as teacher, they reinforce their distance to him.

Further Matthean redaction of the pericope serves to abbreviate the quotation of the Law and the lengthy and convoluted account of the seven brothers in Mark.[87] Matthew also inserts a more personal touch into the pericope. When the Sadducees

---

[86] Gnilka writes: "Die Anfrage der Sadduzäer erfolgt nicht zum Zweck der Belehrung, sondern zur Verteidigung ihrer Meinung, die erwähnt ist und im Gegensatz zur Meinung Jesu steht." Gnilka: *Matthäus*, 2:251.

[87] In v. 24, Matthew replaces ἔγραψεν ἡμῖν with εἶπεν; this change allows for a greater contrast between Μωϋσῆς εἶπεν and ὑπὸ τοῦ θεοῦ λέγοντος (v. 31). Matthew purges the Markan misconstruction of the question which resumes the ὅτι-clause with ἵνα, and abbreviates considerably by leaving out ἀδελφός as well as the middle part of the Markan clause introduced with ἐάν. He uses ἐπιγαμβρεύσει instead of λάβῃ, perhaps inspired by γάμβρευσαι in Gen 38:8. Harrington: *Matthew*, 312. Matthew uses ἀναστήσει instead of ἐξαναστήσῃ. In v. 25 he shifts ἦσαν to the beginning of the sentence. The account of the marriage of the first brother is abbreviated into a participial construction, the death described with ἐτελεύτησεν instead of ἀποθνῄσκων. Then Matthew inserts μὴ ἔχων and introduces γυναῖκα as the direct object of ἀφῆκεν. Finally, Matthew introduces τῷ ἀδελφῷ αὐτοῦ as indirect object. In v. 26 Matthew abbreviates Mark's account of the second and third brother by just mentioning that they did likewise. In v. 27 Matthew changes the word order slightly, replaces καί with δε and ἔσχατον with ὕστερον. In v. 28 inserts οὖν and perhaps abbreviates Mk 12:23; Mark's phrase ὅταν ἀναστῶσιν is not very well attested in the manuscripts. Matthew also substitutes Mark's αὐτῶν with τῶν ἑπτά, οἱ ἑπτά with πάντες. He omits γυναῖκα.

describe the case of the seven brothers, he adds παρ' ἡμῖν (22:25). With this brief insertion Matthew treats the Sadducees with irony.[88] The preposterous case that the Sadducees propose makes them preposterous as well, since it supposedly occurred among them. Where the Markan account of the seven brother suggested a humor that the Sadducees used to make the notion of resurrection laughable, the simple insertion of παρ' ἡμῖν turns that humor against the Sadducees themselves. The *reductio ad absurdum* in Mark went against the concept of resurrection. In Matthew, it reduces the Sadducees to absurdity.

The answer of Jesus is introduced with one of Matthew's favorite formulas for introducing direct discourse (22:29).[89] Before Jesus answers the two questions he points out that his opponents are deceived and do not understand either scripture or the power of God (22:29). What was a rhetorical question in Mark becomes a statement through the omission of οὐ διὰ τοῦτο. Jesus appears more assured in Matthew, and he renders a verdict on the Sadducees; he does no longer invite discussion.[90] He can do so because his opponents have shown repeatedly that they do not know the scriptures at all.[91]

The first question to be answered is the case of one bride and seven brothers (22:30).[92] Jesus' answer is fairly simple. The resurrection entails such a change of life that the idea of marriage after the resurrection becomes moot. The seven brothers and their bride will be like angels. The Sadducees' case study is shown to rest on false premises. While there is life after death, that life is not just a continuation of the life before death.

The second answer of Jesus (22:31–32) gives a proof from scripture for the more general question of the existence of resurrection. With this proof Jesus shows himself to be superior in knowledge of the scriptures and is proven right in accusing

---

[88] Gnilka agrees: "Der vorgetragene Fall von den sieben Brüdern, die alle starben und in peinlicher Befolgung von Dt 25,5 ff – allerdings wirkungslos! – die Schwagerehe an der jeweils hinterbliebenen Witwe vollzogen, ist geeignet, ein schallendes Gelächter auszulösen." Gnilka: *Matthäus*, 2:253. Not so Hagner: "Something of the kind must not have been that unusual given the levirate practices." Hagner: *Matthew 14–28*, 641. Gundry is similarly serious. Gundry: *Matthew*, 445.

[89] In 22:29, Matthew inserts ἀποκριθεὶς and changes ἔφη to εἶπεν. This is one of his favorite combinations. Gundry: *Matthew*, 446. He inserts δε and avoids the Markan asyndeton, and changes the word order slightly.

[90] Gundry points out the intensification of the guilt of the Sadducees. Gundry: *Matthew*, 446. While this is true, the change also enhances the figure of Jesus considerably. Jesus renders judgment here.

[91] Matthew has established the shortcomings of his opponents' exegesis with the phrase οὐκ ἀνέγνωτε. It appeared already in 12:3, 5; 19:4; 21:16; 21:42; the present controversy contains the phrase in 22:31. See also. Hagner: *Matthew 14–28*, 642.

[92] Matthew abridges Mk 12:25 slightly by replacing ὅταν ἐκ νεκρῶν ἀναστῶσιν with the more elegant ἐν τῇ ἀναστάσει. Thus Matthew parallels the question in 22:28. He changes the word order by moving εἰσιν to the end of the sentence and singularizes οὐρανῷ, perhaps to match it with ἀναστάσει.

the Sadducees of being ignorant (22:29). Matthew repeats Mark's οὐκ ἀνέγνωτε, but for Matthew this phrase is by now a formula indicating the particular ignorance of his opponents in the realm of the interpretation of scripture. He keeps the continuity of the passage by repeating the word ἀνάστασις for the fourth time.[93] He also omits Mark's reference to the book of Moses and the passage of the thornbush (12:26) and replaces it with the word spoken by God (τὸ ῥηθὲν ὑμῖν ὑπὸ τοῦ θεοῦ λέγοντος). Matthew emphasizes with this shift how God is a God of the living and excises the Markan reference which is extraneous to the argument at hand. And again Matthew personalizes the argument by inserting ὑμῖν.[94] The insertion emphasizes the hostility and the distance between Jesus and his adversaries.[95] It also recalls the ἡμῖν that the Sadducees related in their account of the seven brothers. Thus the Sadducees are exposed as taking the ridiculous seriously, while neglecting the word of God that is directed towards them. Once more Jesus shows how his opponents are caught up in false perceptions about God and the Law.

Matthew then quotes, following Mark, Ex 3:6. The Matthean redaction assimilates the quotation to the LXX by inserting εἰμι.[96] At the same time, this insertion makes the quotation even more applicable to the present situation.[97] Matthew follows up the quotation with the interpretation given already in Mark, that God is the God of the living and not the dead.[98]

---

[93] Matthew is also more polished than Mk 12:26-27. He omits the clumsy Markan construction τῶν νεκρῶν ὅτι ἐγείρονται in favor of τῆς ἀναστάσεως. This shift allows Matthew a greater thematic continuity with 22:23, 28, 30.

[94] Δ Θ 0102 f[13] 565 omit ὑμῖν, but this is no serious challenge to its original presence.

[95] Again Gundry remarks on the intensification of the guilt of the Sadducees. Gundry: *Matthew*, 446. The argument must extended to the person of Jesus who can make a pronouncement such as this and apply it directly to his opponents.

[96] Apart from the insertion of εἰμι, the Matthean redaction of the quotation is no longer determinable. It can no longer be established whether the second and third occurrence of the definite article ὁ before θεός is due to redaction or not. Some manuscripts omit them from the Matthean version (א) while the presence of this article in Mark is dubious but attested (א A C L Q Ψ f[1.13] and the Majority text). In the LXX, the definite article is absent in all three cases. For Matthew, on balance the article is probably to be assumed for all three places. In the first instance, it is well attested, and in the second and third instance one might assume that Matthew's tendency to use parallels led to the repetition of the article. Hagner considers the insertion of the articles as Matthean redaction. Hagner: *Matthew 14-28*, 642. On the whole the issue cannot be determined with any degree of certainty. For the interpretation of Matthew it is probably marginal.

[97] Gundry: *Matthew*, 446.

[98] Similar to the quotation itself, the only redactional problems are presented by the definite article ὁ. Its presence or absence are equally well attested for Matthew, while its absence in Mark is probable but not assured (present in א A C Ψ f[1] and others). Some minor manuscripts also read in Matthew as well as in Mark ὁ θεὸς θεός. The issue is not really important to the interpretation of Matthew but shows the confusion of the manuscripts.

Matthew closes the controversy with the remark that the crowds were amazed at his teaching. It replaces the Markan repetition that the Sadducees are deceived (12:27b). Matthew uses a formulation that occurred almost exactly already in 7:28.[99] With this change Matthew indicates that the controversy over the resurrection was a public debate. He also keeps his narrative device alive that pictures the series of controversies and parables of chs. 21–22 as a debate over the allegiance of the crowd (21:15, 46). The crowd remains a visible character in the discussion. However, Matthew also leaves the value of the crowd's reaction open.[100] While the teaching of Jesus makes an impression, Matthew does not describe whether this impression is positive or negative. It is a distanced reaction, and as such probably inadequate.[101]

The question of the resurrection itself was not settled in the Judaism of the time of Jesus. The synoptic gospels are not the only witnesses to the Sadducean scepticism concerning the possibility of an afterlife. Josephus mentions it as a distinctive theological difference between them and the Pharisees.[102] Interestingly, Matthew does not use the story to allude to the death and resurrection of Jesus. Consequently, the story does not have the features of a defense of Jesus. It merely raises the general question of a resurrection.[103] The redaction of Matthew focuses

---

[99]   The word order is slightly different. In 7:28, οἱ ὄχλοι appear after ἐξεπλήσσοντο.

[100]   The word ἐξεπλήσσοντο is quite strong in its descriptive force of the crowds being beside themselves. For Matthew, the word does not imply admiration or adulation. It occurs in the first gospel to denote both positive (7:28) and negative reactions (13:54). In 19:25 it seems neutral. Gundry maintains that the crowds are described as disciples and symbolize "the masses of Gentiles coming into the Church." Gundry: *Matthew*, 447. This interpretation goes too far. It does not consider the narrative context, which does not speak of Gentiles, and misses the ambiguous significance of ἐξεπλήσσοντο.

[101]   Walker assumes that the parallel in 7:28–29 expresses a similar "Entsetzen" at the teaching of Jesus that is contrary to the usual teaching of the Scribes. Walker: *Die Heilsgeschichte im ersten Evangelium*, 13. Walker probably stretches the evidence too far. But it is certainly possible to assume in both cases that the reaction of the crowd was not really an adequate response to the teaching of Jesus. Gnilka: *Matthäus*, 2:255.

[102]   Josephus: *J.W.* 2. 14 §§ 162–165; *Ant.* 13. 9 §§ 172–173. Josephus places the teaching of the Sadducees close to Epicureanism. *ARN* A 5 would seem to support the position of Josephus. However, the passage is absent in the earlier *ARN* B. Outside of *ARN* A there is no rabbinic evidence to support Sadducaic disbelief in an afterlife. Saldarini suggests that the position of the Sadducees might be connected with an emphasis on the transcendence of God. Anthony J. Saldarini: *Pharisees, Scribes, and Sadducees in Palestinian Society* (Wilmington: Glazier, 1988), 304. This suggestion is partly directed against an easy assumption that the Sadducees developed their emphasis on the here and now because of their social position as keepers of the status quo. Martin Goodman: *The Ruling Class of Judaea. The Origins of the Jewish Revolt Against Rome 66–70* (Cambridge: Cambridge University Press, 1987), 79. Josephus' attitude towards the Sadducees is not friendly, and one must take this into account when evaluating his reports.

[103]   This feature has led Jeremias to suggest the basic historicity of the controversy. Jeremias: *New Testament Theology*, 1:184 n. 3. Gundry disputes this because "prior to his death Jesus could not refer or be made to refer to his resurrection except by way of prediction, yet until fulfilment

on the features in the story that discredit the opponents and raises the stature of Jesus as a teacher who knows the scriptures and the power of God.

4.1 The Markan Pericope

The Sadducees appear in Mark's gospel only in the pericope of the controversy over the resurrection 12:18–27. As in Matthew, the pericope does not exhibit any allusions to the resurrection of Jesus.[104] Considered together, these elements suggest that the pericope, though perhaps important for the early Christian communities, did not undergo a significant theological development in the light of the resurrection of Jesus and the Christian belief in a resurrection for all believers.[105] It seems possible, then, that Mark preserved a historical reminiscence.[106]

The discrediting of the opponents of Jesus takes place in several steps. They are introduced by Mark as rejecting the resurrection as a group (οἵτινες λέγουσιν 12:18), presumably as part of their interpretation of the Law. It is descriptive of the Sadducees rather than an explicit issue of controversy. Consequently, when Jesus discusses this belief in 12:26–28, this discussion goes beyond the confines of the problem that was originally introduced by the Sadducees. It shows Jesus attacking

---

a prediction does not count as evidence." Gundry: *Mark*, 704. Both arguments are merely hypothetical, though Gundry seems to be quite beside the point. One might imagine Matthew working this controversy into a prediction along the lines of the sign of Jonah, as he has done previously. The pericope could easily have been worked into a prediction without losing the argument from scripture. Yet this has not happened, and to argue for or against historicity because it could or could not have happened is somewhat tedious.

[104] Despite assertions to the contrary by Gnilka and Huber. Gnilka: *Markus*, 161; Huber: *Jesus in Auseinandersetzung*, 292. Both assume that the reader will make the connection to the resurrection of Jesus via the passion predictions. Unfortunately, there are no literary devices or allusions inherent in the story that would encourage the reader to do so.

[105] Hultgren thinks that the pericope reflects the problem of early Christians whose spouses had died and who had remarried. Hultgren: *Adversaries*, 124. But Hultgren must argue from the Lukan expansion of Mk 12:18–25 (Lk 20:34–36). This expansion cannot be used to infer on problems in the community of Mark. Hultgren also argues that Mk 12:26–27 shows an early Christian attempt to prove "that the doctrine of the resurrection of the dead has been swallowed up by the doctrine of the immortality of the soul" of Hellenistic origins (p. 126). His argument is that the immortality of the soul was used as an apology for the resurrection of the body which might have been hard to accept for Hellenistic Christians. But then, Mark uses ἐκ νεκρῶν ἀναστῶσιν (12:25), a language markedly different from that of immortality. The analogies that Hultgren cites (*4 Mac* 7:18–19; 13:17; 16:24–25; *TestXII.Jud* 25:1; *TestXII.Ben* 10:6–8) speak either of a resurrection or an immortality of the soul, but they do not combine them. Consequently, neither the Markan text nor the parallels that Hultgren adduces indicate that Mark tries to combine the teaching of the resurrection with a Hellenistically informed teaching of the immortality of the soul. Mark's text deals only with the question of the resurrection.

[106] Gnilka: *Markus*, 2:161; Pesch: *Markusevangelium*, 2:229. For a full discussion of the arguments, as well as for the suggestion, following Bultmann, that 12:26–28 are secondary additions, see Huber: *Jesus in Auseinandersetzung*, 287–292.

the underlying assumptions inherent in the presentation of the bride of seven brothers.

The answer of Jesus begins with the accusatory question οὐ διὰ τοῦτο πλανᾶσθε. It is only at the end of the pericope that this question is actually transformed into a proper judgment of the Sadducees: πολὺ πλανᾶσθε (12:27). Mark uses the description of the Sadducees to form an inclusion surrounding the argument of Jesus.[107]

The answer itself is surprising in that it actually addresses a question that has not been asked: the question of the doctrine of the resurrection. With this detail Mark perhaps emphasizes the knowledge of Jesus with regard to the underlying problem the Sadducees present. At the same time, Mark returns to Moses whom the Sadducees used as authority to undergird their disbelief. In a sense, Moses is refuted by Moses.[108] Jesus is presented as knowing the Scriptures better that the Sadducees.

The Matthean redaction of this pericope, then, reveals that Matthew only emphasized the points that Mark already made. Matthew's creativity consists mostly in arranging the material to highlight the conflict between the opponents and Jesus, and to draw even more attention to the superiority of Jesus. Matthew achieves this by relating the second answer of Jesus to an actual statement made by the Sadducees, by stating right at the beginning of Jesus' answer that the Pharisees are deceived, and by changing the argument of Jesus slightly so that the Sadducees are refuted by the word of God. The Sadducees are shown to be in opposition to God himself. Furthermore, Matthew personalizes the account to expose the deception of the Sadducees. He inserts "among us" (22:25) and "to you" (22:31).

A very important difference between Matthew and Mark is the changed setting in Matthew. For Matthew, the controversy is a public debate before the crowd, and their reaction is important to him. It is quite possible that Matthew's redaction mirrors the situation which characterized the use of the controversy in Matthew's community. Matthew is not interested so much in transforming or adapting the theological argument concerning the resurrection, as he is in its setting. The importance of the setting, however, may well indicate a situation in the community where it had relevance. It is conceivable that the Matthean version of the controversy over the resurrection mirrors a situation in which the community of the gospel was still interested in winning the crowd away from the Jewish leaders and over to Jesus. The emphasis on the scriptures and the power of God might indicate this. At the same time, the story might have served the attempt to discredit Jewish leaders who were not convinced of Jesus. Therefore, their inadequate understanding of the scriptures and of the power of God is pointed out. To be convincing,

---

[107] Gundry asserts that the inclusion ends with a "powerful putdown of the Sadducees" which is highlighted through the addition and position of πολύ. Gundry: *Mark*, 704.

[108] Gnilka: *Markus*, 2:159.

however, such a reconstruction of the intent behind the redaction of Matthew must be shown to be a consistent feature of the whole gospel.

4.2 Summary of the Matthean Redaction in 22:23–33

Again Matthew provides a story found in Mark with slight but important emphases. He achieves this through stylistic improvements and slight shifts of content:

▸ Stylistically, Matthew creates two questions out of Mark's introduction and one question, and thus can relate them to the double answer of Jesus. With the appearance of the two questions and their answer in form of a chiasm, the conflictual nature of these is emphasized.

▸ Matthew draws attention to the problem of the resurrection by repeating the word throughout the pericope like a *Leitmotiv*.

▸ Matthew turns the ridiculous case study of the seven brothers away from the concept of resurrection and against the Sadducees in an ironic twist.

▸ Matthew turns the irony against the Sadducees into a serious, direct condemnation that they do not understand the word of God.

▸ Jesus appears more assured in Matthew.

▸ Matthew turns the debate public by mentioning the amazement of the crowds.

5. Matthew 22:34–40

The controversy over the great commandment of the Law (22:34–40) follows immediately. Matthew's version follows Mk 12:28–34, but shortens it considerably and creates a new setting for the story. The most striking change Matthew makes concerns the form of the story. In Mark, the story is not a controversy story at all, but a scholastic dialogue[109] between a Scribe and Jesus. The Scribe asks because he wants information for wisdom.[110] Thus in Mark the dialogue ends with the agreement of the Scribe and his being praised by Jesus (12:32–34). Matthew changes the story into a controversy. First, he omits all references that might indicate Jesus and the Scribe in agreement, or that they react positively to one another.[111] Then Matthew omits the Scribe and has the Pharisees return to engage

---

[109] So classified by Bultmann: *History*, 54–55. See also the explanations of Lausberg as "Antwort-Chrie." Lausberg: *Handbuch*, 537–538.

[110] For Bultmann, this is the defining difference between controversy apophthegm and scholastic apophthegm. Bultmann: *History*, 54.

[111] Matthew omits "seeing that he answered them well" (Mk 12:28) and the entire passage 12:32–34: "And the Scribe said to him, 'You are right, Teacher; you have truly said that he is one, and there is no other but he; 33 and to love him with all the heart, and with all the understanding, and with all the strength, and to love one's neighbor as oneself, is much more than all whole burnt

Jesus, and one of them becomes their spokesman and is perhaps further qualified as a lawyer (22:24–35).[112] The Pharisees in Matthew are by now a group known as invariably hostile to Jesus. In a further step, Matthew adds that their representative asked because they wanted to test Jesus (22:35), and that he uses the for Matthew derogatory address "teacher" (22:36). As a result, the setting owes almost nothing to Mk 12:28.[113]

In v. 34 Matthew creates a reference to the preceding controversy. He writes that the Pharisees heard that Jesus had silenced the Sadducees. This statement replaces the friendlier Markan note that the Scribe heard how Jesus answered them well (12:28). The Pharisees, on the defeat of the Sadducees, gather together[114] and question Jesus once more. Matthew may have consciously quoted the messianic Ps 2:2 here.[115] If this is so, the controversial character of the setting is enhanced even further. The participants in the controversy are likewise more clearly characterized. Ps 2:2 speaks of the rise of the foreign kings and rulers against God and his Anointed. In Matthew the Pharisees suddenly are equated with these Gentile kings who plot against God and the Messiah. The setting of the controversy suggests not only that Pharisees, like Gentile kings and rulers, plot against God and his Messiah, but also that their plot will be thwarted. If the allusion to Ps 2:2 makes reference to Jesus as the Anointed of God, it also presages the fate of the Pharisees: "He who sits in the heavens laughs; the Lord takes them in derision" (Ps 2:4). The Pharisees can only enkindle the wrath that will consume them in a disaster they bring upon themselves (Ps 2:12).

---

offerings and sacrifices.' 34 And when Jesus saw that he answered wisely, he said to him, 'You are not far from the kingdom of God.' And after that no one dared to ask him any question."

[112] The description of the Pharisee as a lawyer (νομικός) is somewhat doubtful. Most manuscripts include the word. However, it is absent from family 1 and "widely scattered versional and patristic witnesses." Metzger: *Textual Commentary*, 48–49. In Matthew, the word does not occur elsewhere. The word might have been introduced through the influence of Lk 10:25. Thus, on balance, any judgment on this word is uncertain. However, it also seems likely that for Matthew, if he used the word at all, it was probably more important to characterize the man as one of the Pharisees than as a lawyer.

[113] The only agreements between Mt 22:34–35 and Mk 12:28 are ἀκούσαντες in Mt 22:34 (cf. ἀκούσας in Mk 12:28) and ἐπηρώτησεν ... αὐτόν in 22:35; Matthew keeps the single questioner.

[114] A few manuscripts have instead of ἐπὶ τὸ αὐτό, ἐπ᾽ αὐτόν (D it sy^{s.c}). While this does not put the first reading in any serious doubt, it reflects the setting of hostility which Matthew creates. Harrington points out that the use of the verb συνάγω might refer to the synagogue. Harrington: *Matthew*, 315.

[115] Gundry maintains that "gathered together to the same place" is a typically Matthean allusion to the Old Testament, in this case to Ps 2:2. Gundry: *Matthew*, 447. Indeed, the LXX uses the same phrase there. The full quotation reads: παρέστησαν οἱ βασιλεῖς τῆς γῆς καὶ οἱ ἄρχοντες συνήχθησαν ἐπὶ τὸ αὐτὸ κατὰ τοῦ κυρίου καὶ κατὰ τοῦ Χριστοῦ αὐτοῦ. The parallel is striking. Gnilka suggests that the phrase περὶ τοῦ Χριστοῦ in v. 42 is an additional piece of evidence that Matthew knowingly quoted Ps 2:2. Gnilka: *Matthäus*, 2:259. However, the different prepositions caution against Gnilka's easy association.

In v. 35 Matthew makes it even clearer that the encounter is hostile. The spokesman of the Pharisees is described as πειράζων αὐτόν. In 22:18 this attitude was already rebuked. It marks the question as insincere and recalls previous attempts to entrap Jesus (16:1; 19:3).[116] The atmosphere of hostility is continued into the question of v. 36 by the address "teacher" which the Pharisee uses. The title now occurs for the third time in successive controversies (22:16, 24, 36). As before, the title denotes not only antipathy for Jesus but also irony on the part of Matthew: Those who call Jesus "teacher" never learn from him.

The question itself asks which is the great commandment in the Law. Matthew has changed the question from Mark's version. While Mark was interested in the command that is πρώτη πάντων (12:28), Matthew asks for the command that is μεγάλη ἐν τῷ νόμῳ. The precise meaning of Matthew's phrase depends on the interpretation of "great." On the one hand, it could be taken as a Semitism, where the simple adjective signifies the superlative.[117] However, a definite article is missing, and thus the question might be directed at the quality needed for any commandment to become great.[118] Mark's question aims at the first commandment of them all. Matthew is aware of the impetus of Mark's questions and shows this in 22:38 where he inserts αὕτη ἐστὶν ἡ μεγάλη καὶ πρώτη ἐντολή. Here the definite article is present.[119] The question itself, however, reveals the Matthean intent. Matthew, like Mark, uses the interrogative pronoun ποία. Thus the question is qualitative to begin with. Furthermore, Matthew leaves out the Markan phrase πρώτη πάντων which indicates that Mark's question is aimed at one command that supersedes all others. Given the qualitative nature of the interrogative pronoun and the omission of the Markan specification, Matthew's question is aimed at the kind of commandment that must be considered great. Consequently, Matthew's categorization of commandments differs to a great extent from Mark's. Mark

---

[116] Hagner: *Matthew 14–28*, 646.

[117] Gundry: *Matthew*, 448; Hagner: *Matthew 14–28*, 646; Davies and Allison: *Matthew*, 3:240.

[118] Gnilka maintains that the question aims at the rabbinic practice of weighing commandments against one another as light or heavy. Thus the question about "welche Qualität ein Gebot haben müsse, um unter die großen, wichtigsten gezählt zu werden" would conform more to rabbinical practice and consequently be more Matthean in its intention. Gnilka: *Matthäus*, 2:259. Davies and Allison admit this meaning as a distinct possibility. Davies and Allison: *Matthew*, 3:240.

[119] Davies and Allison use this as the reason to argue for the question to mean "What is the greatest commandment in the Law?" They write: "[I]t is wiser to suppose that question corresponds to answer, and the answer offers 'the greatest and first commandment.'" Davies and Allison: *Matthew*, 3:240. This argument is weighty, but must be qualified by consideration for the second part of the answer of Jesus. Matthew calls the command to love one's neighbor second, yet amplifies it by saying it is like it: δευτέρα δὲ ὁμοία αὐτῇ (22:39). Consequently, while Matthew uses "first" and "second," this use is probably inspired by Mark, while his qualifications of omitting "first" in the question and adding "equal" to the qualify the "second" command indicate that Matthew is interested in the quality that lets one classify the commandments as great. Consequently, ποία should be taken to mean "what sort of."

argues with the category πρώτη and adds δευτέρα. Matthew argues with μεγάλη as a category of commandments and subsumes under this category the Markan distinction between πρώτη and δευτέρα, while at the same time pointing out that they are really the same (ὁμοία 22:39). Consequently, Matthew also omits the further Markan qualification that μείζων τούτων ἄλλη ἐντολή οὐκ ἔστιν (11:31).

With ἐν τῷ νόμῳ Matthew might recall νομικός of v. 36, if that word was present there in the original text. If not, it still represents "Matthew's special diction"[120] and interest (cf. 5:17).

The answer of Jesus is introduced very briefly (22:37).[121] Matthew also reduces Mark's quotation of the introduction to the Shema (Deut 6:4–5). This omission sharpens the focus on the commandment itself.[122] The quotation of Deut 6:5 is different from Mark's version in several respects. Instead of Mark's ἐξ + Genitive Matthew uses the more polished[123] ἐν + Dative. Furthermore, Mark has four elements of the command to love God: with heart, soul, mind and strength (καρδίας, ψυχῆς, διανοίας, ἰσχύας). Matthew takes over the first three elements, but omits the last. On the one hand, this redaction assimilates the Matthean version of the quotation to the text of Deut 6:5 which also has three elements. On the other hand, it is somewhat surprising that Matthew chooses to omit ἰσχύς and keep διάνοια. Both Hebrew text and LXX are, in fact, closer in meaning to ἰσχύς.[124] Perhaps because ἰσχύς does not appear in the LXX either, Matthew chose to retain Mark's first three elements and omit the fourth.

Verse 38 is an addition of Matthew. It echoes v. 36 by repeating μεγάλη and ἐντολή. Matthew asserts that the commandment of Deut 6:5 is the greatest and first commandment. The mention now of πρώτη echoes Mk 12:28–29 and prepares for Matthew 22:39 where the second commandment is introduced.[125] The verse

---

[120] Gundry: *Matthew*, 448. The word νόμος occurs eight times in Matthew, but not in Mark. The phrase ἐν τῷ νόμῳ occurs also in 12:5.

[121] Matthew does not use the Markan introduction to the answer of Jesus ἀπεκρίθη ὁ Ἰησοῦς ὅτι (12:29), but merely notes ὁ δὲ ἔφη αὐτῷ.

[122] Mark's text reads: "The first is, Hear, O Israel: The Lord our God, the Lord is one." Consequent to the abbreviation of Mark is the omission of καί (Mk 12:30). Gundry claims the omission as evidence for Matthew's presumed interest in antinomianism in his community. Gundry: *Matthew*, 449. It must be noted, however, that the context is that of a controversy with opponents who have by now acquired a definite profile in the gospel as opponents of Jesus and the community. Therefore, a transference to presumed antinomians inside the community takes this controversy out of an established narrative context.

[123] Hagner: *Matthew 14–28*, 645.

[124] The Hebrew text reads וּבְכָל־מְאֹדֶךָ while the LXX reads ἐξ ὅλης τῆς δυνάμεώς σου. This departure from the Hebrew text makes it unlikely that Matthew's introduction of the preposition ἐν was motivated by the Hebrew בְּ, as suggested by Gundry: *Matthew*, 449.

[125] Gundry: *Matthew*, 449. Gnilka adds: "Als das größte und erste Gebot ist die Gottesliebe zweimal als das vorrangigste gekennzeichnet." Gnilka: *Matthäus*, 2:260.

emphasizes the importance of the law just mentioned, and together with v. 36 forms an inclusion that heightens the formality of Jesus' declamation of the Shema.

Verse 39 equals the love of neighbor to the love of God. Matthew changes Mark to make this point explicit.[126] He then goes on to quote Lev 19:18 in Mark's version in complete accord with LXX. Matthew emphasizes the second commandment even more in v. 40. He omits Mk 12:31c (μείζων τούτων ἄλλη ἐντολὴ οὐκ ἔστιν) completely. Instead, Matthew summarily mentions the two together and maintains that on these two commandments the whole law the the prophets depend (ἐν ταύταις ταῖς δυσὶν ἐντολαῖς ὅλος ὁ νόμος κρέμαται καὶ οἱ προφῆται). The two commandments are now paired. The commandment to love one's neighbor is no longer, as in Mark, subordinated to the command to love God.[127]

The Matthean formulation has parallels in the rabbinic tradition.[128] The Hebrew and Aramaic equivalents of κρεμάννυμι (תלא‎, תלה‎) are used several times in a way that resembles the Matthean formulation of 22:40. The closest example is the question of Bar Qappara in *b. Ber.* 63a.[129] The formulation is probably Tannaitic. Bar Qappara is a Tanna, though one of the last ones with dates in the early part of the third century. However, the tradition in *m.Hag* 1:8[130] is associated with early Tannaim[131] and possibly dates to the first century.[132]

The parallels in rabbinic literature, as well as the Matthean formulation, are probably part of a wider tendency in Jewish circles to organize the Law by relating individual precepts to more general statements. The saying attributed to Rabbi Hillel is an example of this trend: "Whatever is unpleasant to you, do not do to your neighbor. This is the whole Torah; the rest is interpretation."[133] The purpose for such summaries of the Law in the rabbinic schools seems to have been mostly of a pedagogical nature.[134] These summaries never supersede or abrogate, or are more

---

[126] Matthew changes Mk 12:31 from αὕτη to δὲ ὁμοία αὐτῇ.

[127] Gundry: *Matthew*, 450.

[128] In the LXX, κρεμάννυμι is the most common rendering of תלא/תלה‎. See Terrence A. Donaldson: "The Law That Hangs (Matthew 22:40): Rabbinic Formulation and Matthean Social World," *CBQ* 57 (1995): 689, n. 1.

[129] "What is the smallest portion of scripture from which all essential regulations of the Torah hang (תְּלוּיִין‎)?" The answer is given with Prov 3:6: "In all your ways acknowledge hims, and he will direct your paths." There are similar references in *m.Hag* 1:8; *m.Hag* 1:9; *t.Er* 8:23.

[130] The quote here is: "The rules about release from vows hover in the air and have naught to support them; the rules about the Sabbath, festal offerings, and sacrilege are as mountains hanging (תְּלוּיִין‎) by a hair, for teaching of Scripture thereon is scanty and the rules many."

[131] The rabbis associated with this particular tradition are Joshua ben Hananiah, a pupil of Yohanan ben Zakkai, Eliezer, Isaac, and Tarphon.

[132] Safrai dates this to the first century on the grounds that in 1:9 Abba Yose ben Hanin makes a halakhic statement that is not founded on scripture. Samuel Safrai: *The Literature of the Sages*, CRI 2/3 (Philadelphia: Fortress, 1987), 124, 155–156.

[133] See *b.Shabb.* 31a.

[134] Donaldson: "The Law That Hangs," 692.

binding than, the individual commandments that they supposedly summarize. Their purpose rather was as a pedagogical tool to teach pupils an aid for the memorization of the more detailed individual laws.[135]

For the interpretation of Matthew such a rabbinical use of 22:40 would imply, then, that all precepts of the Law are subsumed under the double command of love, but none of them are abrogated. However, a number of difficulties arise with this interpretation.[136] In several controversies so far, Matthew met a challenge of unlawful behavior with an appeal to mercy (e.g. 12:1–14). There is general agreement among scholars that in several antitheses in the Sermon on the Mount the letter of the Law is set aside.[137] On the other hand, Matthew is not prepared to abrogate the Law (5:17–20; 23:2). The formulation in 22:40 assumes that the double love commandment is the linchpin for the whole law and the prophets. Thus the whole of the Law remains in force.[138] Matthew 22:40 seems to imply not just a memory card for learning the Law, but a hermeneutical principle that allows for the interpretation of the Law.[139]

This difference in emphasis between the Matthean and the rabbinic use of κρέμαται should not be overemphasized.[140] There is only one real conclusion the

---

[135] Birger Gerhardsson: *Memory and Manuscript: Oral Tradition and Written Transmission in Rabbinic Judaism and Early Christianity*, ASNU 22 (Lund, Copenhagen: Gleerup, Munksgaard, 1961), 136–148; John Bowker: *The Targums and Rabbinic Literature* (Cambridge: Cambridge University Press, 1969), 51.

[136] Donaldson: "The Law That Hangs," 691–693.

[137] Generally, the third and the fifth antithesis can be interpreted to set aside a literal interpretation of the Law; for a survey of the pertinent literature see Snodgrass: "Matthew and the Law," 183, n. 21.

[138] Harrington adds: "At least in theory." Harrington: *Matthew*, 316.

[139] Günther Bornkamm: "Das Doppelgebot der Liebe," in: *Neutestamentliche Studien für Rudolf Bultmann zu seinem siebzigsten Geburtstag am 20. August 1954*, ed. W. Eltester, BZNW 21 (Berlin: Alfred Töpelmann, 1954), 93.

[140] Donaldson, e.g., asks the question "why Matthew would use such a characteristically rabbinic formulation in such an anti-Pharisaic passage, and to such unrabbinic ends." Donaldson: "The Law That Hangs," 694. His whole article is devoted to show that in this phrase Matthew exhibits a trend in which a Christian community of both Jews and Gentiles adheres to the Law, but in a manner that fundamentally separates them from the emerging formative Judaism under the leadership of the Pharisees. The central argument for Donaldson is the use of the word κρεμάννυμι. It is, at the same time, his weakest link: He has to assume a fixed and established meaning of the Greek word as translating a *terminus technicus* in Pharisaic circles that is reflected in the later rabbinic writings. Would Matthew have known that he used the formulation to "unrabbinic ends?" It is no longer possible to determine with any certainty that the Matthean use of the double love command as a hermeneutical principle for the interpretation of the Law was entirely unrabbinic at the end of the first century. Such an assumption is hard to uphold since the earliest parallel that exhibits a use of the word similar to that of Matthew is the passage of Bar Qappara. The probably earlier passage in *m.Hag* 1:8 uses the term differently. The passage of Bar Qappara is much too late to infer any significance into Mt 22:40, and the passage from *m.Hag* 1:8 shows that there was no unanimity in the use of the term, at least between *m.Hag* and Matthew.

rabbinic parallels allow for: Matthew used a Greek word which in the LXX translates a Hebrew word employed later on by some rabbis as a *terminus technicus* for summaries of the Law as pedagogical aids. Whether the term was widely used already in Matthew's time can no longer be determined with certainty. Consequently, a fixed use as a *terminus technicus* among the Pharisees contemporary with Matthew seems a presumption. Even more unlikely is the assumption that its Greek translation was such for Matthew himself.[141]

Lk 10:25–28 offers a text that resembles the Matthean version of the controversy over the double love command to some extent.[142] These commonalities have led to various solutions trying to explain them. It has been proposed that

(a) Matthew used only Mark's text, but revised it considerably.[143]

(b) Matthew and Luke used an earlier[144] or a later[145] form of Mark's text.

(c) Matthew conflated parallels in Mark and Q.[146]

This leaves Donaldson with the argument of the general tendency to summarize the Law. But again, the evidence for such summaries among the rabbis is too late to suggest a common and established methodology for such summaries soon after the destruction of the temple. Gnilka summarizes succinctly: "Im Sinne der rabbinischen Ableitbarkeit, für die entsprechend halsbrecherische Exegesen zu Hilfe zu holen wären, werden wir den Satz nicht interpretieren dürfen." Gnilka: *Matthäus*, 2:261.

[141] The word occurs once more in Matthew. In 18:6 it is also a redactional element of Matthew's. The pertinent phrase is: συμφέρει αὐτῷ ἵνα κρεμασθῇ μύλος ὀνικὸς περὶ τὸν τράχηλον αὐτοῦ. This verse represents a redaction of Mk 9:42. When Matthew here uses κρεμάννυμι instead of περίκειμαι the redaction indicates that he is familiar with the word in its normal sense and knows how to use it. If Matthew likes the word in 18:6 in the non-technical sense, it is quite possible that he did not intend the rabbinic *terminus technicus* in 22:39, even if he might have been acquainted with such a use of the word.

[142] Common with Matthew are v. 25: νομικός, though its presence in Matthew 22:34 is in some doubt, cf. above; ἐκπειράζων αὐτόν, though Matthew 22:34 uses the simple form of the verb πειράζων; διδάσκαλε; v. 26: ὁ δέ; there might be a relation between εἶπεν πρὸς αὐτόν and the Matthean ἔφη αὐτῷ; in v. 28 Luke first uses the preposition ἐξ found in Mk 12:30, but then switches to ἐν found in Matthew 22:37. Both Matthew and Luke do not report the conciliatory note of Mk 12:32–34, and both omit the Markan remark that the Scribe saw that Jesus answered the Sadducees well.

[143] Stendahl: *School of St. Matthew*, 75.

[144] Bornkamm: "Doppelgebot," 92.

[145] Ennulat: *Die "Minor Agreements,"* 287.

[146] Bultmann: *History*, 22–23; Bornkamm: "Doppelgebot;" Reginald H. Fuller: "Das Doppelgebot der Liebe," in: *Jesus Christus in Historie und Theologie. FS Hans Conzelmann*, ed. Luise Schottroff (Tübingen: Mohr, 1975), 322; Strecker: *Weg*, 25–26; Arland Hultgren: "The Double Commandment of Love in Mt 22:34–40. Its Sources and Compositions," *CBQ* 36 (1974): 373–378; Hultgren: *Adversaries*, 48–49. There is some disagreement as to whether a supposed tradition common to both Matthew and Luke is to be identified with Q. Bornkamm and Fuller are vague on the point, while Bultmann, Strecker and Hultgren suppose that a version existed within Q. If Matthew and Luke used a common source it is hard to distinguish this tradition from a supposedly different common tradition of Q.

(d) Matthew used and revised an existing conflation of Mark and Q.[147]

(e) Matthew adapted only a text in Q.[148]

(f) all evangelists are independent.[149]

The narrative sequence of Matthew 22:34–40 as well as the considerable amount of verbal agreement with Mark make Matthean independence from Mark highly unlikely. There remains the question whether Matthew might have been influenced by Q as well. The Lukan account of the pericope occurs in a context entirely different, namely as the introduction to the parable of the good Samaritan.[150] While Matthew redacts the account into a controversy story, Luke shapes an interpretation of the love command in the light of Gentile participation in the kingdom of God. Thus the omission of Mk 12:32–34 is explainable for both Matthew and Luke on the basis of their redactional intent. Furthermore, in the Lukan account the double commandment appears on the lips of the lawyer, not of Jesus, while the distinction between a first and a second commandment disappears completely. Luke reports both as if they were one. Finally, Luke's question that gives rise to the quotation does not concern the Law or the commandments, but the gaining of eternal life. Luke is probably dependent here on Mk 10:17.[151]

The verbal agreements between Matthew and Luke[152] must be accounted for from the interest of the Matthew redaction if dependence on Q seems unlikely. The agreement on νομικός cannot really amount to an argument since its presence in Matthew is highly suspect and might be a scribal introduction because of the Lukan parallel. The agreement of πειράζων (Luke: ἐκπειράζων) need not necessarily be attributed to a common source. Matthew likes this word in the context of controversies (16:1; 19:3; 22:18; 22:35) and introduces it at least once into material received from his sources (16:1). Thus it is quite possible that Matthew introduced the word here without a prompt from some source. The same can be said for the address διδάσκαλε. It is by now so familiar as the address that Matthean opponents of Jesus use, that its appearance here cannot be used for source-critical arguments. Matthew merely continues what he found already in Mark in the controversies over taxes and the resurrection (12:14, 19; cf. Mt 22:15, 24). The easy explanation of the verbal agreements in terms of Matthean redaction, and the differences in emphases of Luke and Matthew, make it difficult to sustain a theory of a double

---

[147] Kenneth J. Thomas: "Liturgical Citations in the Synoptics," *NTS* 22 (1975–1976): 209–214.

[148] Klaus Berger: *Gesetzesauslegung*, 203.

[149] Lohmeyer: *Matthäus*, 327–330.

[150] The supposition of the presence of this material in Q ought to account for its location in Q. But as Matthew and Mark agree over its context, and as Luke is usually more reliable for the reconstruction of the sequence in Q, such an account is frought with difficulties. Ennulat: *Die "Minor Agreements,"* 280.

[151] See Fitzmyer: *Luke*, 2:878.

[152] If the material did indeed exist in Q, the verbal agreement between Matthew and Luke is statistically at the low margin. Ennulat: *Die "Minor Agreements,"* 280.

tradition influencing Matthew. It is more likely that the minor agreements between Matthew and Luke are due to their respective redactions of Mk 12:28–31.[153]

5.1 The Markan Pericope

The conversation over the greatest commandment in Mk 12:28–34 is somewhat untypical of Mark in its positive portrayal of the Scribe and the conversation as a whole.[154] The Scribe who approaches Jesus listens to the preceding controversies and perceives that Jesus answers well (12:28).[155] He asks Jesus a question and receives as answer the double commandment of love. The Scribe agrees almost[156] completely with Jesus, repeats the double command, and finally receives praise from Jesus (12:34). The friendliness has prompted the assumption that Mark reports a story that he found in his tradition.[157]

Mark's formulation of the question, and its consequent answer and praise of the Scribe, reveal a treatment of the Law that is markedly different from Matthew. While Matthew asks for the great commandment, Mark asks for the first of all (πρώτη πάντων 12:28). The answer that Jesus gives quotes Deut 6:4–5 in greater

---

[153] Gundry's hypothesis of Matthean influence on Luke is also less than likely. Gundry: *Matthew*, 448. The different settings for Matthew and Luke, their common interest in shaping the pericope into a more hostile atmosphere, and the closer affinity of Luke to Mark in the quotation of Deut 6:5 render his conclusion tenuous. Fitzmyer offers an appealing variation of the double tradition theory. He argues that "the whole form of the episode in the Lukan Gospel is so different from the Markan story that it should be ascribed to 'L.' The use of 'lawyer' instead of 'one of the Scribes' and the omission of the first part of the Shema (Deut 6:4; cf. Mar 12:29b) could easily be explained by Luke's redactional concern for the predominantly Gentile audience for whom he is writing, if these elements were really part of his inherited story. Luke may, however, be influenced by Mk." Fitzmyer: *Luke*, 2:877–878.

[154] Huber: *Jesus in Auseinandersetzung*, 294.

[155] Gundry does not see this approach in a positive light: "We have no good reason to think that the Scribe approaches Jesus any less antagonistically than did the Pharisees or Sadducees." Gundry: *Mark*, 710. However, Gundry's main argument that the remark in 12:34c reflects on the approach of this particular Scribe is less than convincing. After all, there is no need to infer that the καλῶς of 12:28 is an acknowledgment of Jesus' superiority in argument, while in 12:32 it comments on the truthfulness of Jesus' answer.

[156] The Scribe makes a minor correction to the answer of Jesus. In 12:30, Jesus mentions καὶ ἐξ ὅλης τῆς διανοίας σου, while in v. 33 the Scribe amends the answer of Jesus by eliminating διανοίας and substituting συνέσεως. The latter term reflects the LXX version, while the former does not.

[157] Gnilka writes: "Man wird davon ausgehen können, daß dem Evangelisten die Perikope in ihrer vorliegenden Gestalt – von geringfügigen Änderungen abgesehen – vorgegeben war. Die sie bestimmende Intention ist die Werbung um das Judentum mit Hilfe der Schriftargumentation, wie sie in der Übereinstimmung des Schriftgelehrten mit Jesus (32–34a) zum Ausdruck kommt. Diese Intention kann aber kaum als spezifisch markinisch angesprochen werden. Markus bemüht sich nur um die Verklammerung der Perikope nach vorwärts und rückwärts." Gnilka: *Markus*, 2:162–163. Gundry disputes this claim on the grounds that the present story must be analyzed together with the condemnation of the Scribes in 12:35–37a. Gundry: *Mark*, 709.

detail than Matthew by including "Hear o Israel, the Lord our God, the Lord is one" (12:29). But the real meaning of πρώτη πάντων is brought out in the praise that the Scribe heaps on Jesus. The double love commandment "is much more than all whole burnt offerings and sacrifices" (12:33). Jesus then goes on to commend this attitude by answering that the Scribe is not far from the kingdom (12:34).

The double love commandment is interpreted by Mark to imply a critique of the temple cult. Such a critique has its roots in the Hebrew Scriptures, continues through Jewish Hellenistic writings and continues into the Qumran writings.[158] It receives an emphasis through its setting in the temple and its formulation by a Scribe.[159] It is, however, unusual for the critique of the cult to be set in the context of a discussion of a summary of the Law. More usual in the precedents is the setting of the critique of the cult in the context of a critique of people who do not keep the Law. The superiority of the love command over the cult is emphasized by the summary dismissal of the cult (περισσότερόν ἐστιν πάντων … 12:33). In this way, Mark uses Deut 6:4–5 and Lev 19:18 against the commandments governing the cult.

For Mark, the question of the first commandment entails a grading of importance. The function of the cult critique is to allow for precisely such a gradation. Matthew resists this trend. For him, the double commandment provides a summary of the Law that includes all commandments and excludes none. With this intent Matthew is much closer than Mark to the double love commandment found in Philo.[160] It is hard to say whether such a gradation within the Law points to a more Gentile background of Mark. However, the Matthean interpretation of the double commandment shows closer parallels to Jewish literature. It also shows that Matthew felt uncomfortable with such a gradation. Consequently, he did not incorporate it into his account.

The Matthean redaction of the story brings Matthew's argument closer to a Jewish context. This context was, in Matthew's eyes, more controversial; and so Matthew forms a controversy story out of the didactic conversation of Mark. However, the controversy did not center around the interpretation of the great commandment. It focuses on the participants in the debate. Again it seems that Matthew was interested in discrediting the opponents of Jesus among the Jewish leadership, not Judaism as a whole.

---

[158] 1 Sam 15:22; Ps 40:7; 50:8; 51:18–21; Prov 16:7; 21:3; Is 1:11–13; Jer 6:20; 7:21–23; 14:12; Hos 6:6; Am 5:21–27; Mic 6:6–8; Sir 35:1–4; Dan 3:38; *Arist* 234; 1 QS 9:4–5.

[159] Gnilka: *Markus*, 2:167; Huber: *Jesus in Auseinandersetzung*, 303.

[160] Philo: *Special Laws* 2.63: "But among the vast number of particular truths and principles there studies, there stand out practically high above the others two main heads (κεφάλαια): one of duty to God as shewn by piety and holiness, one of duty to men as shewn by humanity and justice, each of them splitting up into multiform branches, all highly laudable."

5.2 Summary of the Matthean Redaction in 22:34–40

Matthew sets the topic of the greatest commandment into the context of a controversy, but remains with his redaction within a clearly Jewish framework.

▸ Matthew constructs a controversy out of the friendly discussion in Mark.

▸ Matthew constructs a setting that reflects extreme hostility of the opponents who are changed to be Pharisees.

▸ The hostility is accentuated by the mention of the motivation of the Pharisees.

▸ The christological implications are drawn out by the possible quotation of the messianic Ps 2:2. Jesus is revealed as the Messiah through the opposition of the Pharisees.

▸ Matthew changes the direction of the discussion from a gradation of the Law to a qualification of specific commandments as great.

▸ Matthew emphasizes the quotation of the Shema though an inclusion and the mentioning of three elements of love instead of Mark's four.

6. Matthew 22:41–46

The last controversy story in the gospel of Matthew (22:41–46) returns to the question of the Son of David. It follows immediately on the discussion of the double love commandment and has a parallel in Mk 12:35–37. Matthew redacts the Markan primitive apophthegm[161] into a controversy story. Matthew creates a setting of a dialogue with Pharisees, who are known to be hostile. Jesus puts a question to the Pharisees, who answer it. Then Jesus utters a pronouncement on the answer of the Pharisees that reduces them to silence.[162] Matthew connects the controversy with the preceding one through a reference to the Pharisees who are gathered

---

[161] In his discussion of the form and history of apophthegms Bultmann notes that Mk 12:35–37 "is a passage the does not appear in Mark in the form of a debate, but in Matt. 22[41–46], it becomes a controversy dialogue in which, on this occasion, Jesus himself launches the attack." Bultmann: *History*, 51. Yet even in this primitive form, Bultmann still recognizes the influence of "the church" (p.66).

[162] Gnilka disputes the form of this story as controversy on the grounds that the opinion that the Christ is the son of David is shared by the opponents in the story. Gnilka: *Matthäus*, 2:263. However, Hultgren rightly points out that the whole story is based on conflict between the Pharisees and Jesus. The story does not wish to deny that the Messiah is the son of David, but points further to the Messiah being the son of God, a conclusion which the Pharisees are unable or unwilling to draw. Hultgren concludes: "In Matthew we have a fully stylized story portraying conflict: opponents, who are identified as a group, are present; they are asked a question by Jesus which is designed to provoke conflict; they answer; and they are refuted by Jesus in an appeal to Scripture and a closing question." Hultgren: *Adversaries*, 46.

together.[163] The Pharisees remain the opponents in this story, though now they are addressed as a group, and not through one of them as their representative (cf. 22:35). For the first time in the entire gospel Jesus himself opens the controversy with a question.

The controversy centers around the identity of Jesus. Although Jesus' question refers to the Christ in the third person (22:42), the gospel has shown already that Jesus is the Christ.[164] The preceding controversy story with its quotation of Ps 2:2 pointed out how Jesus is revealed as Messiah in the opposition of Israel's leaders. Thus the reader knows that Jesus is the Christ, even though within the narrative of the present controversy the opponents of Jesus do not recognize him as such.

The Matthean redaction is extensive in its creation of a new setting for the Markan monologue. Matthew introduces the Pharisees, while in Mark the discourse of Jesus was directed to an indistinct group that was listening to his teaching.[165] The redaction of the setting creates a greater sense of immediacy and urgency to the controversy by focusing on the opponents and binding it more closely to the preceding controversies. This immediacy is underlined by Matthew's change of opponents to the Pharisees, while Mk 12:35 uses the Scribes.

The opening question in Mk 12:35 is redacted into a dialogue by Matthew 22:42. Τί ὑμῖν δοκεῖ is a favorite formula of Matthew.[166] Its insertion renders the rhetorical question of Mk 12:35 as two questions in Matthew, the first introduced with τί, the second introduced with τίνος. The Pharisees' answer is short (τοῦ Δαυίδ) and reflects Mark's rhetorical question.[167]

---

[163] The genitive absolute συνηγμένων δὲ τῶν Φαρισαίων (22:41) recalls οἱ δὲ Φαρισαῖοι | συνήχθησαν (22:34). Mark seems to assume quite a separation from the preceding story since he introduces a new teaching context (διδάσκων ἐν τῷ ἱερῷ). Furthermore, his ἀποκριθείς is quite unconnected. These two features indicate a narrative break that is omitted in Matthew.

[164] Matthew makes this point forcefully from the beginning. The title of the gospel (1:1) mentions that Jesus is the Christ, and the genealogy does so repeatedly (1:16, 17, 18). In the editorial remark 11:2 Matthew calls Jesus Christ, and the confession of Peter (16:16) contains the title, though the disciples are exhorted to keep this a secret (16:20). In the passion narrative the title is extensively used to show how the leaders of Israel rejected the Messiah (26:63–65; 68; 27:17, 22).

[165] Mt 22:41 omits καὶ ἀποκριθείς (Mk 12:35), probably because in Mark the participle is unwarranted; nobody had asked Jesus a question, and the last one speaking had been Jesus, coupled with the express remark that no one dared to ask him any questions (12:34). Instead Matthew inserts συνημένων δὲ τῶν Φαρισαίων. The Markan διδάσκων becomes ἐπερώτησεν αὐτούς, while ἐν τῷ ἱερῷ is omitted. In 22:42 Matthew prefaces the question of Jesus with λέγων that is possibly influenced by Mark's ἔλεγεν. Gundry: *Matthew*, 450.

[166] 17:25; 18:12; 21:28; 22:17; 22:42; 26:66. All these instances are redactional; only in 26:66 does Mk 14:64 have a similar phrase: τί ὑμῖν φαίνεται.

[167] Gundry sees the answer of the Pharisees as a protection of Jesus' later question "from being misunderstood as a denial of Davidic sonship." Gundry: *Matthew*, 451. This reads probably too much into Matthew's purpose. The options for turning the rhetorical question of Mark into a dialogue are limited, and it is hard to see how the mention of Davidic sonship by Jesus in Mark

The introduction of the Davidic sonship of the Messiah sets up the controversy proper. In v. 43 Jesus goes on to challenge the Pharisees to explain why David calls his son "Lord." The Matthean redaction emphasizes the point more strongly than Mk 12:36 by mentioning it already before the actual quotation of Ps 110:1. Jesus' answer begins with πῶς οὖν[168] and substitutes Mark's εἶπεν with καλεῖ αὐτὸν κύριον λέγων. Matthew emphasizes David's calling him "Lord" by moving it to the end of the sentence and pulling ἐν πνεύματι forward.[169] David speaks in the spirit of prophecy, as he does in Mk 12:36.[170]

In v. 44 Matthew quotes Mark's version (12:36) of Ps 110:1. The text follows the LXX with the exception of using ὑποκάτω instead of ὑποπόδιον. Ps 110:1 was popular in early Christianity.[171] It was most often used as a scriptural basis for the assertion of Jesus' exaltation and ascension to God's right hand (Acts 2:34–35; 1 Cor 15:25; Heb 1:3; 8:1; 10:12; Mk 16:19). Here, however, the quotation has the function of making an assertion about the identity of Jesus as Lord and Son of David.[172] Matthew is particularly interested in the relationship between these two titles.[173] The double mention of the κύριος title in Matthew shifts the emphasis precisely to this point. While Mark seems more interested in the paradox of a father calling his son "Lord,"[174] the Matthean redaction draws attention to the connection between the two titles. Matthew connected the "Son of David" with "Lord" already several times previously (15:22; 20:30, 31).[175]

---

lends itself to its denial. Similarly, it seems specious to say that because in Matthew Jesus does not mention Davidic sonship himself it leaves him more open to widen the christology to divine sonship. After all, in Mark Jesus reports Davidic sonship as a teaching of the Scribes.

[168] Probably inspired by Mark's πῶς in 12:35; οὖν is a Matthean favorite.

[169] The omission of Mark's τῷ ἁγίῳ and the anarthrous use of πνεῦμα might be simply an abbreviation. Hagner: *Matthew 14–28*, 650. It could perhaps reflect apocalyptic usage as in Rev 1:10; 4:2; 17:3; 21:10; Ezek 11:24; 37:1. Gundry: *Matthew*, 451. Gundry also recognizes a shift in meaning from Mark's speaking by the Spirit to Matthew's being in the Spirit at the time of speaking.

[170] Harrington: *Matthew*, 317.

[171] For a complete study see David M. Hay: *Glory at the Right Hand. Psalm 110 in Early Christianity*, SBL.MS 18 (Nashville: Abingdon, 1973).

[172] Not so Bornkamm, who sees the quotation as the Matthean legitimation for calling Jesus "Lord." Bornkamm: "Enderwartung," 39.

[173] Strecker writes: "Da der Evangelist 'Davidsohn' durchaus als positive christologische Bezeichnung verwendet, ist von vorneherein ausgeschlossen, daß er … den Titel abgelehnt wissen wollte. Tatsächlich sagt der Wortlaut des Textes nichts von einer Alternative zwischen υἱὸς Δαυίδ und κύριος, sondern fragt nach dem Verhältnis der beiden Messiasprädikationen (vgl. V. 45)." Strecker: *Weg*, 119.

[174] Mark's gospel as a whole views the title "Son of David" as insufficient and superseded by "Son of God." Christoph Burger: *Jesus als Davidssohn*, FRLANT 98 (Göttingen: Vandenhoeck & Ruprecht, 1970), 42–71.

[175] Burger: *Jesus als Davidssohn*, 89.

This interest is further stressed in the redaction of Matthew 22:45. Matthew changes the statement in Mk 12:37 into a conditional clause with the introduction of εἰ and puts this clause in parallel with 22:43b. In this way Matthew also marks an inclusion for the quotation of Ps 110:1. He concludes the conditional clause with the question in what way the Messiah is the Son of David. Matthew changes Mark's πόθεν into πῶς, indicating that he is not interested in the origin of the title "Son of David." Matthew is asking for the manner in which the Messiah can be both Son of David and Lord. The use of πῶς indicates that both claims are true,[176] but their relationship is the matter of this controversy.[177] The title "Son of David" is once again important for Matthew in the context of conflict.[178]

"Lord" is a variegated title. The Greek term κύριος had a wide range of meanings depending on the context. In daily life it could be used as a polite form of address, and often denoted people of high social stature. In the New Testament and some Jewish literature including the LXX, the word was used to translate the *tetragrammaton* יהוה. Furthermore, its equivalent in Aramaic also served to denote God.[179]

Matthew reflects the wide possibilities of the word. He uses κύριος for God several times,[180] but uses the word as well to indicate the more conventional attitude of respect (27:63) or to indicate a relationship between slave and master (10:24). Matthew's most frequent use of the word occurs, however, as an address for Jesus, either by his disciples or by those who seek his help. In this use of the title Matthew shows a great increase over his sources.[181] Thus the title seems of some importance to Matthew.[182] However, it is equally significant that the title is often used in

---

[176] Against Chilton, who argues that Matthew is not at all interested in the title "son of David" for Jesus. Bruce D. Chilton: "Jesus *ben David*: Reflections on the *Davidssohnfrage*," *JSNT* 14 (1982): 88–112. The frequent use of the title in the gospel militates against this position.

[177] Gnilka writes: "Die argumentative Verwendung des Psalmverses in diesem Sinn kommt durch die Wie-Fragen gut heraus." Gnilka: *Matthäus*, 2:266. See also Gundry: *Matthew*, 452; Hagner: *Matthew 14–28*, 651.

[178] See Stanton: *Gospel*, 180–185.

[179] J. Fitzmyer gives a detailed survey and review of the material where κύριος is used for God in Jewish literature around the first century. Joseph A. Fitzmyer: "The Semitic Background For the New Testament *Kyrios*-Title," in: *A Wandering Aramean. Collected Aramaic Essays*, SBL.DS 25 (Missoula: Scholars Press, 1979), 120–123.

[180] See for example 4:7, 10; 5:33; 9:38; 11:25; 21:9; 27:10; 28:2.

[181] As Matthean redaction "Lord" occurs in 8:2, 6; 14:28, 30; 15:22, 25; 16:22; 18:21; etc. Matthew uses "Lord" as it occurs in Q in 8:8 ‖ Q 7:6; 8:21 ‖ Q 9:59. In 15:27 the use of the title is paralleled in Mk 7:28. Often Matthew uses the title in order to substitute another in Mk: 8:25 ‖ Mk 4:38 (teacher); 9:28=20:33 ‖ Mk 10:51 (rabbouni); 17:4 ‖ Mk 9:5 (rabbi); 17:15 ‖ 9:17 (teacher).

[182] Some scholars have argued that the frequency with which the title is applied to Jesus indicates Matthew's most significant title. Bornkamm: "Enderwartung."; Strecker: *Weg*, 123–126; Trilling: *Das wahre Israel*, 21–51.

conjunction with another title for Jesus.[183] It occurs together with "Son of David" (9:27; 15:22), "Son of Man" (24:42), or "Son of God" (14:28, 30). Thus the meaning of the title κύριος was fairly fluid for Matthew.

In the quotation of Ps 110:1 there are two "Lords" mentioned. The first translates יהוה and thus means God, while the second "Lord" (לַאדֹנִי) is the one being enthroned. The second Lord is the one who, according to the interpretation of Ps 110:1 given by Matthew, is also the Son of David. With a wordplay on κύριος Matthew suggests that Jesus is Lord just as God is Lord. The Messiah, the Christ, is both Son of David and Lord, which is developed into denoting Son of God.[184]

The reaction of the Pharisees is described in 22:46, which loosely resembles Mk 12:34b[185] and replaces Mk 12:37b.[186] Matthew states that no one was able to answer Jesus anything at all, nor did anyone dare to ask him any more questions. The victory of Jesus over his opponents is complete, they are silenced utterly and forever. Matthew's use of the controversy stories had the opponents of Jesus come again and again with questions and doubts about his identity. However, Jesus needs only one challenge to send his opponents into stupefaction. This challenge is significant in its exploration of messianic teaching. It shows the Pharisees unable to explain the scriptures concerning the Messiah. Their silence on the matter marks them as people who have not understood their Jewish heritage. Their failure to understand the messianic teaching of the scripture paints them as leaders without legitimacy. At the challenge of Jesus who is Son of David, Lord, and Son of God, their defeat is complete. Their utter failure as leaders of Israel prepares for the teaching against Pharisees and Scribes that is directed towards crowds and disciples (23:1).

It is also perhaps significant that the last group of Jesus' opponents to be silenced are the Pharisees. Matthew changes the Markan Scribes (12:35) into Pharisees (22:41) and makes their evil intent clear from the outset of the controversy (συνηγμένων). Furthermore, he relates specifically that with the silencing of these Pharisees all opposition to Jesus in discussion ended. Because of their failure to reply to Jesus no one dared to ask Jesus any more questions (22:46). Jesus' victory over the Pharisees in this controversy signifies the victory over the entire Jewish leadership. Possibly the redactional work of the evangelist again relates to the social situation of his community. Matthew experienced the opposition of the

---

[183] See especially Jack D. Kingsbury: *Matthew: Structure, Christology, and Kingdom* (Philadelphia: Fortress, 1975), 112.

[184] Gnilka: *Matthäus*, 2:267; Hagner: *Matthew 14–28*, 651; Harrington: *Matthew*, 318.

[185] At the end of the controversy over the resurrection Mark wrote: καὶ οὐδεὶς οὐκέτι ἐτόλμα αὐτὸν ἐπερωτῆσαι. Matthew retains καὶ οὐδείς and uses ἐτόλμησεν ... οὐκέτι. However, the sense is changed considerably.

[186] Mark remarks that "the great throng heard him gladly." The replacement is motivated by the immediately following teaching of Jesus against the Scribes and Pharisees in ch. 23.

Pharisees much more directly than that of the Sadducees or Chief Priests. It is quite possible that the controversies of the Matthean community with the Pharisees were related in some fashion to the identity of Jesus. The first and the final controversy story in Jerusalem form an inclusion with their subject matter being the title "Son of David" applied to Jesus. Thus this final controversy might serve as climax and highlight for the conflict between the Matthean community and the Pharisees after the destruction of the temple. If indeed the Matthean community was as law-abiding as the gospel implies, such controversy probably centered around the person of Jesus and interpretation of him in the community. The last controversy might thus highlight a Jewish community that had accepted Jesus as Messiah, Son of David, and Lord. Such a community would have been quite at odds with the Pharisees and their heirs after the destruction of the temple and during the struggle for the formation of a post-temple Jewish nation and religious identity.

6.1 The Markan Pericope

When compared to the gospel of Matthew, the gospel of Mark uses the title "Son of David" only sparsely, and then only in connection with Jesus' stay in Jerusalem. Bartimaeus, the blind beggar of 10:46–52, meets Jesus on his way from Jericho to Jerusalem. In his request for healing, Bartimaeus calls Jesus "Son of David" (10:47–48), but later on in his conversation with Jesus calls him "Rabbi" (10:50). During the entrance into Jerusalem, the crowds acclaim the coming of the kingdom of David (11:10); while the acclamation is obviously connected with the entrance of Jesus into Jerusalem, it is not made explicit that Jesus is the Son of David. Finally, Jesus ends his teaching in the Jerusalem temple with the teaching on the Son of David, yet again without claiming the title explicitly for himself (12:35–37). Thus the title "Son of David" does not seem to be a major christological theme for the gospel of Mark. This is confirmed by Mk 12:37–40. The title "son of David" is not a proper title for Jesus.[187]

The explanation for such reticence lies to a certain extent in the characteristically Markan lack of interest in a precise outline of the nature of Jesus' identity through titles.[188] Even the much more important title "Son of God" is used sparingly, although at critical junctures in the gospel.[189] For Mark, it was more important to

---

[187] Burger suggests, with reference to Jn 9:41–42, that the thrust of this story is the entire rejection of the title for Jesus. Burger: *Jesus als Davidssohn*, 56. This probably goes too far. Mark is not interested in the title, yet there is not explicit rejection, either. Gnilka: *Markus*, 2:170–171; Gundry: *Mark*, 721–724. The interpretation of the Johannine reference as a rejection of Davidic sonship for Jesus is equally problematic. Raymond E. Brown: *The Gospel According to John*, AncB 29–29A (Garden City: Doubleday, 1966–1970), 2:329–330.

[188] Best: *Mark*, 79.

[189] For this reason, Kee is wrong in attributing to Mark an avoidance of the title. Howard C. Kee: *Community of the New Age: Studies in Mark's Gospel* (Philadelphia: Westminster, 1977), 124.

show what Jesus does than to describe who Jesus is.[190] When the title "Son of David" rises to prominence here, its purpose must be examined. Basically two approaches have been taken.[191]

It is possible to interpret the Markan pericope as an attempt to disprove the need for Davidic descent of the Messiah. Such an explanation assumes that Jesus' origin was not Davidic, and that this origin was used by opponents of the early Christians to dispute the Messianic claim of the early Christians for Jesus.[192] For such a dispute over the origin of Jesus argue Jn 7:40-42 and the development of the title in New Testament writings after Mark. A further piece of evidence for a resistance to the title "Son of David" exists with *Barn* 12:10-11.[193] The theory's linchpin is that Jesus was, in fact, not of Davidic stock. Only then is it possible to assume an early community that needed to defend its Messiah against the charge of fraud because its Messiah was not of Davidic descent.[194] A variation of this theory seeks to show

---

[190] In a sense, Mark is more interested in soteriology than in christology; on this feature of the gospel see, e.g., Tödt: *Son of Man*, 144-147; Kee: *Community*, 116; Best: *Mark*, 79.

[191] A third approach is not widely argued. It insists that the pericope is not designed to make any christological statement but only to end discussion with opponents. The weakness of this approach is that there is no discussion in Mark. To get around this problem, Gagg has suggested that the pericope is the surviving part of an original controversy from the life of Jesus. Jesus had used the paradox in order to end discussion. However, according to Gagg the community then interpreted the saying in the interest of the κύριος acclamation. Robert P. Gagg: "Jesus und die Davidssohnfrage. Zur Exegese von Markus 12,35-37," *ThZ* 7 (1951): 18-30. Yet, the content of the original Jesuanic controversy is not made clear at all. Too much of this reconstruction rests on speculation, not least the idea that the community would have taken a controversy of the life of Jesus and formed it into a κύριος acclamation of questionable effect.

[192] This approach has been taken by Burger. He writes: "Die Überlieferung scheint demnach aus einer Gemeinde zu stammen, die von ihrem Herrn nicht zu sagen wußte, er sei ein Nachkomme Davids gewesen." Burger: *Jesus als Davidssohn*, 71. Burger makes a distinction between the material that Mark used, and between Mark's editorial activity that assumed the Davidic origin of Jesus and therefore inserts it in 10:47-48.

[193] *Barn* 12:10-11 reads: "See, again, Jesus, not as son of man, but as Son of God, but manifested in a type in the flesh. Since therefore they are going to say that the Christ is David's son, David himself prophesies, fearing and understanding the error of the sinners, 'The Lord said unto my Lord sit thou on my right hand until I make thy enemies thy footstool' ... See how 'David calls him Lord' and does not say Son." Barnabas buttresses this argument with a further proof from Is 45:1, not quoted here. Gnilka points out rightly that this is a later christological development that does not so much argue against the Davidic origin of Jesus as move into the direction of Docetism. Gnilka: *Matthäus*, 2:170-171. Against such docetic strains in early Christianity Ignatius of Antioch used the concept of "Son of David" in *IgnEph* 18:2; 20:2; *IgnTrall* 9:1; *IgnSm* 1:1. In each of these passages Ignatius makes the point that Jesus comes from David's house not because it is useful as a christological title, but because it can be used as an argument against docetic claims as a proof of the humanity of Jesus.

[194] The main thrust of Huber's argument against this theory takes aim at precisely this weak point. Huber argues that the Davidic descent of Jesus is sufficiently established to make such a community a phantasm of the imagination. Huber: *Jesus in Auseinandersetzung*, 382.

that Mark found the "Son of David" Messianic concept deficient and sought to displace it with the dignity of the future coming Messiah.[195]

A second line of interpretation sees Mark as affirming the Davidic descent of Jesus but relativizing it. A starting point is the assumption that the apparent paradox of being both "Son" and "Lord" of David has its root in a form of question which quotes two scripture passages that apparently contradict one another. The solution to this paradox is that one assumes these passages to be both true, however in different circumstances. Thus the context of the story points out that the two scripture passages do not allow for a valid comparison.[196] Consequently, Mark could be interested in a relativizing of the title "Son of David," either because he assumed that the title was more relevant to the earthly ministry of Jesus and now superseded by the title "Son of God" or "Lord,"[197] or because he might have been interested in a de-politicizing of the Jewish Messiah-expectations.[198]

The various interpretations offered have in common that they downplay the title "Son of David" as unimportant for Mark in the face of trying to show how Jesus is Lord. All these models of interpretation look at the passage as mainly christological in its thrust. However, the christological niceties of whether or not Mark actually viewed Jesus as "Son of David," and whether this implied a christological title for Mark, are perhaps secondary to Mark's purpose of exposing the Scribes for their lack of knowledge.[199] The anarthrous use of υἱός throughout the pericope might indicate that Mark did not even think of the designation as son of David as a proper Christological title.[200] The interrogative πόθεν (12:37) asks not how David can call his son Lord, but "whence," or "wherefrom" he does so. Gundry makes the astute observation that this question does not aim at the legitimacy of a claim, but its source.[201] Thus quite apart from the issue of Davidic sonship as applicable to Jesus, this question is not about the descent of the Messiah, but about the passages

---

[195] Neugebauer attempts to show that the pericope is not interested in the genealogy of Jesus, nor in the relativizing of this concept, but that Mark's son of man christology seeks a complete renewal of the messianic traditions of the time of Jesus and Mark. Fritz Neugebauer: "Die Davidssohnfrage (Mark xii.35–37 parr.) und der Menschensohn," *NTS* 21 (1975): 81–108. The problem with this interpretation is the complete lack of any reference to the son of man in this pericope and its immediate context. Pesch takes this argument a step further by reconstructing Neugebauer's argument around the concept of the son of God. Pesch: *Markusevangelium*, 2:254–255.

[196] Daube: *The New Testament and Rabbinic Judaism*, 163.

[197] Gnilka's interpretation is one example how an interpretation with Daube's model is done: "Die Konfrontation zweier Schriftstellen in der Haggadafrage legt nahe, daß die Gültigkeit der konfrontierten Meinungen auf verschiedenen Ebenen liegen bzw. die zweite die erste zeitlich ablöst." Gnilka: *Matthäus*, 2:171.

[198] Bastian M. F. van Iersel: "Fils de David et fils de dieu," in *La venue du Messie. Messianisme et eschatologie*, ed. E. Massaux (Paris: Desclée, 1962), 121.

[199] Gundry: *Mark*, 717–724.

[200] So Gnilka: *Matthäus*, 2:170.

[201] Gundry: *Mark*, 722–723.

in the Hebrew Scriptures that would confirm the Messiah to be the son of David. With this question the Scribes are exposed as frauds. They go around and say that the Messiah is the son of David, but they are shown up by Jesus as making claims without any foundation in the Scriptures.

Understood in this way, the purpose of Mark seems to be better understood and well placed in its context. Mark uses the last public teaching of Jesus in the temple to launch a short discourse against Jewish leaders.[202] He begins with the denunciation of the Scribes' inability to understand scripture in 12:35–37, continues with the accusation that they demand honor and oppress the widows (vv. 38–40), and concludes with the offering of the widow's mite as a contrasting example (vv. 41–44).[203]

This also makes the Matthean redaction more understandable. When Matthew changes πόθεν to πῶς he omits the question asking for the source of the Messiah as son of David. Matthew is perhaps aware that no such connection exists in the Scriptures. But Matthew is also decidedly more interested in the "Son of David" as a messianic title than Mark is. Thus when he omits the question of source and replaces it with the question of how David could say what he said he avoids the possible embarrassment of having characterized Jesus with a title that has no foundation in Scripture. Furthermore, Matthew's insistence on Jesus' Davidic descent and the consistent connection between the "Son of David" and the healing ministry of Jesus[204] shows how much he is interested in a portrait of Jesus that includes both aspects. For Matthew, there is no question that Jesus is the Son of David.

6.2 Summary of the Matthean Redaction in 22:41–46

Matthew creates the controversy over the son of David out a Markan public teaching discourse. His redactional highlights are:

▸ Matthew creates a controversy. It is the only controversy initiated by Jesus.
▸ Matthew integrates the controversy tightly into the context and creates an urgency and immediacy of the narrative setting.

---

[202] Here Huber errs in placing the pericope into the context of the Jerusalem controversy dialogues. Huber: *Jesus in Auseinandersetzung*, 339–341. He basically follows Albertz in calling the pericope a controversy story. Martin Albertz: *Die synoptischen Streitgespräche* (Berlin: Trowitzsch, 1921), 19, 34–35. However, the story in Mark is not a dialogue at all, but merely a teaching of Jesus (cf. διδάσκων in 12:35). This feature connects the story with 12:38–40 (ἐν τῇ διδαχῇ αὐτοῦ 12:38).

[203] Smith shows that 12:35–37, together with 12:38–40 and 12:41–44, forms a triad that corresponds to the triad 12:13–17; 12:18–27; 12:28–34 in a chiastic arrangement. Stephen S. Smith: "The Literary Structure of Mark 11:1–12:40," *NT* 31 (1989): 104–124. Smith's analysis convinces Huber that 12:35–37 is somehow different from the previous controversy stories in Mark. However, he still treats it as a controversy story. Huber: *Jesus in Auseinandersetzung*, 441.

[204] Duling: "Therapeutic Son of David."

- ▸ Matthew introduces the Pharisees as opponents.
- ▸ Matthew phrases a double question.
- ▸ Matthew focuses on the relationship between the titles son of David and Lord. With the focus on the title Lord Matthew explores the identity of Jesus as the Son of God.
- ▸ Matthew creates an inclusion for the quotation of Ps 110:1 and thus highlights its christological significance.

7. Summary of the Redaction of the Jerusalem Controversy Stories

Matthew employs patterns in the redaction of the Jerusalem controversy stories that have appeared before. Again Matthew organizes his material better and improves on the style of Mark. While the first story (21:14–17) is entirely constructed by Matthew to fit the pattern of a controversy story, the last story, though found in Mark as a teaching of Jesus, is similarly constructed into a controversy story by Matthew (22:41–46). Both of these stories make reference to Jesus as the "Son of David" and thus form an inclusion for the entire block of the Jerusalem controversies. The other stories are also shaped by Matthew to reflect some of his preferences. Thus the controversy over the authority of Jesus (21:23–27) parallels some of the material in the response of Jesus, in the other stories he abbreviates to some extent. In the controversy over the resurrection (22:23–33) this abbreviation allows Matthew to keep the story together thematically by repeating the word "resurrection."

The whole block of the Jerusalem controversy stories is highly christological in nature. This is already emphasized by the *inclusio* of the outermost stories. The fact that Matthew devotes two controversy stories to Jesus' Davidic sonship, which in Mark does not occur in a controversy story at all, is highly significant. For Matthew, the title "Son of David" seems to have held much more importance than for Mark, and it must have been the origin for acrimonious debates of his community with its opponents. This is emphasized by the context of the first story as taking place in the temple and occasioned by Jesus' healing activity and his cleansing the temple. But the "Son of David" question is not the only christological emphasis that Matthew sets. Matthew clearly sets Jesus up as the rightful leader and teacher in the temple who shows that his opponents make the same claim fraudulently. Thus in the controversy over his authority Jesus is shown to expose the opponents' failure to teach, while at the same time his teaching is validated. Similarly, the controversy over the resurrection shows Jesus as an authoritative teacher with the right to condemn his opponents as not understanding either scripture or the word of God. Finally, the quotations of Ps 8:3 and 2:2 achieve, beyond the Markan quotation of Ps 110:1, a messianic emphasis for the figure of Jesus.

The portrait of Jesus is very tightly intertwined with the portrait of his opponents. The Pharisees, Sadducees, Chief Priests and Elders are shown to be false leaders. They cannot interpret scripture or the word of God over the resurrection, they cannot render a teaching on the ministry of John the Baptist, and when they do render a teaching they cannot explain how the Son of David is also his Lord. Yet in the face of Jesus' ability to do what they cannot do, they exhibit Matthew's usual signs of hostility: they call him teacher and don't learn from him, they try to test him and lay a trap for him. Yet consistently they are shown to be stumped by the questions they themselves put to Jesus. This gives rise to several occasions where Matthew uses heavy irony to discredit the opponents. Finally, in the only story where Jesus poses a question to them as the initiation of the controversy, they are silenced utterly and completely.

As seen before in Matthew's gospel, the controversy stories take place before an audience that sometimes takes an active part. Matthew goes to some lengths to remind the reader of an audience in the temple. He reports the astonishment of the crowds after the controversy over the resurrection, and immediately after the conclusion of the last controversy turns to the attendant crowd (23:1). Furthermore, the first controversy is constructed to show that it is the children in the temple who, by their positive reaction to Jesus, kindle the anger of his opponents. In the controversy over the authority of Jesus Matthew insists that the Elders are "of the people." At the same time, Matthew goes on to show that this claim is really true only for Jesus himself. Thus Matthew keeps up his previous pattern of the controversy stories as a fight for leadership of the crowds. However, Matthew does not use the controversy stories to show the outcome of this struggle.

A final observation concerns several changes Matthew made to the subjects of the controversies. Consistently Matthew shows a greater appreciation for Jewish traditions and ways of interpretation. This explains his interest in the "Son of David" and the change in the question regarding it from "where in scripture" to "how" it might be claimed that the Son of David calls David "Lord." Matthew's attention to the quality of the commands to be called great rather than to an attempt to grade them into a hierarchy reflects a more Jewish environment. Consequently, the context of the Matthean controversy stories presumes Jewish traditions as the common ground between the opposing parties much more than its Markan counterpart.

VI. Matthew's Use of the Controversy Stories as a Literary Form in the Narrative of the Gospel

1. Controversy Stories in Modern Form-Criticism

It has been observed that the Matthean controversy stories form a substantial part of the gospel. Of the 17 stories 16 originated with a parallel in Mark, sometimes amplified with material from Q, while only one story (21:14–17) is an original composition of Matthew's. By incorporating the stories into his gospel Matthew makes certain changes, and these changes can be grouped as recurring patterns: Matthew focuses on the Pharisees, emphasizes the hostility between Jesus and his opponents, integrates community matters into the stories, sharpens the arguments from the Jewish Law, and structures them better. The redaction-critical analysis has focused more on the content of the redaction than on the formal aspects of the Matthean changes. It is to the formal aspects of the Matthean controversy stories we now turn.

This inquiry, then, will consider the literary form of the controversy story. Matthew did not invent controversy story as a literary form, but found the model already in Mark. Thus it must be asked how Matthew consistently works to alter and shape the form of the stories he found in his sources. In order to facilitate such an analysis, the state of critical scholarship on controversy stories will be briefly surveyed. In a second step, the controversy stories will be examined one by one as to their structure in order to isolate the elements critical to the makeup of a controversy story. The examination of the structure of the individual stories will then facilitate the examination of recurring patterns and elements within the construction of the controversy stories. These patterns will finally be examined for their relevance with regard to the particular literary form employed in these stories. They should also provide an answer to the oddity of 13:53–58 among the controversy stories, as it was included only provisionally in the investigation of chapter 4.

The form-critical investigation of the controversy stories is not a new one. Already the early pioneers of the method paid attention to the literary form in which the conflict between Jesus and his opponents was expressed. In the following the views of Albertz,[1] Bultmann,[2] Dibelius,[3] Taylor[4] and Hultgren[5] will be summarized briefly to provide a starting point for the investigation of the Matthean use of the form.[6] These scholars used differing terminologies for controversy stories. Both Bultmann and Albertz used the term *Streitgespräche* (controversy dialogues), Dibelius used *Paradigmen* (paradigms), Taylor used "pronouncement stories." Hultgren went on to call the form "conflict stories." Behind the varied terminology lie differing assumptions concerning the history of the formation and tradition of these stories from oral material to written stories.

1.2 Martin Albertz

Martin Albertz described the form of controversy stories as consisting of two basic parts.[7] The first part comprises an introduction that he called *Exposition* (exposition). Its function is the introduction of the questioner and the setting up of the problem or question (*Streit*). The second part consists of a formal dialogue (*Gespräch*) that might consist of one or more speeches of Jesus and his opponent or opponents. In this second part the main emphasis falls on the dominical saying which often brings the story to a close. Occasionally, concluding observations (*Schlußbemerkungen*) are added which might contain reactions, or the like. Together these elements form the controversy dialogue (*Streitgespräch*).

Albertz did not address the formation of the stories, or the circumstances in the early church which prompted their development and use.[8] He linked their origin to disputes of the historical Jesus and the struggles of certain prophets of the Hebrew Scriptures with their own people and leaders.[9] Jesus' prophetic stance against false leaders in Israel is modeled on prophetic literature.[10] The stories, so Albertz, find their original formal impetus in prophetic conflicts of the Old Testament, but mirror closely the conflicts of the historical Jesus.

---

[1] Albertz: *Die synoptischen Streitgespräche*.

[2] Bultmann: *History*.

[3] Martin Dibelius: *From Tradition to Gospel* (New York: Scribners, 1934).

[4] Vincent Taylor: *The Formation of the Gospel Tradition*, 2nd ed. (London: Macmillan, 1935).

[5] Hultgren: *Adversaries*.

[6] For the analysis of Albertz, Dibelius, Bultmann and Taylor the book of Hultgren provides a summary of their positions. Hultgren: *Adversaries*, 27–38. Hultgren's analysis has been used in the description of their positions.

[7] Albertz: *Die synoptischen Streitgespräche*, 86–87.

[8] Bultmann criticizes this lack as a serious deviation from the form-critical method. Bultmann: *History*, 40, n.2.

[9] Among the examples cited by Albertz are: Amos 8:4–8; Hos 6:1–4; Is 28:7–13; Mic 2:1–11; Jer 28:1–17. The bulk of Albertz' examples comes from Isaiah, Jeremiah, and Ezekiel. Albertz: *Die synoptischen Streitgespräche*, 157–158.

[10] Albertz: *Die synoptischen Streitgespräche*, 163.

1.2 Martin Dibelius

Dibelius argued that the decisive elements of the controversy story do not lie in a dialogue but in the dominical saying or activity concluding the story.[11] Consequently he rejects Albertz's and Bultmann's terminology of controversy dialogues and speaks of paradigms instead.[12] These paradigms were, according to Dibelius, tools of early Christian missionaries in their teaching activity. This use was decisive for the development of the form. Its elements are the rounding off of the story at the beginning and end so that it could be used independently from other narrative contexts; the story was brief, without any development of character or scene; its style was religious, edifying, and didactic, with its final emphasis on the saying of Jesus; an ending useful for homiletic purposes, e.g. a general phrase, and exemplary deed of Jesus, or the admiration of the onlookers.[13] He maintained that the closer a story adheres to such a form, the older it is.[14]

Dibelius saw the origin of the paradigms in the missionary activity of Hellenistic Christianity, with the form indebted to chreia. He marshaled examples from Diogenes Laërtius, Xenophon, Lucian, Philostratus, and the *Philologus*.[15] Dibelius placed the controversy stories within the originally oral Christian kerygma. In making the association with the kerygma he removed the stories from the historical Jesus.

1.3 Rudolf Bultmann

Bultmann treated of the controversy stories as a subset of apophthegms. Under apophthegms Bultmann subsumed controversy dialogues, scholastic dialogues, and biographical apophthegms.[16] They are distinguished from sayings[17] because the saying in the apophthegm is "joined to an already existing situation, whether this were unitarily conceived or compounded of elements."[18] These situations are "ideal" or "imaginary" scenes arising from the church's need.[19] Bultmann agreed with Dibelius that some of the "generating power" leading from saying to apophthegm lies in the saying's brevity and wit.[20] Within the group of apophthegms the controversy stories are distinct by the situation the saying is joined to.

---

[11] Dibelius: *From Tradition to Gospel*, 68.

[12] Martin Dibelius: "Zur Formgeschichte der Evangelien," *ThR* 1 (1929): 195.

[13] Dibelius: *From Tradition to Gospel*, 44–58.

[14] Dibelius: *From Tradition to Gospel*, 61.

[15] Dibelius makes reference to six such stories. Dibelius: *From Tradition to Gospel*, 153–157. The stories form appendix C of Hultgren: *Adversaries*, 213–214.

[16] Bultmann: *History*, 11–69.

[17] On the form of saying see Bultmann: *History*, 69–208.

[18] Bultmann: *History*, 61.

[19] Bultmann: *History*, 39–40.

[20] Bultmann: *History*, 62.

For Bultmann, the controversy stories have three elements rather than the two necessary for scholastic or biographical apophthegms. The first consists of a description of an action or an attitude of Jesus or his disciples. This is the distinguishing feature separating controversy dialogues from scholastic or biographical apophthegms.[21] In the second part, this attitude is attacked by the opponents, either by a question or a direct condemnation. In the third part Jesus replies to the attack.[22] The third part follows a schema: It may consist of a counter question or a metaphor, sometimes both in combination. A scripture quotation is also possible.[23] The third part is the most important.

For Bultmann, then, the origin of the controversy stories lies with the early church as it defined its attitude to the Law. He answered the question of the *Sitz im Leben* of these stories with a reference to Palestinian Jewish Christian communities, although he recognized that the stories he called apophthegms bear resemblance to stories found in Hellenistic literature.[24] As evidence for this setting Bultmann adduced parallels from rabbinic literature.[25] Both Bultmann and Dibelius wrote during a time when scholarship held that Palestinian Judaism and Hellenism were quite distinct and separated. This explains to some extent why both restricted themselves to the investigation of parallels in either Jewish or Hellenistic literature.

1.4 Vincent Taylor

While Dibelius and Bultmann sought the origin of the controversy stories in the early church beginning to form its own traditions, Taylor was more cautious. While he admitted that the communities shaped their material, he maintained that the needs of the communities allowed its members to recall the words and deeds of the historical Jesus.[26] The *Sitz im Leben* of these stories is the particular situation of the community that is answered by a story from the life of the historical Jesus. This approach is fundamentally different from either Dibelius or Bultmann. While they held that the needs of the church created the context for the pronouncements, Taylor submitted that the needs of the church recalled historical events. Consequently, Taylor did not proceed to look for analogies in Hellenistic or Jewish literature. Rather, he concentrated on the form of the stories in the gospels themselves. They consist in his view of a brief narrative of a question or description

---

[21] Bultmann: *History*, 54.

[22] Bultmann: *History*, 39–41.

[23] Bultmann: *History*, 41.

[24] The term "apophthegm" itself comes "from Greek literature, and is least question-begging." Bultmann: *History*, 11.

[25] The 22 stories referred to by Bultmann form appendix B of Hultgren's study. Hultgren: *Adversaries*, 206–212.

[26] Taylor: *Formation*, 37.

which inevitably leads up to the pronouncement of Jesus. Hence Taylor preferred the term "pronouncement stories."[27]

1.5 Arland Hultgren

Hultgren had at his disposal redaction-critical tools that were not yet available to the earlier scholars discussed previously. Through comparison of four controversy stories in the different traditions (Mk 12:13–17 parr.; Mk 12:35–37a parr.; Mk 8:11–12 parr.; Mk 12:28–34 parr.) he discovered that later redactors molded their material more strictly into the form of a controversy story. Hultgren came to the conclusion that there was "a primitive church consciousness of presenting materials in what we have designated the conflict story form."[28] The collection of such stories into units (Mk 2:1–3:6) was for Hultgren a further support for this result. This led Hultgren to the further conclusion that Dibelius' view of older stories as adhering more closely to the form cannot be upheld.[29]

With regard to the actual form Hultgren asserted that the narrative parts of the controversy are more important than the earlier emphasis on the dominical saying would allow one to believe.[30] It is the "dramatic interchange between Jesus and his adversaries" that is of interest to the redactors of the synoptic gospels as much as the concluding dominical saying.[31] Thus Hultgren identified three major and several minor elements in the form of the controversy stories.[32] The major elements are the introductory narrative, the opponents' question or attack, and the dominical saying. Minor elements concern the third major element: The dominical saying can contain a counter-question, it can be partly made up of a scripture quotation, and it can be cast in a parallel structure. Hultgren's structure of the controversy stories is quite similar to Bultmann's analysis described above.

---

[27] "Everything leads up to the final word of Jesus, which for the early Christians must have had the force of a Pronouncement." Taylor: *Formation*, 65.

[28] Hultgren follows Bultmann in this observation, although he suggests that this development is somewhat later than Bultmann assumed. Hultgren: *Adversaries*, 50; Bultmann: *History*, 51.

[29] Hultgren writes: "Traditionists did not compose 'pronouncement stories' to provide a pronouncement of Jesus on an issue, nor did they compose 'paradigms' with a saying useful for preaching. For the pronouncements and sayings useful for preaching were already in the units of tradition prior to the reformation of these units as conflict stories. Rather, the traditionists composed 'conflict stories' by introducing opponents and their questions who enter into dialogue with Jesus as adversaries." Hultgren: *Adversaries*, 50. When Hultgren speaks of traditionists, he means the final redactors of the controversy stories.

[30] Hultgren observes that the closing remarks are not as important for the narrative as is the opening statement as the first step of a controversy story. This would be true even for a passage like Mk 3:6, which he claims is a conclusion not to a conflict story, but to the whole collection found in Mk 2:1–3:6. Hultgren: *Adversaries*, 54.

[31] Hultgren: *Adversaries*, 51.

[32] Hultgren: *Adversaries*, 52–59.

Within the third major element Hultgren made an important distinction. He observed that sometimes the dominical saying seems so embedded in the dialogue that it cannot be imagined apart from the opponents challenge or question. This would be true of a controversy like Mk 11:27–33, where the answer of Jesus cannot be understood without the framework of the challenge to Jesus authority. At other times, the dominical saying seems independent of its present context and quite able to stand on its own. An example of this kind of controversy is the healing of the paralytic (Mk 11:27–33) where the miracle can be separated quite cleanly from the controversy over the forgiveness of sins. Hultgren called the former stories "unitary conflict stories," while he called the latter "non-unitary conflict stories."[33]

As Hultgren proposed a late development of the stories in the formation of the gospels and the importance of their narrative setting, his view of their *Sitz im Leben* varies considerably from the judgment of his predecessors. The stories can no longer be understood as tools of the earliest catechetical or kerygmatic activities, as Dibelius did, nor can they be easily associated with the historical Jesus, as Taylor did. In fact, Hultgren suggested that they do not have a common *Sitz im Leben* at all. He proposed that the stories reflect different situations in different traditions. Some controversy stories were developed in a Jewish context for apologetic purposes among Palestinian churches, e.g. Mk 2:1–12, the healing of the paralytic, or Mk 2:15–17, eating with tax collectors and sinners.[34] A second setting for the controversy stories arises out of their translation into the Gentile and Hellenistic context for catechetical purposes, e.g. Mk 7:1–8 on the tradition of the elders, or Mk 10:2–9 on divorce.[35] For the Matthean controversy stories Hultgren proposes a setting of the church's opposition to Pharisaic Judaism.[36]

1.6 Evaluation of the Form-Critical Studies

The first thing to note after a look at the various approaches proposed so far is their variety. There has been no common approach, description, or even terminology, in

---

[33] See Hultgren: *Adversaries*, 20. The distinction goes back to Bultmann's work. Bultmann uses a different terminology by speaking of stories of "unitary composition" and stories of "secondary construction." Bultmann: *History*, 47. Hultgren classifies as unitary conflict stories: Mk 11:27–33 parr.; Mk 12:13–17 parr.; Mk 12:18–20 parr.; Mk 3:1–5 parr.; Lk 7:36–50. Non-unitary conflict stories are: Mk 3:22–30 parr.; Mk 2:1–12 parr.; Mk 2:15–17 parr.; Mk 2:23–28 parr.; Mk 7:1–8 par.; Mk 10:2–9 par.; Mk 12:18–29 parr.

[34] Hultgren states that: "Christian conduct and belief are justified not by debate after the fashion of the rabbis but, rather, by going behind the rules of juristic procedure to the spirit of the Master himself regarding the oral interpretation of the Torah." Hultgren: *Adversaries*, 197.

[35] Hultgren: *Adversaries*, 197.

[36] He writes: "The evangelist presents Jesus as Teacher over against the Pharisaic opposition on the details of the law by identifying the opponents frequently as Pharisees. The Christians are instructed in the spirit of the Teacher himself to depart from the Pharisaic position." Hultgren: *Adversaries*, 198.

evaluating the controversy stories with regard to their literary form. Beyond this general observation, however, several remarks pertinent to the individual studies are in order.

Albertz' search for parallels in the prophetic literature of the Hebrew Scriptures remains rather unsuccessful. The passages quoted by Albertz mostly contain antitheses of the opponents of the prophets.[37]

However, these antitheses are formulated by the prophets themselves. The element of dialogue is mostly absent form this genre although the speech of the opponents is reported in the words of the prophet. Consequently, the feature of a situation in the controversy stories where Jesus is directly challenged by opponents is largely absent. Thus while it is true to observe that the prophets faced conflict, their conflicts were expressed in literary forms significantly different from the controversy stories.

Bultmann moved away from ancient biblical forms and sought stories of conflict in material related to the first century. Typical of his day, he observed a dichotomy between what was then thought of as Palestinian Judaism and Hellenistic culture. Searching for parallels in Jewish material Bultmann turned towards Rabbinic literature. Bultmann's search for parallels in the rabbinic literature is more successful in finding situations of direct conflict between opponents.[38]

However, since Bultmann major advances in studies of Judaism of the first century[39] have shown that such comparisons with rabbinic materials cannot be used to infer a literary relationship to the writings of the New Testament. Firstly, the rabbinic material is considerably later in its literary development than the synoptic controversy stories. Thus the exact outcome of such a comparison cannot move beyond noting similarities. Secondly, Hultgren makes several arguments to show how the rabbinical stories differ from the synoptic accounts.[40] The rabbinic examples sometimes do not mirror the brevity of the dispute in the synoptic

---

[37] One example, representative for many, is Amos 8:4–8: "Hear this, you who trample upon the needy, and bring the poor of the land to an end, 5 saying, 'When will the new moon be over, that we may sell grain? And the Sabbath, that we may offer wheat for sale, that we may make the ephah small and the shekel great, and deal deceitfully with false balances, 6 that we may buy the poor for silver and the needy for a pair of sandals, and sell the refuse of the wheat?' 7 The Lord has sworn by the pride of Jacob: 'Surely I will never forget any of their deeds. 8 Shall not the land tremble on this account, and every one mourn who dwells in it, and all of it rise like the Nile, and be tossed about and sink again, like the Nile of Egypt?'"

[38] One example of the rabbinic stories he uses (*Gen. Rab.* 10:3 (Gen 2:1)) follows: "The cursed Hadrian asked R. Joshua ben Chanina: 'How did God create this world?' The rabbi shared with him the explanation of R. Chama ben Chanina. 'How then is it possible?' continued the Caesar. The rabbi led him into a small house and told him: 'Stretch out your hand toward the east and toward the west, and toward the north and toward the south. Likewise it happened with the work of creation before God.'" Quote taken from Hultgren: *Adversaries*, 206.

[39] For a cogent statement of the development of rabbinic literature see Strack and Stemberger: *Introduction*.

[40] Hultgren: *Adversaries*, 33.

accounts. Furthermore, one sometimes encounters several parties to the dialogue, not just two parties as in the synoptic controversy stories. The synoptic conflict stories almost always contain an opening question or statement by the opponents of Jesus that is quite openly hostile to the conduct of Jesus or his disciples. The rabbinic stories mentioned by Bultmann sometimes lack this feature. While these arguments are true for a number of the stories that Bultmann quotes, the example also shows that this is not always true. The story is short, hostility is mentioned in the note that Hadrian is cursed, and here there are only two parties to the conflict.

Yet other arguments of Hultgren are somewhat more persuasive. While the rabbinic stories quoted by Bultmann often contain a challenge, they do not really object to the conduct of the one questioned. Finally, as Hultgren points out, the rabbbinic stories follow the established procedures of legal debate to arrive at an authoritative teaching, while the synoptic controversy stories often merely assert the judgment of Jesus and legitimize it with Jesus' authority, as for example in Mk 2:23–28.

Dibelius explored the similarity of controversy stories to the Hellenistic rhetorical form of chreia.[41] However, Dibelius did not quote many of the chreia found in ancient literature. Hultgren used this scarcity of parallels adduced by Dibelius to argue that he failed to some extent to go beyond the mere assertion to the actual demonstration of similarities.[42] In his critique of Dibelius Hultgren used as his starting point the descriptions of chreia by Seneca, Hermogenes, and Quintilian to conclude that the character of chreia is too proverbial and too brief and general to be easily comparable with the Christian conflict stories that are usually made up of a narrative and a dialogue.[43]

Hultgren distanced himself from Albertz, Bultmann, and Dibelius by completely separating the controversy stories from any literary forms of antiquity. In fairness to Hultgren it must be pointed out that the main argument of his book is the discovery of the particular patterns in the development of the controversy stories within the gospels, and their gathering into collections. Thus for him the stories "have no formal dependence on other literary or popular forms of the period"[44] and are thus a literary form *sui generis*. The controversy stories themselves are developed out of a specific need of the early Christian communities. In the discussion of the non-unitary conflict stories, however, Hultgren backed away from this thesis to some extent. He asserts that in these stories the dominical saying is

---

[41] Two examples of the kind of story Dibelius was interested in are taken from Lucian: *Demonax*: (21) "When Peregrinus Proteus rebuked him for laughing a great deal and making sport of mankind saying: 'Demonax, you're not at all doggish!' he answered, 'Peregrinus, you are not at all human.'" (43) "When someone asked him: 'What do you think it is like in Hades?' he replied: 'Wait a bit, and I'll send you word from there!'" Quoted from Hultgren: *Adversaries*, 214.

[42] Hultgren: *Adversaries*, 34.

[43] Hultgren: *Adversaries*, 34–35.

[44] Hultgren: *Adversaries*, 39.

independent of the actual formation of the conflict stories with which they are now connected.[45] This implies that the dominical sayings must have circulated as independent literary forms, perhaps in what Bultmann called "sayings." As a consequence, the absolute independence of the literary form of controversy story is undermined to some extent by the existence of non-unitary controversy stories.[46] Furthermore, the claim that the form developed out of an "early church consciousness" and its needs to present its material looses considerable force if at the same time Hultgren claims that these stories do not have a common *Sitz im Leben*.

The most serious weakness of Hultgren's argument lies in the refusal to recognize the parallels in literature that Bultmann and Dibelius drew. Bultmann clearly defined controversy stories as a subgroup of apophthegms with particular features. Thus when looking at the parallels cited by Bultmann and Dibelius the apophthegmatic character of these stories must be kept in mind. Dibelius pointed to the Greek apophthegms as a parallel, and Bultmann acknowledged as much by taking over the terminology, even when he proceeded to look for parallels in rabbinic literature. Furthermore, Dibelius pointed out, despite the few parallels he cited, just how ubiquitous these stories were in antiquity. And as more recent research into the social setting of first century Christianity has pointed out, the easy division between Palestinian Judaism and Hellenism was artificial. This eliminates the need to decide either for Bultmann's or for Dibelius' parallels. Pronouncement stories were of such nature that they easily adapted to different requirements in terms of context. Thus the earliest Christian writers used apophthegms widely because "they recognized the international nature of their medium."[47] The controversy stories are one vehicle of apophthegmatic composition. As will be seen below, the study of apophthegms since Bultmann and Dibelius has been particularly fruitful in understanding the controversy stories.

The studies of Dibelius and Bultmann in particular have made enormous contributions to the interpretation of the specific literary form of the controversy stories. Just how useful Bultmann's discussion is was shown at the beginning of chapter 2 when his definitions served to establish the parameters for the stories under examination here. Hultgren made a valuable contribution by expanding on

---

[45] See the conclusion to his chapter on non-unitary conflict stories. Hultgren: *Adversaries*, 131–133.

[46] Hultgren discusses Dibelius' claim of dependence on chreia only very briefly. In his discussion, he does not mention the recent research on chreia and pronouncement stories. Consequently, he succeeds in discrediting Dibelius' rather sweeping claims, but fails to convince in proposing his own claims. At this point Hultgren needs to discuss more thoroughly his assumptions concerning apophthegms and chreia. Hultgren: *Adversaries*, 34–35.

[47] The expression is used by Kloppenborg in his study of Q as a sayings collection. Kloppenborg: *Formation*, 261. Kloppenborg places the genre of Q in the context of ancient sayings collections of both Jewish and gentile origin. He recognizes Bultmann's distinction between saying and apophthegm in his survey and points out how widely both forms were used in these collections (pp. 261–316).

Bultmann's discussion of the development and sharpening of the form in the various gospel traditions.

However, the studies did not develop a structural analysis that would obviate the various literary elements within a story.[48] The following pages offer just such an analysis for the Matthean controversy stories. These will first be analyzed for the literary devices and elements that Matthew uses in order to structure the controversy stories. Once these devices are clarified to some extent, and the structure of the individual Matthean stories is established, an examination of recurring patterns in the formal elements of the controversy stories will make an evaluation of the stories as a literary form feasible. Only then can the question of parallels in contemporary literature be profitably asked once again. Some of the conclusions will be applicable to the other gospels as well and will be drawn out where possible.

2. A Structural Evaluation of the Matthean Controversy Stories

The following analysis will search for elements which occur in the Matthean controversy stories with the function of structuring the stories into narrative parts. Each story will be examined separately before a conclusion of the evidence will be drawn. The elements are listed for each story in the form of a table. Words that are proper to the Matthean redaction are underlined. Words that are found in Matthew's sources but repositioned will be enclosed in asterisks (*). Verse numbers are included at the left margin.

The particular Matthean changes to the stories found in Mark and Q have already been detailed in the redaction-critical part of this study. This need not be repeated in the following analysis. Yet attention will be drawn to the particular Matthean characteristics in shaping the structure of these stories when they vary from the sources. The structural patterns which emerge will be summarized briefly at the end of this analysis.

---

[48] Funk has developed this approach for the miracle stories. Robert W. Funk: "The Form of the New Testament Healing Miracle Story," *Semeia* 12 (1978): 57–96. In this article Funk examines the miracle stories for recurring formal patterns within the narrative. These patterns he calls "supersentential narrative grammar" (p. 57) which is broadly based on structuralist theories. The patterns, he claims, need to be verifiable through association with certain literary microforms. These could be recurring phrases, expressions, particles, etc. In the subsequent analysis of the Matthean controversy stories such a supersentential grammar will be evident to some extent. While the method is loosely based on the analysis of Funk, the differences are immediately obvious: In Bultmann's terms, Funk deals with narratives, while the present study considers apophthegms.

2.1 Matthew 9:2–8

In the controversy story occasioned by the healing of the paralytic, Matthew structures his story through the introduction of various parallels.

Table 4: Formal Elements of Matthew 9:2–8

2	καὶ ἰδού ...	setting of the miracle
	καὶ ἰδών ὁ Ἰησοῦς ... εἶπεν	reaction of Jesus to sick man
3	καὶ ἰδού ... εἶπαν	introduction of opponents' objection
4	καὶ ἰδών ὁ Ἰησοῦς ... εἶπεν	introduction of Jesus' answer
	ινατί ...	
5–6	ἵνα δὲ ...	answer of Jesus
	τότε	
7–8	καί ... ἰδοντες	miracle and reaction of crowd

Matthew creates several parallelisms in order to structure his narrative: καὶ ἰδού parallels καὶ ἰδών in v. 2 to signal the narrative setting. The question of the opponents and the introduction to the answer of Jesus parallel this introduction through the repetition of καὶ ἰδού and καὶ ἰδών. The introduction to the objection and Jesus' answer are made even more parallel through the double use of εἶπον which Matthew already inserted to introduce Jesus' reaction to the paralytic. The answer of Jesus itself is divided into three parts, the first two in almost parallel with ἰνατί and ἵνα δὲ, while the third part draws the conclusion with τότε. The conclusion of the pericope introduced with καί and continued with ἰδοντες parallels the various phrases beginning καὶ ἰδού or καὶ ἰδών. As opposed to Mark, Matthew creates parallelisms by inserting ἰδού twice, ἰδών once, and three times a form of εἶπον. Thus in the structure of the story Matthew achieves a contrast between what people see, and how they react by saying something. The omission of the detailed descriptions of the paralytic's arrival enhance the contrasts and parallels.

The parallelizations in 9:2–8 allow a division of the pericope into four narrative elements far more distinct than they appear in Mark: The first narrative element contains the structure of καὶ ἰδού and καὶ ἰδών ὁ Ἰησοῦς. It contains the arrival of the paralytic and Jesus' reaction to him. Since this situation gives rise to the controversy between Jesus and the Scribes, it may be properly called the setting. The second narrative element contains the same structure of καὶ ἰδού and καὶ ἰδών ὁ Ἰησοῦς and contains the objection of the opponents and the introduction of the answer of Jesus. This element will be called the objection. The third element of the narrative contains the answer of Jesus and exhibits a structure of its own. This element will be called the riposte. The fourth element returns in its structure to the parallels of setting and objection through καί ... ἰδοντες and will be called the narrative conclusion.

2.2 Matthew 9:10–13

The structure of the controversy over the meal with sinners reveals itself mainly in the Matthean introduction of particles. However, a single repositioning of a word yields significant structural effects in creating a parallelism.

Table 5: Formal Elements of Matthew 9:10–13

10	καὶ ἰδού	arrival of tax collectors and sinners
11	καὶ *ἰδοντες* ... ἔλεγον τοῖς ...	introduction of objection
	διὰ τί ...	objection
12	*ὁ* δὲ ἀκούσας εἶπεν	introduction of Jesus' answer
12	οὐ ...	answer of Jesus
13	δὲ ...	
	οὐ γάρ ...	

Thus three elements in the narrative can be discerned. The first and second element arise out of the parallel between καὶ ἰδού and καὶ ἰδοντες, while the third element is set in contrast through the introduction of ὁ δὲ ἀκούσας. The contrast of the third element is provided not only by the insertion of the particle δέ, but also by the contrast between seeing and hearing. The first element contains the meal with the objectionable people and provides the setting. The second element contains the arrival of the Pharisees and their discontent at the behavior of Jesus. It is the objection. The third element provides the riposte of Jesus. The riposte itself is divided into three parts through the double use of οὐ which forms an inclusion for the part introduced by δε. The three-partite answer of Jesus is achieved through the introduction of the second part of the answer, the exhortation to go and learn the meaning of Hos 6:6. Its importance is thus underlined.

Again Matthew achieves a tighter structure than Mark. The setting is highlighted with the insertion of ἰδού, the introduction to the riposte is marked with the insertion of δε and the change from λέγει to εἶπεν. The riposte itself is more structured through the divisions achieved with δε and γάρ.

2.3 Matthew 9:14–17

The question about fasting is less securely structured than the two previous stories. Nevertheless, Matthew achieves a two-part controversy story. He highlights the elements of the story that are already present in Mark by introducing parallelisms, as he did in the previous two stories.

Table 6: Formal Elements of Matthew 9:14–17

14	τότε προσέρχονται *αὐτῷ* ... λέγοντες	introduction to question
	διὰ τί ἡμεῖς ...	question
	οἱ δὲ μαθηταί *σου*	

15	καὶ εἶπεν αὐτοῖς	introduction to answer
16	μή	bridegroom
	οὐδεὶς δὲ	garment
17	<u>οὐδέ</u>	wine

Matthew omits Mark's setting of the story (Mk 2:18a) and connects this controversy tightly with the preceding one (τότε). The story's main elements are the objection and the riposte. These two elements are constructed in parallel. Both 14a and 15a begin with a particle + main verb + dative (τότε προσέρχονται αὐτῷ – καὶ εἶπεν αὐτοῖς). Matthew has to change the Markan construction of the first element (2:18) to achieve this parallelism. He inserts τότε, changes the verb to προσέρχονται, and moves αὐτῷ. He can take over the Markan construction of the second element (2:19) in its entirety.

Within the element of objection Matthew contrasts the opponents with the disciples through the parallel construction of the nominative case at the beginning of each part, with the particle δε inserted for emphasis. In the riposte Matthew structures the answer of Jesus loosely into three parts that are mainly distinguished from each other by their content. However, for emphasis Matthew inserts δε into the second part of the answer, and οὐδέ into the third.

Matthew's changes to Mark highlight the introduction to the objection with the use of λέγοντες, thus abbreviating a clumsy Markan construction of three verbs in parataxis. He also marks the tripartite riposte through the insertion of δε and οὐδέ.

2.4 Matthew 12:1–8

Again Matthew constructs parallelisms and uses particles to divide his story of the first Sabbath controversy into elements that make up a controversy story.

Table 7: Formal Elements of Matthew 12:1–8

1	ἐν ἐκείνῳ τῷ καιρῷ ὁ Ἰησοῦς ...	Sabbath
	οἱ <u>δὲ</u> μαθηταί ...	plucking grain
2	οἱ <u>δὲ</u> Φαρισαῖοι <u>ἰδόντες</u> <u>εἶπαν</u> αὐτῷ	introduction to objection
	ἰδού ...	objection
3	ὁ <u>δὲ</u> εἶπεν αὐτοῖς	introduction to answer
	οὐκ ἀνέγνωτε ...	David's men
5	<u>ἢ</u> οὐκ ἀνέγνωτε ...	temple
7	<u>εἰ δὲ ἐγνώκειτε</u> ...	Hos 6:6
8	<u>γάρ</u> ...	Lord of Sabbath

Three elements, already present in Mk 2:23–28, can be distinguished, setting, objection, and riposte. The setting of the story is introduced by ἐν ἐκείνῳ τῷ καιρῷ. It is given in two parts, each introduced by a nominative, the second of which is slightly emphasized through δε. The objection and riposte are constructed in parallel fashion with a nominative definite article + a form of εἶπον + personal pronoun in the dative. The objection introduces the opponents and their disapproval of the meal, highlighted with ἰδού. The riposte of Jesus is subdivided into three accusations against the opponents that each begin with a form of the verb γινώσκω, and a conclusion with γάρ. This parallelism is constructed by Matthew through the insertion of the verb in the second and third instance of its occurrence. In the first two instances it even appears in the same negated compound form οὐκ ἀνέγνωτε. Matthew achieves this through changing οὐδέποτε (Mk 2:25) to οὐκ in the first instance. The answer of Jesus is concluded with an assertion highlighted by the particle γάρ.

As opposed to Mark, Matthew again highlights the parallel nature of the introduction to the objection and the introduction to the riposte by using εἶπαν instead of ἔλεγον (12:2).

2.5 Matthew 12:9–14

The structure of this controversy story owes little to its Markan source (3:1–6). Now the Pharisees ask the question. The opening sentences repeats καί three times. With the answer of Jesus Matthew again goes his own way in structuring the story. He does so by both introducing and omitting material from Mark. Matthew makes this story a proper controversy story.

Table 8: Formal Elements of Matthew 12:9–14

9	καί	Jesus arrives in synagogue
10	καὶ ἰδού	the sick man
	καὶ ἐπηρώτησαν ... λέγοντες	introduction of question
	εἰ ἔξεστιν ...	question
	ἵνα	reason for question
11	ὁ δὲ εἶπεν αὐτοις	introduction to answer
	τίς	qal-wa-ḥomer argument
12	πόσῳ οὖν	
	ὥστε	
13	τότε λέγει	miracle
14	ἐξέλθοντες δε	reaction of opponents

Four elements can be discerned in the Matthean structure of the story, though some better than others. The riposte of Jesus is quite clearly structured. Matthew begins with his usual formula ὁ δὲ εἶπεν αὐτοῖς, changing Mark's historic present and inserting δε. He continues by inserting two questions and drawing a conclusion. Each of these parts of the riposte is clearly marked by Matthean redactions, inserting two interrogative pronouns and the concluding ὥστε. Similarly, the Matthean additions to the narrative conclusion distinguish it as a narrative element quite clearly. Matthew's τότε marks it off from the preceding material. The departure and plot of the Pharisees is set off from the healing of the man with the withered hand through the insertion of δε, a small structural amendment of Matthew's source.

The repetitive καί at the beginning of the story makes it harder to distinguish various narrative elements. However, Matthew changed Mark's statement that the Pharisees observed Jesus closely (3:2) into a question in direct discourse introduced through and added λέγοντες.

This is followed by a statement of their hostile intent, introduced as in Mark with ἵνα. Both of these are grammatically dependent on ἐπηρώτησαν. Thus the question of the opponents paired with their hostile intent can viewed as one formal element in the story, the objection.

Matthew's redaction of the setting of the story uses καί in a parallel construction, once to introduce Jesus into the synagogue, once to introduce the man with the withered hand. In the introduction of the sick man Matthew uses ἰδού, as he has done in previous descriptions of the setting of controversy stories (9:2, 10). The ἰδού alerts to the fact that v. 9, with Jesus' arrival in the synagogue, is not very tightly integrated in the story. It could very well be left out without seriously affecting the controversy itself. It introduces Jesus into the synagogue, but the synagogue is not crucial to the story. Furthermore, if it were left out the structure would be less muddled with the setting beginning with just one καί, and the objection following. However, in this instance Matthew is faithful to his source Mark.

One important structural change is introduced by Matthew into the story: He removes the Markan reference to the man with the withered hand from the controversy proper. In Mark the man appears in the narrative after the Pharisees voice their objection (3:3). In Matthew objection and riposte focus on each other without distraction. Consequently, Matthew achieves a much tighter structure.

2.6 Matthew 12:22–37

The controversy on the occasion of the healing of the blind and dumb demoniac has a sprawling character. Matthew assembles material from varying sources into one narrative, as is shown in the redaction-critical analysis of the story. Partly this is due to the expansive size of the answer of Jesus, combining several topics from various sources. Yet the primary elements of the controversy stories seen so far are still remarkably evident. Matthew again marks these elements through the use of particles as well as parallelisms. The analysis will look only at these major divisions in the story and how they are set off from one another. Within the major divisions Matthew attempts a certain structuring as well, but for the present purposes this is only of minor interest. In particular, the subdivisions of Jesus' answer can be ignored for the purpose of the analysis once it is seen how Matthew parallels objection and riposte.

Table 9: Formal Elements of Matthew 12:22–37

22	τότε προσενέχθη ... καὶ ἐθεράπευσεν ... ὥστε ...	the miracle
23	καὶ ἐξίσταντο ... καὶ ἔλεγον ... μήτι οὗτος ...	reaction of crowds
24	*οἱ* δὲ ... ἀκούσαντες εἶπον οὗτος οὐκ ... εἰ μή .	introduction to objection objection: by Beelzebul
25	εἰδὼς δὲ ... εἶπεν αὐτοῖς	introduction to riposte

The setting of the controversy story begins with the distinctive Matthean τότε + finite verb, followed by three occurrences of καί + finite verb. These four finite verbs follow in quick succession, yet not without interruption. After ἐθεράπευσεν a short subordinate sentence introduced with ὥστε announces the completeness of the miracle, while ἔλεγον is followed by a brief direct discourse relating that the crowds wondered whether Jesus is the Son of David. Thus the setting is constructed symmetrically.

The introductions to the objection of the Pharisees and the riposte of Jesus are constructed to mirror one another. Both revolve around a form of the verb εἶπον, both contain a participle of sensory perception, both contain the particle δε. Their formal relationship is further cemented through a chiastic construction. The objection is constructed with δε + participle, while the riposte is constructed with participle + δε. (24a: οἱ δὲ ... ἀκούσαντες εἶπον – 25a: εἰδὼς δὲ ... εἶπεν). Consequently, the objection and the riposte are quite clearly constructed to formally relate to one another.

This controversy story once again lacks a narrative conclusion. The reaction of onlookers is not reported by Matthew. The controversy story immediately following (12:38–42) reminds the reader that the controversies are not over (τότε ἀπεκρί-θησαν). Consequently, a narrative conclusion would seem out of place.

2.7 Matthew 12:38–45

The first controversy over the demand of a sign follows. It returns in a shorter version in 16:1–4. Again Matthew uses parallelisms and little modifications of his source Mk 8:11–12 and combines this with material taken from Q.

Table 10: Formal Elements of Matthew 12:38–45

38	τότε ἀπεκρίθησαν αὐτῷ ... λέγοντες διδάσκαλε, θέλομεν ...	introduction to objection objection
39	ὁ δὲ ἀποκριθεὶς εἶπεν αὐτοις *γενεὰ* πονηρά καὶ μοιχαλὶς *σημεῖον* ἐπιζήτει *σημεῖον* οὐ δοθήσεται	introduction to answer answer 1: no sign

40	ὥσπερ ... οὕτως ...	answer 2: Jonah
41	*ἄνδρες ... ἰδοὺ πλεῖον ...*	answer 3: men of Nineveh
42	*βασίλισσα ... ἰδοὺ πλεῖον ...*	answer 4: Queen of the South
43	ὅταν ... καί	answer 5: return of evil spirit
44	τότε ... καί ...	
45	τότε ... καί ... <u>οὕτως</u>	

The controversy is introduced with τότε, followed by the introduction of Pharisees and Scribes with their hostile demand for a sign. The adversative δε marks the introduction to the riposte of Jesus. Both introductions are redacted into direct discourse, and are parallel in their use of the combination of ἀποκρίνομαι in connection with λέγω. However, the parallelism is not complete. In the introduction to the demand of the opponents λέγω appears as a participle, while in the introduction to the answer of Jesus it appears in Matthew's usual formula as a finite verb. Nevertheless, it is noteworthy that Matthew goes to the trouble to introduce ἀποκρίνομαι in 12:38.

The answer of Jesus is quite well structured, owing in part to the sources that Matthew used. However, Matthew constructs the parallelism of the evil generation that seeks a sign but will not be given one (39) out of a chiasm in Mk 8:12 (γενεά ... ζήτει; δοθήσεται ... γενεᾷ). Matthew also introduces a new application of the sign of Jonah into the narrative and structures it neatly with the corresponding conjunctions ὥσπερ and οὕτως (40). The obvious and elaborate parallels between the men of Nineveh and the Queen of the South are found also in Q 11:31–32, although in reverse order. Finally, the saying of the return of the evil spirit is structured almost precisely like Luke's parallel in 11:24–26. The only exception is Matthew's conclusion introduced with οὕτως.

The story, then, can be divided into two parts, the objection and the riposte. The riposte is again much longer than the objection. Both a narrative setting and conclusion are absent. The narrative setting is provided by the larger context of the preceding controversy story, and the conclusion is, at least in part, provided by the next story which begins "while he was still speaking" (12:46). Particularly noteworthy is Matthew's attention to phrase the objection in direct discourse. Neither Mk 8:11 not Lk 11:16 exhibit this feature.

2.8 Matthew 13:53–58

The story of Jesus' rejection at Nazareth differs in some features from the controversy stories seen so far. The reaction of the opponents to Jesus' teaching is given much broader space than his reply. The setting of the story is sprawling, and the actual objection to Jesus is given in straight narrative rather than direct discourse.

Table 11: Formal Elements of Matthew 13:53–58

53 καί ἐγένετο ...	end of discourse formula
54 καί ἐλθών ... ἐδίδασκεν ...	Jesus' teaching
ὥστε ... ἐκπλήσσεσθαι ... καί λέγειν	introduction of objection
πόθεν τούτῳ	opponents' acquaintance with
55 οὐχ	the family of Jesus
οὐχ	
56 οὐχί	
πόθεν οὖν τούτῳ	
57 καί ἐσκανδαλίζοντο	opponents take offense
ὁ δέ Ἰησοῦς εἶπεν *αὐτοῖς*	introduction to Jesus' answer
οὐκ ἔστιν ...	answer
εἰ μή ἐν ...	
καί ἐν ...	
58 καί οὐκ ἐποίησεν ...	narrative conclusion: Jesus does not do many miracles

The story begins in v. 53 with the transitional formula that concludes Matthean discourses. Thus the controversy story proper begins in v. 54 with the setting, constructed in parallel fashion. Two verbs describing an activity of Jesus are connected through ὥστε with two verbs describing the reaction of the opponents, introducing the objection. The objection proper is chiastically constructed, with the question concerning the origin of Jesus' wisdom repeated to form the outer ends of the chiasm. Unusually, following the objection in direct discourse, there is a narrative remark attached explaining that the Nazarenes took exception. This interruption of the dialogue is similar to 12:10 where, following the objection, a narrative aside mentioned that the purpose of the objection was to accuse Jesus.

The riposte of Jesus is introduced by the usual formula in abbreviated form. The riposte itself comes in three distinct parts, and is followed by a narrative conclusion, as already in Mk 6:6. Otherwise, the Matthean redaction of this passage reveals established patterns: The introduction to the riposte is redacted to replace ἔλεγεν with εἶπεν, and Matthew inserts δέ, thus achieving a greater contrast between objection and introduction to riposte.

2.9 Matthew 15:1–9

The controversy over ritual purity is part of a longer section which contains not only the controversy (15:1–9) but also an instruction of the crowds (15:10–11) and of the disciples (15:12–20). Yet within this section on purity the controversy is quite distinctly set off from the rest of the section. Matthew again works with particles and parallels in the elements of the controversy. These stand out more clearly than in Mk 7:1–13 because Matthew abbreviates much of Mark's material. Especially the omission of Mk 7:2–4 creates a more concise form of a controversy story. Furthermore, by moving the quotation from Isaiah to the end of the controversy, Matthew can create better parallels.

Table 12: Formal Elements in Matthew 15:1–9

1	τότε προσέρχονται ... λέγοντες	introduction to objection
2	διὰ τί *οἱ μαθηταί σου* ...	objection
	οὐ γάρ ...	reason: unwashed hands
3	ὁ δὲ ἀποκριθεὶς εἶπεν αὐτοῖς	introduction to answer
	διὰ τί καὶ ὑμεῖς ...	answer
4	ὁ γὰρ θεὸς εἶπεν ...	reason
5	ὑμεῖς δὲ λέγετε ...	
6	οὐ μή ... καί ...	
7–8	*ὑποκριταί ...*	Is 29:13

The objection is introduced by the arrival of Pharisees and Scribes marked by τότε. Their question concerning the tradition of the elders is introduced through a redactional λέγοντες and comes in two parts. The first part contains the question proper and begins with the interrogative διὰ τί + nominative, while the second part explains the transgression of the disciples with a redactional οὐ γάρ. The riposte parallels this construction in detail. It is introduced with the Matthean formula beginning the direct discourse of Jesus, paralleled in Mk 7:6 without ἀποκριθείς. The discourse itself begins with διὰ τί + nominative, a Matthean addition which is highlighted with an adversative καί. Just as the objection, the riposte contrasts the διὰ τί with a γάρ clause explaining the action called into question.

The riposte of Jesus is considerably longer than the objection of the opponents. Consequently Matthew has more room to expand on its structure. The phrase ὁ γὰρ θεός εἶπεν is contrasted with ὑμεῖς δὲ λέγετε. The content of what God says is the commandment to honor one's parents, while the content of what the opponents say is the tradition of corban. Thus the δέ has a considerable adversative force.

In v. 6 Matthew draws a conclusion with οὐ μή. This conclusion concerns the incompatibility of the command of God and the tradition of the opponents. A second conclusion concerns the moral standing of the opponents and is introduced with the vocative ὑποκριταί, followed by the quotation of Isaiah.

The structure of this controversy thus falls into two major parts that parallel each other in much of their construction. The objection is a short version of the construction, while the riposte fleshes the construction out a little more and appends the quote from Isaiah. Matthew highlights the parallel construction further through the inversion of the Markan sequence of the riposte. Matthew puts the quotation from Isaiah at the end of the riposte.

2.10 Matthew 16:1–4

The second demand for a sign contains textual problems that influence any structural analysis. In redaction-critical analysis of this pericope it is argued that even though the evidence of the manuscripts in itself is inconclusive, there is good reason to assume that the rules of the weather were not originally part of the pericope. For the analysis of the formal elements in the pericope the verses of the weather shall be included, albeit in square brackets and indentation. After this it is possible to adduce arguments of a structural nature concerning their presence or absence in the original story.

Table 13: Formal Elements in Matthew 16:1–4

1	καί	setting:
	προσελθόντες ...	approaching Jesus
	πειράζοντες ...	to test him
	ἐπηρώτησαν ...	introduction to question
	ἐπιδεῖξαι ...	demand for sign
2	ὁ δὲ ἀποκριθεὶς εἶπεν αὐτοῖς	introduction to answer
2	[ὀψίας ... καὶ πρωΐ ...	[the weather rules and the
3	τὸ μὲν πρόσωπον ... τὰ δὲ σε-μεῖα ...]	signs of the times]
4	*γενεὰ* πονηρά καὶ μοιχαλίς	answer
	σημεῖον ἐπιζήτει	
	σημεῖον οὐ δοθήσεται	
	καί ...	narrative conclusion: Jesus leaves

The objection combines some features of the setting and the objection into one unit. While the main verb clearly marks the demand of the opponents, two preceding participles are dependent on the question and set up the situation of the opponents approaching Jesus and testing him. The demand for a sign is most unusual in that the demand is not framed in direct discourse, but in construction with an infinitive dependent on ἐπηρώτησαν. While Matthew changes Mark's ζητοῦντες and re-orders the Markan construction, he takes over the Markan indirect discourse.

The riposte is introduced with Matthew's typical redactional formula. The verses over the weather seem independent as a unit and not worked tightly into the structure at all. However, in itself the weather unit is tightly woven: Two parallel elements, night and day, precede two adversative elements, the ability of the opponents to read the face of heaven but not the signs of the times. The relative independence of this unit within the narrative context further indicates its later interpolation.

The riposte then contains material that had been used already in 12:39 in exactly the same formulation in all its parts. The only exception is the omission of the description of Jonah as a prophet in 12:39. Matthew adds a narrative conclusion to the pericope. Introduced with καί, it states very briefly that Jesus leaves.

2.11 Matthew 19:3–9

The controversy over divorce is the first of the Matthean controversies which employs a counter-question by the opponents. Other elements in the structure of the story are by now familiar.

Table 14: Formal Elements of Matthew 19:3–9

3	καί προσῆλθον ...	introduction to question
	πειράζοντες ... <u>καὶ λέγοντες</u>	
	εἰ ἔξεστιν ...	question
4–6	ὁ δὲ ἀποκριθεὶς εἶπεν	introduction to answer
	<u>οὐκ ἀνέγνωτε</u>	answer with Gen 1:27
	<u>ὅτι</u> ...	
	<u>ὥστε</u> ...	
	<u>οὖν</u> ...	
7	<u>λέγουσιν αὐτῷ</u>	introduction
	<u>τί οὖν</u> ...	counter-question with Deut 24:1
8	<u>λέγει αὐτοῖς</u>	introduction to answer
	<u>ὅτι Μωϋσῆς</u> ...	answer
9	*ἀπ' ἀρχῆς δε* ...	
	<u>λέγω δὲ ὑμῖν</u> ...	concluding implications

The objection again includes the arrival of the opponents. The description of their arrival is the main verb, while the hostile intention and the inserted λέγοντες are dependent participles. The question itself is brief. The riposte is introduced with Matthew's formula, this time found also in Mk 10:3. The answer of Jesus begins with οὐκ ἀνέγνωτε, seen already in 12:3 and 12:5 as an important redactional element in the structure of a Matthean controversy story. Dependent on the accusation that the opponents did not read the scriptures, Matthew inserts three elements, each introduced with a small particle. The first two of these are redactional.

The counter-question is very brief. Its introduction contains the bare minimum of words. The second riposte also begins with such a minimal introduction, and their parallel structure is obvious. The second riposte parallels the first riposte in its tripartite structure. The second and third elements of this structure are marked off with δε. Matthew went to some length to construct the structure as it is now. In both Matthew and Mark the controversy over divorce is followed by an instruction of the disciples. However, Matthew took some of the material found in the Markan instruction of disciples and inserted it into the controversy. This allowed him to structure both ripostes into consisting of three elements. The redaction-critical analysis of the pericope explains some other reasons of the Matthean transposition of Markan material. Here it may suffice to repeat that the Matthean redaction was probably motivated by a desire to remove the challenge of the counter-question from the disciples and use it to enhance the controversy with the Pharisees.

2.12 Matthew 21:14–17

The controversy over the praise Jesus receives in the temple is in its entirety constructed by Matthew, inserted after Mk 11:17 as a validation of Jesus' authority in the temple protest. Its structure repeats some of Matthew's favorite devices.

Table 15: Formal Elements of Matthew 21:14–17

14	καὶ προσῆλθον αὐτῷ ... καὶ ἐθεράπευσεν αὐτούς	setting: approach of the sick, healings
15	ἰδόντες δέ ... τὰ θαυμάσια καὶ τοὺς παῖδας ... ἠγανάκτησαν	observations of opponents reaction of opponents
16	καὶ εἶπαν αὐτῷ ἀκούεις τί ... ὁ δὲ Ἰησοῦς λέγει αὐτοῖς ναί οὐδέποτε ἀνέγνωτε ὅτι ...	introduction to question question introduction to answer answer 1 answer 2: Ps 8:2
17	καὶ καταλιπὼν αὐτούς ...	narrative conclusion: Jesus' departure

The setting of this controversy is quite elaborate when compared with the other elements of the story, and also when compared to Matthew's usual streamlining of the form. This exception is probably due to the function of this controversy story in underlining the heavenly authorization of Jesus' behavior in the temple. In consists of three finite verbs in sequence. The first describes the approach of those wanting to be healed, the second states briefly the healing activity of Jesus. The third one describes the anger of the opponents at the situation. This third element in the setting is prefaced by a participial construction with an adversative δε that introduces the opponents and their perception of the activity in the temple.

The objection (21:16a–b) is stated briefly as a question, introduced with a resumptive καί and the formula εἶπαν αὐτῷ. The riposte (21:16c–d) is similarly introduced in a formulaic way, somewhat paralleling the introduction to the objection. It is set off from the objection by another adversative δέ. The riposte contains two parts, a brief affirmative particle ναί that corresponds to the question τί, and another instance of the formula "have you not read," this time, however, intensified with οὐδέποτε. In 12:3, 5 and 19:4 the phrase occurred with a simple οὐκ.

The controversy contains a narrative conclusion that is loosely modeled on Mk 11:11. However, Matthew connects the statement that Jesus left more closely with the controversy by omitting that the reason for Jesus' departure was the time of the day.

2.13 Matthew 21:23–27

The form of the controversy over the origin of the authority of Jesus contains several elements that are unusual. The pairing of objection (21:23) and riposte is somewhat broken up because instead of a riposte a counter-question is given (21:24). This counter-question leads to a deliberation among the opponents given in direct discourse, followed by their answer (21:25–26) and a concluding riposte by Jesus (21:27).

Table 16: Formal Elements in Matthew 21:23–27

23	καὶ ἐλθόντος αὐτοῦ ...	return to temple
	προσῆλθον αὐτῷ	approach of opponents
	διδάσκοντι	Jesus' teaching
	οἱ ... λέγοντες	introduction to questions
	ἐν ποίᾳ ἐξουσίᾳ ταῦτα ποιεῖς	question 1
	καὶ τίς ...	question 2
24	ἀποκριθεὶς δὲ ὁ Ἰησοῦς εἶπεν αὐτοῖς	introduction to counter-question
	ἐρωτήσω ὑμᾶς κἀγώ ...	condition of answer
	ὃ ἐάν ...	
	κἀγὼ *ὑμῖν* ἐρῶ	
	ἐν ποίᾳ ἐξουσίᾳ ταῦτα ποιῶ	
25	τὸ βάπτισμα ... πόθεν ἦν	counter question
	ἐξ ... ἢ ἐξ ...	
25	οἱ δὲ ... λέγοντες	introduction to deliberation
	ἐὰν εἴπωμεν ... ἐρεῖ ...	deliberation
26	ἐὰν δὲ εἴπωμεν ... φοβούμεθα ...	
27	καὶ ἀποκριθέντες ... εἶπαν	introduction to answer
	οὐκ οἴδαμεν	answer
27	ἔφη *αὐτοῖς* καὶ αὐτός	introduction to answer
	οὐδὲ ἐγὼ λέγω ὑμῖν	answer
	ἐν ποίᾳ ἐξουσίᾳ ταῦτα ποιῶ	

The setting of the story briefly relates that Jesus went to the temple and was approached by the opponents while teaching there. At the same time, the setting serves to introduce the questions of the opponents since the participle λέγοντες is dependent on the main verb προσῆλθον. However, the subject of the sentence (21:23) is quite elaborate mentioning the chief priests and the elders of the people and comes in between the main verb and the participle introducing the direct discourse. Furthermore, dependent on the main verb is also a genitive absolute mentioning the return of Jesus to the temple, and a dative that is further amplified by a participle. Consequently, the first sentence probably functions as a setting rather than a short introduction to the objection.

The objection itself consists of two questions, of which only the first remains of consequence for the controversy. The phrase ἐν ποίᾳ ἐξουσίᾳ ταῦτα ποι– is repeated throughout the controversy and serves as a *Leitmotiv* for the controversy. It appears in the objection (23), in the first riposte of Jesus (24), and in the final riposte of Jesus (27). Matthew structures the objection by using καί to parallel the two questions of the opponents.

The riposte of Jesus is of a form not seen before in the controversy stories. After the usual formula that opens the direct discourse Jesus answers in two separate elements. Jesus first announces that he asks a counter-question on whose answer his reply will depend. The arrangement of this element is chiastic: ἐρωτήσω ὑμᾶς κἀγώ – κἀγώ ὑμῖν ἐρῶ. The question itself, marked by the interrogative pronoun πόθεν, is a simple either-or question.

A deliberation and an answer of the opponents follow. Both are in direct discourse, each with its own formulaic introduction. The deliberation is structured into two possibilities suggested by the question of Jesus, each introduced with ἐὰν εἴπωμεν. The second occurrence inserts δέ. The structure of the deliberation is quite parallel, and created to be so by Matthew. The answer to Jesus is introduced with καί and quite brief.

The final riposte of Jesus also employs a καί in its introduction to the direct discourse. The answer itself is similarly brief and takes up the οὐκ of the opponents' answer with a slightly more emphatic οὐδέ.

Matthew edited the story only slightly from the one he found in Mk 11:27–33. Noteworthy is that much of the redactional activity focuses on the parallelization in the first riposte of Jesus. A similar trend towards parallelization is evident in the deliberation of the opponents.

Matthew also sets small structural accents: the addition of ἀποκριθείς in v. 24, and the addition of οἱ δέ in v. 25 serves to separate objection and riposte, while in vv. 26 and 27 Matthew is more consistent than Mark through the elimination of the historic present.

2.14 Matthew 22:15–22

The controversy over paying taxes to Caesar introduces elements which were not seen before. A short narrative section intervenes in the dialogue. It relates how the opponents, in answer to a request from Jesus, bring a denarius for inspection (22:19). The resulting structure is similar to that of the preceding story with the double exchange of words.

Table 17: Formal Elements of Matthew 22:15–22

15	τότε ... συμβούλιον ἔλαβον ...	plot to entrap Jesus
16	καὶ ἀποστέλλουσιν ... λέγοντες	introduction to question
	διδάσκαλε	*captatio benevolentiae*
	οἴδαμεν ...	
	εἶ	
	καὶ ... διδάσκεις	
	καὶ οὐ μέλει ...	
	οὐ γὰρ βλέπεις ...	
17	εἰπὲ οὖν ἡμῖν	question
	τί ...	
	ἔξεστιν ... ἢ οὔ	
18	*γνοὺς* δὲ ... εἶπεν	introduction to answer
	τί με πειράζετε ...	rejection of *captatio benevolentiae*
19	ἐπιδείξατέ μοι ...	demand for a coin
	οἱ δὲ προσήνεγκαν αὐτῷ ...	coin brought
20	καὶ λέγει αὐτοῖς	introduction to question
	τίνος	question
	εἰκών ...	
	καὶ ... ἐπιγραφή	
21	λέγουσιν αὐτῷ	introduction to answer
	Καίσαρος	answer
	τότε λέγει αὐτοῖς	introduction to answer
	ἀπόδοτε οὖν	answer
	τὰ Καίσαρος ...	
	καὶ τὰ τοῦ θεοῦ ...	
22	καὶ ἀκούσαντες ἐθαύμασαν	narrative conclusion: reaction of
	καὶ ἀφέντες ... ἀπῆλθαν	opponents: wonder and departure

The setting of this story reveals the purpose of the question as a plot to entrap Jesus. It is distinctly introduced with τότε and tightly connected with the rest of the story. The objection itself begins with a *captatio benevolentiae*. The question proper is marked through the particle οὖν and framed as an either-or question.

The riposte is marked through an adversative δε in the introduction to the answer of Jesus. Then the demand of Jesus to see a tax coin is given in direct discourse, and compliance with the demand is narrated. Jesus asks a counter-question, marked off in the introduction by καί, and the answer is briefly given. The riposte concludes with a conclusion Jesus draws from this exchange in direct discourse. This conclusion is marked by another τότε in its introduction, and by οὖν in the answer. Furthermore, a parallelism concludes the saying.

However, the riposte is not unitary, but broken up into a small dialogue. Its distinctive feature are the three introductions to the various direct discourses of the dialogue following the demand for a coin. They are constructed in parallel and help to structure the dialogue into sub-units: καὶ λέγει αὐτοῖς, λέγουσιν αὐτῷ, τότε λέγει αὐτοῖς. The triple parallelism is already found in Mark. Matthew slightly emphasizes it through the insertion of τότε in v. 21. The lack of Matthean intervention in the dialogue is striking. Matthew's redaction is mainly visible in the setting and the conclusion of the story. Except for εἰπὲ οὖν ἡμῖν Matthew does not change the dialogue or its structure significantly. However, usual Matthean accents like the careful introductions to direct discourse are already in place in Mk 12:13–17.

The narrative conclusion is constructed in two parallel parts, both containing καί + participle + finite verb in the Aorist.

2.15 Matthew 22:23–33

The controversy with the Sadducees over the resurrection of the dead reveals a Matthean redaction that influences the structure of the story to some extent. As seen in the redaction-critical analysis, Matthew shapes two problems out of one in the exposition of the story. While Mk 12:18 mentions generally that the Sadducees as a group do not believe in the resurrection, Matthew makes it part of the problem presented to Jesus.

Table 18: Formal Elements in Matthew 22:23–33

23	ἐν ἐκείνῃ τῇ ἡμέρᾳ προσῆλθον αὐτῷ Σαδδυκαῖοι λέγοντες	introduction to opponents' question 1
	μὴ εἶναι ...	problem 1: resurrection in general
	καὶ ἐπερώτησαν ... λέγοντες	introduction to opponents' question 2
24	διδάσκαλε, Μωϋσῆς εἶπεν ...	problem 2: resurrection on in particular
25–28	*ἦσαν* δέ ... ἐν τῇ ἀναστάσει οὖν ... πάντες γάρ ...	example of two brothers
29	ἀποκριθεὶς δὲ ὁ Ἰησοῦς εἶπεν *αὐτοῖς*	introduction to answer
29	*πλανᾶσθε* μή ... μηδέ ...	answer
30	ἐν γάρ ... οὔτε ... οὔτε ... ἀλλ' *ὡς* ...	answer to problem 2
31		
31–32	περὶ δέ ... οὐκ ἀνέγνωτε ... οὐκ ἔστιν ... ἀλλά ...	answer to problem 1 quotation of Ex 3:6
33	καὶ ἀκούσαντες οἱ ὄχλοι ...	narrative conclusion

Again a narrative setting is largely absent. The introduction to the objection contains the note that Sadducees approached Jesus. The objection itself contains two questions, the first concerning the resurrection in general, the second question concerning a particular case study. Each of these questions has its own introduction, both times with a parallelizing λέγοντες. However, the first question occurs in indirect discourse, while the second appears in direct discourse. Furthermore, the second question is more elaborate, despite Matthean cuts in Mark's story (12:18–27). After the quotation of the Mosaic rule the case study itself is divided in to three parts: the exposition, marked with δε, the statement of the problem, marked with οὖν, and the explication of the problem marked with γάρ.

The riposte of Jesus is introduced with the usual formula. The two problems mentioned in the objection are tackled in reverse order, thus creating a chiasm. Furthermore, the two problems are now revealed as of equal standing in the structure of the argument, even though only the second problem was stated at greater length. The answers to the individual problems are prefaced by the remark that the opponents are deceived, not knowing either scripture or the power of God. Thus the riposte of Jesus contains three distinct parts. The accusation that the opponents are deceived is made on two grounds, parallelized with μή ... μηδέ. The answer to the case study is marked by γάρ, followed by three elements, marked by οὔτε ... οὔτε ... ἀλλ'. The answer to the general problem of the resurrection is set off by a resumptive περὶ δέ. This answer is also has three elements, marked by the οὐκ ... οὐκ ... ἀλλά. The riposte of Jesus is thus parallelized internally. The riposte is followed by a brief redactional narrative conclusion reporting the reaction of the crowds as one of astonishment.

The structure of the story, with the exception of the narrative conclusion, existed already in Mark. Matthew's redaction touches this structure only lightly, mostly to abbreviate the convoluted case study and structure it through the insertion of two particles. Yet noteworthy is the way Matthew draws attention to the riposte of Jesus by amending Mark in order to use a formula seen before: ἀποκριθεὶς δὲ ὁ Ἰησοῦς εἶπεν αὐτοῖς (22:29).

2.16 Matthew 22:34–40

The controversy over the great commandment is, in a sense, another conclusion to the preceding pericope. Its narrative introduction mentions the behavior of the Pharisees as motivated by the way Jesus silenced the Sadducees. Their reaction parallels that of the crowd in the narrative conclusion of the pericope over divorce. The controversy over the great command exhibits a greater succinctness than the previous one. This is of particular importance since it is a controversy that Matthew shaped out of a Markan scholastic debate (12:28–34). Especially the riposte shows how carefully Matthew proceeded with the structuring of the pericope. As the redaction-critical analysis shows, Matthew was interested in the kind of commandment that could be considered great. This interest is probably responsible for shaping at least some of the structures in the Matthean account.

Table 19: Formal Elements in Matthew 22:34–40

34	οἱ δὲ Φαρισαῖοι ἀκούσαντες ...	narrative introduction
35	καὶ *ἐπερώτησεν* ... πειράζων αὐτόν	introduction to question
36	διδάσκαλε, ποία ...	question
37	ὁ δὲ ἔφη αὐτῷ	introduction to answer
	ἀγαπήσεις ...	command to love God
38	αὕτη ... πρώτη	first
39	δευτέρα δὲ ... αὐτῇ	second
	ἀγαπήσεις ...	command to love neighbor
40	ἐν ταύταις ταῖς δυσίν ...	conclusion

The narrative introduction is brief and reports the Pharisaic reaction to the silencing of the Sadducees. The structure of οἱ δὲ Φαρισαῖοι ἀκούσαντες reflects directly the narrative conclusion of the previous story: καὶ ἀκούσαντες οἱ ὄχλοι (22:33).

The objection itself is clarified as such in the introduction to the question. Matthew adds that the question was motivated by putting Jesus to the test. The question is introduced by an interrogative pronoun, ποία, and is brief and to the point.

The riposte is introduced briefly, amending Mark's introduction through the insertion of δε, the omission of Jesus' name, the change of the verb to ἔφη, and the addition of the dative pronoun. The answer itself contains five elements, of which the first four are chiastically arranged, while the fifth contains a concluding observation redacted by Matthew to reflect his understanding of the problem. The table clarifies the intricate chiasm to some extent. This chiasm is then summarized ἐν ταύταις ταῖς δυσίν ... A narrative conclusion is not provided.

Matthew creates the chiasm and its conclusion. It sets the riposte of Jesus apart as a subunit within the controversy story. The particular interest in the question of the kind of law to be considered great might have led Matthew to create a structure that would give each of the quoted commandments equal weight. Thus the structure of the story, and particularly of the riposte, cannot be separated from the Matthean special interest in this story.

2.17 Matthew 22:41–46

The final story under consideration is the controversy over the son of David. It is the only story where Jesus appears as the challenger. Furthermore, the story is constructed by Matthew as a controversy story from a dominical soliloquy in Mk 12:35–37. Because challenger and challenged are suddenly in reversed roles, the structure of the story also becomes unusual. The dialogue is extended with several counter questions, and the riposte seems to be lacking.

Table 20: Formal Elements in Matthew 22:41–46

41	συνηγμένων ... Φαρισαίων	introduction to question
	ἐπερώτησεν ... λέγων	
42	τί ...	question
	τίνος ...	
42	λέγουσιν αὐτῷ	introduction to answer
	τοῦ Δαυίδ	answer
43	λέγει αὐτοῖς	introduction to counter-question
	πῶς οὖν ... καλεῖ ...	counter-question
44	εἶπεν κύριος ...	quotation of Ps 110:1
45	εἰ οὖν ... καλεῖ ...	counter-question repeated
	πῶς ... *ἐστιν*	
46	καὶ οὐδείς ...	narrative conclusion: silencing of op-
	οὐδέ ...	ponents
	οὐκέτι.	

Structurally Matthew observes again his penchant for direct discourse with a proper introduction by a form of the verb λέγω. The introduction to the question posed by Jesus mentions briefly the gathering of the Pharisees. The question itself appears in two parts, the first with τί, the second with τίνος. The first part is an invitation to dispute, while the second part contains the question proper. The answer of the Pharisees follows very briefly, and the counter-question of Jesus is posed at some length. The dialogue is structured through the triple use of the verb λέγω in vv. 41, 42, and 43.

The final counter-question of Jesus is three-partite. The outer parts are chiastically arranged through the use of πῶς, οὖν and καλεῖ in each. Both outer parts pose a question to the opponents. In the center of these questions is the quotation of Ps 110:1.

The narrative conclusion observes the final failure of the opponents to answer Jesus. The failure is underlined through the triple use of an emphatic negation: οὐδείς ... οὐδέ ... οὐκέτι.

All previous stories somehow fitted a division into objection and riposte. In this story, the categories are still appropriate, even though the roles now are reversed. Jesus poses the challenge, and the significance of the story lies in the failure of the opponents to come up with a satisfactory riposte.

2.18 Summary of Formal Features in the Controversy Stories

In the analysis so far several features of the Matthean controversy stories have been identified. All stories contain a central dialogue that can be divided into objection and riposte. These are features occur already in Mark's stories, although Matthew often sharpens them through structural redactions. These include parallelisms and the inclusion of distinguishing particles. Some stories provide an extended narrative setting, while some provide a narrative conclusion. Again this feature is not exclusive to Matthew, but again these elements provide room for Matthew's structural emphases. Both setting and conclusion occur irregularly. Often the narrative setting is so brief that it is integrated with the objection in the introduction to the direct discourse. The narrative conclusion is absent more often than not.

The redaction of these stories indicates that Matthew structures the various elements of the stories more concisely than his sources. He consistently demonstrates deliberate redaction on the form of his sources by using direct discourse and moving to introduce the direct discourse through some form of the verb λέγω. Furthermore, Matthew consistently uses particles like δε to distinguish between the structural parts of the controversy stories. In general these changes do not amount to major reconstructions, yet they emphasize the distinction between the various parts of a controversy story. In keeping with this emphasis Matthew develops a formula to introduce the riposte of Jesus and uses it with variations. The simplest form of this formula is ὁ δὲ εἶπεν αὐτοῖς. As such it occurs in 12:3, 11. In 22:37 it occurs as ὁ δὲ ἔφη αὐτῷ. The formula is sometimes amplified with the mention of Jesus' proper name (9:15; 13:57; 21:16 with λέγει; 21:24; 22:29). It can also be amplified with a participle (9:12 without αὐτοῖς, 12:25 without ὁ; 22:18 without αὐτοῖς). Most often this participle is ἀποκριθείς (12:39; 15:3; 16:2; 19:4 without αὐτοῖς; 21:24; 22:29). The formulaic introduction of Jesus' riposte suggests that for Matthew it is an important structural element.

Yet besides the Matthean emphasis on the introduction to the riposte and the distinction between parts of a controversy story the frequent parallelizations indicate a further structural interest of Matthew. Perhaps not consistently, but frequently, Matthew amends his sources in order to create a better parallel between the various elements of the controversy stories. Most often this appears in the objection and riposte.

Taken together, the redactional elements indicate that Matthew consistently highlights the controversy stories as a dialogue. This might explain why Matthew shaped the sayings material of Mk 12:35–37 into a full-fledged controversy story. This interest in the dialogical nature of the controversy stories will provide further clues about the relationship of these stories to the wider field of the literature of antiquity. Yet before this is explored further, a few summary remarks on the individual parts of the controversy stories and their statistical breakdown are in order.

The results of the analysis of the individual pericopes can be tabulated. Whenever a narrative element is absent, it is represented by "–." For the narrative setting the symbol "■" has been used to indicate that the setting is grammatically not independent of the introduction to the direct discourse of the objection. Under the section "remarks" it has been noted when the dialogue consists of more than one question and one answer. Furthermore, direct quotations of the Hebrew scriptures have been recorded. They occur only in the riposte of Jesus.

Table 21: Summary of Formal Elements of the Matthean Controversy Stories

Pericope	setting	objection	riposte	conclusion	remarks
9:2–8	2	3	4–6	7–8	
9:10–13	10	11	12–13	–	Hos 6:6
9:14–17	◼	14	15–17	–	
12:1–8	1	2	3–8	–	Hos 6:6
12:9–14	9–10a	10b–c	11–12	13–14	
12:22–37	22–23	24	25–37	–	
12:38–45	◼	38	39–45		
13:53–58	53–56	57a	57b–d	58	
15:1–9	◼	1–2	3–9	–	Ex 20:12, 21:17; Deut 5:16; Is 29:13
16:1–4	◼	1	4a–b	4c	
19:3–9	◼	3, 7	4–6, 8–9	–	Gen 1:27; 2:24, extended dialogue
21:14–17	14–15	16a–b	16c–e	17	Ps 8:3
21:23–27	◼	23, 25c–27b	24–25b, 27c–d	–	extended dialogue
22:15–22	15–16a	16b–17, 19b, 21a	18–19, 20, 21b–c	22a–b	extended dialogue
22:23–33	◼	23–28	29–32	33	Ex 3:6
22:34–40	34–35	36	37–40	–	Deut 6:5; Lev 19:18
22:41–46	◼	41–42a, 43–45	42b	46	Ps 110:1, extended dialogue

2.18.1 The Setting

The narrative setting of the controversy stories varies greatly. Nine stories provide a narrative setting independent of the introduction to the direct discourse of the objection. In two instances the setting is provided by a miracle (9:2; 12:9). In other instances the setting is provided by behavior of the disciples (12:1) or by Jesus himself (9:10; 13:53; 22:34). Once the setting merely provides information about the opponents (22:15–16). And twice the setting gives compound information about miracles and an acclamation of Jesus (12:22–23; 21:14–15).

In eight cases Matthew abbreviates the setting to an extent that it loses its grammatical independence in the story. Matthew combines the introduction to the objection with some information about the opponents into one sentence. Typically, Matthew mentions that some opponents arrive and immediately begin the direct discourse of the objection (9:14; 15:1; 16:1; 19:3; 21:23; 22:23; 22:41). In one instance even the arrival of the opponents is missing (12:38). Yet all stories provide at least an identification of the opponents.

Occasionally, Matthew uses the setting of the stories to mention the hostile intent of the opponents. He does this by mentioning that the opponents are testing Jesus (16:1; 19:3; 22:35), or by mentioning that the opponents are plotting against Jesus (22:15) or seeking grounds for accusation (12:9). But again, explicit mention of hostility is not a consistent feature of the setting. Furthermore, it appears only in the later controversy stories.

Taken together, these varying features of the controversy stories indicate that Matthew did not follow a pre-set pattern in the composition of the narrative setting of the controversy stories. The setting occasionally provides the rationale for the controversy story, but not consistently so. Most often, it serves to introduce the opponents. The brevity of many of these introductions suggests that for the literary form of the Matthean controversy story the conflict between Jesus and his opponents did not need to be explained in great detail in the form of a narrative exposition of the problem. Instead, for Matthew it often is enough just to mention the opponents.

2.18.2 The Objection

The objection is always introduced briefly. Most often this introduction consists a mention that the opponents "say" something (9:3; 9:11; 9:14; 12:2; 12:10; 12:24; 12:38; 13:54; 15:1; 19:3; 21:16; 21:23; 22:16; 22:23, 24; 22:41). In two cases this word is substituted by the observation that the opponents "ask" Jesus (16:1; 22:35). Some stories add to this introduction a remark concerning the hostility of the objection in the form of a circumstantial participle πειράζοντες (16:1; 19:3; 22:35). The objection is always voiced by the opponents of Jesus, except in the case of 22:41–46.

This introduction to the objection serves the purpose to introduce the objection proper in direct discourse. All except two stories place the objection in direct discourse. The first exception is the demand for a sign in 16:1, where the demand is placed in indirect discourse. In this instance, the indirect discourse can be considered an abbreviation of the previous occurrence of the same story in 12:38–45. The second exception is the controversy over the resurrection. In this story, the first objection is placed in indirect discourse (22:23), while the second objection is placed in direct discourse (22:24–28). With the exception of 16:1, then, the direct discourse seems to be a fundamental feature of the objection. In most stories, the objection consists only of the introduction and the direct discourse. However, in two stories a brief narrative element is added after the objection: In 12:10 it is expressly stated that the objection serves to be able to accuse Jesus. In 13:57 Matthew mentions after the direct discourse that people were scandalized by Jesus.

The content of the objection varies to some degree. The direct discourse might express in a statement that the opponents find the behavior of Jesus or his disciples objectionable (9:3; 12:2; 13:54–56). Such a statement can turn into an outright accusation (12:24). The objection might contain a question (9:11; 9:14; 12:9; 15:1; 19:3; 21:16; a double question in 21:23; 22:17; 22:28; 22:35; 21:42) or a demand (12:38; 16:1). Quite often the question or statement of the opponents revolves around a point of the Law (12:2; 19:3; 22:17; 22:23–28; 22:36). Closely connected with the Law is the story of the tradition of the Elders (15:2). However, other controversies are quite unconnected with the observation of the Law as such. They sometimes have to do with the legitimation of Jesus himself, as in the controversies over the demand for a sign (12:38; 16:1), the controversies over the Son of David (21:16; 22:42), and over the collusion with Beelzebul (12:24). Yet another possible objection is provided by the teaching and activity of Jesus or the disciples (9:3; 9:11; 9:14; 13:53–56).

Usually the addressee of the direct discourse is Jesus. However, in some of the early controversies Jesus is not accused directly. Instead, the opponents object in the heart (9:3), or to the disciples (9:11). Similarly, the statement that Jesus exorcizes in the name of Beelzebul is directed towards the crowds who wonder if Jesus is the son of David (12:24).

Formally, the objections in the various stories are consistent only in their combination of an introduction and direct discourse. Yet even in this combination exceptions have been noted. The objection itself can be either a question or a statement. Furthermore, neither addressee nor subject matter of the objections are consistent throughout the controversy stories in the gospel.

2.18.3 The Riposte

The riposte in the controversy stories always consists of two parts, a brief introduction and a direct discourse spoken by Jesus directly to his opponents. The introduction to the direct discourse is of such consistency throughout the stories as to be formulaic. In most cases the introduction contains εἶπεν αὐτοῖς. In only three stories the verb form is varied. In 21:16 λέγει and in 22:37 ἔφη appear in place of εἶπεν. The pronoun αὐτοῖς is only occasionally omitted (9:4; 19:4; 22:18) and once put into the singular to fit the situation (22:37). The final controversy story is different because Jesus initiates the exchange. Thus the riposte is introduced with λέγουσιν αὐτῷ. The grammatical subject of the introduction to the riposte is often given as ὁ δέ (9:12; 12:3; 12:11; 12:39; 13:57; 15:3; 16:2; 19:4; 21:16; 21:24; 22:18; 22:29; 22:37). Once the δε is omitted in favor of καί (9:4). Occasionally this subject is amplified by the explicit mention of Jesus' name (9:4; 21:16; 21:24; 22:18; 22:29). Sometimes the subject is qualified by a participle. Most often this participle is ἀποκριθείς (12:39; 15:3; 16:2; 19:4; 21:24; 22:29). In four cases a participle is added to indicate that Jesus is aware of an accusation or implication not made directly to him. The participle can include an object: ἰδών ... τὰς ἐνθυμήσεις αὐτῶν (9:4), ἀκούσας (9:12), εἰδώς ... τὰς ἐνθυμήσεις αὐτῶν (12:25), and γνοὺς ... τὴν πονηρίαν αὐτῶν (22:18).

While the introduction to the riposte is quite consistent in its basic structure, the riposte itself is much less so. All the answers of Jesus are spoken directly to his opponents, regardless whether the opponents addressed him directly or not. However, beyond this observation there is little common ground between the answers. The length of the ripostes ranges from half a verse (13:57) to a sprawling 13 verses (12:25–37). Most of the stories have a riposte in between those two extremes. Slightly more than half the stories use one or more quotations from the Hebrew Scriptures (9:10–13; 12:1–8; 15:1–9; 19:3–9; 21:14–17; 22:23–33; 22:34–40; 22:41–46). But this feature is not consistent enough to be counted as a formal pattern.

Several of the ripostes accuse the opponents of being ignorant of the scriptures (12:3, 5, 7; 15:3; 19:4; 21:16; 22:31). One phrase occurs in this context several times: οὐκ ἀνέγνωτε appears in 12:3, 5; 19:4; 21:16 (with οὐδέποτε instead of οὐκ); 22:31. Again the accusation of not having read the scriptures is a definite theme in the controversy stories, yet it does not constitute a formal pattern.

The answer does not invariably focus on the final or central of a string of sayings of Jesus. This is most obvious in a story like 9:2–8. The compound nature of the story, made up of a miracle that then gives rise to a controversy, revolves around the saying of Jesus to the paralytic that his sins are forgiven (2). The ensuing controversy returns to this saying twice (5, 6). The final saying of Jesus, introduced by τότε, only validates the forgiveness of sins by the miracle, and the narrative conclusion returns to the forgiveness as the central theme. Similarly, in 9:10–13 the riposte contains three pithy sayings of Jesus, about the physician, about Hos 6:6, and about him calling sinners rather than righteous. The text gives no indication that the third saying is more important or weighty than the other two sayings. Similar observations can be made for a number of stories. The sprawling answer of 12:22–37 prohibits any singling out of one saying as the focus of the whole answer. The redaction-critical analysis points to the construction of a *qal-wa-homer* argument in several of the controversy stories. These constructions prohibit a structural or formal separation of the conclusion from the other elements of these arguments. The argument from the lighter to the weightier in fact achieves a better integration of these conclusions into the narrative flow of the ripostes.

In summary, the only formal features of the riposte that constitute a distinctive element in almost all the controversy stories is the introduction, consisting of a form of the verb "say", followed by a personal pronoun in the dative. The answer of Jesus in the stories is directed toward his opponents. It may be structured to a greater or lesser degree, but these structures vary to such an extent that they cannot be interpreted as a formal distinction of the controversy stories.

2.18.4 Extended Dialogues

Four of the stories under consideration go beyond the simple structure of objection and riposte by extending the dialogue further, or by interpolating a brief narrative. In 19:3–9 the answer of Jesus is met with a counter-question by the opponents that occasions a second answer of Jesus. In 21:23–27 the answer of Jesus contains a counter-question that leads to a deliberation by the opponents on how to answer. The deliberation is reported in direct discourse, followed by the opponents' answer to Jesus, again in direct discourse. In 22:15–22 the dialogue over the imperial tax is interrupted by a brief narrative of the examination of a coin, followed by a brief dialogue over the images on the coin consisting of a question by Jesus and an answer by the opponents. The last controversy (22:41–46) contains a question by Jesus, an answer by the opponents, a counter-question by Jesus, and the failure of the opponents to respond.

In each case, the introductions to the direct discourse resemble those in the simple controversy stories, while the discourses themselves are just as varied. These compound stories obscure the easy separation of objection and riposte that was possible in the simple stories by interspersing them. At the heart of these stories is the dialogue between Jesus and his opponents.

2.18.5 The Narrative Conclusion

Slightly more than half of the stories under consideration close with a brief narrative section (9:7–8; 12:13–14; 13:58; 16:4c; 21:17; 22:22; 22:33; 22:46). Of these eight concluding narratives, two deal with the reaction of the bystanders (9:8; 22:33). Three conclusions deal with a reaction of the opponents (12:14; 22:22; 22:46). Three conclusions deal with the reaction of Jesus himself (13:58; 16:4; 21:17). Twice the narrative conclusion weaves in a miracle as well (9:7; 12:13). The reactions are always introduced with καί, except in 12:13, where τότε is used. However, this τότε introduces the direct discourse of Jesus addressing the man with the withered hand. The narrative conclusion of the miracle begins with καί as well.

The reactions of the bystanders are positive in 9:8, and negative in 22:33. The reactions of the opponents are always negative. They plot to kill Jesus (12:14), leave Jesus (22:22), or are struck with a complete inability to answer Jesus (22:46). The reactions of Jesus are usually negative as well. He does not do many miracles (13:58) or leaves the opponents (16:4; 21:17). There is no really common thread to the reactions in the narrative conclusions except that these reactions show that the conflict described in the controversies is not resolved. None of the stories, with the exception of 9:1–8, has a "happy" ending.

The narrative conclusions are not an integral part of the controversy story as a form. Too many of the stories do not have such a conclusion. If such a conclusion is added, it usually connects with the controversy through καί. Furthermore, the conclusions are usually negative in character and do not resolve the conflict.

2.18.6 Summary of the Formal Features of the Controversy Stories

Few formal aspects could be isolated for the establishment of the controversy stories as a literary form. Both the narrative setting and the narrative conclusion do not seem to be necessary parts of a controversy story because of their absence in too many of them. When they are present, they adhere to some rules, like the introduction of the narrative conclusion with καί, or its negative character in general. But all introductions, and all conclusions, also proved to differ greatly from each other. Thus from a form-critical point of view they proved of little help in isolating the controversy story as a literary form.

At the heart of the stories is the conflict that is expressed in the form of dialogue. The introductions to the objection or riposte follow discernible patterns. Since they also are never left out they must be considered a formal element of the stories. The dialogue itself is almost always reported in direct discourse. Thus the direct discourse emerges as another formal element in the construction of the stories. Within the exchange of direct discourse it is the rule that the objection is posed by opponents of Jesus, while the riposte is made by Jesus himself. Notable is, however, the exception of 21:41–46. There Jesus proposes the objection, while the opponents cannot come up with a riposte.

Thus the elements that make up a Matthean controversy story can be summarized as follows: an optional narrative introduction – introduction to the objection – objection in direct discourse – introduction to the riposte – riposte in direct discourse – an optional narrative conclusion.

The controversy stories with an extended dialogue show variances of this structure that defy classification. Consequently, the argument for a literary form of a controversy based on its structure is somewhat weakened. It becomes clear that while Matthew used a certain structure for most of the stories that show Jesus in conflict with opponents, he did not feel bound to it. This argument gains considerable weight through another source as well. The structure that is observed in most of the controversy stories seems to appear in other stories as well. Two examples of the use of this structure in stories from which obvious conflict is absent illustrate the point.

The first story to be considered is the story of the stilling of the storm in 8:23–27. It is one of the nature miracles, and contains a dialogue between Jesus and his disciples. There is no indication of conflict between Jesus and the disciples. The structure of the story is remarkably similar to the controversy stories.

Table 22: Formal Elements in Matthew 8:23–27

23–24	καὶ ... καὶ ἰδού ...	narrative setting
25	καὶ ... λέγοντες	introduction to direct discourse
	κύριε ...	direct discourse
26	καὶ λέγει αὐτοῖς	introduction to direct discourse
	τί ...	direct discourse

	τότε ...	miracle
27	καὶ ... οἱ δὲ ...	conclusion

The table clarifies that most of the elements that were found commonly in the controversy story return in the miracle of the stilling of the storm. The story contains a distinctly structured narrative setting, both introductions to the direct discourses resemble those of the controversy stories, and there is a narrative conclusion. The story's point is, of course, the miracle itself. Consequently it is highlighted with τότε and appears in a narrative and not in direct discourse. However, the narrative conclusion of the story again begins with καί and reports the result of the miracle as well as the reactions of those present.

A second story that exhibits many traits of the controversy stories without the concomitant conflict is reported in 11:2–6. It is the beginning of a small teaching on John the Baptist. John, by now imprisoned, sends a small delegation of his disciples to ask about Jesus.

Table 23: Formal Elements in Matthew 11:2–6

2–3	ὁ δὲ ... εἶπεν αὐτῷ	introduction to direct discourse
	σὺ εἶ ...	question
4	καὶ ἀποκριθεὶς ὁ Ἰησοῦς εἶπεν αὐτοῖς	introduction to direct discourse
	... ἀπαγγείλατε ...	
5	τυφλοὶ ... καὶ χωλοί ...	answer
	λεπροί ... καὶ κωφοί ...	
	καὶ νεκροί ... καὶ πτωχοί ...	
6	καὶ μακάριος ... ὃς ...	

Again some elements seen in controversy stories reappear. The introduction of the question incorporates a small narrative introduction mentioning the imprisonment of John and his awareness of Jesus' deeds in a participial construction. The question itself is brief and to the point. The introduction to the answer of Jesus repeats a formula seen in the controversy stories, while the answer itself is reported in direct discourse and structured by a series of καί. A narrative conclusion is absent, probably because Jesus immediately launches into a teaching of the crowds concerning the Baptist (11:7).

The examination of just two stories has consequences for the form-critical evaluation of the controversy stories. It has been shown that there are rules in the construction of controversy stories that are applied with great consistency. However, these rules have also been shown to apply to other material in the gospel. Consequently, if the controversy stories are a literary form distinct from other forms, their distinguishing feature does not lie in their structural elements. As these appear in other stories as well, the controversy stories are apparently a sub-group of a literary form that shapes stories containing a dialogue as a whole. The controversy stories are defined by the element of conflict that is absent from similar stories containing a dialogue. In other words, while the dialogical form seems constitutive of the controversy stories, their defining feature revolves around content rather than structure.

2.19 The Controversy in the Controversy Stories

At the heart of the controversy stories is the controversy. The objection or the question directed at Jesus is, in each story, made with hostile intent. In consequence, the answer of Jesus responds invariably to this hostility inherent in the question or objection by proving the opponents wrong, misguided, or lacking in some fashion. The story of the healing of the paralytic (9:2–8) illustrates the explication of the conflict quite clearly.

Once Jesus has forgiven the sins of the paralytic the Scribes comment on this action with the objection οὗτος βλασφημεῖ (9:3). Matthew has abbreviated the objection to a considerable extent and concentrates on the charge made against Jesus at the expense of an explanation for the Scribes' discontent.[49] The pronoun οὗτος is derogative, and the accusation of blasphemy tries to put Jesus in opposition to God and, by extension, to those who make the accusation. The hostility of the objection is accentuated in the riposte of Jesus that marks their thoughts as "evil" (9:4). Thus the hostility of the controversy story is expressed in both the objection and the riposte. The narrative framework does not contain a reference to hostilities.

Each of the controversies resembles this scheme. While the actual wording of the hostility in the stories varies to some extent, the hostility as such does not. Matthew includes overt hostility in all his controversy stories. The place for the hostility can be the narrative setting and conclusion, the objection, or the riposte. In a number of stories Matthew combines several references to hostility in their various elements.

Sometimes the narrative surrounding the actual dialogue contains a reference to the animosity between the two parties. Thus Matthew occasionally mentions that the opponents ask a question to test Jesus, or in order to accuse him. He also can include a reference to the hostile reaction of the opponents in the narrative conclusion. This particular form of expressing the conflict occurs in some, but not all stories. The following table illustrates the occurrences. Matthean redaction has been underlined, the actual verse number of the occurrence is given in parentheses.

Table 24: Hostility in the Narrative Context of the Controversy Stories

12:9–13	ἵνα κατηγορήσουσιν αὐτοῦ (9) συμβούλιον ἔλαβον κατ' αὐτοῦ ὅπως αὐτὸν ἀπολέσωσιν (13)

---

[49] See the redaction-critical examination of this story.

13:53–58	καὶ ἐσκανδαλίζοντο ἐν αὐτῷ (57)
16:1–4	πειράζοντες (1)
19:3–9	πειράζοντες (3)
21:14–17	ἠγανάκτησαν (15)
22:15–22	συμβούλιον ἔλαβον ὅπως αὐτὸν παγιδεύσωσιν ἐν λόγῳ (15)
	... τὴν πονηρίαν αὐτῶν ... (18)
22:34–40	συνήχθησαν ἐπὶ τὸ αὐτό (34)[50]
	πειράζων (35)
22:41–46	οὐδεὶς ἐδύνατο ... οὐδὲ ἐτόλμησεν ... (46)

Quite often the hostility is expressed in the objection itself. The wording of this varies to some extent, and some indicators are not immediately obvious. Thus for example the address of Jesus as "teacher" does not at first indicate hostility. It certainly does not do so in Mark. However, Matthew shapes this title to his own purposes. It occurs only as a self-description of Jesus, or in the mouth of his opponents. The disciples never address Jesus as teacher. Thus as an address the title takes on a sinister meaning and indicates in the mouth of people addressing Jesus that their intent is hostile.[51]

The expression of hostility in the objection can also be expressed in other ways. Thus when the Pharisees claim that Jesus can exorcize only because he is aligned with Beelzebul (12:24) they express hostility. Another way of expressing hostility is the accusation that Jesus or his disciples do things that are not allowed (12:2) or contrary to tradition (15:2), or that they do not live up to a standard set by others (9:14). Similarly, when Jesus is asked to legitimize himself the implication is that this legitimation is impossible (21:23). The following table synthesizes the hostilities expressed in the objection.

Table 25: Hostility in the Objection of the Controversy Stories

9:2–7	οὗτος βλασφημεῖ (3)
9:10–13	μετὰ τῶν τελωνῶν καὶ ἁμαρτολῶν ... ὁ διδάσκαλος ὑμῶν (11)
9:14–17	οὐ νηστεύουσιν (14)
12:1–8	ὃ οὐκ ἔξεστιν ποιεῖν ἐν σαββάτῳ (2)
12:22–37	οὗτος ... οὐκ ... εἰ μὴ ἐν τῷ Βεελζεβούλ ... (24)
12:38–45	διδάσκαλε (38)
15:1–9	παραβαίνουσιν ... οὐ γὰρ νίπτονται ... (2)
21:23–27	ἐν ποίᾳ ἐξουσίᾳ ... καὶ τίς σοι ἔδωκεν ... (23)

---

[50] In the redaction-critical examination of this passage it is argued that this phrase is possibly a reference to Ps 2:2. There the rulers of the earth gather together against God and his Anointed. If this assumption is correct, then the hostility inherent in the phrase is highly emphasized.

[51] This feature of Matthew's gospel is explained in greater detail in the redaction-critical section of this study.

22:15–22	διδάσκαλε (16)
22:23–33	διδάσκαλε (24)
22:34–40	<u>διδάσκαλε</u> (35)

Finally, the hostility can be expressed in the riposte of the controversy story. Several expressions are recurring. Thus the riposte contains repeatedly the accusation that the opponents are evil, or think evil. Concomitant with this accusation is the statement that the opponents are hypocrites or resemble the offspring of vipers. Another kind of indictment is the recurring accusation that the opponents have not read the scriptures. Consequently, the opponents are deceived or hard-hearted. Once the opponents are accused of transgressing the Law. It is noteworthy that Matthew spends a considerable amount of his redactional activity on deepening the accusations and the hostility expressed in the ripostes of the controversy stories. In 12:22–37 he even appends a longer section (34–37) to include a prolonged indictment and threat of judgment against the opponents. When compared with the expressions of hostility in the narrative setting and conclusion, or the objection, the expressions of hostility in the riposte appear to be much more severe.

Table 26: Hostility in the Riposte of the Controversy Stories

9:2–8	<u>ἐνθυμεῖσθε πονηρά</u> (4)
12:1–8	<u>οὐκ ἀνέγνωτε</u> (3)
	<u>οὐκ ἀνέγνωτε</u> (5)
	<u>εἰ δὲ ἐγνώκειτε</u> (7)
12:22–37	<u>γεννήματα ἐχιδνῶν ... πονηροὶ ὄντες</u> (34)
12:38–45	γενεὰ πονηρὰ <u>καὶ μοιχαλίς</u> (39)
	<u>τῇ γενεᾷ ταύτῃ τῇ πονηρᾷ</u> (45)
15:1–9	<u>ὑμεῖς παραβαίνετε τὴν ἐντολὴν τοῦ θεοῦ</u> (3)
	<u>ὑποκριταί</u> (7)
16:1–4	γενεὰ πονηρὰ <u>καὶ μοιχαλίς</u> (4)
19:3–9	<u>οὐκ ἀνέγνωτε</u> (4)
	<u>πρὸς τὴν σκληροκαρδίαν ὑμῶν</u> (8)
21:14–17	<u>οὐδέποτε ἀνέγνωτε</u> (16)
22:15–22	<u>τί με πειράζετε, ὑποκριταί</u> (18)
22:23–33	<u>πλανᾶσθε μὴ εἰδότες</u> (29)
	<u>οὐκ ἀνέγνωτε</u> (31)

The feature of overt hostility is proper to the controversy stories. The controversy stories are distinguished as a literary form by the references they make to the hostility between the opponents and Jesus. An integral part of the hostility is its impossibility of resolution.[52] The objection is interpreted as a challenge to Jesus, while the riposte is designed not only to repel the challenge but to discredit the challenger. The hostility inherent in the stories ensures that they are not stories seeking a resolution, but stories of contest.[53]

While Matthew uses the literary structure of a dialogue that can be found in other stories, the dialogue is informed by the hostility between the opposing parties. Consequently, the controversy stories must be viewed as a specific sub-group of a literary form that led to the formation of several kinds of stories. The motif of hostility serves as the distinguishing feature of the controversy stories.[54] The hostility inherent in the controversy stories is expressly verbalized and is not just to be inferred from a larger context.

Hultgren's analysis of the controversy stories is inadequate at this point. Hultgren deals to a large extent with the dialogical structure of the stories as it is embedded in narrative elements. However, the structure has been shown to be inclusive of several stories that are not conflict stories. Hultgren does not seem to be aware of this feature, although he seems to indicate vaguely that the opponents have something to do with the form of the controversy stories.[55] However, Hultgren fails

---

[52] Robert Tannehill has commented upon the lack of resolutions in these and other stories. He writes: "[T]he story remains the servant of the imaginative power of the saying, rather than coming to its own resolution. The story remains open-ended, which invites the reader to make his own response. These encounters begin as stories of men undertaking a quest, but the minor tension involved in their quests is overpowered by the tension of Jesus' words, which reaches beyond the context of the story to the reader." Robert C. Tannehill: *The Sword of His Mouth*, SBL.MS 1 (Missoula: Fortress, 1975), 154–155.

[53] In a review of Hultgren's book Bruce Malina suggested that the stories be called "challenge – riposte stories" or "honor – contest stories." Bruce J. Malina: "Arland J. Hultgren: *Jesus and His Adversaries* (Book Review)," *CBQ* 43 (1981): 132. Neyrey and Malina have suggested that the controversy stories be interpreted with an honor – shame model. This would imply that the controversy stories imply "a challenge in terms of some action ... perception of the action by both the individual to whom it is directed and the public at large ... [and] reaction of the receiving individual and the evaluation on the part of the public." These implications combine to form a story consisting of claim, challenge, riposte, and public verdict. Bruce J. Malina and Jerome H. Neyrey: "Honor and Shame in Luke-Acts: Pivotal Values of the Mediterranean World," in: *The Social World of Luke-Acts. Models for Interpretation*, ed. Jerome H. Neyrey (Peabody: Hendrickson, 1991), 29–30. While the honor – shame model is useful in interpreting the stories and the reasons for the indissolubility of the conflict, the resulting form is less than precise. The Matthean controversy stories suggest that often the claim is absent or implied, and the public verdict is most often absent as well. The verdict probably needs to be re-interpreted in terms of a challenge to take sides, directed towards the reader/hearer of these stories.

[54] This particular observation helps to move beyond the impasse created by Hultgren's assertion that the controversy stories are not dependent on any literary forms in the literature of antiquity. Hultgren: *Adversaries*, 39.

[55] Hultgren writes: "[The opponents] are simply described in the most general terms, usually by sect or office, and that is sufficient to set up the necessary polarity for the conflict dialogue."

to point out how exactly the opponents become such. If the mere identification of the partners in dialogue as Pharisees or Scribes were sufficient, a story like Mk 12:28–34 would have to be classified as a controversy story. But Matthew's redaction of the story in 22:34–40 shows quite clearly that he did not regard it so. Already Bultmann saw this problem and did not rely on the mere identification of the opponents as Scribes or Pharisees as defining a controversy story.[56]

This example leads to a further trait of the Matthean conflict stories. The opponents in the conflict stories are, with the exception of 13:53–58, always Jewish leaders, variously identified as Scribes, Pharisees, Sadducees, Chief Priests, and Elders of the people. These figures are always, as far as Matthew is concerned, opponents of Jesus, even when they are mentioned outside of controversy stories. Thus Matthew consolidates the interpretation of Jewish leaders found in his sources as hostile. For Matthew, it is the Jewish leaders that form the opposition to Jesus and, by extension, to the community. They form a single block that is much more consistent than it is in Mark.

The literary form of the controversy stories has been identified as a narrative which includes a hostile dialogue between Jesus and his opponents, almost always the Jewish leaders. It remains to examine the occurrence of such dialogues in literature outside of the New Testament with a view to placing these narratives within the literary conventions of the first century.

3. Controversy Stories and Chreia

Chreia, or sometimes also called chria, pronouncement stories, apophthegms, or paradigms,[57] are a development of an individual saying (γνώμη, *sententia*) with a concrete narrative context that is bound to a particular person. Consequently, there are two main parts to chreia: the saying and its setting. Individual sayings usually have a general character. Their embedding in a narrative gives the sayings a concrete frame. In a further step, the saying can develop into action through its

---

Hultgren: *Adversaries*, 56. He adds that there is a tendency in the later tradition, notably Matthew, to characterize the opponents as Pharisees and Scribes.

[56] Bultmann writes that Mk 12:28–34 is a scholastic dialogue. "But Matthew and Luke make a controversy dialogue out of it, by deleting the conclusion and imputing to the questioner the motive of 'tempting' Jesus." Bultmann: *History*, 51.

[57] Vincent Taylor coined the name "pronouncement stories," while the term "apophthegms" goes back to Rudolf Bultmann, and the term "paradigms" is used by Martin Dibelius. The term "chreia" is used here as a reflection on the discussion of ancient rhetoricians of these stories. Occasionally, a latinized form of "chria" occurs. Robert C. Tannehill: "Introduction: The Pronouncement Story and its Types," *Semeia* 20 (1981), 1.

narrative context.[58] The particular narrative setting combines with the individual saying to form the chreia.[59] The narrative setting itself can make use of situational descriptions as well as of persons who pose questions, objections, or general observations. Consequently, chreia can take on the form of a dialogue between parties. A few examples illustrate the point. The first is that of a saying embedded into a narrative situation, taken from Plutarch's *Sayings of the Kings and Commanders*, 191A:

> When he [Agesilaus] was about to break camp in haste by night to leave the enemy's country, and saw his favorite youth, owing to illness, being left behind all in tears, he said: "It is hard to be merciful and sensible at the same time."[60]

A chreia from Lucian, *Demonax*, 27, illustrates how the narrative context is provided by a short dialogue:

> When one of his friends said: "Demonax, let's go to the Aesculapium and pray for my son," he replied: "You must think Aesculapius very deaf, that he can't hear our prayers from where we are."[61]

A chreia that substitutes an action for a saying is reported by Diogenes Laërtius, *Lives and Opinions of the Eminent Philosophers*, II 129:

> Not being able to curb the extravagance of someone who had invited him to dinner, he [Menedemus] said nothing when he was invited, but rebuked his host tacitly by confining himself to olives.[62]

---

[58] Theon: *Progymnasmata* 5, gives the following distinctions: πᾶσα γὰρ γνώμη σύντομος εἰς πρόσωπον ἀναφερομένη χρείαν ποιεῖ· καὶ τὸ ἀπομνημόνευμα δὲ πρᾶξίς ἐστιν ἢ λόγος βιωφελής. Quoted by: Klaus Berger: "Hellenistische Gattungen im Neuen Testament," in *ANRW*, ed. W. Haase and H. Temporini, II.25.2:1093. About 450 years later Priscian (*Praeexercitamenta* 3) gives a very similar definition, quoted here from: Lausberg: *Handbuch*, 536: "usus est, quam Graeci χρείαν vocant, commemoratio orationis alicuius vel facti vel utriusque simul, celerem habens demonstrationem, quae utilitatis alicuius plerumque causa profertur." For Priscian's near contemporary Isidore (2,11,2) the distinction between saying and chreia is like the one outlined by Theon: "unde si sententiae persona adiciatur, fit chria; si detrahatur, fit sententia." Lausberg: *Handbuch*, 537. An admirable collection of pronouncement stories containing both actions and sayings as pronouncement is: *Ancient Quotes and Anecdotes: From Crib to Crypt*, ed. Vernon K. Robbins, Foundations and Facets Reference Series (Sonoma: Polebridge, 1989). In this collection, made by the Pronouncement Story Group of the Society of Biblical Literature, pronouncements in form of sayings are the great majority.

[59] Berger: "Gattungen," 1093. While the *apomnemoneuma* is the general remembrance of a historical person, its combination with a *gnome* forms the chreia. Thus already Hermogenes: *Progymnasmata* 3, writes: χρεία ἐστὶν ἀπομνημόνευμα λόγου τινος ἢ πράξεως ἢ συναμφοτέρου.

[60] Quoted by Tannehill: "Introduction," 11.

[61] Quoted by Tannehill: "Introduction," 7.

[62] Quoted by Paula N. Poulos: "Form and Function of the Pronouncement Stories in Diogenes Laërtius' *Lives*," *Semeia* 20 (1981): 59.

A third element constituting chreia is visible from these examples. All these stories serve the purpose of demonstrating that the person giving the response is witty, sharp, superior to the questioner of the situation. Chreia try to elicit admiration for the person to whom the witty saying is attributed. The three elements make it possible to define chreia:

> A pronouncement story is a brief narrative in which the climactic (and often final) element is the pronouncement either in speech or in action or a combination of speech and action. There are two main parts of a pronouncement story: the pronouncement and its setting, i.e., the response and the situation provoking the response. The pronouncement is closely associated with the main character who is the author or the recipient of the speech or action. Both the setting and the pronouncement contribute to the rhetorical goal of the story.[63]

This definition serves admirably to describe the controversy stories in the gospels as well. Closer parallels between chreia and controversy stories can be observed when chreia actually depict a conflict. Again these conflicts can be observed in situations or dialogues. The first of the following examples comes from Diogenes Laërtius, *Lives,* VI 63. It describes a questionable situation to which Diogenes responds to defend himself. The second example describes the situation of conflict in terms of a dialogue. It is taken from Diogenes Laërtius' *Lives,* II 71.

> To one reproaching him for entering unclean places he said: "The sun, too, enters the privies but is not defiled."[64]

> It happened once that he set sail for Corinth and, being overtaken by a storm, he [Aristippus] was in great consternation. Someone said, "We plain men are not alarmed, and are you philosophers turned cowards?" To this he replied: "The lives at stake in the two cases are not comparable."[65]

The similarities between controversy stories and chreia are great. In both forms the saying of a particular person is central to the story and turns up at its end, in direct discourse, as what we called riposte. In the chreia, this answer is usually witty and brief. Mark's controversy stories exhibit the same tendency to brief and witty answers. Thus in Mk 2:27–28 the first Sabbath controversy is clinched by Mark's witty saying: "The Sabbath was made for man, not man for the Sabbath; so the Son of Man is Lord even of the Sabbath." Yet it has also been seen that Matthew is usually uncomfortable with such brief answers, and thus develops them into lengthier arguments. In this particular controversy story, he corrects Mark's previous argument of the loaves that David ate in the temple and expands it with an

---

[63] The definition is given by Vernon K. Robbins. Robbins is closely associated with the Pronouncement Story Group of the Society of Biblical Literature; this definition, so Robbins, "guided members of the Pronouncement Story Group." Robbins: *Ancient Quotes,* xi.

[64] Quoted by Tannehill: "Introduction," 9.

[65] Quoted by Poulos: "Pronouncement Stories," 58.

argument from the innocence of the priest sacrificing on the Sabbath and from Hos 6:6. Then Matthew omits the glib saying about the Sabbath being made for man (12:3–8).

It is furthermore important that the form of chreia incorporates a narrative setting that can contain direct discourse by persons other than the protagonist of the chreia. This coincides with the dialogical form of the controversy stories in which an objection or question is posed to occasion the riposte of Jesus. Thus there is certainly a literary affinity between the chreia and the controversy stories.

The study of chreia has been quite animated in scholarly debates of the last twenty years. One area of discussion concerned the definition of chreia, its distinction from sayings, and the purpose and manner of its elaboration. The second area of scholarly debate focused on ways of classifying chreia. Both discussions are of importance to the understanding of the Matthean controversy stories, but shall be summarized only very briefly here.

Berger distinguishes between apophthegms and chreia. For him, the apophthegm is a saying within a very brief narrative context while the chreia expands the narrative part of the story.[66] While this distinction is useful it has not caught the imagination of subsequent studies. Other scholars who have worked extensively on the chreia admit to the distinction but do not develop it into a working hypothesis.[67] Berger's distinction was not successful in establishing a common terminology,[68] although the issue of elaboration has become a prominent topic in the study of

---

[66] He writes: "Die klassische Form des Apophthegmas ist lediglich: Name/ἐρωτηθεὶς εἶπε (so schon bei Xenophon, Mem. III 13.14) ... Die Worte müssen kurz und scharfsinning sein ... Die Chrie jedoch unterscheidet sich durch die stärkere Bindung an den Einzelfall von den sonst eng verwandten Apophthegmen ..." Berger: "Gattungen," 1093. Berger mentions as evidence the manifold elaborations of the chreia witnessed by the *Progymnasmata* of Hermogenes. He also quotes Quintilian: "Nach Quintilian, Inst. I 9,4 sind die Chrien nach der Einleitung zu gruppieren: *dixit ille* (I), *interrogatus ille* (II), *cum quis dixisset aliquid vel fecisset* (III)" (p. 1094). Berger includes the logia of the *EvThom* in the first group, Mt 18:1–3 in the second group, and Mk 12:41–44 in the third group.

[67] For example, Robert Tannehill writes: "As used here, pronouncement story will correspond rather closely with Rudolf Bultmann's 'apophthegms' ... It also overlaps with the *chreia* discussed by some ancient scholars." Tannehill unfortunately does not proceed to elaborate on the overlap between chreia and apophthegms, and the implicit distinctions. Furthermore, he seems to specifically exclude brevity of story as the distinguishing feature when he writes: "Brevity is a relative matter, of course. In some cases, a pronouncement story is a single sentence ... Descriptive detail can be added, and several exchanges of dialogue can take place. It remains a pronouncement story ..." Tannehill: "Introduction," 1. In a later essay, Tannehill no longer acknowledges his earlier distinction but treats of what he calls apophthegms much in the same way as Berger treats chreia. Robert C. Tannehill: "Types and Functions of Apophthegms in the Synoptic Gospels," in *ANRW*, ed. W. Haase and H. Temporini, II.25.2:1831–1885.

[68] As a witness to this fact consult *Semeia* 64 (1993). The particular issue is entitled "The Rhetoric of Pronouncement." The studies in the volume, however, use chreia and pronouncement story interchangeably.

chreia.[69] An example pertinent to the discussion of Matthean controversy stories is the very visible elaboration of the chreia concerning the plucking of grain on the Sabbath. While Mk 2:23–28 is a story that is dominated by the concluding saying of the Sabbath made for man and the son of Man Lord of the Sabbath, Matthew 12:1–8 has elaborated on the pronouncement by adding considerably to the argumentation preceding the conclusion that the son of Man is Lord of the Sabbath.

For some time the question of the classification of chreia was an important field of study. Basically two approaches were taken, one by Klaus Berger and one by Robert Tannehill. Both authors develop their systems of classification as a modern aid to understand these stories better, without recourse to the work of ancient rhetoricians. Berger proposed that the chreia be categorized according to characteristics of both form and content.[70] With this categorization Berger distinguishes no less than 25 categories of chreia. Tannehill, on the other hand, proceeded with a categorization that was more intuitive and rested mostly on the distinctions of the content of the chreia.[71] Tannehill is more modest in his estimation of six types of chreia.[72] Even though Berger criticized Tannehill extensively as simplistic[73] his own classification is less than helpful because of its distinction

---

[69] In recent study of the chreia, their expansion and elaboration has come under intensified investigation. Thus Hock and O'Neil have argued for a distinction between expanded and elaborated chreia. While expansion of chreia might occur in setting or saying, it does not contain any further argumentative figures. Ronald F. Hock and Edward N. O'Neil: *The Chreia in Ancient Rhetoric*, vol. 1, *The Progymnasmata* (Atlanta: Scholars Press, 1986), 100–103. Elaboration, on the other hand, contains argumentative figures. Hock and O'Neil distinguish between "first-level-elaboration" which expands on one or more individual parts of a chreia, and "second-level-elaboration," which expands the chreia through rhetorical and argumentative devices into a complete argument (pp. 71–74, 176–177). The expansion into complete arguments has been taken up by Burton L. Mack and Vernon K. Robbins: *Patterns of Persuasion in the Gospels*, Foundations and Facets: Literary Facets (Sonoma: Polebridge, 1989), 51–65; Burton L. Mack: *Rhetoric and the New Testament* (Minneapolis: Fortress, 1990), 41–47.

[70] For Berger, the rationale for such an investigation lies in the question of the earlier form critics whether the actual stories as they are found in the gospels belong by nature to the literary form of chreia (Bultmann), or whether they developed from oral material into forms analogous to chreia (Dibelius). In order to press this discussion, Berger suggests "mit textlinguistischen Methoden das Chrienmaterial so zu beschreiben, daß ein Vergleich mit den neutestamentlichen Texten differenzierter erfolgen kann." Berger: "Gattungen," 1096.

[71] Tannehill investigated the chreia and their distinction from a very different starting point. For him the chreia were designed to influence the audience. Thus Tannehill argues that the chreia are a form of rhetorical persuasion. Their categorization reflects this aim. Tannehill: "Introduction," 3–4.

[72] The six types are: correction stories, commendation stories, objection stories, quest stories, inquiry stories, description stories. In his later essay, Tannehill reduced the number to five types by eliminating description stories. Tannehill: "Types and Functions of Apophthegms in the Synoptic Gospels."

[73] Berger points to many of the simplifications necessary in order to apply Tannehill's system. Behind these simplifications lies, according to Berger, a complete lack of criteria for the

between the structure of the question or objection, and the structure of the answer. Thus it is not clear why a story like Mk 12:13–17 should be categorized as a story containing the question to pay taxes[74] and not as a story that contains the elaboration of a small dialogue in the framework of a chreia.[75] Yet both approaches to distinguishing various classes of chreia contain references to stories that have at their heart controversies, or objections, or conflict. Both Tannehill and Berger see controversy stories as a sub-group of chreia.

Using the classification system of Tannehill, Paula Nassen Poulos investigated the *Lives* of Diogenes Laërtius for evidence of chreia.[76] Among the nearly 500 examples investigated the category of correction stories comprised more than half of the chreia. Taken together with the objection stories, the evidence mounted to 70 percent of the entire body of pronouncement stories investigated. If it is true that especially the objection story coincides with Bultmann's form of controversy dialogues,[77] the implications of this study for the examination of controversy stories are great. It would redefine the controversy stories as chreia that were particularly widespread in literature roughly contemporary with Matthew.[78] Three examples of Poulos' analysis of Diogenes' *Lives* shall suffice to illustrate the objections stories:

> Being once reproached for giving alms to a bad man, he [Aristotle] rejoined: "It was the man and not his character I pitied." (V 17)

> To one who accused him of living with a courtesan, he [Aristippus] put the question, "Why, is there any difference between taking a house in which many people have lived before and taking one in which nobody has ever lived?" The answer being "No," he continued, "Or again, between sailing in a ship in which 10,000 people have sailed before and in one in which nobody has ever sailed?" "There is no difference." "Then it makes no difference," said he, "whether the woman you live with has lived with many or nobody." (II 74)

---

classification. Such a lack, Berger rightly points out, "setzt totales Einverständnis über die Exegese der betreffenden Stelle voraus; dadurch rückt die Konsensbildung innerhalb der Zuteilung einer Stelle zu Gattungen jedoch in eine ferne Zukunft." Berger: "Gattungen," 1107–1110.

[74] Berger: "Gattungen," 1099.

[75] To be fair, Berger admits that some stories might be categorized in several of his classes. However, he suggests that such overlaps could be minimized if the classes were to be applied to the "jeweils offenkundig dominierende Element" of the chreia. However, with such a recourse Berger invites the argument that he himself used against Tannehill, namely that of the lacking exegetical consensus. Berger: "Gattungen," 1103.

[76] Poulos gives extensive examples of her research on Diogenes, with extensive quotations of chreia from Diogenes. Poulos: "Pronouncement Stories."

[77] Robert C. Tannehill: "Varieties of Synoptic Pronouncement Stories," *Semeia* 20 (1981): 107.

[78] In the same volume of *Semeia* 20 (1981), other articles come to similar results. Alsup examines Plutarch, while VanderKam examines chreia in the Intertestamental Literature, Greenspon looks at Philo and Josephus, Porton at Tannaitic Literature, Perkins at the Gospel of Thomas, and Stroker at early Christian literature. All the articles cite examples extensively.

He [Heraclitus] would retire to the temple and play at knuckle-bones with the boys; and when the Ephesians stood around him and looked on, "Why, you rascals," he said, "are you astonished? Is it not better to do this than take part in your civil life?" (IX 3)

Yet despite the formal affinities between the chreia, especially the objection chreia, and the controversy stories in the gospels many differences remain. The ancient works that have supplied the above examples are collections of chreia. As such they collect anecdotes of the lives of the philosophers or rulers they purport to portray. However, they are not biographies. Because they are collections of sayings they do not need to develop the characters in their stories. Thus in the objection stories or the corrections stories, the opponents of the philosophers or kings are incidental; they appear for this one story and then are gone from the work. Occasionally they may represent the differences between philosophical schools. But the level of hostility found in the controversy stories of the gospels, and intensified in the gospel of Matthew, cannot be sustained by mere chreia collections. Consequently, the chreia of antiquity are not sufficient to explain the phenomenon of gospel controversy stories. The difference of genre between gospels and chreia collections does not allow for the easy equation between objection chreia and controversy stories. It is probably here that the old dispute between Dibelius and Bultmann can be laid to rest. Dibelius is correct in his assertion that the controversy stories of the gospels are elaborated sayings material. They are this on a formal level. However, Bultmann's claim that these stories are very different from Greek objection chreia is correct as well. The gospel stories can sustain a depth of conflict which goes far beyond the incidental nature of chreia. This is particularly evident in the Matthean elaboration of the Markan controversy stories. Matthew edits and focuses the conflict on Jesus' quarrel with the Jewish leaders. Matthew sharpens the opposition between the two groups, and in some stories refocuses the argument to reflect the conflict better. The example of plucking grain on the Sabbath has already been mentioned. Further examples are Matthew's redaction of the controversy over purity (Matthew 15:1–9 ǁ Mk 7:1–8) or divorce (Mt 19:3–12 ǁ Mk 10:2–12).

In summary, recent investigations into pronouncement stories or chreia have revealed that Hultgren's claim of the uniqueness of the controversy story is, at least on the formal level, quite unfounded. The controversy stories have several affinities with chreia that can be summarized thus: Both are brief stories with a potential for expansion. Both center around a saying, most often in direct discourse, that is ascribed to a person within a concrete context. In both forms the situational aspect is integral to the cohesion of the story as the prompt for the main character's saying. Finally, even though chreia are considerably wider in their possibilities, they can include the capacity to express conflict, controversy, and objection. Similarly, the controversy stories exhibit a structure that can be found in other stories as well.

4. Controversy Stories and Contests in Dialogue

The comparison between the controversy stories and the chreia revealed that while on a formal level the two are quite comparable, the characteristic hostility sustained throughout the narrative of a gospel does not compare well with the incidental and anecdotal character of the chreia. In order to go beyond this impasse Berger suggested that the controversy stories are not just chreia, but are a hybrid between the chreia and the contests in dialogue, the ἀγὼν λόγων.[79] This latter literary form has been analyzed by Wilhelm J. Froleyks and shown to be a wide-spread phenomenon in Greek literature.[80]

The first substantial contests in dialogue appear in the Attic dramas as contests between persons of differing opinions.[81] The form was developed into a contest between persons in general, sometimes personified animals or ideas, or between poets, singers, sages and philosophers.[82] In these contests a tendency to typify the opponents is distinct.[83] Froleyks showed that such contests in dialogue most often contain a dramatic comparison between opponents, or synkrisis,[84] who engage in

---

[79] The *terminus technicus* is attested quite early already in Euripides: *Andromache* 234. An alternative term for the form appears in *Medea* 546: ἄμιλλα λόγων. Michael Lloyd: *The Agon in Euripides* (Oxford: Clarendon Press, 1992), 5. Berger discusses the form in relation to the controversy stories. Berger: "Gattungen," 1305–1310. Berger's suggestion, to my knowledge, has not met with success in the form-critical debate of the controversy stories.

[80] Wilhelm J. Froleyks: "Der Agon Logon in der antiken Literatur," diss (Bonn: Universität Bonn, 1973). There is no consistently used English translation of this term. In the following analysis, the term "contests in dialogue" will be used; The term "agon" is used is some of the secondary literature: Lloyd: *Agon*; Berger: "Gattungen." Froleyks' study is mainly a survey of the occurrence of the form in the literature of antiquity and illustrates how widely it was used.

[81] The earliest examples are found in *Ajax* and *Antigone* of Sophocles, plays of uncertain date but usually thought to be earlier than Euripides' *Alcestis* which can be dated to 438 B.C. For Euripides, the form is already a set-piece literary device appearing in most of his plays. Lloyd: *Agon*, 1.

[82] For a long list of references consult Berger: "Gattungen," 1306, nn. 274–275; Froleyks: "Agon Logon." Froleyks shows how the contest grows from small beginnings into finely crafted rhetorical forms (pp. 20–30). As an example the tree fables may serve. In Aesop's fable 239,1 the felled trees ask the reed how it had survived the storm. The reed answers with a reference to its flexibility. In fable 71 the same topic is explored through a conflict between oak and reed: This time it is mentioned that oak and reed quarrel about who was the stronger of the two. A storm arises, fells the oak, and the reed is left standing. As yet, however, no dialogue is introduced. A fully developed contest in dialogue appears in 263 between pinetree and thornbush. The outside element that decided the quarrel between oak and reed now disappears in favor of an apophthegmatic argument: The pine tree and thornbush quarrel about who is better. The pine argues that the thornbush is useless, while the pine tree is essential in the building of houses and ships. The thornbush answers that it just has to think about axes and saws that will bring an end to the pine in order to prefer being a thornbush.

[83] Berger: "Gattungen," 1307.

[84] Froleyks: "Agon Logon," 396.

a contest by bringing arguments for or against a particular subject. The subject matter itself may sometimes be less important than the actual conflict between the persons engaging in the contest. The winner of the argument, or the truth of the subject matter under discussion, usually is determined already before the contest begins. The opponents of a contest in dialogue engage in a contest over rhetorical art and persuasive argument, but also over the moral weight of their positions.[85] Often the aim of a contest is precisely the exposition of differing moral positions.

Pertinent examples for these characteristics of contests in dialogue can be drawn from Greek tragedies. Euripides uses a contest in dialogue in his *Electra* (988–1138) in order to show the differences between Electra and Clytemnestra.[86] By the time Electra and Clytemnestra engage in this contest, Orestes has already made the decision to kill Clytemnestra, and Electra is aware of this. The contest itself is an extended scene beginning with a chorus (988–997) and an opening dialogue (998–1009):

C   Step from the wain, Troy's daughters; take mine hand, that from this chariot floor I may light down ...

E   May I not then – the slave, the outcast I from my sire's halls, whose wretched home is here, – Mother, may I not take that heaven-blest hand?

C   Here be these bondmaids; trouble not thyself.

E   How? – me thou mad'st thy spear-thrall, haled from home: Captive mine house was led, and captive I, even as these, unfathered and forlorn. This opening is followed by the speech of Clytemnestra who tries to defend her murder of Agamemnon as a just deed (1011–1050), partly quoted here:

C   Such fruit thy father's plottings had, contrived against his dearest, all unmerited. Yea, I will speak; albeit, when ill fame compasseth woman, every tongue drops gall – as touching me, unjustly: Let men learn the truth, and if the hate be proved my due, 'tis just they loathe me; if not, wherefore loathe?

Clytemnestra then goes on to relate the ill treatment she received from Agamemnon and her reasons for killing him (1018–1048). She concludes her speech in 1049–1050 with a plea to Electra:

C   Speak all thou wilt: boldly set forth thy plea to prove thy father did not justly die.

A short dialogue follows (1050–1059) to prepare for Electra's speech:

---

[85] This particular feature of the ἀγών fits well with the suggestion by Malina and Neyrey that the controversy stories should be seen in the light of an honor contest. Malina: "Arland J. Hultgren: *Jesus and His Adversaries* (Book Review);" Malina and Neyrey: "Honor and Shame," 29–32.

[86] Lloyd: *Agon*, 61–69.

E   *Justice* thy plea! – thy "justice" were our shame! The wife should yield in all
        things to her lord, so she be wise. If any think not so, with her mine argument
        has naught to do. Bethink thee, mother, of thy latest words, Vouchsafing me free
        speech to answer thee.

C   Again I say it; and I draw not back

E   Yea mother, but wilt hear – and punish then?

C   Nay: I grant grace of licence to thy mood.

Electra's speech (1060–1099) is insulting in the extreme, especially at the
beginning. The speech ends with a brief saying adduced to condemn Clytemnestra.
A short excerpt from the beginning and end of the speech illustrate this:

E   Then I will speak. My prelude this shall be: – O mother, that thou had'st a
        better heart! This beauty wins you worthy meed of praise, Helen's and thine:
        true sister twain were ye! – Ay, wantons both, unworthy Castor's name! – She,
        torn from home, yet fain to be undone; thou, murderess of Hellas' noblest son,
        pleading that for a daughter's sake thou slew'st a husband! – ah, men know thee
        not as I ...

        Yea, if blood 'gainst blood in judgment rise, I and thy son, Orestes, must slay
        thee to avenge our sire: For, if thy claim was just, this, too, is just.

A dialogue between Clytemnestra and Electra follows that does not add to the
argument, but serves to highlight the hostility between the two women. The contest
in dialogue ends here (1138),[87] and Clytemnestra and Electra pass into the hut
where Orestes is waiting. The scene ends with the chorus condemning Clytemnestra
(1146–1176) while she is killed by her children.

The contest in dialogue does not in any way influence the plot of the play itself,
despite Clytemnestra's conciliatory gestures towards the end of the contest. Thus
it serves only to outline and emphasize different positions. It is not a device to
advance the plot in any manner. On the contrary, the plot is suspended while the
differing positions are outlined. The example of the contest in *Electra* is representative for Euripides' general use of it. It serves to highlight the conflict of the tragedy,
embodied in the contest of dialogue between two protagonists.[88] It is notable that
the speeches between the opponents are of almost equal length.

The contest in dialogue is not a genre of literature by itself, nor is it confined to
dramatic literature. Instead, it is a set-piece which occurs frequently in many genres

---

[87] Lloyd: *Agon*, 3.

[88] Lloyd writes: "The function of the agon remained as consistent as its form. There are many
ways to express conflict in drama, and Euripides' preferred method was to concentrate the conflict
between two important characters so that it could be isolated and expressed formally in a single
scene. This is not a naturalistic method, but it has the advantage of allowing a conflict to be
represented with clarity and explicitness." Lloyd: *Agon*, 131.

beginning with the earliest examples of Greek literature.[89] Herodotus is the first historian to incorporate contests in dialogue systematically into the art of historical writing. A good example is the deliberation before Xerxes concerning war against Greece.[90] Herodotus already formed the contests into longer examples of rhetorical art.[91] He also already exhibits the trend to end the speeches of each of the contestants with a pithy saying.[92] The contest in dialogue still underwent significant development after Herodotus,[93] yet the most important pieces are already in place: the opposition between the opponents of the dialogue, the dialogue itself, the pithy saying that concludes the dialogues, and sometimes the arbiter of the contest.

Often the contest in dialogue has a pronounced didactic or moral character. Two figures in contest symbolize good and evil, virtue and vice.[94] One early example of such a contest is the legend of Heracles having to make a decision between virtue

---

[89] Froleyks analyzes the literary form not chronologically, but by literary genre. His analysis includes fables, philosophical literature, mythological literature, tragedies and comedies, and historical writings among others. His aim is to show the wide use of the literary form of contests in dialogue. He writes in his conclusion: "Die Darlegung der verschiedenen Agontypen hat die Fruchtbarkeit des Agonmotivs und die Vielfalt der Erscheinungsformen deutlich gemacht." Froleyks: "Agon Logon," 440.

[90] Herodotus 7,8–11 reports that Xerxes submits plans for such a war to his council. Mardonius supports the plan, Artabanus warns against it, and finally Xerxes decides in favor. A similar contest also occurs in 8, 140–143.

[91] Before the battle of Plataea a furious debate (λόγων πολλὸς ὠθισμός) arises between Athenians and Tegeans (Herodotus 9,26–27). It begins when the Tegeans demand to be placed on the wing of the army that is not occupied by the Spartans. The Athenians dispute the claim and its implicit suggestion that the Tegeans are more courageous than the Athenians. The Spartans are acknowledged to be the most courageous in Greece, and so they are called to be the arbiters. The Athenians win the contest through rhetorical art and arguments, though, as Froleyks points out, Herodotus stacked the evidence heavily against the Tegeans. Froleyks: "Agon Logon," 296.

[92] Cf. 3,80–82. The section contains the famous dispute over the best form of government. After the assassination of the magi the seven conspirators confer over the best possible future of Persia. Otanes argues for democracy, Megabyzus for oligarchy, and Darius argues for monarchy. The four other conspirators vote for Darius. All three speakers end their discourse with a pithy saying: Otanes says ἐν τῷ πολλῷ ἔνι τὰ πάντα; Megabyzus concludes ἀρίστων ἀνδρῶν οἶκος ἄριστα βουλεύματα γίνεσθαι; finally Darius concludes with ἀνδρὸς γὰρ ἑνὸς τοῦ ἀρίστου οὐδὲν ἄμεινον ἂν φανείη.

[93] Froleyks mentions that Thucydides, for example, tends to give the opponents more balanced speeches and thus achieves that the arbitration is actually more arbitrary rather than self-evident before the speeches even begin. Froleyks also mentions that the characteristics of the contest in dialogue remain important for many of the Roman historians as well through the introduction of the Greek tradition of historiography into Roman traditions through Polybius: "Polybios selbst hat durch die Verwendung dieses Stilmittels in seinem Geschichtswerk den jüngeren römischen Historikern Sallust, Livius und Tacitus starke Impulse gegeben, und der ἀγὼν λόγων läßt sich in der rhetorischen Geschichtsschreibung bis in die Spätantike verfolgen." Froleyks: "Agon Logon," 318–319.

[94] Froleyks subsumes these under allegorical agones. Froleyks: "Agon Logon," 133–379.

and vice (ἀρετή and κακία).[95] Heracles seeks solitude to make the big decisions of life when two women approach him, one dressed virtuously without adornment, the other with much makeup in the transparent garments of a lewd woman. Two lengthy speeches follow. Vice promises Heracles an easy life without toil:

> When they drew nigh to Heracles, the first pursued the even tenor of her way: but the other, all eager to outdo her, ran to meet him, crying: 'Heracles, I see that you are in doubt which path to take towards life. Make me your friend; follow me, and I will lead you along the pleasantest and easiest road. You shall taste all the sweets of life; and hardship you shall never know' ... (II 1, 23).

> 'My friends call me Happiness (Εὐδαιμονίαν),' she said, 'but among those that hate me I am nicknamed Vice (Κακίαν)' (II 1, 26).

Virtue the draws near and makes her offer. She begins by complimenting Heracles on his family and character and proceeds to outline a life that would be in keeping with choosing Virtue over vice:

> Meantime the other had drawn near, and she said 'I, too, am come to you, Heracles: I know your parents and I have taken note of your character during the time of your education. Therefore I hope that, if you take the road that leads to me, you will turn out a right good doer of high and noble deeds, and I shall be yet more highly honoured and more illustrious for the blessings I bestow. But I will not deceive you by a pleasant prelude: I will rather tell you truly the things that are, as the gods have ordained them. For of all things good and fair, the gods give nothing to man without toil and effort ...' (II 1, 27–28).

Vice answers with a very brief remark (II 1, 29) comparing the sweat and toil that Virtue promises to the easy life she has to offer. Virtue then launches into another long speech attacking Vice directly first revealing Vice's promises as empty and then proceeds to extol her own propensity to make him happy. The denunciation of Vice and the extolling of Virtue are clearly related to one another:

> And Virtue said: 'What good thing is thine, poor wretch, or what pleasant thing dost thou know, if thou wilt do nothing to win them? Thou dost not even tarry for the desire to pleasant things, but fillest thyself with all the things before thou desirest them, eating before thou art hungry, drinking before thou art thirsty ... Immortal art thou, yet the outcast of the gods, the scorn of good men. Praise, sweetest of all things to hear, thou hearest not ... Who will believe what thou dost say? who will grant what thou dost ask? Or what sane man will dare join thy throng? ... But I company with gods and good men ... I am first in honour among the gods and among the men that are akin to me ...To my friends meat and drink will bring sweet and simple enjoyment: for they wait till they crave them ... through me they are dear to the gods, lovely to friends, precious to their native land ... O Heracles, thou son of goodly parents, if thou wilt labour earnestly on this wise, thou mayest have for thine own the most blessed happiness' (II 1, 30–33).

---

[95] Xenophon, *Mem.* II 1, 21–33, retells the myth ascribed to the Sophist Prodicus.

Xenophon does not relate the decision Heracles makes, but the inference is clear, and he does not need to spell out where his sympathies lie. This kind of contest in dialogue with ethical implications remained popular and received a number of variations.[96] Philo reports such a contest in an allegory explaining some details of the Mosaic Law,[97] and Lucian of Samosata satirizes the genre quite successfully.[98] The situation of contest is often enhanced by the use of invectives. Thus virtue chastises vice in the fable of Prodicus related by Xenophon: "What good thing is thine, poor wretch?" and other choice invectives relating to the shame she brings to herself and those who follow her. Electra calls Clytemnestra wanton, unworthy, murderess. During Herodotus' account of Xerxes' council Artabanus accuses Mardonius of calumny and foolishness (VII 10). The conclusion can culminate in a pithy saying and the silencing of the opponents who do not know how to answer. The loser of the argument often considers the loss unjust, and reacts with dejection, silence, or sometimes vents his frustration on the innocent.[99]

Several characteristics of the contest do not show up in the controversy stories: the appearance of an arbiter of the contest, like the chorus in *Electra* or Xerxes in the war council,[100] and the initial self-praise of the party that goes on to lose the

---

[96] A rather humorous variation is the contest between Tragedy and Elegy for the poet Ovid. Ovid: *Amores*, III, 1. Ovid rests in a mythical region when Tragedy and Elegy approach him, each with their proper attire. Tragedy speaks first to induce Ovid to leave the lightweight erotic elegies to turn his mind to Roman tragedies. Elegy counters with irony, pointing out that despite the serious and stormy character of Tragedy she has used Elegy's verse meter. Ovid finally decides for Elegy, yet promises Tragedy a later work. Silius Italicus: *Punica*, 15.18–20, ascribes such an allegorical contest between Virtus and Voluptas to the young Scipio Africanus, quite extensively molded on the temptation of Heracles. Thus Scipio is portrayed as somebody like Heracles, a luminous example of virtue to the Romans of Silius' times as Heracles became the example of cynic and stoic ethics. Froleyks: "Agon Logon," 147.

[97] Philo: *De Sacrificiis*, 20–45. His setting is not the lad who makes decisions for life, but the explanation of Deut 21:15–17, on the right of heritage of a firstborn son from a hated first wife. Philo proceeds to explain that each human being is wedded to two wives who hate each other and fill the house of the soul (τὸν ψυχικὸν οἶκον) with their clamor. This leads to the contest between pleasure (ἡδονή) and virtue (ἀρετή) who speak to the mind (νοῦς). Thus Philo uses the form as an allegory to explain the Mosaic law. His conclusion reveals, however, how as the arguments progress, the law recedes from view more and more, and the allegory ends up with merely the ethical conclusion that one ought to choose virtue.

[98] The young Lucian is destined to become a sculptor. But during his first day in his uncle's shop he receives such a beating for some mishap that he comes home crying and falls asleep, having a dream of a contest between Ἑρμογλυφικὴ Τέχνη and Παιδεία. Needless to say, Lucian decides for the art of letters, without even waiting for her to finish her discourse. Lucian: *Life*, 6–14.

[99] Froleyks: "Agon Logon," 396.

[100] Although Froleyks agrees that the arbiter is not a constitutive element of the contest. In some literary genres the arbiter almost never appears, as for example in fables. Similarly, the comedies which Froleyks examines reveal a tendency to omit the arbiter, especially in works later than Aristophanes. Froleyks: "Agon Logon," 20–39, 320–334. See also the example of Heracles

argument.[101] Furthermore, while the contest in dialogue can be quite lengthy, the controversy stories usually are not. Matthew, as has been seen, develops a tendency to elaborate the answers that Jesus give his opponents. However, there is no concomitant elaboration of the opponents statement. In the one case with a lengthy question, the controversy over divorce (Mt 19:3–9 || Mk 10:2–12), Matthew abbreviates it.

In other respects, however, the analogies of the contest in dialogue to the controversy stories are noticeable. Both forms engage in a contest that is already pre-determined in its outcome. The contest itself centers around issues of deeper significance than the anecdotal chreia can sustain. Furthermore, a connection between the contests in dialogue and the controversy stories can account better for the sustained hostility encountered between Jesus and his opponents than a sole reference to chreia.

The evidence of the contests in dialogue does not offer enough similarities to pose a direct literary relationship between the controversy stories and such contests. However, the contests in dialogue show evidence that there were many different ways to express hostility between opponents in the literature of antiquity. Furthermore, the contests draw attention to several features of the Matthean redaction of the controversy stories. As has been seen, Matthew has a propensity to elaborate on the answer of Jesus, to present a fuller argument, sometimes amplified by scripture quotations. Matthew exhibits a tendency to refine Jesus' answer rhetorically by making *qal-wa-ḥomer* arguments. Furthermore, Matthew focuses the controversies more directly on the Pharisees as the main opponents of Jesus in debate. At the same time the hostility inherent in the stories is amplified. These features of the Matthean redaction are not explainable with a reference to chreia. Chreia emphasize brevity and wit in the response. Matthew emphasizes a well argued response. For this purpose Matthew draws together material from different sources. The extensions of the ripostes in the controversy over plucking grain on the Sabbath (12:1–8), over the healing on a Sabbath (12:9–13), or the extensive expansion of the controversy over the collusion with Beelzebul (12:22–37) are examples of this trend. Furthermore, Matthew also shows that he likes to take material from Mark and redact it into controversy stories, as in the question over fasting (9:10–13), or the great commandment (22:34–30).

The tendency to typification of the opposing parties in the contest is also important in its relation to the assessment of the controversy stories. In the Markan controversy stories, various groups of Jewish leaders are presented as opposing

---

deciding between Vice and Virtue. Even though he is present at the contest in order to decide between the two, his decision is not transmitted.

[101] Berger also includes the invectives among the featured items in an ἀγών that are omitted in the controversy stories. Berger: "Gattungen," 1306. However, this is only partly correct. Matthew uses "hypocrites" several times in the controversy stories (e.g. 22:18). Furthermore, "offspring of vipers" (12:34) should be counted in this category.

Jesus.[102] Matthew focuses more clearly on the Pharisees as the main opposition. Thus Matthew uses the Pharisees in order to typify the opposition of Jesus more succinctly. They become the representatives of those opposing Jesus, of those who choose not to follow him.

Similarly, Jesus typifies more than just himself. He is the representative of God who can announce the arrival of the kingdom (4:17). But he is also the spokesman for those who decide to follow Jesus. Jesus represents his community, as, e.g., in the controversy over the authority to forgive sins (9:2–8), or over fasting (9:14–17), purity (15:1–9), or divorce (19:3–9). As a consequence, the controversy stories have a moral and didactic character similar to the contests in dialogue of which the story of Heracles is an example, and the story of Lucian a satire. The controversy stories need an audience to which both sides in the contest appeal to make a decision. By showing Jesus consistently besting his opponents, and by showing Jesus consistently as representing the way of life of the community, Matthew uses the controversy stories to make an ethical and moral appeal to his audience to follow the way of Jesus.

As in many of the ancient contests in dialogue, the Matthean controversy stories exhibit characteristics of set-pieces. They do not advance the plot in significant ways, but serve to exhibit a conflict between Jesus and his opponents that does not vary, despite the different issues that are discussed. The conflict is always deep seated, and the stories do not make room for any rapprochement between Jesus and his opponents. They serve to emphasize the conflict through various dramatic situations, but they do not offer a resolution. This feature of the controversy stories likens them to the contests found in the ancient tragedies. Although the conflict between Jesus and his adversaries is spread out over the gospel rather than compressed into a single scene, the various controversy stories highlight the conflict rather than solve it. The origin of these stories in the form of the chreia makes for the repetitive appearance of controversy stories, while their affinity with the contests in dialogue provides for the static nature of the conflict. As a consequence, the controversy stories can be viewed as an extended ἀγὼν λόγων between Jesus and his opponents. The outcome of this contest is pre-determined, while its function is the ethical demand for adjudication by the audience.

Because these contests in dialogue were such a widespread phenomenon in the literature of antiquity, it is unlikely that Matthew was not aware of them. Yet it is much harder to pinpoint the exact influence these contests might have had on

---

[102] Berger suggests that the typification of the contests is observable in the controversy stories as well: "Der 'jüdische' Weg wird so abgegrenzt von dem durch Jesus verkündigten neuen Weg." Berger: "Gattungen," 1307. Thus Berger uses the typification found in the contests to argue for the Jewish leaders as typifying the whole of Israel in the controversy stories. Furthermore, Berger makes a general remark concerning all the gospels; he makes no distinctions between the gospels. As has been seen so far, for Matthew the Jewish leaders do not represent Judaism. They typify just what they are: Jewish leaders.

Matthew. But a tentative conclusion can be drawn, nevertheless. Matthew mirrors the trend of these contests to move beyond the constricting form of chreia with their demand for brevity and wit. This makes it likely that Matthew's controversy stories exhibit a literary influence rather more complex and elusive than the mere appeal to chreia can sustain. Perhaps these contests offered Matthew some necessary elements to enhance the significance and rhetorical dignity of the stories he found in Mark. Matthew's controversy stories move beyond the form of the chreia in order to achieve a greater forensic power. The contests in dialogue are a likely model for the enhanced style of Matthew. As such there is a distant literary relationship between the contests in dialogue and Matthew's controversy stories.

5. Summary

The form-critical analysis of the controversy stories in Matthew's gospel has produced several results. The Matthean controversy stories are consistent in their redacted structure and development. However, their structure is applicable to other stories in the gospel as well. This is explained by the dependence of the controversy stories on the literary form of chreia. However, as the controversy stories depend on the chreia, Matthew also develops the literary form to a considerable extent.

The distinguishing mark of the controversy stories is their explicit mention of the motif of hostility between the opposing parties. This motif is presented in Matthew with an intensity that goes beyond the scope of chreia in other contemporary literature. To account for this feature, attention has been drawn to several points of contact with the form of contests in dialogue. As a consequence, the controversy stories are viewed as a literary form that combines the formal aspects of chreia with the influence of contests in dialogue. This combination makes the Matthean controversy stories a distinguishable variation of the literary form of chreia.

This form-critical analysis has departed to a large degree from the intentions of the early form critics. Unlike Bultmann or Dibelius, this analysis is not concerned with a possibility of discovering literary forms as revealing the stories' *Sitz im Leben* for the early Christian communities, but the relationship of the forms found in the gospel to its literary environment. Yet, perhaps not surprisingly, the results overlap to some extent. While it has been shown that the results of Bultmann and Dibelius needed refinement, some of their observations still have validity.

The most important result for this study is the establishment of parameters for the inquiry into controversy stories. As the controversy stories have been shown to have unique literary and formal characteristics, they can be grouped and investigated as a group. The problem of 13:53–58 can also be resolved. The story exhibits the literary characteristics of a chreia as well as the feature of hostility between the opponents necessary to qualify it as a controversy story. It is unique because it is the only controversy story that does not feature Jewish leaders as opponents.

Consequently, the story is not part of the extended contest in dialogue between Jesus and his opponents. Thus while the hostility of the people in Nazareth designate it as a controversy story,[103] its omission of Jewish leaders as opponents sets it apart within the group.

---

[103] Against Bultmann: *History*, 31.

VII. The Narrative Setting and Characters of the Controversy Stories in Matthew's Gospel

Following the analysis of their form and redaction the Matthean controversy stories can now be examined for their overall role and function in the gospel of Matthew. A thoroughgoing narrative analysis of the controversy stories in Matthew's gospel would take up more space than this chapter can allow for. Only a few selectively chosen arguments can be presented here. These will be presented in two steps.

The first will try to situate the controversy stories within the narrative framework of Matthew. It has already been seen that Matthew tends to present his controversy stories in blocks. The Jerusalem controversies basically follow the narrative sequence of Mark, although the Markan sequence is amplified to some extent. Furthermore, Matthew presents some material as controversy stories that appears in Mark in a different form. The controversies of chs. 9 and 12 depart even further from the Markan narrative thread. Here Matthew breaks up the sequence to a considerable extent to suit his own purposes. The examination of the narrative situation of the Matthean controversy stories will attempt to account for these phenomena.

In a second step the controversy stories will be analyzed for their theological implications. This will include a look at the opponents of Jesus in the stories. Furthermore, implications for the portrait of the various witnesses will be pointed out. Finally, the role of the christology implied in the controversies will be summarized. After this it will be possible to return to the initial question of this investigation. The controversy stories will be examined for the clues they offer as to the state of the discussion between the Matthean community and its Jewish contemporaries. It will be asked once more whether the controversy stories allow for a judgment on the question whether the Matthean community can be considered *intra* or *extra muros* of Judaism.

1. The Narrative Function of the Controversy Stories in Matthew's Gospel

With the exception of four stories scattered throughout the narrative between chs. 13 and 19, the Matthean controversies usually occur in distinct blocks. In order to place the stories into their narrative framework these blocks must be examined within their immediate context. The controversy stories in chs. 9, 12 are paralleled in Mark as a single block (2:1–3:6). Any investigation into the Matthean controversies of chs. 9 and 12 must take into account the breakup of the Markan sequence. Consequently, the following analysis will treat the controversies of these chapters together. Thus a first section will look at the controversies of chs. 9 and 12, a second section will look at the scattered controversies of chs. 13–19, and a third section will look at the Jerusalem controversies. A fourth and final section will summarize the findings.

1.1 The Controversies of Chapters 9 and 12

Within Mk 2:1–3:6 there are five controversy stories,[1] sometimes called the "Galilean controversies" and compared with the "Jerusalem controversies" of 11:27–12:37.[2] The theory that the controversy stories in this section were collected into a written form previous to Mark has found some success,[3] although not unanimously so.[4] Variations of this theory also abound.[5] These various theories bear

---

[1] The healing of the paralytic: 2:1–12; eating with tax collectors and sinners: 2:15–17; the question about fasting: 2:18–20; the first Sabbath controversy: 2:23–28; the second Sabbath controversy: 3:1–5, followed by the plot to destroy Jesus: 3:6.

[2] As Gundry rightly points out, the comparison suffers greatly from the fact that 12:28–37 are not really controversies, but a scholastic dialogue followed by a soliloquy of Jesus. Gundry: *Mark*, 105. See also: Huber: *Jesus in Auseinandersetzung*, 12–17.

[3] Among the scholars who propose 2:1–3:6 as a pre-Markan collection are: Albertz: *Die synoptischen Streitgespräche*, 5; Bultmann: *History*, 349; Taylor: *Formation*, 68. Taylor later corrected himself stating that the collections might have been compiled by Mark himself. Taylor: *Mark*, 92. The theory is most staunchly defended by Hultgren: *Adversaries*, 151–174.

[4] Dewey, following a trend to interpret Mark's gospel in terms of ancient conventions of rhetoric, sees a careful construction of concentric parallelism in the section Mk 2:1–3:6. Her study is quite restrained and detailed, and she is suitably hesitant in proposing her argument. Joanna Dewey: *Markan Public Debate*, SBL.DS 48 (Chico: Scholars Press, 1980). Some of the details that lead her to suggest concentric parallelisms are subject to controversy. Ernest Best: *Mark. The Gospel as Story* (Edinburgh: T. & T. Clark, 1983), 104–106. Dewey's case for concentric parallelism as constructed by Mark leads her to argue against prevailing scholarship that 2:1–3:6 is not a pre-Markan collection (pp. 52–55). Dewey's argument is important in its implication that within this block there is no increase in tension. Matthew breaks out of this possibly concentric circle through his interpolations in 9–11. This makes the Matthean increase in tension more obvious. Gundry also opposes the pre-Markan theory, although his arguments differ considerably from Dewey and concentrate on the thematic and narrative unity of the collection with the entire gospel. Gundry: *Mark*, 105–10.

[5] Thus Gnilka wants to shorten the collection considerably by eliminating the stories containing a miracle. His collection runs from 2:15–28. Gnilka: *Markus*, 1:132. Kee advances the same theory on the argument that 2:1–12 and 3:1–5 should be regarded as miracle stories in their original form that Mark adapted to form into controversy stories. He takes these two stories and groups them with the miracle stories of ch. 1 as a cycle of miracle stories collected before the gospel was written. Howard C. Kee: *Community of the New Age: Studies in Mark's Gospel* (Philadelphia: Westminster, 1977), 34–37. Some wish to extend the collection. Kertelge suggests that 12:13–17 might have been part of the earlier collection. Karl Kertelge: *Die Wunder Jesu im*

witness to the narrative unity of the section, regardless of its possible history before its current appearance. At the beginning and the end of the collection stand two pericopes (Mk 2:1–12; 3:1–6) which contain, apart from their controversial character, a miracle of Jesus that demonstrates the validity of the argument in the controversy. Together they form an *inclusio*.[6] This *inclusio* interrupts the narrative flow of Mark to some extent.[7] Within the *inclusio* the motif of controversy is prominent.[8] Thus the Markan collection of controversy stories in 2:1–3:6 gives an impression of independence precisely because of its internal cohesion.[9] Its narrative place within the gospel of Mark is explainable as a section that contrasts vividly the success of Jesus in ch. 1 with the opposition he faced in 2:1–3:6. Jesus' preaching, healing, and exorcisms reach a climax with the end of ch. 1 and the spread of Jesus' fame throughout the Galilean towns.[10] In a sense, the conflict beginning in 2:1 marks a new section that comes to a similar climax in 3:6. In 1:45 the former leper

---

Markusevangelium. Eine redaktionsgeschichtliche Untersuchung, StANT 33 (München: Kösel, 1970), 83. Further variations on the pre-Markan collection theory are listed by Gnilka: *Markus*, 1:131–132; Gundry: *Mark*, 105–110.

[6] Gnilka suggests that these two pericopes cannot be part of the original pre-Markan collection because they differ in form by including a miracle. Gnilka: *Markus*, 1:131. Yet if in their present position the healing of the paralytic and the healing of the man with the withered hand are an *inclusio*, then their difference in form cannot be used as the only argument against their being part of the collection. However, Gnilka also adduces other arguments. He maintains that the middle three controversies are "als konkrete Gemeindefragen unschwer zu erkennen" because they contain references to the disciples which are missing in the outer two stories (p. 1:132).

[7] In 1:45 Mark writes: "Jesus could no longer openly enter a town." But in 2:1 Jesus then enters Capernaum, although Mark adds "after some days." However, in 3:7 Jesus withdraws from the town toward the sea. Furthermore, in 1:45 Mark reports people from every quarter coming to Jesus, while in 3:7 a great multitude follows him when he withdraws. Thus there could be a narrative connection between 1:45 and 3:7 that is interrupted by 2:1–3:6. Hultgren: *Adversaries*, 152. Gundry maintains that 3:7 follows just as easily upon 3:6 as it does on 1:45. The withdrawal would then be a direct reaction to the plot of the Pharisees and Herodians. Gundry: *Mark*, 105. Thus it is not very clear whether 2:1–3:6 is an interruption of the narrative, or whether it is part of it. It is possible to lift the entire section out of the narrative flow of Mark without having to adjust the surrounding material. This speaks for a degree of independence of the section.

[8] For Best the fact that controversy stories are collected here points to a pre-Markan collection. Regarding the traditions behind Mark he writes: "Mark was tied in another way by the tradition; some of it was already gathered into 'complexes' of material of similar nature, e.g. controversy stories (2.1–3.5), parables (4.3–32)." Best: *Mark*, 129.

[9] Joanna Dewey's argument of concentric parallelism points to this cohesion of the collection. Dewey: *Markan Public Debate*. Because she finds such parallelisms in other sections of Mark's gospel, she concludes that the collection is not pre-Markan.

[10] Gnilka writes: "Da die außergewöhnliche Heilung eines Leprösen jetzt in der ersten galiläischen Tätigkeit stattfindet, markiert sie einen ersten Höhepunkt in der Öffentlichkeitsbewegung, die Jesus auslöst. Sein Ruf breitet sich nicht nur aus, sondern er wird jetzt auch durch einen von ihm vom Aussatz Befreiten ins Land getragen." Gnilka: *Markus*, 1:94. Gundry argues similarly for a climax reached in 1:45. Gundry: *Mark*, 109.

spreads the news about Jesus with the consequence that people come to him from everywhere. In 3:6 Pharisees and Herodians begin to plot the death of Jesus.

Mark, then, presents a narrative picture of the Galilean controversies that is quite cohesive both as a unit and within the larger Markan sequence. Matthew decides to break up the sequence altogether. Although he uses the Markan material to a large extent Matthew significantly rearranges it. Of the five controversies in Mk 2:1–3:6 Matthew uses the first three in ch. 9 and defers use of the last two until ch. 12.

In order to explain this considerable redactional activity, most commentators refer to the narrative unity of chs. 8–9.[11] The reason for this is a general agreement that chs. 8–9 form "the second half of a two–panel presentation which typifies Jesus' ministry. In 5–7 Jesus speaks. In 8–9 he acts."[12] Thus chs. 8–9 are seen as a sample anthology of miracles, arranged by topic.[13] Yet an examination of scholarly opinions concerning the structure and content of chs. 8–9 reveals that the agreement ends with the declaration of these chapters as a unit.

The suggestion that chs. 8–9 are an allusion to the 10 miracles Moses works in Egypt (Ex 7–12) is grounded in the observation that Jesus works 10 miracles in 8–9.[14] Yet while there are distinctive Mosaic allusions in the portrait of Jesus in the gospel of Matthew,[15] such a proposition for 8–9 meets with several improbabilities. Firstly, even though there are ten miracles, there are only nine miracle stories. The story of the ruler's daughter and the woman with the issue of blood (9:18–26) is a unit. Secondly, and more importantly, the miracle stories are divided into three different groups (8:2–15, 8:23–9:8; and 9:18–34) that have no correspondence in Exodus. Finally, the miracles of Moses are fundamentally different from the miracles of Jesus in the sense that they are miracles which are directed against the oppression of Pharaoh while the miracles of Jesus are healings.[16]

Gerd Theissen's approach to the structure of chs. 8–9 connects the recurring and distinct geographical references with the prophecy of 4:15–16. The scene begins in

---

[11] As a sample, Briscoe might be quoted here: "Clearly, any attempt to explain Matthew's reasons for separating 9:1–17 from 12:1–14 involves an explanation of the compositional arrangement of chs. 8–9 and the placing of 9:1–17 within that composition." Peter Briscoe: "Faith Confirmed Through Conflict – The Matthean Redaction of Mark 2:1–3:6," in: *Back to the Sources. Biblical and Near Eastern Studies in Honour of Dermot Ryan*, ed. Kevin J. Cathcart and John F. Healey (Dublin: Glendale, 1989), 108–109.

[12] Davies and Allison: *Matthew*, 2:1.

[13] Most influential in proposing this thesis has been Held. He believed that 8:1–17 are primarily concerned with Jesus as savior, 8:18–9:17 with discipleship, and 9:18–31 with faith. Held: "Interpreter," 246-253.

[14] Erich Klostermann: *Das Matthäusevangelium*, HNT 4 (Tübingen: Mohr, 1927), 72; Hans J. Schoeps: *Theologie und Geschichte des Judenchristentums* (Tübingen: Mohr, 1949), 93.

[15] Dale C. Allison: *The New Moses. A Matthean Typology* (Minneapolis: Fortress Press, 1993).

[16] Davies and Allison: *Matthew*, 2:1–2.

Galilee (8:1 takes up 4:23), then moves out across the sea (8:23), and finally returns to Galilee (9:1).[17] However, the chapters are not structured primarily on the principle of geography. Similarly a common theme is not obvious, nor can it explain the structure.[18] A thematic structure separates 8–9 into three distinct parts, each with its own subject. The first unit is composed of 8:2–17 and focuses mainly on christology, the second unit contains 8:18–9:17 with discipleship as its subject, the third unit on faith consists of 9:18–38.[19] Behind this structure stands the literary insight that the miracle stories fall into three separate sections.[20] In this case a triadic structure based on the nine miracle stories with some complementary material can be detected.[21]

---

[17] Theissen: *Stories*, 210. While the geographical arrangement pointed out by Theissen is possible, the correspondence to 4:15–16 is less convincing. There is no mention of Capernaum in the prophecy. Furthermore, Theissen's theory explains only the movement in ch. 8, because in ch. 9 Jesus is back in Galilee and does not travel any more. Thus a structure based solely on the geographical arrangement would make 8–9 rather lopsided. Davies and Allison point out, among other arguments against Theissen, that a real difficulty ensues when the formula quotation of 4:15–16 is seen as fulfilled in the structure of chs. 8–9. This would be the only place in Matthew where such a quotation is not fulfilled in its immediate context. Davies and Allison: *Matthew*, 2:2. Furthermore, while the geographical arrangement seems similar, no real parallels in wording are apparent: Capernaum is not said to be "by the sea," the Gadarenes are not said to be Gentiles, the Jordan is never mentioned in 8–9.

[18] Cope suggested Hos 6:6 as the mid–point text that states the theme of mercy as opposed to Torah piety as central to this section. Cope: *Matthew*, 65–73. Cope focuses this interpretation mainly on the contact of Jesus with uncleanness. However, from 9:18 onwards uncleanness or Torah piety are not an issue, and Matthew does not point out explicitly that the dead child and the issuing woman are unclean. Furthermore, Cope entirely ignores the fact that Hos 6:6 returns in the first controversy of ch. 12. Consequently, the quotation from Hosea probably functions more as a bridge between the Markan material separated by the Matthean redaction than it does as a glue holding chs. 8–9 together.

[19] This was first proposed by Held and subsequently adopted by Thompson. Held: "Interpreter," 246–253; William G. Thompson: "Reflections on the Composition of Mt 8:1–9:34," *CBQ* 33 (1971): 365–388. The major disadvantage of this theory is the inconsistency with which the supposed themes occur. While two miracle stories of section three mention faith (9:22, 28) this theme also occurs in 8:26 and 9:2. The theme of christology may be the driving force behind 8:16–17 with the fulfilment of Is 53:4, but how does this shape the whole section? And while two stories in the second section treat of discipleship in an obvious sense (8:18–27; 9:9–13) the other two stories seem unaffected by this theme. Thus a division according to themes is fraught with too many inconsistencies.

[20] For this reason the division into four thematic parts, proposed by Burger and Kingsbury, fails. Christoph Burger: "Jesu Taten nach Matthäus 8 und 9," *ZTK* 70 (1973): 272–287; Jack D. Kingsbury: "Observations on the 'Miracle Chapters' of Matthew 8–9," *CBQ* 40 (1978): 559–573. Similar to the proposal by Held, their supposed themes do not stand up to closer scrutiny.

[21] In the first part a leper is healed (8:1–4), the centurion's servant is healed (5–13), Peter's mother–in–Law is healed (14–15). The first part concludes with a summary report and some words of Jesus (16–22). The second part begins with the calming of the storm (8:23–27), relates the story of the Gadarene demoniac (28–34), includes the healing of the paralytic (9:1–8), and concludes with the call of Levi and words of Jesus (9–17). The third part begins with the story of

In yet another proposal for a division of the material in 8–9 Luz suggests four parts of roughly equal length.[22] These parts define themselves not through literary characteristics so much as through narrative progression.[23] The first part, 8:1–17, has Jesus on the move from the descent from the mountain (8:1) into Capernaum (8:5) and into a house (8:14). Similarly in the second part (8:18–9:1) Jesus suggests a trip across the sea (8:18), the trip takes place (8:24–28), and Jesus returns to Capernaum (9:1). The third part (9:2–17) finds Jesus in controversy in the house, while in the fourth part he leaves the house (9:19) to follow the ruler, and from there moves on (9:27).

While this division of the chapters by Luz owes some of its arguments to Theissen, Luz does not try to tie this progression to the prophecy of 4:15–16. Luz points out, however, a certain repetitiveness in the miracle stories, in the recurring thoughts on discipleship, and the conflict with Israel's leaders. Thus two dimensions of the narrative thread of chs. 8–9 become apparent. On the surface level a consecutive narrative of miracle and controversy stories are geographically and chronologically linked and become "Teil der Geschichte Jesu mit seinem Volk, die mit seiner Hinrichtung und Auferstehung enden wird."[24] On a deeper level Matthew tells the story of his own community, beginning with the ministry of Jesus, leading to the separation of Israel and the mission to the Gentiles.[25]

The proposal by Luz has much to recommend it, despite its looseness compared to the proposal of a triadic structure. It ties the narrative of 8–9 into the whole gospel according to a narrative progression.[26] As a consequence chs. 8–9 are much

---

the ruler's daughter and the woman with a hemorrhage (9:18–26), continues with the two blind men (27–31) and the dumb demoniac (32–34) and concludes with a summary report and words of Jesus (35–38). Davies and Allison: *Matthew*, 1:102. But the three parts that Davies and Allison propose are of rather unequal length, the last part with only 20 verses being the shortest, while the middle part with 29 verses is much longer. Furthermore, what does this structure explain beyond the fact that Matthew likes triads? This structural analysis does nothing to elucidate any particular purpose of the triadic structure. For this reason this explanation is not sufficient despite its obvious attractiveness.

[22] These parts are 8:1–17; 8:18–9:1, with 9:1 as a transition that leads into the third part (9:2–17), and the fourth part 9:18–35). Luz: *Matthäus*, 2:5–7. Luz refrains from trying to subsume these parts under common theological themes with reference to the failed attempts by Held, Kingsbury, and Burger.

[23] A similar approach to the structure of Matthew through narrative devices is proposed by Bauer. He finds seventeen such devices that help to structure the narrative of Matthew's gospel. David R. Bauer: *The Structure of Matthew's Gospel: A Study in Literary Design*, JSNT.S 31 (Sheffield: The Almond Press, 1989), 13–20.

[24] Luz: *Matthäus*, 2:6.

[25] Luz: *Matthäus*, 2:7. Luz sees here a recurrence of an underlying theme present in the infancy narrative. There Jesus' birth was miraculous, but at the same time elicited opposition from Herod and all the people in Jerusalem, and led to a manner of discipleship by the magi. Luz is careful in suggesting that his proposal is only a "Vermutung," not an established fact.

[26] Senior suggests that such an approach has much more to recommend it than a restriction of the structure to just one literary device. He writes: "As Matthew moves the reader through his

less a distinct unit in the gospel than the other approaches to their structure claim. Luz also takes into account that because of this narrative progression the story of Jesus has moved on to become more complex. This conclusion is strengthened by a further analysis of chs. 8–12 in the light of the controversy stories. As Luz relates the structure of 8–9 to the wider context of the gospel he points to another shortcoming of the attempts to view them as a tightly woven unit: A restriction to the supposed narrative unity of chs. 8–9 also remains unsuccessful in explaining the Matthean breakup of the Markan collection of controversy stories.

Further evidence for the relationship of these chapters to the material surrounding it can be found in the summary at the end of the unit (9:35–38).[27] This summary makes explicit reference to the fact that Jesus travels throughout the villages and cities, teaching, preaching, and healing in "their synagogues" (4:23; 9:35). While this summary echoes 4:23–25 and almost certainly forms an *inclusio* together with the earlier summary statement, it also moves beyond the earlier summary through the geographical extension and heightening of the abandonment of the people. While in 4:23 Jesus moves around Galilee, and people from other areas are said to follow him (4:24–25), in 9:35 Jesus is no longer restricted to Galilee. While the people in 4:23 are infirm, in 9:36 the crowds are harassed and outcast.[28] The summary of 9:35–38 gives some understanding of how the preceding chapters need to be read. The frequent geographical descriptions given in the chapters are not accidental, but an intrinsic element of the narrative progression which shows Jesus' ministry of mercy to the people.[29] While the disciples gather around the master, and while the storm clouds gather over Jesus and the Jewish leaders, the as yet undecided crowds are described as alienated by the increasing discrepancy between miracle and controversy, between Jesus and the Jewish leaders.

The summary, then, points to the importance of the miracles of Jesus. But it also points explicitly to the material following the summary. In 9:35 Jesus is portrayed in his ministry to the cities and villages of Galilee. In 9:36 Matthew presents one of the results of this activity: Jesus knows the condition of the people as sheep without

---

story there are several devices and motifs that carry the plot ... To these should be added reactions to the material provided by his sources." Donald Senior: *What Are They Saying About Matthew?* 2nd ed., (New York, Mahwah: Paulist Press, 1996), 35.

[27] Luz misses this important evidence in his analysis.

[28] The RSV translates ἐρριμμένοι as "helpless." However, the verb in the active carries the meaning of throwing, or ripping. The compound ἀπορρίπτω occurs regularly denoting outcasts. Liddell and Scott: *A Greek–English Lexicon*, 216. Matthew uses this word also in 27:5 to denote how Judas returns the blood money to the temple. In 15:30 it is used to describe how the sick are deposited at the feet of Jesus for him to heal them. While the Matthean evidence is not conclusive it is probable that the people described in the present pericope are perceived as rejected, not just helpless.

[29] This leads to further scepticism concerning the triadic theory of the structure of Mt 8–9 proposed by Davies and Allison. Their proposal neglects the geographic arrangement completely.

a shepherd. In 9:37–38 the conclusion of this situation is drawn: the disciples are told of the harvest and the few laborers available for it. This statement leads naturally into the mission that the disciples are to undertake in ch. 10.[30]

Consequently, several themes overlap in this summary. Matthew reflects on the miracles and Jesus' general activity in chs. 8–9. But he interprets them as signs of compassion on the side of Jesus and notes at the same time that the people are still confused, harassed, and outcast (9:36). Furthermore, Matthew gives this summary, and consequently the following mission to "the lost sheep of the House of Israel" (10:5), an eschatological sub-text by referring to it as a harvest.[31] The disciples are asked to prepare the people for the end of time.

But beyond the themes of the powerful deeds of Jesus and the eschatological gathering of Israel the central statement of the summary affirms that the people are like sheep without a shepherd (9:36). This image of Israel is a recurring topic in the literature of the Hebrew Scriptures.[32] It describes a people which suffers from oppressive leadership. The first thing of note in Matthew's version of this saying is that he transposed it from its place in Mk 6:34 to the present position before the missionary discourse. Matthew augments the saying with two passive participles describing the plight of the people: they are harassed and outcast. The transposition and amplification of the saying show that Matthew considers it vital in this context. Matthew then combines this impression of Israel with the prayer for workers in the vineyard, thus combining Mk 6:34 with a saying from Q (Lk 10:2). This combination leads to a more vivid portrayal of Israel as without proper leadership[33] and also serves to introduce the mission of the disciples. Thus what began as a summary in 9:35 continues also to evaluate the ministry of Jesus, his judgment about Israel and her leaders, and the mission of the disciples.

The observation that the people resemble sheep without a shepherd is probably a direct attack against the Jewish leaders that Jesus encountered in the controversies of ch. 9.[34] The Jewish leaders have so far been shown to oppose Jesus. But in these

---

[30] Davies and Allison call this summary a presentation of "three images of Jesus ... Notice that the three images become increasingly contracted ... The task that the twelve are to perform ... is rooted in Jesus' compassion for the multitude ... and results from the need for the ministry of teaching, preaching, and healing to be carried out by more than one individual." Davies and Allison: *Matthew*, 2:146.

[31] Elsewhere in the synoptic tradition, the harvest is a metaphor for eschatological judgment: Mt 3:12; 13:30, 39; Mk 4:26–29; 13:27. See also Rev 14:14–20. The eschatological connotations of this metaphor is probably rooted in the prophetic tradition (Is 18:4; 27:12; Jer 51:53; Hos 6:11; Joel 3:13) and finds parallels in *4 Ezra* 4:26–37; 9:17; *2 Bar* 70:1–2. Davies and Allison: *Matthew*, 2:149; Luz: *Matthäus*, 2:81.

[32] See for example Num 27:17; 1 Kings 22:17; 2 Chron 18:16; Ezek 34:5; Zech 13:7.

[33] Overman: *Church and Community*, 139.

[34] There is no scholarly consensus on this point. Luz thinks that because ποιμήν is used in the singular no direct polemic is intended. Luz: *Matthäus*, 2:81. Davies and Allison suggest that such polemic is intended. Davies and Allison: *Matthew*, 2:148. See also: Overman: *Church and*

controversies they have also shown that they do not have regard for those who need direction and ministry. Thus they have no regard for sinners, they show none of the pity that Jesus shows, and when Jesus heals they accuse him of collusion with Beelzebul (9:34). The latter reference is especially poignant for three reasons: Firstly, it directly precedes the present summary. Thus the last impression of the wonderful deeds of Jesus is the opposition of the Pharisees. And secondly, the same incident returns in 12:22–30 to become a matter of a controversy story. Thirdly, the accusation that Jesus works by the power of Beelzebul is also taken up in the missionary discourse (10:25). There Matthew explains that as Jesus has been called Beelzebul, so will his disciples be maligned. The reason for this is that the disciples will actually go to the lost sheep of the house of Israel (10:6–8), just as Jesus did.

Consequently, the summary of 9:35–38 cannot be viewed just as a narrative conclusion to chs. 8–9. It is perhaps true that Matthew begins a new section with the mission of the twelve.[35] But these verses also provide an account of how the great deeds of Jesus tie in with the following chapters on mission and controversy. He explains that the wonderful deeds of Jesus contrast with a desperate situation of a leaderless people. This situation occasions the mission of the disciples to the lost sheep of the house of Israel. The summary, then, looks both backward and forward in the narrative.

Matthew locates the first controversies within this assessment of Israel. Kingsbury points out that the controversies of ch. 9 prove to be preliminary in several respects.[36] They do not immediately move the opponents to organize themselves for a concerted action against Jesus. None of the early controversies involves an intricate discussion of the Law, and even though one of the charges leveled against Jesus is the quite serious accusation of blasphemy, the arguments remain outside of legal debates.

Kingsbury's observations apply to the Markan sequence as well as to the Matthean sequence. It seems probable that Matthew viewed Mark as intending a progressive animosity between Jesus and his opponents in the sequence Mk 2:1–3:6. Matthew, however, tried to provide an explanation for the progression.[37] Through the interruption of the Markan account of the controversies with miracle stories of ch. 9 and the discourses of chs. 10 and 11 Matthew shows how the

---

Community, 139. It seems unlikely that the saying concerning a lack of a shepherd in Israel is completely void of any polemic. Even if the attack is not direct but merely a claim of Jesus to assume this leadership, the implications of such a claim still contain a judgment on those who claim leadership of Israel.

[35] Luz maintains that Matthew begins "einen neuen Hauptteil." Luz: *Matthäus*, 2:80.

[36] Kingsbury: *Matthew as Story*, 119.

[37] Even though Kingsbury maintains that he undertakes a literary-critical study of Matthew as a story, he fails to acknowledge the significance of the material between the blocks of controversy stories in Matthew. He jumps immediately from a discussion of the controversies in ch. 9 to the analysis of 12:1–14. Thus he can describe the development of the hostility, but cannot account for the break in the Markan narrative sequence. Kingsbury: *Matthew as Story*, 119–121.

Pharisees take exception to the teaching, healing, and preaching of Jesus. It also explains that this opposition is not just directed against Jesus, but also against his disciples who share in this mission. If this is correct, Matthew's explanation for the progressive sharpening of the controversies between Jesus and his opponents is the mission to the lost sheep of the house of Israel. Consequently, Matthew elaborates this mission before he goes on to report the remaining stories of Mark's block.

A look at the sequence of Mt 8–13 as compared with Mark gives support to this suggestion. The following table illustrates how Matthew displaced Markan material, and how he inserted other material. For the sake of emphasis, the controversy stories are framed in the table.

Table 27. The Matthean Dislocations of Markan Material

MATTHEW'S SEQUENCE		CONTENT	MARK	
from Mark	*additions, doublets*		*same se-quence*	*dislocations*
8:1–4		the leper	1:40–45	
	8:5–13	the centurion		
8:14–15		Peter's mother–in–law		1:29–31
8:16		summary		1:32–34
	8:17	Is 53:4		
	8:18–22	on discipleship		
8:23–27		calming of the storm		4:35–41
8:28–34		Gadarene demoniacs		5:1–20
9:1–8		forgiveness of sins	2:1–12	
9:9–13		tax collectors and sin-ners	2:13–17	
9:14–17		fasting	2:18–22	
9:18–26		two healings		5:21–43
	9:27–31 ‖ 20:29–34	two blind men		[10:46–51]
	9:32–34 ‖ 12:22–24	demoniac		
	9:35–38	summary		[6:6b] 6:34
	10	missionary discourse		[6:7; 3:13–19a; 6:8–9; 9:10–11]
	11:1	Jesus teaches		
	11:2–19	John the Baptist		
	11:20–24	woes over the cities		
	11:25–30	the great thanksgiving		
12:1–8		Sabbath controversy 1	2:23–28	
12:9–14		Sabbath controversy 2	3:1–6	
12:15–16		Jesus withdraws	3:7–12	
	12:17–21	Isaiah fulfilled		
12:22–32		Beelzebub controversy	3:22–30	
	12:33–37	good fruit		
	12:38–45 ‖ 16:1–4	demand for a sign		[8:11–12]

MATTHEW'S SEQUENCE		CONTENT	MARK	
from Mark	*additions, doublets*		*same sequence*	*dislocations*
12:46–50		the family of Jesus	3:31–35	
13:1–35		parables of the kingdom	4:1–34	
	13:36–52	parables of the kingdom		
13:53–58		Jesus' own country	6:1–6a	

The table clarifies the relationship between the Markan and the Matthean narrative sequences to some extent. It is after the healing of the leper that Matthew departs from Mark's sequence to a considerable extent. However, Matthew also leaves significant pieces in place. These are the five controversy stories of Mk 2:1–3:6. After the last controversy of this sequence (12:9–14 || Mk 3:1–6) Matthew then begins to follow Mark again more closely. Although he inserts material like the fulfillment quotation (12:17–21) and fleshes out the controversy over the accusation of collusion with Beelzebul, in the process adding another controversy over the demand for a sign, Matthew no longer displaces Markan material. Thus the major change that Matthew makes to the Markan sequence concerns the interweaving of Mk 1:40–2:22 and 4:35–5:43, with interpolations from Q and the duplication of a miracle story from Mk 10:46–52 in Matthew 9:27–31.

The controversies are heightened in their initial surprise because Matthew shows a Jesus who works miracles and heals and works powerful signs. In order to show the upsetting response of Jesus' opponents more clearly, Matthew makes the first major change in the Markan sequence. He cuts Mk 1:23–28 and 1:35–39 and places 1:29–34 after the healing of the centurion's servant. This results in the sequence of the centurion's servant (8:5–13) from Q, the healing of Peter's mother-in-law (8:14–15 || Mk 1:29–31) and a suitable summary (8:16 || Mk 1:32–34) which is amplified by the fulfilment quotation of Is 53:4 (8:17). Matthew then inserts two sayings about discipleship (8:18–22) which anticipate the division between those who are called by Jesus to follow him and those who are rejected by Jesus. Finally, Matthew anticipates the material from Mk 4:35–5:20 which results in the calming of the storm in 8:23–27 and the Gadarene demoniacs (8:28–34). The two latter stories already develop a christological focus (8:27; 8:29) that builds on the question of discipleship. The story of the Gadarene demoniacs prepares for a rejection of Jesus as the Gadarenes ask Jesus to leave their territory.

This builds up to the first controversies in ch. 9. The opponents of Jesus now come from the midst of Israel. After these preliminary controversies Matthew inserts more miracle stories, one from Mk 5:21–43, and two others which are doublets from later material in Matthew. After a suitable summary Matthew assembles the missionary discourse of ch. 10 and the various teachings of ch. 11.

With ch. 12 Matthew returns to the sequence found in Mark, though now he has to make adaptations for the material that he already used earlier.

This places 12:1–8 at a crucial point in the Matthean narrative. The care with which Matthew redacts this story reflects this to some extent. The mission to Israel sets the stage for Israel's answer. The discourse over the ministry of John the Baptist and the woes over the cities of Galilee prepare for the heightened opposition of the Pharisees. But the great thanksgiving also intimates that the ministry of Jesus is not to be futile. The disciples of Jesus still follow him, because he reveals the Father to them (11:27). They accept the challenge to learn from Jesus (11:29), just as the opponents do not (12:7).

Matthew 12:1–8 focuses these different narrative threads into one controversy story. The followers of Jesus give scandal to the Pharisees. But as they object, and as Jesus answers them, the struggle between them is not one over the practice of the disciples any longer. The dispute over the Sabbath regulations reveals the rift between the authority of Jesus and the intransigence of the Pharisees to accept the better and more righteous interpretation of the Law which Jesus offers. While the Pharisees object to the behavior of the disciples they reject the authority of Jesus. They refuse to learn from Jesus. The renewed reference to Hos 6:6 in 12:13 makes this abundantly clear. At the same time, it ties the controversy stories of chs. 9 and 12 together. Matthew uses the repetition of Hos 6:6 as a major structural element holding together chs. 9 and 12 by pointing out that the narrative thread is not suspended but continuing.

With the emphasis on the controversy stories the rationale for the disruption of the Markan sequence and the construction of the Matthean sequence becomes clear. Matthew is obviously interested in fashioning a coherent narrative. Each incident follows directly upon the other, sometimes with surprising results.[38] But an "internal principle"[39] in this sequence can be detected. Jesus begins his public ministry among the people, calls his disciples from among them, and sends his disciples out to mission to them and make him present to them (10:40). At the same time, the first tensions begin to rise with the leaders of Israel.[40] These tensions increase after the missionary discourse and the thanksgiving of Jesus for the revelation to the little ones and his promise to reveal himself (11:25–27). His invitation to all the burdened

---

[38] When Jesus comments in 8:10 that nowhere in Israel had he found faith like the centurion's he does so without previous mention of the theme of faith, either presence or lack of it. The subsequent withdrawal in 8:18 seems unmotivated since he had given some attention to the crowd previously. The Pharisaic response to the healing of the demoniac in 9:34 seems surprising since it lacks any preparation. Until this point, Jesus has not expelled any demons. In 10:1 Jesus calls 12 disciples even though only five have been mentioned so far.

[39] The term is used by Luz. He considers this principle to be the conflict with Israel. Luz: *Theology*, 64. However, the crowds at this point are still the observers of the conflict. Consequently, so Luz, a mission to them (ch. 10) is still possible.

[40] Kingsbury points out the preliminary nature of the conflict in Mt 9. Kingsbury: *Matthew as Story*, 118–120.

(11:28–30) is immediately followed by the onset of the controversies of ch. 12 with their increase in the severity of mutual hostility between Jesus and the Jewish leaders. The tension inherent already in the Markan block of the controversy stories is amplified through the interspersion and contrast with the healings, the teaching and the preaching of Jesus and his disciples. The often positive reaction of the crowds sets the controversy stories into even starker relief.

For Matthew the block of Markan controversy stories was important. He perceived the increase in tension inherent in them. Consequently, he arranged his narrative to flesh out this increase in tension and give it a reason: Jesus and his disciples' mission to the house of Israel served to alienate the Jewish leaders further and further. The arrangement of the controversy stories of chs. 9 and 12 finds its explanation, then, in the claim of the Matthean community to bring Jesus to the lost sheep of Israel. The controversy stories found in Mk 2:1–3:6 remain the mainstay of the Matthean structure in 8:1–13:52. Around them Matthew builds a narrative that gives credence to the increase in tension between Jesus and the Jewish leaders.

1.2 The Controversy Stories of Chapters 13–19

Beginning with the rejection of Jesus in Nazareth (13:53–58) Matthew follows the narrative sequence of Mark closely. The controversy stories of this section no longer occur in blocks but singly. But the patterns of contrast established in the controversy stories of chs. 9 and 12 are still important. As a consequence, the opposition of Jesus' adversaries continues the narrative tension.

Chapter 13 begins with the parable discourse. It follows the same day upon the controversies of ch. 12 (13:1) and is addressed to the crowds (13:2). But after the parable of the sower (13:3–9) the conversation is restricted to the disciples (13:10). The reason for this is a growing alienation of the crowds from Jesus. They do not understand what he is saying (13:14).[41] On the other hand, the disciples are called blessed because they do understand the teaching of Jesus (13:17). Consequently they receive an explanation of the parable of the sower (13:18–23). The pattern of public parable and private explanation is repeated (13:34–36). Finally, three parables are given to the disciples alone (13:44–50). The discourse ends with the question of Jesus whether the disciples have understood all that was said. The disciples answer in the affirmative, and are compared to a Scribe trained for the kingdom (13:51–52).

---

[41] According to Kingsbury, the parable discourse is a turning point in Matthew's gospel. Jack D. Kingsbury: *The Parables of Jesus in Matthew 13: A Study in Redaction Criticism* (Richmond: John Knox, 1969), 130. After the Jews rejected Jesus in Mt 12 Jesus now rejects them in the parable discourse of Mt 13. Kingsbury especially refers to 13:36–37. Yet even before 13:36 Matthew used language of judgment (11:16–24; 12:22–45). And even after the turning point Jesus still ministers to the crowds. Luz concludes that the rejection of Israel is a more protracted affair than Kingsbury admits. Luz: *Matthäus*, 2:292.

In Mark's parable discourse (4:1–32) the disciples do not seem to understand what Jesus is saying (4:13), even though the secret of the kingdom of God is given to them (4:11). The contrast between the understanding disciples and the crowds that hear but do not understand is a Matthean creation. Matthew further enhances this contrast with the story of the rejection of Jesus in his own town.[42] Immediately following the assertion that the disciples have understood all, and after their commendation as Scribes trained for the kingdom, Matthew reports the rejection of Jesus at home. The people who listen to him at home may marvel at the wonderful things that Jesus has to say (13:54), but shortly it becomes clear that they marvel at his eloquence while still taking offense at himself (13:57). Similar to the mission discourse in ch. 10 Matthew reports contrasting reactions to the parable discourse. While the disciples understand, the people in Jesus' town do not.

The contrast between those who believe and those who challenge Jesus remains a prominent feature in the remaining controversy stories before Jerusalem. Chapter 14 ends with the story of the storm and Pater walking on the water. The pericope concludes with the worship of those in the boat (14:33). This positive evaluation of Jesus is followed by a summary (34–36) which speaks of healings, of people bringing every sick person to Jesus, and it ends with the statement that everyone who touched only the fringe of Jesus' garment was made well (14:36). Into this positive atmosphere of worship and healing the controversy over the tradition of the elders (15:1–9) intrudes. Matthew clarifies this contrast against his source Mark. In Mark, the same sequence occurs, yet without the studious contrast between the understanding disciples and the excited crowds on the one hand, and the opposing Jewish leaders on the other. In Mark's calming of the storm the disciples remain with hardened hearts (6:51–52). The summary is much the same (6:53–56), while the ensuing controversy (7:1–13) again reveals a different Markan emphasis. While Matthew appends an instruction to the crowds and reports the disciples' worry about offended Pharisees (15:12) Mark explicitly mentions again that the disciples are without any understanding (7:18). Consequently, Matthew heightens the contrasting nature of the opposition to Jesus by restricting it entirely to the Pharisees and eliminating the Markan theme of the lack of understanding among the disciples.

A similar observation can be made for the controversy over the demand for a sign (16:1–4). After the controversy over the tradition of the elders Matthew follows Mark in reporting the faith of the Canaanite woman (15:21–28) and amends the ensuing summary of healings (15:29–31 ‖ Mk 7:31–37) to report explicitly that the crowds "glorified the God of Israel" (15:31). Their devotion to Jesus leads to his compassion for them and the feeding of the four thousand (15:32–39 ‖ Mk

---

[42] In Mark the parable discourse and the rejection in Nazareth (6:1–6) do not follow each other immediately. The intervening material has been used already by Matthew to frame the controversy stories of ch. 9.

8:1–10).[43] Again Matthew contrasts the devotion of the crowd quite abruptly with the opposition of Pharisees and Sadducees and their demand for a sign. It is the contrast between the crowd on which Jesus has compassion and the Jewish leaders whom he designates an evil and adulterous generation (15:4), between those who give glory to the God of Israel and those who demand a sign from heaven.

On a somewhat smaller scale the same contrast can be observed for the last controversy before the entrance into Jerusalem. It is set after the discourse to the disciples of ch. 18. Matthew creates some narrative distance from the discourse by having Jesus move from Galilee into Judea (19:1–2 ‖ Mk 10:1). Again Jesus attracts crowds, and Matthew marks two significant changes against the same account in Mark. First, Matthew insists that the crowds are large, and that they follow Jesus. The word "follow" is a key word for Matthew and indicates that the crowds are very positively inclined towards Jesus.[44] Secondly, Matthew departs from Mark in describing that Jesus healed them. Yet again the following controversy story breaks up this harmonious picture through the intrusion of the Pharisees and their antagonistic question about divorce.

An important element of the redaction of this controversy story limits the actual opposition to the Jewish leaders. While in Mk 10:10 the disciples seemingly do not understand the explanation of Jesus on divorce and ask him again about it, Matthew concludes the controversy with the explanation to the Jewish leaders and then continues with an additional instruction to the disciples on the issue of celibacy (19:10–12).

The Matthean controversy stories of chs. 13–19 thus serve as a narrative device to keep up the contrast between those who oppose and those who follow Jesus which Matthew established in earlier chapters. Matthew shapes this tension by restricting the opposition to the Jewish leaders who confront Jesus with questions that are designed to test him. This restriction shapes a narrative which derives its flow from contrasting reactions to the ministry of Jesus. Jesus' activity of teaching and healing leads to positive reactions from disciples and crowds, but at the same time provokes the opposition of the Jewish leaders. Matthew uses this contrast as a recurring narrative pattern. It continues the contrast established in the earlier blocks of controversy stories. In ch. 9 the controversy stories were used as a negative response to the teaching and miracles of Jesus. In ch. 12 the controversy stories were used to focus the opposition more clearly as a response to the mission

---

[43] Matthew omits the description in Mk 8:1a in order to create a closer connection between the feeding of the four thousand and the material preceding it. Instead of ἐν ἐκείναις ταῖς ἡμέραις πάλιν ... (Mk 8:1) Matthew connects καὶ ἐδόξασαν τὸν θεὸν Ἰσραήλ (15:31) with the following material through the use of δέ as if reporting a reaction of Jesus to the devotion of the crowd: ὁ δὲ Ἰησοῦς ... εἶπεν (15:32).

[44] On the importance of the work ἀκολουθέω see Jack D. Kingsbury: "The Verb *Akolouthein* ('To Follow') as an Index of Matthew's View of His Community," *JBL* 97 (1978): 56–73; Strecker: *Weg*, 230–232.

of Jesus and his disciples to Israel. This resulted in much more acrimonious debates. The controversy stories of chs. 13-19 build upon this foundation. The conflict, however, does not come to a resolution and is continued in Jerusalem. But Matthew maintains the crowds as a key feature of the controversy stories. Matthew retains the crowds and their reaction to Jesus as a key to understanding the harshness of the controversies. As Jesus wins the admiration of the crowds and leads them to give praise to the God of Israel, the leaders of Israel refuse to acknowledge the authority of Jesus. As a consequence, the narrative context of the controversy stories reveals that the struggle over the authority of Jesus and his interpretation of the Law in the individual stories is only the surface of the deeper struggle over rightful leadership of the people of Israel. Matthew's arrangement of the Jerusalem controversies supports this assessment.

1.3 The Jerusalem Controversy Stories

The Jerusalem controversy stories are part of a section in the gospel of Matthew that includes chs. 21–23.[45] The unity of the chapters as a section is established through three elements.[46] The first of these is the location. With the entry into Jerusalem Matthew has Jesus move immediately into the temple, where most of the following narrative takes place. The exception to the setting of the location is the night spent in Bethany with the cursing of the fig tree on the return to Jerusalem.[47] Yet Matthew has minimized the Markan arrangement of several trips between Bethany and Jerusalem.[48] With its concentration on the temple the local setting of the section is much more coherent than its counterpart in the gospel of Mark.

---

[45]   This is by no means a generally held thesis. Sometimes ch. 23 is grouped with 24–25 as a discourse. This theory goes back to Bacon: "The 'Five Books' of Matthew Against the Jews," 56–66. More recently it is proposed by Gundry: *Matthew*, 453. However, the discourse of ch. 23 is quite distinct from what follows in 24–25, since it concludes with Jesus and the disciples moving out of Jerusalem and away from the crowds (24:1). Thus both setting and audience of ch. 23 are different from chs. 24–25. Davies and Allison propose a structure that is ordered according to topics and breaks up the unity of 21–23. Their outline is: 19:1–20:28 (instruction for a Christian household); 20:29–21:22 (miraculous deeds and prophetic acts near Jerusalem); 21:23–22:46 (hostile encounters with Jewish leaders); 23:1–39 (woes against Pharisees and Scribes, lamentation over Jerusalem). Davies and Allison: *Matthew*, 3:2–3. This outline suffers from the neglect of the geographical features of the section they describe. Furthermore, they ignore the presence of a controversy story in the second part (21:14–17). The material of the second section in itself does not hold up well to forming a section of its own because of its variety of miracles, entry, controversy and the cursing of the fig tree.

[46]   Rollin Grams: "The Temple Conflict Scene: A Rhetorical Analysis of Matthew 21–23," in: *Persuasive Artistry. Studies in New Testament Rhetoric in Honor of George A. Kennedy*, ed. Duane F. Watson, JSNT.S 50 (Sheffield: JSOT Press, 1991), 47.

[47]   Grams fails to mention this exception. Grams: "Temple Conflict Scene," 47.

[48]   Mark's arrangement includes two trips between Jerusalem and Bethany (11:11–15; 19–20). Both trips include an account of the fig tree and sandwich the report of the cleansing of the temple (11:15–18).

A second unifying element in these chapters is the concentration on the conflict with the Jewish leaders. When other people enter the scene, like the people who spread their garments at the entry of Jesus into Jerusalem, or the people that are healed in the temple, they serve to give rise to a controversy between Jesus and his opponents. Jesus' authority is at stake in this section and is repeatedly questioned by his opponents (21:16; 21:23). Even the parables of this section become a tool in the ongoing dispute between Jesus and his opponents (21:32; 21:45–46). In ch. 23 Jesus closes these controversies with his final verdict over his opponents.[49] Consequently, the section exhibits a remarkable unity of persons and topics.

A further unifying element is the christological dimension of the section. Besides the question of the authority of Jesus, Matthew creates an *inclusio* between the first and the last actual controversy story in its reference to the Son of David (21:15; 22:42). The importance of this title is further underlined by its use in the ceremonial entry of Jesus into Jerusalem (21:9). A second *inclusio* exists between the entry into Jerusalem and the statement that Jesus will not return until Jerusalem says "Blessed is he who comes in the name of the Lord" (23:39).[50] Another christological element continuing throughout much of the section is the prophetic nature of the public ministry of Jesus in Jerusalem. He is acclaimed as prophet upon his entry (21:11). In the temple cleansing he quotes two prophets (21:13). Jesus brings up John the Baptist in one of the controversies, who is held to be a prophet by the crowds (21:26). Similarly, Jesus is held to be a prophet by the crowds (21:46). The woes

---

[49] This is held by Grams: "Temple Conflict Scene," 47. It should be noted, however, that the history of interpretation of Mt 23 is divided over whether to interpret it as a discourse regarding advice and warnings for the community against its own or against Jewish leaders. Those interpreters who wish to place ch. 23 with 24–25 as one discourse tend to view the Jewish leaders addressed in 23 as transparent for "falsely professing Jewish–Christian leaders." Gundry: *Matthew*, 453. Such views are also held by Kilpatrick: *Origins*, 109–111; Simon Légasse: "L'Antijudaïsme dans l'évangile selon Matthieu," in: *L'évangile selon Matthieu. Rédaction et Théologie*, ed. M. Didier, BEThL 29 (Louvain: Gembloux, 1971), 417–428; Schweizer: *Matthäus*, 430; Beare: *Matthew*, 461. A modified view of this thesis is held by Garland. He believes that Mt 23 is an attempt to explain the apparent rejection of Israel. David E. Garland: *The Intention of Matthew 23*, NTTS 52 (Leiden: Brill, 1979), 215. Yet this interpretation of Mt 23 is not convincing. The community is given direct advice only in vv. 8–12. But this can hardly be transformed into the central thrust of the chapter. Kenneth G. Newport: *The Sources and Sitz im Leben of Matthew 23*, JSNT.S 117 (Sheffield: Sheffield Academic Press, 1995), 69. The final judgment concerns the opponents of Jesus, not the Matthean community or its leaders, however errant they may or may not be. Furthermore, if the references to the killing of the prophets can be interpreted as allusions to the killing of Jesus himself, as they should be given the recurring prophetic motif in chs. 21–23, then a paradigmatic interpretation of the leaders as errant Christians collapses. The agenda behind many of the paradigmatic approaches is the defusion of the vituperative language in ch. 23. But this language does not become less embarrassing because it is redirected, as Newport astutely observes (p. 73). This language must be explained otherwise, e.g. with a reference to the historical context in which such language was more common than it is today as done by Johnson: "Slander and Polemic," 419–441.

[50] This latter *inclusio* is pointed out by Grams: "Temple Conflict Scene," 47.

of ch. 23 resemble prophetic speech.[51] And the opponents of Jesus are finally castigated for killing the prophets then and now (23:29–36, 37; see also 21:35–38; 22:6). All these elements combine to unify chs. 21–23 in terms of location, persons, and topic.

If chs. 21–23 form a continuous section of the gospel, the function of this unit must be explained. Rollin Grams employed rhetorical criticism in a comparison between these chapters and the judicial rhetoric of a trial scene. He sees an analogy to these chapters in the rhetorical form of a trial speech.[52] His outline begins with the *narratio* of three parabolic actions of Jesus which display him as Son of David and judge (21:1–22). The trial moves on to the first stage of proof with the question over authority (21:23–27) and the counter–argument of Jesus of three parabolic questions challenging the Jewish leaders' authority (21:28–22:14). The second stage of proof contains three questions asked for the sake of entrapping Jesus in order to test his authority (22:15–40). The third stage of proof contains the closing question of Jesus on the authority of the Messiah (22:41–46). With the conclusion of proofs Matthew then moves to a *peroratio* that contains Jesus' verdict in an epideictic speech against Pharisees and Scribes (23:1–39). Grams concludes that the arrangement of chs. 21–23 is "an assertion of Jesus' authority throughout his public trial ... and judgment of the Jewish leaders."[53]

For several reasons this outline must be judged as too simplistic. While the section does contain speech material, in and of itself it is not a speech but a composite of narrative, dialogue, and a speech in ch. 23. It is not convincing to structure a composite part of the gospel according to the analogy of a speech. Furthermore, the *narratio* is more complicated than Grams admits. Apart from the three actions mentioned by Grams there is a further one in the healing of the sick in the temple. This healing activity and the ensuing praise by the children give rise to a controversy story (21:14–17). Consequently, what Grams perceives as *narratio* is, in fact, a compound of narrative and controversy story. Thus the public trial of

---

[51] The woes occur also in other Matthean contexts: 11:21; 18:7; 24:19; 26:24. In these instances the woe takes a particular form: Woe + address + reason for woe + future punishment. In ch. 23 the future punishment is omitted, but it is possible to explain this with the section concerning judgment in 23:32–39. Gnilka: *Matthäus*, 2:281. In the LXX there are more than sixty woes; in Is 5:8–22 a collection of woes appears, similarly Hab 2:6–20; prophets used the woes to proclaim social injustice and moral depravity: Hos 7:13; Hab 2:6, 12, 19; Is 5:8–22; 10:1, etc.

[52] Grams: "Temple Conflict Scene," 51.

[53] Grams: "Temple Conflict Scene," 65. Grams summarizes the rhetorical structure as follows: "The arrangement of the Temple Conflict Scene is highly rhetorical. Two questions over authority, at the beginning by the chief priests and elders and at the end by Jesus, form an *inclusio* for the whole conflict. The sequence of events fits into groupings of three, a typical feature of Matthew's rhetoric: three action parables, three stages to the conflict scene, three parables, three questions for entrapment, three stages to the speech in ch. 23, three reasons for not following the Pharisees' example, three groupings of six examples of how the Pharisees do things for show, and three concluding enthymemes" (pp. 51–52).

Jesus begins already before 21:23. This breaks up the *inclusio* that Grams perceives between 21:23 and 22:42. That very *inclusio* is not convincing for another reason. Grams views 22:41–46 as a contest over authority like 21:23–27. However, the topic is not mentioned in 22:41–46. Instead it appears that the story is concerned with the relationship between the Messiah and the Son of David, a relationship which the opponents of Jesus cannot explain. Consequently, the passage more likely forms an *inclusio* with 21:14–17 where the Son of David already gave rise to a controversy. Finally, the parables which Grams supposes to be part of the first stage of proof contain judgment sayings (21:31, 43) that draw the proof to its conclusion already before ch. 23. Thus the structure of these chapters is more complex than Grams' outline suggests.

Despite these criticisms much of Grams' work remains helpful. Clearly the chapters are dominated by the theme of authority. The symbolic actions[54] at the beginning of the section indicate this setting quite clearly. With the entry into Jerusalem Jesus claims kingship, and the crowds acknowledge this claim.[55] Matthew makes it explicit with the quotation of Zech 9:9 (21:9). The cleansing of the temple prophetically proclaims divine disfavor.[56] This disfavor is highlighted by Matthew through the insertion of the healings of the blind and lame in the temple. The infirm are contrasted with those peddling their wares in the temple as Jesus shows in his actions which side God takes. The cursing of the fig tree similarly declares Jesus' prophetic power.[57] Thus all four actions of Jesus in ch. 21 proclaim the power and authority of Jesus, yet they do so with the help of complex patterns. Jesus appears as the royal Son of David, but also as healing Son of David and as prophet. In the last controversy story Matthew brings up the image of the Messiah as well (22:42).

---

[54] Ed P. Sanders: *The Historical Figure of Jesus* (Allen Lane: Penguin, 1993), 251.

[55] Davies and Allison comment on the irony between the crowds acknowledging the claim of Jesus by spreading their garments and the city that asks "who is this?" Davies and Allison: *Matthew*, 3:128–129.

[56] Sanders highlights, although in a different context, the eschatological nature of the cleansing of the temple with a number of parallels discussing the eschatological new temple in contemporary Jewish thought. Ed P. Sanders: *Jesus and Judaism* (Philadelphia: Fortress Press, 1985), 77–90.

[57] Although the precise meaning of this deed remains elusive. In Mark the action demonstrates the judgment that is to befall Israel. Mark's account (11:12–14, 20–25) brackets the cleansing of the temple (11:15–19). Thus it might be termed a "Strafwunder." Gnilka: *Markus*, 2:123. Matthew removes the sandwich technique. Thus the action loses even more its judgmental character, particularly since the following instruction occasioned by the fig tree teaches about faith. Saldarini writes: "Matthew probably sees and rejects the natural thrust of the fig tree symbol, that Israel is cursed and rejected, and his awkward use of the event to teach a lesson on faith and prayer is a testimony to his discomfort with any rejection of Israel as a whole." Saldarini: *Matthew's Christian-Jewish Community*, 54–55. Gnilka offers that the cursing of the fig tree is the "Abschluß der Etappe der Heilsgeschichte mit Israel." Gnilka: *Matthäus*, 2:214. Davies and Allison refer to the passage as "a prophetic act of power, something like a *semeion* in the Johannine sense," yet remain inconclusive with regard to the meaning of this sign. Davies and Allison: *Matthew*, 3:148.

Furthermore, the authority of Jesus is undergirded by his continuing success at besting his opponents in the arguments of the controversy stories.

The theme of the authority of Jesus finds a corresponding motif in the presumed authority of the Jewish leaders that is subsequently exposed as fraudulent. This motif pervades the whole section of Matthew 21–23. It takes several forms. In 21:13 the accusation of Jesus implies that the Jewish leaders are responsible for the sorry state of the temple. The Jewish leaders challenge Jesus repeatedly. Their challenge implies that they have the authority to do so. Matthew plays on this fact with irony when the leaders challenge the authority of Jesus and yet fail to answer a question he puts to them (21:23–27). The parable of the wicked tenants refers to a presumed authority of the leaders in a number of ways. They are described as tenants who feel themselves above the authority of the owner of the vineyard (21:38) and as the builders who reject the cornerstone (21:42). Later on, they are likened to invited guests who feel themselves above the authority of the king who invited them (22:3–6). They perceive that Jesus speaks about them and plot to arrest Jesus, but fail to do so for fear of the crowd (21:45–46). Repeatedly they engage Jesus in controversy in order to test him (22:15, 35). They are acknowledged to sit on the seat of Moses (23:2) with the power to shut people out of the kingdom (23:13), only to be revealed as blind guides (23:16). Finally, the false authority of the leaders makes them murderers (23:34). With these two conflicting claims Matthew creates a theme that pervades the public ministry in Jerusalem.

People other than Jesus and his opponents flesh out this contrast to a degree. Yet they remain marginal to the progression of these chapters. Two disciples appear briefly at the outset to procure the donkeys before Jesus enters Jerusalem (21:1, 6). Crowds proclaim Jesus with shouts of "Hosanna to the Son of David" as a prophet (21:8–11). The blind and lame appear, only to be healed by Jesus (21:14), while children proclaim his praise (21:15). The disciples reappear after the cursing of the fig tree as the object of an instruction on the power of faith (21:20). The crowds reappear when the leaders are frightened of them (21:46). They are astonished at the teaching of Jesus on the resurrection (22:33). Together with the disciples they form the audience for the discourse on the Jewish leaders (23:1).

When one groups the crowds, the blind and the lame, and the children together, they appear more important for the narrative than the disciples. These people provide by their acclamations of Jesus the starting point for much of the discussion that follows. They influence the narrative when fear of them prevents the leaders from arresting Jesus. The image of the crowds is basically rather positive here. On the other hand, the crowds are never addressed directly. They are not engaged in the dialogue, and only a few remarks concerning their reactions alert the reader to the fact that the whole debate of 21–23 is public. When in ch. 23 Jesus turns directly to the crowds to explain to them why the Jewish leaders are so deficient, as they are shown to be in the controversy stories, their reactions are not recorded.

Chapters 21–23 thus concentrate on the conflict between Jesus and his opponents. The recurring issue is that of authority. The authority of Jesus is asserted in the different themes of prophecy, royal kingship, as Son of David, and finally as Messiah. The presumptive authority of the opponents is the object of the discourse in ch. 23. There the leaders are reported to sit on Moses' seat (v. 2), to bind up burdens for others (v. 4), to demand the seats and greetings of honor (vv. 6–7), have the authority to prevent people from entering the kingdom (v. 13), to teach (v. 16–18). They are "blind guides" (23:24). The three parables[58] of the two sons (21:28–32), of the wicked tenants (21:33–46), and of the marriage feast and the guest without the proper garment (22:1–14) indicate the conflicting claims to authority that stand behind the controversies between Jesus and his opponents.[59]

The first parable concerns two sons, one of whom does not do the will of the father even though he says he will, while the other does what is asked of him even though he at first refuses. It is not found in either Mark or Luke.[60] The application of the parable to the reception of John the Baptist links the parable closely with the preceding material.[61] It implies that the message of John the Baptist concerning the imminence of the kingdom fell on deaf ears with the Jewish leaders. The feature that unites the parable with the one immediately following is the task that the father is asking of his sons: to work in the vineyard. The image has appeared before

---

[58] These parables have often been taken to mean the rejection of Israel as a whole. For a survey of these arguments, as well as a refutation of it, see: Akira Ogawa: "Paraboles de l'Israel véritable? Reconsidération critique de Mt 21,28–22,14," *NT* 21 (1979): 121–149. Ogawa interprets these parables as a warning against the church, a claim just as improbable as that of a rejection of all Israel. The parables are directed against and reacted to by the Jewish leaders who recognize themselves in them. Consequently, the parables are part of the ongoing conflict between Jesus and his adversaries in 21–23.

[59] Davies and Allison summarize the features that connect the three parables to a remarkable extent through both a cohesion of grammatical constructions and vocabulary, and overarching themes. Davies and Allison: *Matthew*, 3:188–190. All three parables share the theme of failure of the religious leaders. This failure is interpreted in all three parables as the failure to receive the messengers sent to them.

[60] The origin of the parable is a matter of some debate. Some have argued for its presence in a pre-Matthean collection of dominical sayings. Gnilka: *Matthäus*, 2:219–220. Yet close examination reveals a striking similarity to the vocabulary of the two following parables, which leads Tilborg to claim that the three parables circulated independently before Matthew. Tilborg: *The Jewish Leaders in Matthew*, 47–48. This claim seems to impose too much on the texts, one of which only occurs in Mark, while another perhaps existed in Q. Consequently, Gundry argues for a redactional origin of the parable. Gundry: *Matthew*, 421–424. Certainty about the source of this parable is probably no longer attainable. It is possible, but unprovable, that Matthew used a dominical parable, found in oral tradition, and redacted it into its present place. Davies and Allison: *Matthew*, 3:165. Whatever source one assumes to lie behind the parable, Matthew has integrated it into the context. However, the integration is labored. The parable in itself is oriented towards doing the will of the father by working in the vineyard. This orientation has ethical conduct in view. Matthew interprets the parable in v. 32 in terms of faith in the witness of the Baptist. The logical break between the parable and its interpretation leads me to believe that the parable of the two sons was part of the traditions Matthew inherited.

[61] Harrington: *Matthew*, 299.

(20:1–16) and now becomes the main feature of the parable of the wicked tenants immediately following. Thus it is quite possible that the parable of the two sons appears in its present context because of the connection with the vineyard of the following parable.[62]

One prominent feature of the parable of the two sons is the labored interpretation accorded it by Matthew. The parable itself speaks of two sons who are asked to work in the vineyard. Its conclusion in 21:31 brings the work into focus again by asking which of the sons did the will of the father. Thus the parable itself seems to be ethically oriented in its focus on the work in the vineyard. But this ethical interest is completely abandoned in the interpretation of the parable. Matthew tries to historicize the parable by applying it to the ministry of John the Baptist (21:32). The dominant theme in this interpretation is no longer based on works, but concentrates on faith. Three times Matthew mentions it: When John came in righteousness, the opponents of Jesus did not believe, but tax collectors and harlots believed, and even with this strong evidence the opponents did not believe.

Matthew's use of the parable of the two sons thus is directed against the opponents of Jesus because they did not believe John as the forerunner of Jesus. The redaction shows how he labored to make the parable fit his intent. This makes it all the more likely that Matthew had a direct attack against the Jewish leaders in view when he incorporated it.

This would preclude any conclusion that Matthew envisioned the separation of Jews and Gentiles in this parable.[63] The evidence is borne out by the relationship that is made between the work in the vineyard of the parable and its consequent application to the ministry of John the Baptist (21:32). The problem as related by Matthew is not that the leaders are Jews, but that the leaders of Israel did not believe the message of the Baptist, a prophet sent to the people of Israel. The accusation made against the leaders is their failure to listen to John and thus their failure to provide adequate leadership for Israel. Quite the opposite: The leaders are outdone even by tax collectors and harlots.

The following parable reveals a similar pattern. Again the topic revolves around work in the vineyard. The tenants prove worthless by not delivering the fruit to the owner and killing his emissaries and son. Ironically, the Jewish leaders condemn themselves by condemning the wicked tenants (21:41). Again this parable is often

---

[62] In 21:33 Matthew interprets the vineyard as Israel by an allusion to Is 5:1–2. It is possible that this identification might be implied in the parable of the two sons. Yet this is by no means certain. It is probable that the image is more fluid for Matthew. If 21:39 is read as a prediction of the death of Jesus, which it surely is, then the vineyard can be interpreted as Jerusalem. In 21:43 it seems to be the kingdom. This fluid interpretation of the vineyard might lie behind the conclusion of the parable of the two sons with its reference to who will enter the kingdom.

[63] Davies and Allison cite a number of church fathers holding this position. Davies and Allison: *Matthew*, 3:172 n.29. Among modern authors the position is held by, e.g., Clark: "The Gentile Bias of Matthew," 166; Walker: *Heilsgeschichte*, 104; Meier: *Vision*, 149–150.

interpreted as an image of Christianity superseding Judaism.[64] Such an interpretation depends to a large extent on the interpretation of the saying that "the kingdom will be taken from you and given to a people (ἔθνει) bearing its fruit" (21:43). In such an interpretation, "you" needs to refer to Israel as a whole, while ἔθνει must mean a nation different from Israel.

However, the word ἔθνος is used by Matthew in a wide variety of meanings[65] that does not always refer to non–Jews, or consistently to the same group of people.[66] And if Matthew were to refer to Gentiles, one would expect him to use the plural rather than the singular.[67] Consequently, this word alone does not make a case for the implied rejection of all of Israel. Furthermore, the reaction of the Jewish leaders shows that they apply both this parable and its predecessor to themselves (21:45). With this redactional addition Matthew shows his own interests in the parables: They apply first and foremost to the Jewish leaders who are in conflict with Jesus. This interpretation fits well with the logical argument made in the parable of the wicked tenants: The vineyard which is Israel remains outside of the judgment of the householder. It is fruitful, but the tenants withhold the fruit from its rightful owner. It is the tenants who kill the son, who are judged, and finally replaced. The vineyard gives its fruit which is now rendered to the householder by the new tenants.[68]

A further indication to the indictment of the Jewish leaders is the interpretation of the parable through Psalm 118:22–23 (21:42).[69] It concerns the wrong judgment

---

[64] For a review of the scholarship on this parable see: Klyne Snodgrass: *The Parable of the Wicked Tenants*, WUNT 27 (Tübingen: Mohr, 1983). As a sample of such an interpretation, Strecker writes that "in der Zeit des Matthäus ist die Übertragung der βασιλεία auf das nachfolgende ἔθνος erfolgt; die βασιλεία ist gegenwärtig, ähnlich ihrer Gegenwart in der heilsgeschichtlichen Vergangenheit des jüdischen Volkes." Strecker: "Das Geschichtsverständnis des Matthäus," *Evangelische Theologie* 26 (1966): 218, n. 40.

[65] Saldarini argues that the variations of meaning of the word are consistent with Hellenistic Greek usage. Saldarini: *Matthew's Christian-Jewish Community*, 68–81.

[66] Sometimes the word and its concomitant adjective ἐθνικός are used in a pejorative sense to refer to outsiders of the Matthean group (5:47; 6:7, 32). Sometimes the use is ambiguous in its inclusion of Jews and/or non–Jews (4:12–17; 28:19). In the sense of "nation" it occurs in 20:25 and might include Jews. In 24:7 the nations will rise against the Matthean community. This probably includes Jews as well (cf. 10:17), as it does in 10:6 and 15:24.

[67] See on this point Davies and Allison: *Matthew*, 3:189.

[68] Saldarini points out that a similar judgment might lie behind the prophecy of Is 5:1–2, quoted by Matthew in 21:33. He writes: "Even in Isaiah, the prophetic condemnation of Judah and Jerusalem is focused and limited. It does not mean that all Israel is rejected. Some in Israel are suffering a lack of judgment and justice are crying out to God. Others, presumably the powerful and wealthy, are acting contrary to judgment and justice and shedding blood. Thus there is an implication that the leaders of the house of Israel are at fault." In support of this thesis Saldarini adduces Is 3:13–15 as a further example of such a technique. Saldarini: *Matthew's Christian-Jewish Community*, 61.

[69] This interpretation is already made in Mk 12:10–12. However, Mark does not make Matthew's immediate connection with the Jewish leaders that Matthew makes in 21:43, 45.

of the builders in selecting a cornerstone.[70] The image of the builders directly refers to the Jewish leaders.[71] The reaction of the leaders with the plot to arrest Jesus confirms this assessment. The logic that has the leaders defer their plan because of their fear of the crowds makes it unlikely that a wholesale rejection of Israel is implied.[72]

As with the previous parable of the two sons, the interpretation of the parable of the wicked husbandmen through the saying of the builders (21:42–43) is not immediately logical. There is little connection between the ethical dimensions of a parable of vineyard, its tenants who do not do their duty with their destruction by the owner, and the parable's interpretation that focuses on stone rejected by the builders but elevated by the marvelous deed of God. Matthew is not the author of the parable's connection with the saying. The redaction shows, however, that he tries to make this connection more logical. He inserts 21:43 and forges a strong link with the preceding saying of the builders by inserting διὰ τοῦτο. Because the leaders have rejected the cornerstone the kingdom will be taken from them. It will then be given to a nation ποιοῦντι τοὺς καρποὺς αὐτῆς. Thus he reverts back to the image of the vines and their fruit. Matthew makes it very clear that the parable of the vineyard needs to be applied to the Jewish leaders.

The following parable of the wedding banquet (22:1–14) solidifies the attack on the Jewish leaders. Matthew integrates the parable into his context of conflict between Jesus and the Jewish leaders.[73] The theme of authority is brought to

---

[70] The Lukan version of the parable adds a saying concerning the one who falls on this stone (Lk 20:18). In Matthew, this verse appears as 21:44 in some but not all manuscripts. Between these two versions there are a few minor discrepancies in wording. Most scholars regard the verse in Matthew as an accretion from Luke's parallel. Metzger: *Textual Commentary*, 47. The verse is omitted in D 33 it sy^s and thus belongs to the group of Western-non-interpolations. Part of the reason for regarding the verse as an interpolation is its awkward position in the text. This seems convincing.

[71] A similar image of the Jewish leaders as builders can be found in *CD* 8:12. Gundry points out that the Matthean change in v. 42 from Mark's "have you not read even this scripture?" to "have you never read in the scriptures?" serves to intensify the religious leaders' guilt. Gundry: *Matthew*, 429. This is only marginally convincing because Matthew uses a formula here that occurs elsewhere (12:3; 12:5; 19:4; 21:16; 21:42; 22:31). Matthew uses οὐδέποτε ἀνέγνωτε in 21:16 and 21:42, otherwise he uses οὐκ ἀνέγνωτε However, it is only here that Matthew also inserts ἐν ταῖς γραφαῖς into the formula, prompted by Mark's τὴν γραφὴν ταύτην (12:10).

[72] Carter: *Matthew*, 239.

[73] The source for this parable is often assumed to be Q because of its parallel in Lk 14:15–24. Yet the differences between the two versions are as remarkable as the similarities. Consequently a source-critical evaluation only leads to suggestions. For a review of the relevant scholarship see: Eugene E. Lemcio: "The Parables of the Great Supper and the Wedding Feast: History, Redaction and Canon," *HBT* 8 (1986): 1–26. Harrington suggest a source in Q that was extensively redacted by Matthew. Harrington: *Matthew*, 307. Davies and Allison resign the material to the Matthean special source, although they admit that the Lukan and Matthean parables are two versions of the same original parable. Davies and Allison: *Matthew*, 3:194. Gnilka suggests a common source for Matthew and Luke and *EvThom* 64 without specifying it further. Gnilka: *Matthäus*, 2:235. Tuckett

prominence through the insertion of a king as host (22:2), the increased shameful treatment of the messengers (22:6), and through the added detail of the punitive expedition of the king (22:7).[74] The latter two incidents serve clearly to establish a connection with the preceding parable of the wicked tenants. The insertion of the king allows Matthew to keep the wedding feast as one in which only the subjects of the king are invited, while Luke's account specifically mentions those outside the city as invitees (14:23). Thus Luke makes reference to those outside of Judaism invited to the kingdom in a second gathering of guests, while Matthew does not have this extension, as he does not have a second gathering of guests.[75] Matthew's first invitees are the honored in the kingdom, yet the fail to accept the invitation. Their failure brings about the destruction of their city.

The original invitees in Matthew represent the Jewish leaders. Matthew makes this clear in the setting of the parable which is again addressed to the leaders (22:1). But the details that Matthew adds to the parable also make it clear how he views the obstreperousness of the Jewish leaders. As in the parable, they and their city Jerusalem are destroyed as a consequence to their failure to accept Jesus.

All three parables fit well into the overarching narrative context created by Matthew for chs. 21–23. In all parables the Jewish leaders are specifically attacked for their failures. They fail to go to the vineyard, they fail to submit its fruits to the rightful owner, and they finally fail to follow the invitation issued by their king. On the "allegorical" level, all three failures are caused by the leaders' failure to attend to the messengers of God. These messengers are John the Baptist, the prophets, and finally Jesus himself.[76] Matthew delegitimizes the Jewish leaders and exposes them as blind guides (23:16).[77] The object of this delegitimation is to win the people of Israel away from its leaders.[78] The crowds and children that appear throughout the

---

points out the varying level of verbal agreements in the Synoptics. He writes: "Within the triple tradition, the agreement between Matthew and Mark, or between Luke and Mark, is rarely verbatim, and hence too the level of Matthew's agreement with Luke when both are using Mark is correspondingly lower. In actual fact, the overall level of verbal agreement between Matthew and Luke in Q passages is slightly higher than the level of agreement between them in Mark passages. If then one accepts the literary dependence of Matthew and Luke on Mark, there is no need to doubt literary dependence on a written Q simply because at times Matthew and Luke are not verbally identical." Tuckett: *Q*, 93. Thus Tuckett makes a convincing case for the parable as part of Q. For the purpose here it is enough to state that Matthew's version develops its own concerns and themes to a largely independent extent.

[74] The Lukan account centers around the issues of wealth rather than power. For a lucid interpretation of the social issues behind the Lukan parable see: Richard L. Rohrbaugh: "The Pre-Industrial City in Luke-Acts: Urban Social Relations," in: *The Social World of Luke–Acts*, ed. Jerome H. Neyrey (Peabody: Hendrickson, 1991), 125–149.

[75] Saldarini: *Matthew's Christian-Jewish Community*, 63.

[76] Davies and Allison: *Matthew*, 3:189.

[77] Anthony J. Saldarini: "Delegitimation of Leaders in Matthew 23," *CBQ* 54 (1992): 649–680.

[78] Saldarini: *Matthew's Christian-Jewish Community*, 64.

section as the audience of the conflict between Jesus and the Jewish leaders are the "vineyard" that is claimed by Jesus and his disciples. They in turn are the son who goes into the vineyard, the new tenants, and the servants who go and invite to the feast of the king. The conflict between Jesus and his adversaries is a conflict over rightful leadership of the people of Israel. As a consequence of their intractability, the leaders will face their own destruction as well as that of their city.

After the conclusion of the three parables Matthew resumes with the remaining four controversy stories (22:15–41). These culminate in the complete silencing of the opponents. No one dares to ask more questions (21:41). With the silencing of the opponents Matthew then moves to the final reckoning with the Pharisees and Scribes. He then inserts a lengthy discourse on the judgment of the opponents presented in the three parables of 21:28–22:14. The opponents are indicted for the abuse of their leadership position. While they sit on Moses' seat (23:2) they use their authority aggrandize themselves (23:6–7). Their teaching is hypocritical because they do not do what they preach (23:3). Their hypocrisy results in the murder of the prophets (23:31, 35). Finally, they will murder Jesus, and the consequences will be on this generation (23:36). The foil for this indictment is the crowd that they mislead. The indictment is grounded on the leaders' habit of teaching what they themselves are not prepared to do. In other words, they bind up heavy burdens for others while not lifting a finger themselves (23:4).

The narrative sequence of Matthew 21–23, then, focuses on the conflict between Jesus and the Jewish leaders. In his final reckoning with the leaders Matthew uses controversy stories and parables to illustrate the leaders' shortcomings. Throughout the section the leaders are shown to act out of spite against Jesus. Matthew insists that the leaders recognize that Jesus teaches about them (21:45). But the recognition is fruitless. Like the preaching of John the parables and controversies of Jesus do not lead to repentance (21:32). They return to their attacks against Jesus in more controversy stories. Finally they are described as completely overcome by Jesus in argument (22:41). When they are silenced, Matthew moves on to render his final judgment on the leaders as hypocrites.

Consequently, the controversy stories of chs. 21–22 are only one of the elements Matthew uses to delegitimize the leaders. In themselves Matthew did not judge them sufficient to make his point. However, they are the necessary proof that substantiates Matthew's judgment of ch. 23. Throughout the public ministry of Jesus in Jerusalem the Jewish leaders have challenged Jesus, and throughout this ministry Jesus has shown himself superior in argument. The public ministry in Jerusalem shows the context in which the controversy stories need to be understood. The Jewish leaders converge on Jesus to examine him and challenge him without reprieve. One after another different groups of leaders come and go to examine Jesus. Matthew inserts three parables into these comings and goings to alert the reader to the purpose of the leaders: They are questioning and rejecting the messenger sent by God. Even though Jesus bests these opponents throughout the stories, they still conspire against him. Chapter 23 draws the consequences of this behavior in the final saying of judgment (23:34–36). The leaders have proven that they kill the prophets, and they will not stop at Jesus. But the consequences of this are dire: It is the destruction of Jerusalem (23:36).

1.4 Summary of the Narrative Function of the Controversy Stories

Throughout his gospel Matthew uses the controversy stories to develop a narrative contrast between Jesus' powerful deeds and teaching and the reaction of his opponents to them. This contrast is developed in the blocks of controversy stories in chs. 9 and 11, and continued through the individual controversy stories of chs. 13–19. In the block of Jerusalem controversy stories this contrast comes to a head with the ultimate judgment on the Jewish leaders in ch. 23 as a direct result of their opposition to Jesus.

The stories of ch. 9 serve as a preparation for the unfolding of the conflict as the Jewish leaders react with misgivings to the forgiveness of sins offered to the paralytic and the table fellowship with sinners. Their opposition is then extended to the disciples who do not fast as expected. When the disciples are given the mission to Israel with the express reference that Jesus himself is present to Israel as she receives the disciples and their message, the conflict escalates. In the controversy stories of ch. 12 both the disciples and Jesus are accused of transgression of the Law in an attempt to delegitimize this mission to Israel. Furthermore, Jesus is accused of collusion with Beelzebul and asked to show the legitimacy of his ministry through a sign. At the same time, they begin to plot against Jesus. As the accusations of the opponents become more pointed, the denunciation of the Jewish leaders increases. They are now called evil, offspring of vipers, and an evil and adulterous generation.

The controversies that uphold the narrative tension in chs. 13–19 continue to call the contrast between the wonderful deeds of Jesus and the antagonism of the opponents to mind. Again Jesus' opponents include his disciples in their opposition to him by the accusation that they do not adhere to the tradition of the elders. The accusations against the Jewish leaders are repeated and amplified. They are again called an evil and adulterous generation, they are accused of transgressing the commandments of God, and of being hard–hearted. These eruptions of conflict are surrounded by references to the ministry of mercy that Jesus extends to the people of Israel.

The final conflict scene in Jerusalem (21–23) reaffirms this result. The Jerusalem controversies center the conflict of Jesus and the Jewish leaders as one over authority in Israel. The authority of Jesus is affirmed against the opposition of the leaders. As the leaders claim to have authority themselves, their claim is proven to be fraudulent. They fail to assert their authority over Jesus, and finally are exposed for their malice and hypocrisy. They are proven to be blind guides who lead Israel astray and are responsible for the fate that befell her in the aftermath of the Jewish revolt. The leaders are held responsible for the destruction of Jerusalem because they rejected the rightful claim of Jesus.

Matthew takes great care to set the controversy stories with in the framework of Jesus' inner-Jewish ministry. Through the missionary discourse and the repeated references to disciples in the controversy stories this framework is extended to include the ministry of the disciples. This context explains why Matthew takes so much more care in phrasing legal questions and arguments in the controversy stories. The claim of Jesus and his disciples to leadership in Israel precludes a cavalier attitude to the Law as is sometimes shown by Mark. Matthew is interested in showing that Jesus and his disciples are claimants to the position to the position of Israel's leaders. Jesus' opponents are acknowledged as holding this position, but also exposed as doing so without justification and approval from God. Furthermore, their misguided leadership is finally blamed for the destruction of Jerusalem.

2. The Characters in the Controversy Stories

Inevitably the assessment of the controversy stories as a reflection on the ministry to Israel raises further questions. Matthew's descriptions of conflict are not just an explanation for the death of Jesus, they also provide an explanation for the destruction of Jerusalem. While Matthew gives an explanation for the death of Jesus, he does so with a view to the consequences of Jesus' rejection. Yet this assessment raises further questions: Did Matthew see the Jewish rejection of Jesus as final, or did he see his community as continuing the ministry to the lost sheep of the house of Israel? In other words, are the opponents of Jesus only historical figures responsible for the death of Jesus, or are they also transparent representatives of the opposition that a Matthean community faced?[79]

Before these questions can be answered with some degree of satisfaction, a final investigation into the controversy stories is in order. With the evidence of form criticism, redaction criticism, and narrative criticism at hand, it is now possible to draw a portrait of each of the participants in the controversy stories. A first step will draw out the portrait of the opponents of Jesus. A second step will look at the audience of these controversies. A final step will draw out the christological implications of these stories for the portrait of Jesus. Finally, a conclusion will return to the question whether the controversy stories reflect on the history of the Matthean community or on its present situation.

---

[79] This question can be asked for any of the characters appearing in the gospel. In a seminal article Luz defined this problem with a view to the interpretation of the disciples. Ulrich Luz: "Die Jünger im Matthäusevangelium," first published in *ZNW* 62 (1971) 141–171, in: *Das Matthäusevangelium*, ed. Joachim Lange (Darmstadt: Wissenschaftliche Buchgesellschaft, 1980), 377–414.

2.1 The Opponents of Jesus

A cursory glance at the gospel of Matthew shows that it is fond of grouping the leaders of Israel in pairs.[80] Often Scribes and Pharisees appear together, or chief priests and elders are grouped together.[81] Only occasionally Matthew groups the leaders in a triad.[82] This tendency of Matthew has sometimes led to the assumption that the Jewish leaders are portrayed without any attempt to maintain distinctions between the social and political groups that make up the Matthean cluster of Jewish leaders.[83] Beyond the association of the various groups, Kingsbury observes that their function in the narrative is unified in their unequivocal opposition to Jesus. The Jewish leaders are, according to Kingsbury, thus essentially a single or corporate character for the purpose of the narrative.[84]

Despite this assessment of the leaders as a single character a few distinctions must be made. The controversy stories show a remarkable tendency to avoid the grouping of opponents. Of the seventeen controversy stories that have been investigated, only seven present the opponents as comprised of several subgroups (9:14–17; 12:38–45; 15:1–9; 16:1–4; 21:14–17; 21:23–27; 22:15–22). The redaction–critical analysis has shown that the first and the last of these controversies concentrate on the Pharisees. In 9:14–17 the disciples of John the Baptist recede into the background in the controversy over fasting. In 22:15–22 the Pharisees are named as the chief perpetrators of the attempt to entrap Jesus, and so they send their disciples with the Herodians. Both the disciples of John the Baptist and the Herodians do not occur elsewhere in such a hostile context. In the remaining controversies of this group the Pharisees are paired with the Scribes (12:38; 15:1)[85]

---

[80]   Tilborg: *The Jewish Leaders in Matthew*, 1.

[81]   Tilborg gives a list of such pairs. Tilborg: *The Jewish Leaders in Matthew*, 1–7. Anderson has completed the listing. Anderson: *Web*, 97, n. 1. The occurrences of the leaders in pairs are: Pharisees and Scribes, or Scribes and Pharisees: 5:20; 12:38; 15:1; 23:2, 13, 15, 23, 25, 27, 29. The chief priests and elders (of the people) is an expression particular to Matthew and occurs in: 21:23; 26:3, 47; 27:1, 3, 12, 20; 28:11–12. The chief priests and Pharisees: 21:45; 27:62. The chief priests and Scribes: 2:4, 20:18; 21:15. Chief priests and the whole Sanhedrin: 26:59. Scribes and elders: 26:57, with Caiaphas the High Priest also there.

[82]   Elders, chief priests, and Scribes are grouped together in 16:21 and 27:41.

[83]   Again Tilborg has been an influential proponent of this position in his treatment of the Jewish leaders. He writes that "Matthew looks upon the representatives of Israel as a homogeneous group. The many names he eventually gives the Jewish leaders are not meant as further historical information. He does not want to introduce a distinction between Pharisees, Sadducees, Scribes, high priests, and elders." Tilborg: *The Jewish Leaders in Matthew*, 1. Anderson states that because of these groupings "there are no sharp distinctions between the subgroups." Anderson: *Web*, 98.

[84]   Kingsbury writes: "Because all of these groups are presented in Matthew's story as forming a united front opposed to Jesus, they can be treated as a single character." Kingsbury: *Matthew as Story*, 18.

[85]   For Matthew this pairing is frequent: see also 5:20, and seven occurrences in ch. 23. Only in 15:1 are the Pharisees named before the Scribes. The pairing of Scribes and Pharisees is not

or the Sadducees (16:1), while the chief priests are paired with the Scribes (21:15) or the elders (21:23). Thus in the controversies where several groups of opponents appear Matthew shows a distinct preference to use the Pharisees as one of the constituents.

In the ten controversies which show only one group of opponents the Pharisees appear most frequently (9:10–13; 12:1–8; 12:9–13; 12:22–37; 19:3–9; 22:34–40; 22:41–46). Other groups appearing singly are the Scribes (9:2–8), the people of Jesus' home simply identified as "they" (13:53–58), and the Sadducees (22:23–33). Again here Matthew seemingly favors the Pharisees as the opponents of Jesus. Thus the controversies as a whole exhibit a heavy tendency towards naming the Pharisees as the chief opponents of Jesus. They occur in twelve controversies, while the Scribes occur four times. Sadducees and chief priests each occur twice, while the elders, the disciples of John the Baptist, the Herodians, and "they" occur once each.

The focus of the controversy stories on the Pharisees occurs already in Matthew's sources, although Matthew has sharpened this focus to some extent. In 9:10–13 he replaces "Scribes of the Pharisees" (Mk 2:16) with the Pharisees. Matthew replaces the Scribes of Mk 3:22 with the Pharisees in 12:24. He clarifies the involvement of the Pharisees in 22:15–22 through the insertion of 22:15, and he inserts the Pharisees into his construction of 22:34–40. Similarly, the controversy of 22:41–46 is directed against the Pharisees, while Mk 12:35 speaks of Scribes. Yet on the other hand, Matthew inserts the Scribes next to the Pharisees in 12:38–45. In the doublet of this controversy Matthew places the Sadducees next to the Pharisees (16:1–4). And when Matthew constructs a controversy in 21:14–17, he names as opponents the chief priests and Scribes.

The distinctions of the various groups of leaders seem motivated by their role in Mark's story of Jesus.[86] Thus the Sanhedrin is referred to stereotypically by the phrase "the chief priests and the elders,"[87] and the Scribes are mentioned as part of the Sanhedrin several times.[88] It is these groups that are chiefly held responsible for the death of Jesus. The Pharisees do not appear at all either in the trial of Jesus or under the cross as the chief priests, Scribes and elders mock Jesus (27:41).[89] Similarly, the Pharisees do not occur in the passion predictions, again a trait present

---

found exactly like this in Mark's gospel. There they appear together in 2:16 and 7:1. However, the formulaic "Scribes and Pharisees" is not used by Mark.

[86] Kingsbury assumes that the grouping goes back to the historical Jesus. Kingsbury: *Matthew as Story*, 18. Here it is sufficient to note that Matthew chose not accept Mark's view of who is responsible for the passion of Jesus, and who is involved in most of the controversy stories.

[87] See 21:23; 26:3, 47; 27:1, 3, 12, 20; 28:11–12. The elders are called "of the people" in 21:23; 26:3, 47; 27:1.

[88] See 26:57; 27:41; probably also in 16:21. Perhaps 2:4 should be counted among these references as well, particularly since the Scribes here are mentioned in a phrase mentioning the "chief priests and the Scribes of the people."

[89] In Mark the Pharisees are similarly absent from the trial and death of Jesus. Mark's last occurrence of the Pharisees is in 12:13, the controversy over paying taxes to Caesar.

already in Mark (16:21 ‖ Mk 8:31; 17:12d, 22–23 ‖ Mk 9:31; 20:18–19 ‖ Mk 10:33–34; 26:2). The Pharisees all but disappear from the gospel after ch. 23. Their only reappearance after this is in the company of the chief priests to ask for a guard for the tomb (27:62). Yet when the guard reports on its failed mission the Pharisees are absent again (28:11–12). Thus the Pharisees as the main opponents of Jesus in the controversies are absent from Matthew's trial and execution of Jesus, as they are in Mark.

The characterization of the opponents of Jesus is quite simple.[90] They are generally described as evil.[91] This is their "root trait"[92] which is spelled out through various attributes which are often repeated.[93] They are called "brood of vipers"[94] or "hypocrites,"[95] and are described as "blind guides."[96] They are described as producing evil fruit, or no fruit at all.[97] They are shown as ignorant about the scriptures.[98] They take counsel against Jesus[99] and tempt him repeatedly.[100] They accuse him of collusion with Beelzebul[101] and request a sign while ignoring the signs given already.[102] The characterization of the Jewish leaders never varies from these parameters. As such they are "flat characters" in the narrative[103] and function like types. There is no development of the character of the opponents, it is stated at the outset and does not vary.

---

[90] The issue of characters, or figures, in the gospel is mainly taken from Kingsbury: *Matthew as Story*, 9–28. Kingsbury uses Chatman's methodology to a large extent. In this scheme, a narrative consist not only of plot and events, but also of various characters, persons or groups of persons appearing in a narrative. Seymour Chatman: *Story and Discourse. Narrative Structure in Fiction and Film* (Ithaca: Cornell University Press, 1978), 107–138. Characterization of the Jewish leaders takes place through epithets or descriptions given by "reliable characters" in the gospel narrative, such as Jesus, John the Baptist, or the narrator. Anderson: *Web*, 102. For the description of characters, Kingsbury adapts a scheme of Edward M. Forster: *Aspects of the Novel* (New York: Harcourt, Brace & World, 1954). See also Meyer H. Abrams: *A Glossary of Literary Terms*, 4th ed., (New York: Holt, Rinehart & Winston, 1981).

[91] They think evil thoughts (9:4); consequently they are evil themselves (12:34, 39; 16:4).

[92] Kingsbury: *Matthew as Story*, 19.

[93] Anderson has explored the repetitive nature of the descriptions given the opponents of Jesus. Anderson: *Web*, 97–132.

[94] Cf. 3:7; 12:34; 23:33.

[95] Cf. 6:2, 5, 16; 15:7; 22:18; 23:13, 15, 23, 25, 27, 29; 24:51.

[96] Cf. 15:14; 23:16, 34.

[97] Cf. 3:7–10; 7:19 (this verse does not directly refer to Jewish leaders; however, it is an exact re-statement of 3:10 directed against Pharisees and Sadducees); 12:33–34; 21:43.

[98] Cf. 12:3, 5; 19:4; 21:16; 21:42; 22:29, 31.

[99] Cf. 12:14; 22:15; 26:3–4; 27:1. See also the reference in 27:7 where the chief priests and elders take counsel on what to do with the blood money of Judas.

[100] Cf. 16:1; 19:3; 22:18, 35.

[101] Cf. 9:34; 10:25; 12:24.

[102] Cf. 12:38; 16:1.

[103] "Flat" characters in a narrative possess only very few traits and thus are highly predictable in their behavior. Kingsbury: *Matthew as Story*, 10.

The controversy stories bear this out to a large extent. Already in the first of the controversies the leaders are described as having evil thoughts (9:4), and there are no redeeming features ever mentioned thereafter. When Mark has a scholastic dialogue of a very positive nature with a Scribe, Matthew takes great care to form this into a highly charged controversy (22:34–40; cf. Mk 12:28–34).

Whenever Matthew uses an epithet or a description of the Jewish leaders where there is a direct reference to a subgroup, the Pharisees emerge prominently.[104] When Matthew speaks about the brood of vipers, the hypocrites, the blind guides, when he uses the fruit imagery, when he mentions the tempting of Jesus by his opponents or reports that Jesus is thought to work in collusion with Beelzebul, or when the opponents ask for a sign, the Pharisees are always present. When Matthew draws attention to the fact that the opponents are not well versed in the scriptures, the Pharisees are almost always present.[105] The only instances where the absence of the Pharisees in the negative description of the Jewish leaders is conspicuous is in the plotting of the death of Jesus, where the chief priests and elders appear prominently.[106] Similarly, the passion predictions do not mention the Pharisees. Thus again Matthew shows that he can make distinctions among the Jewish leaders. The use of polemic, invective, and epithets bears out what was observed in the controversy stories: Matthew decidedly favors the Pharisees as opponents of Jesus, easily associates the Scribes with them, and does not connect the Pharisees with the trial of Jesus.[107]

As a consequence, within the flat character of the Jewish leaders as the opponents of Jesus the Pharisees play a particular role. They appear as the chief opponents of Jesus in the controversy stories, and most of the invective of the gospel is directed towards them. Matthew inserts ch. 23 as a critique of the

---

[104] As direct recipients of epithets or invective or polemic the Pharisees appear alone in 9:34; 12:3–5, 14, 24, 34–39; 19:3–4; 22:15, 35. To this one might add 22:16–18 where they appear together with the Herodians, but where the emphasis is most strongly on the Pharisees. With the Scribes they appear in 9:4; 12:38; 15:7, 14, and throughout ch. 23. With the Sadducees they appear in 3:7–10 and 16:1. Once they appear with the chief priests in 21:43–45.

[105] The two exceptions are 21:14–17 and 22:23–33. The latter reference easily explains the absence of the Pharisees because they actually do believe in the resurrection and thus cannot be part of the controversy over it.

[106] Matthew describes the Pharisees only once as plotting directly against Jesus, in 12:14. There the Pharisees plot how to destroy (ἀπολέσωσιν) Jesus. This verse is a quotation of Mk 3:6, though Matthew omits the Herodians. The Pharisees plot once more, but only how to entrap Jesus in his talk (22:15). When the chief priests and elders plot, they plot the death of Jesus in much clearer terms. In 26:4 they conspire "to arrest him by stealth and kill him," (ἀποκτείνωσιν) while they plot "to put him to death" (θανατῶσιν) in 27:1.

[107] The only time the Pharisees are seemingly linked with the death of Jesus is in the verses following the parable of the wicked tenants (21:45). Yet the Pharisees here are mentioned after the chief priests, who figure prominently in the trial of Jesus. Furthermore, here there is only an attempt to arrest Jesus, not yet to kill him. Finally, the attempt fails because they fear the crowds.

Pharisees[108] and heightens the attention to the Pharisees in other places as well. Matthew continues a trend already found in his sources. However, this trend is noticeably intensified by Matthew. This intensification needs explanation.

The increased attention to the Pharisees points to a particular Matthean interest that cannot be explained with reference to the Pharisees as the historical figures that antagonized Jesus.[109] It seems more plausible that Matthew was interested in the Pharisees because he and his community knew them. This implies that the controversies between Jesus and the Pharisees reflect at least some of the contemporary relationship between the Matthean community and the Pharisees and their heirs.

This assessment is borne out by the controversy stories to some extent. As has been seen, Matthew redacted many of these stories to reflect more pointedly an objection of the opponents that has some bearing on the practical life of the community. The controversy over the forgiveness of sins (9:1–8) is redacted in this way. The first Sabbath controversy (12:2–8) links the accusation of the opponents with a comparison between the priests in the temple and the disciples plucking grain, while the second Sabbath controversy emphasizes the interpretation of the Sabbath observance within the framework of the community's interpretation of doing good. The first controversy over the demand for a sign contrasts the opponents as the evil spirits among Israel with the community. The story of the washing of hands before meals (15:1–9) contrasts the tradition of the elders with

---

[108] This statement makes no judgment about the controversial source-critical evaluation of ch. 23. For a recent evaluation of the scholarship on this problem and a defense of ch. 23 as a pre-Matthean literary construct see Newport. He argues that the chapter consists of a main source (23:2–31, Sermon on the Mount) that predates the fall of Jerusalem and reflects a discussion with Judaism *intra muros*. The gospel itself reveals a gentile bias. Consequently, Matthew 23 and the Sermon on the Mount "reveal a layering of material ... not explained by the two–document hypothesis, unless, that is, one is prepared seriously to qualify that hypothesis by allowing for an M – Q overlap or the possibility of Luke's knowledge of Matthew's redactional activity." Newport: *Matthew 23*, 177.

[109] The role of the Pharisees in the story of the historical Jesus has recently come under renewed investigation. Serious doubts have been raised that the Pharisees were actually the chief opponents of Jesus as they are depicted in the gospels. Thus Berger proposes that the oldest traditions behind some of the controversy stories in Mark's gospel is the contrast *logion*. In particular he observes this for Mk 2:16–17, 18–20, 23–28; 3:1–4; 7:1–23; 10:1–12; 12:13–17. Berger argues that these early Christian traditions were made biographical through the insertion of the figures of Jesus and Pharisees as antagonists, and are thus representative for the controversies between the early Christian communities and the Pharisees. Berger: *Gesetzesausle-gung*, 576–578. Hultgren makes a similar point when he argues that the pre-Markan collection 2:1–3:6 received its current references to Scribes and Pharisees through the influence of 3:6 which was inserted by the pre-Markan compiler. Hultgren: *Adversaries*, 159. Smith probably goes too far by arguing that there were no Pharisees in Galilee during Jesus' lifetime. Morton Smith: *Jesus the Magician* (San Francisco: Harper & Row, 1978), 153–157. For a summary argument in favor of the Pharisees as a post–resurrection opposition to the early Christians see also Sanders: *Jesus and Judaism*, 287–293.

the command of God and warns the community against any attraction that such traditions might hold for them. A similar point is made with the controversy over divorce (19:3–9).

But beyond the direct comparison between the Jewish leaders and the community all the controversy stories are geared towards the delegitimation of the opponents as rightful leaders of Israel. Their objections against Jesus and his disciples do not hold up under the arguments made by Jesus. Their interpretation of the law is shown to be faulty in the extreme whenever they bring it up. Matthew uses irony to show how inept the opponents are in their attempts to justify themselves (22:15–33). The repeated quotation of Hos 6:6 casts serious doubts on their covenant loyalty. They are portrayed as blind guides who are responsible for the dissolution in the temple cult and ultimately bring about the downfall of Jerusalem (23:16, 35–36). Matthew holds the opponents of Jesus responsible for the events that led to the destruction of Jerusalem because they plot against God and his Messiah like the Gentile rulers (22:34). Their rejection of Jesus and of the Matthean community makes them unfit to lead Israel. With the fate they brought upon Jerusalem through this rejection they have shown that their claim to leadership is pretentious without foundation. They are hypocrites.

While Matthew draws this portrait for all groups of Jewish leaders, his added emphasis on the Pharisees mirrors a situation after 70 A.D. In the wake of the destruction of the temple the Pharisees were one of the groups trying to assert leadership over Israel.[110] Matthew's attempts to delegitimize them and blame them for the disastrous war against Rome (23:35–36; 27:24) show that he viewed their claims as illegitimate. Furthermore, the frequent allusions to the Matthean community in the controversy stories suggests that the community claimed such leadership for itself. Such a claim to leadership, however, must be evaluated against the portrait that Matthew draws of the audience of his controversies. To this we now turn.

2.2 The Audience of the Controversy Stories

Only very few controversy stories in Matthew's gospel distinguish an audience. However, whenever Matthew does make a reference to an audience in the controversies, it is heavily redacted.

While the controversy over the forgiveness of sins (9:1–8) mentions the reaction of the crowds, Matthew edits their reaction to reflect on the community. In Mk 2:12 all (πάντας) are utterly amazed at the sight of the healing of the paralytic and give praise to God. In Matthew 9:8 however, the crowds (οἱ ὄχλοι) are afraid and give praise to God for giving such authority as the forgiveness of sins to human

---

[110] See the discussion of the situation after the destruction of the temple in Overman: *Matthew's Gospel*, 35–71.

beings. Matthew shapes the reaction of the crowds into a reaction which reflects on the practice of the community forgiving sins.

The controversy over Jesus' collusion with Beelzebul contains a further reference to the crowds (πάντες οἱ ὄχλοι 12:23). They react to a healing of a blind and dumb demoniac with amazement. While Matthew probably found this reference in Q[111] he redacts it considerably. He inserts that the crowds held Jesus to be the son of David. This statement becomes the driving force behind the accusation of the Pharisees that Jesus works by the power of Beelzebul. As a consequence, the acclamation of the crowds leads to the objection of the Pharisees and opens a rift between the two groups.

A further reference to an audience of a controversy is found in 21:14, the first confrontation in the temple which is constructed by Matthew. Jesus heals the blind and the lame, and the children acclaim him as the Son of David. To this the opponents react by initiating a controversy. Thus the function of the audience in this controversy is similar to that of 12:23.

A fleeting reference to an audience is made in 21:33. Matthew reports in a redactional remark that Jesus is teaching in the temple when the opponents approach him to question his authority. Such teaching presumably implies that at least some people were listening to the ensuing debate. This is confirmed when in 22:33 the crowds appear again and are astonished at Jesus' teaching on the resurrection. Matthew does not make further references to an audience in the controversy stories.

In the stories where an audience appears there is not much distinction in their reactions. They react to Jesus with astonishment and acclamation. At least within the controversy stories the crowds appear as "stock characters."[112] Yet for all the scarcity of the appearance of an audience in the controversy stories, the redactional attention given them seems rather lavish. Matthew has characterized the audience in such a way as to put the opposition to Jesus in stark relief because of its positive reaction to Jesus. And the positive reaction to Jesus in turn gives the substance to at least some of the controversies. The controversy following the miracle of the blind and dumb demoniac (12:22–37) is occasioned by the question of the crowds whether Jesus might be the son of David. The first Jerusalem controversy (21:14–17) revolves around the acclamation of Jesus by the children as son of David.

---

[111] The parallel in Mark does not contain a miracle. Lk 11:14–15 gives an account of this miracle and reports the amazement of the crowd (οἱ ὄχλοι). However, Luke goes on to report dissension among the crowds (τινὲς δὲ ἐξ αὐτῶν), while Matthew reports the accusation of collusion with Beelzebul made by the Pharisees. For a complete analysis of the source-critical problems of this passage see the redaction-critical examination of this passage in chapter 3.

[112] Kingsbury differentiates between flat characters who posses only few predictable traits and stock characters who possess only one trait. Kingsbury: *Matthew as Story*, 10.

A further element in the characterization of the audience is the public nature of the controversies. Even though the reactions of the crowds are mentioned infrequently, none of the controversy stories takes place in a private setting. The larger context of the controversies invariably reveals that the conflict between Jesus and his opponents takes place in public.

Such a narrative device seems to indicate that Matthew intends the audience of the controversy stories to reflect a group that turns from the fraudulent leadership of the opponents of Jesus towards an acknowledgment of the Matthean community as the rightful leaders of Israel. Yet before this conclusion is drawn from the scarce evidence of the controversy stories, the role of the crowds in the whole gospel must be taken into account.

Most often the crowds appear in Matthew as the audience of Jesus. They are described as following Jesus,[113] listening to him,[114] reacting with astonishment and praise to his teaching and miracles.[115] Sometimes just their presence is noted.[116] They appear as sheep without a shepherd (10:6). Jesus has compassion on them.[117] Conversely, the crowds react to Jesus by identifying him as a prophet and Son of David.[118] Generally this portrait of the crowds is mildly positive. But their distance from Jesus is clear as well. Unlike the disciples, Jesus dismisses them on occasion.[119] While the disciples are instructed clearly, the crowds are taught only in parables and do not understand.[120] Sometimes the crowds jeer at Jesus (9:23–25), or they rebuke those that would come to him (20:31).

On the whole, however, Matthew depicts the crowds mostly positively. The crowds are attracted to Jesus, and he continues to instruct them throughout his public ministry, ending with ch. 23. Yet the response of the crowd is never as committed as that of the disciples. Matthew describes them "as a shifting, unorganized, but interested group"[121] that lacks proper leadership. Their presence throughout the public ministry of Jesus speaks against a suggestion that the crowds reject Jesus already in ch. 13.[122] Furthermore, throughout the public ministry in

---

[113] Cf. 4:25; 8:1; 12:15; 14:13; 15:30; 19:2; 20:29.

[114] Cf. 5:1; 11:7; 12:46; 13:2, 34; 15:10; 22:33; 23:1.

[115] Cf. 7:28; 9:8; 9:33; 12:23; 15:30–31; 21:8–9, 11; 22:33.

[116] Cf. 8:18; 9:23, 25; 17:14; 20:31.

[117] Cf. 9:36; 11:25–27; 14:13–15; 15:32–33.

[118] Cf. 12:23; 21:8–9, 46.

[119] Cf. 8:18; 13:22–23, 36; 14:22–23; 15:39.

[120] Cf. 13:2, 10–17, 34–36.

[121] Saldarini: *Matthew's Christian-Jewish Community*, 39.

[122] Kingsbury writes: "Repudiated by all segments of Israel, Jesus reacts by declaring that Israel has become hard of heart (13:13–15)." Kingsbury: *Matthew as Story*, 75. A similar argument is brought by Hare and Hill, among others. Hare: *Persecution*, 149–151; Hill: *Matthew*, 227. Meier writes that in 13:13 "Jesus draws the veil of the parables over his teaching. For the outsiders, who for Matthew and his church equal the Jews, everything is now taught in unintelligible riddles." Meier: *Vision*, 90. If this were indeed so, the continued attention given to

Jerusalem there is the recurring motif of the leaders being afraid of the crowds (21:26, 46; 26:3–5), while the people seem still positively inclined towards Jesus. Right to the end of the gospel, the leaders are afraid that the people might be won away from them by Jesus and his disciples (27:64). Thus while the crowds' relationship to Jesus is never positively committed, they are always attracted to Jesus. Only in the scene before Pilate do the leaders finally manage to persuade the crowds against Jesus (27:20).

The central question remains, however, whether the people in the end reject Jesus completely, even if they seemingly don't do so during his public ministry. The pivotal text often cited in support of such a rejection is the redactional episode 27:20–26. It has already been discussed briefly in chapter 1. Pilate asks whether the crowd in front of the praetorium wants Barrabas or Jesus. The chief priests and elders persuade the crowds (τοὺς ὄχλους) to demand the release of Barrabas and the conviction of Jesus (27:20). When Pilate protests his innocence Matthew writes that all the people (πᾶς ὁ λαός) declare: "His blood be on us and our children" (27:25).[123]

Saldarini argues that λαός is used in Matthew's gospel with varying meanings, not all of them implying a comprehensive reference to Israel.[124] As a consequence, Saldarini suggests that ἔθνος and λαός are synonymous. Yet a comparison of the semantic fields in which both words occur generally in Greek literature does not bear this out.[125] And Matthew's gospel does not offer the same range of meaning

---

the crowds and the compassion Jesus has on them would not make any sense at all. Furthermore, in 15:10 Jesus explicitly calls the crowds to him, teaches them, and exhorts them to listen and understand an instruction that is not given in parables.

[123] Such an interpretation is offered already by McNeile: *Matthew*, 413. Hill emphasizes the prophetic character of this story and notes that 27:25 functions as a Matthean prophecy of future judgment. Hill: *Matthew*, 228. As examples for scholars arguing the reference to all the people as a *theologoumenon* signifying the rejection of all Israel see Trilling: *Das wahre Israel*, 72–73; Joseph A. Fitzmyer: "Anti–Semitism and the Cry of 'All the People' (Mt 27:25)," *TS* 26 (1965): 668; Strecker: *Weg*, 116–117; Frankemölle: *Jahwebund und Kirche Christi*, 210–211; Meier: *Vision*, 199–200; Mora: *Le refus*; Gnilka: *Matthäus*, 2:458–459; Gundry: *Matthew*, 565.

[124] Saldarini: *Matthew's Christian-Jewish Community*, 28–32. Davies and Allison take up the argument. Davies and Allison: *Matthew*, 2:592 n. 57. The references to λαός in Matthew are: 1:21; 2:4; 2:6; 4:16; 4:23; 13:15; 15:8; 21:23; 26:3; 26:5; 26:47; 27:1; 27:25; 27:64. Of these, 5 appear in scripture quotations: 1:21; 2:6; 4:16; 13:15; 15:8. Five more appear in the formula "elders of the people:" 2:4; 21:23; 26:3, 47; 27:1. In these ten occurrences it does not seem likely that the word is used to refer to a small crowd, or to only a section of the people of Israel. Matthew uses the word to refer to the whole of Israel in 4:23. Questionable are the uses in 26:5, a warning against tumult among the people, and 27:64, where the leaders tell Pilate that there is the danger that the disciples might tell the people of the resurrection. Both cases do not argue decisively that the word must be understood in terms of a small section of Israel.

[125] See Liddell and Scott: *A Greek–English Lexicon*, 480, 1029–1030. They note how the meaning of λαός changes in later antiquity to mean "nation." In this sense it is used exclusively in the LXX.

for λαός as it does for ἔθνος. In Matthew 15:8 Jesus cites Isaiah to infer an attack on the Jewish leaders who void the commandment of God for their own traditions. The quote from Isaiah is then used to make an *ad hominem* argument against the hypocritical leaders (15:7) who are said to be ὁ λαός of the Isaiah quotation (15:8) which perverts the scriptures by their teaching of traditions. A similar argument can be made for 13:15, again a quotation from Isaiah. Yet both these occurrences are in scripture quotations, and they should not be pressed too far by inferring that Matthew referred in 27:25 only to the probably small, selected crowd in attendance at the trial of Jesus. The extension of such an assumed variety of meanings for the word to 27:25 is unlikely for another reason as well. Throughout the trial of Jesus Matthew refers to the attendant people as ὄχλοι. But in 27:25 he switches to πᾶς ὁ λαός. This change is significant and probably means more that just the people who happened to be there.[126] The explicit mention of πᾶς in connection with λαός works against this. The context of this change is decidedly hostile. This also precludes an interpretation of the cry of the people as a Matthean ironic reference to a salvation of Israel through the blood of Jesus.[127] The cry of all the people is hostile.

As a consequence, it seems likely that in the cry of 27:25 Matthew had the people of Israel in view. He uses their condemnation of Jesus to highly dramatic effect.[128] The narrative setting of this verse makes it clear that the people act under the influence of the chief priests and elders (27:20). The opponents of Jesus have won over the people of Israel in order to put Jesus to death. The people accept the responsibility for the death of Jesus[129] and include in this their children. In this way Matthew portrays the repudiation of Jesus as directly responsible for the destruction of Jerusalem.[130]

It is highly unlikely, however, that Matthew implied with the cry of the people a view of salvation history in which the people of Israel are excluded from the kingdom permanently. The Jewish leaders are still afraid of the people even after

---

[126] Gnilka: *Matthäus*, 2:458; Harrington: *Matthew*, 392.

[127] Cargal has argued that Matthew might imply both the culpability of Israel and the offer to salvation in the blood of Jesus. Timothy B. Cargal: "'His Blood Be Upon Us and Our Children': A Matthean Double Entendre?" *NTS* 37 (1991): 101–112. The problem with such an interpretation is that the gospel does not offer a theology of redemption of "all the people."

[128] Brown calls the Matthean treatment of all the people "dramatizing theology." He writes: "Taken together with previous episodes about Judas' guilt over innocent blood and the tormenting dream of Pilate's wife about this just man, [the episode of Pilate washing his hands and the cry of all the people] raises Matt's PN to the level of supplying the most effective theater among the Synoptics, outclassed only by the Johannine masterpiece." Brown: *Death*, 1:832.

[129] Davies and Allison: *Matthew*, 3:591.

[130] This view is commonly held. This interpretations takes "and our children" in the literal sense as a reference to the generation that witnessed the destruction of Jerusalem. For a recent summary of this view see: Davies and Allison: *Matthew*, 3:592, with references in n. 57. For a full argument supporting this thesis, and for relevant background, see: Mora: *Le refus*, 156–165.

this incident (26:64) and continue to deceive them (28:13). Finally, there is no evidence that the mission of the community to Israel comes to an end with the death of Jesus.[131] Quite the opposite: The great commission of 28:16–20 is inclusive of Jews and gentiles.

Matthew used the cry of all the people as an explanation for the destruction of Jerusalem. Matthew makes an argument from an inner-Jewish perspective. This argument is made by other groups as well, e.g. *2 Bar* (e.g. 4:1; 13; 54:14–19; 78) and *4 Ezra* (e.g. 1:20–27; 5:23–30; 9:29–37). In their quest for an explanation of the disaster of 70 A.D. they affirm the responsibility of the Jewish people.[132] By demonstrating the ruinous consequences of the rejection of Jesus Matthew once more tries to delegitimize the Jewish leaders and those they persuade to reject Jesus. By continuing the mission to Israel even after the trial before Pilate Matthew extends the image of the people as misled by their fraudulent leaders, as sheep without a proper shepherd. Matthew probably realized how severely limited Jesus' success was among the people of Israel. At the same time, Matthew's own community was in dispute with the Jewish leaders. Thus with the cry of all the people Matthew reaches for an explanation of the widespread rejection of Jesus and his message among the people of Israel. At the same time, he continues to seek the identity of his community in the Jewish context and thus does not abandon the mission to Israel.

The controversy stories reflect this ambivalent nature of the crowds to a large extent. While the crowds acknowledge the power of Jesus in his teaching and miracles, they remain unreliable and in need to be won over. The mission to Israel provided some of more acrimonious debates between Jesus and his opponents. The horizon of the mission to Israel is never lost, and the controversies remain a contest between Jesus and his adversaries over the adherence of the people.

2.3 Jesus in the Controversy Stories

Matthew's gospel is the story of Jesus first and foremost. The gospel's story, its characters, and its theology ultimately relate to the person of Jesus as its defining point of reference.[133] The Matthean controversy stories are no exception. They highlight the figure of Jesus from the particular viewpoint of the conflict with the

---

[131] It is possible to view the great commission of the disciples in 28:16–20 as a commission to the gentiles only. Douglas R. Hare and Daniel J. Harrington: "'Make Disciples of All the Gentiles' (Mt 28:19)," *CBQ* 37 (1975): 359–369. However, it is unlikely that 28:19 ought to be read as excluding Israel. John P. Meier: "Nations or Gentiles in Matthew 28:19?" *CBQ* 39 (1977): 94–102.

[132] The same topic is also treated, with similar results, in the *ApcAbr* and *3 Baruch*. For a larger treatment of these themes in the literature after the destruction of Jerusalem see: George W. E. Nickelsburg: *Jewish Literature Between the Bible and the Mishnah. A Historical and Literary Introduction* (Philadelphia: Fortress, 1981), 277–309.

[133] Senior: *What Are They Saying About Matthew?* 74.

Jewish leaders. Consequently, the controversy stories do not give a complete picture of Jesus as Matthew wanted to portray him. In addition, the Jesus of the controversy stories does not stand isolated in the gospel, but is connected with the other strands of Matthean christology.

It is not the aim of this section to give an exhaustive account of the christology of Matthew's gospel. This would go beyond the confines of a subsection within a chapter of this thesis. Nevertheless, a few issues that have shaped recent scholarship on the christology of Matthew must be raised because they relate to the christology found in the controversy stories. These issues concern methodological observations on the trend from a christology of titles to a christology of actions. They also include some notes on the content of Matthean christology.

A number of Matthean christological studies in recent years have emphasized the importance of titles applied to Jesus. These titles certainly are expressions of an early Christian reflection on the experience of Jesus.[134] Among Matthean studies the work of Kingsbury has dealt extensively with Matthew's use of titles for Jesus.[135] Kingsbury claims that the preeminent title for Jesus is "Son of God" under which all other titles must be subsumed. It expresses the divine authority of Jesus and touches on all aspects of his ministry. Kingsbury's study is highly influential, even though it has not had unqualified success.[136] Particularly his attempt to qualify the

---

[134] For a general survey of christological titles as early Christian expressions of faith in Jesus see, among many others: Raymond E. Brown: *An Introduction to New Testament Christology* (New York: Paulist Press, 1994); James D. G. Dunn: *Christology in the Making* (Philadelphia: Westminster, 1980).

[135] Kingsbury's most comprehensive study of the titles of Jesus is a redaction–critical analysis. Jack D. Kingsbury: *Matthew: Structure, Christology, and Kingdom* (Philadelphia: Fortress, 1975). More recently he has integrated narrative criticism into his approach to the christology of Matthew. Jack D. Kingsbury: "The Figure of Jesus in Matthew's Story: A Literary-Critical Probe," *JSNT* 21 (1984): 3–36; Kingsbury: *Matthew as Story*. Kingsbury was not the first to concentrate on titles, however. Otto Michel approached Matthean christology from the great commission of 28:16–20 and came to the conclusion that Matthean christology can be summed up in a "Son of Man" theology. Otto Michel: "Der Abschluß des Matthäusevangeliums," *Evangelische Theologie* 10 (1950): 16–26. Since Michel there has been general agreement that the verses are crucial for the Matthean christology, although their evaluation has varied to a considerable extent. Günther Bornkamm: "Der Auferstandene und der Irdische. Mt. 28, 16–20," in: *Zeit und Geschichte. Festschrift Rudolf Bultmann*, ed. E. Dinkler (Tübingen: Mohr, 1964) 171–191; Lange: *Erscheinen*; Benjamin J. Hubbard: *The Matthean Redaction of a Primitive Apostolic Commissioning: An Exegesis of Matthew 28:16–20*, SBL.DS 19 (Missoula: Scholars, 1974); John P. Meier: "Two Disputed Questions in Matt. 28. 16–20," *JBL* 96 (1977): 407–424.

[136] A direct response to Kingsbury, Meier contends that the "'Son of Man' christology influences the final scene of the gospel and thus cannot be subsumed under the 'Son of God' christology." Meier concludes that no single title expresses the entire christology of Matthew. Meier: *Vision*, 210–219. Stanton agrees with this evaluation through the analysis of the title "Son of David" as a somewhat neglected title in Matthean scholarship. Stanton: *Gospel*, 169–191.

title "Son of God" as the most important in Matthew has met with resistance.[137] On the other hand, Kingsbury's assertion of a comparatively "high" christology in Matthew's gospel has won widespread support.[138] Other christological studies concerned themselves less with titles than with recurring motifs. One of the proposed motifs is wisdom,[139] although this particular approach did not gain widespread support.[140] Other approaches concentrate on Jesus as the New Moses,[141] or as healer.[142] These studies emphasize a "low" christology.

The apparent failure of Matthean scholarship, however, to settle on one dominant title or category for Matthew's christology reflects the extraordinary richness of the gospel's portrait of Jesus. Thus the gospel is not a philosophical or theological treatise but "a story, a narrative in which Old Testament reflection, christological titles and vignettes of Jesus in action are all blended to convey [Matthew's] experience of Jesus' presence within the community."[143]

Behind this observation lies the insight that Matthew uses titles for Jesus to some extent. But these titles do not always offer a fixed take on Jesus. In other words, when Matthew uses a title for Jesus he does not always and invariably intend the

---

[137] One important opponent of Kingsbury's scheme is Stanton. In his analysis of the accusations against Jesus to work in collusion with Beelzebul and the title "Son of David" Stanton claims that it is these passages which must have been very important to Matthew because of their connection with the controversies of the gospel. Stanton goes on to claim that these issues were much more contentious than the claim that Jesus is the Son of God. Stanton: *Gospel*, 169–170.

[138] See the argument and references in Davies and Allison: *Matthew*, 3:719.

[139] Thus proposed by M. Jack Suggs: *Wisdom, Christology, and Law in Matthew's Gospel* (Cambridge: Harvard University Press, 1970). The starting point for Suggs is that Matthew used Q. This document, according to Suggs, was in turn influenced by wisdom motifs and a lost Jewish Wisdom apocalypse containing oracles about Wisdom sending its emissaries on a mission to Israel. When this mission failed, Wisdom brought judgment on Israel. Jesus would be one of Wisdom's rejected messengers in Q. Matthew redacted Jesus into Wisdom herself.

[140] Criticisms concerning Sugg's argument centered around the hypothesis of the Wisdom apocalypse and the speculation that wisdom motifs might have developed into a full-blown myth of Wisdom sending emissaries. Furthermore, since Q itself is no longer extant, the whole approach is highly speculative. Marshall D. Johnson: "Reflections on a Wisdom Approach to Matthew's Christology," *CBQ* 36 (1974): 44–64. However, others have continued to explore the motif. Fred W. Burnett: *The Testament of Jesus–Sophia: A Redaction–Critical Study of the Eschatological Discourse in Matthew* (Washington: University Press of America, 1981); Celia Deutsch: "Wisdom in Matthew: Transformation of a Symbol," *NT* 32 (1990): 13–47.

[141] Allison: *New Moses*.

[142] This thesis was first proposed in a very influential study by Held: "Interpreter." Kingsbury has incorporated this approach to emphasize his "Son of God" christology. Kingsbury: "Observations." Birger Gerhardsson advanced the study of the Matthean miracle stories considerably in a comprehensive study of all miracles in Matthew, going beyond chs. 8–9. He argues that many different titles are connected with Jesus in the miracle stories. Consequently, no one of them should be singled out as *the* christology of Matthew. Matthew's portrait of Jesus in the miracle stories is "illustrated with many kinds of material." Birger Gerhardsson: *The Mighty Acts of Jesus According to Matthew* (Lund: C. W. K. Gleerup, 1979), 82.

[143] Senior: *What Are They Saying About Matthew?* 86.

same meaning for this title. Matthew uses such titles in specific contexts. An example of the shifting use of titles is the repeated assertion that Jesus is the "Son of David." Several scholars have noted that even though the title is connected with Jewish expectations of a royal messiah of Davidic lineage, Matthew actually uses the title quite frequently in association with the healing ministry of Jesus.[144] Furthermore, as will be examined more closely below, the title crops up quite often in material that deals with the conflict between Jesus and the Jewish leaders.[145] Thus the background of the title as well as the Matthean narrative setting and associations all contribute to a cluster of meanings associated with the title and not to one univocal meaning. From one passage to another any one of these associations or contexts might be more dominant than another. Jesus appears as a "round character."[146]

This rather cursory look already reveals that in order to grasp Matthew's portrait of Jesus more fully, the story of the first gospel is more important than the various individual titles applied to Jesus. And again it cannot be overemphasized that in different narrative situations Matthew applied different titles to Jesus. As a consequence, no one of them can be said to encompass the others. Matthew's portrait of Jesus remains complex. The controversy stories confirm this assessment. The portrait of Jesus drawn in these stories of conflict with the Jewish leaders is as complex as it is in the rest of Matthew's gospel. However, a few traits are repeated and emerge as patterns.

One of the more obvious implications for the christology of Matthew is the shape of the controversy stories. All except the last begin with an objection or question by the opponents to which Jesus gives an answer. And in all of these stories Jesus remains victorious in the contest in dialogue. This victory is, however, of no consequence to the opponents of Jesus. As such none of the controversy stories really changes the relationship between Jesus and his opponents. The hostility between Jesus and the Jewish leaders remains unaffected by Jesus' persuasive arguments in these contests. Thus the victory of Jesus in contest is a moral one,[147] yet it does not affect the narrative progression to a noticeable extent.

---

[144] Burger: *Jesus als Davidssohn*, 72–106; Jack M. Gibbs: "Purpose and Pattern in Matthew's Use of the Title 'Son of David,'" *NTS* 10 (1963–1964): 446–464; Jack D. Kingsbury: "The Title 'Son of David' in Matthew's Gospel," *JBL* 95 (1976): 591–602; Dennis C. Duling: "The Therapeutic Son of David. An Element in Matthew's Christological Apologetic," *NTS* 24 (1977–1978): 392–410.

[145] See Stanton: *Gospel*, 180.

[146] Kingsbury writes: "'Round' characters are those who possess a variety of traits, some of which may even conflict, so that their behavior is not necessarily predictable ... Jesus is a round character because although he is always cast in a positive light, he nonetheless exhibits such a great number and variety of traits that he effectively becomes a 'real person' for the reader." Kingsbury: *Matthew as Story*, 10.

[147] Berger writes: "Die synoptischen Streitgespräche sind eine Verbindung der paganen Gattung der Chrie und der paganen und auch hellenistisch–jüdischen Gattung des 'dualistischen'

As has been seen in the previous chapter, the contests in dialogue, specifically those found within Greek tragedies, exhibit these same formal characteristics consistently.

On the other hand, the reader or hearer of these stories is always aware of the superiority of Jesus' arguments. On occasion the reaction of bystanders in the stories confirms this, and sometimes the opponents' frustration manifests itself in their departure. But more often the persuasiveness of the argument is evident from the failure of the opponents to respond to Jesus' arguments, and its sometimes apophthegmatic conclusion. But beyond this general statement Jesus' superiority in contests in dialogue also manifests itself in a variety of other ways.

In the controversies of ch. 9 in particular, Jesus emerges as the defender of the Matthean community. The first controversy (9:2–8) centers around the authority of Jesus to forgive sins, but in the final redactional verse this authority is predicated of the community as well. As a consequence, Jesus' argument from the power to perform the healing miracle as a validation of the forgiveness of sins is applied to the community as well. The appeal to the authority of Jesus becomes the legitimation for the community to grant forgiveness of sins as well.

The meal with the sinners (9:10–13) confirms this. While the opponents object to the table fellowship of Jesus with sinners, Matthew also puts the disciples in a prominent place next to Jesus. Jesus replies that he came to call sinners and not the righteous. On one level this is most certainly an ironic allusion to 5:21 where the community is supposed to be more righteous than the Pharisees and Scribes. Thus now Jesus and his disciples exhibit the greater righteousness in the table fellowship. On the other hand, Jesus is portrayed as calling the sinners as a physician treats the sick. Thus Jesus again is the authority by which his disciples continue this practice of calling sinners (9:10). Taken in conjunction with the previous pericope, Jesus is the model for a community which has table fellowship with sinners and extends the forgiveness of sins to them.

The discussion over the practice of fasting (9:14–17) again shows the close association between Jesus and the community. While the opponents attack the disciples for their perceived failure to follow fasting practices, Matthew explains this practice from the close association between Jesus and his disciples. He then goes on to expound on the nature of the community and its newness through the images of the patch and the cloth, and the new wine in new skins.

The two Sabbath controversies of ch. 12 repeat this point. The first controversy shows the Pharisees objecting to an action of the disciples (12:2–8), while in the second controversy the same objection is leveled against Jesus himself (12:9–14). In a redactional emendation in second controversy makes it even clearer that the

---

Streitgesprächs zwischen einem typisch gerechten und einem typisch ungerechten Partner, die für beide divergierenden Wege stehen. Es geht daher weniger um die Beeinflussung durch den paganen Streitdialog als um die *confutatio* des von Anfang an im Unrecht stehenden Gegners. Es geht damit gewissermaßen um absolute Gegensätze ..." Klaus Berger: "Gattungen," 1310.

community is still in view even though the attack is overtly directed against Jesus. The question is not about healing on the Sabbath as much as about doing good.

Matthew establishes early on that the attacks on the community are attacks on Jesus himself who is present, both to his community (28:20) and through his community (10:40). Conversely, if the opponents wish to attack the Matthean community they have to face the authority of Jesus himself. By extension, then, the following controversies must be seen against the background of the congruence of the ministries of Jesus and his community. Just as in the mission of ch. 10 the disciples make Jesus present to Israel, the opponents' attacks on Jesus are attacks on the community as well. The opponents make this point forcefully themselves when they hold Jesus responsible for the break of the disciples with the tradition of the elders (15:1–9).

Yet with the beginning of ch. 12 the controversy stories take on a further dimension. While the identification of community and Jesus in conflict remains in view, the conflict comes to revolve around the interpretation of the Mosaic Law. Eight of the seventeen conflict stories deal with the Law, although in different ways. Two controversies deal directly with the accusation that either Jesus or his disciples break the Law (12:2–8, 9–14). The controversy over the tradition of the elders (15:1–9) is at first about Pharisaic customs. Yet in the riposte Jesus turns the controversy into one over the correct interpretation of the Law as he shows that the traditions of the Pharisees are in direct contradiction with what God commanded. In the conflict over divorce Jesus shows the mistaken interpretation of the Law by his opponents. Similarly the question of the resurrection is exposed as a frivolous misinterpretation of the Law. Conversely Jesus can also show that the imperial tax his opponents presume to be a matter of the Law is in fact not of interest to the Law at all (22:15–22). Finally, the opponents can only ask Jesus for an explanation of the great commandment without an interpretation of their own (22:34–40), and when the opponents are asked to explain Psalm 110:1 they fall silent (22:41–46).

In all these controversy stories Jesus appears as the superior interpreter of the Law. In some of the controversies it has been observed that the Matthean redaction takes greater care with arguments about the Law, and that the Matthean Jesus exhibits greater familiarity with it, than Mark does. Matthew's Jesus does not countermand the Law in the controversy stories. On the contrary, he exhibits a refinement in its interpretation that is absent from Matthew's sources. Jesus' ability to interpret the Law would seem to lend itself to the motif of Jesus as the New Moses.[148] Yet none of the controversy stories exhibits such a tendency. Even though Matthew's Jesus appears as the authoritative interpreter of the Law in conflict with the Jewish leaders, a connection with Moses is never made explicit in these stories.

---

[148] On Jesus as the New Moses see Allison: *The New Moses. A Matthean Typology.*

Matthew approaches the authority of Jesus in several ways. The first of these is a negative one. Even though Jesus teaches throughout the gospel, and even though many of the controversies are concerned with Jesus' teaching of the Law, Matthew indicates that to call Jesus a teacher is a failure to grasp what he is about. He redacts Mark to this end.[149] The opponents consistently call Jesus a teacher (9:11; 12:38; 19:16; 22:16, 24, 36). Other people who call Jesus a teacher are people who stand at a distance from the community, such as the rejected Scribe (8:19) and the collectors of the temple tax (17:24). While Jesus describes himself once as a teacher in relation to his disciples (23:8) his disciples do not call him that. Rather, the address teacher seems to be a convenient identification of Jesus to outsiders: When the disciples go to prepare the last supper they are to say that the teacher needs the room (26:18). As a consequence Matthew gives the impression that even though Jesus acts as a teacher with unprecedented authority (7:29) the title "teacher" is not an adequate description of Jesus. It most often indicates hostility to Jesus.

Matthew spells out Jesus' authority in a different manner. Several controversy stories exhibit a direct challenge to the authority of Jesus. All of them reveal much redactional activity. The first of these challenges appears in the controversy following the miracle of the blind and mute man (12:22–37). Matthew had used the material of the challenge in an earlier story (9:32–34); here he creates a doublet to use it in the context of a controversy story. The crowds ask whether the miracle reveals Jesus as the Son of David. The opponents respond to the identification of Jesus with the Son of David by charging that he works by the power of Beelzebul. The opponents recognize the power of Jesus, yet they ascribe it to an evil origin. Immediately following (12:38–45) a controversy arises when the opponents want to see a sign that would legitimize Jesus. The importance of this demand for legitimation is enhanced when the controversy is repeated in an abbreviated form (16:1–4).

A similar challenge to the authority of Jesus is contained in the controversy in Nazareth (13:53–58). The audience in Nazareth recognizes the wisdom and the powerful deeds of Jesus. However, they completely lack any explanation concerning the origin of this wisdom and power. The first of the Jerusalem controversies (21:14–17) revolves around the acclamation as Son of David. Yet the opponents complain about this acclamation again, this time to Jesus personally. The following controversy makes the challenge even more succinct when the opponents ask with which authority Jesus acts, and where it comes from (21:23–27). The final controversy story (22:41–46) takes up Jesus' authority in the question of the Son of David and the Messiah.

---

[149] The twelve occurrences of διδάσκαλος in Mark offer a wide variety of uses. The disciples call Jesus a teacher, as do some who request a healing from Jesus. The opponents of Jesus do so as well. Consequently, the Matthean redaction of this title is much more consistent. Mark's references are: 4:38; 5:35; 9:17; 9:38; 10:17; 10:20; 10:35; 12:14; 12:19; 12:32; 13:1; 14:14.

Especially prominent in these controversies is the acclamation of Jesus as Son of David. When crowds or children suggest that Jesus might be the Son of David, the opponents immediately seize on this title in order to confront Jesus. For Matthew the title seems more important than for Mark.[150] It has been claimed that for Matthew the title is important particularly in connection with healing miracles,[151] and indeed in four of the redactional passages healings play a part.[152] Yet this interpretation does not by itself account for "the evangelist's strong emphasis on this particular Christological theme."[153] Matthew also points repeatedly to the opposition this title elicits from the Jewish leaders.[154]

Stanton attempts to explain the Matthean use of the title as "an early form of the 'two parousias' schema."[155] However, he has to presuppose that Matthew always thinks about a humble servant when he calls Jesus the Son of David. This is not persuasive. When the title is mentioned in the controversy stories, it appears in the context of power and authority. Similarly, the connection of the title with healing miracles does not support a view of a "Son of David" christology that appeals to the humility of Jesus. The Beelzebul controversy illustrates this point admirably. The occasion is the healing of the blind and mute man, already redacted by Matthew to increase the healing power of Jesus. The healing is emphasized in its completeness (12:22). The reaction of the crowd is exaggerated (23), and they refer to Jesus as the Son of David. The Jewish leaders accuse Jesus of collaboration with Beelzebul. In the ensuing riposte of Jesus the issue of power and authority is prominent. Jesus "sees their thoughts" and replies with the images of kingdom, city, and house (25), he asserts that the kingdom of God has come upon them (28) and that he has bound up the strong man (29). Prominent as well is the theme of judgment (27, 31–32, 36–37).

---

[150] Matthew has nine references to the Son of David compared to Mark's three: 1:1; 9:27; 12:23; 15:22; 20:30, 31 (cf. Mk 10:47, 48); 21:9, 15; 22:42 (cf. Mk 12:35).

[151] Burger: *Jesus als Davidssohn*, 72–106; Kingsbury: "The Title 'Son of David' in Matthew's Gospel;" Duling: "Therapeutic Son of David."

[152] These are: 9:27; 12:23; 15:22; 21:15.

[153] Stanton: *Gospel*, 180.

[154] In addition to the passages cited above, Stanton also thinks that the hostility of Herod to Jesus in the infancy narrative is provoked by the association of the title "Son of David" in 1:1 with the royal Messiahship alluded to in 2:2, 6. Stanton: *Gospel*, 181–182. If this is correct, then the Matthean pattern of positive response and violent opposition to the claim could be observed in the Magi and Herod.

[155] The theory of the two advents of Christ is a theological construct that tries to explain why the ministry of the earthly Jesus, the first parousia, was so unlike the Jewish expectations of a powerful Messiah. It holds that while Jesus first came as a humble Messiah, the second parousia will reveal him as the powerful Messiah. Stanton quotes Justin and Origin to explain the theory and goes on to postulate that Matthew constructs an early form of this theory in the ministry of the humble Son of David while awaiting the "Son of Man seated at the right hand of power and coming on the clouds" (26:64). Stanton: *Gospel*, 185–191.

A similar association of the power of Jesus and the acclamation as "Son of David" appears in 21:15. In the first Jerusalem controversy the acclamation of the children in the temple repeats the acclamation of Jesus by the crowds during his entry into Jerusalem, while it is also associated with the θαυμάσια of entry and cleansing of the temple. And again the riposte of Jesus contains a high christological claim with the quotation of Psalm 8:2 and its application to Jesus. Jesus is validated as the son of David with the reference to God bringing out perfect praise from the mouth of mere children. Finally, in the last controversy the title is associated with that of Messiah (22:42). As a consequence, it seems unlikely that Matthew viewed the title "Son of David" as a title expressing the humility of Jesus' earthly ministry. On the contrary, the title expresses the claim of Jesus to displace the Jewish leaders from their position of authority in Israel.

Several controversies are also redacted by Matthew to express the claim to a position of leadership within Israel on the part of the disciples invested with the authority of Jesus' teaching. The first occurrence of this theme is visible in the redaction of the first Sabbath controversy (12:2–8). Matthew inserts the argument of the priests in the temple as guiltless despite the performance of their duties on the Sabbath. He then goes on to compare his disciples with these priests as equally guiltless and to state that with the presence of Jesus there is something greater than the temple. The Pharisees, on the other hand, have falsely condemned the guiltless and thus forfeited any claims to leadership. And they have done so because they did not take to heart Hos 6:6 and have thus become unfaithful to the covenant.

A similar argument occurs when the opponents demand a sign from Jesus (12:38–45). Scribes and Pharisees are excoriated for not repenting at the teaching of Jesus while he is greater than either Jonah or the Queen of the South. The appended parable of the evil spirit returning to the swept house with his seven friends is then used to describe the situation of Israel under the leadership of Jesus' opponents: Israel is in a worse state than ever before. Similarly the tradition of the elders reveal the bad stewardship of the opponents who substitute the commandments of God with their own teaching (15:3), while their interpretation of the divorce laws only serves to exhibit their hardheartedness (19:8).

The cleansing of the temple and the subsequent controversy over the acclamation of the temple repeat the theme of the displacement of the leaders and now tie it together with the claim that Jesus is the Son of David. While the leaders let the marketeers into the temple and transform it into a den of robbers (21:13) Jesus drives out the traders and moneychangers and heals the blind and lame, thereby restoring the temple as well as its people (21:14). The children in the temple recognize this and proclaim as a consequence that Jesus is the Son of David. To all this the leaders take exception and challenge Jesus over it (21:16). They question the authority of Jesus again (21:23), and finally are likened to the Gentile rulers who plot against God and his Messiah (22:34). The last controversy ties the Messiahship of Jesus together with his Davidic sonship (22:42). Thus Matthew enhances the controversial nature of the title to a considerable extent.

The christological implications of the controversy stories are complex. But Matthew ordered these implications within the framework of the controversies with one overarching aim. The authority of Jesus to teach and heal, his continuing superiority in argument, his masterful interpretation of scripture and Law, all serve the purpose of establishing Jesus as the true Messiah of Israel and his disciples as her true leaders. For Matthew, the title "Son of David" served as one convenient focus for this claim. The christological claims of the controversy stories imply that the Matthean community was in direct competition with others for Israel's leadership shortly after the destruction of the temple. As such, the controversy stories of the gospel of Matthew also lend credence to the hypothesis that the Matthean community struggled and competed within the walls of Judaism.

2.4 Summary of the Characters in the Controversy Stories

The characters appearing in the Matthean controversy stories seem to serve one overarching aim, the establishment of Jesus and his community as the rightful leaders of Israel. It seems unlikely that Matthew viewed this claim as a purely historical explanation of what led to the death of Jesus. While Matthew indeed holds the Jewish leaders responsible for the death of Jesus, and while he admits that a large portion of Israel followed these leaders in their rejection of Jesus as the Messiah, Matthew goes to some length to establish that this conflict is not yet resolved. His identification of the Pharisees as the chief opponents of Jesus confirms this. Matthew intensified the focus on the Pharisees as the fiercest opponents of Jesus and went to some lengths to extend this animosity toward the community as well. Furthermore, they remain absent from the passion narrative. This adds up to the conclusion that, for Matthew's community, the conflict with the Jewish leaders as represented by the Pharisees has not yet reached a conclusion. In other words, Matthew adapts the controversy stories to fit the conflicts which his own community experienced.

Other characteristics in the controversy stories bear out this judgment. Matthew's attention to the crowds as one of the circumstances that precipitates controversy stories and his extension of the objection beyond a criticism of Jesus to a practice of the community are recurring patterns. Furthermore, many of the individual controversy stories as well as their narrative framework suggest the mission to Israel as the underlying rationale for much of the conflict.

That the conflict is ongoing may also be inferred from the minor importance of the controversy stories with regard to the narrative plot of the whole gospel. While the Pharisees occur in most of these stories, and while they plot to destroy Jesus (12:14), their plot comes to naught. They are ultimately irrelevant in bringing about the death of Jesus. Furthermore, no solution to the conflict is ever suggested. While Jesus remains insistent that his opponents convert, they remain ultimately silent. While the mission to Israel provided a reason for the conflict, the mission is reaffirmed and extended at the end of the gospel (28:19). In this lack of resolution of conflict the controversy stories resemble the contests in dialogue of the Attic tragedies. As seen in chapter 6, this literary form serves to highlight opposing positions, not to reconcile them. Similarly, Matthew does not indicate that the conflict between Jesus and his opponents is resolved at the end of the gospel. As a consequence, the controversy stories resemble a drawn out contest in dialogue between Jesus and his opponents.

VIII. The Matthean Controversy Stories as Reflections of a Struggle *Intra Muros* of Judaism

The present investigation began with the question of the Jewishness of the gospel of Matthew. This question led to a detailed examination of the controversy stories as one of the focal points detailing some of the relationship between Matthew's community and the Jewish leadership of the time. The examination included methodological considerations prompted by an overview of critical scholarship on the issue of Matthew's Jewishness. Subsequently, a redaction-critical analysis investigated specific Matthean patterns in the treatment of these stories. These patterns were then applied to a form-critical investigation which included a literary-critical look at extra-biblical literature of possible influence on Matthew. Finally, a narrative-critical investigation tried to place the individual controversy stories within the larger framework of the entire gospel, both in terms of a narrative progression and in terms of the characters employed in the controversy stories. Now it is possible to try and draw the results of this investigation together.

The examination of the critical literature revealed that it is no longer possible to approach the problem of Matthew's Jewishness with just one method. Redaction criticism was able to distinguish various layers in the gospel. But subsequent attempts to assign these layers to different sources and concomitant interest groups in the tradition of the gospel failed to be entirely convincing because the method lacked the critical controls which would have made these reconstructions plausible. Subsequent scholarship tried to remedy this failure by extending redaction criticism into composition criticism and literary criticism, while others implemented models of social stratification to explain the phenomenon of Matthew's relationship to Judaism. One result of these studies was the realization that a clear cut distinction between Judaism and Matthean Christianity is probably wrongheaded. The differences between formative Judaism and Matthew's community are less clearly defined than the early redaction critics thought.

Furthermore, whatever conclusions are drawn about the nature of the conflict between Matthew and formative Judaism are almost exclusively based on the gospel of Matthew and lack the view from the opposition. The first gospel is the only source on which to base judgment on the issue. Consequently, any judgment on the relationship between these two groups is from the outset skewed. The polemics of Matthew's gospel may reveal a conflict, but the precise nature and extent of this conflict is also hidden by the one-sidedness of the polemic rhetoric. James Dunn's formulation of the issue reveals the problem precisely. He asks: "Are Matthew and his community outside the walls of Judaism, or did they still regard themselves as inside?"[1] A conceivable answer to this question is that both alternatives could be correct.

Granted these limitations, the examination of the controversy stories yielded several important results. The redaction-critical analysis showed that Matthew is not just taking these stories over from his sources, but that he is clearly interested in them. This interest shows itself on several levels. First of all, to some extent the appearance of the opponents concentrates on one particular group, the Pharisees. Concomitant with the emphasis on the Pharisees as the main opponents in the controversies, Matthew also redacts the stories to reflect more clearly that the conflict is not just between Jesus and his opponents, but that it involves Jesus' disciples as well. This indicates that Matthew's interest in the controversy stories went beyond simply repeating his sources. The development of the interest in the community with the concomitant interest in the Pharisees probably reflects on a social situation of the Matthean group marked by conflict with the Pharisees and their successors after the destruction of Jerusalem.

This assessment is supported by another feature of the Matthean redaction. As in Mark, the stories assert the authority of Jesus. But the assertion is made quite differently from the way Mark does. When Mark simply states that Jesus has authority, as e.g. in the Sabbath controversies, Matthew feels compelled to buttress this claim with an argument which shows Jesus as the superior interpreter of scripture and Law. On the other hand, when Mark dismisses all regulations concerning clean food, Matthew eliminates this passage. Similarly the controversies which Matthew constructs, either from material in Mark or from other material, use the Jewish scriptures to support or buttress the argument in the controversy. Central to these particular controversies is the claim that Jesus is the Son of David. In these ways Matthew appears much more interested in and committed to the Jewish traditions than Mark.

Yet the closeness of Matthew to the Jewish traditions, and his respect for the Law, does not finally settle the issue of Matthew's place within or without Judaism. It merely shows that Matthew saw his community within the tradition of the Jewish scriptures. For Matthew the scriptures were fulfilled with the appearance of Jesus and the gathering of his community.

Israel's place in Matthew's view of fulfillment through Jesus remains open. The controversy stories indicate that on occasion conflict is provoked by positive reactions to Jesus. These stories seem to indicate a distinction between the Jewish leaders on the one hand, and the Jewish people on the other hand. Matthew realized that the majority of the people of Israel did not accept Jesus as their Messiah. However, for Matthew the mission to Israel continues, and the portrait of the

---

[1] James D. G. Dunn: *The Parting of the Ways* (Philadelphia: Trinity, 1991), 152.

crowds as attracted but not committed might reflect on the hope Matthew had for a final conversion of Israel.

The examination of the integration of the controversy stories into the narrative context of the entire gospel, however, sheds further light on the nature of the conflict between Jesus and his adversaries. Matthew creates a framework for the controversy stories with the references to Israel as lost sheep without proper leadership. He goes on to insert the disciples' mission to Israel as a catalyst for the increasing hostility of the controversy stories. The eschatological tendencies of the mission discourse of ch. 10 heighten the sense that Matthew viewed the mission to Israel as the ongoing project of the community. The combination of the mission to Israel with the denunciation of her leaders indicates that Matthew saw his own community of believers in Jesus taking the place of the hypocritical leaders attacked in the controversy stories. Furthermore, Matthew also holds the failure of the Jewish leaders to respond positively to the mission of Jesus responsible for the catastrophe of the destruction of Jerusalem. Consequently, the controversy stories are part of the Matthean agenda to delegitimize the Jewish leaders.

Yet the gospel does not just present a mission to Israel and the attempt to displace the Jewish leaders. Concomitant with the mission is also a new conception of the community as a group of Jewish believers in Jesus as the Messiah and Son of David. The Matthean indictment of the established Jewish leaders is not just one of failed stewardship. It includes the recognition that the promises of the Jewish scriptures came to fulfillment in Jesus. The claim of the Matthean community rests on the insight that all power and authority has been given to the risen Christ (28:18). And in a further step, the Matthean community realizes that this authority extends not just to the people of Israel but to all nations (28:19).

The Gentile mission never becomes a matter of controversy, nor does Matthew ever spell out its concrete practicality for a law-abiding community. It is introduced only at the end of the gospel as the mandate of the risen Christ, and it comes as somewhat of a surprise.[2] But if Matthew's community took this mandate seriously, this perhaps alienated it even further from the Judaism of its time.[3] Thus the

---

[2] Schuyler Brown: "The Matthean Community and the Gentile Mission," *NT* 22/3 (1980): 193–221; David C. Sim: "The Gospel of Matthew and the Gentiles," *JSNT* 57 (1995): 19–48.

[3] There has been a lively debate whether Judaism in the first century was engaged in a mission to the Gentiles. Schürer and Juster were instrumental in propagating the view that Jews in the first century were actively seeking proselytes. This position has been taken up subsequently by, e.g., Stern and Jeremias. More recently the theory was propagated by McKnight. Emil Schürer: *The History of the Jewish People in the Age of Jesus Christ (175 B.C. – A.D. 135)*, 4 vols., ed. Geza Vermes, Fergus Millar and Martin Goodman (Edinburgh: T. & T. Clark, 1973–1987); Jean Juster: *Les juifs dans l'Empire romain: Leur condition juridique, économique et sociale*, 2 vols., 2nd ed. (New York: B. Franklin, 1965); Menahem Stern: *Greek and Latin Authors on Jews and Judaism*, 3 vols. (Jerusalem: Israel Academy of Sciences and Humanities, 1974–84); Joachim Jeremias: *Jesus' Promise to the Nations*, 2nd ed., trans. S.H. Hooke (London: SCM Press, 1967); Scot McKnight: *A Light Among the Gentiles. Jewish Missionary Activity in the Second Temple Period*

Matthean claim to leadership within Judaism does not just seek to displace the Pharisees from their position of prominence. It seeks to introduce a form of Judaism that is radically different from that of its opponents.

It seems probable, then, that Matthew's community saw itself within Judaism, yet at odds with the leaders of the Judaism it encountered. It remains unclear, however, whether its opponents saw the Matthean community in the same light. Most certainly the opposition resisted the Matthean claim to leadership. This much is obvious from the controversy stories, and from the grudging respect that Matthew pays these leaders on occasion (e.g. 23:2). Yet it is not clear that the opposition would have seen the Matthean community as a group within Judaism, perhaps at variance with the main body, but still connected with it. The various scholarly approaches that deal with the Matthean community as a sect within Judaism evade this question.[4] To a certain extent this is not surprising. If the Matthean community was indeed a sect within Judaism, it was perhaps one among several.[5] However, Matthew's gospel identifies the Pharisees as chief opponents. By the time the final version of Matthew's gospel was edited, the Pharisees had

---

(Minneapolis: Fortress, 1991). Opponents to this theory include: Johannes Munck: *Paul and the Salvation of Mankind* (Richmond: John Knox, 1959); David Rokéah: *Jews, Pagans and Christian in Conflict* (Jerusalem: Magnes Press, 1982); Shaye J. D. Cohen: "Was Judaism in Antiquity a Missionary Religion?" in: *Jewish Assimilation, Acculturation and Accommodation. Past Traditions, Current Issues and Future Prospects*, ed. M. Mor, Studies in Jewish Civilization (Lanham: University Press of America, 1992), 14–23; Martin Goodman: *Mission and Conversion. Proselytizing in the Religious History of the Roman Empire* (Oxford: Clarendon Press, 1994). There was certainly a Jewish expectation of conversion of the Gentiles at the end of times. However, this expectation does not imply an active mission to the Gentiles. The existence of proselytes does not in itself prove an active mission, either. A summary of the arguments for and against a Jewish mission to the Gentiles is given by Goodman, with a cogent argument against the prevalence of such a mission (pp. 60–90). Goodman examines the evidence that is usually cited in support of an active Gentile mission in first century Judaism. He goes on to claim that it supports the view that writings like those of Philo and Josephus had an "apologetic mission" (p. 86). Such a mission was intended to win Gentile sympathizers rather than converts. Thus recognition from sympathizers "may well have been political or social rather than theological" (p. 87).

[4] As one of the most vigorous proponents of the theory that Matthew's community is a Jewish sect Overman falls short in this respect. He argues that "sectarian groups feel alienated from those in authority and often openly denounce or oppose them. They, in contrast to the leaders or "parent group," understand the truth, possess it, and will one day be vindicated by God." Overman: *Matthew's Gospel*, 8–9. A little further on Overman admits that such sects not only rejected the parent group, but often were rejected by the parent group themselves (p. 15). Yet he does not elaborate how this might affect the interpretation of Matthew.

[5] Throughout the period from the Maccabean revolt to the end of the first century C.E. political and religious leadership changed frequently. Impulses for the fragmentation of Judaism were provided by the Maccabean, Hasmonean, and Roman rulers, by the various Jewish groups exerting influence at one time or another, splinter groups like the Qumran community, and by the rise and subsequent dissolution of the revolutionary movement that led to the destruction of Jerusalem.

begun the task of preserving and reforming Judaism in order to facilitate its survival of the catastrophe of the destruction of the temple in Jerusalem. Part of the reform probably centered on the gradual unification of the various Jewish movements in existence before 70. This was perhaps helped by the disappearance of Sadducees[6] and Essenes[7] after the war. The *birkat-hamminim* offers evidence of the unifying trend of formative Judaism, even if its exact date cannot be fixed.[8]

The Pharisees' reaction to Matthean Christianity and its claim to leadership within Judaism obviously cannot be reconstructed with any certainty. Yet Matthew's group, though claiming to be Jewish, may have proved a stumbling block to the quest for unity in the early phases of formative Judaism. Thus at some point Matthew's group may have been forced to either conform or "leave." As both Judaism and Christianity were in a formative stage, and thus transitional, it can no longer be established with certainty whether Matthew's claim to Jewishness was acknowledged by other Jewish groups. It is probable that Matthew did not want to part company with Judaism; but perhaps formative Judaism had already parted company with Matthew.

The controversy stories are only one possible window into the richly complex story of Jesus and his community in Matthew's gospel. They place this story firmly within the Jewish tradition and witness to the claim of Matthean Christianity within the community of Jewish groups. However, Matthew's community is probably more complex than its analysis as a Jewish sect admits. While this is not the place to extend the study even further, three characteristics of the gospel must be mentioned which are deserving of further study.

---

[6] Saldarini: *Pharisees, Scribes, and Sadducees*, 298–308.

[7] VanderKam: *Scrolls*, 108.

[8] Davies argued forcefully for the importance of a council at Yavneh around the year 90. Davies: *The Setting of the Sermon on the Mount*, 256–315. More recently both Saldarini and Schäfer have argued that the tradition surrounding the flight of Yohanan ben Zakkai from Jerusalem to Yavneh, and the subsequent foundation of a rabbinic school there, is a rabbinic legend being read back into the events surrounding the fall of Jerusalem. Saldarini: *ARN B*; Schäfer: "Jabne." Concerning the growing authority of rabbinic schools Saldarini writes: "The story [of Yohanan's flight and] the meeting with Vespasian explains this gradual development by means of one, crucial meeting" (p. 204). Overman uses this research in order to claim that the symbol of Yavneh was the "beginning of the end of sectarianism" in Jewish circles. Overman: *Matthew's Gospel*, 38. This is an unconvincing argument. It states that the formulation of the *birkat-hamminim* mark the beginning of anti-sectarian tendencies. But it could equally well be argued that these tendencies were present much before and gave rise to the formulation, notwithstanding the fact that implementation might have been still long in coming. In fact, Overman admits as much when he writes: "To speak of the beginning of the end of sectarianism is not to suggest that an authoritative body suddenly appeared ... It is true that the Yavneh tradition gives this impression, but this is a sociological improbability. The formation and establishment of guidelines and authoritative figures or bodies would be part of a lengthy process of social construction within formative Judaism" (p. 41). Given this lengthy process it seems ingenious to argue that this process only began with the symbol of Yavneh and not before.

The first of these is quite simple. Matthew tells a story of a Jewish community of believers in Jesus. Yet he begins with a source that is quite obviously of a gentile orientation. Matthew uses Mark, and not only as a reservoir for stories that he then shapes to his own purposes. Matthew's use of Mark is quite respectful in following much of its plot, in using almost all the material in Mark even when it seems at first quite contrary to his purpose, as in the controversy over purity (15:1–9 ‖ Mk 7:1–7). Matthew has two sources at his disposal. One of these, Q, has a friendly attitude towards the Law. In Q the attitude to the Law is "strongly conservative,"[9] while challenges to the authority of the Law are firmly countered. The only exception to this pattern seems to be Q 9:60. Mark, on the other hand, incorporates many traditions critical of the Law. Matthew is a "Neufassung des Markusevangeliums und nicht eine Neufassung von Q."[10] In a sense this is perhaps not surprising, since Matthew wrote a gospel, and Mark rather than Q was the source that used this literary form before. Yet it still seems significant that Matthew chooses to draw so extensively on a gentile writing.

A further area of study is somewhat connected with this issue. It concerns the gentile mission in the gospel of Matthew. It has already been remarked how little the gentile mission of 28:19 seems to retroject into the narrative. There is little doubt that the commission of 28:16–20 is a pivotal text for the gospel. And the argument that for Matthew there was no gentile mission[11] does not convince at all. The gentiles are the first to worship Jesus (2:11) while the Jewish leaders already plot persecution (2:16). Both the centurion (8:5–13) and the Canaanite woman (15:21–28) are significant gentiles in the gospel. And yet the disciples mission is restricted to Israel (10:5), while Jesus himself never actively seeks out gentiles. The gospel seems content to tell almost all of its story in the context of Israel, and to make all its argument in the context of inner-Jewish debates. This makes the gentile mission all the more surprising. If it is right to interpret the Matthean group in terms of a Jewish sect, the mission to the gentiles breaks the pattern of a supposedly tightly inward looking group.[12]

A final observation concerns the portrait of Peter. He has not been a concern in this study so far. But he is quite important in Matthew's gospel. Matthew receives from Mark the singling out of Peter from among the group of disciples. But Matthew goes on to enhance this portrait even more (e.g. 16:18–19). It is curious, to say the least, that Peter would become a figure on which the gentile community of Mark as well as the Jewish community of Matthew focused. The traditions in Acts similarly show Peter as central in the development of gentile Christianity with the baptism of Cornelius and the subsequent speech (Acts 10) and his radical position at the council of Jerusalem (Acts 15:7–11). While there is no sign that

---

[9] Tuckett: *Q*, 424. See also Catchpole: *Quest*, 232.

[10] Luz: *Matthäus*, 1:58.

[11] Sim: "The Gospel of Matthew and the Gentiles," 48.

[12] Overman: *Matthew's Gospel*, 8–19.

Matthew ever knew the Peter traditions in Acts it seems at least curious that Peter should become a focal point for the communities of Mark, of Matthew, and of Luke.

These three points only indicate that the present study does not exhaust Matthew's gospel. The position of Matthew with regard to Jews and gentiles is probably much more complex than a simplified theory of a sect within Judaism can encompass.

Little is known about the subsequent history of the Matthean community.[13] Matthean influence can possibly be detected in writings like the Didache, 5 Ezra, perhaps the Preaching of Peter.[14] Already by the time Ignatius of Antioch appropriated Matthew's gospel, its Jewish community had all but disappeared and its gospel appropriated into gentile circles. Yet during its brief flowering Matthew's community crafted a richly satisfying theology which combined the saving experience of Jesus as the Messiah of all nations with the traditions of its Jewish heritage.

---

[13] For an attempt at a reconstruction of the subsequent Matthean history see Raymond E. Brown and John P. Meier: *Antioch and Rome. New Testament Cradles of Catholic Christianity* (New York, Ramsey: Paulist Press, 1983), 45–86.

[14] The history of the Matthean community subsequent to the gospel is no longer traceable. However, some influences of the gospel on subsequent writings can be recognized. See: Klaus Berger: *Theologiegeschichte des Urchristentums*, 2nd ed. (Tübingen, Basel: Francke Verlag, 1995), 733–754; Overman: *Matthew's Gospel*, 162. A more comprehensive overview of Matthew's reception is: Edouard Massaux: *The Influence of the Gospel of Saint Matthew on Christian Literature Before Saint Irenaeus*, trans. J. Bellinzoni, 3 vols., New Gospel Studies 5, (Macon: Mercer, 1990).

Bibliography

Texts

Ancient Quotes and Anecdotes: From Crib to Crypt. Edited by Vernon K. Robbins. Foundations and Facets Reference Series. Sonoma: Polebridge Press, 1989.

Aristotle: *"Art" of Rhetoric*. Translated by J. H. Freese. LCL. Cambridge: Harvard University Press, 1926.

Babrius: *Aesopi Fabulae*. Edited by Maria J. Luzzatto and A. la Penna. BSGRT. Leipzig: B. G. Teubner, 1986.

Biblia Hebraica: 12th ed. Edited by R. Kittel. Stuttgart: Württembergische Verlagsanstalt, 1937.

Dio Chrysostom: *Works*. 5 vols. Translated by J. W. Cohoon and H. L. Crosby. LCL. London: Heinemann, 1932–1951.

Diogenes Laërtius: *Lives of the Eminent Philosophers*. 2 vols. Translated by R. D. Hicks. LCL. Cambridge: Harvard University Press, 1925.

Epictetus: *Dissertationes ab Arriani digestae*. Edited by H. Schenkl. BSGRT. Stuttgart: Teubner, 1965.

Euripides: *Electra. Orestes. Iphigenia in Taurica. Andromache. Cyclops*. Translated by A. S. Way. LCL. Cambridge: Harvard University Press, 1939.

Eusebius: *The Ecclesiastical History*. 2 vols. Translated by Kirsopp Lake. LCL. Cambridge: Harvard University Press, 1926–1932.

I Clement. II Clement. Ignatius. Polycarp. Didache. Barnabas. Translated by Kirsopp Lake. LCL. Cambridge: Harvard University Press, 1912.

Irenaeus: *Adversus Haereses*. Edited by W. W. Harvey. Cambridge: Cambridge University Press, 1857.

Jerome: *Commentaire sur S. Matthieu. Texte Latin, introduction, traduction, et notes*. Translated by Emile Bonnard. Paris: Cerf, 1977.

—: *Liber de Viris Illustribus*. Edited by Jaques-Paul Migne. PL XXIII, 602–718.

Josephus: *Works*. 10 vols. Translated by H. S. Thackeray. LCL. Cambridge: Harvard University Press, 1926–1965.

Lucian of Samosata: *Works*. 8 vols. Translated by A. M. Harmon, K. Kilburn and M. D. MacLeod. LCL. Cambridge: Harvard University Press, 1913–1967.

Martinez, F. García: *The Dead Sea Scrolls Translated. The Qumran Texts in English*. 2nd ed. Leiden, New York, Cologne, Grand Rapids: E. J. Brill, Eerdmans, 1996.

The New Oxford Annotated Bible with the Apocryphal/Deuterocanonical Books. Edited by B. M. Metzger and R. E. Murphy. New York: Oxford University Press, 1991.

The Old Testament Pseudepigrapha. 2 vols. Edited by James H. Charlesworth. New York, London, Toronto, Sydney, Auckland: Doubleday, 1983–1985.

Ovid: *Works*. Translated by F. J. Miller. LCL. Cambridge: Harvard University Press, 1916–1971.

Philo: *Works*. 11 vols. Translated by F. H. Colson, G. H. Whitaker and J. W. Earp. LCL. Cambridge: Harvard University Press, 1929–1962.

Philostratus: *The Life of Apollonius of Tyana, the Epistles of Apollonius, and the Treaties of Eusebius*. 2 vols. Translated by F. C. Conybeare. LCL. New York: Heinemann, 1912.

Pindar: *Pindare. Texte établi et traduit*. 4 vols. Reprint of the 1922–1923 edition. Translated by A. Puech. Paris: Societé d'Edition "Les belles lettres," 1970.

Plutarch: *Lives*. 11 vols. Translated by B. Perrin. LCL. Cambridge: Harvard University Press, 1914–1926.

—: *Moralia*. 15 vols. Translated by F. C. Babbitt, W. C. Helmbold, et al. LCL. Cambridge: Harvard University Press, 1927–1969.

Quintilian: *Institutiones Oratoriae*. 4 vols. Translated by H. E. Butler. LCL. London: Heinemann, 1921–1922.

Septuaginta. Edited by A. Rahlfs. Stuttgart: Deutsche Bibelgesellschaft, 1979.

Suetonius: *Works*. 2 vols. Translated by J. C. Rolphe. LCL. Cambridge: Harvard University Press, 1914.

Synopsis Quatuor Evangeliorum. 2nd ed. Edited by K. Aland. Stuttgart: Württembergische Verlagsanstalt, 1964.

Tertullian: *Opera*. 2 vols. CChr.SL. Turnholti: Typographi Brepols, 1953–1954.

Xenophon: *Memorabilia and Oeconomicus*. Translated by E. C. Marchant. LCL. Cambridge: Harvard University Press, 1923.

Secondary Literature

Aarde, Andries van: *God-With-Us: The Dominant Perspective in Matthew's Story and Other Essays*. HTS.S 5. Pretoria: Hervormde Teologiese Studies, 1994.

Abrams, Meyer H.: *A Glossary of Literary Terms*. 4th ed. New York: Holt, Rinehart & Winston, 1981.

Albertz, Martin: *Die synoptischen Streitgespräche*. Berlin: Trowitzsch, 1921.

Albright, William F., and Christopher S. Mann: *Matthew*. AncB 26. New York: Doubleday, 1971.

Allen, Ward C.: *A Critical and Exegetical Commentary on the Gospel According to St. Matthew*. 3rd ed. ICC. Edinburgh: T. & T. Clark, 1912.

Allison, Dale C.: "Two Notes on a Key Text: Matthew 11:25–30." *JThS* 39 (1988): 477–485.

—: *The New Moses. A Matthean Typology*. Minneapolis: Fortress Press, 1993.

—: "Anticipating the Passion: The Reach of Matthew 26:47–27:56." *CBQ* 56 (1994): 701–714.

Amram, David W.: *The Jewish Law of Divorce According to the Bible and Talmud*. 4th ed. New York: Hermon, 1968.

Anderson, Janice C.: *Matthew's Narrative Web: Over, and Over, and Over Again*. JSNT.S 91. Sheffield: JSOT Press, 1994.

Bacon, Benjamin W.: "The "Five Books" of Matthew Against the Jews." *Exp* 25 (1918): 56–66.

—: *Studies in Matthew*. New York: Holt, 1930.

Barth, Gerhard.: "Das Gesetzesverständnis des Evangelisten Matthäus." In: *Überlieferung und Auslegung im Matthäusevangelium*, edited by Gerhard Barth, Günther Bornkamm and Heinz Joachim Held, 54–154. WMANT. Neukirchen: Neukirchener Verlag, 1960.

Barton, Stephen C.: *Discipleship and Family Ties in Mark and Matthew*. MSSNTS 80. New York: Cambridge University Press, 1994.

Bauer, David R.: "The Interpretation of the Gospel of Matthew in the 20th Century." *ATLA.P* 42 (1988): 119–145.

—: *The Structure of Matthew's Gospel: A Study in Literary Design*. JSNT.S 31. Sheffield: The Almond Press, 1989.

Bauer, Johannes B.: "Bemerkungen zu den matthäischen Unzuchtsklauseln (Mt 5,32; 19,9)." In: *Begegnung mit dem Wort: Festschrift für Heinrich Zimmermann*, edited by J. Zmijewski and E. Nellessen, 23–33. BBB 53. Bonn: P. Hanstein Verlag, 1980.

Bauer, Walter, William F. Arndt, et al.: *A Greek-English Lexicon of the New Testament and Other Early Christian Literature*. Chicago: University of Chicago Press, 1961.

Baumgarten, Albert I.: "The Pharisaic-Sadducean Controversies about Purity and the Qumran Texts." *JJS* 31 (1980): 157–170.

—: "*Korban* and the Pharisaic Paradosis." *JANES* 16 (1984): 5–17.

—: "The Pharisaic *Paradosis*." *HThR* 80 (1987): 63–78.

Beare, Francis W.: "The Sabbath Was Made for Man?" *JBL* 79 (1960): 130–136.

—: *The Gospel According to Matthew*. Oxford: Blackwell, 1981.

Becker, Hans-Juergen: *Auf der Kathedra des Mose. Rabbinisch-theologisches Denken und antirabbinische Polemik in Matthäus 23,1–12*. ANTZ 4. Berlin: Institut für Kirche und Judentum, 1990.

Bellinzoni, Arthur J.: *The Sayings of Jesus in the Writings of Justin Martyr*. NT.S 17. Leiden: E. J. Brill, 1967.

Benoit, Pierre: "Les épis arrachés (Mt 12,1–8 et par)." *SBFLA* 13 (1962/63): 76–92.

Berger, Klaus: *Die Gesetzesauslegung Jesu: Ihr historischer Hintergrund im Judentum und im Alten Testament. Vol. I: Markus und Parallelen*. WMANT 40. Neukirchen-Vluyn: Neukirchener Verlag, 1972.

—: "Hellenistische Gattungen im Neuen Testament." In: *ANRW* II.25.2, edited by W. Haase, 1031–1432. Berlin, New York: Walter de Gruyter, 1984.

—: *Theologiegeschichte des Urchristentums*. 2nd ed. Tübingen, Basel: Francke Verlag, 1995.

Berger, Peter L.: "The Sociological Study of Sectarianism." *Social Research* 21 (1954): 467–485.

—: *The Social Construction of Reality. A Treatise in Sociological Knowledge*. Garden City: Doubleday, 1966.

—: *The Sacred Canopy. Elements of a Sociological Theory of Religion*. Garden City: Doubleday, 1967.

Best, Ernest: "The Miracles in Mark." *RExp* 75 (1978): 539–554.

—: *Mark. The Gospel as Story*. Edinburgh: T. & T. Clark, 1983.

Betz, Hans Dieter: *The Sermon on the Mount. A Commentary on the Sermon on the Mount, Including the Sermon on the Plain (Matthew 5:3–7:27 and Luke 6:20–49)*. Hermeneia. Minneapolis: Fortress, 1995.

Bird, Charles H.: "Some Γάρ-Clauses in St. Mark's Gospel." *JThS* 4 (1953): 171–187.

Black, Matthew, ed.: *An Aramaic Approach to the Gospels and Acts*. 3rd ed. Oxford: Oxford University Press, 1967.

Blau, Ludwig: *Die jüdische Ehescheidung und der jüdische Scheidebrief: Eine historische Untersuchung*. 2 vols. Straßburg: Trübner, 1911–1912.

Blenkinsopp, Joseph: "Interpretation and Sectarian Tendencies: An Aspect of Second Temple History." In: *Jewish and Christian Self-Definition*, edited by E. P. Sanders, 2:1–26. Philadelphia: Fortress Press, 1981.

Bonnard, Pierre: *L'évangile selon Saint Matthieu*. CNT 1. Neuchatel, Delachaux & Niestle, 1963.

Borg, Marcus J: *Conflict, Holiness, and Politics in the Teaching of Jesus*. New York: E. Mellen, 1984.

Bornkamm, Günther: "Das Doppelgebot der Liebe." In: *Neutestamentliche Studien für Rudolf Bultmann zu seinem siebzigsten Geburtstag am 20. August 1954*, edited by W. Eltester, 85–93. BZNW 21. Berlin: Alfred Töpelmann, 1954.

—: "Der Auferstandene und der Irdische. Mt. 28, 16–20." In: *Zeit und Geschichte. Festschrift Rudolf Bultmann*, edited by E. Dinkler, 171–191. Tübingen: Mohr, 1964.

—: "Die Binde- und Lösegewalt in der Kirche des Matthäus." In: *Die Zeit Jesu: Festschrift für Heinrich Schlier*, edited by Günther Bornkamm and Karl Rahner, 93–107. Freiburg, Basel, Wien: Herder, 1970.

—: "Enderwartung und Kirche im Matthäusevangelium." In: *Das Matthäusevangelium*, edited by J. Lange, 224–264. Darmstadt: Wissenschaftliche Buchgesellschaft, 1980. First published in: *The Background of the New Testament and its Eschatology (Studies in Honor of C. H. Dodd)* Cambridge 1956.

—: "Die Sturmstillung im Matthäusevangelium." In: *Das Matthäus-Evangelium*, edited by J. Lange, 112–118. Darmstadt: Wissenschaftliche Buchgesellschaft, 1980. First published in: *WuD* (1948) 49–54.

Bornkamm, Günther, Gerhard Barth, and Heinz Joachim Held: *Tradition and Interpretation in Matthew*. Translated by Percy Scott. NTLi. Philadelphia: Westminster Press, 1963.

Bowker, John: *The Targums and Rabbinic Literature*. Cambridge: Cambridge University Press, 1969.

Briscoe, Peter: "Faith Confirmed Through Conflict – The Matthean Redaction of Mark 2:1–3:6." In: *Back to the Sources. Biblical and Near Eastern Studies in Honour of Dermot Ryan*, edited by Kevin J. Cathcart and John F. Healey, 104–128. Dublin: Glendale, 1989.

Brooke, George: "The Feast of New Wine and the Question of Fasting." *ET* 95 (1983–1984): 175–176.

Brooks, Stephenson H.: *Matthews' Community: The Evidence of his Special Sayings Material*. JSNT.S 16. Sheffield: JSOT Press, 1987.

Brown, Raymond E.: *The Gospel According to John*. AncB 29–29A. Garden City: Doubleday, 1966–1970.

—: *The Birth of the Messiah: A Commentary on the Infancy Narratives in the Gospels of Matthew and Luke*. 2nd ed. AncB.RL. New York: Doubleday, 1993.

—: *The Death of the Messiah: From Gethsemane to the Grave. A Commentary on the Passion Narratives in the Four Gospels*. 2 vols. AncB.RL. New York: Doubleday, 1994.

—: *An Introduction to New Testament Christology*. New York: Paulist Press, 1994.

Brown, Raymond E., and John P. Meier: *Antioch and Rome. New Testament Cradles of Catholic Christianity*. New York, Ramsey: Paulist Press, 1983.

Brown, Schuyler: "The Matthean Community and the Gentile Mission." *NT* 22/3 (1980): 193–221.

Brown, Francis, et al.: *The Brown-Driver-Briggs Hebrew and English Lexicon. With an Appendix containing the Biblical Aramaic* (Peabody: Hendrickson Publishers 1997; reprinted from the 1906 edition).

Buck, Erwin: "Anti-Judaic Sentiments in the Passion Narrative According to Matthew." In: *Anti-Judaism in Early Christianity*, edited by Peter Richardson and David Granskou, 165–180. Waterloo: Wilfrid Laurier University Press, 1986.

Bultmann, Rudolf: *The History of the Synoptic Tradition*. 2nd ed. Translated by John Marsh. New York: Harper, 1968.

Burger, Christoph: *Jesus als Davidssohn*. FRLANT 98. Göttingen: Vandenhoeck & Ruprecht, 1970.

—: "Jesu Taten nach Matthäus 8 und 9." *ZThK* 70 (1973): 272–287.

Burnett, Fred W.: *The Testament of Jesus-Sophia: A Redaction-Critical Study of the Eschatological Discourse in Matthew*. Washington: University Press of America, 1981.

—: "Exposing the Anti-Jewish Ideology of Matthew's Implied Author: The Characterization of God as Father." *Sem* 59 (1992): 155–191.

Cargal, Timothy B.: "'His Blood Be Upon Us and Our Children': A Matthean Double Entendre?" *NTS* 37 (1991): 101–112.

Carter, Warren: *Households and Discipleship: A Study of Matthew 19–20*. JSNT.S 103. Sheffield: JSOT Press, 1994.

—: *Matthew: Storyteller, Interpreter, Evangelist*. Peabody: Hendrickson, 1996.

Catchpole, David R.: *The Quest For Q*. Edinburgh: T. & T. Clark, 1993.

Chatman, Seymour: *Story and Discourse. Narrative Structure in Fiction and Film*. Ithaca: Cornell University Press, 1978.

Chilton, Bruce D.: "Jesus *ben David*: Reflections on the *Davidssohnfrage*." *JSNT* 14 (1982): 88–112.

Chow, Simon: "The Sign of Jonah Reconsidered: Matthew 12:38–42 and Luke 11:29–32." *Theology and Life* 15–16 (1993): 53–60.

Clark, Kenneth W.: "The Gentile Bias of Matthew." *JBL* 66 (1947): 165–172.

Cohen, Boaz: *Jewish and Roman Law: A Comparative Study*. 2 vols. New York: Jewish Theological Seminary of America, 1966.

Cohen, Shaye J. D.: "Was Judaism in Antiquity a Missionary Religion?" In: *Jewish Assimilation, Acculturation and Accomodation. Past Traditions, Current Issues and Future Prospects*, edited by M. Mor, 14–23. Studies in Jewish Civilization. Lanham: University Press of America, 1992.

Cohn-Sherbok, Daniel M.: "An Analysis of Jesus' Arguments Concerning the Plucking of Grain on the Sabbath." *JSNT* 1979 (1979): 31–41.

Collins, John J.: "The Son of Man in First Century Judaism." *NTS* 38 (1992): 448–466.

Collins, Raymond F.: *Divorce in the New Testament*. GNS 38. Collegeville: Glazier, 1992.

Cook, Michael J.: "Interpreting 'Pro-Jewish' Passages in Matthew." *HUCA* 54 (1983): 135–146.

Cope, O. Lamar: *Matthew. A Scribe Trained For the Kingdom of Heaven*. CBQ.MS 5. Washington: The Catholic Biblical Association, 1976.

Coser, Lewis A.: *The Functions of Social Conflict*. New York: Free Press, 1964.

Cotter, Wendy J.: "For It Was Not The Season For Figs." *CBQ* 48 (1986): 62–66.

Dahl, Niels A.: "Die Passionsgeschichte bei Matthaeus." In: *Redaktion und Theologie des Passionsberichtes bei den Synoptikern*, edited by Meinrad Limbeck, 205–225. WdF. Darmstadt: Wissenschaftliche Buchgesellschaft, 1981. First published in: *NTS* 2 (1955/56) 17–32.

Danby, Herbert: *The Mishnah*. Oxford: Oxford University Press, 1933.

Daube, David.: "Rabbinic Methods of Interpretation and Hellenistic Rhetoric." *HUCA* 22 (1949): 239–264.

—: *The New Testament and Rabbinic Judaism*. Peabody: Hendrickson, 1956.

—: "The Responsibilities of Master and Disciples in the Gospels." *NTS* 19 (1972): 1–15.

Davies, Margaret: *Matthew*. Readings: A New Biblical Commentary. Sheffield: JSOT Press, 1993.

Davies, William D.: *The Setting of the Sermon on the Mount*. Cambridge: Cambridge University Press, 1966.

Davies, William D., and Dale C. Allison: *A Critical and Exegetical Commentary on the Gospel According to St. Matthew*. 3 vols. ICC. Edinburgh: T. & T. Clark, 1988–1997.

Delling, Gerhard.: "Ehescheidung." In: *RAC* 4, edited by T. Klausner, 707–719. Stuttgart: Hiersemann, 1959.

Derrett, John D.: "'Render to Caesar...'." In: *Law in the New Testament*, 313–338. London: Longman & Todd, 1970.

Deutsch, Celia: "Wisdom in Matthew: Transformation of a Symbol." *NT* 32 (1990): 13–47.

Dewey, Joanna: *Markan Public Debate*. SBL.DS 48. Chico: Scholars Press, 1980.

Dibelius, Martin: "Zur Formgeschichte der Evangelien." *ThR* 1 (1929): 191–198.

—: *From Tradition to Gospel*. New York: Scribners, 1934.

—: *Die Formgeschichte des Evangeliums*. 3rd ed. Tübingen: Mohr, 1959.

Dobschütz, Ernst von: "Matthäus als Rabbi und Katechet." *ZNW* 27 (1928): 338–348.

Dodd, Charles H.: *The Parables of the Kingdom*. New York: Scribner, 1961.

Donaldson, Terrence A.: "The Law That Hangs (Matthew 22:40): Rabbinic Formulation and Matthean Social World." *CBQ* 57 (1995): 689–709.

Downing, F. Gerald: "Towards a Rehabilitation of Q." *NTS* 11 (1964): 169–181.

Doyle, B. Rod: "A Concern of the Evangelist: Pharisees in Matthew 12." *ABR* 34 (1986): 17–34.

Duling, Dennis C.: "The Therapeutic Son of David. An Element in Matthew's Christologi-
    cal Apologetic." *NTS* 24 (1977–78): 392–410.
Dunn, James D. G.: *Jesus and the Spirit. The Religious and Charismatic Experience of
    Jesus and the First Christians According to the New Testament.* Philadelphia:
    Westminster, 1975.
—: *Christology in the Making.* Philadelphia: Westminster, 1980.
—: *Unity and Diversity in the New Testament. An Inquiry into the Character of Earliest
    Christianity.* 2nd ed. Philadelphia: Trinity Press International, 1990.
—: *The Parting of the Ways.* Philadelphia: Trinity, 1991.
Edwards, James: "Matthew's Use of Q in Chapter Eleven." In: *Logia: Les paroles de
    Jésus. The Sayings of Jesus. Mémorial Joseph Coppens,* edited by J. Delobel and
    T. Baarda, 257–275. BEThL 59. Leuven: Uitgeverij Peeters, 1982.
Edwards, Richard A.: *Matthew's Story of Jesus.* Philadelphia: Fortress, 1985.
—: *Matthew's Narrative Portrait of Disciples. How the Text-Connoted Reader is
    Informed.* Harrisburg: Trinity Press International, 1997.
Ellis, Peter F.: *Matthew: His Mind and His Message.* Collegeville: Glazier, 1974.
Ennulat, Andreas: *Die "Minor Agreements": Untersuchung zu einer offenen Frage des
    synoptischen Problems.* WUNT 2/62. Tübingen: Mohr [Siebeck], 1994.
Eppstein, Victor: "Historicity of the Gospel Account of the Cleansing of the Temple." *ZNW*
    55 (1964): 42–58.
Evans, Craig A.: "Jesus' Action in the Temple: Cleansing or Portent of Destruction?" *CBQ*
    51 (1989): 237–270.
Farmer, William R.: *The Synoptic Problem: A Critical Analysis.* New York: Macmillan,
    1964.
Feldtkeller, Andreas: *Identitätssuche des syrischen Urchristentums: Mission, Inkulturation
    und Pluralität im ältesten Heidenchristentum.* Freiburg, Göttingen: Universitäts-
    verlag, Vandenhoeck & Ruprecht, 1993.
Fenton, John C.: *The Gospel of St. Matthew.* PGC. Baltimore: Penguin, 1964.
Fitzmyer, Joseph A.: "Anti-Semitism and the Cry of 'All the People' (Mt 27:25)." *TS* 26
    (1965): 667–671.
—: "Matthean Divorce Texts and Some New Palestinian Evidence." *TS* 37 (1976):
    197–226.
—: "Divorce Among First-Century Jews." *ErIs* 14 (1978): 103–110.
—: "The Semitic Background For the New Testament *Kyrios*-Title." In: *A Wandering
    Aramean. Collected Aramaic Essays,* 120–123. SBL.DS 25. Missoula: Scholars
    Press, 1979.
—: *The Gospel According to Luke.* 2 vols. AncB 28–28A. New York, London, Toronto,
    Sydney, Auckland: Doubleday, 1983.
Foerster, Werner: "ἔξεστιν κ.τ.λ.," *TDNT* 2:560–575.
Forster, Edward M.: *Aspects of the Novel.* New York: Harcourt, Brace & World, 1954.
The Four Gospels: A New Translation. Edited and translated by Charles C. Torrey. New
    York: Harper & Row, 1933.
Frankemölle, Hubert: *Jahwebund und Kirche Christi.* NTA 10. Münster: Aschendorff,
    1974.

—: "'Pharisäismus' in Judentum und Kirche. Zur Tradition und Redaktion in Matthäus 23." In: *Biblische Handlungsanweisungen. Beispiele pragmatischer Exegese*, edited by H. Frankemölle, 133–190. Mainz, 1983.

—: *Das Matthäusevangelium*. 2 vols. Düsseldorf: Patmos, 1997, 1999.

Fridrichsen, Anton: "Le péché contre le Saint-Esprit." *RHPhR* 3 (1923): 367–372.

—: "*Excepta fornicationis causa.*" *SEÅ* 9 (1944–1945): 54–58.

Friedrich, Gerhard: "Die formale Struktur von Mt 28, 18–20." *ZThK* 80 (1983): 137–183.

Froleyks, Wilhelm J.: "Der Agon Logon in der antiken Literatur." diss, Bonn: Universität Bonn, 1973.

Fuller, Reginald H.: *The Mission and Achievement of Jesus. An Examination of the Presuppositions of New Testament Theology*. SBT 12. Chicago: Allenson, 1954.

—: "Das Doppelgebot der Liebe." In: *Jesus Christus in Historie und Theologie. FS Hans Conzelmann*, edited by Luise Schottroff, 317–329. Tübingen: Mohr, 1975.

Funk, Robert W.: "The Form of the New Testament Healing Miracle Story." *Semeia* 12 (1978): 57–96.

Gaechter, Paul: *Das Matthäusevangelium. Ein Kommentar*. Innsbruck: Tyrolia, 1963.

Gager, John G.: *Community and Kingdom. The Social World of Early Christians*. Englewood Cliffs: Prentiss, 1983.

Gagg, Robert P.: "Jesus und die Davidssohnfrage. Zur Exegese von Markus 12,35–37." *ThZ* 7 (1951): 18–30.

Garland, David E.: *The Intention of Matthew 23*. NTTS 52. Leiden: Brill, 1979.

—: *Reading Matthew: A Literary and Theological Commentary on the First Gospel*. Reading the New Testament. New York: Crossroads, 1993.

Gaston, Lloyd: "The Messiah of Israel as Teacher of the Gentiles." *Interp* 29 (1975): 24–40.

Geist, Heinz: "Jesusverkündigung im Matthäusevangelium." In: *Jesus in den Evangelien*, edited by W. Pesch, 105–126. Stuttgart: Katholisches Bibelwerk, 1970.

Gerhardsson, Birger: *Memory and Manuscript: Oral Tradition and Written Transmission in Rabbinic Judaism and Early Christianity*. ASNU 22. Lund, Copenhagen: Gleerup, Munksgaard, 1961.

—: *The Mighty Acts of Jesus According to Matthew*. Lund: C. W. K. Gleerup, 1979.

—: "Die Passionsgeschichte bei Matthaeus." In: *Redaktion und Theologie des Passionsberichtes bei den Synoptikern*, edited by Meinrad Limbeck, 263–291. WdF. Darmstadt: Wissenschaftliche Buchgesellschaft, 1981. First published as "Utlämnad och övergiven. Till förståelsen av passionshistorien i Matteusevangeliet." In: *SEÅ* 32 (1967) 92–120.

Gibbs, James M.: "Purpose and Pattern in Matthew's Use of the Title "Son of David"." *NTS* 10 (1963–1964): 446–464.

Giblin, Charles H.: "'The Things of God' in the Question Concerning Tribute to Caesar." *CBQ* 33 (1971): 510–527.

Glasson, T. Francis: "The Ensign of the Son of Man (Matt XXIV.30)." *JThS* 15 (1964): 299–300.

Gnilka, Joachim: *Das Evangelium nach Markus*, 2 vols. EKK II,1–2. Zürich, Einsiedeln, Köln, Neukirchen: Benziger, Neukirchener, 1978–1979.

—: *Das Matthäusevangelium*, 2 vols. HThKNT 1. Freiburg, Basel, Wien: Herder, 1986–1988.

358   Bibliography

Goldin, Judah: *Abot de Rabbi Natan A*. YJS X. New Haven: Yale University Press, 1955.
Goodman, Martin: *The Ruling Class of Judaea. The Origins of the Jewish Revolt Against Rome 66–70*. Cambridge: Cambridge University Press, 1987.
—: *Mission and Conversion. Proselytizing in the Religious History of the Roman Empire*. Oxford: Clarendon Press, 1994.
Goodspeed, Edgar J.: *Matthew, Apostle and Evangelist*. Philadelphia: Winston, 1959.
Goppelt, Leonhard: *Die Freiheit zur Kaisersteuer: Christologie und Ethik*. München: Kaiser, 1968.
Goulder, Michael D.: *Midrash and Lection in Matthew*. London: SPCK, 1974.
Grams, Rollin: "The Temple Conflict Scene: A Rhetorical Analysis of Matthew 21–23." In: *Persuasive Artistry. Studies in New Testament Rhetoric in Honor of George A. Kennedy*, edited by Duane F. Watson, 41–65. JSNT.S 50. Sheffield: JSOT Press, 1991.
Green, H. Benedict: *The Gospel According to Matthew*. New Clarendon Bible. New Testament. London: Oxford University Press, 1975.
—: "Matthew 28:19, Eusebius, and the *lex orandi*." In: *The Making of Orthodoxy: Essays in Honor of Henry Chadwick*, edited by Rowan Williams, 124–141. Cambridge: Cambridge University Press, 1989.
Greeven, Heinrich: "'Wer unter Euch...?'." *WuD* 3 (1952): 86–101.
—: "Die Heilung des Gelähmten nach Matthäus." *WuD* 4 (1955): 65–78.
Grundmann, Walter: *Das Evangelium nach Matthäus*. ThKNT. Berlin: Evangelische Verlagsanstalt, 1968.
—: *Das Evangelium nach Markus*. ThHK 2. Freiburg: Herder, 1974.
Guelich, Robert: *The Sermon on the Mount: A Foundation For Understanding*. Waco: Word Books, 1982.
Gundry, Robert H.: *The Use of the Old Testament in St. Matthew's Gospel*. Leiden: Brill, 1967.
—: *Mark. A Commentary on His Apology For the Cross*. Grand Rapids: Eerdmans, 1993.
—: *Matthew. A Commentary on His Handbook for a Mixed Church Under Persecution*. 2nd ed. Grand Rapids: Eerdmans, 1994. First ed. 1982.
—: "Εὐαγγέλιον: How Soon a Book?" *JBL* 115 (1996): 321–325.
Hagner, Donald A.: *The Jewish Reclamation of Jesus*. Grand Rapids: Zondervan, 1984.
—: *Matthew 1–13*. Word Biblical Commentary 33A. Dallas: Word Books, 1993.
—: *Matthew 14–28*. Word Biblical Commentary 33B. Dallas: Word Books, 1993.
Hare, Douglas R.: *The Theme of Jewish Persecution of Christians in the Gospel According to St. Matthew*. Cambridge: Cambridge University Press, 1967.
Hare, Douglas R., and Daniel J. Harrington: "'Make Disciples of All the Gentiles' (Mt 28:19)." *CBQ* 37 (1975): 359–369.
Harnack, Adolf von: *Die Mission und Ausbreitung des Christentums in den ersten drei Jahrhunderten*. 4th ed. Leipzig: Hinrich'sche Buchhandlung, 1924.
Harrington, Daniel J.: "Matthean Studies Since Joachim Rohde." *HeyJ* 16 (1975): 375–388.
—: *The Gospel of Matthew*. Sacra Pagina 1. Collegeville: Liturgical Press, 1991.
—: "The Rich Young Man in Mt 19,16–22: Another Way to God for Jews." In: *The Four Gospels 1992. Festschrift Frans Neirynck*, edited by Frans van Segbroeck,

Christopher M. Tuckett, et al., 1425–1432. Leuven: Leuven University Press & Uitgeverij Peeters, 1992.

Haut, Irwin H: *Divorce in Jewish Law and Life*. Studies in Jewish Jurisprudence 5. New York: Sepher-Hermon, 1983.

Hay, David M.: *Glory at the Right Hand. Psalm 110 in Early Christianity*. SBL.MS 18. Nashville: Abingdon, 1973.

Hay, Lewis S.: "The Son of Man in Mark 2,10 and 2,28f." *JBL* 89 (1970): 69–75.

Hays, Richard B.: *The Moral Vision of the New Testament. A Contemporary Introduction to New Testament Ethics*. San Francisco: Harper, 1996.

Held, Heinz J.: "Matthew as Interpreter of the Miracle Stories." In: *Tradition and Interpretation in Matthew*, edited by G. Bornkamm, Gerhard Barth and Heinz Joachim Held, 165–300. Philadelphia: Westminster, 1963.

Hicks, John M.: "The Sabbath Controversy in Matthew: An Exegesis of Matthew 12:1–14." *RestQ* 27 (1984): 79–91.

Hilgenfeld, Adolf: *Die Evangelien nach ihrer Entstehung und geschichtlichen Bedeutung*. ATLA monograph preservation program 1986–3547. Leipzig: S. Hirzel, 1854.

Hill, David: *The Gospel of Matthew*. NCeB. London: Marshall, Morgan & Scott, 1972.

—: "False Prophets and Charismatics: Structure and Interpretation in Matthew 7,15–23." *Bib* 57 (1976): 327–348.

—: "On the Use and Meaning of Hosea VI. 6 in Matthew's Gospel." *NTS* 24 (1977): 107–119.

Hirunuma, Toshio: "Matthew 16, 2b–3." In: *New Testament Textual Criticism: Its Significance for Exegesis. Essays in Honor of Bruce M. Metzger*, edited by Eldon J. Epp and Gordon D. Fee, 35–45. New York: Oxford University Press, 1981.

Hock, Ronald F., and Edward N. O'Neil: *The Chreia in Ancient Rhetoric*. Vol. 1, *The Progymnasmata*. Atlanta: Scholars Press, 1986.

Hodgson, Robert: "The Testimony Hypothesis." *JBL* 98 (1979): 361–378.

Holtzmann, Heinrich Julius: *Die synoptischen Evangelien: ihr Ursprung und geschichtlicher Charakter*. ATLA monograph preservation program 1987–1158. Leipzig: Wilhelm Engelmann, 1863.

—: *Lehrbuch der neutestamentlichen Theologie*. 2 vols. Edited by Adolf Jülicher and Walter Bauer. Sammlung theologischer Lehrbücher. ATLA monograph preservation program 1987–0091. Tübingen: J.C.B. Mohr (Paul Siebeck), 1911.

Hooker, Morna D.: *The Son of Man in Mark. A Study of the Background of the Term "Son of Man" and Its Use in St. Mark's Gospel*. Montreal: MacGill University Press, 1967.

Howell, David B.: *Matthew's Inclusive Story. A Study in the Narrative Rhetoric of the First Gospel*. JSOT.SS 42. Sheffield: JSOT Press, 1990.

Hubbard, Benjamin J.: *The Matthean Redaction of a Primitive Apostolic Commissioning: An Exegesis of Matthew 28:16–20*. SBL.DS 19. Missoula: Scholars, 1974.

Huber, Konrad: *Jesus in Auseinandersetzung. Exegetische Untersuchungen zu den sogenannten Jerusalemer Streitgesprächen des Markusevangeliums im Blick auf ihre christologischen Implikationen*. fzb 75. Würzburg: Echter, 1995.

Hultgren, Arland: "The Double Commandment of Love in Mt 22:34–40. Its Sources and Compositions." *CBQ* 36 (1974): 373–378.

—: *Jesus and His Adversaries: The Form and Function of the Conflict Stories in the Synoptic Tradition*. Minneapolis: Augsburg, 1979.

Hummel, Reinhart: *Die Auseinandersetzung zwischen Kirche und Judentum im Matthäusevangelium*. München: Kaiser, 1963.

Iersel, Bastian M. F. van: "Fils de David et fils de dieu." In: *La venue du Messie. Messianisme et eschatologie*, edited by E. Massaux, 113–132. Paris: Desclée, 1962.

Jeremias, Joachim: *The Parables of Jesus*. Translated by S. H. Hooke. New York: Scribner, 1963.

—: *Jesus' Promise to the Nations*. 2nd ed. Translated by S. H. Hooke. London: SCM Press, 1967.

—: *New Testament Theology*. Translated by S. H. Hooke. New York: Scribner, 1971.

Johnson, Luke T.: "The New Testament's Anti-Jewish Slander and the Conventions of Ancient Polemic." *JBL* 108 (1989): 419–441.

Johnson, Marshall D.: "Reflections on a Wisdom Approach to Matthew's Christology." *CBQ* 36 (1974): 44–64.

Juster, Jean: *Les juifs dans l'Empire romain: Leur condition juridique, économique et sociale*. 2 vols. 2nd ed. New York: B. Franklin, 1965.

Kee, Howard C.: *Community of the New Age: Studies in Mark's Gospel*. Philadelphia: Westminster, 1977.

Kennedy, George A.: "Classical and Christian Source Criticism." In: *The Relationships Among the Gospels: An Interdisciplinary Dialogue*, edited by W. O. Walker, 125–155. TUMSR 5. San Antonio: Trinity University Press, 1978.

—: *A New History of Classical Rhetoric*. Princeton: Princeton University Press, 1994.

Kertelge, Karl: *Die Wunder Jesu im Markusevangelium. Eine redaktionsgeschichtliche Untersuchung*. StANT 33. München: Kösel, 1970.

Kilpatrick, George D.: *The Origins of the Gospel According to St. Matthew*. Oxford: Clarendon, 1946.

Kimbrough, Stephen T.: "The Concept of Sabbath at Qumran." *RdQ* 5 (1966): 483–502.

Kingsbury, Jack D.: *The Parables of Jesus in Matthew 13: A Study in Redaction Criticism*. Richmond: John Knox, 1969.

—: "The Composition and Christology of Matt 28:16–20." *JBL* 93 (1974): 573–584.

—: *Matthew: Structure, Christology, and Kingdom*. Philadelphia: Fortress, 1975.

—: "The Title "Son of David" in Matthew's Gospel." *JBL* 95 (1976): 591–602.

—: "Observations on the "Miracle Chapters" of Matthew 8–9." *CBQ* 40 (1978): 559–573.

—: "The Verb *Akolouthein* ("To Follow") as an Index of Matthew's View of His Community." *JBL* 97 (1978): 56–73.

—: "The Figure of Jesus in Matthew's Story: A Literary–Critical Probe." *JSNT* 21 (1984): 3–36.

—: "The Developing Conflict Between Jesus and the Jewish Leaders in Matthew's Gospel: A Literary-Critical Study." *CBQ* 49 (1987): 57–73.

—: *Matthew as Story*. 2nd ed. Philadelphia: Fortress, 1988.

Klauck, Hans-Josef: "Die Frage der Sündenvergebung in der Perikope von der Heilung des Gelähmten (Mk 2.1–12 parr.)." *BZ* 25 (1981): 223–248.

—, ed.: *Weltgericht und Weltvollendung: Zukunftsbilder im Neuen Testament*. QD 150. Freiburg: Herder, 1994.

Kloppenborg, John S.: *The Formation of Q. Trajectories in Ancient Wisdom Collections*. Studies in Antiquity and Christianity. Philadelphia: Fortress, 1987.

—: *Q Parallels. Synopsis, Critical Notes & Concordance*. Foundation and Facets Reference Series. Sonoma: Polebridge Press, 1988.

Klostermann, Erich: *Das Matthäusevangelium*. HNT 4. Tübingen: Mohr, 1927.

Koch, Dietrich A.: *Die Bedeutung der Wundererzählungen für die Christologie des Markusevangeliums*. Berlin: De Gruyter, 1975.

Krentz, Edgar: "The Extent of Matthew's Prologue." *JBL* 83 (1964): 409–414.

Kunzel, Georg: *Studien zum Gemeindeverständnis des Matthäus-Evangeliums*. CThM.BW 10. Stuttgart: Calwer Verlag, 1978. 295 pp.

Kürzinger, Josef: "Das Papiaszeugnis und die Erstgestalt des Matthäusevangeliums." *BZ* 4 (1960): 19–38.

—: "Irenäus und sein Zeugnis zur Sprache des Matthäusevangeliums." *NTS* 10 (1963): 108–115.

Lambrecht, Jan: *The Sermon on the Mount: Proclamation and Exhortation*. GNS 14. Wilmington: Glazier, 1985.

Lange, Joachim: *Das Erscheinen des Auferstandenen im Evangelium nach Matthäus. Eine traditionsgeschichtliche und redaktionsgeschichtliche Untersuchung zu Mt 28, 16–20*. Würzburg: Echter, 1973.

Lausberg, Heinrich: *Handbuch der Literarischen Rhetorik. Eine Grundlegung der Literaturwissenschaft*. 3rd ed. Stuttgart: Franz Steiner, 1989.

Lemcio, Eugene E.: "The Parables of the Great Supper and the Wedding Feast: History, Redaction and Canon." *HBT* 8 (1986): 1–26.

Légasse, Simon: "L'Antijudaïsme dans l'évangile selon Matthieu." In: *L'évangile selon Matthieu. Rédaction et Théologie*, edited by M. Didier, 417–428. BEThL 29. Louvain: Gembloux, 1971.

Liddell, Henry George, and Robert Scott: *A Greek-English Lexicon*. 9th ed. Oxford: Clarendon, 1996.

Liebers, Reinhold: *"Wie geschrieben steht": Studien zu einer besonderen Art frühchristlichen Schriftbezuges*. Berlin, New York: De Gruyter, 1993.

Lienemann, Wolfgang, ed.: *Die Finanzen der Kirche*. München: Kaiser, 1989.

Lindars, Barnabas: *New Testament Apologetic: The Doctrinal Significance of the Old Testament Quotations*. London: SCM Press, 1973.

—: *Jesus Son of Man*. London: SCM Press, 1982.

Lloyd, Michael: *The Agon in Euripides*. Oxford: Clarendon Press, 1992.

Loader, William R.: "Christ at the Right Hand – Ps. CX.1 in the New Testament." *NTS* 24 (1978): 199–217.

Lohmeyer, Ernst: "Das Gleichnis von den bösen Weingärtnern (Mark 12:1–12)." *ZSTh* 18 (1941): 242–259.

—: *Das Evangelium des Matthäus*. KEK.S. Göttingen: Vandenhoeck & Ruprecht, 1956.

Luz, Ulrich: "Jesus in der vormarkinischen Tradition." In: *Jesus Christus in Historie und Theologie. Neutestamentliche Festschrift für Hans Conzelmann zum 60. Geburtstag*, edited by Georg Strecker, 347–374. Tübingen: Mohr (Siebeck), 1975.

—: "Die Jünger im Matthäusevangelium." In: *Das Matthäusevangelium*, edited by Joachim Lange, 377–414. Darmstadt: Wissenschaftliche Buchgesellschaft, 1980. First published in: *ZNW* 62 (1971) 141–171.

—: *Das Evangelium nach Matthäus*. 4 vols. EKK I. Zürich: Benziger, Neukirchener, 1985–.

—: *Matthew in History. Interpretation, Influence, and Effects*. Philadelphia: Fortress, 1994.

—: *The Theology of the Gospel of Matthew*. New Testament Theology. Cambridge, New York: Cambridge University Press, 1995.

Mack, Burton L.: *Rhetoric and the New Testament*. Minneapolis: Fortress, 1990.

—: "Persuasive Pronouncements: An Evaluation of Recent Studies on the Chreia." *Semeia* 64 (1994): 283–287.

McConnel, Richard J.: *Law and Prophecy in Matthew's Gospel: The Authority and Use of the Old Testament in the Gospel of Matthew*. Basel: Kommissionsverlag Friedrich Reinhardt, 1969.

McKnight, Scot: *A Light Among the Gentiles. Jewish Missionary Activity in the Second Temple Period*. Minneapolis: Fortress, 1991.

MacMullen, Ramsay: *Roman Social Relations*. New Haven: Yale University Press, 1974.

McNeile, Alan H.: *The Gospel According to St. Matthew*. London: Macmillan, 1915.

Mack, Burton L., and Vernon K. Robbins: *Patterns of Persuasion in the Gospels*. Foundations and Facets: Literary Facets. Sonoma: Polebridge, 1989.

Mahoney, Aidan: "A New Look at the Divorce Clauses in Mt 5:32 and 19:9." *CBQ* 30 (1968): 29–38.

Maier, Gerhard: *Das Matthäusevangelium*. 2 vols. Bibel-Kommentar. Neuhausen, Stuttgart: Hänssler, 1979.

Maisch, Ingrid: *Die Heilung des Gelähmten. Eine exegetisch-traditionsgeschichtliche Untersuchung zu Mk 2,1–12*. SBS 52. Stuttgart: Katholisches Bibelwerk, 1971.

Malina, Bruce J.: "The Literary Structure and Form of Matt. XXVIII. 16–20." *NTS* (1970): 87–103.

—: "Arland J. Hultgren: *Jesus and His Adversaries* (Book Review)." *CBQ* 43 (1981): 131–133.

Malina, Bruce J., and Jerome H. Neyrey: *Calling Jesus Names: The Social Value of Labels in Matthew*. Sonoma: Polebridge, 1988.

—: "Honor and Shame in Luke-Acts: Pivotal Values of the Mediterranean World." In: *The Social World of Luke-Acts. Models for Interpretation*, edited by Jerome H. Neyrey, 25–65. Peabody: Hendrickson, 1991.

Manson, Thomas W.: "Mark 2:27f." *CNT* 11 (1947): 141–152.

—: *The Sayings of Jesus, as Recorded in the Gospels According to St. Matthew and St. Luke*. London: SCM Press, 1949.

Marco, Mariano H.: "Las espigas arrancadas es sábado (Mt 12,1–8 par)." *EstB* 28 (1969): 313–348.

Martin, Ralph P.: *Mark: Evangelist and Theologian*. Grand Rapids: Zondervan, 1973.

Massaux, Edouard: *The Influence of the Gospel of Saint Matthew on Christian Literature Before Saint Irenaeus*. 3 vols. Translated by J. Bellinzoni. New Gospel Studies 5. Macon: Mercer, 1990.

Meeks, Wayne A.: *The First Urban Christians. The Social World of the Apostle Paul*. New Haven: Yale University Press, 1983.

Meier, John P.: *Law and History in Matthew's Gospel*. AnBib 71. Rome: Biblical Institute Press, 1976.

—: "Nations or Gentiles in Matthew 28:19?" *CBQ* 39 (1977): 94–102.

—: "Two Disputed Questions in Matt. 28. 16–20." *JBL* 96 (1977): 407–424.

—: *The Vision of Matthew. Christ, Church and Morality in the First Gospel.* Theological Inquiries. New York, Ramsay, Toronto: Paulist, 1979.

—: *A Marginal Jew. Rethinking the Historical Jesus.* 3 vols. AncB.RL. New York, London, Toronto, Sydney, Auckland: Doubleday, 1992–.

Menninger, Richard E.: *Israel and the Church in the Gospel of Matthew.* AmUSt.TR 162. New York: Peter Lang, 1994.

Metzger, Bruce M.: *A Textual Commentary on the Greek New Testament.* 2nd ed. New York: United Bible Societies, 1994.

Michel, Otto: "Der Abschluß des Matthäusevangeliums." *EvTh* 10 (1950): 16–26.

Moiser, Jeremy: "The Structure of Matthew 8–9: A Suggestion." *ZNW* 76 (1985): 117–118.

Moloney, Francis J.: "Matthew 19, 3–12 And Celibacy. A Redactional And Form Critical Study." *JSNT* 2 (1979): 42–60.

Mora, Vincent: *Le refus d'Israël. Matthieu 27,25.* LeDiv 124. Paris: Cerf, 1986.

Morris, Leon: *The Gospel According to Matthew.* Pillar Commentary. Grand Rapids: Eerdmans, 1992.

Moule, Charles F. D.: "St. Matthew's Gospel: Some Neglected Features." In: *Studia Evangelica II,* 91–99. TU 88. Berlin: Akademie-Verlag, 1964.

Munck, Johannes: *Paul and the Salvation of Mankind.* Richmond: John Knox, 1959.

Myers, Ched: *Binding the Strong Man.* Maryknoll: Orbis, 1988.

Negoita, Athanase, and Constantine Daniel: "L'enigme du levain." *NT* 9 (1967): 306–314.

Neirynck, Frans: "La rédaction matthéenne et la structure du premier évangile." *EThL* 43 (1967): 41–73.

—: "Les accords mineurs et la rédaction des évangiles. L'épisode du paralytique (Mt IX 1–8 / Lc V 17–26, par. Mc II 1–12)." *EThL* 50 (1974): 15–30.

Nepper-Christensen, Poul: *Das Matthaeusevangelium. Ein judenchristliches Evangelium?* AThD 1. Aarhus: Universitetsforlaget, 1958.

Neugebauer, Fritz: "Die Davidssohnfrage (Mark xii.35–37 parr.) und der Menschensohn." *NTS* 21 (1975): 81–108.

Neusner, Jacob: "The Formation of Rabbinic Judaism: Yavneh from 70–100." In: *ANRW* II,19,2, edited by W. Haase and H. Temporini, 3–42. Berlin: De Gruyter, 1979.

—: *Judaism: The Evidence of the Mishnah.* Chicago: University of Chicago Press, 1981.

—: *Formative Judaism.* 5 vols. Chico: Scholars Press, 1982–1985.

Newport, Kenneth G.: *The Sources and Sitz im Leben of Matthew 23.* JSNT.S 117. Sheffield: Sheffield Academic Press, 1995.

Nickelsburg, George W. E.: *Jewish Literature Between the Bible and the Mishnah. A Historical and Literary Introduction.* Philadelphia: Fortress, 1981.

Norton, David: *A History of the Bible as Literature.* 2. vols. Cambridge: Cambridge University Press, 1993.

Ogawa, Akira: "Paraboles de l'Israel véritable? Reconsidération critique de Mt 21,28–22,14." *NT* 21 (1979): 121–149.

Orton, David E.: *The Understanding Scribe: Matthew and the Apocalyptic Ideal.* MSSNTS 25. Sheffield: JSOT Press, 1989.

Osten-Sacken, Peter von der: "Streitgespräch und Parabel als Formen Markinischer Christologie." In: *Jesus Christus in Historie und Theologie. Neutestamentliche Festschrift für Hans Conzelmann zum 60. Geburtstag*, edited by Georg Strecker, 375–394. Tübingen: Mohr (Siebeck), 1975.

Overman, J. Andrew: *Matthew's Gospel and Formative Judaism. The Social World of the Matthean Community*. Minneapolis: Fortress Press, 1990.

—: *Church and Community in Crisis. The Gospel According to Matthew*. The New Testament Message in Context. Valley Forge: Trinity Press International, 1996.

O'Neill, John C.: "The Source of the Parables of the Bridegroom and the Wicked Husbandmen." *JThS* 39 (1988): 485–489.

Patte, Daniel: *The Gospel According to Matthew. A Structural Commentary on Matthew's Faith*. Philadelphia: Fortress, 1987.

Perrin, Norman: *Rediscovering the Teaching of Jesus*. New York: Harper & Row, 1967.

Persuasive Artistry: Studies in NT Rhetoric in Honor of George Kennedy. Edited by Duane F. Watson. Sheffield: JSOT Press, 1991.

Pesch, Rudolf: *Das Markusevangelium*. 2 vols. HThK. Freiburg: Herder, 1977.

Pesch, Wilhelm: "Theologische Aussagen der Redaktion von Matthäus 23." In: *Orientierung an Jesus. Für J. Schmidt*, edited by Norbert Brox, Paul Hoffmann and Wilhelm Pesch, 286–299. Freiburg, Basel, Wien: Herder, 1973.

Plummer, Alfred: *An Exegetical Commentary on the Gospel According to St. Matthew*. London: R. Scott, 1915.

Poulos, Paula N.: "Form and Function of the Pronouncement Stories in Diogenes Laërtius' *Lives*." *Semeia* 20 (1981): 53–64.

Powell, J. Enoch: *The Evolution of the Gospel: A New Translation of the First Gospel with Commentary and Introductory Essay*. New Haven, London: Yale University Press, 1994.

Powell, Mark A.: *What is Narrative Criticism?* Philadelphia: Fortress, 1990.

—: "The Plot and Subplots of Matthew's Gospel." *NTS* 38 (1992): 187–204.

—: "Do and Keep What Moses Says (Matthew 23:2–7)." *JBL* 114 (1995): 419–435.

—: "A Typology of Worship in the Gospel of Matthew." *JSNT* 57 (1995): 3–17.

Przybylski, Benno: *Righteousness in Matthew and His World of Thought*. Cambridge, New York: Cambridge University Press, 1980.

—: "The Setting of Matthean Anti-Judaism." In: *Anti-Judaism in Early Christianity*, edited by Peter Richardson and David Granskou, 181–200. Waterloo: Wilfrid Laurier University Press, 1986.

Rengstorf, Karl Heinz: *Kirche und Synagoge: Handbuch zur Geschichte von Christen und Juden I*. Stuttgart: Klett, 1968.

Reuss, Eduard: *Geschichte der heiligen Schriften, Neuen Testamentes*. Braunschweig: C. A. Schwetschke und Sohn (M. Bruhn), 1860.

Rist, John M.: *On the Independence of Matthew and Mark*. MSSNTS 32. Cambridge; New York: Cambridge University Press, 1978.

Robbins, Vernon K.: *Jesus the Teacher. A Socio-Rhetorical Interpretation of Mark*. Philadelphia: Fortress Press, 1984.

—: "Rhetorical Composition and the Beelzebul Controversy." In: *Patterns of Persuasion*, edited by Burton L. Mack and Vernon K. Robbins, 161–193. Sonoma: Polebridge, 1989.

—: "Introduction: Using Rhetorical Discussion of the Chreia to Interpret Pronouncement Stories." *Semeia* 64 (1994): vii–xvii.

Robinson, James M.: "The International Q Project Work Sessions 12–14 July, 22 November 1991." *JBL* 111 (1992): 500–508.

Rohde, Joachim: *Rediscovering the Teaching of the Evangelists*. NTLi. Philadelphia: Westminster Press, 1968.

Rohrbaugh, Richard L.: "The Pre-Industrial City in Luke-Acts: Urban Social Relations." In: *The Social World of Luke-Acts*, edited by Jerome H. Neyrey, 125–149. Peabody: Hendrickson, 1991.

Rokéah, David: *Jews, Pagans and Christian in Conflict*. Jerusalem: Magnes Press, 1982.

Roloff, Jürgen: *Das Kerygma und der irdische Jesus. Historische Motive in den Jesuserzählungen der Evangelien*. Göttingen: Vandenhoeck & Rupprecht, 1970.

Rothfuchs, Wilhelm: *Die Erfüllungszitate des Matthäus-Evangeliums: Eine biblisch-theologische Untersuchung*. BWANT 5/8. Stuttgart: Kohlhammer, 1969.

Safrai, Samuel: *The Literature of the Sages*. CRI 2/3. Philadelphia: Fortress, 1987.

Saldarini, Anthony J.: *The Fathers According to Rabbi Nathan (Abot de Rabbi Natan) Version B*. SJLA 11. Leiden: Brill, 1975.

—: *Pharisees, Scribes, and Sadducees in Palestinian Society*. Wilmington: Glazier, 1988.

—: "The Gospel of Matthew and the Jewish-Christian Conflict." In: *Social History of the Matthean Community: Cross-Disciplinary Approaches*, edited by David L. Balch, 38–61. Minneapolis: Fortress Press, 1991.

—: "Delegitimation of Leaders in Matthew 23." *CBQ* 54 (1992): 649–680.

—: *Matthew's Christian-Jewish Community*. Chicago, London: University of Chicago Press, 1994.

Sand, Alexander: *Das Gestz und die Propheten*. Regensburg: Pustet, 1974.

—: *Das Evangelium nach Matthäus*. RNT. Regensburg: Pustet, 1986.

Sanders, Ed P.: *The Tendencies of the Synoptic Tradition*. Cambridge: Cambridge University Press, 1969.

—: "Priorités et dépendances dans la tradition synoptique." *RSR* 60 (1972): 519–540.

—: "Jesus and the Constraint of the Law." *JSNT* 17 (1983): 19–24.

—: *Jesus and Judaism*. Philadelphia: Fortress Press, 1985.

—: *Judaism. Practice and Belief 63 BCE–66 CE*. London, Philadelphia: SCM Press, Trinity Press International, 1992.

—: *The Historical Figure of Jesus*. Allen Lane: Penguin, 1993.

Sato, Migaku: *Q: Prophetie oder Weisheit?* WUNT 2.29. Tübingen: Mohr, 1988.

Schaberg, Jane: *The Father, the Son, and the Holy Spirit. The Triadic Phrase in Matthew 28:19b*. SBL.DS. Chico: Scholars, 1982.

Schäfer, Peter: "Die sogenannte Synode von Jabne. Zur Trennung von Juden u. Christen im ersten/zweiten Jh. n. Chr." *Jud* 31 (1975): 54–64; 116–124.

Schenk, Wolfgang: ""Den Menschen" (Mt 9,8)." *ZNW* 54 (1963): 272–275.

Schenke, Ludger: *Die Wundererzählungen des Markusevangeliums*. Stuttgart: Katholisches Bibelwerk, 1974.

Schiffman, Lawrence H.: "The New Halakhic Letter (4QMMT) and the Origins of the Dead Sea Sect." *BA* 53 (1990): 64–73.

—: "Origin and Early History of the Qumran Sect." *BA* 58 (1995): 37–48.

Schlatter, Adolf von: *Der Evangelist Matthäus. Seine Sprache, sein Ziel, seine Selbstständigkeit: Ein Kommentar zum ersten Evangelium.* 6th ed. Stuttgart: Calwer, 1963.

Schleiermacher, Friedrich: *Einleitung ins Neue Testament. Aus Schleiermachers handschriftlichem Nachlasse und nachgeschriebenen Vorlesungen, mit einer Vorrede von Dr. Friedrich Lücke.* In: Friedrich Schleiermachers sämmtliche Werke; 1. Abt., 8. Bd. Edited by G. Wolde. ATLA Monograph Preservation Program 1989–3032. Berlin: G. Reimer, 1845.

Schmidtke, Alfred: *Neue Fragmente und Untersuchungen zu den judenchristlichen Evangelien.* TU XXXVII. Leipzig: Teubner, 1911.

Schnackenburg, Rudolf: *Das Matthäusevangelium.* 2 vols. NEB.NT. Würzburg: Echter, 1985, 1987.

Schoeps, Hans J.: *Theologie und Geschichte des Judenchristentums.* Tübingen: Mohr, 1949.

Scholtissek, Klaus: *Die Vollmacht Jesu: Traditions- und redaktionsgeschichtliche Analysen zu einem Leitmotif markinischer Christologie.* NTA 25. Münster: Aschendorff, 1992.

Schulz, Siegfried: *Die Stunde der Botschaft.* Hamburg: Furche, 1967.

—: *Q – Die Spruchquelle der Evangelisten.* Zürich: TVZ, 1971.

Schürer, Emil: *The History of the Jewish People in the Age of Jesus Christ (175 B.C. – A.D. 135).* 4 vols. Edited by Geza Vermes, Fergus Millar and Martin Goodman. Edinburgh: T. & T. Clark, 1973–1987.

Schweizer, Eduard: *The Good News According to Mark.* Translated by Donald H. Madvig. Richmond: John Knox, 1970.

—: *Das Evangelium nach Matthäus.* NTD 2. Göttingen, Vandenhoeck & Ruprecht, 1973.

—: *Matthäus und seine Gemeinde.* SBS 71. Stuttgart: Stuttgarter Bibelgesellschaft, 1974.

—: *Die Bergpredigt.* KVR 1481. Göttingen: Vandenhoeck & Ruprecht, 1984.

Senior, Donald: *What Are They Saying About Matthew?* 2nd ed. New York, Mahwah: Paulist Press, 1996.

Shuler, Philip L.: *A Genre for the Gospels: The Biographical Character of Matthew.* Philadelphia: Fortress, 1982.

Sim, David C.: "The Gospel of Matthew and the Gentiles." *JSNT* 57 (1995): 19–48.

—: *Apocalyptic Eschatology in the Gospel of Matthew.* MSSNTS 88. Cambridge; New York: Cambridge University Press, 1996.

Smith, Morton: *Jesus the Magician.* San Francisco: Harper & Row, 1978.

Smith, Stephen S.: "The Literary Structure of Mark 11:1–12:40." *NT* 31 (1989): 104–124.

Snodgrass, Klyne: *The Parable of the Wicked Tenants.* WUNT 27. Tübingen: Mohr, 1983.

—: "Matthew and the Law." In: *Treasures New and Old. Recent Contributions to Matthean Studies*, edited by David R. Bauer and Mark Allan Powell, 179–196. Atlanta: Scholars Press, 1996.

Stambaugh, John E., and David L. Balch: *The New Testament in Its Social Environment.* LEC. Philadelphia: Westminster Press, 1986.

Stanton, Graham N.: "The Origin and Purpose of Matthew's Gospel. Matthean Scholarship from 1945 to 1980." In: *ANRW* II.25.3, edited by W. Haase, 1889–1951. Berlin, New York: Walter de Gruyter, 1985.

—: "Matthew." In: *It is Written: Scripture Citing Scripture. Essays in Honour of Barnabas Lindars, SSF*, edited by D. A. Carson and H. G. Williamson, 205–219. Cambridge, New York, New Rochelle, Melbourne, Sydney: Cambridge University Press, 1988.

—: "Matthew as a Creative Interpreter of the Sayings of Jesus." In: *The Gospel and the Gospels*, edited by Peter Stuhlmacher, 257–272. Grand Rapids: Eerdmans, 1991.

—: "The Communities of Matthew." *Interp* 46 (1992): 379–391.

—: "Matthew's Christology and the Parting of the Ways." In: *The Parting of the Ways A.D. 70 to 135. The Second Durham-Tübingen Research Symposium on Earliest Christianity and Judaism (Durham, September 1989)*, edited by James D. G. Dunn, 99–116. WUNT 66. Tuebingen: Mohr (Siebeck), 1992.

—: *A Gospel for a New People*. Louisville: John Knox, 1993.

—: "Revisiting Matthew's Communities." In: *SBL.SP 1994*, edited by E. H. Lovering, 9–23. Atlanta: Scholars Press, 1994.

—: "Matthew's Gospel: A Survey of Some Recent Commentaries." *BiTr* 46 (1995): 131–140.

Stauffer, Ethelbert: *Christus und die Caesaren. Historische Skizzen*. 7th ed. München: Kaiser, 1966.

—: "Jeschu ben Mirjam: Kontroversgeschichtliche Anmerkungen zu Mk 6:3." In: *Neotestamentica et Semitica: Studies in Honor of Matthew Black*, edited by E. Ellis and M. Wilcox, 119–128. Edinburgh: T. & T. Clark, 1969.

Steck, Odil H.: *Israel und das gewaltsame Geschick der Propheten*. WMANT 23. Neukirchen-Vluyn: Neukirchener, 1967.

Stemberger, Günther: "Die sogenannte "Synode von Jabne" und das frühe Christentum." *Kairos* 19 (1977): 14–21.

—: *Jewish Contemporaries of Jesus. Pharisees, Sadducees, Essenes*. Translated by A. W. Mahnke. Minneapolis: Fortress, 1995.

Stendahl, Krister: *The School of St. Matthew and its Use of the Old Testament*. ASNU XX. 2nd edition. Lund: CWK Gleerup, 1968.

Stern, Menahem: *Greek and Latin Authors on Jews and Judaism*. 3 vols. Jerusalem: Israel Academy of Sciences and Humanities, 1974–1984.

Stock, Klemens: *Jesus – die frohe Botschaft. Meditationen zu Markus*. Innsbruck: Tyrolia, 1983.

Strack, Hermann Leberecht, and Paul Billerbeck: *Kommentar zum Neuen Testament aus Talmud und Midrasch. Bd. I: Das Evangelium nach Matthäus*. München: Beck, 1956.

Strack, Hermann Leberecht, and Günther Stemberger: *Introduction to the Talmud and Midrash*. Translated by M. Bockmuehl. Minneapolis: Fortress, 1992.

Strecker, Georg: "Das Geschichtsverständnis des Matthäus." *EvTh* 26 (1966): 219–230.

—: *Der Weg der Gerechtigkeit. Untersuchung zur Theologie des Matthäus*. 3rd ed. Göttingen: Vandenhoeck & Ruprecht, 1971.

—: "The Concept of History in Matthew." In: *The Interpretation of Matthew*, edited by Graham N. Stanton, 67–84. Philadelphia: Fortress, 1983.

—: *Die Bergpredigt: Ein exegetischer Kommentar*. Göttingen: Vandenhoeck & Ruprecht, 1984.

Suggs, M. Jack: *Wisdom, Christology, and Law in Matthew's Gospel*. Cambridge: Harvard University Press, 1970.

Tannehill, Robert C.: *The Sword of His Mouth*. SBL.MS 1. Missoula: Fortress, 1975.

—: "Introduction: The Pronouncement Story and its Types." *Semeia* 20 (1981): 1–13.

—: "Varieties of Synoptic Pronouncement Stories." *Semeia* 20 (1981): 101–119.

—: "Types and Functions of Apophthegms in the Synoptic Gospels." In: *ANRW* II.25.2, edited by W. Haase, 1831–1885. Berlin, New York: Walter de Gruyter, 1984.

Taylor, Vincent: *The Formation of the Gospel Tradition*. 2nd ed. London: Macmillan, 1935.

—: *The Gospel According to St. Mark*. London: Macmillan, 1952.

Theissen, Gerd: *Miracle Stories of the Early Christian Tradition*. Translated by F. McDonough. Philadelphia: Fortress, 1983.

Thomas, Kenneth J.: "Liturgical Citations in the Synoptics." *NTS* 22 (1975–1976): 209–214.

Thompson, William G.: *Matthew's Advice to a Divided Community. Mt. 17, 22–18, 35*. AnBib 44. Rome: Biblical Institute Press, 1970.

—: "Reflections on the Composition of Mt 8:1–9:34." *CBQ* 33 (1971): 365–388.

Thysman, Raymond: *Communauté et directives éthiques: la catéchèse de Matthieu*. Paris: Gembloux, 1974.

Tilborg, Sjef van: *The Jewish Leaders in Matthew*. Leiden: Brill, 1972.

Tisera, Guido: *Universalism According to the Gospel of Matthew*. EHS.T 23. Frankfurt, Bern, New York: Lang, 1993.

Tödt, Heinz Eduard: *The Son of Man in the Synoptic Tradition*. Translated by D. Barton. London: SCM Press, 1965.

Trilling, Wolfgang: *Das wahre Israel: Studien zur Theologie des Matthäus-Evangeliums*. 3rd ed. StANT 10. München: Kösel, 1964.

—: *The Gospel According to St. Matthew*. Translated by K. Smyth. New York: Herder & Herder, 1969.

Tuckett, Christopher M.: *Q and the History of Early Christianity. Studies on Q*. Peabody: Hendrickson, 1996.

Twelftree, Graham: "Jesus in the Jewish Traditions." In: *The Jesus Tradition Outside the Gospels*, edited by D. Wenham, 289–341. Sheffield: JSOT Press, 1985.

VanderKam, James C.: *The Dead Sea Scrolls Today*. Grand Rapids: Eerdmans, 1994.

Vermes, Geza: *Jesus the Jew*. Philadelphia: Fortress, 1973.

Veyne, Paul: *The Roman Empire*. Translated by A. Golhammer. Cambridge: Belknap Press of Harvard University Press, 1997.

Via, Dan O.: "Narrative World and Ethical Repsonse: The Marvelous and Righteousness in Matthew 1–2." *Semeia* 12 (1978): 123–149.

Viviano, Benedict T.: "Where Was the Gospel According to Matthew Written?" *CBQ* 41 (1979): 533–546.

Wahlde, Urban C. von: "*Wiederaufnahme* as a Marker of Redaction in Jn 6:51–58." *Bib* 64 (1983): 542–549.

Walker, Rolf: *Die Heilsgeschichte im ersten Evangelium*. FRLANT 10. Göttingen: Vandenhoeck & Ruprecht, 1967.

Watson, Francis B.: *Paul, Judaism, and the Gentiles, A Sociological Approach*. MSSNTS 56. Cambridge: Cambridge University Press, 1986.

Weaver, Dorothy J.: *Matthew's Missionary Discourse: A Literary Critical Analysis*. JSNT.S 38. Sheffield: JSOT, 1990.

—: "Power and Powerlessness: Matthew's Use of Irony in the Portrayal of Political Leaders." In: *Treasures New and Old. Recent Contributions to Matthean Studies*, edited by David R. Bauer and Mark Allan Powell, 179–196. Atlanta: Scholars Press, 1996.

Weber, Max: *On the Methodology of the Social Sciences*. Translated by E. A. Shils and H. A. Finch. Glencoe: The Free Press of Glencoe, 1949.

Weiss, Bernhard: *Das Matthäus-Evangelium*. ATLA monograph preservation program 1987–2274. Göttingen: Vandenhoeck und Ruprecht, 1898.

Wellhausen, Julius: *Einleitung in die drei ersten Evangelien*. ATLA monograph preservation program 1986–3594. Berlin: Georg Reimer, 1905.

Wernle, Paul: *Die synoptische Frage*. ATLA monograph preservation program 1986–0463. Freiburg i. B.: J.C.B. Mohr (Paul Siebeck), 1899.

White, L. Michael: "Grid and Group in Matthew's Community: The Righteousness/Honor Code in the Sermon on the Mount." *Semeia* 35 (1986): 61–90.

—: "Shifting Sectarian Boundaries in Early Christianity." *BJRL* 70 (1988): 7–24.

Witherington, Ben: "Matthew 5.32 and 19.9 – Exception or Exceptional Situation?" *NTS* 31 (1985): 571–576.

Wolff, Hans Julius: *Written and Unwritten Marriages in Hellenistic and Post-Classical Roman Law*. Haverford: American Philological Association, 1939.

Wouters, Armin: *"... wer den Willen meines Vaters tut": Eine Untersuchung zum Verständnis vom Handeln im Matthäusevangelium*. BU 23. Regensburg: F. Pustet, 1992.

Wrede, William: "Zur Heilung des Gelähmten (Mc 2.1ff.)." *ZNW* 5 (1904): 354–358.

Zahn, Theodor: *Das Evangelium des Matthäus*. Reprint of the 4th edition 1922. Wuppertal: R. Brockhaus Verlag, 1984.

Zumstein, Jean: "Matthieu 28:16–20." *RTL* 22 (1972): 14–33.

—: *La condition du croyant dans l'évangile selon Matthieu*. OBO 16. Fribourg: Editions universitaires, 1977.

Index of Modern Authors

Biblisch-theologische Schwerpunkte

11: Herbert Ulonska
Streiten mit Jesus
Konfliktgeschichten in den
Evangelien

1995. 208 Seiten, kartoniert
ISBN 3-525-61347-4

Der Streit mit und um Jesus wird
anhand der Konfliktgeschichten in
den synoptischen Evangelien rekon-
struiert und nach thematischen
Schwerpunkten interpretiert.
Zum besseren Verständnis des zeit-
geschichtlichen Hintergrundes
werden die Streitpartner Jesu und
der Urgemeinde gesondert darge-
stellt.

14: Reinhard Feldmeier (Hg.)
„Salz der Erde"
Zugänge zur Bergpredigt

1998. 265 Seiten mit 6 Abbildungen,
kartoniert
ISBN 3-525-61358-X

Wie verstehen Christen an der
Schwelle zum 21. Jahrhundert die
Bergpredigt? Worin besteht die
zentrale Botschaft? Welche „Lebens-
formen des Glaubens" ergeben sich
aus der Bergpredigt? Läßt sich die
Bergpredigt in eine realistische
Politik umsetzen? Wie kann die
Bergpredigt unterrichtlich erschlos-
sen werden?

17: Gisela Kittel
Befreit aus dem Rachen des Todes
Tod und Todesüberwindung
im Alten und Neuen Testament

1999. 207 Seiten, kartoniert
ISBN 3-525-61364-4

In diesem Buch werden die biblischen Texte vorgestellt und interpretiert, in denen sich, zunächst
noch andeutend und verhalten,
dann aber immer deutlicher, die
Hoffnung auf eine Überwindung
auch der letzten Grenze, des Todes,
artikuliert.

Dabei kommt ein Erkenntnisprozeß
in den Blick, der – beide Testamente
übergreifend – von den Psalmen
und prophetischen Texten des Alten
Testaments bis zu den neutestamentlichen Auferstehungsaussagen führt.

Vandenhoeck
& Ruprecht

Forschungen zur Religion und Literatur des Alten und Neuen Testaments

Herausgegeben von Wolfgang Schrage und Rudolf Smend. Eine Auswahl:

V&R

Vandenhoeck & Ruprecht